A PRACTICAL APPROACH TO

LANDLORD
AND TENANT

A PRACTICAL APPROACH TO

LANDLORD AND TENANT

SEVENTH EDITION

Simon Garner

MA, BARRISTER

Alexandra Frith

LLB, BARRISTER

OXFORD
UNIVERSITY PRESS

Great Clarendon Street, Oxford, OX2 6DP,
United Kingdom

Oxford University Press is a department of the University of Oxford.
It furthers the University's objective of excellence in research, scholarship,
and education by publishing worldwide. Oxford is a registered trade mark of
Oxford University Press in the UK and in certain other countries

British Library Cataloguing in Publication Data

Data available

ISBN 978–0–19–966251–7

Printed in Great Britain by
Ashford Colour Press Ltd, Gosport, Hampshire

PREFACE

The seventh edition of *A Practical Approach to Landlord and Tenant* has been comprehensively updated to cover all recent developments in landlord and tenant law. This edition considers in particular the impact of the Localism Act 2011 on existing landlord and tenant legislation, including important changes to the law on tenancy deposits and the introduction of the flexible tenancy regime for social landlords in England. Also included is coverage of recent developments in Human Rights Act defences in possession proceedings following the Supreme Court decisions in *Manchester City Council v Pinnock* and *Houndslow LBC v Powell*.

This edition is dedicated to the BPTC team at Kaplan Law School with thanks for their support.

Simon Garner and Alexandra Frith
October 2012

CONTENTS SUMMARY

DETAILED CONTENTS

TABLE OF CASES

TABLE OF STATUTES

TABLE OF SECONDARY LEGISLATION

What does the client want?

IN.05 Because a landlord comes to you complaining that the tenant is in arrears with his or her rent it does not necessarily mean that the landlord wants possession of the property. A tenant with a disrepair problem may want the repairs done as quickly as possible; another may be happy with a reduction in the rent, or may be more interested in claiming compensation because he or she wants to leave the property in any event.

IN.06 Similarly, a business tenant who has been served with s 25 notice may wish to discuss its options—there may be no point in involving the tenant in costly negotiations for a new tenancy if it is likely that the rent under the new tenancy will be more than the tenant can afford.

IN.07 All clients should be advised to consider the cost implications of any course of action at this stage of the claim. For example, is there any point in issuing a complicated claim for damages against an impecunious tenant when the client would be best served by obtaining early possession under the accelerated possession procedure?

Documents

IN.08 Establish what further documents are needed from the client or from the other side. Be wary of giving firm advice until you have seen all of the agreements and notices that may exist.

The tenancy agreement

IN.09 You must see a copy if one exists. The first point to establish is whether the agreement the client has in his or her possession is the first agreement. If your client was the original tenant or lessor check that he or she has provided you with all agreements and notices that have been issued.

IN.10 If the landlord is a successor, find out the details of the original landlord and check that he or she has provided your client with all relevant notices and agreements.

IN.11 Note that it is not uncommon to find that the original tenancy was protected (eg under the Rent Act 1977) and that a previous landlord has entered into an unenforceable surrender and re-grant with the tenant. Your client may present you with an assured shorthold tenancy agreement but further investigation may show that the tenant was originally a Rent Act protected tenant and has retained that status.

IN.12 If there is no written agreement, you must establish:

- the date the tenancy or occupation began;
- the rent payable and how it is paid (eg weekly or monthly);
- the name and address of the landlord and the names of the tenants;
- the type of property that is being occupied, the extent to which it is occupied by the tenant, and the purpose for which it is occupied;
- whether it is occupied by anyone besides the tenant.

Licences

IN.13 If either party asserts that the occupation agreement is a licence, check the details of the agreement thoroughly. Remember: an agreement may be a tenancy even if both parties have agreed that it is to be a licence.

Which statutory code applies?

Following on from this, establish what type of tenancy (or licence) exists, and what statutory code will apply (see the chart at 12.12). **IN.14**

Notices

If your client tells you that a notice (eg under the Housing Act 1986, s 20 or 21) has been issued make sure you can obtain a copy and check it carefully for errors. Make sure you can establish that any notices have been properly served. **IN.15**

Deposits

If you act for a landlord or a tenant where the tenancy is an assured shorthold, check to see that any deposit taken in respect of that tenancy after 6 April 2007 has been properly secured with an approved deposit scheme (see 15.133 to 15.160). **IN.16**

C BEFORE ISSUING PROCEEDINGS

In rent arrears cases it is important to establish whether the landlord has proof of the arrears and can produce an accurate schedule of arrears. You should also check that the tenant has been served with notice of the name and address of the current landlord. Unless this has been done, the tenant has no obligation to pay rent and a claim for rent arrears will automatically fail. Arrears will become due once such a notice has been served. **IN.17**

Where either party alleges a breach of the tenancy agreement, it is important to identify any relevant clause in the tenancy agreement and check the exact wording of that clause. It is not uncommon for a party alleging that he or she has a particular right under the agreement to find on closer examination that that right is subject to provisos, or does not clearly exist. In particular, if your client wishes to obtain possession during the fixed term of a tenancy, check that there is a forfeiture clause in the lease that allows them to do this (see 11.18 to 11.19). **IN.18**

Notices and time limits

You must check that the correct notices have been served and that the statutory time limits have been adhered to. There is no point in advising a client to issue proceedings if the notice to quit has not been properly completed, or has not expired. **IN.19**

If notices need to be served make sure you have enough information from your client to enable you to set out any breaches of the tenancy agreement in sufficient detail. If there is a dispute as to which statutory code applies to the tenancy you may need to consider serving two notices (for example, in possession claims, one under s 8 and one under s 21 of the Housing Act 1988). **IN.20**

Protocols

The conduct of disrepair claims is governed by a mandatory pre-action protocol, which has been incorporated into the Civil Procedure Rules. Unless a claim needs to be issued in **IN.21** an emergency (for example, a claim for an injunction where urgent repair works are necessary) the claimant must adhere to the protocol or face possible costs sanctions. Some other types of claim (currently dilapidations claims and business tenancy renewals) are covered by voluntary draft protocols which you are advised to follow for guidance.

Letter before action

IN.22   In many types of proceedings it may be advisable to issue a letter before action before issuing proceedings (in addition to serving notice). This letter will set out the client's allegations and request that whatever breach is alleged is remedied within a certain period of time and/or set out proposals for resolving any dispute. Failure to issue such a letter before action may result in the client incurring costs unnecessarily, particularly where it emerges that the claim could have been settled without recourse to litigation.

Is there scope for negotiation?

IN.23   You should also consider with the client whether there is any room for negotiating with the other party before proceedings are issued. This will be of particular relevance where both parties are alleging that there have been breaches of the agreement (eg where a landlord claims rent arrears and the tenant alleges that the landlord is in breach of his or her repairing obligations).

D   IF PROCEEDINGS ARE TO BE ISSUED

The county court

IN.24   Be aware that all types of proceedings require a specific claim form to be used. The form of most notices is also prescribed by regulations. The procedure to be followed in most landlord and tenant claims is as set out in the Civil Procedure Rules. In particular CPR 55 and 56 apply specifically to landlord and tenant claims. Nowadays it is extremely rare in practice for any simple landlord and tenant claim to be brought in the High Court.

The leasehold valuation tribunal or residential property tribunal

IN.25   You should also be advised that the jurisdiction for many claims involving long leases is increasingly being moved to the leasehold valuation tribunal (LVT) or the residential property tribunal (RPT). Before issuing proceedings, the practitioner must check to see whether the claim must be heard before a court or a LVT or RPT or, if there is a choice, consider with the client which tribunal would be the most suitable for his or her claim.

E   PREPARING FOR THE HEARING

IN.26   In advance of the hearing, consider what your client will need to prove and ensure that the person who is to attend court is able to do this. For example, in a possession claim based on rent arrears under Ground 8 of the Housing Act 1988 (see 16.46) your client will need to provide proof of service of the s 8 notice and give evidence as to the amount of the arrears at the date of the notice and the date of the hearing. It may be that the notice was served by a process server and a managing agent has been collecting the rent. In that case an affidavit from the process server should be produced at the hearing and the agent should attend court to give evidence of the arrears.

If the claim was not served by the court you will need to prove service of the proceedings. **IN.27**
At the possession hearing your client should also be in a position to provide evidence of the landlord's title to the property.

If you act for a landlord who wishes you to represent him or he at a possession hearing for **IN.28**
which fixed costs are likely to be awarded (CPR r 55.7.8 and r 45.1), make sure he or she
is aware that he or she will not be able to recover the full cost of representation.

F CHECKLIST FOR INITIAL INTERVIEW WITH CLIENT

All claims

- What type of agreement exists? **IN.29**
- Who is/are the landlord(s) and who is/are the tenant(s)?
- What does the client want to achieve?
- What further documents are needed?
- What evidence is needed to prove or disprove any alleged breach?
- Should a letter before action be sent? If so, what terms for resolving the claim should be set out and what time limit for compliance should be specified?
- Have all relevant notices been correctly completed and served? If not, what notices are needed? Will these be drafted and served by the advisor or by the client?
- What are the possible cost implications of any course of action that is being considered?
- If a claim is to be issued, should it be issued in the county court, High Court, or LVT?

G FURTHER CHECKLISTS FOR PARTICULAR TYPES OF CLAIMS

Claims for possession

(a) On grounds of arrears of rent

- Has the tenant been served with notice of the name and address of the landlord? **IN.30**
- Has the landlord produced a schedule of arrears? Are these arrears disputed and if so what is the tenant's proof of payment?
- Is there a housing benefit problem which has caused the arrears?
- Has the landlord complied with the pre-action protocol?
- Does the tenant have any proposals for paying off the arrears?
- Have all relevant notices been correctly completed and served?
- Have the notices been served within the correct time limits and have the notices expired?
- In the case of long leases, is there a proviso for re-entry by the landlord without the need for a formal demand?

(b) On grounds of other breaches

- Check the exact wording of the tenancy agreement to establish whether a breach has **IN.31**
occurred.
- Have all relevant notices been correctly completed and served?

- Have the notices been served within the correct time limits and have the notices expired?

(c) Generally

IN.32 • Have there been any previous proceedings? If so, what orders have been made?
- Is there a potential counterclaim?

Claims for disrepair

IN.33 • Has the client complied with the pre-action protocol? If not, which steps need to be completed?
- Is there a need for an expert surveyor? If so, can a joint expert be agreed and how is he or she to be paid?
- Is the disrepair sufficiently serious to merit an immediate claim for a mandatory injunction?

Business tenancies—termination or renewal

IN.34 • Does the tenant qualify for a new tenancy?
- Does the landlord have sufficient grounds to argue that a new tenancy should not be granted?
- If there is to be a new tenancy, what terms would the client agree to?
- If no new tenancy is granted, is the tenant entitled to compensation?
- Does the landlord have a claim for dilapidations?
- Does the client need to serve a notice or make an application to the court? If so, when does the time limit expire?

Claims for enfranchisement, leasehold extension, or creation of a commonhold

IN.35 • Can the tenants satisfy the requirements for entitlement?
- Is the advisor sufficiently experienced to advise fully on all aspects of such a claim (eg the setting-up of a company or the relevant conveyancing matters)?
- What time limits apply to any application your client needs to make?

PART I

THE COMMON LAW

1

THE BASICS

A INTRODUCTION

The law of landlord and tenant is concerned with the legal rights and obligations that arise **1.01** between people when they enter into a relationship to do with land. The first part of this book covers the general principles which govern the relationship of landlord and tenant; the second part deals with the various statutory codes which apply to certain types of occupiers. This first chapter is concerned with defining the different ways in which a person can occupy land. First, however, the most important concept of all needs to be introduced—an estate in land.

B AN ESTATE IN LAND

Example Paul lives in a self-contained, one-bedroom flat which he has rented from James **1.02** for a year. When Paul talks about this flat he refers to it as his. James too, if asked, will speak of the same flat as his. If James has in fact rented the flat from Peter in the first place, Peter will also describe the flat as his. It would be most unlikely to find three different individuals all honestly claiming simultaneous ownership of a car or a TV set. What each of them means when they talk about their 'ownership' of the flat is that they hold an *interest* in the flat. Land itself cannot be owned. A person can acquire only an interest in the land which confers upon him or her certain rights and obligations in relation to that land for a particular period of time. Such an interest is known in English land law as an *estate in land*.

By virtue of s 1 of the Law of Property Act 1925 (LPA 1925) there are only two estates in **1.03** land which are recognized at law:

(a) an estate in fee simple absolute in possession;
(b) a term of years absolute.

An estate in fee simple absolute in possession

An estate in fee simple absolute in possession is an estate of indefinite duration. The holder **1.04** of the fee simple absolute thus has an unlimited amount of time in the land. The fee simple absolute is therefore the closest thing to absolute ownership of land that is possible under English land law. The word 'possession' does not mean that the holder of the fee simple must be in actual physical possession of the land, but merely that the estate must be current, ie not an interest to start at some time in the future. 'Possession' is defined by LPA 1925, s 205(1)(xix) as including 'the receipt of rents and profits or the right to receive the same'. A holder of the fee simple is therefore entitled to carve a smaller estate out of his or her interest by renting out the land for a fixed period of time. The holder of an estate in fee simple absolute in possession is commonly known as a 'freeholder'.

A term of years absolute

1.05 A term of years absolute is an estate of fixed maximum duration. Being of definite duration, a term of years absolute is always of necessity a lesser estate than the fee simple. A term of years absolute exists within an estate in fee simple in the sense that the shorter fixed term is carved out of the longer indefinite term. A term of years absolute is more commonly known as a lease or a leasehold estate. Whenever a term of years absolute is carved out of a freehold estate a relationship arises between the holder of the fee simple and the holder of the term of years absolute; this is the relationship of landlord and tenant. It is this relationship that forms the core subject matter of this book.

1.06 In our example Paul, James, and Peter all hold estates in the same piece of land. Each estate consists of a bundle of rights and obligations in relation to that piece of land which enable each of them to speak of the flat as 'theirs'. If we look at the arrangement in a cold legal light we can see that each estate consists of a different set of rights and obligations:

(a) Paul has the right to occupy the flat and use it as his home for a year; during this time he also has the obligation to pay rent to James. The flat is 'his' in the sense that he can live in it for that period.

(b) James does not have the right to use the flat as his home at the moment because he has given that right to Paul for a year. At the end of the year he will recover the right to live in the flat if he wants to. However, he does have the right to collect rent from Paul. He has the obligation to repair and maintain the flat. He also has the obligation to pay rent to Peter. The flat is 'his' in the sense that he can collect rent and he will have the right to occupy the flat or to rent it out again once Paul's rights over the flat have expired.

(c) Peter likewise does not have the right to live in the flat, but he does have the right to collect rent from James. When James's rights over the flat have expired, Peter will again acquire the right to occupy the flat or to rent it out again.

1.07 Each of them thus refers to the flat as theirs in a different sense. Each of them holds a different estate in the flat, and each of those estates is capable of existing concurrently with the other estates. From this it should be clear that although landlord and tenant law may seem ostensibly to be about the relationship between a person (the occupier) and his or her flat, it is in fact really concerned with the relationship between individuals in respect of that flat. The nature of Paul's right to occupy 'his' flat is defined in contrast to other people's rights over the same flat. Landlord and tenant law is therefore concerned with analysing the relative claims different people have to the same piece of land.

C CLASSES OF OCCUPIER

1.08 A person can occupy land in a variety of ways. Consider the simple situation of a student, Paul, coming to London and looking for somewhere to live. Depending upon finance and availability he will have a considerable range of accommodation open to him. He could, for example, find himself in any of the following situations:

(a) Living in a room in a hall of residence.
(b) Living in a room in a private house as a lodger with the landlord supplying breakfast.
(c) Living in a bedsitting room with shared use of a bathroom.
(d) Living in a self-contained flat.
(e) Getting together with a group of friends and sharing a house.
(f) Finding a room in a shared house where there are already other tenants.
(g) Sleeping on a friend's sofa.
(h) Staying in the parental home and commuting to college.
(i) Squatting in an empty house.
(j) Obtaining a flat through a housing association.
(k) Obtaining a flat through a housing co-operative.
(l) Obtaining a local authority flat.
(m) Staying in a bed and breakfast hotel.
(n) Purchasing a freehold house.
(o) Purchasing a leasehold flat.
(p) Purchasing a leasehold flat with a share of the freehold (see Chapter 24).
(q) Purchasing a share of the commonhold of a property (see Chapter 25).

Whatever happens, each of the situations in the list in 1.08 falls into one of the following   **1.09**
four broad categories:

(a) **Freehold owner** Paul might be given the whole thing. The owner of the property might hand over the whole estate for a sum of money, renouncing any rights he or she might have over the property in the future ((n) and (q) in the list).
(b) **Tenant** Paul might be given a slice of time in the land, the landlord handing over to Paul possession of the property for a limited period of time while retaining his right to regain possession at some point in the future ((c), (d), (e), (f), (j), (k), (l), and (o) in the list). In (p) Paul would be a tenant of his flat, although by purchasing a share of the freehold he is also to a certain extent his own landlord.
(c) **Licensee** Paul might be given permission to use the land for a period of time. The landlord does not hand over possession of the property but retains his or her right to use it ((a), (b), (g), (h), and (m) in the list).
(d) **Trespasser** Paul could simply occupy the premises without permission by moving in and using the property as his home ((i) in the list).

These are the four categories of occupation at common law. Every occupier falls into one of   **1.10**
these categories. It is not always easy to distinguish between them. The first stage of analysis when confronted with any landlord and tenant problem will always be to determine to which category the occupier belongs. As we shall see, the majority of the statutory codes considered in the second part of this book will apply to tenants but not to freeholders, licensees, or trespassers.

The freehold owner

As a holder of the greatest estate in land (an estate in fee simple absolute in possession),   **1.11**
the freeholder has the greatest freedom to carve lesser estates out of his or her interest by renting out his or her property. In the context of a landlord and tenant relationship the freehold owner will therefore invariably be the landlord. Many people, however, purchase the freehold of a property with the intention of living in that property themselves, in which

case the freeholder is an occupier with the same fundamental concerns as any other, namely to provide himself or herself with a secure home. The occupier who owns the freehold of his or her own home is in principle the most secure of all occupiers. The estate is unlimited in time; there is no landlord with a superior interest who will reclaim the property at some point in the future. In fact the freehold owner-occupier is outside of the relationship of landlord and tenant altogether: he or she has the greatest rights and the least obligations; he or she does not have to pay rent; and provided he or she complies with local authority regulations, can do what he or she likes with the property. Nevertheless, the freehold owner is not completely unassailable. A local authority might purchase the house compulsorily to make way for a road or new development. If the property is allowed to fall into extreme disrepair, the local authority might make a demolition order. If the freeholder goes bankrupt, the trustee-in-bankruptcy might force the sale of the property or, as a result of the break-up of a relationship, a court might order the property to be sold or transferred to one of the partners outright.

Tenant

1.12   The second class of occupier, the tenant or leaseholder, forms the core of the subject matter of this book. It is therefore necessary at this point to define the essential elements of a lease.

For a tenancy to arise the following must be satisfied:

(a) there must be a landlord and a tenant;
(b) there must be exclusive possession;
(c) there must be identifiable land;
(d) the grant must be for a definite period;
(e) the lessor must retain a reversion.

Identifiable landlord and tenant

1.13   For a lease to be created there must be separate and identifiable legal persons capable of granting and of receiving the tenancy. It is not strictly necessary that the tenant must know the identity of the landlord—in many cases where an agency grants a tenancy on behalf of a landlord the landlord's identity is unknown to the tenant. Neither is it necessary that either party be an individual—a 'legal person' such as a corporate body can grant or receive a lease provided it is empowered to do so by the company constitution. A tenancy can also be granted to a group of people as joint tenants. A minor (ie a person under the age of 18) is not legally competent to hold an estate in land and neither is a body, such as an unincorporated association, which does not have a legal personality. Furthermore the owner of land cannot grant a lease to himself (*Rye v Rye* [1962] AC 496), although a person can be the tenant of a company of which he or she is a director or of a partnership of which he or she is a partner. The company or partnership has a separate legal identity from the tenant.

Exclusive possession

1.14   It is fundamental to a tenancy that the tenant must have been granted a sufficient degree of control over the premises for the tenant to be able lawfully to exclude others from those premises. 'Others' in this context includes the landlord, although a tenant will still have exclusive possession if the landlord retains only a restricted right to enter the premises for a specific purpose, such as inspecting the premises' state of repair:

> The tenant possessing exclusive possession is able to exercise the rights of an owner of land, which is in the real sense his land albeit temporarily and subject to certain restrictions. A tenant

armed with exclusive possession can keep out strangers and keep out the landlord unless the landlord is exercising limited rights reserved to him by the tenancy agreement to enter and view and repair. (*Street v Mountford* [1985] AC 809 *per* Lord Templeman at 816)

Exclusive possession is an essential requirement for a lease. If the occupier does not have **1.15** exclusive possession, the right to use the premises cannot amount to a lease, although the occupier may have a lesser right in the land, such as a licence. This question will be considered in detail in Chapter 2 (see 2.25 to 2.69).

Identifiable land

The premises which are the subject matter of the tenancy must be defined with certainty. **1.16** Normally this requirement is easily satisfied: a house can be adequately defined by giving the address, a room can be defined either by numbering the room or describing it (eg the front second-floor room). However, difficulties can arise if two or more individuals are given separate agreements to occupy the same premises; each individual may not have been granted an identifiable portion and may not therefore be capable of holding a tenancy (see 2.57 to 2.69).

A definite period

A lease must be granted for a period that is definite or capable of definition. We have **1.17** already seen how a lease or a term of years absolute is of fixed duration and is thereby distinguished from the fee simple which is of indefinite duration. The fact that the LPA 1925, s 1 refers to a lease as a 'term of years' does not mean that the length of the lease must be measured in years. Section 1 is further defined by s 205(1)(xxvii), which provides that 'the expression "term of years" includes a term for less than a year, or for a year or years and a fraction of a year or from year to year'. A lease therefore can be for virtually any period; it can be for 100,000 years or for a couple of days, or even for three successive bank holidays (*Smallwood v Sheppards* [1895] 2 QB 627). The important point is that it must have a definable beginning and a definable end.

However, in many leases the duration of the term is not expressly specified. Consider the **1.18** following situations:

(a) Maurice is granted a 99-year lease of a house by Peter, the freeholder, in exchange for a sum of £75,000.
(b) Jane is granted a tenancy of a flat by Simon in exchange for a rent of £300 per month payable in advance.

The period of occupation granted to Maurice is clearly defined; it will last 99 years **1.19** and has a fixed beginning and a fixed end and is therefore known as a *fixed-term tenancy*. Jane's situation is not so clear; there is a fixed beginning, but although the lease she signed sets out the ways in which either she or the landlord can end the tenancy by giving notice there is no reference to any fixed date on which the tenancy is to end and, provided neither party decides to end the relationship, it could go on forever. Such a tenancy is known as a *periodic tenancy*. Nevertheless, like Maurice's 99-year lease, Jane's monthly tenancy is regarded as being for a term that is capable of definition. Each time a monthly term expires the term is automatically renewed and it can be terminated by either party giving a specified amount of notice to quit. The nature of a periodic tenancy (ie whether it is to be weekly, monthly, yearly, or for some other period) will normally be specified in the tenancy agreement. If it is not specified it will be determined by reference to the period used to calculate the rent. If the period of the notice to quit is not specified in the agreement this will similarly be determined according to the rent period (see 10.36).

1.20   It should be noted that if the terms of the periodic tenancy agreement actually prevent either the landlord or the tenant from terminating the tenancy or allow a party to terminate the tenancy only in the event of a circumstance that may never arise (for example a term that allows the landlord to give the tenant notice to quit only if he or she fails to pay the rent) the position becomes more complicated as there cannot then be said to be a definable period on the face of the agreement. In such a case, provided that the tenant is an individual, the periodic tenancy will take effect as a tenancy for a term of 90 years terminable on the death of the tenant (by virtue of s 149(6) of the LPA 1925). However, if the occupier is not an individual, such a restriction on the parties' ability to give notice to quit will mean that the agreement is not for a definable period and cannot be a tenancy (see 10.33 and *Berrisford v Mexfield Housing Co-operative Ltd* [2011] UKSC 52).

The lessor must retain a reversion

1.21   For a lease to be created it is essential that the term held by the tenant is for a shorter period than the term held by the landlord. We have seen that the freeholder's estate is for an unlimited duration. A freeholder is therefore able to grant a lease for any period he likes. Any fixed period of time will of necessity be for a lesser period than an indefinite period. In the example given, Peter, the freeholder, grants Maurice a lease for 99 years, but it could be for 999 years or longer.

1.22   A leaseholder too is able to grant a lease. This is possible only provided that the term granted is shorter than the term held by the leaseholder. Maurice, for example, as the holder of a 99-year lease, would be able to grant to Philip a 98-year lease. Despite the fact that Maurice has handed over the right of actual occupation of the flat for 98 years, there are still rights and obligations outstanding on either side: Philip has the right to occupy the flat as his home but also the obligation to pay rent; Maurice does not have the right to occupy the flat but he does have the right to collect rent. In 98 years' time the right to occupy the flat will revert to him. Maurice therefore still retains an interest in the flat. It is this interest that is known as the reversion.

1.23   If Maurice sought to grant a lease for 99 years or more, he would be handing over the whole of his interest to Philip and would retain no reversion. There would be no rights or obligations outstanding and therefore the relationship of landlord and tenant would not arise between Maurice and Philip. Instead Philip would acquire Maurice's rights in their entirety and the grant would function as an assignment (see 9.15 to 9.23).

1.24   Strictly speaking, because Maurice is a leaseholder and not the freeholder, the lease acquired by Philip is known as a sub-lease. Unless he is precluded from doing so by the terms of the agreement with Maurice, Philip too can grant a further lease of the flat (technically known as an underlease) to Mary. Philip may, for example, grant Mary a monthly periodic tenancy, but in theory he could grant a lease for any period provided that the period granted is for less than 98 years.

1.25   If we now consider this flat we find that there are four people who possess a legal estate in it. The freeholder has the fee simple absolute in possession, Paul has a lease for 99 years, Philip has a 98-year sub-lease, and Mary has a monthly periodic underlease. All three of these leases fall within the definition of a term of years absolute.

Rent

1.26   Surprisingly enough, rent is not an essential requirement of a lease. Section 205(1)(xxvii) of the LPA 1925 defines a lease as a term of years 'whether or not at a rent'. In *Ashburn Anstalt v Arnold* [1988] 2 WLR 706, it was held that an agreement giving the occupier exclusive possession of premises for a certain term created a tenancy despite the fact that no rent was payable under the agreement. Nevertheless, it is usual for rent to be paid under a tenancy. As we shall see in Chapter 2 (see 2.11), Lord Templeman in *Street v Mountford* [1985] AC 809 includes rent in his definition of a tenancy. Lord Templeman's position can perhaps be explained by the fact that *Street v Mountford* was a case dealing with Rent Act eligibility. While rent is not a requirement for the creation of a tenancy, it is essential to bring that tenancy within the protection of the residential statutory codes (see Chapters 12 to 18).

The owner-occupier

So far we have considered the two categories of occupier whose interests are capable of amounting to an estate in land under s 1 of the LPA 1925: the freeholder and the tenant. Existing within both of these categories is a sub-category of occupier that is generally known as the owner-occupier. The distinctive feature of owner-occupation is that the right of occupation will be paid for in a large lump sum on the transference of the estate rather than by regular payments of rent.   **1.27**

In the strict sense only the freehold estate owner is really an owner-occupier. Once the free-   **1.28** holder has paid the purchase price of the property he or she has no outstanding obligations, the entire estate is his or hers to do with what he or she will. In many ways, and certainly in common parlance, the holder of a long lease is also an owner-occupier. The holder of a 99-year lease shares many of the same concerns as a freehold owner. Nevertheless, the leaseholder does not acquire the entire estate; the owner of the freehold retains an interest in the property in that he or she is the holder of the reversion. There are rights and obligations outstanding between the freeholder and the leaseholder; they are in a relationship of landlord and tenant. It is normal for the leaseholder to pay a nominal 'ground rent' to the freeholder. In general, however, a long leaseholder acquires considerably greater rights over his or her home than a periodic tenant or a tenant holding a short-term lease. In particular a long leaseholder is unlikely to be evicted by the freeholder during the currency of the lease. Furthermore, the long leaseholder may have the right to compel the landlord to sell him or her the freehold of the property (see Chapter 24).

Home ownership is therefore a very attractive prospect to many people; it offers consider-   **1.29** ably greater freedom of choice than the rented sector and considerably greater freedom from eviction. In recent years home ownership has also been promoted by legislation. The Housing Acts of 1980 and 1985 introduced the 'Right to Buy' (see 17.137 to 17.170), thus giving local authority tenants the opportunity to purchase their local authority homes at reduced rates, and the Housing Act 1996 has more recently extended the right to buy to tenants of registered social landlords (formerly housing associations). However, even at reduced rates few people can afford to raise the often considerable purchase prices without borrowing substantial sums of money. This money is usually raised by way of mortgage. A mortgage is a contract which can contain restrictions in the same way as a lease. If owner-occupiers fall into arrears with mortgage payments the building society or bank may be able to evict them from their homes.

Commonhold

The Commonhold and Leasehold Reform Act 2002 introduced a new type of owner occu-   **1.30** pation. It is now possible for a number of occupants of separate flats to own the freehold of the whole property. This provision is different from the enfranchisement system (see Chapter 24). Under that scheme long lessees remain lessees but they share the freehold ownership of the common parts. In contrast, when a commonhold is created all of the pre-existing leases cease to exist. The occupiers (through their membership of a commonhold association) are the registered freehold owners of the whole property. They will of course retain mutual obligations and restrictions on their rights to occupy parts of the property. A guide to the provisions of the Act is contained in Chapter 25.

The licensee

1.31 It is unlawful to drive a car on the public highway: if you possess a driving licence this act becomes lawful. It is unlawful to sell alcohol to the public: if you possess a licence to do so it becomes lawful. The meaning of the word 'licence' in these two examples is exactly the same meaning it holds within the law of landlord and tenant. When an occupier is granted a licence he or she is not given an estate or an interest in the land, but simply permission to use the land. This permission makes occupiers' presence on the land lawful; before the granting of the licence their presence would have been unlawful and therefore trespass.

1.32 In the majority of cases permission to occupy land is granted with the minimum of formality. Permission can be express or implied. If friends invite you round for coffee you have their express permission to enter their flat. If you enter a shop to buy some milk, permission to enter is implied from the fact that the door is open. In both cases you are a licensee until you leave the premises or permission to be on the premises is withdrawn. Such a licence is known as a *bare licence*. At the other end of the scale a licence can be a formal arrangement granting an individual permission to occupy a room or a flat as his or her home in return for regular payments, in which case a licence can give rise to rights and obligations that may seem to be indistinguishable from the rights and obligations acquired under a tenancy. This type of licence is known as a *contractual licence*.

A bare licence

1.33 A bare licence is a licence granted without any valuable consideration to support it. A person who stays on a friend's sofa while looking for somewhere else to live is a bare licensee; likewise a child staying in the parental home. A person will still be a bare licensee even if a financial contribution is made if, as is frequently the case in family arrangements, there is no intention to create binding legal relations between the parties (*Hannaford v Selby* (1976) 239 EG 811).

1.34 A fundamental feature of the bare licence is that the licensor can revoke the licence at any time. Once permission is withdrawn the licensee has a reasonable time to leave the premises. Once that period has expired he or she becomes a trespasser. In *Robson v Hallet* [1967] 2 QB 939 police officers knocked on the door of a house. The officers had no warrant or other authority to be there and were therefore merely implied licensees of the householder. The householder withdrew permission. The court implied into the licence a term that the officers should be given a 'reasonable time to leave the premises by the most appropriate route' (at 954D).

1.35 A person occupying a house or room under a bare licence has no protection against eviction. Once that person has been told the licence has been revoked he or she will become a trespasser as soon as a 'reasonable period' has elapsed. What will be a reasonable period of time will depend on the circumstances, and the situation of both parties will be considered. In family arrangements the period of time regarded as 'reasonable' to leave the premises after the revocation of a bare licence can be as much as six months (*Hannaford v Selby*). Where land was occupied under a licence for over 26 years, 12 months was held to be a reasonable period (*E&L Berg Homes Ltd v Gray* (1980) 253 EG 473).

Contractual licence

In many situations permission is granted to enter a premises in return for valuable consid- **1.36**
eration. In such a case the holder of the permission is regarded as a contractual licensee.
Clearly purchasers of tickets to view Buckingham Palace will not have a tenancy, but they
do hold some sort of right to be on the land. If, five minutes after paying for a ticket, a
security guard throws him or her back out onto the street the licensee will have some form
of redress. By purchasing a ticket the licensee enters into a contract with the occupiers of
Buckingham Palace; in exchange for valuable consideration the occupiers have contracted
to permit the licensee to view the interior of the building. If the occupiers break their side of
the agreement the licensee will have a remedy in contract. However, as the case of *Wood v
Leadbitter* [1845] 13 M&W 838 illustrates, a remedy in contract is not always satisfactory.
The key question is whether the licensee has any sort of right to remain on the land.

In *Wood v Leadbitter* a racegoer paid a guinea to enter the racecourse and watch the rac- **1.37**
ing. He was forcibly ejected by the race steward soon after arriving and sued the steward
for damages for battery and false imprisonment. The suit was unsuccessful and it was held
that, since the racegoer had been asked to leave and had refused, he had become a trespasser and reasonable force could be used to remove him. The view of the court was that a
licence, whether or not granted for valuable consideration, was revocable at the will of the
grantor. Nevertheless, the racegoer got his guinea back as damages for breach of contract.

Thirty years later the Supreme Court of Judicature Acts 1873 and 1875 made equitable **1.38**
remedies available in all courts, and in 1915 the issue fell to be considered again in *Hurst v
Picture Theatres Ltd* [1915] 1 KB 1. In this case a cinema goer was forcibly ejected from a
cinema by the management who mistakenly believed that he had not paid for his ticket. In
contrast to *Wood v Leadbitter*, where damages for breach of contract were seen as the only
remedy, the court took the view that the further equitable remedies of an injunction or of
specific performance would have been available to the cinema goer to prevent the cinema
management from breaching their contract. The reasoning behind this decision is that the
courts have implied a term into the contract that the licensor will not revoke the licence
during the currency of the contract. Thus it can be said that a contractual licence cannot be
revoked by the grantor until the contractual period has expired.

Trespasser

A person is a trespasser whenever he or she enters the land or premises of another without **1.39**
permission. A burglar is a trespasser, likewise an old lady who comes into your garden
and walks around admiring your flowers; neither of them have your permission to be on
your land. A person is also a trespasser if he or she has permission to be on someone else's
premises for one purpose but uses it for another. A postman, who has an implied licence to
walk up your garden path in order to deliver letters, would become a trespasser if he went
wandering into your garage. From the point of view of landlord and tenant law a more
appropriate example is that of a landlord, who, having reserved the right to enter his or her
tenants' premises to collect rent and inspect for repairs, uses the occasion to harass the tenants and to interfere with their belongings. The fact that a landlord holds an estate in the
premises does not prevent him or her from being a trespasser if he or she has no permission
to be in the premises. We saw earlier how exclusive possession is an essential element of a
tenancy and how a person with exclusive possession has the right to exclude everyone from
his or her premises, even the landlord.

In all of these examples the trespasser occupies the land for only a short period of time. **1.40**
However, in a time of housing shortage when many flats and houses remain unoccupied

it is a common occurrence for people to move into an empty property without permission and to occupy that property as their home. It should be noted that the term 'squatter' has no real legal significance; an occupier is either a trespasser or a licensee depending upon whether that occupier has permission to be on the premises. In the eyes of the law a squatter is simply a type of long-term trespasser. In *McPhail v Persons, Names Unknown* [1973] Ch 447 at 456 Lord Denning defined a squatter as 'one who without any colour of right, enters on an unoccupied house or land, intending to stay there as long as he can'. It is not uncommon for individuals who have entered empty local authority housing as squatters to be granted a short-term licence by the local authority. The term 'licensed squat', which is generally applied to such accommodation, is really a contradiction in terms. The occupiers have permission to be there and are therefore licensees.

KEY DOCUMENTS

Law of Property Act 1925

Printed copies of all legislation can be ordered from The Stationery Office at <http://www.tsoshop.co.uk>. All legislation from 1988 onwards and most pre-1988 primary legislation is available online at <http://www.legislation.gov.uk>.

2

THE DISTINCTION BETWEEN
A LEASE AND A LICENCE

A INTRODUCTION

The modern decisions of the courts on the distinction between a lease and a licence must **2.01** be seen in their historical context. The first Rent Act was enacted in 1915 as a temporary measure in response to tenants' protests at rising rents (the Increase of Rent and Mortgage Interest (War Restrictions) Act). Over the next 60 years, legislation protecting tenants' rights developed into a comprehensive statutory code culminating in the Rent Act 1977. The Rent Acts sought to protect the tenant in two key ways, first by restricting landlords' right to evict and secondly by restricting their ability to increase rent arbitrarily. As a result many landlords sought different ways to evade the Rent Acts. The most obvious way was to grant a licence rather than a lease, as licensees were not afforded Rent Act protection.

The Rent Acts will be dealt with in detail in later sections of this book, but a short example **2.02** at this stage will make clear the consequences to both landlord and tenant of the tenant's eligibility for statutory protection.

Example In 1985 Harry rents a bedsit to Jane. Jane is a protected tenant under the Rent Act **2.03** 1977. Jane contacts the Rent Officer and registers a fair rent. Because he cannot increase the rent, Harry decides to evict Jane. To do this he must first terminate the tenancy at common law (see Chapter 10) and then satisfy one of the statutory grounds of possession contained in the Rent Act (see 14.25 to 14.69). Jane, however, is a good tenant and she has not breached any of the terms of her tenancy agreement. The court therefore refuses to grant Harry a possession order.

If Jane's bedsit is held under a licence the situation is radically different. The Rent Acts do **2.04** not apply to her licence at all. Harry raises the rent which Jane can no longer afford to pay. Jane falls into arrears and Harry decides to evict her. All Harry has to do is terminate her licence by giving her four weeks' notice in writing although he may also need to obtain a court order before he can require her to leave the property (Protection from Eviction Act 1977, s 3; see 19.18).

Thus it can be seen that in certain situations the granting of a tenancy can result in the **2.05** occupier acquiring what is sometimes called the status of virtual irremovability. In marked contrast the granting of a licence provides the occupier with only minimal security and permits the licensor to regain possession of the premises at short notice and without having to establish reasons before the court.

2.06 The situation, from the landlord's point of view, is no longer quite so acute as it was. Since 15 January 1989 it has no longer been possible (except in certain exceptional circumstances) to create a Rent Act protected tenancy. The new regime, contained in the Housing Act 1988, while containing similar provisions with regard to security for the tenant, has done away with the Rent Act's system of rent control. It also provides the landlord with several broader grounds of possession than under the old Act. Most significantly, however, it introduced a means of granting short-term tenancies without security of tenure in the form of assured shorthold tenancies, a type of letting that has proved so popular with landlords that its significance was further extended by the Housing Act 1996 (see 15.108 to 15.132). Thus a landlord of residential property who wishes to avoid the risk of the tenant acquiring protection under a statutory code can now do so without having to claim that the occupier is holding under a licence. This does not mean that the importance of the distinction between a lease and a licence is in any way diminished. It simply means that certain residential landlords no longer need to employ the device of granting a licence rather than a tenancy to avoid the consequences of statutory protection.

B GRANTING A LICENCE

2.07 To grant a licence instead of a tenancy effectively is not as easy as it sounds. Consider the situation where a landlord simply takes a standard form tenancy and blanks out the word 'Tenancy' and replaces it with 'Licence'. He goes through the whole agreement substituting the words 'licensor' and 'licensee' for 'landlord' and 'tenant'. For good measure, he adds an extra declaration at the end of the agreement which states, 'I understand and accept that a licence in the above form does not and is not intended to give me a protected tenancy under the Rent Acts'.

2.08 Two things can be said about this agreement:

(a) It contains a clear statement that it is intended to create only a licence.
(b) Changing the labels does not alter the rights and obligations contained in the agreement.

2.09 In such a situation the courts are confronted with a dilemma. On one hand stands the long-established principle of freedom of contract. Parties to an agreement should be free to contract as they wish upon any terms they can agree between themselves. The courts have no right to interfere simply because they dislike the nature of the bargain struck. On the other hand parties should not be permitted to contract out of a statute and thereby defeat the intention of Parliament. Parliament, by enacting the Rent Acts, intended to provide protection for the tenant; landlords, finding that the Rent Acts worked against their interests, should not be able to evade them by the simple device of getting the prospective occupier to sign a clause stating that the Rent Acts did not apply to the agreement. It could, of course, be argued that a tenant, confronted with such a clause, is perfectly free to refuse to sign the agreement, but such an argument would not accord with the reality of the situation. In a time of housing shortage there is considerable inequality of bargaining power between a house owner and a prospective occupier.

Street v Mountford

In *Street v Mountford* [1985] AC 809 at 819, Lord Templeman gave short shrift to the **2.10**
argument on behalf of the landlord that freedom to contract should prevail:

> My Lords, Mr Street enjoyed freedom to offer Mrs Mountford the right to occupy the rooms
> comprised in the agreement on such lawful terms as Mr Street pleased. Mrs Mountford
> enjoyed freedom to contract or not to contract and both parties exercised that freedom
> by contracting on the terms set forth in the written agreement and on no other terms. But
> the consequences in law of the agreement, once concluded, can only be determined by
> consideration of the effect of the agreement. *If the agreement satisfied all the requirements
> of a tenancy, then the agreement produced a tenancy* and the parties cannot alter the effect
> of the agreement by insisting they only created a licence. The manufacture of a five pronged
> implement for manual digging results in a fork even if the manufacturer, unfamiliar with
> the English language, insists that he intended to make and has made a spade. (emphasis
> added)

To see whether an agreement is a tenancy it is necessary to determine whether the effect **2.11**
of the agreement is to confer all the elements of a tenancy on the occupier. In *Street v
Mountford* Lord Templeman concentrated primarily on the issue of whether or not exclusive possession has been granted as the test for distinguishing between a lease and a licence.
Following *Marchant v Charters* [1977] 1 WLR 1181, he agreed with Lord Denning that it
is necessary to ascertain the nature and quality of the occupancy, but disagreed with him
that the way to do that was to look at all the circumstances including the intention of the
parties:

> [I]n my opinion in order to ascertain the nature and quality of the occupancy and to see
> whether the occupier has or has not a stake in the room or only permission for himself
> personally to occupy, the court must decide whether upon its true construction the
> agreement confers on the occupier exclusive possession. If exclusive possession at a rent for
> a term does not constitute a tenancy then the distinction between a contractual tenancy and
> a contractual licence becomes wholly unidentifiable. (at 825)

Thus it can be said that: **2.12**

(a) where there is a grant of exclusive possession to an occupier for a definable term at a
     rent a tenancy will usually be created (although it should be noted that strictly speak-
     ing rent is not an essential characteristic of a tenancy. It is only necessary to bring the
     tenancy within the protection of the residential statutory codes, see 1.26);
(b) where exclusive possession is not granted there cannot be a tenancy;
(c) these principles apply irrespective of the actual intention of the parties.

Although the grant of exclusive possession normally creates a tenancy, there are a number **2.13**
of exceptions to this rule. In certain situations an occupier who has been granted exclusive
possession will hold only a licence.

Exceptions

The basis for these exceptions was set out by Denning LJ in *Facchini v Bryson* **2.14**
[1952] 1 TLR 1386 at 1389–1390, and is referred to by Lord Templeman in *Street v
Mountford*:

> In all the cases where an occupier has been held to be a licensee there has been something in
> the circumstances, such as a family agreement, an act of friendship or generosity, or such like,
> to negative any intention to create a tenancy.

2.15 According to Lord Templeman there are three categories which consist of circumstances of legal significance which would negative a grant of a tenancy:

(a) Where there is no intention to create legal relations.

(b) Where there is some other relationship than landlord and tenant.

(c) Where the grantor has no power to grant a tenancy.

No intention to create legal relations

2.16 In *Booker v Palmer* [1942] 2 All ER 674, the owner allowed a number of evacuees to stay in his cottage rent free for the duration of the war (an act of friendship or generosity). It was held that the parties here did not intend to contract at all: 'The law does not impute intention to enter into legal relationships where the circumstances and the conduct of the parties negative any intention of the kind' (*per* Lord Greene MR at 677). Likewise in *Cobb v Lane* [1952] 1 All ER 1199, [1952] 1 TLR 1037, CA, where the owner of a house allowed his brother to live there rent free (a family arrangement) there was no tenancy because there was no intention to enter into legal relations (see also *Heslop v Burns* [1974] 1 WLR 1241, [1974] 3 All ER 406, CA).

2.17 The question as to whether the parties entered into a legal relationship is not always straightforward. In *Marcroft Wagons v Smith* [1951] 2 KB 496, the statutory tenant having died, his daughter, upon the death of his widow, claimed to be a statutory tenant by succession. The landlords refused to recognize her claim, but accepted payments from her while they considered the matter. The Court of Appeal held that there was no intention to create legal relations and no tenancy had arisen upon the payments made by the daughter. This case, however, was decided on its own particular facts.

Some other legal relationship

2.18 The right to exclusive possession may arise in a legal relationship other than a tenancy.

2.19 **Vendor and purchaser** A person who is allowed to occupy property pending completion of the sale to him or her of the property will occupy as a licensee. In *Errington v Errington and Woods* [1952] 1 KB 290, [1952] 1 All ER 149, a father bought a house by paying £250 in cash and borrowing £500 from the building society. He gave the building society book to his son and daughter-in-law and told them that the £250 was a present, and if they paid the instalments on the loan the house would be theirs. The father died and left the house to his wife who sought to gain possession from the daughter-in-law (the son had moved back to his mother's home). It was held that the daughter-in-law and son were not tenants but licensees, notwithstanding that they had exclusive possession of the property. They were said to be 'in a position analogous to purchasers' (*per* Denning LJ at 154). (It should be noted that the view expressed in this case, that a contractual licence could bind third parties, was overruled in *Ashburn Anstalt v Arnold* [1989] 1 Ch 1.)

2.20 Occupation whilst the parties are negotiating the possibility of granting a lease may also not amount to a tenancy. For example in *Cameron Ltd v Rolls Royce Plc* [2007] EWHC 546 (Ch) the tenant was allowed to occupy the property whilst the landlord sought the consent of a superior landlord to the granting of the lease. As both parties had agreed that no security would attach to the occupation until the lease was granted, the potential tenant was held to have occupied as a licensee.

2.21 **Master and servant** The fact that an occupier happens to be employed by his or her landlord does not mean that that occupier cannot be a tenant. Where, for example, the owner of a factory also owns housing in the area, it may be convenient for both parties if a worker at the factory lives in a house owned by the factory owner. This is no reason why the worker should not be a tenant; there is no necessity that the worker should live there and not elsewhere. On the other hand, where an au pair lives in a room in his or her employer's house there is a much stronger connection between the au pair's employment and accommodation. If the au pair is dismissed the landlord/employer will wish to employ a new au pair. The landlord will also want the room to be available for the new employee. In this case it can be said that the accommodation 'goes with the job' in that it is necessary for the employee to live in this particular accommodation to perform the duties involved in his or her employment. Such a person is known as a service occupier or a service licensee.

Where a person occupies accommodation as a service licensee and has exclusive posses-   **2.22**
sion of that accommodation no tenancy will be created. Whether or not a person is a service licensee or a tenant will be a question of fact. If the employee is genuinely required to occupy the premises for the better performance of his or her duties, he or she will be a service licensee (*Norris v Checksfield* (1991) 23 HLR 425, CA).

No power to grant a tenancy

If it is not within the landlord's power to create a lease a tenancy cannot arise. In *London*   **2.23**
Borough of Camden v Shortlife Community Housing et al. (1993) 25 HLR 330, the question arose whether Camden had granted a lease or a licence to a housing association which provided housing for young single people in London. By virtue of certain sections of the Housing Act 1980, Camden was forbidden to 'dispose' of land without ministerial consent. The sort of agreement entered into between Camden and the housing association would have been *ultra vires* if had been held to be a lease. Millet J found that on its true construction the agreement entered into was a licence and not a lease. The word 'dispose' includes a lease, but not a licence, and therefore, because Camden did not have the power to grant a lease, the housing association had acquired a licence and not a lease. It would be a licence regardless of the fact that the housing association had acquired exclusive possession (which was not accepted by the judge). (See also *Bruton v London Quadrant Housing Trust* [1997] EGCS 125, CA.)

The deductive process undertaken to distinguish a tenancy from a licence follows the fol-   **2.24**
lowing pattern:

(a) Is there a grant of exclusive possession? If not, it cannot be a tenancy.
(b) If there is a grant of exclusive possession, does the grant fall into one of the exceptions? If it does there is no tenancy; if it does not there is a tenancy.

C EXCLUSIVE POSSESSION

Of course in many cases, as in *Street v Mountford*, none of the exceptions considered above   **2.25**
applies, in which case determining whether the occupier has a lease or a licence is decided purely by reference to the first step in the analysis: whether there is a grant of exclusive possession to the occupier. If there is no grant of exclusive possession, the occupier's claim to be a tenant will fall at the first hurdle. In *Street v Mountford* it was accepted by both parties that exclusive possession had been granted, but despite the fact that Lord Templeman reinstated exclusive possession as the touchstone of a tenancy he failed to provide a definition or consider the nature of exclusive possession in depth. In later cases, however, the issue has been of prime importance.

What then is a grant of exclusive possession? We have seen that it is no longer to be deter-   **2.26**
mined by looking at the intention of the parties. Nevertheless, this does not mean that the agreement reached between the owner and the occupier is now to be disregarded. Parties

are free to contract as they wish, but the courts will be careful to look at the true nature of the bargain.

2.27 In determining whether exclusive possession had been granted the decisive consideration is the degree of control over the premises and their use which is retained by the owner. We shall start our study of this topic by looking at a long-established category of occupier who does not have exclusive possession: the lodger.

The lodger

2.28 An occupier of residential accommodation for a term at a rent is either a lodger or a tenant:

> The occupier is a lodger if the landlord provides attendance or services which require the landlord or his servants to exercise unrestricted access to and use of the premises... any express reservation to the landlord of limited rights to enter and view the state of the premises and to repair and maintain the premises only serves to emphasize the fact that the grantee is entitled to exclusive possession and is a tenant. (*Street v Mountford*, *per* Lord Templeman at 818)

2.29 The lodger is the paradigm of a licensee. In reading many of the cases the term 'lodger' is used interchangeably with the term 'licensee' without causing undue confusion. A lodger is always a licensee, although as we have seen a licensee is not always a lodger. Traditionally, however, the term 'lodger' does have a reasonably precise meaning. A lodger is an individual who occupies a room in another person's home; he or she has shared use of facilities such as the kitchen and bathroom and traditionally is provided with certain services and attendances by the owner, such as breakfast and/or supper, clean linen, and having the room cleaned regularly (see *Marchant v Charters* [1977] 1 WLR 1181, [1977] 3 All ER 981; *Bassairi v London Borough of Camden* [1999] L&TR 45). The provision of these services is usually included in the fee paid for the accommodation. It is also common for the owner to impose further restrictions on the lodger which interfere with the lodger's occupancy of the room. For example, the lodger may be permitted guests only between certain hours, or may not be permitted guests without the prior permission of the owner.

2.30 If attendances and services are provided they indicate that the owner retains a degree of control over the premises which is incompatible with exclusive possession, because they require unrestricted access in order to provide the services which are part of the contract (*Crancour v Da Silvaesa* (1986) 18 HLR 265, CA). Whether the rights retained by the owner interfere with the occupancy of the room to such an extent that it cannot be said that the occupier has exclusive possession will often be a complicated question of fact. Each case must be looked at in the light of its own individual peculiarities (see for example *Uratemp Ventures v Collins* [2000] 1 EGLR 156).

Old people's homes and hostels

2.31 The provision of attendances and services is not confined to the traditional lodger. In *Abbeyfield (Harpenden) Society Ltd v Woods* [1968] 1 WLR 374, the occupier of a room in an old people's home was held to be a licensee despite the fact that he had exclusive possession of his room. The elderly person was provided with two meals per day and there was a resident housekeeper. Lord Denning decided he was a licensee (despite the fact that the word 'rent' was used to describe his weekly payments) on the basis that the whole agreement was 'personal in nature', not on the grounds that the occupier did not have exclusive possession. Nevertheless, Lord Templeman approved of this case in *Street v Mountford* by saying simply that the court came to the conclusion that the occupier was a lodger. He did not explain the reasoning that led him to this conclusion. Following the decision in *Westminster City Council v Clarke* (1992) 24 HLR 360, HL (see 2.32), it is probable that if this case were to be decided today it would not be the personal nature of the relationship that was decisive; more likely it would be held that the owner of the old people's home in fact retained a degree of control over the premises such that the occupier could not be said to have exclusive possession.

In *Westminster City Council v Clarke* a man who was vulnerable and homeless was given **2.32** a room in a hostel for single men. This particular hostel numbered among its occupants men with personality disorders and physical disabilities. There was a resident warden and also a team of social workers who provided support for the occupiers, the hope being that after a period of rehabilitation at the hostel each occupier would be able to move on to permanent accommodation where they would be able to look after themselves. Meals were not provided by the hostel and all the rooms had basic facilities for cooking. When the council tried to regain possession of Mr Clarke's room he claimed to have exclusive possession and therefore to be protected under the Housing Act 1985. Lord Templeman stated (at 368) that '[f]rom the point of view of the council the grant of exclusive possession would be inconsistent with the purposes for which the council provided the accommodation...'. In providing accommodation for vulnerable homeless people the council needed to retain possession of every room so that it could provide the occupiers with supervision and assistance. For example, it needed to be able to move an occupier to a different room if he or she was causing a nuisance to his or her neighbours, or if the room became uninhabitable. The provisions in the licence agreement were not inserted to enable the council to avoid the creation of a statutory tenancy, but to enable it to discharge its responsibilities to the vulnerable people housed in the hostel.

Keys

Whether or not an owner grants exclusive possession is looked at by the courts in a broad **2.33** way, taking into account not merely the nature of the accommodation provided but also the surrounding circumstances. A particular example of this is the question of the retention of a key by the owner. It has been argued by many owners in various cases that the retention of a key denies the occupier exclusive possession, but the courts have refused to take such a simple view. Exclusive possession of premises is not to be equated with exclusive possession of the keys to those premises. The retention of a key has no magic in itself; what has to be considered is the underlying reason for the retention of the key:

> A landlord may well need a key, in order that he may be able to enter quickly in the event of an emergency, fire, burst pipes or whatever. He may need a key to enable him or those authorised by him to read meters or to do repairs which are his responsibility. (*Aslan v Murphy (Nos 1 and 2), Duke v Wynne* [1989] 3 All ER 130 at 135)

In *Family Housing Association v Jones* (1990) 22 HLR 45, the Housing Association retained **2.34** a key in order to inspect the premises and to provide the occupier with help and advice. This was held not to interfere with her exclusive possession of the property. Of course if the key was retained in order for the owner to fulfil an obligation to provide services of some sort, such as to clean the room or to change the sheets, it might well be inferred that the occupier was a licensee and not a tenant.

Sham agreements

2.35 Let us go back to the example of Jane and Harry (see 2.03). Harry knows enough about the law to realise that merely changing labels will not change a tenancy into a licence. He knows that exclusive possession is the decisive factor and so he tries to avoid granting exclusive possession to Jane by inserting the following two clauses into their agreement:

(1) The licensor licences the licensee to use (but not exclusively) the room on each day between the hours of midnight and 10.30 am and between noon and midnight, but at no other times.

(2) The licensor shall at all times have the right to decide the use and occupancy of the room and each part of the room together with the positioning of the furniture in the room.

2.36 Jane reluctantly signs the agreement and moves in. She is never asked to vacate the room or to share the room. Harry enters the room only once and knocks on the door before entering. The reason he gives is that he needs to inspect the paintwork on the window frames. Can Harry rely on these clauses to claim that Jane is a licensee? Given that Harry has never acted upon those clauses, can it be said that he never had the intention to do so? In other words, are the clauses part of the true bargain between the parties, or pretences? (See *Aslan v Murphy per* Lord Donaldson of Lymington at 133.) The word 'sham' is generally used to describe clauses such as these and the agreements that contain them.

2.37 The classic definition of a sham comes from *Snook v London & West Riding Investments Ltd* [1967] 1 All ER 518. In discussing the meaning in law of the word 'sham', Diplock LJ said (at 528):

> ... if it has any meaning in law, it means acts done or documents executed by the parties to the 'sham' which are intended by them to give to third parties or to the court the appearance of creating between the parties legal rights and obligations different from the actual legal rights and obligations (if any) which the parties intend to create.

2.38 In determining whether the actual legal rights are different from the rights set out in the document the courts must take 'due account of how the parties have acted in performance of their apparent bargain' (*Aslan v Murphy* at 133). The starting point, however, will be the document itself. In *Crancour v Da Silvaesa and another* and *Same v Merola and another* [1986] 1 EGLR 81, Purchas LJ (at 88F) set out the correct approach as follows:

> ... to construe the document as a whole in order to determine the nature and quality of the occupancy under the terms of the agreement reached between the parties. To this end the use of the words such as licence or lease in the agreement is not definitive, nor indeed is the *de facto* intention of either or both of the parties. Subject to the agreement on its face appearing to be a sham, the effect in law of the agreement must depend upon its construction in accordance with the normal rules in the context of its factual matrix and genesis.

2.39 It is important to note that sham clauses cannot be detected simply by looking at what happened after the grant. It is a combination of looking at the clause itself to see whether it makes sense in the context of a grant of residential accommodation, and looking at the surrounding circumstances for supporting evidence. Subsequent conduct is not relevant as an aid to construction of the document, but it is relevant in determining whether the document gives effect to the true intention of the parties (see *Antoniades v Villiers and another* [1988] 3 WLR 1205).

2.40 In *Aslan v Murphy* a clause in the agreement drafted in similar terms to clause (1) in our example was held to be totally unrealistic and a pretence and therefore was not part of the true bargain between the parties. It was held that Mr Murphy had been granted exclusive possession and was a tenant.

The deductive process here is as follows: **2.41**

(a) Prima facie does the clause make sense in the context of a grant of residential accommodation (eg forbidding the occupation of a room for 90 minutes per day)?

(b) If not, what supporting evidence is there for asserting that the clause makes no sense (eg does the landlord in fact act upon the clause)? If, however, two parties with equal bargaining power, each having the benefit of legal advice, enter into an agreement which is expressly designed to exclude exclusive possession, it will be extremely difficult for either of the parties to argue that this is not the true effect of the agreement (*Clear Channel UK v Manchester City Council* [2005] EWCA Civ 1034, [2006] 1 EGLR 27).

Multiple occupation

We have seen that without exclusive possession there can be no tenancy. The occupier of   **2.42**
a flat with exclusive possession has the right to exclude all others from that flat, including the landlord. However, if an occupier shares that flat with one or more people, the sharers too have a right to be there. In what sense then can an occupier who shares a flat with other people be said to have exclusive possession?

Harry, our notional landlord, has inherited a large flat consisting of four bedrooms, a   **2.43**
sitting-room, a kitchen, and a bathroom. He does not want to live there himself and decides to rent it out. The flat would be ideal for four people to share. There are various different ways in which he can permit a group of people to live in his property.

First we shall consider the ways that Harry could actually grant exclusive possession to   **2.44**
the occupiers.

Example 1: Tenancy of an individual room Harry numbers the bedrooms one to four and   **2.45**
then advertises in the local paper, 'rooms to rent in shared house'. Over the next few weeks four applicants come to view the house. Harry grants each of them a tenancy of an individual room together with the right to share the common areas of the flat. Each occupier therefore has exclusive possession of the room he or she has been allocated.

Such an arrangement has certain advantages. Each tenant has the right to exclude the other   **2.46**
sharers from his or her room. Each tenant is also only individually liable for the rent for that room, so if one or more of the other sharers fail to pay their rent Harry can take action only against the defaulting tenant(s). There is however the disadvantage that the tenant of one room has no control over the occupancy of the other rooms. If one sharer moves out, Harry can move someone else into the vacant room without consultation. Sharers cannot change rooms without consulting Harry and entering into a new agreement.

From Harry's point of view the granting of individual tenancies of each room is somewhat   **2.47**
labour intensive. He has to deal with each occupier separately, to enter into four separate agreements, and collect rent from four different people. If one of them moves out he will obtain no rent for that room until he has found a new tenant. On the other hand he is able to specify which occupier should have which room and is able to take action against one occupier without affecting the other sharers.

Example 2: Joint tenancy A less complex arrangement would be for Harry to grant a single   **2.48**
tenancy to a group of people. Such a tenancy is known as a joint tenancy. There would be only one agreement signed by all the tenants and only one rent which would be for the

whole property. The principle behind a joint tenancy is that although the rights granted by the landlord are in fact granted to a group of people, this group is treated by the law as if it was a single person. Therefore for a joint tenancy to exist it is necessary that the individuals who make up the group must be, at least as far as the law is concerned, intimately connected. In other words, the four unities must be satisfied. The four unities are:

(a) time—the tenancy must start at the same time for each occupant;

(b) title—the tenancy must be created by one act or document;

(c) interest—the interests of each sharer must be of the same nature, duration, and extent;

(d) possession—each sharer must be equally entitled to possession of the whole.

2.49   In many ways a joint tenancy is a very sensible way for an owner to rent out property to a group of people; it has advantages for both the landlord and the tenant. Certainly it has the benefit of simplicity. The group of sharers is treated as one entity and so it is necessary only to draw up one agreement specifying one rent for the whole property. The landlord need not be concerned with deciding who is to occupy which room. The tenants all hold the whole of the property equally and can organize their living arrangements between themselves. Of course it has the disadvantage that if the landlord objects to one of the occupiers there is no means of terminating just that occupier's tenancy; there is only one tenancy so either the landlord terminates the tenancy for all of the occupiers or not at all. However, the landlord's lack of recourse against one of the occupiers is amply compensated for by the fact that each occupier is jointly and severally liable for the obligations contained in the tenancy. If one occupier breaches the terms of the agreement the landlord's remedy is against all of them. This is of particular significance when it comes to the payment of rent. If a flat is let to four occupiers at a rent of £400 per month, it is probable that between themselves each of the occupiers will arrange to contribute £100 per month. If one of them leaves, the remaining three are still liable to the landlord for £400 and will have to make up the rest of the rent themselves. On the other hand, provided the remaining tenants continue to pay the whole rent the landlord cannot terminate their tenancy or bring in a new occupier.

2.50   Of course one possible disadvantage to Harry of both of the above arrangements is that in each example all of the occupiers are tenants and will therefore be eligible for statutory protection. As we have seen, Harry cannot avoid the consequences of statutory protection by granting licences in respect of the individual rooms if the reality of the situation is that he has granted his occupiers exclusive possession of a specified room for a term at a rent. What, however, would be the situation if Harry granted individual occupiers separate licences to occupy his flat but did not specify which rooms they were to occupy? It would not be possible for any one of the occupiers to argue that he or she had exclusive possession of any part of the flat. Exclusive possession, as we have seen, is an essential feature of a tenancy. The only option open to the sharers would be to argue that together they held exclusive possession of the whole flat, ie that they had a joint tenancy. We shall now look at this situation in more detail.

2.51   **Example 3: Licence to occupy with no specified share** Harry advertises his flat in the paper as being suitable for four sharers. Andrew, Belinda, Charles, and Denise each read the advert and come and view the property separately. Andrew arrives first. Harry shows him the flat and explains that he is intending to move in four people. Andrew likes the flat. Harry gives him an agreement to sign. The agreement is granted as a licence and contains the following clauses:

(1) The licensor grants to the licensee the right to use in common with others who have or may from time to time be granted the like right the flat known as…

(2) The licensee agrees with the licensor to share the use of the said flat peaceably with and not to impede the use of the said flat by such other persons [not exceeding three in number at any one time] to whom the licensor has granted or shall from time to time grant licence to use the said flat in common with the licensee...

(3) The licensee agrees to pay the licensor the sum of £100 per month for the right to share in the use of the said flat.

Andrew signs the agreement and moves into the largest bedroom. It cannot be said that **2.52** Andrew has exclusive possession because Harry has reserved the right to move in other occupiers. A week later Belinda views the flat, she likes it, signs an agreement identical to the one signed by Andrew, and moves into the second largest bedroom. A couple of months later Charles and Denise also sign the same agreement and move in. Six months later Andrew moves out. Belinda, as the most senior resident, moves into his old room, and both Charles and Denise shift up to more desirable rooms leaving the smallest one vacant. Harry re-advertises and after a week Edward moves in having signed an agreement the same as the others, except that because of inflation Harry has put the rent up to £110 per month.

A year later Harry decides to sell the flat and gives notice to all the occupiers. They refuse **2.53** to move out, claiming that they are joint tenants and therefore eligible for statutory protection.

As we have seen, in determining the relationship between the parties the courts will look **2.54** to the 'substance and reality of the transaction entered into by the parties' (*AG Securities v Vaughan* [1988] 3 WLR 1205 *per* Lord Ackner at 1219). In our example it is probable that the agreements will be seen to be genuine. In determining whether a clause is a pretence the court will consider the surrounding circumstances. In *Antoniades v Villiers and another* [1988] 3 WLR 1205, Lord Templeman stated (at 1213) that surrounding circumstances will include, 'any relationship between the prospective occupiers, the course of negotiations and the nature and extent of the accommodation and the intended and actual mode of occupation of the accommodation'. The surrounding circumstances here are unlikely to be able to support a claim that the agreement was a pretence: the four occupiers did not know each other before they moved into the flat; the negotiations did not suggest that there was any intention to grant a joint tenancy and the situation was clear to each occupier when he or she moved in; the flat is large and suitable for four sharers, and Harry has in fact subsequently exercised his right to move in a new occupier. In fact it is probable that the courts may well see the arrangement as 'a sensible one which suited both the owner of the flat and a shifting population of occupiers' (*Stribling v Wickham and others* [1989] 2 EGLR 35).

The question then arises whether, under the agreement as it stands, all or any of the occu- **2.55** piers can be said to have exclusive possession. Certainly so long as at least one room remains vacant none of the occupiers can be said to have exclusive possession because Harry has reserved the right to move in a new licensee. If all four rooms are occupied, can it be said that between them the four occupants collectively have exclusive possession? In *AG Securities v Vaughan* the House of Lords answered this question in the negative: 'The landlord is not excluded because he continues to enjoy the premises through his invitees, even though he may have precluded himself by contract with each from withdrawing the invitation' (*per* Lord Oliver of Aylmerton at 1224). If, for example, one of the occupiers died, the other three occupiers would not be able to claim exclusive joint possession of the whole flat and prevent Harry moving in a new occupier. On the other hand, Harry could not claim that the remaining tenants should make up the missing share of the rent as would be the case if they occupied under a joint tenancy.

2.56 The House of Lords also pointed out various other reasons why, when one looked at the reality of the arrangement, it could not be a joint tenancy. Under a joint tenancy the individual occupants must be connected by more than merely just living in the same flat at the same time; the four unities must be satisfied. In our example there was no unity of title, the individual licences being created by separate documents; no unity of time, the licences started at different times; no unity of interest, each had an individual liability to Harry for the rent, and all the rents were not for the same amount. It is possible, however, that there was unity of possession.

2.57 **Example 4: Licence to occupy with no specified share granted to a couple** Harry is also the owner of a small, one-bedroom flat. He wants to rent it out, but again he wants to be sure that he can obtain vacant possession relatively quickly if he needs to sell the property. He advertises the flat in the local paper as suitable for two sharers. Peter and Sue, a young couple, see the advert and arrange to view the flat. They come together and Harry, who has not finished furnishing the flat, asks them if they would like two singles or a double bed. They tell him they would like a double bed and that they would like to take the flat. They ask him how much the rent will be and he tells them it will be £200 per month payable in advance. Both Peter and Sue separately sign identical agreements each containing the clauses:

(1) Use of the rooms is to be in common with the licensor and such other licensees or invitees as the licensor may permit from time to time to use the said rooms.

(2) The licensee shall use his best endeavours amicably and peaceably to share the use of the rooms with the licensor and with such other licensees or invitees whom the licensor shall from time to time permit to use the rooms and shall not interfere with or otherwise obstruct such shared occupation in any way whatsoever.

(3) The licensee agrees to pay the owner the sum of £100 per month for the right to share in the use of the said flat.

2.58 Peter and Sue then move into the flat. Throughout the currency of their occupation Harry has never sought either to use the rooms himself or to authorize any other person to use the rooms. He decides that he wants to sell the flat and gives Peter and Sue notice. They refuse to leave saying that they are joint tenants and therefore have statutory protection.

2.59 Can the clauses Harry has inserted into the agreement serve to deprive Peter and Sue of exclusive possession? As we saw in the previous example, the court will reject any clause it considers to be a pretence by considering whether the clause represented the true bargain between the parties. In determining whether a clause is a pretence the court will consider the surrounding circumstances. In our present example the surrounding circumstances indicate that at least clauses (1) and (2) may be sham. Sue and Peter were a couple when they came to view the flat, and it was clear that they intended to occupy the flat as a couple since they asked Harry to provide a double bed. They were told by Harry that the rent would be £200 even though the agreements stated that it was to be £100 each. The accommodation itself is small and not suitable for strangers to share. Harry never tried to move in another occupier or to use the flat himself. In *Antoniades v Villiers* the House of Lords decided, on facts virtually identical to our example, that '[i]t was quite implausible that the landlord had ever seriously intended either to move in himself or to authorize a stranger to share the property'.

2.60 Nevertheless, one difficulty still remains. Peter and Sue together have exclusive possession of the flat. If exclusive possession for a term at a rent is granted to a single occupier that occupier has a tenancy. For Peter and Sue to have a joint tenancy we saw above that the four unities must be satisfied. What, then, is their status given that they have both signed separate agreements which hold them individually liable for half of the rent? On the face of it, it seems that there is no unity of interest, in which case they cannot have a joint tenancy. What would happen if Peter decided to leave the flat? Would Sue become liable to Harry for the full £200 per month, or would she be able to continue paying £100 per month?

This is a difficult question and present authority seems to suggest that without a joint **2.61** liability to pay the whole of the rent there cannot be a joint tenancy. Consequently it may be the case that a couple can share a flat together under two agreements which entitle them to joint exclusive possession of the flat at a rent for a term but, because each agreement states that each occupier is to pay half the rent, they will not be joint tenants and therefore will not be eligible for statutory protection. It is not possible to argue that they are each individual tenants because they do not individually have exclusive possession of the flat; they hold exclusive possession jointly but not as against each other.

In *Antoniades v Villiers* Lord Templeman avoided this consequence by saying that the two **2.62** agreements signed were interdependent: 'The grant of a tenancy to two persons jointly cannot be concealed accidentally or by design, by the creation of two documents in the form of licences' (at 1212). He went on to give the following example:

> If the owner of a one-bedroom flat granted a licence to a husband to occupy the flat provided he shared the flat with his wife and nobody else and granted a similar licence to the wife provided she shared the flat with the husband and nobody else, the court would be bound to consider the effect of both documents together. If the licence to the husband required him to pay a licence fee of £50 per month and the licence to the wife required her to pay a further licence fee of £50 per month, the two documents read together in the light of the property to be occupied and the obvious intended mode of occupation would confer exclusive occupation on the husband and wife jointly and a tenancy at the rent of £100.

And further: **2.63**

> A tenancy remains a tenancy even though the landlord may require each of two joint tenants to agree expressly to pay one half of the rent. (at 1214)

Therefore, if one moves out, the other is liable for the full rent. **2.64**

In subsequent cases, however, the courts have been less willing to construe two separate **2.65** documents as constituting one agreement. On two occasions the Court of Appeal has taken a strict line and concluded that 'by no process of "legal alchemy" could the separate agreements be fitted into the mould of a joint tenancy' (*Stribling v Wickham*).

In *Mikeover v Brady* (1989) 21 HLR 313, [1989] 3 All ER 618, CA a couple occupied **2.66** a two-room flat. The court was satisfied that 'the layout of the flat was such that it was clearly only suitable for occupation by persons who were personally acceptable to each other'. Both occupiers signed identical agreements, each of which contained the clauses: (1) 'The owner grants to the licensee the right to use in common with others who have been granted the like right the rooms on the second floor...'; and (1.4) 'The licensee agrees... not to impede the use of the said rooms... by such other persons not exceeding one in number to whom the Owner shall grant licence'. In this case, however, the Court of Appeal did not hold either of these clauses to be a sham. The clauses were interpreted to mean merely that each sharer had acquired the right to share the flat with the other sharer and the obligation not to interfere with the other sharer's use of the flat. The court did not think that either of the clauses gave the owner the right to move another occupier into the flat during the currency of the agreements. The agreements represented the true nature of the bargain between the parties.

2.67　The court was at least partially persuaded towards this conclusion by the fact that the agreements did not contain a clause permitting either of the licensees to terminate their agreement within the currency of the six-month term. If either of the occupiers had left before the expiry of the term the owner would still have been able to hold that occupier responsible for his or her share of the payment, in which case the owner would have no need to move in a replacement occupier because he would not be out of pocket. The court thought that the arrangement had business efficacy. It also thought that the agreements should be construed against the owner, and if he had intended to reserve the right to move in an alternative occupier he should have done so in much clearer terms. Neither clause was a pretence. Neither clause served to deprive the occupiers of exclusive possession. The effect of the agreements was to confer on each occupier a right of joint exclusive occupation of the property.

2.68　Nevertheless, the court held that there could not be a joint tenancy because there was no unity of interest:

> Interest in this context must, in our judgment, include the bundle of rights and obligations representing that interest... the two agreements instead of imposing a joint liability on him [Mr Brady] and Miss Guile to pay a deposit of £80 and monthly payments of £173.32, on their face, imposed on each of them individual and separate obligations to pay only a deposit of £40 and monthly payments of only £86.66.
>
> Counsel for the occupiers argued that in so far as the two agreements purported to make both occupiers individually liable for £86.66 they were shams. The true intention of the parties was that they should be jointly liable for the full rent of £173.32. The court, stating that the onus was on the occupiers to prove a sham, rejected this argument finding no evidence to support it.

2.69　To return to our example, two comments can be made in the light of the decision in *Mikeover v Brady*:

(a)　Exclusive possession will not be destroyed by a clause entitling an owner to move in another occupier. If it is clear from the surrounding circumstances that the flat is not suitable, such a clause would not reflect the true nature of the bargain.

(b)　Even if the owner does grant exclusive possession jointly to the two occupiers, they still will not have a joint tenancy if the agreement holds them separately liable for rent, unless they can show that this part of the agreement is a sham.

3

CREATING A TENANCY

A INTRODUCTION

In Chapter 1 we saw that a tenancy is fundamentally a relationship between people. It is **3.01** a particular sort of relationship; a relationship where one party, the landlord, has granted to the other party, the tenant, exclusive possession of identifiable premises for a definite period while retaining a reversion. How then are two people to get into this particular type of relationship? On a basic level, at least, the answer to this question is simple: the parties enter into the relationship of landlord and tenant by making an agreement. Consider the following three situations; in each of them the parties involved are seeking to make an agreement with regard to the use of land:

Example 1 Tim is about to start a college course in London and needs somewhere to live. **3.02** He contacts his old school friend James, who moved to London a few years ago, to see if he can help him. James tells Tim that he has a sofa-bed in the sitting room. 'You can stay here until you find a place of your own', James says. 'Just pay me some money towards the bills when your grant comes through.' The following weekend Tim moves in with James.

Example 2 Paul's friend John lives at Flat B, 32 Cranley Gardens. John's landlady, Christine, **3.03** who owns the whole house, lives in the upper maisonette (Flat C). John tells Paul that the basement (Flat A) is currently vacant. John introduces Paul to Christine who shows him the basement flat. Paul likes it and he and Christine go out for a drink. Christine tells him the rent is £600 per month, he can move in on Saturday, and he can have the flat for a year. Paul thinks that this is reasonable and accepts, they shake on it, and Paul buys Christine a drink to celebrate. He moves in the following Saturday and gives Christine one month's rent in advance.

Example 3 Sandra has recently received a substantial raise in salary. She decides that it **3.04** is time to consider buying her own home. First she goes to a building society. The building society agrees to give her a mortgage of up to £270,000. She then visits various estate agents in her area. After several months of searching she finds a flat she likes. The flat has recently been renovated by Plusstyle Developments Ltd who own the freehold of the whole building. Plusstyle wish to sell all of the flats in the building on 99-year leases. The flat

Sandra is interested in is advertised at an asking price of £270,000. She puts in an offer of £260,000, which Plusstyle reject. She thinks about it for a few more days and then raises the offer to £265,000. Plusstyle accept this second offer. Sandra puts the purchase in the hands of a local solicitor who contacts Plusstyle and makes preliminary enquiries about the lease and the building; the solicitor also puts in hand a search of the local land charges register. Sandra employs a surveyor to carry out a structural survey of the flat and building. The building society also instructs a surveyor to carry out a valuation. The results of the survey, valuation, and searches are all satisfactory and four weeks after making the original offer Sandra exchanges contracts with Plusstyle. Two weeks after exchange of contracts the purchase is completed and Sandra moves in on the same day.

Example 1: an informal arrangement

3.05 Let us look first at the situation between Tim and James. In their conversation the two of them have certainly come to an agreement of sorts, but the arrangement they have made between them is very informal. Virtually nothing has been established beyond the fact that Tim has James's permission to stay. James has not specified any rent, he has not specified any definite period, nor is it clear that Tim will have exclusive occupation of any part of James's flat. The arrangement they have agreed falls far short of exhibiting all the essential characteristics of a tenancy (see Chapter 1). At the very most such an arrangement might amount to a contractual licence, but in Tim and James's case their conversation is unlikely to be seen as exhibiting an intention to create binding legal relations and, furthermore, in the absence of any definite arrangement for payment there is no valuable consideration for such a contract. This agreement has created nothing more than a bare licence (see 1.33).

Example 2: an informal agreement

3.06 At first sight the arrangement between Christine and Paul does not seem that dissimilar from that reached between Tim and James. In both cases the agreement was reached in a relatively informal manner, and in neither case has anything been put in writing. However, certain matters have been clarified between Christine and Paul, albeit orally. The rent has been specified, as has the term, and although no precise definition has been agreed Christine has shown Paul round the flat and indicated the premises available. In fact the agreement they have reached exhibits all the essential characteristics of a tenancy. As we shall see, the fact that the agreement is not contained in a written document is no bar to it amounting to a tenancy. Christine and Paul have created a fixed-term tenancy for one year.

Example 3: a formal agreement

3.07 The procedure by which Sandra and Plusstyle have created a tenancy is as long and complex as Christine and Paul's agreement is brief. Both sides have employed solicitors, many letters have been exchanged, negotiations entered into and concluded, building societies and surveyors have been involved. The final result of these dealings is a document of about 40 pages containing detailed provisions which has been signed and witnessed by both sides. Throughout the process detailed formalities have been observed. The reason for Plusstyle and Sandra's caution is obvious. The agreement that they are entering into involves the handing over of an estate in land for 99 years and the payment of a large sum of money. Neither side wants to make a mistake or find that they have agreed to be bound by an obligation that they are going to find difficult or expensive to keep for the next 99 years. The result of the process is that Sandra and Plusstyle have created a 99-year fixed-term lease.

It is important to remember that where a tenancy has been created it will be subject to the **3.08** provisions of one or more of the statutory codes. The applicable code will imply certain terms into the agreement and will provide the framework within which the landlord can regain possession of the property. The application of these codes is considered in Part II of this book.

B CREATING A TENANCY—A TWO-STAGE PROCESS

An agreement for a lease

One of the first things to notice about the procedure followed by Sandra and Plusstyle in **3.09** Example 3 is that the lease has been created by a two-stage process. Following their initial negotiations the parties first entered into a contract to grant the lease (exchange of contracts) before the lease was actually granted (completion). Both the contract to grant a lease and the lease itself are contracts. A contract to grant a lease (or an agreement for a lease) does not create the lease; it is instead an agreement between the parties that at a point in the future one party will grant the lease and the other party will take it.

It should be noted here that the term 'lease' is used to refer both to the written document **3.10** that creates the lease and to the interest in land itself. Likewise 'tenancy agreement' refers to the document that creates the interest in land, while a 'tenancy' normally means the interest itself. A tenancy and a lease mean exactly the same thing, but in practice the word 'tenancy' is usually used to refer to periodic and shorter-term interests. An 'agreement for a tenancy' should not be confused with a 'tenancy agreement'. An 'agreement for a tenancy' is the same as an agreement or a contract for a lease; it does not create the tenancy but is an agreement to create a tenancy at a point in the future.

There is in fact no legal requirement that the parties wishing to create a tenancy should first **3.11** enter into a contract to grant a tenancy. In Christine and Paul's case (Example 2), where the term is short and the amount of money involved relatively small, both parties proceeded straight to the grant of the tenancy. However, if the grant is to be of a lengthy term of a valuable estate in land, where the tenancy itself may involve a considerable number of complicated terms, it is normal to enter into a contract to grant the lease first. The reason for this is that the grant of a lengthy term takes time and money. Neither party wants to find that, at a late stage in the process, the other side has decided to pull out. By entering into a contract for a lease at an earlier stage of the process the dealings between the parties are put onto a contractual basis. If one party reneges on his or her obligations the other party will have a contractual remedy.

This does not mean that once an agreement for a lease has been entered into the grant **3.12** of the lease is an inevitable consequence. In some cases, having entered into a contract to grant a lease, the parties may never proceed to the actual grant. This may be because the situation changes such that the parties no longer wish to enter into the tenancy, or it may be a mistake, an oversight or even a deliberate attempt to avoid paying stamp duty which becomes due only on the actual grant of the lease. In some cases one party may even enter into occupation of the premises and start paying rent as if the agreement for a lease was the lease itself. We shall be considering the legal consequences of this situation in more detail later in this chapter. First, however, we shall consider the formalities that must be observed in order successfully to grant a tenancy.

Formalities for a valid tenancy

3.13 In this section we shall be considering the formalities that must be fulfilled to create a valid tenancy. It should be noted at the outset that, beyond these formalities, the law does not prescribe any particular form for a tenancy agreement. A tenancy agreement can take a wide variety of forms: it can be oral; it may be in writing drafted by a solicitor or taken from a wide range of available precedents; or it may be a ready-printed form bought from a legal stationers.

3.14 Whatever form the tenancy agreement takes, it will be a document of crucial importance if any dispute arises with regard to the tenancy. The task of the housing adviser, and of the court if the problem cannot be settled, will be to consider the facts of the case in the light of the tenancy agreement. The adviser, or court, will generally be trying to ascertain whether one party is acting within the agreement. If the original agreement was oral it will not always be easy to ascertain the exact content of that agreement and the court's task will be made harder. This is one reason why the law demands that the majority of tenancy agreements must be made not only in writing but by deed (see 3.16). As with any dispute over a contract, it is important to know the terms of that contract to reach a resolution.

3.15 A further reason for the requirement of formalities is that a tenancy is an estate in land. The tenancy may be created by a contract, but once created it possesses qualities that run beyond the purely contractual. In particular an estate in land is binding on all persons, whether or not they were parties to the contract that created it. The formalities required to create a tenancy are therefore often greater than those required to create a binding contract.

Creation by deed

3.16 The fundamental rule is that a legal estate must be created by deed. The LPA 1925, s 52(1) states:

> All conveyances of land or of any interest therein are void for the purpose of conveying or creating a legal estate unless made by deed.

3.17 There is nothing mysterious about a deed; it is simply a document that has been created in accordance with particular formalities in order to ensure that its validity can be proved if necessary. The traditional rules were that a deed had to be 'signed, sealed and delivered', the seal originally being a device that enabled the authenticity of the document to be established in an age when many people could not read or write. In more recent years the actual seal became more symbolic than functional and was replaced by a representative red sticker; even a printed circle containing the letters 'LS' (standing for '*locus sigilli*') would be sufficient (*First National Securities v Jones* [1978] Ch 109). Nowadays a person's signature is regarded as sufficient authentication and the requirement of a seal was dispensed with altogether by s 1 of the Law of Property (Miscellaneous Provisions) Act 1989, which came into force on 31 July 1990. Section 1 of this Act provides:

> (2) An instrument shall not be a deed unless—
>   (a) it makes it clear on its face that it is intended to be a deed by the person making it or, as the case may be, by the parties to it (whether describing itself as a deed or expressing itself to be executed or signed as a deed or otherwise); and
>   (b) it is validly executed as a deed by that person or, as the case may be, one or more of those parties.
> (3) An instrument is validly executed as a deed by an individual if, and only if—
>   (a) it is signed—
>   (i)   by him in the presence of a witness who attests the signature; or

(ii) at his direction and in his presence and the presence of two witnesses who each attest the signature; and

(b) it is delivered as a deed by him or a person authorised to do so on his behalf.

Provided that Sandra and Plusstyle complied with these formalities they will have created a legal estate. If a lease that should be made by deed is created orally it will take effect as a tenancy at will (see 3.30) (LPA 1925, s 54(1)). **3.18**

Exceptions to the rule

Despite the fundamental rule that a lease should be created by deed, the majority of rented accommodation (ie accommodation held on a short tenancy rather than on a long lease) in England and Wales is held under tenancies that are not created by deed. Often the tenancy is created using a mass-produced form and frequently there is no written document at all, just an oral agreement between the parties. Nevertheless, as in Paul and Christine's case (Example 2), such relatively informal agreements can create a legal lease. **3.19**

The LPA 1925 contains two important exceptions to the rule that a lease must be created by deed. The first is in respect of short leases and the second applies to leases created by social landlords. **3.20**

Short leases Section 54(2) provides that: **3.21**

(2) Nothing in the foregoing provisions of this Part of this Act shall affect the creation by parol of leases taking effect in possession for a term not exceeding three years (whether or not the lessee is given power to extend the term) at the best rent which can be reasonably obtained without taking a fine.

Thus certain short leases can be created without formalities provided they satisfy the following conditions: **3.22**

(a) The lease must be for a fixed term of less than three years or a periodic tenancy. Periodic tenancies fall within this class regardless of the fact that the final duration of the term may exceed three years. It is the initial period of the term that matters in determining whether a tenancy is for a term of less than three years. A two-year fixed tenancy with an option to extend the term to four years will fall within s 54(2); a four-year fixed term with an option to terminate the tenancy after two years will not (see *Kushner v Law Society* [1952] 1 KB 264, [1952] 1 All ER 404; the nature of an option is considered at 6.113 to 6.123).

(b) The lease must be at a full market rent (*Fitzkriston LLP v Panayi* [2008] EWCA Civ 283, [2008] L&TR 26) without taking a fine. A fine is a lump sum payable at the beginning of the lease resulting in reduced rental payments.

(c) The lease must begin at the date of the grant. A lease granted to take effect at a date in the future (a reversionary lease) will not fall within the section (*Long v Tower Hamlets LBC* [1996] 2 All ER 683). This is what the section means by requiring the tenancy to take effect 'in possession'. Possession does not mean that the tenant must actually move into the premises for, as we saw in Chapter 1, under the LPA 1925, s 205(1)(xix), 'possession' includes the receipt of rent and profits (see 1.04).

Thus Paul and Christine's oral agreement in Example 2 will be sufficient under s 54(2) to create a legal estate in land. **3.23**

Leases granted by registered providers of social housing in England Section 52(2)(d) (inserted by the Localism Act 2011, s 156) provides that the requirement that leases be created by deed does not apply to flexible tenancies (see 17.40) or assured tenancies of dwelling houses in England that are granted by private registered providers of social housing (see **3.24**

Chapter 21) and are not long tenancies (tenancies for a term of over 21 years) or shared ownership leases. This provision was enacted to simplify the procedure for social landlords who wish to take advantage of their ability under the Localism Act 2011 to grant fixed-term flexible tenancies.

Registration of a lease

3.25 Since the Land Registration Act 2002 came into force on 13 October 2003, all leases granted for a term of more than seven years must be registered. This rule will also apply where the remainder of a lease is transferred if the unexpired term exceeds seven years. A lease of any length must also be registered if it is granted more than three months in advance of the date on which the lessee is to take possession. The Localism Act 2011 has, again, simplified the procedure for registered providers of social housing in England by amending the 2002 Act to provide that the transfer or grant of a leasehold interest under a relevant social housing tenancy is not required to be registered (Land Registration Act 2002, s 4(5A)). Relevant social housing tenancies are flexible tenancies or assured tenancies of dwelling houses in England that are granted by private registered providers of social housing and are not long tenancies or shared ownership leases.

Implied grant

3.26 In certain situations the law will imply the existence of a tenancy even where there has been no agreement between the parties. It should, however, always be borne in mind that a tenancy arises as the result of 'a consensual arrangement between two parties' (*Javid v Aqil* [1991] 1 All ER 243 *per* Nicholls LJ at 247h). A tenancy will therefore be implied only where it can be inferred from the parties' behaviour that they intended to create a tenancy.

3.27 Consider the situation where a person occupies a house with the consent of the owner and pays the owner £300 a month. From these basic facts it will be inferred that the parties intended to create a tenancy and a periodic tenancy will be implied. This is the interpretation 'which best fills the vacuum which the parties have left' (*Cardiothoracic Institute v Shrewdcrest Ltd* [1986] WLR 368 *per* Knox J at 378). The absence of a written agreement is no bar to the implication because, as we saw earlier, a periodic tenancy can be created without formalities. The type of periodic tenancy will be determined by reference to the way in which the rent is calculated; thus, in this case a monthly periodic tenancy will be implied.

3.28 In reality, however, few situations will be quite so straightforward. In that case, whether or not a tenancy should be implied will depend upon consideration of all the circumstances. For example, while Steve and Emma are negotiating the terms of a tenancy that they are intending to create, Emma might let Steve into occupation in return for monthly payments. In this case it cannot be said that because Steve has entered into possession and is paying rent a tenancy should be implied, for the actual grant of the tenancy is still under discussion (see *Javad v Aqil*; also *Brent LBC v O'Bryan* [1993] 02 EG 113).

3.29 Another common situation in which a tenancy may be implied is where, after a fixed-term tenancy has expired, the tenant remains in occupation and continues paying rent. Again, whether a periodic tenancy will be implied will depend upon the facts. If a tenancy is implied it will be assumed to be on the same terms as the previous tenancy so far as they are compatible with a periodic tenancy. It is also possible for a tenancy to be implied where a person takes possession of a premises under an agreement for a lease or under an invalid lease (we shall be considering this situation in more detail below).

Tenancy at will

In the previous section we saw how a person who occupies land with the permission of the owner and pays rent may acquire an implied tenancy. Such a tenancy will even be a legal tenancy, because a legal tenancy can be created without formalities. What, however, is the situation where a person occupies land with the permission of the owner but does not pay any rent? Clearly such a person is not a trespasser. The law classifies this situation as a tenancy at will. A tenancy at will has been described as the lowest estate known to the law (*per* Parke B in *Doe d Gray v Stanion* [1836] 1 M&W 700). A tenancy at will is not a legal estate. It does not fall within the definition of a term of years absolute as provided by the LPA 1925; it can be terminated at any time by the landlord withdrawing permission for the occupier to be on the premises and is therefore for an uncertain duration. This is in marked contrast to the situation under an implied tenancy, which has a defined duration and must be terminated by giving the appropriate notice (see Chapter 10). **3.30**

A tenancy at will can be created by express agreement (see *Manfield and Sons Ltd v Botchin* [1970] 2 QB 612, [1970] 3 All ER 143), but usually it will arise by implication. This will most commonly be where a tenant holds over at the end of a fixed-term tenancy, or where, before the actual grant of a tenancy or sale of a freehold, the owner allows the prospective tenant or purchaser into possession of the premises. If a tenant at will begins to pay rent the tenancy at will may be converted into an implied tenancy. This will be the case only provided that the intention to create a tenancy can be inferred between the parties; if the circumstances indicate that there is no intention to create a tenancy the tenant will remain a tenant at will. **3.31**

It should be noted that in some situations it may be difficult to distinguish a tenancy at will from a licence, and the courts may well decide to opt for the latter interpretation (see *Heslop v Burns* [1974] 1 WLR 1241, [1974] 3 All ER 406, CA and *Street v Mountford* [1985] AC 809 at 824). **3.32**

Tenancy at sufferance

A tenancy at sufferance is an even more precarious form of occupation than a tenancy at will. It will arise when a tenant holds over at the end of his or her tenancy without the permission of the landlord. In fact a tenancy at sufferance is not really a tenancy at all. A tenant at sufferance lies somewhere between a tenant at will and a trespasser (in that if the landlord gave permission for the occupier to be on the premises that occupier would be a tenant at will, while if the landlord actively objected the occupier would be a trespasser). However, like a tenancy at will, a tenancy at sufferance may be converted into an implied periodic tenancy if the landlord accepts rent. **3.33**

C THE POSITION OF AN OCCUPIER UNDER AN INVALID LEGAL LEASE

The consequences of the provisions discussed are best understood with the aid of an example. Say that John is offered a five-year contract for a job in the US. He decides to let his colleague Peter have his house for this period, and together they draft a written agreement to this effect which they both sign, but it is not witnessed. Under the agreement Peter is to pay John £12,000 per year for the five-year period. John leaves for the US and Peter enters into possession, duly paying the rent in instalments of £1,000 on the first of every month. **3.34**

The first thing to note about John and Peter's arrangement is that it was not made by deed and has therefore not fulfilled the requirements demanded by the LPA 1925, s 52(1). **3.35**

Furthermore the lease they have tried to create is for a period of five years and so it does not fall within the exception created by the LPA 1925, s 54(2). Thus the transaction is ineffective to convey to Peter a legal lease for a term of five years. However, Peter may have acquired an equitable interest in the property. The difference between an equitable and a legal interest is that, while a legal interest may be enforced as of right, an equitable interest can only be enforced at the discretion of the court. Let us then consider first Peter's position at law.

The position at law

3.36   As previously explained, Peter has no formally valid lease; nevertheless, he is in possession of the property, he has John's permission to be there, and he is paying regular rent. We saw earlier how a periodic tenancy can arise by implication and this is exactly what will happen here. The facts of Peter's possession of the property and of the regular payment and acceptance of rent would, in the absence of any evidence to the contrary, lead the court to imply a periodic tenancy. A periodic tenancy falls under the LPA 1925, s 54(2), and therefore the fact that Peter and John's agreement was not made by deed does not invalidate the implied periodic tenancy—it is a legal estate.

3.37   The term of the implied periodic tenancy will be determined with reference to the period by which the rent is calculated. The document Peter and John drew up, although invalid to create a five-year lease, would be sufficient to determine the terms of a periodic tenancy. The rent is expressed as an annual sum, so the implied tenancy would be a yearly periodic tenancy. If Peter and John had in fact reached no agreement about the payment of rent, or had failed to write an agreement, it would be inferred from the monthly payment of rent that a monthly tenancy had been created. The result of this is that although John and Peter tried to create a five-year fixed-term tenancy, they have in fact created a legal yearly periodic tenancy.

3.38   The consequences of this conclusion can be seen if after a year John decides not to return from the US and instead to sell his house to James. James wants to gain possession of the house; Peter, however, wishes to remain in occupation for the remaining four years of his original agreement with John. Unfortunately for Peter this agreement, being formally invalid, is not legally binding on James. However, the implied yearly tenancy, being a legal lease, is binding on James. Nevertheless, since it is a periodic tenancy James will be able to terminate it by giving Peter a half year's notice to quit the premises (see 10.35 to 10.53).

The intervention of equity

Contract to grant a lease

3.39   Understandably the courts are reluctant to override an agreement which had been voluntarily created between two adults simply because it fails to comply with the correct formalities. We mentioned earlier how the process of creating a lease is frequently a two-stage process: first, a contract for a lease is agreed and then, at a later date, the lease itself is granted. The LPA 1925, s 52(1) applies only to an actual conveyance of land and so the contract itself does not have to be made by deed. The courts therefore will regard the formally invalid lease as in fact being a valid contract to convey the legal estate at a later date when the technical error has been corrected. To understand the significance of this it is necessary to look at the remedies which might be available to Peter if John seeks to break this contract.

3.40   At common law Peter's remedy for John's breach of contract would be damages. However, the subject matter of the contract is land, and the established view of land is that it is unique and irreplaceable and therefore cannot be adequately compensated for in money terms. For breach of a contract to convey an interest in land equity will usually grant specific performance of the contract (however, specific performance is a discretionary remedy and may not always be available, see 3.60).

Thus Peter's position can now be described as follows. He has a formally invalid lease for five years that is void at law. However, he has: **3.41**

(a) a legal periodic lease that is valid and can be enforced;
(b) an agreement to grant a lease which may be specifically performed by the courts under their equitable jurisdiction.

The best way to think of the situation in (b) is as a legal fiction. Equity looks upon the relationship between Peter and John in the knowledge that if a dispute arose between them the contract would be specifically enforced. In other words, it assesses the rights and obligations of both parties as if the contract had already been performed; a good example of the maxim that 'equity regards as done that which ought to be done'. **3.42**

The result of this legal sleight of hand is that equity regards Peter as holding a five-year lease of the house on the terms contained in the agreement which was ineffective to create a five-year legal lease. Of course it cannot be said that Peter has in fact acquired a legal five-year lease—to do so would mean that the required formalities set out in the LPA 1925, s 52(1) had been completely bypassed—so it is said that Peter has a five-year *equitable lease*. **3.43**

Formalities for creating a contract for a lease

An equitable lease will not arise in every situation where there is a formally invalid lease. A contract for a lease, like a lease itself, is a legal document which has to comply with certain formalities. The formalities that apply will depend upon whether the contract was made before or after 27 September 1989, this being the date when the relevant provisions of the Law of Property (Miscellaneous Provisions) Act 1989 came into force. **3.44**

The position pre-27 September 1989   Any contract to grant a lease made before 27 September 1989 had to comply with the LPA 1925, s 40(1): **3.45**

> (1) No action may be brought upon any contract for the sale or other disposition of land or any interest in land, unless the agreement upon which such action is brought, or some memorandum or note thereof, is in writing, and signed by the party to be charged or by some other person thereunder by him lawfully authorised.

Section 40(1) is based on the Statute of Frauds 1677. Prior to this there was no requirement for an agreement for a lease to be in any particular form, but it was very difficult for the courts to establish if the parties had an agreement at all (and what its terms were) when the only evidence was oral. Therefore the requirement was introduced that the person seeking to enforce the agreement should produce some documentation of the agreement signed by the other side. Unlike the current provisions under s 2 of the 1989 Act, it is not necessary that the contract itself be in writing; all that is required is that there be some written evidence of the contract. **3.46**

If Peter and John agreed the lease between them orally one evening, and then the next day John wrote a letter confirming what they had agreed and sent it to Peter, this letter would be enough to satisfy s 40 provided it contained the essential terms of the contract (ie the address of the property, the length of the term, the date on which the term is to commence, and the rent payable). Even a letter signed by John, setting out the essential terms of the contract and sent to his own solicitor, could be sufficient (see *Smith-Bird v Blower* [1939] 2 All ER 406). If the essential information is not contained in one document it is even possible for several **3.47** related documents to be combined to satisfy the requirement (*Timmins v Moreland Street Property Co. Ltd* [1958] Ch 110, [1957] 3 All ER 265). The written agreement entered into by Peter and John has been signed by both of them and contains all the terms, so although it was not made by deed it will almost certainly satisfy the requirements of s 40(1).

3.48 **The doctrine of part performance**   It should be noted that the effect of s 40(1) of the LPA 1925 is simply to make an agreement not conforming to its requirements unenforceable by action. An oral contract for a lease is not void because of the absence of writing; it is a valid contract, but if a dispute arises between the parties the courts will not enforce it.

3.49 Consider the result if, in our example, John and Peter reached a purely oral agreement for the five-year lease. As part of this agreement Peter promises to repair the structure of the house and to redecorate the interior. He then moves into the house and, as agreed, carries out the required repairs. Six months later John returns from the US and seeks to evict Peter. He argues that because there was no written memorandum or note of the contract to satisfy s 40, the courts will not enforce the oral agreement. Therefore, he says, he is free to regain possession of the house complete with the improvements made by Peter, regardless of the fact that Peter has fulfilled his side of the bargain.

3.50 Clearly this is a most unsatisfactory situation: John is using the statute to enable him to breach the terms of the oral agreement. The courts will therefore seek to enforce the contract in equity under the doctrine of part performance. The doctrine of part performance is closely related to that of estoppel. Where one party to an agreement has carried out that agreement (whether in part or completely) and acted to his or her detriment in reliance on the promise of the other party, it would be inequitable to allow the other party to evade the consequences of that agreement by relying upon the fact that the agreement does not comply with a technical requirement.

3.51 Therefore, if Peter can show that he has performed sufficient acts of part performance in pursuance of the original agreement, he may be able to get the courts to enforce that agreement by specific performance. Essentially Peter will have to show that he did particular things (eg repairing the property, paying rent) which he would not have done if there had not been a binding agreement. Actions which have been held to be sufficient acts of part performance are:

(a) carrying out improvements to the land (*Rawlinson v Ames* [1925] Ch 96);

(b) the giving up of a former home to move into an employer's home (*Wakeham v Mackenzie* [1968] 1 WLR 1175); or leaving the former matrimonial home on a promise that the husband would pay a portion of the proceeds of sale (*Liddell v Hopkinson* (1974) 233 EG 512);

(c) payment of money if combined with other actions (*Steadman v Steadman* [1976] AC 536).

3.52 A claim for specific performance can be brought in the county court if the value of the property does not exceed the county court limit (currently £30,000). Damages may be awarded instead of, or as well as, specific performance. It is also possible to ask the court for a declaration that there is a binding agreement between the parties to take or grant a lease.

3.53 **Formalities after 27 September 1989**   Any contract to grant a lease made after 27 September 1989 must comply with the provisions of the Law of Property (Miscellaneous Provisions) Act 1989, s 2, which states:

(1) A contract for the sale or other disposition of an interest in land can only be made in writing and only by incorporating all the terms which the parties have expressly agreed in one document or, where contracts are exchanged, in each.

(2) The terms may be incorporated in a document either by being set out in it or by reference to some other document.

(3) The document incorporating the terms or, where contracts are exchanged, one of the documents incorporating them (but not necessarily the same one) must be signed by or on behalf of each party to the contract.

Section 2(1) does not apply in relation to a contract to grant such a lease as is mentioned **3.54** in s 54(2) of the LPA 1925 (ie short leases) (s 5(5)). Thus, if the agreement reached by John and Peter was made after 27 September 1989, it must be a written contract incorporating all the terms of the agreement and signed by both the parties (although the terms themselves may be contained in a separate document referred to in the contract, and if contracts are exchanged it is sufficient if each party signs one of the documents). Provided they have fulfilled these requirements Peter and John may have created an equitable lease. If these requirements were not fulfilled, however, then the agreement between them cannot amount to a contract to convey land.

We noted earlier that the effect of s 40 of the LPA 1925 was to make an agreement unen- **3.55** forceable if it did not comply with the specified formalities. Section 2(1) of the 1989 Act states in contrast that an agreement can only be made in writing, so if there is no writing there is no contract. Thus the basis of the doctrine of part performance is effectively removed. Under the old law an oral agreement to convey land was unenforceable, but it was still a contract. If there were sufficient acts of part performance to indicate the existence of a contract the courts would enforce that contract. Under the new law an oral agreement cannot amount to a contract at all. If the agreement fails to satisfy s 2 it is void *ab initio*. Thus, while under the old law an oral agreement could create an equitable tenancy for a term of more than three years this is no longer possible after 27 September 1989. It should be noted, however, that if a person goes into occupation under an invalid contract for a tenancy and makes regular payments to the owner the courts may imply a periodic tenancy (see 3.36).

The conflict of equity and law

We started with John attempting to grant Peter a five-year lease. The grant failed because **3.56** it was not by deed and was for a period of more than three years, and therefore did not comply with the formalities demanded by the LPA 1925, s 52(1). We then saw how there were two ways in which the defective grant might be rescued:

(a) at law Peter may hold an implied periodic tenancy;

(b) in equity because Peter and John's agreement amounts to a contract to create a lease which may be specifically enforceable, Peter may hold an equitable five-year fixed-term tenancy.

The next question we have to consider is which of these two leases should prevail.   **3.57**

This question was conclusively answered in *Walsh v Lonsdale* [1882] 21 Ch D 9. The facts **3.58** of this case were as follows:

L granted W a seven-year lease of a mill. The grant was formally invalid because it was made in writing and not by deed. Under the terms of the agreement W was to pay each year's rent in advance. W entered into possession of the mill and paid rent in arrear for a period, thereby becoming a legal periodic tenant by implication. L then demanded one year's rent in advance. W refused to pay and L distrained for it (by seizing W's goods, see 6.35). W then took the matter to court, seeking damages for trespass and a decree of specific performance for the yearly periodic tenancy. The question before the court was whether W held the mill under a legal periodic tenancy, in which case L's distraining for the rent would be illegal, or whether W held the mill under an equitable seven-year lease on the terms drawn up in the agreement, in which case W was liable to pay the rent in advance. The answer given was clear. The court held that in consequence of the Judicature Acts 1873–1875 equity was to prevail. Lord Jessel MR said (at 14f):

> He [W] holds, therefore, under the same terms in equity as if a lease had been granted… he cannot complain of the exercise by the landlord of the same rights as the landlord would have had if a lease had been granted.

3.59 If we apply this principle to Peter and John, we can see that Peter holds an equitable five-year fixed-term tenancy. If John returns from America and seeks to regain possession of the house he will only be able to do so in accordance with the rules that apply to fixed-term tenancies (see Chapter 10); in fact he may not be able to terminate the tenancy at all until the term has expired.

Is a contract for a lease as good as a lease?

Specific performance not always available

3.60 As we have seen, an equitable lease depends on the presumption that the contract to grant a lease will be specifically performed by the courts. Specific performance is a discretionary remedy and will not be ordered in all situations. The person seeking specific performance must have acted fairly and ethically; this is usually expressed in the maxim 'he who comes to equity must come with clean hands'.

3.61 This is illustrated in the case of *Coatsworth v Johnson* [1886] 55 LJ QB 220. Here the landlord agreed to grant the tenant a 21-year lease of a farm. The agreement was not executed by deed. A term of the agreement was that the tenant would cultivate the farm properly. The tenant entered into possession. Before the tenant had paid any rent the landlord sought to repossess the farm because the tenant had failed to cultivate it properly and had therefore breached one of the covenants that would have been inserted into the lease had it been executed. The court held that specific performance would not have been granted in this case because the tenant had not behaved properly by breaching a term of the agreement. Thus there could be no equitable lease. Because no rent had been paid the law would not imply a legal periodic lease. The tenant was merely a tenant at will and the landlord was entitled to possession. It is also possible that the court would not make an order if it would be impractical, or if damages would be an adequate remedy.

Third parties

3.62 We considered earlier, by way of illustration, the position if John decided to stay in the US and to sell his house to James (see 3.38). This needs to be addressed in a little more detail. We have seen how, provided the formalities are observed, the contract for a lease will be binding on John if it is specifically enforceable (for a more detailed account of what happens when either the landlord or tenant disposes of his or her interest to a third party, see Chapter 9). In this section we shall see that unlike a legal lease, an equitable lease will bind a third party only in certain circumstances. If Peter wants to be secure against third parties there are certain steps he should take.

3.63 **Unregistered land** An equitable lease will bind a purchaser only if it was registered as a class C(iv) land charge (as an estate contract) under the Land Charges Act 1972, s 2(4). If not registered, even if James had notice of the agreement between Peter and John, it will not bind him.

Registered land In registered land an equitable lease is a minor interest and should be noted on the register as such if it is to bind a purchaser. It cannot be an overriding interest under the Land Registration Act 1925, s 70(1)(k), because that applies only to legal leases. It can be an overriding interest under s 70(1)(g) of that Act if the tenant is in actual occupation at the time of the transfer to the third party. The position for Peter is thus a little more secure than it would be with unregistered land. However, if his equitable lease is not noted on the register and he is not in actual occupation at the time of the sale to James then the equitable lease will not bind James. If Peter's interest has not been registered and does not bind James, Peter's only protection will be to fall back on his legal implied yearly tenancy.   **3.64**

No privity of estate The concept of privity of estate will be discussed later in Chapter 9. For now it is only necessary to note that under a contract for a lease there can be no privity of estate. Because of the absence of privity of estate, some obligations entered into by the original parties to a contract for a lease may not be enforceable against a third party who later acquires an interest in the property.   **3.65**

The LPA 1925, s 62 contains a useful provision which ensures that on the conveyance of an estate in land most of the rights enjoyed with that land (such as easements) will be transferred with the estate. Section 62 will not apply to a contract for a tenancy, however, because it is not a conveyance as defined by s 205(1)(ii) of the LPA 1925.   **3.66**

D SUMMARY

A legal lease may be created validly in the following ways: **3.67**

(a) by deed;
(b) in writing, if for less than three years;
(c) orally, if for less than three years;
(d) by implication, if the tenant entered into possession with the consent of the landlord and paid rent regularly.

An equitable lease for more than three years may be created in the following ways provided that specific performance would be granted: **3.68**

(a) if made in writing;
(b   if evidenced in writing and made before 27 September 1989;
(c) if made orally but with sufficient acts of part performance before 27 September 1989;
(d) if it fulfils the provisions of s 2(1) of the Law of Property (Miscellaneous Provisions) Act 1989 if made after 27 September 1989.

KEY DOCUMENTS

Law of Property Act 1925

Law of Property (Miscellaneous Provisions) Act 1989

Localism Act 2011

Printed copies of all legislation can be ordered from The Stationery Office at <http://www.tsoshop.co.uk>. All legislation from 1988 onwards and most pre-1988 primary legislation is available online at <http://www.legislation.gov.uk>.

4

INTRODUCTION TO OBLIGATIONS IN LEASES

A INTRODUCTION

All legally binding relationships consist of a series of obligations. At root an obligation **4.01** is a promise to behave in a particular way in the future. When two people enter into the relationship of landlord and tenant they make a variety of such promises. For example, the tenant may promise to pay £100 per week to the landlord, while the landlord may promise to let the tenant live in the premises for one year. The opposite side of an obligation is a right. If a tenant promises to pay £100 rent per week then the landlord has the right to receive this rent. If a landlord promises to let a tenant live in the property for one year then the tenant has the right to live there for that period.

The promises that are made between a landlord and tenant define the nature of the ten- **4.02** ancy; they set out the various rights and obligations that are held by each of the parties. If there were no obligations it could not be said that a relationship of landlord and tenant existed at all. In this and the following chapters we shall be considering these rights and obligations and how they arise, for, as we shall see, not every obligation comes about as a result of a promise made by one of the parties.

In theory these promises can cover any aspect of the landlord and tenant relationship, rang- **4.03** ing from the essential to the seemingly trivial. The following list gives an idea of the types of issues that landlords and tenants will seek to resolve between them by use of promises:

(a) The amount of rent payable.
(b) The time and manner of payment.
(c) What happens if rent is not paid.
(d) How long the tenant can live in the premises.
(e) Whether the landlord can evict the tenant before the term of the tenancy has expired.
(f) Who is to be responsible for bills.
(g) Who is to be responsible for insurance.
(h) Who is to be responsible for external maintenance and repair.
(i) Who is to be responsible for internal decoration and repair.
(j) Whether the tenant can have a lodger.
(k) Whether the tenant can sub-let.
(l) Whether the tenant can assign the lease.
(m) Whether the landlord has a right of access.

(n) Whether the tenant can keep a pet.
(o) Whether the tenant can alter the premises.
(p) Whether the tenant can use the premises for business purposes.

4.04 At the beginning of Chapter 3 three examples were considered: Tim, Paul, and Sandra (see 3.02 to 3.07). Tim failed to acquire a tenancy, but both Paul and Sandra entered successfully into the relationship of landlord and tenant. Paul's tenancy was created by an oral agreement between himself and his landlady, Christine. Sandra's lease, on the other hand, was drafted by solicitors and was contained in a detailed and lengthy document. The question we are now concerned with is the nature and extent of the rights and obligations that arise between the parties to these two agreements.

4.05 Sandra is very pleased with her new home and relieved to escape from rented accommodation where she always felt her landlord was watching over her. She is therefore surprised, and a little amused, when she browses through her lease, to find it contains, among others, the following provisions:

(1) Not to throw or permit to be thrown any dirt or rubbish rags or other refuse into the sinks, baths, lavatories, cisterns, or waste or soil pipes in the demised premises.
(2) Not to permit the practising of any singing in the demised premises between the hours of 11.00 pm and 8.00 am.
(3) Not to keep any bird, dog, or other animal in the demised premises.
(4) Not to hang or expose in or upon any part of the demised premises so as to be visible from the outside any clothes or washing of any description or any other article.

4.06 Sandra has just expended a considerable amount of money on what is likely to be the most expensive purchase of her life, and yet her lease prohibits her from performing some actions that no reasonable owner-occupier would entertain. A casual observer reading through Sandra's lease would probably first laugh, make a disparaging comment about the pedantry of lawyers, and then say, 'That goes without saying'. The unfortunate truth, however, is that in the relationship of landlord and tenant very little goes without saying. The general rule is that if a lease is silent on some matter then there is no obligation on the parties to the lease. If it fails to say who is responsible for repairing the roof then no one is responsible for repairing the roof; if it fails to say that you may not keep crocodiles then (provided you do not cause a nuisance or a danger, or are not restricted by any statute) you may keep crocodiles. Seen in this light the draughtsman's fervour is perfectly understandable. The aim of the lease is to attempt to be as comprehensive as possible. Unlikely though it is that Sandra will buy a crocodile, stuff rags down the toilet, rent the back room to a male voice choir, and wave her knickers out of the window, the landlord wants to be sure that if she does any of these things he or she will be able to stop her.

4.07 A long lease, such as Sandra's, is the clearest example of how a landlord and tenant may expressly allocate their respective rights and obligations. Many tenants, however, do not hold a long lease: they may have a shorter fixed term granted to them by use of a smaller document containing only a few covenants; they may have a periodic tenancy expressed in a standard form bought ready-printed from a legal stationers; or, like Paul, they may not even have a written agreement at all. This does not mean that there are no obligations on either party. If there were no obligations it could not be said that a relationship of landlord and tenant had arisen at all. The common law regards certain obligations as being so essential to the relationship of landlord and tenant that, in the absence of any express provision, these obligations will be implied into every lease.

So while it may seem that Sandra, as the holder of a long lease, should enjoy the greater **4.08** freedom of action within her new flat as compared with Paul, legally speaking at least, the obverse is in fact true. Aside from the few terms agreed orally with Christine, the only obligations placed upon Paul will be those which are implied into the tenancy either by common law or by statute. Sandra will be bound by all the many and various obligations included in her lease. On the other hand, the fact that Sandra holds a detailed and comprehensive lease means that she will also be able to benefit from any rights that have been granted to her in that lease, rights that may well be more extensive than those implied by the common law or statute.

B TYPES OF OBLIGATION

Express obligations

When we speak of obligations and rights arising as a result of promises made between **4.09** landlord and tenant we are talking about contractual obligations and rights. Contractual obligations and rights arise as a result of an express agreement between the landlord and the tenant. These contractual obligations and rights are not all of the same type; they can differ because the way they are expressed means that different consequences flow from their being breached.

Express covenants

Strictly speaking the term 'covenant' should be applied only to a contractual promise con- **4.10** tained in a tenancy made by deed. However, as we saw in the previous chapter, the law does not require leases for less than three years to be made by deed. As a result many shorter leases are simply made in writing. To be terminologically correct the terms of such an agreement should be referred to as 'contractual obligations'. Nevertheless, the word 'covenant' is so commonly used to refer to obligations created in this manner, and also to obligations that are implied into the lease, that it has acquired a broader meaning.

Seen in this light it is possible to say that covenants are the terms of the contract between **4.11** landlord and tenant. However, a covenant, even a covenant in the broader sense, cannot be truly equated with a contractual term. A contractual term will bind only parties to that contract: a covenant can continue to impose obligations and rights upon people who have acquired an interest in the land after the original parties to the agreement have departed. Covenants can 'run with the land' (see Chapter 9).

What distinguishes a covenant from a condition (see below) are the consequences that flow **4.12** from the breach of that covenant. If a covenant is breached by the tenant, the landlord will have a variety of remedies at his or her disposal. For the moment, however, it is necessary only to mention the most draconian of these remedies, namely that the landlord may be able to terminate the tenancy. In the case of a breach of covenant the right to terminate does not arise automatically. The landlord can terminate the tenancy only if he or she has expressly reserved a right to do so in the agreement (see Chapter 11 on forfeiture).

Express covenants will commonly include: **4.13**

(a) Landlord's covenants:
    (i) a covenant for quiet enjoyment (see 6.42);
    (ii) a covenant to repair (see 7.07);
    (iii) a covenant to insure (see 6.43);

    (iv) a covenant permitting the tenant to renew the tenancy or to purchase the land-lord's interest (see 6.116 and 6.128).
(b) Tenant's covenants:
    (i)   a covenant to pay rent (see 6.09);
    (ii)   a covenant to pay taxes;
    (iii) various covenants regarding user (see 6.52);
    (iv) a covenant prohibiting assignment and/or sub-letting (see 6.81).

Express conditions

4.14 A landlord may regard a term of the contract as so essential that he or she may wish to make the continuation of the tenancy conditional upon the observance of this term. In such a case the landlord will seek to include an express condition in the lease. A well-drafted condition will give the landlord an automatic right to terminate the tenancy if it is broken. For the tenant the consequences of breaching a condition can be very harsh—so harsh, in fact, that when the court comes to interpreting a lease it will in general assume the terms to be covenants unless it is made very clear by the wording of the lease that the obligation in question is intended to be a condition (*Doe d Henniker v Watt* [1828] 8 B&C 308 at 315).

Collateral contracts

4.15 A third type of promise is known as a collateral contract. This is where the promise does not form part of the lease itself, for example where a landlord promises to a tenant before the lease is entered into that the drains of the house are in working order (*De Lassalle v Guildford* [1901] 2 KB 215, CA). If, on the strength of this promise, the tenant enters into the tenancy agreement but finds when he or she moves in that the drains are not in fact functional, there will be a breach of collateral contract. Here the tenant's remedy is an action for misrepresentation and the tenant may be able to rescind the tenancy agreement or claim damages. Because a collateral contract is not part of the tenancy we shall not consider this topic any more in this chapter.

Implied obligations

4.16 Not all obligations in a tenancy arise directly from express promises made between the landlord and tenant. A tenancy such as Paul's (see Example 2 at 3.03) can be created without the formalities that accompany the creation of a longer lease, leaving plenty of scope for future disputes to arise between the parties. In such a case the law will imply certain obligations into the agreement.

Covenants implied by the common law

4.17 These are the covenants which although not expressly set out in the tenancy agreement will be implied by the common law to be a part of that contractual agreement. They provide a basic minimum of protection for both landlord and tenant where the express terms fail to cover the allocation of basic obligations between the parties.

4.18 Covenants implied by the common law include:

(a) Landlord's covenants:
    (i)   a covenant for quiet enjoyment (5.01);
    (ii) a covenant not to derogate from grant (5.32);
    (iii) an implied contractual duty of care to keep the common parts in repair (7.64).

(b) Tenant's covenants:
    (i)   a covenant to pay rent (5.44);
    (ii) a covenant to pay taxes (5.45);
    (iii) a covenant to allow the landlord entry (5.47);
    (iv) a covenant not to deny the landlord's title (5.48);
    (v) a covenant to use the premises in a tenant-like manner (7.75).

Covenants implied by statute

These are the covenants which although not expressly set out in the tenancy agreement will **4.19** be implied by statute to be part of that contractual agreement. They augment the minimum standard of protection provided by the common law. Covenants implied by statute include certain obligations to repair (see 7.81 to 7.104).

Implied conditions

These are conditions which although not expressly set out in the tenancy agreement will be **4.20** implied into that contractual agreement.

The only implied condition is an implied condition of fitness for human habitation at the **4.21** commencement of the tenancy imposed upon the landlord (see 7.60).

Obligations arising in tort

These are obligations based on the principle of a duty of care existing between the parties. **4.22** Such obligations arise independently of contract and so it is not necessary for the parties involved to be in the relationship of landlord and tenant. Tortious obligations can arise either at common law in the law of negligence or nuisance, or for breach of a statutory duty (see Chapter 8).

Usual covenants

These are a particular class of covenants that are implied by the common law into a con- **4.23** tract for a lease. Where the parties to a contract to a lease fail to specify what terms the actual lease should contain, a term will be implied into the contract for a lease that the actual lease, when it is granted, will contain 'the usual covenants'. (This can be of particular importance when the grant never takes place and the tenant holds under an equitable lease, see 3.34 to 3.59.)

Whether or a covenant is a 'usual covenant' not is a question of fact and may vary depend- **4.24** ing upon the nature of the premises, the locality, the purpose of the letting, and local conveyancing customs (*Flexman v Corbett* [1930] 1 Ch 672). However, certain basic covenants will be implied in every case:

(a) Landlord's covenants:
    (i)   to allow the tenant quiet enjoyment;
    (ii) not to derogate from grant;
    (iii) a right of re-entry for non-payment of rent (a condition).
(b) Tenant's covenants:
    (i)   to pay rent;
    (ii) to pay taxes;
    (iii) to keep and deliver up the premises in repair;
    (iv) to allow the landlord access to view and carry out repairs if the landlord has expressly covenanted to repair.

C REMEDIES—AN OVERVIEW

4.25 To understand fully the nature of any of the obligations listed it is necessary to consider what the consequences would be if one of those obligations were breached. An obligation that cannot be enforced would be of little use to either party. Therefore, before moving on to consider in detail the nature of the various obligations we shall briefly run through the remedies that may be available to either a landlord or a tenant if the other party fails to honour its obligations.

Remedies for breach of covenant

Damages

4.26 The basic common law remedy for breach of a covenant is damages. An award of damages is suitable when the losses incurred by the wronged party are quantifiable in money and where money can be a sufficient compensation for the wrong suffered. For example, where a tenant damages the fixtures and fittings in a flat the landlord may recover from the tenant damages of a sufficient sum to replace or repair the damaged fixtures and fittings. We shall see later that the principles governing the measure of damages for a breach of covenant to repair the premises are different depending on whether it is the landlord or the tenant who has suffered the damage.

Equitable remedies

4.27 If the court thinks it appropriate it may order either *specific performance* or an *injunction*. Both remedies are discretionary.

4.28 Specific performance is an order compelling a party to fulfil its side of a contract. It is suitable where there is no doubt about what would need to be done to remedy the breach. Specific performance is therefore particularly appropriate to a situation where a party to a tenancy agreement promises to do something and then fails to do it, for example where a landlord promises to keep the structure of a building in repair and then allows it to fall into disrepair. Specific performance can be ordered under the ordinary equitable jurisdiction of the court. It is also provided by the Landlord and Tenant Act 1985, s 17, that where a tenant alleges that a landlord has breached a repairing covenant relating to any part of the premises in which the dwelling is comprised, the court may, at its discretion, order specific performance of that covenant. It has been long established, however, that a landlord cannot get specific performance of a tenant's repairing covenant (*Hill v Barclay* [1810] 16 Ves 402).

4.29 An injunction is an order which restrains someone from doing an act (or in some cases compels someone to do a positive act in order to end a state of affairs that amounts to a breach of contract or a tort). An injunction may therefore be appropriate where a party to a tenancy agreement has promised not to do something but then goes ahead and does it. For example, if a tenant covenants not to play loud music after 11.00 pm but persists in doing this, the landlord may be able to obtain an injunction to prevent recurrence of the breach.

Special remedies available only to landlords

4.30 The most drastic remedy a landlord can use against a tenant if the tenant breaches a covenant is to end the tenancy. This is done through the procedure known as forfeiture. Since the effect of forfeiture (if successful) can be to deprive the tenant of his or her home, this remedy is subject to strict conditions which will be considered in detail in Chapter 11. It should be noted that while a landlord can forfeit a lease a tenant has no corresponding right once the lease has been executed, no matter how disreputable the landlord's conduct may be. The Law Commission has recommended the introduction of a termination scheme for tenants (Law Com No. 142: *Forfeiture of Tenancies* [1985]).

Another remedy peculiar to landlords is distress. Distress is an old self-help remedy for the **4.31** non-payment of rent and involves the landlord entering the premises and seizing goods to the value of the unpaid rent. The common law remedy of distress is to be abolished and replaced with a statutory system that can only be used in respect of arrears of rent under commercial leases (see 6.35 to 6.38).

Remedies in tort

Damages are the primary tortious remedy and the measure will be calculated on tortious **4.32** principles. It is also possible that an injunction may be awarded to prevent harm arising from a tort.

5

IMPLIED OBLIGATIONS

A LANDLORD'S IMPLIED OBLIGATIONS

Covenant for quiet enjoyment

An implied covenant for quiet enjoyment protects the tenant from interference with the **5.01** most fundamental of his or her rights as a tenant—the right to exclusive possession. Of all the implied obligations placed upon the landlord by the common law it is of the most practical importance. It can provide the tenant with a cause of action in a great variety of situations, ranging from harassment by the landlord to the landlord's failure to keep the property in repair.

One thing a covenant for quiet enjoyment cannot normally do, despite its moniker, is to **5.02** provide a remedy for noise pollution. The words 'quiet enjoyment' used in a legal context do not mean noise-free enjoyment, but enjoyment without interruption of possession. Nevertheless, if on the facts, the noise created by the landlord is so excessive as to prevent the tenant's enjoyment of possession it could be a breach of covenant for quiet enjoyment (*Sampson v Hodson-Pressinger* [1981] 3 All ER 710).

All that is required for a covenant for quiet enjoyment to be implied into a tenancy is that **5.03** there should be a contract of letting. Any contract of letting will do—an informal oral agreement, a written document, or a deed. Even an agreement for a tenancy will give rise to an implied covenant for quiet enjoyment provided it creates an equitable tenancy (see *Markham v Paget* [1908] 1 Ch 697).

A covenant for quiet enjoyment will not be implied where the tenancy agreement already **5.04** contains an express covenant for quiet enjoyment. If we consider the cases of Paul and Sandra (see Examples 2 and 3 in 3.03 to 3.07), we can see that the implied covenant will be of particular significance to Paul. Paul has no written tenancy agreement. His landlord, Christine, has not signed any document which places her under any express obligation to Paul. Nevertheless, Paul will be able to benefit from a covenant for quiet enjoyment implied by virtue of the contract of letting. Sandra's lease, on the other hand, is by deed and will almost certainly contain an express covenant for quiet enjoyment (see 6.42). However, if through an oversight the draftsman has failed to include an express provision, a covenant for quiet enjoyment will be implied by the common law.

5.05 Despite the fact that the implied covenant for quiet enjoyment is normally spoken of in the singular, it in fact is a composite of three closely related obligations:

(a) a qualified undertaking as to title;
(b) an undertaking to put the tenant into possession;
(c) a qualified undertaking to allow the tenant quiet enjoyment of the premises.

5.06 *A qualified undertaking as to title*   The essence of a qualified undertaking as to title is that the landlord undertakes that he or she has sufficient interest in the property to be able to put the tenant into possession. This is in contrast to an absolute undertaking as to title, by which a landlord undertakes that he or she has sufficient interest to be able to grant the whole of the tenant's term.

5.07 For example, Paul moves in to the basement flat in Cranley Gardens on 1 February 2010. Unbeknown to him, Christine in fact rents the whole house from Mrs Green and her tenancy expires on 7 February 2010. On 14 February, Paul receives a letter from Mrs Green demanding that he moves out of the flat by the end of the month. Paul will have no remedy against Christine. On 1 February, Christine possessed sufficient interest in the land to put Paul into possession; this is all that is demanded by a qualified undertaking as to title. Once her estate expires on 7 February, she has no further liability to Paul. The situation would be very different if Christine had signed a written agreement containing an absolute undertaking as to title.

5.08 *An undertaking to put in possession*   This aspect of the covenant for quiet enjoyment is so closely related to the undertaking as to title as to be virtually indistinguishable. It requires that the landlord must permit the tenant to be put into possession of the premises. Clearly a landlord cannot claim to grant a person a tenancy and then refuse to allow him or her into possession. To do so would be to deprive the tenant of exclusive possession. (See *Miller v Emcer Products Ltd* [1956] Ch 304.)

5.09 *An undertaking to allow the tenant quiet enjoyment*   The third aspect of the implied covenant for quiet enjoyment is of far more practical importance. Its essence is that, having entered into the relationship of landlord and tenant with the tenant, it is implied that the landlord has undertaken not to do acts that would tend to deprive the tenant of the full benefit of the right of possession (*Kenny v Preen* [1963] 1 QB 499).

5.10 There are three important limitations on the covenant for quiet enjoyment:

(a) it applies only to 'substantial interference' with the tenant's 'ordinary reasonable' enjoyment;
(b) it applies only to acts done by landlords themselves, or by their servants or agents, and to the lawful acts of people deriving title from the landlord;
(c) it applies only to tenants and not to licensees.

5.11 *Acts which can amount to substantial interference with the tenant's quiet enjoyment* Originally it was thought that for an act of the landlord to amount to a breach of the covenant for quiet enjoyment there had to be some physical interference with the tenant's enjoyment of the demised premises: for example, where the landlord engaged in mining activities under the house that caused the basement to subside (*Markham v Paget* [1908] 1 Ch 697); where the landlord entered the tenant's premises and removed the windows and doors (*Lavender v Betts* [1942] 2 All ER 72); and where the landlord failed to repair a culvert on neighbouring land and, as a result of the lack of repair, water escaped from the culvert and physically damaged the tenant's property (*Booth v Thomas* [1926] Ch 397, CA).

Physical interference is not to be equated with physical damage to the property, however. **5.12** The key point is not whether the acts cause physical damage to the property, but whether they physically disturb the tenant's enjoyment of possession. Thus when the landlord cuts off the tenant's gas and electricity supplies that also amounts to physical interference although no actual physical damage is done to the property (*Perera v Vandiyar* [1953] 1 WLR 672).

In more recent years there has been some retreat from the principle that there needs **5.13** to be some physical interference. In *Kenny v Preen* [1963] 1 QB 499, [1962] 3 All ER 814, CA, a landlord sent threatening letters, banged on the door, and shouted abuse at the tenant. This was held to be a breach of covenant for quiet enjoyment. In *Southwark LBC v Mills* [1999] UKHL 40, [1999] 3 WLR 939, regular excessive noise from an adjoining flat was held to be capable of amounting to a breach of covenant for quiet enjoyment. The crux of the matter is that the acts done must interfere with 'the tenant's freedom of action in exercising his rights as a tenant' (*per* Lord Denning MR in *McCall v Abelesz* [1976] QB 585, [1976] 1 All ER 727 at 730; also *Sampson v Floyd* [1989] 2 EGLR 49, (1989) 33 EG 41, CA). The tenant's key right as a tenant is possession of the premises; a landlord who seeks to intimidate a tenant into leaving the premises clearly is interfering with this right even though he or she may be causing no physical interference (such behaviour may also amount to unlawful eviction and harassment, see 19.05 to 19.14).

The covenant for quiet enjoyment does not, however, apply to things done before the **5.14** grant of the tenancy, even if they have continuing consequences for the tenant. The tenant in *Southwark v Mills* did not succeed in showing that there had actually been a breach of the covenant, because the excessive noise could only be heard as a result of poor soundproofing that had been in existence at the date the tenancy was granted. Similarly in *Long v Southwark LBC* [2002] EWCA Civ 403, [2002] HLR 56, a build-up of rubbish in a building was not a breach of the covenant for quiet enjoyment because it was caused as a result of the faulty design of the original rubbish chutes (the presence of the rubbish was, however, found to be a nuisance for which the landlord was liable, see 8.14).

Whether substantial interference has taken place is a question of fact depending on the **5.15** individual circumstances of the case. Acts which cause inconvenience to tenants but which do not actually disturb their enjoyment of possession will not be breaches: for example, where the landlord built an external staircase past the tenant's bedroom window which destroyed the tenant's privacy (*Brown v Flower* [1911] 1 Ch 219); or where the landlord made noise which merely inconvenienced the tenant (*Kelly v Battershell* [1949] 2 All ER 830, CA). However, where a landlord erected scaffolding outside a shop which obstructed the shop's entrance this was held to be substantial interference (*Owen v Gadd* [1956] 2 QB 99). Similarly, a temporary disturbance which is unlikely to be repeated will probably not amount to a breach of covenant for quiet enjoyment (see *Manchester, Sheffield and Lincolnshire Rly Co. v Anderson* [1898] 2 Ch 394, CA; *Phelps v City of London Corpn* [1916] 2 Ch 255).

Where a landlord has to enter the tenant's premises to undertake repairs in accordance **5.16** with the terms of the lease this will not be a breach of the covenant for quiet enjoyment provided that the landlord takes all reasonable precautions to minimize disturbance to the tenant (*Goldmile Properties v Lechouritis* [2003] EWCA Civ 49, (2003) 15 EG 143, CA).

Even if the acts complained of by the tenant amount to substantial interference on the cri- **5.17** terion discussed at 5.11, they will still not be a breach of the covenant for quiet enjoyment unless they are done by a person for whom the landlord may be held responsible. The landlord is responsible for:

(a) acts done by the landlord, whether the acts are done on or off the premises and regardless of whether the acts are lawful or unlawful;

(b) acts done by the landlord's servants or agents acting under the landlord's authority, whether lawful or unlawful (when another person performs such an act it is effectively the act of the landlord because the person is acting as the landlord's agent);

(c) lawful acts of persons claiming title under the landlord, for example other tenants of property owned by the landlord.

5.18   The landlord is *not* responsible for:

(a) unlawful acts of persons claiming title under the landlord. Where a single landlord rented three neighbouring farms to three tenants, one of the tenants complained of flooding on his farm caused by drains running from the farms let to the other two tenants. The landlord was held to be in breach of covenant in respect of one of the farms, where the drains were defective and flooded despite the fact that the tenant was using them within the scope of his legal rights. The landlord, however, was not held liable for the flooding caused by the drains from the second farm. The drains on this farm were in good working order but were flooding because the tenant was using them in excess of his legal rights (*Sanderson v Berwick-upon-Tweed Corp* (1984) 13 QBD 547);

(b) an act of disturbance done by a third party;

(c) an act of disturbance done by a person who had superior title to the landlord, for example by the head landlord where the tenant is a sub-lessee.

5.19   **Example** Several weeks after Paul moves into his new flat a firm of builders begins substantial renovation work on the whole house. Scaffolding is erected which obstructs access to the front door. To make matters worse, the next door neighbour also undertakes building work on his property, which causes a lot of dust that penetrates into Paul's flat. Furthermore, John, in the flat above, allows some friends of his who are in a band to use his back room to rehearse; the noise caused is excessive and prevents Paul from studying and sleeping. When he tells John about the trouble this is causing him, John tells Paul that Christine gave him permission to use his back room as a rehearsal studio.

5.20   With regard to the builders, the first question is to ascertain who they are working for. If they are employed by Christine then Paul may have a remedy against her. (This is assuming, of course, that Christine's tenancy has not expired.) If they are employed by Mrs Green, the head landlord, then Paul will not be able to hold Christine responsible, for Mrs Green possesses a title superior to Christine's tenancy. Secondly, it will be necessary to consider whether the acts of the builders, as servants of Christine, amount to substantial interference with Paul's right of possession. We saw earlier that obstructing access to a premises can be a breach of the covenant for quiet enjoyment, but Paul's case would have to be considered on its own facts. Much will depend upon how long the scaffolding is to stay in place; if it is only for a short period it is unlikely that Christine will be in breach.

5.21   Paul will have no remedy against Christine for the disturbance caused by the neighbour's building work. Christine is not liable for acts of disturbance done by third parties. To prevent the disturbance Paul would have to pursue an action in tort against the neighbour.

5.22   With regard to the noise from John's flat, Paul may be more successful. John is also Christine's tenant and as such he derives his title from her. Christine has further given John permission to use the back room as a rehearsal studio; John is therefore acting legally. If the studio causes excessive noise so as to interfere with Paul's enjoyment of the basement flat (which will be a question of fact), Christine will be in breach of covenant. However, if John has set up the studio without permission and is acting in excess of his legal rights, Christine will not be liable for his interference. A tenant who has complained to his or her landlord about the behaviour of third parties using the common parts of the building may, however, be able to bring a claim against the landlord for nuisance if the landlord does not take reasonable steps to prevent the behaviour from continuing (*Brumby v Octavia Hill Housing Trust* [2010] EWHC 1793 (QB)).

Damages An action for breach of covenant for quiet enjoyment is an action for breach   **5.23**
of contract. Damages for the breach will normally be calculated on contractual principles. Contractual damages are limited to losses which flow naturally from the breach. Thus a tenant can recover damages for inconvenience, for damage to his or her property, and for the cost of any court proceedings. If the breach of covenant for quiet enjoyment has been so severe as to force the tenant to leave the property, the tenant will also be able to recover removal costs.

Many activities by a landlord can constitute a breach of covenant for quiet enjoyment.   **5.24**
Where, for example, a landlord's building work causes damage to the tenant's possessions, contractual damages will cover the replacement or repair of these articles. However, where a landlord seeks to drive a tenant from the property by conducting a prolonged campaign of harassment, contractual damages may seem rather limited. The tenant may well want to recover aggravated damages for injured feelings and mental distress, or exemplary damages as a punitive measure against the landlord.

In many cases, however, damages have not been kept within the contractual parameters.   **5.25**
Because a covenant for quiet enjoyment can cover a very wide range of action by the landlord the breach of covenant will also frequently involve a tort; most commonly trespass or nuisance. The damages awarded under tortious principles can be significantly higher than contractual damages, for they may include damages for mental distress and exemplary damages.

Exemplary damages may be awarded where a landlord has calculated that he or she will   **5.26**
make a profit by performing a tortious act. This is not an uncommon occurrence—the value of possession to a landlord may be considerable and outweigh any damages that would have to be paid to the tenant as a result of the wrongdoing. For example, where a tenant has a rent controlled tenancy an unscrupulous landlord may feel that it is financially viable to intimidate that tenant into leaving, because having gained possession of the property the landlord will then be able to let it out at a higher rate. The purpose of exemplary damages is essentially punitive. Exemplary damages will be awarded only where the landlord has committed a tort such as trespass, for example where the landlord enters the tenant's flat, throws out the tenant's belongings, and refuses to let him or her back in. It is not, however, essential that the tenant should pursue an action for trespass. Where the tenant's claim was for breach of covenant for quiet enjoyment but the claim included allegations of trespass, exemplary damages were awarded (*Drane v Evangelou* [1978] 1 WLR 455).

Aggravated damages are different from exemplary damages; they are awarded to compen-   **5.27**
sate the tenant for injury to feelings and mental distress resulting from the aggravation caused by the landlord's actions (see *Ramdath v Daley* (1993) 25 HLR 273).

Damages for breach of contract can, in certain circumstances, extend to damages for men-   **5.28**
tal distress. This will be the case only where the object of the contract is to provide pleasure, peace of mind, or freedom from molestation (see *Jarvis v Swan Tours Ltd* [1973] QB 233, [1973] 1 All ER 71). Despite attempts to argue that a covenant for quiet enjoyment falls within this category, the Court of Appeal has stated (albeit *obiter*) that such a covenant

is not within this exception to the general rule (*Branchett v Beaney* [1992] 3 All ER 910). This means that a tenant pursuing a claim solely for breach of covenant for quiet enjoyment will not be able to recover for mental distress. However, if the tenant is also able to pursue an action in trespass or nuisance, damages for mental distress will be available.

5.29   Where the actions performed by the landlord result in the tenant having to give up occupation of the premises, this may constitute a statutory tort of unlawful eviction under s 27 of the Housing Act 1988. Damages under the Housing Act 1988 are calculated on a different basis to those in contract; their aim is to deprive the landlord of any profit he may make by virtue of the commission of the unlawful act rather than simply to compensate the tenant for any damage done. The award will be based upon the difference between the value of the landlord's interest with the tenant in occupation and the value of the property to the landlord with vacant possession (s 28). In general, awards under the Housing Act 1988 are significantly higher than those awarded for breach of contract, trespass, or nuisance. (In *McSpadden v Keen* [1999] EWCA Civ 1515 the tenant was awarded £90,500.) An action under s 27 should be brought in the county court (Housing Act 1988, s 40).

5.30   A breach of covenant for quiet enjoyment may also amount to the criminal offence of harassment under s 1(3) of the Protection from Eviction Act 1977 (see 19.09). If this is the case an order for criminal compensation may be made. It is only necessary for the tenant to prove that the landlord's actions constituted harassment; the tenant does not have to show that the acts amounted to a breach of covenant (see *R v Burke* [1990] 2 All ER 385, HL).

5.31   *Injunction*   As well as damages, the court may grant an injunction restraining the landlord from breaching a covenant for quiet enjoyment. If the tenant has been forced out of the premises by the activities of the landlord the court may even grant an injunction requiring the tenant to be put back into possession (see *Drane v Evangelou*, 5.26). If the landlord persists in the breach after an injunction has been granted, he or she will be in contempt of court and may even be committed to prison. It should always be remembered that an injunction is an equitable remedy and the grant of an injunction is therefore discretionary. In deciding whether to grant an injunction the court will consider a wide variety of factors, including the conduct of both sides, whether the injunction would act oppressively upon the landlord, the nature of the breach, and whether it is likely to be repeated.

Covenant not to derogate from grant

5.32   The essence of the covenant not to derogate from grant is the principle that 'a grantor having given a thing with one hand is not to take away the means of enjoying it with the other' (*per* Bowen LJ in *Birmingham, Dudley and District Banking Co. v Ross* (1888) 38 Ch D 295 at 313). The most common application of the covenant not to derogate from grant is with regard to easements. If a tenant is granted a right (eg a right of way over the landlord's land) the landlord must not do anything which prevents the tenant from exercising this right (eg by erecting a fence). However, a landlord may also breach the covenant not to derogate from grant if:

(a)   he or she retains land adjacent to the tenant's premises; and

(b)   the landlord or someone deriving title under the landlord (a tenant or an assignee) then performs some action on the retained land that renders the tenant's land substantially less fit for the purposes for which it was let (*Aldin v Latimer, Clark, Muirhead & Co.* [1894] 2 Ch 437); and

(c)   at the time of the letting the landlord knew of the purpose to which the tenant was going to put the land (*Robinson v Kilvert* (1889) 41 Ch D 88).

It should be noted that if the landlord's actions merely make the tenant's land less profit-   **5.33**
able, as, for example, when the landlord uses the neighbouring land for a business similar
to that of the tenant, this does not necessarily make the tenant's land substantially less fit
for the purposes for which it was let (*Port v Griffith* [1938] 1 All ER 295; *O'Cedar Ltd v
Slough Trading Co.* [1927] 2 KB 123; *Romulus Trading Co. Ltd v Comet Properties* (1996)
48 EG 157). Where, however, a lease contained a covenant that a landlord would not
permit the setting-up of a competing business within the same building as the tenant the
landlord was held to be in breach of the covenant not to derogate from the grant when he
set up a competing business immediately next to the building (*Oceanic Village v Shirayama
Shokusan Co Ltd* [2001] EGCS 20 (Ch), [2001] L&TR 35).

If the lease does not contain any specific restrictions on the landlord's use of the retained   **5.34**
land they may be implied from the circumstances of the letting:

> The exercise of determining the extent of the landlord's implied obligation not to derogate
> from a grant involves identifying what obligation, if any, on the part of the grantor can fairly
> be regarded as necessarily implicit, having regard to the particular purpose of the transaction
> when considered in the light of the circumstances subsisting at the time the transaction was
> entered into. (*Johnson & Sons Ltd v Holland* [1988] 1 EGLR 264 *per* Sir Donald Nicholls V-C
> at 268A)

In *Platt v London Underground Ltd* [2002] 2 EGR 121 the landlord granted a tenancy of   **5.35**
a kiosk adjacent to the exit at an underground station. The landlord subsequently decided
to restrict the times that the exit was open, thus depriving the tenant of passing trade. The
landlord was held to have derogated from the grant because during negotiations for the
lease both parties had contemplated that the exit would be open at all times that the station was open.

The covenant not to derogate from grant will often be exactly the same as the covenant   **5.36**
for quiet enjoyment. To interfere with a tenant's quiet enjoyment is also to do something
incompatible with the rights granted in the agreement. A claim that the landlord has
breached the covenant not to derogate from grant may, however, be more appropriate in
situations where tenants put their land to a particularly sensitive use.

The classic illustration of a breach of covenant not to derogate from grant is to be found in   **5.37**
Aldin v Latimer, Clark, Muirhead & Co. (see 5.32). Here the premises were let to a tenant
for the purposes of running a timber yard and the landlord retained neighbouring land.
One of the buildings let to the tenant was a wood drying shed which required the free flow
of air to function properly. The landlord erected buildings on the neighbouring land which
interrupted the flow of air to the drying shed. The interruption of air effectively rendered
the drying shed useless for the purposes for which it had been let, so there was held to be a
breach of the covenant not to derogate from grant.

In *Harmer v Jumbil (Nigeria) Tin Areas Ltd* [1921] 1 Ch 200, the premises were let for the   **5.38**
purposes of storing explosives. To store explosives the tenant had to have a licence, and
one of the conditions of this licence was that there should be no buildings within a specified
distance of the storage area. The landlord, who retained neighbouring land, erected buildings on this land. The erection of buildings would result in the tenant losing his licence to
store explosives and render the land useless for the purposes for which it had been let. The
landlord was therefore in breach of his covenant not to derogate from grant.

If a landlord breaches a covenant not to derogate from a grant the tenant may be entitled   **5.39**
to damages or an injunction. The principles applied will be roughly the same as where a
tenant seeks damages for a breach of the covenant for quiet enjoyment (see 5.23 to 5.30).

Repairing obligations

5.40 The landlord will also be under several implied obligations relating to the condition and repair of the property, namely:

(a) Implied condition of fitness for human habitation at the commencement of the tenancy.
(b) Implied contractual duty of care to keep the common parts in repair.
(c) Certain statutory repairing obligations.
(d) A tortious duty of care.

5.41 We will deal with these in Chapters 7 and 8 on repair.

B TENANT'S IMPLIED OBLIGATIONS

5.42 The relationship of landlord and tenant is a reciprocal arrangement. In the same way that the common law implies certain basic obligations onto the landlord, it will also imply a basic minimum of obligations onto the tenant when there are no express covenants in the lease.

Not to assign or sub-let

5.43 The Housing Acts 1985 and 1988 imply covenants into secure and assured periodic tenancies that the tenant cannot assign or sub-let the premises without the consent of the landlord (Housing Act 1985, s 91, Housing Act 1988, s 15; see 17.75 and 15.74).

To pay rent

5.44 In practice, the one obligation that the parties are unlikely to forget, even when entering into an informal oral tenancy, is the obligation to pay rent. In the absence of any express agreement the law will normally imply an obligation to pay rent onto the tenant. The implication of an obligation to pay rent will not be automatic, for as we have seen the payment of rent is not essential to create a tenancy (see 1.26). Nevertheless, it will nearly always be the intention of the parties that rent should be paid, and it can safely be said that the instances where the common law will not imply a covenant to pay rent will be very rare. The courts have even held the personal representative of a deceased tenant liable to pay the rent due on a property for the period between the death of the original tenant and service of a notice to quit, even though the personal representative did not occupy the property and took no benefit from it (*Youngmin v Heath* [1974] 1 WLR 135, [1974] 1 All ER 461, CA). (The remedies for non-payment of rent are dealt with at 6.35 to 6.41.)

To pay taxes

5.45 The general rule was that unless the landlord was expressly liable under the tenancy agreement or under statute, the tenant was under an implied obligation to pay rates and taxes. Fundamentally this obligation still stands, but since the introduction of the community charge and then the council tax, both of which levy the charge on the resident and not on the property, the situation is governed by statute (currently the Local Government Finance Act 1992).

5.46 One point where a dispute may arise is regarding liability for water rates. If there is no express term in the agreement stating that the landlord is liable for water rates, it will be implied that it is the tenant's responsibility to pay.

To allow the landlord entry

Exclusive possession, as we have seen, grants the tenant the right to exclude the landlord **5.47** from the premises. If the landlord enters without permission or without a right to do so he or she commits trespass. If, however, the landlord has covenanted to be responsible for repair of the premises, in the absence of any express provision to the contrary, it will be implied that the tenant has granted the landlord the right to enter to inspect and carry out repairs. This right must, of course, be exercised reasonably—the landlord can enter to carry out the work he or she has covenanted to do but is not entitled to go beyond this. If, for example, the landlord attempts to carry out major renewals when the covenant entitles him or her only to repair, the landlord will be exceeding the right (*Plough Investments Ltd v Manchester City Council* [1989] 1 EGLR 244). A right of entry will also be implied in weekly tenancies even if there is no express covenant to repair (see *Mint v Good* [1951] 1 KB 517, CA and *McAuley v Bristol City Council* [1991] 2 EGLR 64, CA). Similarly, the landlord will not be entitled to enter the premises to carry out works which amount to improvements rather than repairs unless the lease expressly allows for this (*Yeomans Row Management Limited v Meyrick* [2002] EWCA Civ 860, [2002] 2 EGLR 39).

Not to deny landlord's title

For a tenant to deny that the landlord has an interest (or a sufficient interest) in the land, **5.48** for example by suggesting that the land is in fact vested in a third party other than the landlord, is, in essence, to deny the existence of the tenancy altogether; it would amount to repudiation of contract. If there is no contract the relationship of landlord and tenant will not exist between the parties. The consequences of denying the landlord's title can be serious for the tenant; if there is no tenancy the landlord will be entitled to repossess the premises. However, a partial disclaimer of the landlord's title will not amount to an unequivocal or a clear repudiation of the relationship of landlord and tenant (see *WG Clark (Properties) Ltd v Dupre Properties Ltd* [1992] 1 All ER 596).

Use

A tenant may not use the premises for illegal purposes (*Gas Light and Coke Co. v Turner* **5.49** [1840] 6 Bing NC 324). There is, however, no implied covenant against using premises for immoral purposes (*Edler v Auerbach* [1950] 1 KB 359; *Hill v Harris* [1965] 2 QB 601).

Repairing obligations

There are further implied obligations on the tenant with regard to the repair and mainte- **5.50** nance of the premises:

(a) to use the premises in a tenant-like manner;
(b) not to commit waste (this is a tortious obligation).

Again, we shall deal with these in Chapters 7 and 8 on repair. **5.51**

KEY DOCUMENTS

Civil Procedure Rules 1998

Form N1—Part 7 Claim

Forms N9B and N9D defence and counterclaim.

Form N208—Part 8 Claim

Form N208A—Part 8 Claim (notes for claimant)

Form N208B—Part 8 Claim (notes for defendant)

Printed copies of all legislation can be ordered from The Stationery Office at <http://www.tsoshop.co.uk>. All legislation from 1988 onwards and most pre-1988 primary legislation is available online at <http://www. legislation.gov.uk>.

The Civil Procedure Rules are available online from <http://www.justice.gov.uk/courts/procedure-rules>.

Court forms are available online from the HM Courts and Tribunals Service at <http://www.justice.gov.uk/forms/hmcts>.

6

EXPRESS OBLIGATIONS

A INTRODUCTION

Conflict between express and implied covenants

The covenants implied by common law are generally intended to provide a basic mini- **6.01** mum standard of protection where the parties have failed to create an express agreement. If the parties have reached an express agreement which is in conflict with the implied common law covenant, the general rule is that it is the express agreement that will prevail. In the case of covenants implied by statute the situation is somewhat different; the aim of the statute is often to prevent the exploitation of one party by the other when there is an inequality of bargaining power and to ensure a minimum level of protection across the board. Most statutory provisions therefore provide that the parties cannot contract out of the statute by express agreement. The tenant's implied obligation not to commit waste (see 7.77 to 7.79) cannot be excluded by an express covenant because it is a tortious and not a contractual duty.

Balance of bargaining power

6.02   In virtually every case it will be the landlord (or the landlord's lawyer) who draws up the tenancy agreement. The agreement therefore will tend to serve the landlord's interests. Of course, tenants are free to object to any term in an agreement which they regard as too harsh or unsuitable, but in reality they are unlikely to try and drive too hard a bargain. Frequently, they will not have the money to pay for a lawyer to check through the terms, and in any case they will be all too aware of the fact that if they refuse to accept the terms of a lease the landlord can simply find someone else who, eager to find somewhere to live, will go along with the terms. It is precisely this inequality of bargaining power that has led to the introduction of the statutory codes considered in Part II of this book.

Construction of covenants

6.03   The majority of covenants in a lease will be drafted using standard expressions, and so in most cases there will be little difficulty in interpretation. Nevertheless, the wording of a covenant should always be checked carefully. In creating a lease the parties are free to include any terms upon which they can agree and so, in theory, the range of possible covenants is infinite.

6.04   If a court is asked to interpret a covenant its starting point will always be the wording. If the wording is clear and unambiguous the court will give effect to the covenant even if it seems to produce an unfair result. The court cannot depart from that meaning just because one of the parties dislikes the bargain struck (*Marks v Warren* [1979] 1 All ER 29). If there are difficulties in interpretation the court will try to discover the mutual intention of the parties. If the parties' intentions are not clear from the words used the court may take into account the factual background known to the parties at the time the lease was created. Other covenants or words used in the lease may be used to help clarify an unclear term. When appropriate—and particularly when dealing with vague rent review clauses (see 6.22 to 6.34)—the court may take into account the underlying purpose of the lease. If the landlord wishes to include a clause that limits a tenant's common law rights it is incumbent on him or her to do it in clear, unambiguous language; if it is unclear the covenant will be construed against the landlord.

6.05   It is possible that the provisions of the Unfair Terms in Consumer Contracts Regulations 1999 can be applied to protect tenants from onerous contract terms. Where a tenancy agreement has been prepared for widespread use (for example by a public sector landlord or a letting agency) the Office of Fair Trading may intervene if any provision is deemed to be unfair to the tenant. The Regulations will not normally apply to core terms of the tenancy (ie the rent payable, details of the property, and length of the term), but may be invoked to remove other terms. For example, a term requiring the tenant to pay a penalty if the rent is overdue or a term allowing the landlord to impose rules or restrictions at will may be challenged as being an unfair contract term (*Guidance on Unfair Terms in Tenancy Agreements*, OFT, 2005).

6.06   Anti-discrimination legislation may also make a term of a tenancy unlawful (and therefore unenforceable) if the term makes it unreasonably difficult or impossible for a particular person to occupy or enjoy the premises because of his or her sex, race, or physical ability. This will be particularly relevant with regard to disability discrimination. The relevant provisions are to be found in Part 4 of the Equality Act 2010.

B ABSOLUTE AND QUALIFIED COVENANTS

Covenants which prohibit the tenant from doing something (eg sub-letting, changing the **6.07** use of the premises, keeping a pet) can be absolute or qualified. An absolute covenant is a complete prohibition against the doing of whatever has been forbidden; a qualified covenant states that the act is not to be done 'without the consent of the landlord'. A qualified covenant can be tempered further by adding that the landlord's consent is not to be unreasonably withheld, such a covenant sometimes being known as a 'fully qualified covenant'.

C CONDITIONS PRECEDENT

Performance of one party's covenant may be a condition precedent to the performance **6.08** of the other party's covenant. For example, where a landlord covenants to put the drains of a property into repair before the commencement of a tenancy and fails to do so, he or she cannot enforce the tenant's express obligation to keep the drains in repair. Whether a condition can be held to be a condition precedent depends on whether it is material to the performance of the other party's subsequent obligations. If it is not, the covenants will be construed as independent. This will be the case even if a covenant is expressed as being subject to the performance of the other party's obligations. Thus, where a landlord enters into a covenant to carry out repairs subject to the tenant 'paying his rent and performing his covenants', the fact that the tenant does not pay his rent will not excuse the landlord from carrying out repairs as the two covenants are not mutually dependent (see *Yorkbrook Investments v Batten* (1985) 52 P&CR 51, [1985] 2 EGLR 100, CA).

D TENANT'S COVENANT TO PAY RENT

We saw in Chapter 5 how, in the absence of an express covenant to pay rent, the common **6.09** law will almost certainly imply such a covenant into the lease. In real terms, while negotiating a tenancy, rent is probably going to be the one factor that neither the landlord nor the tenant is likely to ignore, so the vast majority of leases will contain an express covenant as to rent.

The amount of rent payable, and the time and manner of payment, are normally set out **6.10** (reserved) in the section of the lease called the 'reddendum'. The reddendum is then followed by a list of the tenant's covenants, the first of which is normally a covenant to pay the rent reserved in the reddendum.

Example Jane entered into a five-year lease with Harry on 1 February 2010. Her lease **6.11** reads as follows:

THIS LEASE made the 1st day of February 2010 between HARRY BRIGGS of 17 Ashlands Road (hereinafter called the landlord) of the one part and JANE SMITH of 44 Park Crescent (hereinafter called the tenant) of the other part.

NOW THIS DEED WITNESSETH as follows:

1. The landlord demises unto the tenant the premises known as Flat 2, 24 Mountview Road (hereinafter called the demised premises) which premises for the purposes of identification only are outlined in red on the plan attached hereto, TO HOLD the same unto the tenant from the 1st day of February 2010 for the term of five years YIELDING AND PAYING during the term hereby granted the yearly rent of £9,600 by equal monthly payments to be made in advance on the first day of each month.

2. The tenant hereby covenants with the landlord as follows:
   (1) To pay the reserved rents on the days and in the manner aforesaid without any deductions whatsoever.

What is rent?

6.12   Today, rent is generally regarded as a contractual sum payable by the tenant to the landlord as compensation for the tenant's right to possession of the land for the term of the tenancy. This contractual view of 'rent', however, grew out of the medieval concept of 'rent service' which was rooted in a tenurial rather than a contractual approach to the relationship of landlord and tenant. Rent service was performed by the tenant not as compensation for the use of the land but as an acknowledgement of the landlord's right to the reversion.

6.13   One surviving result of the old tenurial view is that the tenant is still under an obligation to pay rent even if the premises rented are destroyed or otherwise made uninhabitable. Many leases therefore contain an express clause suspending the tenant's obligation to pay rent in such circumstances.

What is not rent?

6.14   Capital sums payable at the commencement of the tenancy (or on its assignment) are not rent. Thus where a tenant acquires a long lease on a flat the lump sum payable at the commencement of the term is not rent. Such a tenant will normally pay a 'ground rent' throughout the term (usually about £50 per year) and this rent will be expressly reserved in the lease.

6.15   Other monies payable to the landlord, such as service charges or payments for insurance, do not, at common law, count as rent. The landlord may, however, expressly reserve such charges as rent in the lease. For the landlord this has the advantage that in the event of the tenant failing to pay a service charge or other sum, the landlord can treat the outstanding monies as rent arrears and use the remedies applicable to rent arrears to recover the sums owed (in particular the old remedy of distress, which is only available for rent arrears, see 6.35–6.38). It should be noted however that a landlord's ability to recover service charges in this manner is becoming increasingly restricted (see Chapter 23).

Certainty of rent

6.16   The rent expressed to be payable must be either certain or capable of being calculated with certainty at the date when payment becomes due. There is no necessity that rent should be expressed to be in money terms; it is quite possible, in principle, for rent to be paid in the form of services in kind or in chattels. There is also no necessity for a particular sum to be stated in the lease provided the lease contains some mechanism by which a definite sum can be ascertained. The courts cannot enforce an uncertain agreement, but at the same time they are reluctant to reject an agreement that has been worked out between the parties simply because it is poorly drafted or imprecise, and they will therefore seek to give effect to the intentions of the parties if they can.

6.17   An option to renew a lease 'at a rent to be fixed at a price to be determined having regard to the market valuation of the premises at the time of exercising the option' has been held to be sufficiently certain (*Brown v Gould* [1972] Ch 53, [1971] 2 All ER 1505). It can also be sufficient if the parties set out some machinery by means of which the rent can be determined, eg that it should be fixed by a person chosen by the President of the

Royal Institution of Chartered Surveyors (*Lloyds Bank Ltd v Marcan* [1973] 1 WLR 1387, [1973] 3 All ER 754). If the machinery set out in the agreement is inadequate the court may, provided it does not regard the machinery as constituting an essential term of the contract, substitute its own mechanism for calculating the rent (*Sudbrook Trading Estate Ltd v Eggleton* [1983] 1 AC 444, [1982] 2 All ER 1). Nevertheless, an option to renew a tenancy which stated that the new tenancy should be 'at such a rental as may be agreed upon between the parties hereto in writing' and failed to provide any formula by which the rent could be calculated was not sufficiently certain (*King's Motors (Oxford) Ltd v Lax* [1970] 1 WLR 426).

Time and manner of payment

The tenant's covenant for rent should also state the date on which the rent is payable and the manner in which it should be paid (see our example reddendum at 6.10). If rent is not paid by midnight on the specified day then it is held to be in arrears (*Dibble v Bowater* [1853] 2 E&B 564). Rent may be paid to the landlord or to the landlord's agent. If the lease does not specify the date on which the rent should be paid it becomes due at the end of each period by reference to which the rent has been calculated. So in the case of a weekly periodic tenancy, rent falls due at the end of each week, but in the case of a term of years it does not become due until the end of each year of the term. **6.18**

Demands for rent

Where premises consist of residential property a landlord is obliged to give written notice to the tenant of a name and address in England or Wales where the tenant can serve notices on the landlord. If the landlord has not given such a notice no rent or service charge is lawfully due from the tenant until the landlord has complied (Landlord and Tenant Act 1987, s 48). A tenant facing possession proceedings on grounds of rent arrears may rely on this provision to prevent a possession order being made. **6.19**

A tenant under the long lease of a dwelling is not liable to pay ground rent unless the landlord has given the tenant notice stating the amount due and the date for payment (Commonhold and Leasehold Reform Act 2002, s 166). The form and content of the notice is prescribed by the Landlord and Tenant (Notice of Rent) Regulations 2004, SI 2004/3096, WSI 2005/1355. **6.20**

Deductions and set-off

The tenant can deduct sums from the rent due in respect of certain liabilities that are clearly the responsibility of the landlord but which have been paid by the tenant because of the landlord's default (for example, where the tenant pays the landlord's gas or electricity bills to avoid disconnection). The tenant may also deduct from the rent the cost of repairs which were the responsibility of the landlord but were paid for by the tenant (see 7.117). A claim to set-off of any deductible amounts against the rent claimed may be raised as a cross claim in proceedings for arrears of rent and may provide a partial or complete defence in possession proceedings for rent arrears. **6.21**

Rent review clauses

From the early 1970s the increasing level of inflation in Britain made it difficult for landlords to predict what a market rent for a property would be in the future. Clearly, **6.22** landlords letting property on a commercial basis did not want to find themselves lumbered with a tenant paying a rent that had been fixed several years ago and was now well below current market values. It is therefore common, particularly in commercial leases but also in some residential leases, for the landlord to include a rent review provision in the agreement. The aim of these rent review provisions is to give the landlord the opportunity to raise the rent to market value at regular intervals during the tenant's term, usually every five or seven years. In general, rent review clauses provide only for an upwards variation in the rent.

6.23   If a landlord wishes to take advantage of a rent review clause he or she will first have to 'trigger' the rent review procedure by serving notice of intention upon the tenant (although in some cases the review process may be automatic). The tenant must then respond within a certain time limit by serving a counter-notice upon the landlord stating the tenant's intentions. The rent review provision in the lease should provide a timetable setting out the dates and time limits within which the parties should act.

6.24   Where a rent review provision provides a timetable setting out the dates by which a landlord should serve notice on the tenant and vice versa, a particular problem has arisen. The courts have had to consider what happens if a landlord fails to serve notice of his or her intention to implement a rent review by the time specified in the lease; does the landlord thereby lose the right to have the rent reviewed? In other words, is 'time of the essence'? In *United Scientific Holdings v Burnley BC* [1978] AC 904, [1977] 2 All ER 62, the House of Lords overruled earlier authority and held that the general presumption is that time is not of the essence. Time will be held to be of the essence only if:

(a)   the terms of the lease expressly provide that time should be of the essence (see *Bradley Ltd v Telefusion Ltd* (1981) 259 EG 615);

(b)   the terms of the lease indicate that time is to be of the essence, for example where the rent review clause is linked to a clause providing an option and that option must be taken up within strict time limits (*Al Saloom v Shirley James Travel Services Ltd* (1981) 42 P&CR 181);

(c)   the surrounding circumstances indicate that time is to be of the essence.

6.25   Thus, in *United Scientific Holdings*, where the landlord triggered the rent review clause two months late, the landlord was held still to be entitled to a rent review. The House of Lords has confirmed this position in relation to a rent review clause in a housing association tenancy (*Riverside Housing Association v White* [2007] UKHL 20, [2007] HLR 31), again overturning the Court of Appeal's attempt to impose time limits on the implementation of rent review clauses. In exceptional circumstances the rent review may even be implemented 13 years after the review date (*Bello v Idealview* [2009] EWHC 2808 (QB)).

6.26   The new rent decided under a rent review clause will take effect retrospectively from the date the rent review was allowed under the lease. If the rent is increased, any 'arrears' do not have to be paid by the tenant until the next rent day after the new rent is agreed or awarded, unless the lease specifically provides otherwise. A landlord cannot, therefore, issue proceedings to recover the back payments of the increased rent until the next rent day, even if this day will not occur until some time after the new rent has been agreed (*South Tottenham Land Securities v R & A Millett (Shops)* [1984] 1 WLR 710, (1984) 48 P&CR 159).

6.27   As we saw earlier, the fact that there may be a provision in the lease allowing the landlord to vary the rent is not necessarily a bar to the rent being certain provided the amount of rent due can be calculated properly at the date of payment. A rent review provision should therefore provide a procedure for establishing what the new rent should be. This is by no means an easy task—whoever is called upon to perform the valuation has to try to determine the hypothetical value the property would have if it was to be let on the open market. There is a variety of factors which may affect the hypothetical value.

Consider the case of a 15-year business tenancy being assessed in the tenth year of the term. **6.28** What length of term should the valuer consider when assessing the value of the tenancy: a 15-year term the same as the original tenancy, or a five-year term, this being the remainder of the tenant's current tenancy? If the tenant has made improvements to the property or built up goodwill for the business, should these be taken into account or disregarded? If the tenancy contains a covenant restricting the use of the premises, should the valuation be on the basis that this covenant will be included in the hypothetical tenancy or on the basis that a new tenant might be able to change the use of the premises? Should the valuer assume that the hypothetical tenancy will contain a rent review clause the same as the one in the current tenancy?

A well-drafted rent review provision should attempt to resolve these problems in advance **6.29** by setting out what assumptions the valuer should make, what factors should be taken into account, and what factors should be disregarded. It should also state who is to make the valuation (eg an independent surveyor) and provide a procedure to be followed in the event of a dispute (eg the appointment of an arbitrator).

Unfortunately not all rent review provisions are well drafted and in the last 20 years or **6.30** so there has been a huge amount of case law on this subject, a detailed consideration of which is beyond the scope of this book. The following points, however, should provide some guidance as to the assumptions that will be made by the courts in dealing with rent review clauses.

The duration of the lease

Unless the clause states otherwise the duration of the hypothetical lease will generally **6.31** be taken to be the length of the unexpired term (*Lynnthorpe Enterprises Ltd v Sidney Smith (Chelsea) Ltd* [1990] 2 EGLR 148, CA). However, in the case of a long lease this assumption might not be made (see *Prudential Assurance Co. Ltd v Salisburys Handbags Ltd* (1992) 23 EG 117); instead the term may be held to be one which the landlord might reasonably be expected to grant and the tenant expected to take (*Milshaw Property Co. v Preston BC* [1995] EGCS 186). The fact that a tenant may acquire security of tenure under Pt II of the Landlord and Tenant Act 1954 (see business tenancies, Chapter 26) will be taken into account unless expressly excluded (*Pivot Properties Ltd v Secretary of State for the Environment* (1979) 39 P&CR 386).

Improvements

Usually a rent review clause will make it clear that the tenant's improvements to a property **6.32** should be disregarded in the valuation (unless they were carried out by the tenant as part of an obligation under the terms of the lease). Certainly, not to disregard improvements seems unfair to the tenant, who may well end up paying an increased rent because of improvements that he or she paid for in the first place. Nevertheless, if there is no express provision requiring improvements to be disregarded and the rent review clause states that the rent should be valued as a 'reasonable rent for the demised premises' it seems that the clause will be taken literally. The improvements are part of the premises and the valuation will include them (see *Ponsford v HMS Aerosols Ltd* [1979] AC 63, [1978] 2 All ER 837, HL). It is also likely that improvements will be disregarded only if they were undertaken with the landlord's consent.

The terms of the tenancy

6.33 Generally the terms of the hypothetical tenancy will be assumed to be the same as the terms of the current tenancy (*Basingstoke and Deane BC v Host Group Ltd* [1988] 1 WLR 348, [1988] 1 All ER 324). Where the current tenancy contained a strict user clause the valuation was made on the basis that this clause would be included in the hypothetical tenancy (*Plinth Property Investments v Mott, Hay and Anderson* (1978) 38 P&CR 361). Likewise, unless there is a provision to the contrary, the hypothetical tenancy will be assumed to contain a rent review clause (*British Gas Corpn v Universities' Superannuation Scheme Ltd* [1986] 1 WLR 398, [1986] 1 All ER 978).

Sham clauses

6.34 A rent review provision which purports to allow the landlord to increase the rent dramatically may be disallowed by the court even if the tenant has agreed to it. This will be the case where the increase is obviously intended to bring a tenancy outside the ambit of protection of one of the statutory codes. In *Bankway Properties Ltd v Penfold Dunsford* [2001] EWCA Civ 528, [2001] 1 WLR 1369, a rent review provision in an assured tenancy agreement allowed the rent to rise to a sum above £25,000 per year. At the time this increase would have meant that the tenancy ceased to be protected by the security of tenure provisions of the Housing Act 1988 (see 15.23). It was held that the object of the rent review clause was explicitly to deny the tenant ongoing security of tenure. The clause was therefore unenforceable, as it is not possible for parties to contract out of the security of tenure afforded by the statutory codes.

Remedies for non-payment of rent

Distress

6.35 Distress in an old self-help remedy; it can only be used to recover unpaid rent and not to recover outstanding service charges or insurance premiums unless these sums are reserved as rent in the lease. The right to distrain arises as soon as rent falls into arrears.

6.36 Distress entitles a landlord, without any legal process at all, to enter the premises and seize the tenant's goods. The landlord can do this himself or herself, or he or she can employ a certified bailiff. The tenant's goods must be kept for five days, and if, at the end of that period, the tenant has not paid off the rent arrears, the goods can be sold. The landlord should seize goods only to the value of the rent owed and certain items are not permitted to be seized, eg the tools of the tenant's trade, goods in actual use, loose money, and perishable goods.

6.37 Sections 71 to 87 of the Tribunals, Courts and Enforcement Act 2007 (which are not in force at the date of writing) will abolish the common law right to distress for rent and replace it with a new modified regime called Commercial Rent Arrears Recovery (CRAR). This regime will apply only to the recovery of rent arrears due under leases of commercial premises. Landlords of premises that are wholly or partly residential will no longer be able to levy distress for rent. CRAR is considered in more detail in Chapter 26.

6.38 Until the new CRAR provisions come into force the common law rules will continue to apply, subject to the current statutory modifications. If a landlord wishes to distrain against a tenant with Rent Act 1977 or Housing Act 1988 protection, it is necessary to obtain leave from the county court (Rent Act 1977, s 147(1); Housing Act 1988, s 19(1)). It has been held that where a tenant withholds rent because of the landlord's breach of covenant and the landlord then claims to levy a distress against the tenant for rent arrears, the tenant may set off the claim for breach of covenant against the claim to levy a distress (*Eller v Grovecrest Investments* (1994) 27 EG 139, CA).

Action for rent

An action for rent is an action for debt on the covenant to pay rent. Where a landlord **6.39** seeks to recover rent without making a claim for possession the general provisions of the Civil Procedure Rules will apply. Claims for less than £50,000 should normally be brought in the county court using the CPR Part 7 procedure. Claims for less than £5,000 will be brought on the small claims track. Claims for over £50,000 and more complicated claims for sums over £25,000 may be brought in the High Court. If the claim for rent also includes a claim for possession the provisions of CPR Part 55 will apply (see 16.74 to 16.76).

Action for use and occupation

Where a person occupies premises and there is no covenant to pay rent, the landlord may **6.40** bring an action for compensation for use and occupation of the premises. If there is no covenant to pay rent the landlord cannot bring an action for debt, for example where, after a fixed-term tenancy has expired, the tenant holds over without an express or implied agreement to pay rent, or where a person enters into possession.

Forfeiture

Provided the landlord has reserved right of re-entry, he or she may seek to forfeit the lease **6.41** for a breach of covenant to pay rent. The law of forfeiture is dealt with in Chapter 11.

E EXPRESS COVENANT FOR QUIET ENJOYMENT

We saw in Chapter 5 that a covenant for quiet enjoyment will be implied into every tenancy. **6.42** Nevertheless most leases will contain an express covenant for quiet enjoyment. The vast majority of express covenants for quiet enjoyment will be qualified covenants and will not therefore confer on the tenant any rights in excess of those conferred by an implied covenant for quiet enjoyment (see 5.01 to 5.22), in which case the landlord is liable only for acts done by the landlord or by persons deriving title under the landlord. The landlord will not be liable for the acts of a person claiming by title paramount, such as a superior landlord, or for the acts of strangers. An express covenant, however, can be drafted so as to include liability for the acts of named or identifiable strangers (see *Queensway Marketing Ltd v Associated Restaurants Ltd* [1988] 2 EGLR 49, CA). Where an express covenant for quiet enjoyment is included in the lease it overrides an implied covenant for quiet enjoyment. (The remedies for a breach of covenant for quiet enjoyment have been considered earlier at 5.23 to 5.31.)

F COVENANTS TO INSURE

Clearly it is in the interest of all parties to keep a property adequately insured. If a building **6.43** is destroyed by fire or other calamity and found to be uninsured, the losses can be very serious for both sides; the landlord will lose the reversion, while the tenant will lose his or her home. The tenant may even find that despite the destruction he or she is still liable for rent to the landlord for the rest of the term (unless there is an express term in the lease suspending the obligation to pay rent in the event of the premises being rendered uninhabitable). Most long leases, therefore, are careful expressly to allocate the responsibility for insurance on either the landlord or the tenant.

Short leases

6.44 In short leases it is less usual to include an express covenant to insure. Where the tenant's interest in the property is only short term, the financial loss suffered in the case of destruction of the building will fall mainly upon the landlord. It is therefore up to the landlord to protect his or her interest by insuring adequately. Such insurance cover will of course extend only to the building and the fixtures and fittings; if tenants wish to protect their own belongings they will have to take out their own contents insurance.

6.45 Where a landlord insures a property he or she will want to ensure that the tenant does not do anything on the premises that might raise the insurance premium or invalidate the policy (such as storing dangerous goods). It is therefore common for a covenant to this effect to be included in the tenancy agreement, even when there is no obligation on the landlord to insure the premises.

Long leases

Responsibility on the landlord

6.46 The landlord may covenant to insure the premises. Usually when this is the case there will also be provision entitling the landlord to recover the cost of the insurance premiums from the tenant by way of a service charge. Frequently the landlord will also undertake to send the tenant a copy of the insurance particulars annually and to inform the tenant if there is any change in the policy. This is perhaps the most common arrangement in long leases.

6.47 A problem for the tenant when the landlord organizes the insurance policy may be that the landlord, anxious to have the best cover to protect his or her interest in the property but also aware that it is the tenant's money that is going to be paying the premiums, might take out an excessively expensive policy of insurance. If such a situation arises the court will not normally imply a term that the insurance should not place an unnecessarily high burden on the tenant, even where the same insurance cover might have been obtained at a lower price (*Bandar Property Holdings Ltd v J S Darwen (Successors) Ltd* [1968] 2 All ER 305). Possibly, however, the tenant may be protected against the undue inflation of insurance costs under the general principle that service charges are not to be raised by unreasonable expenditure on behalf of the landlord (see *Finchbourne v Rodrigues* [1976] 3 All ER 581, CA).

Responsibility on tenant

6.48 The tenant may covenant to insure the premises. In such a case the tenant will have to organize insurance at his or her own expense. The landlord may require the tenant to insure with a specified company, or with a company approved by the landlord. If the covenant states that the landlord must approve the insurance company, the landlord can refuse his or her approval without having to give reasons (*Viscount Tredegar v Harwood* [1929] AC 72, HL). If the tenant fails to insure with a company approved by the landlord, or fails to take out adequate cover as specified in the lease, the tenant will be in breach of covenant. However, if the tenant takes out a policy with a specified company or with a company approved by the landlord and this policy excepts damage for certain risks (eg war damage), it is not a breach of covenant to fail to insure against those risks provided that the policy obtained by the tenant is the normal policy issued by that company (*Upjohn v Hitchens, Upjohn v Ford* [1918] 2 KB 48, CA).

Application of insurance monies

If either the landlord or the tenant voluntarily takes out insurance cover without being **6.49** obliged to do so by the terms of the lease and the premises are subsequently destroyed, the party who took out the policy is not bound to spend the insurance monies on reinstating the premises. Where there is an express covenant to insure it will usually provide that if the premises are damaged or destroyed then the insurance monies must be applied to reinstating the building. If the landlord has covenanted to insure the premises and is entitled to reclaim the cost of insurance from the tenant then, in the absence of an express undertaking to reinstate the building, the court will imply such a term, for the insurance was clearly intended to benefit both parties and not just the landlord (*Mumford Hotels Ltd v Wheeler* [1964] Ch 177, [1963] 3 All ER 250).

Breach of covenants to insure

It is a breach of a covenant to insure if the premises (or even any part of the premises) **6.50** are uninsured for any period, irrespective of whether any damage occurs. It will also be a breach if the premises are not insured in accordance with the covenant, for example where they have not been insured to the value specified, or even if they are not insured in the names specified in the covenant (*Denise Green v 180 Archway Road Management Co Ltd* [2012] UKUT 245 (LC)).

Remedies for breach of covenants to insure

Damages will be the usual remedy for a breach of a covenant to insure. The damages **6.51** recoverable will be the actual loss incurred. If the building was damaged while uninsured, the damages will be the cost of reinstatement. If one party has failed to insure the building in breach of covenant and the other party has therefore had to take responsibility for insurance, the wronged party will be able to recover the cost of the insurance premiums. Where a tenant is in breach of a covenant to insure the landlord may seek to forfeit the lease, but provided the tenant remedies the breach it is likely that relief will be granted (see Chapter 11).

G COVENANTS REGARDING USER

The general rule at common law is that a tenant may use the demised premises for any **6.52** lawful purpose. The doctrine of waste (see 7.77) prevents the tenant actively damaging the premises, and planning legislation and statutory provisions with regard to overcrowding imply certain restrictions onto the tenant. Otherwise, if the landlord wants to retain any control over the use to which the premises are put, he or she will have to include express provisions in the lease. Any covenant prohibiting a particular type of user can be either absolute or qualified (see 6.07). The burden of proof will be on the landlord to prove breach of covenant.

Nuisance, damage, or annoyance

Many leases will contain a variety of specific prohibitions preventing the tenant from per- **6.53** forming particular acts (eg see Sandra's lease at 4.05). The problem with such specific prohibitions is that it is not possible for the landlord to cover everything that a tenant may do on the premises. It is common, therefore, for tenancy agreements to contain a general covenant prohibiting the tenant from doing or permitting to be done upon the premises any act which may be a nuisance, damage, or annoyance to the landlord or to the tenants or occupiers of any of the adjoining premises.

6.54 'Nuisance' in such a context means a nuisance in law and will not necessarily include acts that might be regarded as a nuisance in the everyday sense of the word. 'Annoyance', however, has a broader, non-technical meaning and will cover the majority of acts that cause disturbance to neighbours. The meanings of 'nuisance' and 'annoyance' are considered in more detail in Chapter 14 on the Rent Act 1977 (at 14.33).

Business use

6.55 A covenant may also serve to restrict to a certain type of user the purposes to which the premises are put. The majority of residential leases will contain a covenant requiring the tenant to use the property only as a private dwelling-house and not to carry on or permit any trade, profession, or business use upon the premises. In such cases even a partial or minor business use of the premises will be a breach of covenant, but in each case it will be a question of fact as to whether the activity amounts to business use (*German v Chapman* [1877] 7 ChD 271, CA). A tenant who takes in lodgers on a commercial basis would be in breach of such a user covenant, but not a tenant who takes in a lodger who lives with the tenant as part of the family (*Segal Securities Ltd v Thoseby* [1963] 1 QB 887, [1963] 1 All ER 500). Business use of premises is considered in more detail in Chapter 26 on business tenancies. It should be noted that the fact that a particular use of premises amounts to a breach of covenant not to use the premises for business purposes does not necessarily mean that that tenancy will count as a business tenancy for the purposes of Pt II of the Landlord and Tenant Act 1954 (see *Lewis v Weldcrest* [1978] 1 WLR 1107, [1978] 3 All ER 1226, CA).

6.56 In business leases the landlord may also include a covenant prohibiting the tenant from undertaking particular sorts of trade or business, or requiring that the premises be used only for a particular trade or business. Such covenants are generally included for commercial reasons, for example the landlord may be the owner of a nearby shop and does not want the tenant to take customers away by opening up a shop trading in the same sort of goods. A positive obligation to use a premises for a particular purpose does not always mean that the tenant must use the premises for that purpose; the tenant will not necessarily be in breach of covenant if he or she makes no use of the premises at all (*Pulleng v Curran* (1980) 44 P&CR 58 at 68). It is possible, however, for a covenant specifically to provide that the tenant must make use of the premises. Where there is doubt as to the effect of the covenant it must be construed in the context of the particular lease (*Blumenthal v Church Commissioners for England* [2004] EWCA Civ 1688, [2005] 1 EGLR 78, CA). A covenant may also be included on the part of the landlord not to let adjoining premises for a particular use, such as a business that competes with that of the tenant.

Change of use

6.57 Most business leases will contain a covenant prohibiting the tenant from changing the use of the premises. If this covenant is absolute, a tenant who wishes to change the use of the premises can do nothing to compel the landlord to agree to the prospective change other than enter into negotiations with the landlord. The landlord may either flatly refuse to allow the change of use, or he or she may demand that the tenant pay any sum that can be agreed between them in return for the landlord waiving the right to rely upon the covenant.

Where a lease contains a restriction on the use of a property and the landlord is aware **6.58** that that use has never been observed, or has not been observed for a number of years, it may be possible to argue that the restrictions have been released by implication and cannot be enforced (*Southwark Roman Catholic Diocesan Corporation v South London Church Fund and Southwark Diocesan Board of Finance* [2009] EWHC 3368 (Ch)).

A qualified covenant which requires the tenant to obtain the landlord's consent for a change **6.59** of use is not subject to an implied term that such consent is not to be unreasonably withheld. Such a term may however be expressly included in the wording of the covenant. Where this is the case the principles governing the interpretation of the word 'reasonable' will be similar to those concerning covenants against assigning and sub-letting (see 6.96 to 6.104).

Where the right to manage premises has been acquired by a right to manage (RTM) com- **6.60** pany (see 23.149), the request for the approval should be made to the company but the company must not grant an approval without giving the landlord 30 days' notice in writing (Commonhold and Leasehold Reform Act 2002, s 98(4)). The RTM company can only grant the approval with the landlord's written consent or, if the landlord objects, in accordance with a determination of the leasehold valuation tribunal (s 99).

If the covenant against change of use is a qualified covenant, the tenant is offered some **6.61** assistance by s 19(3) of the Landlord and Tenant Act 1927. Provided that the proposed change of use does not involve any structural alteration of the premises, s 19(3) implies into the covenant a provision that 'no fine or sum of money in the nature of a fine, whether by way of increase of rent or otherwise, shall be payable for or in respect of such licence or consent [of the landlord to that change]'. Thus a landlord who has included in a lease a covenant that permits a tenant to change the use of the premises with the landlord's consent is not permitted to charge the tenant for the granting of that consent. The implied provision will override any express provision to the contrary, but the landlord is permitted to recover from the tenant a reasonable sum by way of compensation for any damage to the landlord's reversion and for any legal or other expenses.

Remedies for breach of use covenant

Unless the landlord has waived a breach of covenant, his or her remedies will consist of an **6.62** injunction to restrain a breach of a covenant not to put the property to a particular use, or damages to compensate for the tenant's breach of a positive covenant to use the property in a particular way. As the breach will be of a continuing nature (see 11.39) any waiver will have to be of a positive nature, such as giving consent for alterations which are obviously specifically designed to facilitate the wrongful use.

If the wording of the covenant specifies that consent is not to be unreasonably withheld, **6.63** and the landlord has refused to consent, the tenant may apply to the county court for a declaration that consent has been unreasonably withheld, and that he or she is entitled to change the use of the premises. An application may be made using the procedure set out in Part 8 of the CPR. If the tenant has been required by the landlord to pay compensation as a result of a change of use and that sum appears to be excessive, he or she may apply to the court for a determination of the sum to be paid. Such an application can be brought in the High Court or the county court depending on the rateable value of the property. CPR Part 7 or Part 8 procedure may be used, depending on the complexity of the case.

Discharge and modification

It is possible for the holder of a long lease of over 40 years to apply to the Lands Tribunal **6.64** for the discharge or modification of a restrictive covenant once 25 years of the term of the lease have expired (LPA 1925, s 84). A more recent restrictive covenant may also be discharged if the tenant can show that it does not confer any practical benefit on the lessor (*Graham v Easington DC* [2008] EWCA Civ 1503).

H ALTERATIONS AND IMPROVEMENTS

6.65 In the same way that a landlord may wish to retain some control over the use to which a property is put, the same landlord may also want to retain some control over the structure of the building. A landlord does not want to rent out a house and receive back, at the end of the term, a house that has been converted into four separate flats. Of course, it may well be the case that the value of the house converted into flats is greater than the value of the unconverted house at the beginning of the lease, but this will not necessarily meet with the landlord's approval. The landlord may have had his or her own plans to develop the house when the lease expired; and in any case, even if the landlord has no objection to the conversion in principle, he or she will want to be able to ensure that any major works are carried out properly and in keeping with his or her own plans for the building.

6.66 It is therefore common for a landlord to include a covenant in the lease prohibiting a tenant from carrying out any alterations to the premises (although at common law the landlord may have a remedy under the doctrine of waste, see 7.77). Such a covenant can be phrased however the parties wish, depending upon the length of the lease and the nature of the premises. Some covenants may prohibit any alterations, while others may prohibit alterations to the structure or fabric of the building. Such covenants may be absolute or qualified, and if qualified they may contain provisions requiring the tenant to submit plans of the proposed alterations to the landlord for approval before consent will be granted.

6.67 A term that the tenant will not make any improvements without the consent of the landlord and that such consent shall not be unreasonably withheld is implied into protected and statutory tenancies by virtue of s 81(1) of the Housing Act 1980 and into secure tenancies by s 97 of the Housing Act 1985 (see 17.89 and 6.74).

Improvement?

6.68 If an alteration constitutes an improvement, s 19(2) of the Landlord and Tenant Act 1927 will apply (see 6.69 to 6.70). Deciding whether an alteration is an improvement is not always easy. Certainly an improvement is an alteration which makes the premises better in some way, but whether an alteration is an improvement is not to be judged by considering simply whether the alteration increases the value of the premises. The question has to be considered from the tenant's point of view. If, for example, a tenant rents two neighbouring shops and wishes to remove a dividing wall in order to create a larger shop space, this will count as an improvement even though, from the landlord's point of view, the letting value of the two separate shops would be more than the letting value of one larger shop (see *Woolworth & Co. Ltd v Lambert* [1937] Ch 37, [1936] 2 All ER 1523, CA).

Consent for improvements

6.69 Section 19(2) of the Landlord and Tenant Act 1927 provides that where a lease contains a covenant or condition against the making of improvements without licence or consent (ie a qualified covenant), such a covenant or condition shall be deemed, notwithstanding any express provision to the contrary, to be subject to a proviso that such licence or consent is not to be withheld unreasonably. Thus any qualified covenant against improvements is converted into a fully qualified covenant.

Section 19(2) does not preclude the landlord from requiring, as a condition of his or her licence or consent: **6.70**

(a) the payment of a reasonable sum in respect of any damage to or diminution in the value of the premises or any neighbouring premises belonging to the landlord;

(b) the payment of any legal expenses properly incurred in connection with such licence and consent;

(c) in the case of an improvement which does not add to the letting value of the holding, the right to require as a condition of such licence or consent, where such a requirement would be reasonable, an undertaking on the part of the tenant to reinstate the premises in the condition in which they were before the improvement was executed.

Reasonableness

The general principles to be applied in assessing reasonableness of a landlord's decision **6.71** to refuse consent under a fully qualified covenant were set out by the Court of Appeal in *International Drilling Fluids Ltd v Louisville Investments (Uxbridge) Ltd* [1986] Ch 513. In applying these principles to refusal of consent for alterations or improvements in *Iqbar v Thakrar* [2004] EWCA Civ 592 the Court of Appeal gave the following guidance:

(1) The purpose of the covenant against alteration is to protect the property of the landlord from damage by the tenant. Refusal of consent should therefore not be for a reason that does not relate to the landlord's property interests.

(2) It is for the tenant to prove that the refusal of consent is unreasonable. The tenant must have made his or her proposals sufficiently clear so that the landlord could be sure what he or she was being asked to consent to.

(3) The landlord's reasons for refusal will be reasonable if they were based on conclusions that a reasonable landlord would have reached in the particular circumstances of the case.

(4) Refusal will not automatically be unreasonable if the purpose is to convert the premises to a proposed use allowed under the terms of the lease, but the landlord's knowledge of the tenant's plans at the commencement of the tenancy will be relevant.

(5) A landlord need not usually consider any interest other than his or her own. However, where the adverse effect on the tenant in refusing the consent would be disproportionate to the minor adverse effect on the landlord of allowing consent, this should be taken into consideration.

(6) Refusal would not be reasonable where the loss to the landlord is purely pecuniary and he or she could ask for compensation from the tenant.

(7) In each case it is a question of fact, depending on all the circumstances, whether a landlord, having regard to the actual reasons that impelled him or her to refuse consent, acted unreasonably.

As we have seen, where a tenant wishes to argue that the landlord has unreasonably with- **6.72** held consent to an improvement, the burden of proof is on the tenant. However, if the landlord simply refuses consent without giving reasons for the refusal, the burden of proof is on the landlord to justify the refusal. This is illustrated by two cases involving Woolworths. In the first case (*Woolworth & Co. Ltd v Lambert* (see 6.68) L's consent to the improvements was made conditional upon Woolworths either paying £7,000 in damages or reinstating the premises at the end of the term. The court held that Woolworths had failed to establish on the facts that by imposing such conditions L had unreasonably withheld consent.

Woolworths tried a second time to get L to give its consent. This time L flatly refused. The court held that L had unreasonably refused consent (*Lambert v FW Woolworth* & *Co. Ltd* (*No. 2*) [1938] Ch 883).

6.73   Where the property is managed by an RTM company the request for approval should be made to the company in the same way it would be made where an approval for a change of use is sought (see 6.60).

6.74   It should be noted that the principles set out in *International Drilling Fluids* do not apply to protected or statutory tenancies (for example, assured and secure tenancies). Instead these are governed by statutory provisions. Section 82 of the Housing Act 1980 (HA 1980) and s 98 of the Housing Act 1985 (HA 1985) place the burden of proof on the landlord to show that consent was not unreasonably withheld. In determining this question the court shall, in particular, have regard to the extent to which the improvement would be likely:

(a) to make the dwelling-house, or any other premises, less safe for occupiers;

(b) to cause the landlord to incur expenditure which it would be unlikely to incur if the improvement were not made; or

(c) to reduce the price which the dwelling-house would fetch if sold on the open market or the rent which the landlord would be able to charge on letting the dwelling-house (HA 1980, s 82(1); HA 1985, s 98(2)).

6.75   Where the tenant has applied in writing for consent and the landlord refuses to give consent the landlord must give the tenant a written statement of the reasons why consent was refused. If the landlord fails to either give or refuse consent within a reasonable time consent is taken to be withheld (HA 1980, s 82(3); HA 1985, s 98(4)). If consent is given subject to an unreasonable condition it is taken to be unreasonably withheld (s 82(3), s 99(2)).

Disability discrimination

6.76   Section 20 of and Sch 4 to the Equality Act 2010 impose a duty on the manager or controller of let premises to make reasonable adjustments to the premises to prevent a disabled person being disadvantaged in using the premises. Where the manager or controller is itself a tenant, the duty to make reasonable adjustments will not extend to the removal or alteration of a physical feature (Sch 4, para 2(8)) but may include other matters that might ordinarily be classed as alterations (for example, the installation of a door entry system to allow easier access for an occupier who uses a wheelchair). It may be that the manager or controller would normally be prohibited from making such an alteration under the terms of its own lease because the lease contains an absolute or qualified covenant against the making of such an alteration. Schedule 21 to the Equality Act 2010 provides that in such circumstances a fully qualified covenant against making alterations will be incorporated into the lease. A structure is then set out for the making of a written request for consent to make an alteration by the tenant and for the giving of a response by the landlord. If a landlord unreasonably refuses to give consent in these circumstances, he or she may be joined as a party in a complaint of discrimination and may be liable to compensate the complainant.

6.77   For disabled tenants or occupiers of dwelling-houses who do not occupy under secure or statutory tenancies (long leaseholders for example) the Equality Act 2010, s 190 provides that where a tenant applies to the landlord for consent for an improvement that is necessary because of the disability, consent is not to be unreasonably withheld. Unlike the position under s 19(2) (see 6.71) the burden of proof is on the landlord to show that the refusal of consent was reasonable. Similar provisions for statutory and secure tenants, whether or not disabled, are contained in the HA 1980, s 82 and the HA 1985, s 98(1) (see 6.74 and 17.90).

Schedule 4, para 2(7) to the 2010 Act also requires the landlord to change any term of **6.78** the lease that prohibits the making of any alterations that may be reasonably necessary to allow a disabled person properly to use the premises (exceptions are made for certain small dwellings where part is occupied by the landlord or the landlord's family (Sch 5)).

Remedies for breach of covenant against alterations

If a tenant breaches a covenant against alterations or improvements a landlord may seek **6.79** damages. However, if the alterations have not caused the value of the premises to depreciate the landlord will not be able to recover damages. The landlord may seek to forfeit the lease provided there is a right of re-entry in the lease (see 11.15 to 11.19), or seek an injunction requiring the tenant to reinstate the premises.

If the tenant is of the opinion that the landlord has unreasonably withheld consent to **6.80** an alteration or improvement, the tenant may seek a declaration under s 53(1)(b) of the Landlord and Tenant Act 1954. The application can be made in the county court using the CPR Part 8 procedure. The tenant can then go ahead and carry out the alteration without the need to seek consent. Alternatively the tenant can go ahead with the alteration without a declaration, in which case the tenant runs the risk of forfeiture proceedings.

I COVENANTS RESTRICTING THE RIGHT TO ASSIGN AND SUB-LET

It is a long-established principle of English land law that an estate in land is freely alienable. **6.81** When a tenant acquires the bundle of rights that amount to an interest in land, one of the rights that the tenant receives is the right to dispose of that estate as he or she wishes. Quite understandably this is not a right that is particularly popular among landlords.

Landlords can spend a long time trying to find a tenant they regard as suitable. Usually **6.82** they will interview potential tenants, and frequently they take references from employers and previous landlords. In many cases they may hand over the responsibility of finding a tenant to an accommodation agency, in which case the vetting procedure is likely to be even more stringent. Having found a suitable tenant the landlord will want that tenant to remain in occupation.

If the tenant hands over the right to occupy the premises to another person the landlord **6.83** will have several major concerns. First, the new occupier may well be a complete stranger. The landlord will have had no chance to interview the new occupier or take references and the new occupier may prove to be undesirable. Secondly, even if the occupier is not undesirable he or she may want to put the property to a use to which the landlord may object. Thirdly, it is possible that the new tenant may acquire statutory protection that the original tenant did not have and thus may make it difficult for the landlord to regain possession of the property.

By far the most common way of preventing a tenant from handing over the right of occu- **6.84** pation to a third party is to insert an express covenant into the tenancy agreement prohibiting the tenant from sub-letting or assigning. A covenant against assigning or sub-letting restricts a right that the tenant would have at common law and acts to the benefit of the landlord. It is therefore up to the landlord to draft the covenant as carefully as possible to include all ways in which the tenant may part with possession, for any ambiguity in the wording could be resolved in favour of the tenant.

6.85 A covenant 'not to assign' is not broken by sub-letting (*Crusoe d. Belencowe v Bugby* [1771] 3 Wils 234; *Russell v Beecham* [1924] 1 KB 525, CA). A covenant 'not to sub-let' the premises will not prevent the tenant sub-letting a part of the premises (*Cook v Shoesmith* [1951] 1 KB 752). However, a covenant 'not to assign or underlet any part of the premises' will prohibit an assignment or sub-letting of the whole, the reasoning being that an assignment or a sub-letting of the whole of the premises necessarily means that every part of the premises has been assigned or sub-let (*Field v Barkworth* [1986] 1 WLR 137, [1986] 1 All ER 326).

6.86 In an attempt to cover all the possibilities a landlord will often draft a covenant requiring the tenant 'not to assign, sub-let or part with possession of the demised premises or any of part thereof'. Even this wording may prove insufficient if the tenant permits other people to use the premises, provided that the tenant is not completely excluded from legal possession of the premises (see *Lam Kee Ying Sdn Bhd v Lam Shes Tong* [1975] AC 247, [1974] 3 All ER 137). Whether or not the tenant has actually given up legal possession is a question of fact which may be inferred from surrounding circumstances (eg transferring the telephone, water, and electricity bills into the new occupier's name, paying the rent with a cheque drawn on the new occupier's bank account, or where the new occupier erects a notice board outside the premises).

6.87 A provision prohibiting a tenant from parting with possession of the premises will not prevent the tenant from taking in a lodger or otherwise allowing another person to share occupation. It is therefore common to include a provision forbidding the tenant 'from permitting another person to occupy or share occupation of the premises'. It should also be noted that a covenant against sub-letting will effectively prevent the tenant creating a mortgage by sub-demise (*Sergeant v Nash, Field & Co.* [1903] 2 KB 304, CA). To prevent a tenant creating a mortgage by way of charge the landlord will have to include an express covenant against charging.

6.88 A covenant against assignment and sub-letting will automatically be implied into assured tenancies (see 15.74) and secure tenancies (see 17.75 and 17.83).

Absolute and qualified covenants

6.89 A covenant against assigning or sub-letting may be drafted in one of three ways:

(a) A covenant not to assign or sub-let the property (an absolute covenant).
(b) A covenant not to assign or sub-let the property without the landlord's consent (a qualified covenant).
(c) A covenant not to assign or sub-let the property without the landlord's consent, and that consent is not to be unreasonably withheld (sometimes called an absolutely qualified covenant).

Absolute covenants

6.90 An absolute covenant is a complete prohibition against assigning or sub-letting. If a tenant under a lease containing an absolute covenant wishes to assign or sub-let the property, the tenant's only option is to negotiate with the landlord to try to gain his or her consent. The tenant is in a very weak bargaining position, however; the landlord is under no compulsion to permit the assignment or sub-letting and can quite simply refuse. The landlord may grant the tenant a licence to assign or sub-let, but there is nothing to stop him or her requiring payment for the granting of such permission.

Qualified covenants

Prior to the introduction of the statutory provisions discussed later, a tenant under a lease **6.91** containing a qualified covenant was not really in a much better position than a tenant under an absolute covenant. The tenant could ask for the landlord's consent, but again the landlord could quite simply refuse to grant it. There was nothing to stop the landlord acting capriciously.

Absolutely qualified covenants

The Landlord and Tenant Act 1927, s 19(1)(a) provides that in all leases containing a **6.92** covenant against assigning, underletting, charging, or parting with the possession of the demised premises without licence or consent, that covenant shall, notwithstanding any express provision to the contrary, be deemed to be subject to a proviso to the effect that such licence or consent is not to be withheld unreasonably. The effect of this provision is to convert all qualified covenants into absolutely qualified covenants. The section will not apply to assured periodic tenancies or secure tenancies where assignment is prohibited by statute (see 6.88). Section 19(1A) allows the parties to agree to specific circumstances in which the landlord may refuse to consent to an assignment.

Where the property is managed by an RTM company consent should be sought from the **6.93** RTM company, which is effectively construed as being the landlord (CLRA 2002, Sch 7, para 1).

Section 144 of the LPA 1925 further provides that in the case of a qualified (or fully quali- **6.94** fied) covenant, a proviso will be implied that unless the lease contains an express provision to the contrary, no fine or sum of money in the nature of a fine will be payable for or in respect of a licence or consent. This section, however, does not preclude the right of the landlord to require the payment of a reasonable sum in respect of any legal or other expense incurred in relation to such licence and consent.

Tenant must seek consent

It is important to note that despite the fact that a landlord cannot unreasonably withhold **6.95** consent to a sub-lease or an assignment, it is still vital that the tenant who seeks to sub-let or assign should seek the landlord's consent before proceeding. A tenant who fails to seek consent, even if the landlord in the circumstances could not reasonably have withheld such consent, will be liable to have the lease forfeited (see *Wilson v Fynn* [1948] 2 All ER 40 and *Barrow v Isaccs & Son* [1891] 1 QB 417, CA).

Reasonable refusal of consent

The general principles set out in *International Drilling Fluids Ltd v Louisville Investments* **6.96** *(Uxbridge) Ltd* and *Iqbar v Thakrar* (see 6.71) apply to the assessment of reasonableness in refusing consent to sub-let or assign.

Consideration should be had to the fundamental purpose of the covenant, namely to **6.97** enable the landlord to retain some control over the occupation of the premises. The covenant should protect the landlord from having the premises occupied by an undesirable tenant or occupied in an undesirable way (*per* AL Smith LJ in *Bates v Donaldson* [1896] 2 QB 241 at 247). A landlord, therefore, is not entitled to refuse consent to an assignment for reasons which are not connected to the subject matter of the particular lease in question.

6.98   For example, where a landlord refused consent in order to gain a surrender of the lease because this would lead to better estate management of the whole building, the landlord was seen as trying to gain some collateral advantage for himself and the refusal was unreasonable (*Bromley Park Garden Estates Ltd v Moss* [1982] 1 WLR 1019, [1982] 2 All ER 890, CA). Likewise in *Holder Bros & Co. v Gibbs* [1925] Ch 575, CA, the proposed assignee was also a tenant of the landlord; the landlord refused consent because if the assignment took place the assignee's old flat would become empty and it would be difficult to find a new tenant. This refusal of consent was unreasonable, the landlord's objections not being based upon the undesirability of the new tenant or upon the use to which he would put the property but on difficulties that the landlord might encounter with another flat. Such considerations were unrelated to the particular lease in question; they did not relate to the personality of the tenant (who was presumably acceptable to the landlord being, as he was, already one of his tenants) or to the use to which the tenant would put the premises.

6.99   Refusal may be reasonable, however, when the landlord objects to the purpose for which the proposed assignee intends to use the premises, even though that purpose is not forbidden in the lease (*Bates v Donaldson*, 6.97). The landlord has to show only that the conclusions which led him or her to refuse consent were conclusions which might be reached by a reasonable person in the circumstances, not that the conclusions themselves were justified.

6.100 It is common for a landlord to insist that the terms of any under-lease are exactly the same as those contained in the head lease. If the tenant and the sub-tenant propose to enter into a private collateral agreement which contains different terms the landlord may be entitled to use this as a reason to refuse consent (*Allied Dunbar Assurance v Homebase* [2002] EWCA Civ 666, (2002) 27 EG 144 CA).

6.101 In *Pimms Ltd v Tallow Chandlers Co.* [1964] 2 QB 547, [1964] 2 All ER 145, the landlords' refusal to give consent to grant an assignment of the end of a lease of a restaurant in an area which was shortly to be redeveloped was held to be reasonable. The potential assignees were a development company whose only reason for taking the remaining term was to try to force the landlord to let them into the redevelopment scheme.

6.102 Because assignment and sub-letting have very different legal and practical consequences for the landlord, it may be that the refusal of consent to sub-let may be unreasonable but in the same circumstances a refusal to allow an assignment would be reasonable (*NCR v Riverside Portfolios No. 1 Ltd (No. 2)* [2005] EWCA Civ 312, [2005] 2 EGLR 42).

6.103 The landlord's objection need not relate only to concerns about detriment to the reversion. A landlord is entitled to refuse consent if it has genuine concerns about the ability of the proposed assignee to meet the obligations in the lease (*Royal Bank of Scotland Plc v Victoria Street (No. 5) Ltd* [2008] EWHC 3052 (Ch)). A landlord is entitled to insist on a guarantor for the assignee; however the landlord cannot reasonably require a guarantee for a term extending beyond the period during which the assignee is the tenant (*Landlord Protect Ltd v St Anselm Development Co. Ltd* [2009] EWCA Civ 99).

Detriment to the tenant

6.104 In general the landlord needs to consider only his or her own relevant interests. However, where there is a great disproportion between the benefit to the landlord and the detriment to the tenant, the detriment to the tenant may be taken into account. In *International Drilling Fluids Ltd v Louisville Investments (Uxbridge) Ltd* (6.71) the landlords, in refusing to grant consent for the tenants to assign, considered only the detriment to their own reversion. There was evidence that this damage would not cause great inconvenience to the landlords because there was no prospect of the landlords wishing to realize their reversion; it was simply a diminution in the 'paper value'. On the other hand, if the tenants, who had already moved to other premises, were not allowed to assign, they would still remain liable under the lease and would continue to have to pay rent even though the property was empty. It was held that in this case it was unreasonable for the landlords to withhold consent.

Discrimination

In most circumstances it is also unlawful to refuse to allow permission for the disposal of   **6.105**
premises by assignment or sub-letting to a person on grounds of that person's sex, race, religion, sexual orientation, disability, or gender reassignment (see Equality Act 2010, ss 4, 32, and 34).

Statutory tenancies

In some cases landlords have refused consent to an assignment because it would create a   **6.106**
statutory tenancy that did not exist when the original tenancy was granted (and was not enjoyed by the original tenant). The landlords' fear was that if an assignee acquired statutory protection the value of their reversion might be adversely affected because they might find it difficult to get vacant possession of the property at the end of the term.

From the earlier cases on this issue it seemed that a general principle could be discerned,   **6.107**
namely that it was reasonable for a landlord to refuse to grant consent to an 'abnormal' assignment. An abnormal assignment was one which usually took place towards the end of a lease, which the courts regarded as being designed to gain for the assignee protection which the assignor did not have, eg where a company, which as a company could not have Rent Act protection, sought to assign a lease to a director of that company, who as an individual could enjoy Rent Act protection (*Lee v K Carter Ltd* [1949] 1 KB 85, [1948] 2 All ER 690); or where a tenant was not in actual occupation of a property and sought near the end of the term to assign the lease to someone who could occupy the premises and thereby gain Rent Act protection (*Swanson v Forton* [1949] Ch 143, [1949] 1 All ER 135, CA).

Now, however, it seems that there is no such general doctrine and each case is to be consid-   **6.108**
ered on its own individual facts. In *Bickel v Duke of Westminster* [1977] QB 517, [1976] 3 All ER 801 and *Norfolk Capital Group Ltd v Kitway Ltd* [1977] QB 506, [1976] 3 All ER 787, it was held reasonable for a landlord to refuse consent to 'normal' assignments that would entitle assignees to acquire the freehold of the property under the Leasehold Reform Act 1967 because the assignments would adversely affect the landlord's interest. Likewise in *Leeward Securities Ltd v Lilyheath Properties Ltd* (1983) 271 EG 279, a refusal to grant consent to a sub-letting which would attract Rent Act protection was held to be reasonable because the sub-letting would affect the value of the landlord's reversion. The covenant protected the landlord against a danger that was different from that contemplated at the start of the lease. However, on the principles set out in *International Drilling Fluids*, it may be unreasonable for the landlord to refuse consent in certain situations where the detriment to the tenant caused by the refusal would far outweigh the detriment to the landlord's interest (see *Deverall v Wyndham* (1988) 21 HLR 260, [1989] EGLR 57):

> It must not be thought that, because the introduction of a Rent Act tenant inevitably has an adverse effect upon the value of the reversion, that that is a sufficient ground for the landlords to say that they can withhold consent and that the court will hold that that is

reasonable. (O'Connor LJ in *Leeward Securities* at 283, cited in *International Drilling Fluids* at 587)

Landlord's reasons

6.109 The landlord is obliged to provide written reasons for his or her refusal to give consent (Landlord and Tenant Act 1988, s 1). He or she will be confined to these written reasons should the matter come to be considered by a court (*Footwear Corporation v Amplight Properties* [1999] 1 WLR 551). The landlord is also required to reach a decision within a reasonable time. What is a reasonable time has to be assessed having regard to all the circumstances of the case (*Go West Ltd v Spigarolo* [2003] EWCA Civ 17). In *Mount Eden Land Ltd v Folia Ltd* [2003] EWHC 1815 (Ch), a case where the tenant had requested a decision as a matter of urgency, 24 days was held not to be reasonable.

Burden of proof

6.110 Originally it was a general principle that the onus of proving that consent had been withheld unreasonably was on the tenant. This presumption was reversed by the Landlord and Tenant Act 1988, s 1(6)(b) and (c). The 1988 Act also requires a landlord who receives a written request for consent to an assignment or sub-letting to respond in writing, to give reasons for his or her refusal, and to respond within a reasonable time. It also entitles the tenant to damages if the landlord unreasonably withholds consent.

Remedies for breach of covenant not to assign or sub-let

6.111 Where a tenant has breached a covenant not to assign or sub-let the landlord may sue for damages. The measure of damages will be the loss flowing from the breach. The landlord may seek an injunction to prevent a proposed assignment or sub-letting, or, if a right of re-entry has been reserved in the lease, bring proceedings for forfeiture (see Chapter 11).

6.112 Where a tenant is of the opinion that a landlord has withheld consent to an assignment or sub-letting unreasonably, the tenant may go ahead with the assignment or sub-letting. This is clearly a risky path for the tenant to take, for if the landlord has reserved a right of re-entry in the lease it may result in forfeiture proceedings. However, if consent was withheld unreasonably the tenant will probably be granted relief from forfeiture. A more cautious tenant might prefer to apply to the county court for a declaration that consent was withheld unreasonably under the Landlord and Tenant Act 1954, s 53(1). The declaration should also provide that he or she is entitled to assign or sub-let under the proposed terms. The tenant may also be able to seek an order of specific performance. Where a tenant makes a written application for consent under the Landlord and Tenant Act 1988, s 3, and the landlord fails to comply with the requirement of the Act, then the tenant may sue for damages for breach of statutory duty.

J OPTIONS

6.113 So far the majority of the covenants we have looked at serve to enable the landlord to continue to exercise some control over the property, even though the landlord has handed over the possession of that property to the tenant. Covenants do this by restricting the tenant's common law rights by way of a prohibition (not to sub-let or assign, not to use for particular purposes), by compelling the tenant to do something that he or she would not be under a common law obligation to do (to repair, to insure), or by allowing the landlord to retain a right over the property that he or she would not have at common law (to allow the landlord to enter to inspect, right of re-entry in case of breach).

Options are different; they do not restrict the tenant's rights, rather they give the tenant **6.114**
the right to do something in the future, a right which the tenant would not have had under
the common law. There are three common rights which the tenant may acquire by way of
option:

(a) the right to take the tenancy for a further term (an *option to renew*);
(b) the right to end the tenancy (this right can be given to either or both parties) (an *option
     to determine*);
(c) the right to purchase the landlord's interest in the property (an *option to purchase*).

These options normally take the form of a covenant by the landlord in which the landlord **6.115**
promises, on the occurrence of a certain event or at a particular time, and if the tenant so
wishes, that the landlord will perform the content of the covenant.

Option to renew

The landlord may choose at the start of a fixed-term tenancy to promise the tenant the **6.116**
grant of another tenancy when the first one expires. Of course, at the end of a fixed-term
tenancy a tenant can ask the landlord to enter into another term, but the landlord can
always refuse. If an option is included in the lease it means that the landlord must grant the
tenant a further tenancy if the tenant so wishes. Effectively the tenant will have a guarantee
that the tenancy will be renewed. Such a promise by a landlord can make a property much
more desirable to a tenant.

Renewal will rarely be automatic, however. A landlord does not want to be obliged to grant **6.117**
a further tenancy to a badly behaved tenant. Renewal will therefore normally be made
conditional on two factors:

(a) that the tenant gives the landlord notice of his or her desire to renew the lease at a
     specified time and in a specified manner (eg in writing at least six months before the
     expiry of the term);
(b) that the tenant is not in breach of any of the covenants in the lease.

To exercise the option, therefore, the tenant must comply strictly with the notice require- **6.118**
ments. If notice is not served in the specified form or is served outside of the designated
period it will be invalid unless the landlord waives the error (*Multon v Cordell* [1986]
1 EGLR 44). If no requirement of prior written notice is set out in the lease, the fact that
the tenant remains in occupation of the premises beyond the end of the term is sufficient to
indicate that the tenant wishes to exercise the option. If the landlord then accepts rent from
the tenant, this will be regarded as consent to the exercise of the option (*Gardner v Blaxill*
[1960] 1 WLR 752, [1960] 2 All ER 457).

A requirement that there be no existing breach of covenant at the time of the exercise of **6.119**
the option is also strictly applied. Even a trivial breach of covenant will render the tenant
unable to exercise the option; for example, where a tenant had failed to observe a covenant
to repaint at fixed intervals (*West Country Cleaners (Falmouth) Ltd v Saly* [1966] 1 WLR
1485, [1966] 3 All ER 210, CA). However, if the breach is not current at the point in
time when the tenant wishes to exercise the option the tenant will not be prevented from
exercising the right. In *Bass Holdings Ltd v Morton Music Ltd* [1987] 2 All ER 1001, CA,
the landlord had, in the past, tried to forfeit the lease for breach of covenant. The court
had granted the tenant relief and the tenant had complied with all the conditions of relief.
When, later in the same year, the tenant tried to exercise an option to renew, the court
regarded the past breaches as 'spent' and they did not entitle the landlord to refuse to
renew the tenancy.

Terms of the new lease

6.120   If the tenant chooses to opt for a further term the lease is normally renewable on the same terms as the original lease, and this will be specified in the landlord's covenant to renew. Nevertheless, there will usually be two variations in the terms of the new lease:

(a) The covenant will usually provide that the new lease will not contain the option to renew. The inclusion of this exception is prudent of the landlord, for if the new lease contains a further covenant for renewal it would mean that the tenant could continue to renew the lease *ad infinitum*. (Such perpetually renewable leases are converted into terms of 2,000 years by the LPA 1925, s 146, Sch 15.)

(b) It is also common for provision to be made for the rent to be varied. Usually the new rent will be agreed between the parties, or by some mechanism that is set out in the lease.

6.121   In the absence of such express terms the new lease will be on the same terms as the old lease, for the same period and at the same rent.

Option to determine

6.122   Unlike an option to renew, an option to determine (often called a break clause) can, and frequently does, apply to both parties. The option gives the party who wishes to exercise it the right to end the tenancy at a specified time, or on the occurrence of a specified event. Break clauses are more often to be found in business leases than in residential leases. Commonly an option to determine will give the tenant (and sometimes the landlord) the right to end a fixed-term tenancy at certain points during the term. For example, a six-year tenancy may contain a provision enabling the tenant to terminate the tenancy at the end of the second and fourth years. Similarly a provision may be included in the lease permitting the landlord to terminate the tenancy in a specified circumstance.

6.123   As with an option to renew, the party wishing to exercise the break clause will have to comply strictly with the requirements set out in the lease. For example in *Claire's Accessories UK Ltd v Kensington High Street Associates LLC* [2001] PLSCS 112 a landlord's notice of intention to exercise the option (break notice) that was sent to the tenant's employees at the premises was held to be invalid because the lease provided that such a notice must be sent to the tenant's registered office. Usually the lease will demand that a written break notice must be served upon the other party six months (or other period) prior to the date upon which the option is to be exercised. If there are joint tenants, a break notice will not be valid unless it is served by all of them (*Prudential Assurance Co Ltd v Exel UK Ltd* [2009] EWHC 1350 (Ch)).

Conditions

6.124   It is common for landlords' break clauses to be subject to conditions that must be met before a break notice can be served, for example a condition that the clause can only be operated if the landlord intends to redevelop the property, or that it can be operated if the premises are destroyed or seriously damaged. Tenants' break clauses often contain conditions that the option cannot be exercised unless the tenant has paid the rent up to date and there are no current breaches of any of the terms of the lease.

Effect of exercising the option to determine

6.125   **Tenant's break notice**   If the tenant exercises an option to determine the lease, this will end the contractual term. In the case of a business tenancy, service of a break notice will also remove the tenancy from the protection of the Landlord and Tenant Act 1954. This means that the tenant will not be entitled to remain in the property after the break notice has expired and will not have the right to request a new tenancy (see 26.119).

Landlord's break notice A landlord's break notice will also end the tenant's contractual term **6.126** but it will not end the tenant's statutory right to occupy the property (see, for example, 15.46 on the position of an assured tenant). A business tenant who has the protection of the 1954 Act will be entitled to remain in occupation and will have the right to request a new tenancy unless the tenancy is terminated in accordance with the provisions of that Act (see 26.62).

Effect on sub-tenants If a landlord or a tenant exercises a break clause this will also end **6.127** any sub-tenancy. The sub-tenants will, however, then become the immediate tenants of the head landlord and will have the same statutory protection they had under the sub-lease. In the case of business tenancies this means that the former sub-tenant will have rights of continuation and renewal under the 1954 Act (*PW & Co. v Milton Gate Investments Ltd* [2003] EWHC 1994 (Ch), [2004] 3 EGLR 103, Ch D).

Option to purchase

An option to purchase gives the tenant the right to buy the landlord's interest in the premises **6.128** at a point in the future. Like an option to renew, an option to purchase normally takes the form of a covenant by the landlord in which the landlord undertakes, on being given notice by the tenant and on the payment of a specified sum, to convey the landlord's interest in the property to the tenant. The option may state a price to be paid, or it may set out a valuation procedure by which the price can be ascertained.

An option to purchase is not regarded as being part of the lease; it is instead an agreement **6.129** collateral to the lease. An option to purchase affects the parties as vendor and purchaser and not as landlord and tenant (which is important, as we shall see later, because it means that it does not touch and concern the land and therefore does not run with the land as a matter of course, although the option may be registered as a charge under the Land Charges Act 1972, s 2(4): see 9.80). It is not in itself a contract, for until it is exercised the landlord is not obliged to sell; rather, it is an offer to sell which the landlord had precluded himself or herself from revoking. If the tenant chooses to exercise the option and serves notice in accordance with the provisions of the lease, the offer will be accepted and the option will then become a binding contract.

Validity of notices

As a general rule, minor errors in notices will not invalidate the notice provided that the **6.130** reasonable recipient of the notice would have understood the notice and not been misled by the error (*Mannai Investment Co. Ltd v Eagle Star Life Assurance Co. Ltd* [1997] AC 749, [1997] 2 WLR 945). Thus a notice to exercise a break clause that gave the wrong date of termination was held to be valid because the lease did not require a date to be given on the notice and it would have been clear to the landlord that it was a mistake (*Peer Freeholds Ltd v Clean Wash International* [2005] EWHC 179 (Ch), (2005) 17 EG 124). However, a notice to exercise an option that gave the wrong date of expiry was not valid as it left doubt as to how and when the notice was intended to operate (*Peaceform Ltd v Cussens and Greengrass* [2006] EWHC 2657 (Ch), (2006) 47 EG 182). Where the information to be provided in a notice is prescribed by statute, failure to provide any or all of that information will generally make the notice invalid (*Speedwell Estates Ltd v Dalzeil* [2001] EWCA Civ 1277, [2002] HLR 43; *Burman v Mount Cook Land Ltd* [2001] EWCA Civ 1712, [2002] WLR 1172).

KEY DOCUMENTS

Landlord and Tenant Act 1925

Law of Property Act 1925

Landlord and Tenant Act 1927

Civil Procedure Rules 1998

Forms N9B and N9D defence and counterclaim

Form N1—Part 7 Claim

Form N208—Part 8 Claim

Form N208A—Part 8 Claim form (notes for claimant)

Form 208B—Part 8 Claim form (notes for defendant)

Printed copies of all legislation can be ordered from The Stationery Office at <http://www.tsoshop. co.uk>. All legislation from 1988 onwards and most pre-1988 primary legislation is available online at <http://www. legislation.gov.uk>.

The Civil Procedure Rules are available online from <http://www.justice.gov.uk/courts/ procedure-rules>.

Court forms are available online from the HM Courts and Tribunals Service at <http://www.justice. gov.uk/forms/hmcts>.

Guidance on Unfair Terms in Tenancy Agreements, Office of Fair Trading 2005, is available online from <http://www.oft.gov.uk>.

7

REPAIR—CONTRACTUAL OBLIGATIONS

A INTRODUCTION

Even the most modern and well-built houses will deteriorate if left to their own devices. To **7.01** keep a house in a habitable, let alone good, condition, constant maintenance is needed. A building is a complex interdependent structure; a fault in any of its components can lead to more extensive damage to other parts of the building. Something as simple as a blocked gutter can lead to serious damp penetration if it is not remedied and rainwater is allowed to run down a section of wall.

Whether the landlord or the tenant is to be responsible for the maintenance and repair of **7.02** a property is a question of considerable significance for both parties. In an ideal world the interests of tenant and landlord would coincide. Both would want to see that the property was well maintained: the landlord so that at the end of the tenant's term he or she would recover a property that had not deteriorated in value, the tenant so that throughout the term he or she has somewhere satisfactory to live. In reality, however, the situation is nowhere near so simple and disputes over disrepair are commonplace. Proper maintenance requires both time and money and can, in some cases, be exceedingly expensive. Unsurprisingly, both landlords and tenants will often seek to avoid their responsibilities.

7.03 Unfortunately the law has not developed a coherent system to deal with the problems of repair. Long-established common law principles, which are frequently of dubious relevance to contemporary residential housing situations, have been subject to scrappy, piecemeal reform by various disparate statutes and case law. The result is a heterogenous body of law spanning both contract and tort, partially encoded in a wide variety of different statutes and partially to be found in case law.

B THE PRINCIPLE OF *CAVEAT LESSEE*

7.04 As with the majority of the covenants we considered in the last chapter, the basic principle is that, in the absence of any express agreement between the parties, neither party is responsible for repairs. This approach is epitomized by the old principle of *caveat emptor* and *caveat lessee*, the ghost of which still haunts the law relating to repair.

7.05 Literally, *caveat emptor* means 'let the buyer beware' and *caveat lessee* 'let the lessee beware'. Under the principle of *caveat lessee* the onus is on the person entering into a tenancy agreement to satisfy himself or herself of the condition of the property to which the tenancy relates. The tenant is assumed to take the property as it stands. If, for example, the tenant moves into the property and discovers that it suffers from such severe damp as to render it virtually uninhabitable, in the absence of any express agreement to the contrary the tenant cannot complain to the landlord that the flat is not fit for the purpose for which it was rented. This is in marked contrast to the position when a customer goes into a shop and buys a computer. If that computer turns out to be defective the customer has a remedy against the shop. The shop has to guarantee that what it sells is fit for the purpose for which it is intended. In English law, land does not come with a guarantee.

7.06 To grant the landlord such comprehensive immunity from any obligation as to the condition of the property let is so clearly at odds with the demands of modern housing requirements that the law has sought, albeit in a fragmentary fashion, to temper the harshest consequences of the principle of *caveat lessee*. The much quoted maxim, 'Fraud apart, there is no law against letting a tumble down house' (*Robbins v Jones* [1863] 15 CB (NS) 221 at 240) is no longer strictly true. There are plenty of laws against renting a tumble down house, but the majority of them are either statutory in origin or have developed in the law of negligence. At common law in contract the landlord retains a considerable degree of immunity from obligations to repair.

C EXPRESS AGREEMENT

7.07 Where there is a written tenancy agreement, the parties to that agreement will normally include an express provision dealing with repair. The parties are free to allocate the responsibility for repairs between them in any way upon which they can agree. Frequently, the responsibility may be split between both parties, the landlord undertaking to repair and maintain the structure and exterior of the premises while the tenant undertakes to keep the internal decorations in repair. In practice, because it is usually the landlord who draws up the agreement, there is a tendency for express covenants to lean towards placing that responsibility upon the tenant.

7.08 Who is to be responsible for repairs and maintenance will usually depend on the length of a lease. As a general rule it can be said that the shorter the term of lease the more likely it is that the landlord will take responsibility for repairs. Clearly, a tenant with a six-month lease will be unlikely to agree to pay for any substantial repairs to a property in which he or she has no long-term interest. With a longer lease the tenant will probably shoulder the burden of responsibility for repairs (at least financially, although the landlord or management company may actually arrange for the work to be done). In the case of a long lease it is the tenant who will benefit directly from the premises being in good condition. However, the landlord will also wish to ensure that repairs are properly carried out in order to protect the value of the reversion. Where the lease could be construed as imposing a repairing obligation on both landlord and tenant the Court of Appeal has held that the court must attempt to find an interpretation that places liability on one party only, rather than creating overlapping repairing obligations (*Petersson v Pitt Place (Epsom) Ltd* [2001] EWCA Civ 86, [2002] HLR 52).

Where there is a dispute as to the exact meaning or extent of an express repairing covenant   **7.09** the court will adopt a common sense approach by looking at the 'factual matrix' of the case, the natural and ordinary meaning of the words to be interpreted, and the objectives of the parties (*Holding & Barnes Plc v Hill House Hammond* [2001] EWCA Civ 1334, [2002] L&TR 7).

Construction

An express covenant to repair can be worded in any way the parties desire, but in practice   **7.10** there are certain common expressions that are frequently found in leases.

'To put in repair'

This expression is used when the premises are out of repair at the commencement of the   **7.11** lease. It imposes on the burdened party an obligation to perform work upon the premises to bring them up to standard. (For the standard of repair, see 7.41 to 7.50.)

'To leave (deliver, yield up) in repair'

This expression imposes an obligation on the tenant to have the premises in repair at the   **7.12** end of the term when they are given back to the landlord. Unless there is also an obligation to keep in repair then no liability will arise until the end of the term. If the property falls into disrepair during the course of the tenancy, the landlord will not be able to compel the tenant to make repairs until the term expires. So long as the tenant gives back the property in good condition he or she will not have breached the covenant.

'To keep in good condition'

The use of this expression will, again, impose a more extensive standard than a covenant   **7.13** to keep in repair. In *Welsh v Greenwich LBC* (2000) 49 EG 118, CA, a covenant to keep in good condition was held to trigger an obligation to remedy condensation dampness. This work would be beyond the scope of an obligation to keep in repair (see 7.14).

'To keep in repair'

This is a common expression used in many agreements and requires the tenant (or land-   **7.14** lord) to ensure that the premises are kept in good condition throughout the term. If at any time during the term the premises fall into a state of disrepair, this will be a breach of covenant. Liability will arise once the premises have fallen into disrepair and thus the landlord (or tenant) will be able to compel repair work to be undertaken during the course of the tenancy. Such a covenant will also require the tenant (or landlord) to leave the premises in repair, and also to put them into repair at the beginning of the term if they are out of repair (*Proudfoot v Hart* (1890) 25 QBD 42).

'To keep in tenantable condition'

7.15 A covenant to put and keep in tenantable condition will go further than a covenant to keep in repair: there does not have to be actual disrepair to give rise to an obligation under such a covenant (*Credit Suisse v Beegas Nominees Ltd* [1994] 4 All ER 803).

'To repair and renew'

7.16 Unless clearer words are used such a covenant does not impose any wider obligation on the burdened party than a covenant simply to repair (*Collins v Flynn* [1963] 2 All ER 1086). The difference between repair and renewal is considered at 7.32.

'To carry out structural repairs'

7.17 We shall discuss later what amounts to 'structure' (see 7.96). In general it means repairs to the fabric of the building such as the roof, walls, floors, and foundations as opposed to repairs to decorations and fixtures and fittings. Such repairs can be very expensive, and in short leases it is therefore more common for them to be imposed on the landlord. In long leases, however, the financial burden at least is often placed upon the tenant.

'Fair wear and tear excepted'

7.18 This is a clause most commonly found in short leases. It excludes the tenant from liability to repair damage which occurs due to the natural process of ageing. Such damage could be caused by action of the elements, or by the tenant's normal and reasonable use of the premises for the purposes for which they were let. The scope of such a clause is limited and will not extend to the following situations:

(a) If the tenant uses the premises in a way not envisaged when they were let which puts greater strain on the building and accelerates wear and tear, eg by storing very heavy items on a warehouse floor (*Manchester Bonded Warehouse Co. v Carr* [1880] 5 CPD 507).

(b) If the damage is caused by extraordinary natural events such as earthquakes or floods.

(c) Where the cause of the damage can be traced back to a defect which was originally due to fair wear and tear but the damage itself is not directly caused by fair wear and tear: for example, where a tile falls off a roof due to the natural process of ageing but the leak caused by the missing tile becomes so serious as to render the whole top floor of the house uninhabitable. In such a situation the tenant is regarded as being under an obligation to do work 'to prevent the consequences flowing originally from wear and tear from producing others which wear and tear would not directly produce' (*Haskell v Marlow* [1928] 2 KB 45 *per* Talbot J at 59; see also *Regis Property Co. Ltd v Dudley* [1959] AC 370, [1958] 3 All ER 491). Talbot J contrasted the example of a missing tile with that of a stone floor or a staircase which gradually wears away over years of use; this, he says, would be fair wear and tear and the tenant would not be liable for it.

'To rebuild'

7.19 A landlord is under no obligation to rebuild the premises if they are destroyed unless he or she has expressly covenanted to do so. A tenant, on the other hand, who has covenanted to keep the premises in repair will be obliged to rebuild the premises if they are destroyed unless this obligation is expressly excluded by the terms of the lease.

Conditions precedent to repair

7.20 It is common for a lease to contain a provision that the landlord's obligation to repair arises provided the tenant pays all rents and service charges. It is important to note that a landlord cannot use the tenant's breach of an obligation to pay rent or service charges as an excuse not to carry out repairs (see 6.08). The payment of rent cannot form a condition precedent to the obligation to repair (*Yorkbrook Investments v Batten* (1985) 52 P&CR 51, [1985] 2 EGLR 100, CA).

D WHEN WILL A LIABILITY TO REPAIR ARISE?

An obligation to repair will arise when: **7.21**

(a) there is disrepair; and
(b) the party under an obligation to repair has notice of the disrepair.

Disrepair

To say that there must be some disrepair before an obligation to repair will arise may seem   **7.22**
to be stating the obvious. Clearly, if something is not broken there is no need to fix it. The law, however, uses a strict definition of 'disrepair'. For a condition of disrepair to exist two factors must be satisfied:

(a) there must be some deterioration of a part of the premises from a previous better condition;
(b) the burdened party must be under an obligation (either express or implied) to repair that part which has deteriorated.

Disrepair cannot therefore be equated with damage. A house may fall into a very bad con-   **7.23**
dition because of a leaky roof, but if no one has covenanted to repair the roof there is no disrepair. Likewise a basement may be prone to flooding and the tenant may be under an obligation to repair, but if the structure of that basement has not deteriorated from a previous better condition there is no disrepair (see *Post Office v Aquarius Properties Ltd* [1987] 1 All ER 1055, CA and *Janet Reger International v Tirtree Ltd* [2006] EWHC 1743 (Ch)).

The strict application of these principles to the practical realities of modern housing has   **7.24**
led to something of a lacuna in the law of repair. The problem has centred around condensation dampness. Unlike dampness caused by a hole in the roof or a leaking down-pipe, condensation dampness arises when the water vapour in the air condenses on contact with a cold surface. It is prone to arise when there is insufficient ventilation and inadequate insulation. It tends to affect more modern buildings, with their large windows with metal frames and thinner walls.

The most striking example of this was in *Quick v Taff Ely BC* [1985] 3 WLR 981, where   **7.25**
severe condensation was caused largely by big, metal-framed windows. The dampness caused by the condensation caused damage to the tenant's furniture, bedding, clothes, and decorations and rendered some rooms of the flat uninhabitable. The court agreed that the condensation 'rendered the living conditions of the plaintiff and his family appalling' (*per* Dillon LJ at 985). The tenant, however, had no remedy against the landlord. The landlord had covenanted to repair only the 'structure and exterior' of the flat (implied by the Landlord and Tenant Act 1985, s 11, see 7.87). Such a covenant includes a liability to repair walls and windows. Unfortunately for the tenant, the walls and windows themselves were undamaged and so, despite the fact that the flat was virtually unfit for human habitation, there was no disrepair. 'The key factor ... is that disrepair is related to the physical condition of what had to be repaired, and not to questions of lack of amenity or efficiency' (*per* Dillon LJ at 987C). If there was no condition of disrepair, there could be no liability to repair.

7.26   The result in *Quick v Taff* can be contrasted with *Staves and Staves v Leeds City Council* (1992) 29 EG 119, CA. Here, damp and condensation caused small parts of plaster to perish and the tenant was held able to recover because the structure and exterior of the flat had itself deteriorated (see also *Grand v Gill* [2011] EWCA Civ 554).

7.27   As condensation dampness is a very common problem it is often a significant feature of potential disrepair claims. The matter was considered in two further cases. In *Southwark LBC v McIntosh* [2002] 1 EGLR 25 it was upheld that there is no disrepair when a property suffers from damp unless damp arises from disrepair to the structure or exterior of the dwelling or unless the damp itself has caused damage to the structure or exterior. (Damage to the tenant's possessions or decorations caused by condensation dampness will not provide a cause of action.) In *Lee v Leeds City Council* [2002] EWCA Civ 6, [2002] 1 WLR 1488, the Court of Appeal affirmed this view, ruling that *Quick v Taff* had been correctly decided. Interestingly, however, the court raised the proposition that very serious levels of condensation dampness in a property let by a local authority might constitute a breach of the tenant's rights to family and private life under Article 8 of the European Convention on Human Rights.

Notice

7.28   No liability can arise under a repairing covenant, be that covenant express or implied, until the landlord has actual knowledge of the need for repair. It makes no difference that the landlord may have reserved the right to enter to inspect the premises. A tenant who becomes aware of a defect should notify his or her landlord or the landlord's agent immediately. To establish liability the tenant must prove that the landlord had knowledge of the defect. If the tenant has not directly informed the landlord of the defect, he or she may be able to establish liability if it can be shown that the landlord knew about the defect through a reliable source such as a caretaker, a workmen employed by the landlord, or even an independent environmental health officer (*Dinefwer BC v Jones* (1987) 19 HLR 445). The tenant must show that the landlord received information about the defect that would be sufficient to put a reasonable person on enquiry as to whether work was necessary (*O'Brien v Robinson* [1973] AC 912). However, in *Brewer v Andrews* [1997] EGCS 19, CA, it was held that vague complaints of disrepair given to the landlord's managing agent were not sufficient. The complaints must relate to specific items of disrepair. Until recently *O'Brien v Robinson* was also authority for the fact that a landlord's liability did not arise immediately the disrepair became apparent but only after a reasonable period had elapsed. This view was rejected by the Court of Appeal in *British Telecom v Sun Life Assurance* [1995] 4 All ER 44, CA. The general rule now seems to be that a covenant to keep in repair creates an obligation to keep the premises in repair at all times; this obligation will be breached the moment a defect occurs. In *British Telecom v Sun Life* the defect occurred to a common part of the building which was under the landlord's care and control and so the landlord was assumed to have notice of the defect. In such a case, however, it may be appropriate to allow the landlord a reasonable time to carry out repairs when he or she becomes aware of the defect, for example where the landlord is required to consult with the lessees before commencing major works or where the landlord needs access through a tenant's flat in order to carry out repairs (*Charalambous v Earle (Addendum to judgment)* [2006] EWCA Civ 1338, [2007] HLR 8, CA).

Access to carry out works

7.29   Where a landlord has an express or implied duty to carry out repairs he or she will have a correlative common law right to enter the tenant's premises to carry out those works (see

5.47). This right is subject to an obligation on the part of the landlord to give the tenant reasonable notice that access will be needed, and an obligation to behave reasonably in exercising the right to access (*Granada Theatres v Freehold Investments (Leytonstone) Ltd* [1959] Ch 592, [1959] 2 All ER 176, see 7.114). The tenant can only be required to vacate the property during the course of the works if this is essential because of the nature or extent of the works, rather than simply being cheaper or more convenient (*McGreal v Wake* (1984) 13 HLR 107, CA).

Where a landlord is undertaking repairs according to his or her statutory obligations under **7.30** s 8 or s 11 of the Landlord and Tenant Act 1985 the Act specifically provides that the tenant allow the landlord entry (s 8(2) and s 11(6)). Similar rights are found in the Rent Act 1977, s 148 (relating to protected or secure tenancies) and the Housing Act 1988, s 16 (relating to assured tenancies).

E WHAT IS REPAIR?

In *Calthorpe v McOscar* [1924] 1 KB 716, CA, it was said that repair means 'making good **7.31** damage so as to leave the subject as far as possible as though it had not been damaged'. So far so good, but when an attempt is made to apply this legal principle to the complex and infinitely variable practicalities of repairing and maintaining a house, certain difficulties manifest themselves; after all, it is never truly possible to repair a building so as to leave it exactly as it was before it was damaged.

Repair or renewal

When a tenant is granted a lease, particularly a lease of an old property, the components **7.32** of the house will not be in perfect condition: they will have already suffered from the effects of use, misuse, ageing, weather, and neglect. If one of the components becomes defective and requires replacement it will normally be replaced by a new component. Cracked and defective guttering will be replaced by new guttering, worn out flooring will be replaced with a new floor. All repair will of necessity involve renewal (*Lurcott v Wakely and Wheeler* [1911] 1 KB 905 *per* Buckley LJ at 923). It will still be repair even if, over a period of time, each individual part of a building falls into disrepair and is replaced until in due course the whole building has been renewed (*per* Fletcher Moulton LJ at 917).

On the other hand, what would be the situation if the condition of a house was so bad that **7.33** the only way to repair it would be by rebuilding the whole structure? Clearly, this would not be the subordinate renewal of parts, but rather the renewal of the whole. In *Lister v Lane* [1893] 2 QB 212 at 216, Lord Esher stated:

> However large the words of the covenant may be, a covenant to repair a house is not a covenant to give a different thing from that which the tenant took when he entered into the covenant. He has to repair that thing which he took; he is not obliged to make a new and different thing, and moreover, the result of the nature and condition of the house itself, and the result of time upon that state of things, is not a breach of the covenant to repair.

In between these two extremes the courts have been faced with the near impossible task of **7.34** deciding whether the work required amounts to repair or renewal. Each case has its own particular facts, and the range of possibilities when it comes to considering the condition of a building is virtually infinite. It is not surprising that the courts have been unable to come up with one simple principle with which to draw the line. In *Brew Bros Ltd v Snax Ltd*

[1970] 1 QB 612 at 640, Sachs LJ considered the various phrases that had been put before him in an attempt to express the distinction and concluded:

> ... it is really not much use looking at individual phrases which necessarily deal with only one of the infinitely variable sets of circumstances that can arise.

> For my part I doubt whether there is any definition—certainly not a general definition—which covers the above distinctions: nor will I attempt to provide one ... It seems to me that the correct approach is to look at the particular building, to look at the state which it is in *at the date of the lease*, to look at the precise terms of the lease, and then to come to a conclusion as to whether, on a fair interpretation of those terms in relation to that state, the requisite work can fairly be called repair. However large the covenant it must not be looked at in vacuo.

> Quite clearly this approach involves in every instance a question of degree ... .

7.35 In *Holding Management Ltd v Property Holdings Plc* [1990] 1 All ER 938 at 945, Nicholls LJ set out some of the factors that may be taken into account:

> ... the nature of the building; the terms of the lease; the state of the building at the date of the lease; the nature and extent of the defect sought to be remedied; the nature, extent and cost of the proposed remedial works, at whose expense the proposed remedial works are to be done; the value of the building and its expected lifespan; the effect of the works on such value and lifespan; current building practice; the likelihood of a recurrence if one remedy rather than another is adopted; and the comparative cost of alternative remedial works and their impact on the use and enjoyment of the building by the occupants. The weight to be attached to these circumstances will vary from case to case.

> This is not a comprehensive list. In some cases there will be other matters properly to be taken into account.

7.36 Each case will turn upon its own particular facts. Where the 24-ft-wide front wall of a building that went back 100 ft required rebuilding, it was held to be repair rather than renewal (*Lurcott v Wakely and Wheeler* [1911] 1 KB 905, CA). On the other hand, where the two outside walls of a triangular building needed rebuilding this was held to be renewal rather than repair (*Torrens v Walker* [1906] 2 Ch 166). Likewise, when the wooden foundations of a house built on soft ground rotted, the remedy would have involved digging down 17 ft to solid gravel and putting in new foundations; this was held to be renewal (*Lister v Lane & Needsham* [1893] 2 QB 212, CA). The installation of a modern and expensive damp proof course in a 150-year-old house was held to go beyond repair as it would have turned the house into a very different property from the one that was let (*Trustees of the Eyre Estate v McCraken* (2000) 80 P&CR 220 CA).

Inherent defects

7.37 If, as we saw earlier, repair means 'making good damage so as to leave the subject as far as possible as though it had not been damaged', what then is the position when the disrepair is caused by an inherent fault in the design or construction of the building? It has been argued that an obligation to repair did not include the obligation to remedy defects in the construction of the building, because a building without an inherent defect is in fact a wholly different thing from a building with an inherent defect. It has been suggested that this reasoning leads to what has been called 'the doctrine of inherent defect', namely that the remedying of inherent defects does not fall within the ambit of a repairing covenant.

7.38 Support for such a view is said to be found in cases such as *Collins v Flynn* [1963] 2 All ER 1068. Here, due to inadequate foundations, a structure supporting part of the back and side wall of a house collapsed. It was held that to replace the foundations and rebuild the structure would be an improvement of the premises and that the covenant to repair did not extend to the remedying of an inherent defect (see also *Sotheby v Grundy* [1947] 2 All ER 761). However, as with the majority of repair cases, this case turned on its own facts. The house in question was over 100 years old and had been condemned. It would be wrong to assume, from the fact that in this case the court found that to undertake the repairs would be to give back to the landlord a wholly different thing from the premises as demised, a doctrine that a covenant to repair never covers inherent defects.

The doctrine of inherent defect was finally laid to rest in *Ravenseft Ltd v Davstone Ltd*   **7.39** [1980] 1 QB 12. Here the stone cladding on a large block of flats cracked and became detached from the building itself due to the failure to install expansion joints. Relative to the value of the building the cost of the work required to remedy the inherent fault was small. Forbes J (at 21) found himself unable to accept that the doctrine of inherent defect 'has any place in the law of landlord and tenant':

> The true test is, as the cases show, that it is always a question of degree whether that which the tenant is being asked to do can properly be described as repair, or whether on the contrary it would involve giving back to the landlord a wholly different thing from that which he demised.

The remedying of an inherent defect can therefore be repair regardless of the fact that   **7.40** the defect was due to an error in design or construction. In *Elmcroft Developments Ltd v Tankersley Sawyer* (1984) 270 EG 1289, the original slate damp course in a block of flats had been installed too low, with the result that the lower flats were subject to damp. To remedy the damp it was necessary to install a new silicon damp course. The court held that this was repair. This case should however be contrasted with *Eyre v McCraken* (see 7.36). In that case there was no existing damp proof course. Installing one was held to go beyond what constitutes repair.

F STANDARD OF REPAIR

Like human beings, buildings have a life-span. As they age their condition will deterio-   **7.41** rate. A fit 70-year-old will not be expected to be able to perform the same tasks as a fit 21-year-old, despite the fact that a doctor would classify both as being in good health. It is the same with buildings. A Victorian property that needed to have some windows replaced would not be regarded as being in bad condition, but a new flat that needed new windows would be a cause for concern for a prospective purchaser.

How, then, is the standard of repair of a building to be assessed? Clearly, it has to be a flex-   **7.42** ible criterion that can adjust itself to properties of various types and ages. The following rule was set out in *Proudfoot v Hart* (1890) 25 QBD 42:

> good tenantable repair is such repair as, having regard to the age, character, and locality of the house, would make it reasonably fit for the occupation of a reasonably-minded tenant of the class who would be likely to take it.

The judge in this case illustrated his three factors. Age was important because a 200-year-old   **7.43** house could not be expected to be in the same condition as a new one; character because a palace would demand a different standard of repair from a cottage; and location because a house in Grosvenor Square would demand a different standard of repair from a house in Spitalfields. The benchmark was subjective: what would be expected by the incoming tenant?

7.44   In certain situations such a criterion can prove too flexible. For example, a tenant takes a long lease of a new property in a fashionable area. Over the years the neighbouring properties fall into a state of disrepair and the neighbourhood deteriorates, so that at the end of the lease the only likely tenants are people looking for short-term lets. Is the standard of repair to be demanded of the outgoing tenant at the end of his term the relatively low standard of the potential incoming tenant looking for a short-term let?

7.45   This was the situation in *Calthorpe v McOscar* [1924] 1 KB 716. Three new houses had been let on 99-year leases. At the beginning of the term they had been country houses in a good area: at the end of the term the area had deteriorated to such a degree that the only tenants likely to take the houses would be short-term tenants. It was not disputed that the houses were out of repair and that the outgoing tenants should pay damages to the landlord sufficient to put the properties back into repair. The problem arose when it came to calculating the amount of damages. What standard of repair should be adopted? An arbitrator was appointed to assess the damages and he came up with two figures, one substantially lower than the other. The lower figure was calculated on the basis of executing such repairs as, in view of the age, character, and locality of the houses, would make them reasonably fit to satisfy the requirements of reasonably minded tenants of the class then likely to occupy them, ie under the criterion set out in *Proudfoot v Hart*. The higher figure was calculated on the basis of putting the houses into a state of repair in which they would be found if they had been managed by a reasonably minded owner, having regard to their age, character, and ordinary uses, or to the requirements of tenants of the class likely to take them at the time of *the demise or at the commencement of the term*.

7.46   The Court of Appeal agreed unanimously that it should be the higher figure that should be awarded as damages. *Proudfoot v Hart* was distinguished; to accept the *Proudfoot* test in the case of a long lease would be, in the words of Atkin LJ at 732, 'to expose both landlord and tenant to possibilities of the most astonishing variation of obligations and rights'. If the standard of repair was dependent upon the class of tenant likely to take the property at the end of the lease then, if the area deteriorated, the repairing obligation on the burdened party would be lessened; if the area went up in the world it would be increased: this could not be what the parties had in their contemplation when the lease was entered into, and to impose the *Proudfoot* test would be 'to substitute a different standard of obligation for the one to which the parties did agree'.

7.47   The position is then that the standard of repair is determined by the character of the premises at the beginning rather than at the end of the term. Age, however, is to be taken into account for the tenant cannot be expected to be under an obligation keep a property as if it was new; 'the words "keep in good condition" will have a different meaning according to the nature and age of the house' (*per* Fletcher Moulton LJ in *Lurcott v Wakely* at 917). If the property turns out to have a shorter life expectancy than that anticipated at the date of the tenancy, the original, higher standard of repair will continue to be appropriate (*Ladbroke Hotels Ltd v Saudhu* (1995) 72 P&CR 498, [1995] 2 EGLR 92). The standard to which the tenant must repair is to keep the premises in such condition as if they had 'been managed by a reasonably minded owner, having full regard to the age of the buildings, the locality, the class of tenant likely to occupy them, and the maintenance of the property in such a way that only an average amount of annual repair would be necessary in the future ...' (arbitrator's report, quoted in Bankes LJ's judgment in *Calthorpe v McOscar* at 725). This was perhaps more simply put by Fletcher Moulton LJ in *Lurcott v Wakely* at 916, when he said: 'What is the meaning of keeping old premises in good condition? ... It means that, considering that they are old premises, they must be kept in good condition as such premises.'

A point to note is that because the standard of repair is judged by the condition of the prop-   **7.48**
erty at the commencement of the lease, it can mean that two leases of the same property
with identical wording but entered into at different times can impose different standards
of repair. For example, John is granted a lease of a brand new flat on 1 January 1980. He
is offered a job abroad and on 1 January 1995 he moves out, granting a sub-lease to Tom.
The sub-lease contains identical repairing covenants to the original lease. The standard of
repair, however, will depend upon the condition of the property at the date of the lease.
The standard of repair demanded of John will be assessed with reference to a brand new
flat and will be higher than that imposed upon Tom, because at the date of Tom's lease the
flat was already 15 years old.

In certain cases it may be possible to carry out patching work to remedy disrepair, but such   **7.49**
works would need to be continually repeated. In such cases the court has been prepared
to order substantial work to be carried out to a property, which works may arguably
amount to renewal, in order to prevent repeated episodes of disrepair and patch repairs by
the landlord (*Elmcroft v Tankersley Sawyer* (1984) 270 EG 140; *Stent v Monmouth DC*
(1987) 19 HLR 269). In *Gibson v Chesterton Plc* [2002] EWHC 19 (Ch) the court ordered
the replacement of a lift in circumstances where repair work, whilst possible and certainly
cheaper, would have been a waste of time as the work would need repeating in the future.
The court held that in certain circumstances an obligation to repair will not be met unless
the works done will remedy the problem once and for all. Where the obligation to repair
falls on the tenant and repair and renewal are both viable options, the tenant is entitled
to choose which course to take (*Riverside Property Investments v Blackhawk Automotive*
[2005] 1 EGLR 114).

The situation might arise where the landlord intends to carry out work which goes beyond   **7.50**
repair and actually amounts to improvement, or chooses to carry out necessary repairs to a
very high standard using expensive materials. For leaseholders of short leases this will not
usually be a problem provided the work does not interfere with their use of the property;
however, long leaseholders who are obliged to pay a proportion of the cost of works done
to the property might have grounds to object. In *Fluor Daniels Properties v Shortlands
Investments* [2001] 2 EGLR 103 the court held that the landlord is obliged to have regard
to the amount a tenant can fairly be expected to pay when choosing what works to carry
out and the standard of works adopted. If the landlord chooses to carry out works to a
standard beyond that which it would be reasonable to expect the tenant to pay the landlord must bear the additional cost himself or herself.

Redecoration

The landlord's obligation to effect repairs carries with it an obligation to make good any   **7.51**
consequential damage to decoration. It is possible that this may involve the landlord putting
the premises in a substantially better state of decoration than they were in before the repair
works were carried out. Where repairs cannot sensibly be carried out without an element
of betterment (for example, the decoration of the whole ceiling where only one part was
repaired) the landlord is not allowed to make a deduction for this betterment (*McGreal v
Wake* (1984) 13 HLR 107, CA, a case where the tenant sued the landlord for the cost of
redecorations). Redecoration must be undertaken utilizing good quality materials and a
good standard of workmanship (*Vukelic v Hammersmith & Fulham LBC* [2003] EWHC
188 (TCC); *Legal Action*, November 2003).

The situation is different where the works carried out are outside the terms of the repairing   **7.52**
covenant because they constitute improvements rather than repairs. Even if such works

are carried out at the request of the landlord there will be no obligation on the part of the landlord to redecorate at the conclusion of the works unless he or she has expressly agreed to do so (*McDougall v Easington DC* (1989) 21 HLR 310, CA).

G SUMMARY

7.53 Before we examine the specific obligations imposed by the common law on landlord and tenant, it may prove useful to summarize the points discussed previously.

7.54 In the absence of any express agreement no one is responsible to do repairs.

7.55 An express covenant is normally included in every lease. Such covenants can be worded in a variety of ways and thereby increase or decrease the obligations on the burdened party, but the key point is that they express an intention that the premises are to be kept in repair.

7.56 Before an obligation to repair can arise there must be some disrepair to the premises themselves, not just loss of amenity.

7.57 Repair is a difficult concept to define. It involves the renewal of subordinate parts, but it does not extend to the creation of a wholly different thing from the premises originally demised. It can also involve the remedying of inherent defects. It is always a question of degree to be decided upon the individual facts.

7.58 The standard of repair is determined by the condition of the property at the start of the term, but age is to be taken into account.

H IMPLIED COMMON LAW OBLIGATIONS ON LANDLORDS

7.59 Despite the general rule that in the absence of an express agreement no one is to be responsible for repairs, the common law imposes certain limited obligations to repair upon the landlord.

Implied condition of fitness for human habitation at commencement of a tenancy of furnished premises

7.60 *Smith v Marrable* [1843] 11 M&W 5, established a significant exception to the rule of *caveat lessee*. In the case of *furnished* premises it was held that the common law will imply into a tenancy of such premises a condition that the premises are fit for human habitation at the start of the tenancy. In *Smith v Marrable*, Parke B said that premises were unfit for human habitation 'if the demised premises are incumbered with a nuisance of so serious a nature that no person can reasonably be expected to live in them'. Infestation with bugs (*Smith v Marrable*) has been held to render premises unfit, as has inhabitation by a tubercular patient when the premises were not disinfected afterwards (*Collins v Hopkins* [1923] 2 KB 617), defective drains (*Wilson v Finch Hatton* [1877] 2 Ex D 336), and an insufficient water supply (*Chester v Powell* [1885] 53 LT 722).

7.61 The implied condition of fitness for human habitation is concerned with fitness at *common law*. Case law concerning the Defective Premises Act 1972, s 1, however, provides useful guidance: see for example *McMinn Bole & Van Den Haak v Huntsbuild Ltd & Money* [2009] EWCA 483 (TCC); *Legal Action*, December 2009 (unfitness for habitation relates to defects rendering the dwelling dangerous or unsuitable for its purpose and not to minor defects; the effects of the defects as a whole must be considered).

The implied condition of fitness for human habitation is limited in the following ways: **7.62**

(a) It applies only to furnished premises (see *Cruse v Mount* [1933] Ch 278). The Court of Appeal has indicated that if a condition of fitness for human habitation is to be extended to unfurnished accommodation, the decision should be made by Parliament rather than by the courts (*McNerny v London Borough of Lambeth* (1988) 21 HLR 188 at 195).

(b) It applies only to residential tenancies and does not apply to tenancies of social housing let by local authorities (*Lee v Leeds City Council* [2002] EWCA Civ 6, [2002] 1 WLR 1488).

(c) It applies only at the commencement of the tenancy; if the premises later fall into a state of disrepair which renders them unfit for human habitation the landlord is not liable. However, the landlord will be liable if the premises were unfit for human habitation at the start of the tenancy but the defect did not become apparent until later on in the tenancy (*Harrison v Malet* [1886] 3 TLR 58).

(d) It covers only fitness for human habitation and does not make the landlord liable for the structural condition of the premises. (Although today the courts may be prepared to take a broader view of what constitutes fitness for human habitation and consider the statutory definition of 'unfitness' in the Housing Act 1985.)

(e) The landlord's liability arises from the contract and so only the tenant can bring an action under the implied condition.

(f) The condition may be excluded from the tenancy by an express term to the contrary (subject to the requirements of the Unfair Terms in Consumer Contracts Regulations 1999, SI 1999/2083).

If the premises are not fit for human habitation the tenant is entitled to quit and will not be   **7.63**
liable for rent; he or she will also be able to recover damages. The implied term is a *condition* and not a covenant. Breach of covenant does not entitle the tenant to quit. It should be noted that the landlord's breach of this implied condition does not enable the tenant to require the landlord to put the premises into a habitable condition, which in a time of housing shortage is probably the remedy which would be most useful to the tenant.

Implied contractual duty of care to keep the common parts in repair

Blocks of flats present their own special problems when it comes to the allocation of   **7.64**
responsibility between the landlord and the tenants. Frequently, there are common areas which the tenants have a right to use (usually in the nature of an easement), but which do not actually form part of the premises leased to each tenant. Particularly in high-rise blocks, these common parts can be quite extensive and require frequent maintenance; there may be lifts, staircases, hallways, storage areas, rubbish chutes, and other facilities. In many cases there will be an express agreement allocating responsibility. Usually, the responsibility for repair and maintenance of the common parts will be on the landlord, but he or she will be entitled to recover the costs of this maintenance from the tenants in the form of a service charge. There may, however, be no express agreement allocating responsibility for the common parts.

If the tenancy was granted on or after 15 January 1989, a term will be implied into the ten-   **7.65**
ancy requiring the landlord to keep in repair the structure and exterior of any part of a building in which the landlord has an estate or interest (Landlord and Tenant Act 1985, s 11(1A) as supplemented by the Housing Act 1988, s 116(1)). Thus the landlord will generally be under a statutory duty to keep the structure and exterior of the common parts of a block in repair (see 7.87 to 7.102 for a consideration of s 11). However, for tenancies granted before 15 January 1989, a contractual duty of care may be implied into the contract.

7.66 In *Liverpool City Council v Irwin* [1977] AC 239, [1976] 2 All ER 39, the tenants of a
15-storey high-rise block rented from the council. There was no proper tenancy agreement,
only a document entitled 'Conditions of Tenancy' which, although it set out certain obligations to be observed by the tenants, did not refer to any obligations undertaken by the landlord council. Due to a large extent to vandalism there was continual failure of the two lifts,
frequently both at the same time, which required the tenants of the upper floors to use the
staircases, which were themselves, also largely due to vandalism, dangerous and often unlit.
The court considered the incomplete agreement between the parties. It concluded that as a
matter of necessity a contractual obligation upon the landlord should be implied into the
contract, namely that the landlord was under a duty of care to take reasonable care in all the
circumstances to repair and maintain the common parts. To leave the landlord free of such
an obligation would be 'inconsistent totally with the nature of this relationship. The subject
matter of the lease (high-rise blocks) and the relationship created by the tenancy demand, of
their nature, some contractual obligation on the landlord' (*per* Lord Wilberforce at 254G).

7.67 It should be noted that this implied duty of care is closely related to the implied duty not
to derogate from grant (see 5.32). If a landlord rents a top floor flat to a tenant and then
refuses or fails to maintain the means of access to that flat, effectively the landlord would
be depriving the tenant of the means of enjoying the flat.

7.68 A contractual duty of care to keep the common parts in repair will be implied only in limited situations. Its application is restricted as follows:

(a) It applies only to the common areas of a building which are kept within the landlord's possession and control. In fact, Lord Wilberforce's words seem to indicate that
it applies only to the letting of high-rise blocks of flats. Certainly, the courts have
been reluctant to extend the principle to other situations, although in *King v South
Northamptonshire DC* [1992] 1 EGLR 53, where a house had a rear path that was to
be used for deliveries, it was held that the landlords had an implied duty to keep the
path in repair.

(b) The term will be implied only in circumstances where it is necessary and where not to
imply the term would render the contract 'inefficacious, futile and absurd' (*per* Lord
Salmon in *Liverpool City Council v Irwin* at 262A–B). Thus, where there was a formal lease which seemed on the face of it to set out the complete bargain between the
parties, the court would not imply a duty to repair a drain (*Duke of Westminster v
Guild* [1985] QB 688, [1984] 3 All ER 144; see also *Gordon v Selico Co. Ltd* (1986)
18 HLR 219, [1986] 1 EGLR 71). Likewise, the court would not imply a duty to the
landlord to enforce a nuisance clause contained in the lease to prevent a noisy neighbour disturbing the other tenants (*O'Leary v LB of Islington* (1983) 9 HLR 81). The
implication of the duty was not necessary to the agreement; the other tenants would
have an adequate remedy in tort.

(c) It is not an absolute duty of care; the landlord need take only reasonable care in all
the circumstances. In *Liverpool City Council v Irwin*, it was held that on the facts
the landlord had in fact discharged this duty by making considerable efforts to keep
the common parts of the block in repair and that it would have been unreasonable to
demand more in the difficult circumstances created by continual vandalism.

(d) The duty of care can be excluded simply by the inclusion of an express term into the
contract.

(e) The duty is owed only to parties to the contract.

7.69 It should be noted that because the common parts are regarded as being within the landlord's care and control, it would seem that the tenant does not need to give the landlord
notice of the disrepair before the obligation to repair arises.

Correlative obligations/business efficacy

In certain situations one party may find it impossible to comply with its side of the bar-   **7.70**
gain unless the other party is placed under a correlative obligation. In *Barrett v Lounova*
[1982] Ltd [1988] 2 EGLR 54, the tenancy contained express covenants requiring that
the tenant should keep the interior of a house in good repair and that the landlord should
have access to the house for any reasonable purpose. No express obligation was placed on
either party to keep the outside of the property in repair. The structure and exterior of the
house fell into disrepair, causing extensive water penetration which damaged the internal
plasterwork of the house, thereby preventing the tenant from complying with the covenant
to keep the interior in good repair. The court held that in these circumstances 'as a matter
of business efficacy to make this agreement workable' (at 56) the obligation to repair the
structure and exterior of the building should be imposed on the landlord.

As with the case of an implied obligation to keep the common parts in repair, this exception   **7.71**
to the general rule of *caveat lessee* is severely limited. An obligation will be implied only
where it is *necessary* to do so to make the contract work, not, as Lord Denning MR suggested
in his dissenting judgment in *Liverpool City Council v Irwin*, if it was reasonable to do so.

Other implied covenants

In cases where the tenant cannot take advantage of express or implied repairing covenants it is   **7.72**
possible that he or she may be able to rely on the landlord's implied covenant for quiet enjoyment or the covenant not to derogate from a grant (see Chapter 5). The covenant for quiet
enjoyment applies to all lettings regardless of length or type. One or both of these implied
covenants might apply where there is no actual disrepair to the tenant's premises but the landlord's use or neglect of other premises has caused damage or inconvenience to the tenant.

I IMPLIED COMMON LAW OBLIGATIONS ON TENANTS

When renting out a property a landlord will obviously be concerned to ensure that the   **7.73**
tenant looks after that property well. Even in a short lease where the landlord is under
an obligation to perform the repairs relating to the structure and exterior of the building,
that landlord will still want to prevent the tenant from damaging the interior decoration,
fixtures and fittings, and any furniture supplied with the tenancy. It should come as no
surprise then to find that the majority of express tenancy agreements will include a clause
requiring the tenant to keep the interior of the property, the decorations, and the fixtures,
fittings, and appliances in good repair and condition.

If, however, such express terms are absent, the common law will imply certain basic obliga-   **7.74**
tions onto the tenant: first, in contract, through an implied covenant for *tenant-like user*
and, secondly, through the *doctrine of waste*. Waste is a special tort peculiar to the law of
landlord and tenant and therefore independent of any express or implied term of the contract. If a landlord wishes to take action against a tenant, he or she can choose whether to
sue for breach of contract or to pursue an action in tort. However, if the landlord gives a
tenant permission to breach the contract and then changes his or her mind, that landlord
cannot then seek a remedy for the breach in tort.

Implied covenant to use the premises in a 'tenant-like manner'

The words 'tenant-like manner' are not easy to define precisely, but it seems that they mean   **7.75**
that the tenant must perform the everyday tasks around the home that a reasonable tenant

would. Each case must be judged on its own facts. Guidance as to what this means was set out by Denning LJ in *Warren v Keen* [1954] 1 QB 15 at 20, [1953] 2 All ER 1118 at 1121:

> The tenant must take proper care of the place. He must, if he is going away for the winter, turn off the water and empty the boiler. He must clean the chimneys, when necessary, and also the windows. He must mend the electric light when it fuses. He must unstop the sink when it is blocked by his waste. In short, he must do the little jobs about the place which a reasonable tenant would do. In addition, he must, of course, not damage the house, wilfully or negligently; and he must see that his family and guests do not damage it: and if they do, he must repair it.

7.76 This implied covenant remains limited; it does not extend to replacing or repairing things which become defective through age or the everyday actions of the elements. As Denning LJ stated, 'if the house falls into disrepair through fair wear and tear or lapse of time, or for any reason not caused by him, then the tenant is not liable to repair it'.

Obligation not to commit waste

7.77 To commit waste means doing (or failing to do) any act which alters or changes the land. 'Waste' is a broad term which includes carrying out alterations which improve the land; this is known as ameliorating waste. For our present purposes, however, we are concerned with behaviour by the tenant that causes the property to deteriorate. This falls into two categories:

(a) Voluntary waste—where the tenant causes damage to the premises by doing something that should not be done.

(b) Permissive waste—where the premises fall into disrepair because the tenant fails to take action to prevent the deterioration.

7.78 For example, if a tenant knocks down an internal wall in the flat between the kitchen and the sitting room in order to give himself or herself more space, this would be voluntary waste. If, however, the wall was in bad condition and it collapsed because the tenant had failed to take action to repair it, this would be permissive waste.

7.79 The extent of the implied obligation imposed upon the tenant varies with the nature of the tenancy. In general it can be said that the longer the tenancy the greater the obligation that lies on the tenant:

(a) A tenant for a fixed term of years is liable for both voluntary and permissive waste.

(b) A yearly tenant is liable only for voluntary waste, with the additional obligation that he or she should keep the premises wind and water tight (*Wedd v Porter* [1916] 2 KB 91). However, a yearly tenant will not be liable for 'fair wear and tear' (see *Warren v Keen*, 7.75 at 20).

(c) A tenant with a shorter periodic tenancy is liable only for voluntary waste.

Obligation to allow the landlord entry

7.80 If the landlord is under an obligation to repair it will be implied, in the absence of any express provision, that the tenant has granted the landlord the right to enter to inspect and carry out repairs (see 7.29 and 5.47).

J COVENANTS IMPLIED BY STATUTE

7.81 We have already seen that the general rule is that, in the absence of any express provisions and subject to certain common law exceptions considered earlier, no covenant will be implied that the premises let will be fit for human habitation, or that the landlord will be liable to keep the premises in repair. Contained in the Landlord and Tenant Act 1985 there are two provisions concerning:

(a) houses at a low rent;
(b) houses let on a short lease.

Houses at a low rent

The Landlord and Tenant Act 1985, s 8(1) provides that where a house is let on very low rent there is implied on the part of the landlord: **7.82**

(a) a condition that at the commencement of the tenancy the house is fit for human habitation;
(b) an undertaking that during the course of the tenancy the house will be kept in all respects reasonably fit for human habitation.

These terms will be implied regardless of any express stipulation to the contrary. However, if the house is let for a term of three years or more upon the terms that the tenant is responsible to put it into a condition reasonably fit for human habitation, and the lease is not determinable by either party before the expiration of three years, s 8 will not apply. For the purposes of s 8, 'house' includes a part of a house and so these provisions will also apply to flats and bedsits (s 8(6)). A 'tenancy' includes both sub-tenancies and an agreement for a tenancy (s 36(2)), but s 8 will not apply to a licence.   **7.83**

The rent levels set by statute as defining a 'low rent' are so low as to make this provision of little practical importance. Section 8 will apply only if the property is let at a rent not exceeding £80 per annum in London and £52 per annum elsewhere; if the letting was made before 6 July 1957 the levels are even lower (s 8(4)). It should be noted that it is the rent at the commencement of the tenancy that defines whether a tenancy will fall within s 8, not the current rent.   **7.84**

Section 8(2) entitles the landlord to enter the premises for the purpose of viewing their state and condition on giving the tenant 24 hours' written notice. As with practically every provision relating to the landlord's obligation to repair, an obligation under s 8(2) will not arise until the landlord has knowledge of the disrepair.   **7.85**

In determining whether a house is unfit for human habitation, regard shall be had to its condition in respect of the following matters: repair, stability, freedom from damp, internal arrangement, natural lighting, ventilation, water supply, drainage and sanitary conveniences, and facilities for preparation and cooking of food and for the disposal of waste water. The house will be regarded as unfit for human habitation only if it is so far defective in one or more of those matters that it is not reasonably suitable for occupation in that condition (Landlord and Tenant Act 1985, s 10). However, if a landlord can establish that the house is in such condition that it could not be made fit for human habitation at reasonable expense, the landlord will not be liable under s 8 of the 1985 Act (*Buswell v Goodwin* [1971] 1 WLR 92, [1971] 1 All ER 418, CA).   **7.86**

Houses let on a short lease

For the majority of residential tenants holding under a short or periodic tenancy, the obligations implied by s 11 of the Landlord and Tenant Act 1985 will constitute their repairing covenant. It is unlikely that the landlord will wish to impose upon himself or herself any more onerous repairing duty than that contained in s 11. In fact it is quite common for a clause to be included in the tenancy agreements stating that the tenancy takes effect subject   **7.87** to the provisions of s 11. In any case, regardless of any express provisions contained in the tenancy agreement, s 11 will imply a basic repairing covenant into the lease. It is not possible for a landlord to contract out of the obligations imposed by s 11 except with the consent of the tenant and the approval of the court (s 12).

Tenancies to which s 11 applies

7.88 Section 11 applies to any lease of a dwelling-house, granted after 24 October 1961, for a term of less than seven years (s 13(1)). The term 'dwelling-house' includes a building or part of a building (s 16(b)) and so s 11 can apply to a flat or bedsit just as well as it can apply to a whole house. Section 11 will not apply to business tenancies (tenancies to which Pt II of the Landlord and Tenant Act 1954 applies) (s 13(3)), to tenancies of agricultural holdings (s 14(3)), to tenancies granted after 3 October 1980 to local authorities and certain other public bodies (s 14(4)), or to tenancies granted after 3 October 1980 to the Crown (s 14(5)).

7.89 In calculating whether a lease is a lease for less than seven years, any part of the term falling before the grant will be left out of account (s 13(2)(a)). A landlord cannot therefore avoid s 11 by backdating the start of the tenancy to create a term of more than seven years. A lease which is determinable at the option of the lessor before the expiration of seven years from the commencement of the term shall be treated as a lease for a term of less than seven years (s 13(2)(b)). Thus, a 12-year lease containing a break clause entitling the landlord to terminate the tenancy after six years will fall within s 11. If a lease gives the tenant an option to renew the tenancy, it shall not be treated as a lease for a term of less than seven years if it confers on the tenant an option for renewal for a term which, together with the original term, amounts to seven years or more (s 13(2)(c)). Thus, a five-year term containing an option to renew the tenancy for a further five years will not fall within s 11.

7.90 Periodic tenancies count as leases for a term of less than seven years regardless of the fact that the total length of the term may amount to more than seven years.

Social housing

7.91 Exceptions to the seven-year limit exist in respect of certain social housing tenancies. Section 13(1A) and (1B) of the 1985 Act (as amended by the Localism Act 2011, s 166) provide that s 11 will also apply to:

(a) a secure tenancy (see 17.05) granted for a fixed term of more than seven years; and

(b) an assured tenancy (see 15.03) granted for a fixed term of more than seven years which is not a shared ownership lease and which is granted by a private registered provider of social housing (see 21.04).

The new provisions will only apply to tenancies granted on or after 1 April 2012.

The nature of the covenant

7.92 The Landlord and Tenant Act 1985, s 11(1) states:

(1) In a lease to which this section applies … there is implied a covenant by the lessor—

(a) to keep in repair the structure and exterior of the dwelling-house (including drains, gutters and external pipes),

(b) to keep in repair and proper working order the installations in the dwelling-house for the supply of water, gas and electricity and for sanitation (including basins, sinks, baths and sanitary conveniences, but not other fixtures, fittings and appliances for making use of the supply of water, gas or electricity), and

(c)   to keep in repair and proper working order the installations in the dwelling-house for
      space heating and heating water.

Section 11 imposes an obligation to 'keep in repair'. As we saw at 7.14, this will include   **7.93**
an obligation to put the dwelling-house into repair if it is out of repair at the start of
the tenancy. The meaning of disrepair is not extended by s 11. It does not impose an
obligation to carry out maintenance works to remove a potential hazard where there
is no actual disrepair, for example by removing moss from steps (*Brunskill v Mulcahy*
[2009] EWCA Civ 686). No obligation to repair will arise until the landlord has actual
knowledge of the disrepair. As under s 8 of the 1985 Act, the landlord is given the right
to enter the premises for the purpose of viewing their state and condition on giving the
tenant 24 hours' written notice (s 11(6)). The standard of repair will be the same as for
express covenants (see 7.41 to 7.50) and will be assessed with regard to age, character,
and prospective life.

Section 11 does not impose a duty on the landlord: **7.94**

(a)   to carry out works or repairs for which the lessee is liable by virtue of his duty to use
      the premises in a tenant-like manner (s 11(2)(a)). Thus, the tenant will still be respon-
      sible for performing minor everyday repairs about the house (see 7.75);
(b)   to rebuild or reinstate the premises in the case of destruction or damage by fire, or by
      tempest, flood, or other inevitable accident (s 11(2)(b));
(c)   to keep in repair or maintain anything which the lessee is entitled to remove from the
      dwelling-house (s 11(2)(c)).

The meaning of 'structure and exterior'

There is no statutory definition of 'structure and exterior' and these terms are not always   **7.95**
easy to interpret. A building is a complex whole where supporting beams, walls, and roofs
are frequently shared between neighbouring flats or rooms. The courts have adopted a
common-sense approach and will ask whether, in the ordinary use of words, the part of the
house in question would be regarded as structure and exterior (see *Campden Hill Towers
v Gardner* [1977] QB 823).

'Structure' was said in *Irvine v Moran* [1991] 1 EGLR 261 not to include the entire   **7.96**
dwelling-house but only those elements which give it its essential appearance, stability, and
shape. It is important to note that under s 11(1)(a) the implied covenant extends only to
the structure and exterior of the dwelling-house. If Sally occupies a flat on the third floor of
a six-storey block of flats, s 11 will extend only to the structure and exterior of her flat; it
will not include the structure and exterior of the whole building. In *Campden Hill Towers
v Gardner*, the structure and exterior of a flat was held to include: the outside walls of
the flat, the outside of the interior party walls, the outer sides of the horizontal divisions
between the flat and the flats above and below and the ceilings and walls of the flat, and the
structural framework and beams directly supporting the floors, ceilings, and walls of the
flat. These parts will count as 'structure and exterior' regardless of whether they were actually demised to Sally under the tenancy. However, other essential parts of the building will
not form part of the structure and exterior of Sally's flat. If, for example, the roof falls into
disrepair, Sally will be unable to compel the landlord to carry out the required work under
the covenant implied by s 11. Tim, on the other hand, lives on the top floor of the block.
Provided that, on the facts, the roof forms part of the structure and exterior of his flat, he
will be able to enforce the s 11 covenant against the landlord (see *Douglas-Scott v Scourgie*
[1984] 1 WLR 716, [1984] 1 All ER 1086, CA; compare with *Rapid Results College Ltd v
Angell* [1986] 1 EGLR 53, CA).

7.97   The difficulties encountered by tenants such as Sally have now been partially resolved by s 11(1A) which was introduced into the 1985 Act by the Housing Act 1988, s 116(1). Section 11(1A)(a) will imply into any tenancy granted after 15 January 1989 to which s 11 applies a covenant that the landlord will keep in repair the structure and exterior of 'any part of the building in which the lessor has an estate or interest'. A tenant, however, will be able to rely upon s 11(1A) only where the disrepair is such as to affect the lessee's enjoyment of the dwelling-house or of any common parts which the lessee is entitled to use (s 11(1B)).

7.98   Windows are generally regarded as part of the exterior (*Ball v Plummer* [1879] 2 TLR 877, CA); and in some cases, eg where a plate-glass window forms a substantial part of the front of a building, windows can be seen as part of the structure (*Boswell v Crucible Steel Co. of America* [1925] 1 KB 119). Steps and flagstones which are necessary as a means of access to the premises can be part of the exterior (*Brown v Liverpool Corp* [1969] 3 All ER 1345 at 1346) but not the paving in a back yard (*Hopwood v Cannock Chase DC* [1975] 1 WLR 373). Internal plasterwork has been held to be part of the structure (*Staves & Staves v Leeds City Council* (1992) 29 EG 119; *Grand v Gill* [2011] EWCA Civ 554). Floor joists situated entirely within a tenant's flat may also be regarded as part of the structure as they are integral to the structure of the whole building (*Marlborough Park Services v Rowe* [2006] 2 EGLR 27, CA).

Installations

7.99   Section 11 of the 1985 Act states specifically that the landlord must keep in repair and proper working order all the installations for the supply of water, gas, and electricity, and for sanitation; and also installations for space heating and heating water. Section 11 will therefore cover water and gas pipes, water tanks, wiring, radiators, boilers, heating ducts, etc. The obligation to keep installations in proper working order may include remedying faults in design that would not normally amount to disrepair. For example, in *Liverpool City Council v Irwin* [1977] AC 239 a landlord was obliged to replace cisterns which caused lavatories to overflow. The cisterns were not out of repair but the problem was caused by their design. However, in *O'Connor v Old Eton Housing Association* [2002] EWCA Civ 150, [2002] 2 WLR 1133, CA, a temporary problem caused by a drop in water pressure which meant that the narrow pipe-work in a building did not work properly was held on appeal not to be disrepair. Section 11 is limited to installations which are actually in the tenant's dwelling-house. Problems can arise when considering blocks of flats. Sally's flat is heated by a communal heating system run from a central boiler in the basement. While the landlord will be under an obligation to repair a leaky radiator in Sally's flat, he will be under no obligation by virtue of s 11(1)(b) to repair the boiler if it breaks down.

7.100   If Sally's tenancy was granted after 15 January 1989, s 11(1A)(b) now provides a solution to this problem. The landlord is placed under an obligation to keep in repair and proper working order an installation which serves the dwelling-house and either:

(a)   forms any part of the building in which the lessor has an estate or interest; or
(b)   is owned by the lessor or under his or her control.

7.101   As with s 11(1A)(a), this obligation will arise only if the failure to repair affects the lessee's enjoyment of the dwelling-house or any common parts.

7.102   It should be remembered that the requirement that the landlord has notice of disrepair is also applicable where a tenant relies on a s 11 obligation to repair (see 7.28). The definitions of disrepair and the standards of repair discussed at 7.31 to 7.50 apply equally to an implied covenant as to a similarly worded express covenant.

Gas appliances

The Gas Safety (Installation and Use) Regulations 1998, SI 1998/2451, impose additional **7.103** duties on landlords under certain leases. Regulation 36 provides that where the tenant occupies residential property under:

(a) a lease for less than seven years;
(b) a periodic tenancy; or
(c) a statutory tenancy arising after either (a) or (b),

the landlord is obliged to maintain any gas fitting on the premises and any flue serving any gas fitting so as to prevent risk of injury to anyone lawfully occupying the premises.

The gas appliances and flues in the property must be checked at least 12 months before a **7.104** property is let out and again every 12 months thereafter by a registered gas fitter. The land-lord must always be able to produce a record of safety going back over the last two years. This record must be produced to the tenant within 28 days of each check or, in the case of a new tenant, within 28 days of the tenant occupying the building. The Regulations also require the landlord to ensure that any room occupied as sleeping accommodation does not contain a gas fitting that is not room sealed and/or does not incorporate safety controls (reg 36(11) and reg 30(2) and (3)). Additional regulations apply in respect of houses in multiple occupation (see 20.102).

K REMEDIES

Landlord's remedies against a non-repairing tenant

Forfeiture

Provided that a landlord has expressly reserved a right of re-entry in the tenancy agree- **7.105** ment, he or she may be able to forfeit the tenant's lease for a breach of covenant to repair. Forfeiture is dealt with in detail in Chapter 11. The landlord will have to serve notice upon the tenant in accordance with s 146 of the LPA 1925, and the tenant will have the right to apply for relief from forfeiture. In the case of leases granted for a term of seven years or more with more than three years of the term left to run, the landlord will also have to comply with the provisions of s 1 of the Leasehold Property (Repairs) Act 1938 (see 7.109). Forfeiture proceedings will usually be combined with a claim for damages.

Damages

When a landlord brings an action for damages during the currency of the tenancy, the **7.106** landlord can recover a sum representing the diminution of the value of the reversion which results from the breach. In practical terms this means the amount by which the market value of the reversion has been reduced by the tenant's failure to repair. If a tenancy has many years to run before it expires the value of the reversion will be relatively low; consequently, the amount of damages recoverable by the landlord will depend to a considerable degree upon the length of the unexpired term. (The more obvious measure of damages, ie the cost of putting the premises into repair, is not used during the currency of the tenancy because there is no guarantee that the landlord would use the money to carry out the repairs, and in order to carry out the repairs the landlord would require the tenant's permission to enter.)

When the landlord brings an action for damages after the tenancy has been terminated, the **7.107** measure of damages is the cost of carrying out the repairs necessary to put the premises into the state of repair required by the covenant. Here the landlord will be suing on the tenant's covenant to leave the premises in repair rather than on the covenant to keep the premises in repair. (We saw earlier that a covenant to keep in repair will also include a covenant to leave in repair.)

7.108   Regardless of which measure of damages is used, the total amount of damages recoverable by the landlord will be subject to the limits imposed by s 18 of the Landlord and Tenant Act 1927. Section 18 states that the damages recoverable by the landlord are in no case to exceed the amount (if any) by which the reversion (whether immediate or not) in the premises is diminished owing to the breach. This will apply whether the covenant is express or implied. Thus, if the actual cost of putting the premises into repair at the end of the term is greater than the amount by which the breach of covenant has reduced the market value of the premises, the landlord will be able to recover only the lesser of these two sums. If, because the market is running high, there is no diminution in the market value of the premises despite the fact that they are out of repair, the landlord may not be able to recover any damages at all (see *Landeau v Marchbank* [1949] 2 All ER 172). Similarly, if the tenant can show that any repairs carried out would be valueless because the landlord intends to demolish or alter the premises at or shortly after the end of the tenancy, s 18(1) specifically provides that no damages can be recovered. In most claims for damages for disrepair, however, it will not usually be practical or cost effective to obtain valuation evidence before bringing the claim. In such cases the court will usually accept the cost of the repair as being a reliable guide to the amount of damage to the value of the reversion (*Latimer v Carney* [2006] EWCA Civ 1417, [2006] 3 EGLR 13).

Long leases

7.109   The Leasehold Property (Repairs) Act 1938 imposes special restrictions upon a landlord wishing to take forfeiture proceedings or seeking damages for breach of a covenant to repair against a tenant holding a long lease. The Act will apply where the lease was granted for a term of more than seven years and there are more than three years of the term unexpired (s 7(1)). The aim of the Act is to prevent a landlord from terminating a long lease mid-term by seeking to enforce a repairing covenant with which the tenant cannot easily comply.

7.110   Where a landlord wishes to take action on a repairing covenant in a lease to which the 1938 Act applies, he or she will have to comply with strict procedural requirements. Whether the action is for forfeiture or for damages, the landlord will have to serve an LPA 1925, s 146 notice upon the tenant informing the tenant of his or her rights under the Act (s 1(4)). The tenant may then, within 28 days of receiving the notice, serve counter-notice on the landlord claiming the benefit of the Act. If the tenant serves such a counter-notice the landlord is not permitted to proceed further without obtaining the leave of the court (s 1(3)).

7.111   Leave will be granted only if the landlord can establish to the normal civil standard of proof (see *Associated British Ports v CH Bailey Plc* [1990] 1 All ER 929) one of the five grounds set out in s 1(5) of the 1938 Act:

(a)   that the value of the reversion has been substantially diminished by the breach, or that the breach must be immediately remedied to prevent the value of the reversion being substantially diminished;

(b)   that the breach must be immediately remedied in order to comply with a by-law, an Act of Parliament, a court order, or the requirement of a local authority;

(c)   that if the tenant is not in occupation of the whole premises the breach must be immediately remedied in the interests of an occupier of the premises or part of the premises;

(d)   that the breach can be immediately remedied at relatively small expense in comparison with the probable cost of the work that would be needed if the repairs were postponed;

(e) that there are special circumstances which in the opinion of the court render it just and equitable to grant leave.

Entering to carry out repairs

We have seen that where the landlord is under an obligation to repair, that landlord will **7.112** also acquire an implied right to enter and carry out those repairs for which he or she is liable. Some leases may also include a provision entitling the landlord to enter and carry out repairs for which the tenant is responsible and then charge the tenant with the cost. Such a provision usually entitles the landlord to recover the cost of the repair work from the tenant as a debt due (*Jervis v Harris* [1996] Ch 195, [1996] 1 All ER 303, CA). The amount recoverable by the landlord is not restricted by s 18(1) of the Landlord and Tenant Act 1927, which applies only to a claim for damages.

Specific performance

It was previously accepted that specific performance was not available as a remedy for the **7.113** breach of a tenant's repairing covenant. The High Court reviewed the subject and held that specific performance can be ordered in appropriate circumstances (*Rainbow Estates v Tokenhold* [1998] 2 All ER 860). The need for caution was however emphasized. The tenant must be aware of exactly what works need to be done and a workable agreement for supervision of works should be in place. It is expected that this remedy will be used rarely.

Protocol for terminal dilapidations

Tenants of business premises whose leases contain a repairing covenant are usually required **7.114** to compensate the landlord for any outstanding matters of disrepair when they hand back the property at the end of the term (referred to as terminal dilapidations). A pre-action protocol for claims for damages for terminal dilapidations has been incorporated into the Civil Procedure Rules (CPR). The aims of the protocol are to encourage and facilitate early settlement of dilapidation claims or to ensure the efficient management of proceedings if litigation becomes inevitable. Landlords and managing agents would be advised to follow the protocol when dealing with terminal dilapidation claims as failure to do so may mean that they are unable to recover all of their legal costs (or may have to pay increased costs) if the claim goes to court.

Tenant's remedies against a non-repairing landlord

Damages

The aim of damages is to restore the tenant to the position he or she would have been **7.115** in had there been no breach of repairing covenant. The tenant will therefore be able to recover financial compensation for losses which result from the landlord's failure to repair (provided, of course, that these losses are reasonably foreseeable). Damages will be recoverable regardless of whether the landlord's repairing covenant is express or implied. A tenant, however, will not be able to recover damages for any losses incurred before the landlord had knowledge of the disrepair. Once the tenant has given the landlord notice of the disrepair the tenant must allow the landlord a reasonable period in which to carry out the required repairs. If the tenant refuses to give the landlord access to the premises to carry out the work then no damages will be recoverable (*Granada Theatres Ltd v Freehold Investment (Leytonstone) Ltd* [1959] Ch 529, [1959] 2 All ER 176).

How the amount of damages to be awarded is calculated will depend upon the circumstances **7.116** of the case. The court must look at the facts of the case and work out what losses the tenant has actually suffered. Thus, where a periodic tenant occupies a flat as his or her home and the landlord fails to carry out repairs in breach of covenant, the tenant will be able to recover the cost of carrying out the repairs, the cost of restoring internal decoration, compensation for the inconvenience of living in premises that were out of repair, compensation for injury to health, the cost of moving to and occupying alternative accommodation, and the cost of storing furniture. The measure of damages would be different, however, if the tenant was a long leaseholder who had purchased the tenancy as a speculative investment. In this case the measure of damages would be the difference between the capital value of the property as it stands and the capital value the property would have had if the landlord had performed the repairs. Likewise if the tenant held the tenancy in order to sub-let the premises; in this case the damages could be calculated as the loss of rental value to the tenant while the premises were out of repair (see *Calabar Properties Ltd v Stitcher* [1984] 1 WLR 287, [1983] 3 All ER 759, CA and *Mira v Aylmer Square Investments Ltd* [1990] 1 EGLR 45, CA).

Self-help

7.117   Where a landlord is in breach of his or her repairing obligations, the tenant may carry out the repairs and then deduct the cost of the repairs from the future rent (*Lee-Parker v Izzet* [1971] 1WLR 1688, [1971] 3 All ER 1099). Before taking such action the tenant must be sure that the landlord has notice of the disrepair and that the disrepair in question falls within the scope of the landlord's repairing obligations. The tenant should inform the landlord in advance of his or her intention to carry out the works. Care should be taken to ensure that a competitive tender is obtained for the works and that the works are carried out by a properly qualified contractor. The tenant must also make sure that he or she has copies of all receipts and invoices before making a claim for reimbursement. If the landlord then sues the tenant for rent arrears, the tenant may counter-claim for the cost of the repairs (see *British Anzani (Felixtowe) Ltd v International Marine Management (UK) Ltd* [1980] QB 137, [1979] 2 All ER 1063). Before undertaking repair works a prudent tenant may be well-advised to obtain a declaration from the county court stating that the landlord is in breach of a repairing obligation, and that the tenant is entitled to do the works and deduct the cost from future rent. Such an application may be made under CPR Part 25 and before proceedings are commenced.

7.118   The tenant is not legally entitled to withhold rent on the grounds that the premises are in disrepair and may face possession proceedings if he or she does so. A tenant may, however, set off damages for disrepair against a landlord's claim for rent arrears.

Interim injunctions

7.119   In extreme cases of disrepair it may be possible for the tenant to obtain an interim injunction requiring the landlord to carry out works. This remedy will only be available in exceptional circumstances as it requires the landlord to take action before the case has been fully argued at trial. Some guidance has been given by the Court of Appeal. In *Parker v Camden LBC* [1986] Ch 162 it was held that before granting an interim injunction the court should be satisfied that there is an immediate need for the work to be done (eg because there is an obvious risk to health and safety), and it must be clear what work needs to be done.

7.120   An application for an injunction should usually be made on notice to the landlord following the procedure set out in CPR Parts 23 and 25. It will normally be necessary for the tenant to provide a surveyor's report or other expert evidence stating what works are needed. An interim injunction may be granted before proceedings have even been commenced (CPR r 25.2).

Specific performance

Section 17 of the Landlord and Tenant Act 1985 provides that in any proceedings **7.121**
in which a tenant of a dwelling-house alleges a breach on the part of a landlord of a
repairing covenant relating to any part of the premises in which the dwelling is comprised, the court may order specific performance of that covenant. Thus, a residential
tenant may obtain an order for specific performance compelling the landlord to fulfil
his or her repairing obligations not only with regard to the tenant's flat, but also with
regard to the common parts of the building. Specific performance is an equitable remedy, however, and will be ordered only at the discretion of the court. A court is unlikely
to make an order of specific performance where it is not clear what specific work has
to be done.

Section 17 of the 1985 Act will not apply to business tenants. Nevertheless, in an appropri- **7.122**
ate case, a tenant may obtain an order of specific performance under the general equitable
jurisdiction of the court. Business tenants will only be able to obtain an order for specific
performance in respect of works to the common parts of the building that remain in the
possession of the landlord (as they could not do these works themselves without trespass-
ing on the landlord's property). Such relief will also only be granted where the covenant in
the lease is sufficiently clearly worded so that the necessary works can be clearly defined.
The claimant must also have a substantial interest in the works being completed so that
damages would not be an appropriate remedy (see *Jeune v Queens Cross Properties Ltd*
[1974] Ch 97, [1973] 3 All ER 97).

An order for specific performance can be enforced by the granting of a mandatory injunc- **7.123**
tion. The obvious advantage to the tenant of obtaining an injunction is that, if the landlord
then fails to carry out the works, he or she could be committed to prison for contempt of
court. This may provide a powerful incentive to do the work properly.

Appointment of receiver

In certain situations a landlord may neglect his or her duties as a landlord to such an **7.124**
extent that it makes it fruitless for a tenant to take action against that landlord to remedy
a condition of disrepair: for example, where a landlord has failed to collect rent or to carry
out repairing obligations for a number of years (see *Hart v Emelkirk* [1983] 1 WLR 1289,
[1983] 3 All ER 15), or where the landlord cannot be traced. In such cases, where it appears
just and convenient to do so, the court may appoint a receiver to take over the landlord's
duties under the Supreme Court Act 1981, s 37(1) (also the County Courts Act 1984, s 38
and the County Court Rules 1981, Ord 32). The court, however, will not appoint a receiver
to take over the management of local authority housing (*Parker v Camden LBC* [1986] Ch
162, [1985] 2 All ER 141, CA).

Appointment of a manager

Under Pt II of the Landlord and Tenant Act 1987 (as amended by the Housing Act 1996, **7.125**
ss 85 and 86), the tenant may apply to a leasehold valuation tribunal for the appointment
of a manager where a landlord persistently fails to maintain a block consisting of two or
more flats (see 23.110 to 23.122). The tenant must first serve notice upon the landlord
warning that such an application is about to be made. If the landlord then fails to take
action to remedy the disrepair, the tribunal may appoint a manager to take over the running of the block provided that it is satisfied that the landlord is in breach, that that breach
is likely to continue, and that it is just and convenient in all the circumstances to make the
order. These provisions do not apply if the landlord is a local authority or registered social
landlord, a resident landlord, or if the tenant is a business tenant (s 21(3)).

Proceedings

7.126 Claims for disrepair will normally be brought under the procedure set out in Part 7 of the CPR. A request for specific performance can be included in the claim. Applications made before proceedings have been commenced should be made following CPR Part 23 procedure.

Limitation periods

7.127 The limitation period for bringing a claim involving a breach of a repairing obligation will normally be six years (Limitation Act 1980, s 5). It should, however, be remembered that if the claim includes a claim for damages for personal injury the limitation period will be three years (Limitation Act 1980, s 11). The date from which the period will run is the date on which the breach occurred. If notice of disrepair is required this date will be the date the landlord should reasonably have commenced work after receiving notice of the disrepair. If no notice is required the relevant date will be the date that the disrepair occurred.

Disrepair protocol

7.128 The pre-action protocol for housing disrepair cases has been incorporated into the CPR and applies to all disrepair claims commenced after 8 December 2003. The protocol sets out clear guidance for tenants wishing to bring proceedings against their landlord for disrepair and is aimed at encouraging early resolution of cases or facilitating the efficient management of proceedings. The protocol includes provisions requiring the tenant to provide the landlord with an early and detailed letter notifying him or her of disrepair, requirements for a full letter of claim to be served before proceedings are issued, guidelines for the instruction of a joint expert, and guidance for the landlord in responding to a claim.

7.129 The protocol is lengthy and cannot be reproduced here; a full text, including draft letters and notices, is available online at <http://www.dca.gov.uk>. It is essential that tenants wishing to bring claims, and landlords defending an action for disrepair, follow the protocol as any unreasonable failure to comply may result in costs orders or other sanctions (*Birmingham City Council v Lee* [2008] EWCA Civ 891). In urgent cases of serious disrepair, however, it will still be possible for the tenant to issue injunction proceedings without first following the protocol. It should also be noted that use of the protocol will not extend the limitation period.

Expert evidence

7.130 There will be very few disrepair cases where it would be sufficient for the tenant to rely solely on his or her own evidence of disrepair without providing expert evidence in support of the claim. Care must be taken in the choice of an expert. The expert must have sufficient expertise on the matters in dispute and must be able to give his or her evidence impartially (CPR r 35.3). It should be remembered that the purpose of an expert is to provide technical information to the court that would normally be outside the knowledge of the parties, the lawyers, and the judge. It is preferable, wherever possible, for the parties in a disrepair dispute to instruct one expert who will provide the court with an unbiased and conclusive report on the issues before it. These issues may include whether there is disrepair, the cause of any disrepair, the remedial action necessary, and the probable cost of repair. The cost of instructing the expert will normally be recovered by the successful party at the conclusion of the case but those contemplating bringing an action for disrepair should bear in mind that before the case is concluded they may have to fund half or all of the cost of instructing the expert.

Complaints to the ombudsman or Homes and Communities Agency

Tenants of social landlords have an alternative method of complaint in cases of disrepair. **7.131**
Tenants of local authorities may bring a complaint to the Local Government Ombudsman;
tenants of registered social landlords can approach the Housing Ombudsman Service (from
April 2013 these will be replaced by one single housing ombudsman). Both ombudsmen
can investigate complaints about housing conditions or maladministration by the landlord
and may award compensation to the tenant. Before approaching the ombudsmen the tenant must have exhausted the landlord's own internal complaints procedure, otherwise the
complaint must be referred to the ombudsman by a 'designated person' rather than directly
by the tenant (Localism Act 2011, s 180). A 'designated person' is a member of Parliament,
a member of the local housing authority, or a designated tenant panel (s 180(3)).

In cases involving serious disrepair tenants of social landlords in England are also able **7.132**
to use the services of the Regulatory Committee of the Homes and Communities Agency
(HCA), a body created by the Housing and Regeneration Act 2008 (as amended by the
Localism Act 2011), to set and monitor standards in social housing (see 8.46 and Chapter
21). This body will also be able to award compensation to the tenant (although not if the
ombudsman has already done so) and it will not be necessary for the tenant to have used
the landlord's internal complaints procedure before approaching the HCA.

The ombudsmen and/or the HCA may be of more use to tenants than the civil courts sim- **7.133**
ply because they will be much cheaper to use. In particular they are able to appoint a sur
veyor to investigate complaints of disrepair so the tenant does not need to commission an
expert report. They are also able to adjudicate on matters that would be outside the scope
of a disrepair claim, for example complaints of condensation dampness.

KEY DOCUMENTS

Housing Act 1985

Landlord and Tenant Act 1985

Gas Safety (Installation and Use) Regulations 1998, SI 1998/2451

Civil Procedure Rules 1998

Form N1—Part 7 Claim

Form N16A—Application for Injunction

Pre-action protocol for disrepair including draft notices and letters; available from <http://www.dca.gov.uk>

Printed copies of all legislation can be ordered from The Stationery Office at <http://www.tsoshop.co.uk>. All legislation from 1988 onwards and most pre-1988 primary legislation is available online at <http://www.legislation.co.uk>.

Parts 55 and 56 of the Civil Procedure Rules are available online from <http://www.justice.gov.uk>.

Court forms are available online from <http://www.hmcourts-service.gov.uk>. The pre-action protocol for disrepair including draft notices and letters is available from <http://www.dca.gov.uk>.

8

REPAIR—COMMON LAW AND STATUTORY DUTIES

A INTRODUCTION

We have already seen in the previous chapters that in many cases there will be a contractual **8.01** liability between a landlord and a tenant. In this chapter, we shall be looking at disrepair from the perspective of the law of tort. The question we are concerned with is whether and to what extent a landlord may be liable for injury or damage caused to an occupier of a property by the condition of that property.

Tort has one very obvious advantage over the law in contract, namely that to pursue an **8.02** action in tort the claimant does not have to be a party to the contract. People, such as neighbours or a tenant's family, friends, or visitors, who are not within a contractual relationship with the landlord, may nevertheless be able to pursue a claim in tort against the landlord if they or their property are damaged.

Tortious liability can arise either at common law as negligence or nuisance, or it can arise **8.03** under statute.

B LANDLORD'S LIABILITY AT COMMON LAW

Negligence

Liability in negligence is founded on the notion of a duty of care. If one person owes **8.04** another a duty of care, and then through some act or omission fails to take reasonable care to observe this duty of care with the result that the other person suffers injury or damage, the wronged party can recover damages. A duty of care arises when the person under the duty of care ought reasonably to have foreseen that another person might be affected by his or her actions or omissions. These principles were set out by Lord Atkin in the famous case of *Donoghue v Stevenson* [1932] AC 562.

If the manufacturer of a fizzy drink (in that case) owes a duty of care to the consumer of **8.05** that drink, it may seem obvious that on the same principles the landlord should owe a duty of care to the occupiers of his or her property. To jump to this conclusion, however, would be premature. As we have seen, the law of landlord and tenant does not necessarily follow innovations in consumer law. Principles that apply to goods will not always apply to an estate in land. In comparison to the long history of land law, the extension of the principle of negligence that occurred with *Donoghue v Stevenson* is a relatively modern phenomenon. The long-established principle of *caveat lessee* has survived the development of the law of negligence with the result that, rightly or wrongly, a landlord retains a basic immunity from an action in negligence for injury or damage caused by the condition of the property let. This is the principle as set out in *Cavalier v Pope* [1906] AC 428 at 430, where Lord MacNaghten cited *Robbins v Jones* (1863) 15 CB (NS) 221:

> A landlord who lets a house in a dangerous state is not liable to the tenant's customers or guests for accidents happening during the term: for fraud apart, there is no law against letting a tumbledown house; and the tenant's remedy is upon his contract, if any.

8.06 This does not mean, however, that a landlord can never be liable in negligence for the condition of his or her property. The principle of *Cavalier v Pope* still stands but 'must be kept in close confinement' (*Rimmer v Liverpool City Council* [1984] 1 All ER 930 *per* Stephenson LJ at 935, citing Denning LJ in *Green v Chelsea BC* [1954] 2 QB 127 at 138).

When will a landlord be liable in negligence?

8.07 In recent years the law of negligence has expanded to cover the people involved in the construction and design of a building. Builders, developers, architects, surveyors, designers, and local authorities who have failed to exercise reasonable care in the work they have carried out on a building have been held to be liable to the occupiers of that building for injury or damage resulting from their negligence. If the builder or developer of a property is also the landlord of that property, it will not be able to escape liability for negligent construction simply because it is the landlord. As Lord Salmon stated, albeit *obiter*, in *Anns v Merton LBC* [1977] 2 All ER 492 at 511:

> The immunity of a landlord who sells or lets his house which is dangerous or unfit for habitation is deeply embedded in our law. I cannot, however, accept the proposition that a contractor who has negligently built a dangerous house can escape liability to pay damages for negligence to anyone who, eg, falls through a shoddily constructed floor and is seriously injured, just because the contractor happens to have been the owner of the land upon which the house stands.

8.08 Lord Salmon's view was confirmed in *Rimmer v Liverpool City Council* [1984] 1 All ER 930. Here the tenant of a flat was injured when he stumbled and put his hand through a glass panel in an internal wall of the flat. The council, as well as being the tenant's landlord, had designed and built the block of flats in which he lived. The court held that the council, in its capacity as designer/builder, owed a duty of care, not just to the tenant but to all persons who might reasonably be expected to be affected by the design or construction of the premises.

Liability when carrying out repairs or improvements

8.09 A landlord will also have a duty when carrying out repairs or improvements to premises to ensure that those works do not cause injury or damage to the tenants or their property. Where the landlord employs others to carry out works to the premises, the landlord may be vicariously liable for any negligence on the part of the workmen if the landlord has sufficient control over the works. If the landlord does not retain sufficient control (for example where works are carried out by an independent contractor) the tenant's remedy may lie against the contractor responsible for the works rather than the landlord.

Liability for common parts

Where a landlord retains control of parts of the building such as staircases, corridors, **8.10** roofs, or guttering, the landlord is under a duty of care to keep these parts of the building in condition so they do not cause injury to the tenant or damage to the tenant's property (*Cockburn v Smith* [1924] 2 KB 119). This duty of care extends to cover any person lawfully upon the premises, such as the tenant's visitors or family.

When will a landlord not be liable in negligence?

Rimmer v Liverpool City Council did not go so far as to overrule *Cavalier v Pope.* **8.11** Stephenson LJ expressed the view (at 939) that 'to impose a duty on all landowners who let or sell their land and dwellings, whether or not they are their own designers or builders' might be such a great change in the law as to require legislation. Where the landlord is not responsible for the construction or design of the building, the landlord's immunity remains. Such a landlord is sometimes known as a 'bare landlord' (*McNerny v London Borough of Lambeth* (1988) 21 HLR 188).

Act of third parties

In *King v Liverpool City Council* [1986] 1 WLR 890, the tenant lived in a block of flats **8.12** owned by the council. The flat above her flat became vacant. The tenant requested that the council make the flat secure, but no effective steps were taken. On three occasions vandals broke into the empty flat and damaged the water system causing water to flood the tenant's flat underneath. The court stated that there is no principle of law excluding the landlord from liability for the acts of third parties, but held that the council was not under a duty of care: liability would arise only where there was some special relationship between the defendant and the third party (*Dorset Yacht Co. Ltd v Home Office* [1970] 2 WLR 1140), or where the injury was 'the inevitable and foreseeable result of the defendant's act or omission'.

Nuisance

Where a landlord retains part of the building and disrepair of that part causes interfer- **8.13** ence with the tenant's enjoyment of the part let, the landlord may be liable in nuisance, for example, if the landlord has retained control of the roof and guttering and fails to maintain them so that water penetrates to the tenant's property beneath (*Tennant Radiant Heat Ltd v Warrington Development Corp* (1988) 11 EG 71). Only a person in possession of the premises has *the right* to sue in nuisance (in contrast with the position in negligence, where a tenant's family, friends, or visitors may acquire the right to sue).

A claim in nuisance will often be very similar to a claim for breach of covenant for quiet **8.14** enjoyment (see 5.01 to 5.31); however, there will be cases where nuisance is the only remedy available to the tenant. In *Long v Southwark LBC* [2002] EWCA Civ 403, [2002] HLR 56 the tenant complained that the communal facilities for the disposal of rubbish were inadequate as the rubbish chutes were too narrow. As a result tenants were leaving rubbish bags at the side of the chute and this rubbish was not cleared away regularly. In this case the lease contained an express condition whereby the landlord would take reasonable steps to keep the common parts tidy, and it was found to be in breach of this obligation. The Court of Appeal, however, went on to consider the tenant's alternative claims of disrepair, breach of the covenant for quiet enjoyment, and nuisance. It found that there was no disrepair: the criticism of the chute was that it was too narrow, not that it was in want of repair. It also held that there was no breach of the covenant for quiet enjoyment as this covenant does not amount to a warranty for the fitness of the premises and does not apply to problems caused by faults in the design of the building. The presence of the rubbish bags did, however, constitute a nuisance for which the landlord was liable, as it had failed to take reasonable steps to abate the nuisance.

8.15 A claim in nuisance may also be available to tenants in cases where they cannot rely directly on the landlord's obligations in the lease, for example where disrepair in another flat in the building is causing damage to the tenant's flat. A claim in nuisance may be brought against the landlord in order to oblige him or her to take remedial action, or, if the landlord has no right or duty to remedy the disrepair, a claim may be brought directly against the offending tenant.

8.16 In cases of ongoing nuisance the landlord will not be liable if the cause of the nuisance existed before the granting of the lease (see *Jackson v JH Watson Property Investment Ltd* [2008] EWHC 14 (Ch) where the landlord was not liable in nuisance for long-standing water penetration caused by faulty construction work that was carried out before the lease was granted).

C LIABILITY UNDER STATUTE

8.17 While a bare landlord will not be liable in tort at common law, two statutory provisions, the Occupiers' Liability Act 1957 and the Defective Premises Act 1972, provide that in certain circumstances a duty of care may be imposed upon a landlord.

Occupiers' Liability Act 1957

8.18 The Occupiers' Liability Act 1957, s 2 provides that:

(1) An occupier of premises owes the same duty, the 'common duty of care,' to all his visitors, except in so far as he is free to and does extend, restrict, modify or exclude his duty to any visitor or visitors by agreement or otherwise.

(2) The common duty of care is a duty to take such care as in all the circumstances of the case is reasonable to see that the visitor will be reasonably safe in using the premises for the purposes for which he is invited or permitted by the occupier to be there.

(3) The circumstances relevant for the present purpose include the degree of care, and of want of care, which would ordinarily be looked for in such a visitor, so that (for example) in proper cases—

(a) an occupier must be prepared for children to be less careful than adults; and

(b) an occupier may expect that a person, in the exercise of his calling, will appreciate and guard against any special risks ordinarily incident to it, so far as the occupier leaves him free to do so....

8.19 'Occupier' for the purposes of the Act means the person who has control of the premises. Clearly, a tenant, who will have exclusive possession of the premises demised, is an occupier in this sense. The landlord, having given up exclusive possession, cannot be under a duty of care to visitors to the tenant's house or flat, nor can he or she be under a duty to the tenant. However, when the landlord retains control of parts of a building, for example the entrance hall, staircases, lifts, roof, forecourt, and other common areas in a block of flats, he or she will be an occupier in the terms of the Act and will be under the common duty set out in s 2(2).

8.20 'Visitor' is a broad term which covers any person to whom the occupier has given implied or express permission to enter. Clearly, the tenant and his or her family and friends are visitors when they make use of the common parts of the building.

Whether the landlord has discharged his or her duty to a visitor will depend upon the facts   **8.21** of the case in all the circumstances. The Act itself gives some guidance in s 2(3) by stating that the 'occupier must be prepared for children to be less careful than adults' and that the occupier 'may expect that a person, in the exercise of his calling, will appreciate and guard against any special risks ordinarily incident to it'. Section 2(4) goes on to state that a warning given by the occupier will not 'without more' absolve the occupier from responsibility 'unless in all the circumstances it was enough to enable the visitor to be reasonably safe', and likewise that the occupier will not be regarded as absolved from responsibility for an independent contractor unless he or she had acted reasonably in entrusting the work to the contractor.

If the tenancy agreement binds the occupier to permit third parties to the contract to   **8.22** enter the premises, the occupier is prevented from excluding or reducing his or her liability to such a third party by inserting a clause into the contract (s 3(1)) (eg, where, with regard to a block of flats, the tenancy agreement binds the landlord to permit the tenant's visitors to use the common areas such as staircases and hallways).

It should be noted that, for business occupiers, the Unfair Contract Terms Act 1977   **8.23** demands that any exclusion of liability be shown to be reasonable and that liability for death or personal injury cannot be excluded.

Despite the fact that the Occupiers' Liability Act 1957 imposes a broad liability upon an   **8.24** occupier, it is of limited use when it comes to trying to compel a landlord to do repairing work. First, it applies only to those parts of a building which remain in the landlord's occupation. Secondly, no liability will arise until an injury actually takes place. If a friend comes to visit you and on the way out is injured by falling down a dangerous stairwell, the landlord will be liable for the injury. The Act cannot force the landlord to make the stairwell safe before an accident happens, except in the sense that if the landlord knows that he or she could well be liable for any injury occurring on the premises he or she may be more diligent about getting the work done.

Defective Premises Act 1972

Section 1 of the Defective Premises Act 1972 imposes a duty on persons who undertake   **8.25** work for, or in connection with, the provision of a dwelling:

(a) to do the work in a professional or workman-like manner;
(b) to use proper materials;
(c) to ensure with regard to that work that the dwelling will be fit for habitation when completed.

This duty will apply both to builders and to professionals such as architects and engineers,   **8.26** as well as to property developers and local authorities involved in the provision of housing. The duty owed is somewhat stricter than that owed at common law, for it is owed both to the person for whom the building was provided and to anyone subsequently acquiring a legal or equitable interest in the property, such as a subsequent purchaser or a tenant.

However, s 2 provides that s 1 will not apply to dwellings which are covered by an 'approved   **8.27** scheme' of purchaser protection. In practice the vast majority of private developments will be covered by such a scheme (eg, the National House Building Council scheme). Section 1 is also restricted by the six-year limitation period which begins to run when the building is completed (s 1(5)) and it will apply only to work carried out after the commencement of the Act (1 January 1974).

8.28 Section 3 of the 1972 Act applies to works carried out prior to a sale or letting. It imposes a duty of care in negligence upon anyone carrying out a work of construction, repair, maintenance, or demolition. The duty is owed to anyone who might reasonably be affected by the defects created by the doing of the works and will therefore cover not only the tenant but also his or her family and visitors. The duty also continues to be owed if the property is sold or let. However, s 3 will not apply to work done prior to the commencement of the Act and will function only where the landlord (or other person) has negligently done work on the property. If the defect is due to a failure to perform work, s 3 cannot provide a remedy.

8.29 Section 4 is, from the point of view of landlord and tenant law, the most important provision in the Defective Premises Act 1972:

> (1) Where premises are let under a tenancy which puts on the landlord an obligation to the tenant for the maintenance or repair of the premises, the landlord owes to all persons who might reasonably be expected to be affected by defects in the state of the premises a duty to take such care as is reasonable in all the circumstances to see that they are reasonably safe from personal injury or from damage to their property caused by a relevant defect.

Landlord under a repairing obligation

8.30 The Act takes a broad view of what it means to be under a repairing obligation; it includes an obligation implied into the contract by the common law or by statute as well as an express covenant to repair. Furthermore, by s 4(4), a landlord who has a right, express or implied, to enter the premises in order to carry out any description of maintenance and repair is treated for the purposes of s 4 as if he or she were under a repairing obligation. The obligation is only in respect of premises that are let and will not, therefore, extend to the common parts of the building. These parts, however, will usually be covered by the implied duty to keep the common parts in repair (see 7.64 to 7.69) and/or the Occupiers' Liability Act 1957 (see 8.18).

8.31 It should be noted that where the landlord is under an obligation to repair, s 4 will not expand this obligation. In *McNerny v London Borough of Lambeth* (1988) 21 HLR 188, a flat suffered from condensation dampness. The landlord was under an implied obligation to repair the structure and exterior of the flat (Landlord and Tenant Act 1985, s 11) but the tenant was unable to establish disrepair (see 7.22 to 7.27). An argument that the landlord was liable in negligence under s 4 of the 1972 Act failed. Section 4 is 'geared to the landlord's obligation to repair the premises. It goes no wider than that' (*McNerny v London Borough of Lambeth per* Dillon LJ at 193). Similarly, a landlord has no duty to make premises safe where there is no actual disrepair (for example, by installing safety glass in a front door) (*Alker v Collingwood Housing Association* [2007] EWCA Civ 343, [2007] HLR 29, CA).

Knowledge of defect

8.32 The Defective Premises Act 1972, s 4(2), provides:

> (2) The said duty is owed if the landlord knows (whether as a result of being notified by the tenant or otherwise) or if he ought in all the circumstances to have known of the relevant defect.

8.33 The landlord does not need to have actual knowledge of the defect. In *Clarke v Taff Ely BC* (1984) 10 HLR 44, a tenant was injured when a floor collapsed. The tenant had not informed the council of the state of the floor. The council, however, was under an obligation to repair and had the right to enter and inspect the premises. The council was held to be liable. In the circumstances it ought reasonably to have known of the defect; the house in question was old and the state of the floorboards should have been inspected. (See also *Smith v Bradford Metropolitan Council* (1982) 44 P&CR 171, CA.)

Even where there is no express provision entitling the landlord to repair, such a right may **8.34** be implied. For example, in *McAuley v Bristol City Council* [1992] 1 QB 134, CA, the tenant was injured falling from a defective step in the garden. The tenancy agreement placed no repairing obligation on either party, but there was a provision requiring the tenant to give the council access to the premises for any purposes which might from time to time be required by the council. It was accepted, however, that the tenancy agreement placed no obligation on the council to repair the step. Nevertheless, the court decided (relying on *Mint v Good* [1951] 1 KB 517, [1950] 2 All ER 1159) that in order to give business efficacy to the tenancy agreement, the landlord had an implied right to enter in order to carry out repairs and remedy any defects which might expose visitors to the premises (or the tenant himself) to the risk of injury. Thus, by virtue of s 4(4) (8.30) the council was held to be liable for the injury. In *Sykes v Harry* [2001] EWCA Civ 167, [2001] QB 1041 it was held that a landlord's statutory duty to inspect gas appliances annually gave rise to an obligation to inspect, and therefore repair, under s 4. For the purposes of s 4 this implied right is limited to repair work. In *Dunn v Bradford MDC* [2002] EWCA Civ 1137, [2002] HLR 41, CA, it was held that the fact that an express covenant in the lease allowed the landlord access to carry out repairs and improvements did not give rise to an obligation to carry out improvements.

Meaning of 'relevant defect'

A duty of care will arise under s 4 only when the defect in question is a 'relevant defect'. **8.35** By s 4(3), a relevant defect is:

> a defect in the state of the premises existing at or after the material time and arising from, or continuing because of, an act or omission by the landlord which constitutes or would if he had had notice of the defect, have constituted a failure by him to carry out his obligation to the tenant for the maintenance or repair of the premises ...

The material time is 1 January 1974 for a tenancy which was in existence before the com- **8.36** mencement of the Act. In all other cases it will be the earliest of the following times:

(a) the time when the tenancy commences;
(b) the time when the tenancy agreement is entered into;
(c) the time when possession is taken of the premises in contemplation of the letting.

D REMEDIES

Remedies for breach of a tortious obligation will be roughly the same as those for contrac- **8.37** tual breaches discussed in the previous chapter. Damages will be awarded to put the tenant in the position he or she would have been in if the landlord had not been negligent or in breach of a statutory duty. In practice this will include the same heads of damage as those arising using the contractual measure of damages. It should be remembered that the tenant can rely on obligations in tort and contractual obligations within the same claim. Breaches of either type of obligation may be pleaded together, or in the alternative. The disrepair protocol discussed at 7.128 will also apply to claims for breach of a tortious obligation.

Limitation periods

8.38   The limitation period for a claim in tort is six years from the date of damage (Limitation Act 1980, s 2). If the damage came to the claimant's attention at a later date the period will be three years from the date of knowledge (subject to a total limitation period of 15 years). Again, if the claim includes a claim for personal injury it must be brought within three years of the claimant's knowledge of the injury.

E ENFORCEMENT OF HOUSING STANDARDS

Housing Act 2004

8.39   Part 1 of the Housing Act 2004 introduced a new duty for local housing authorities to monitor private sector housing in their area with a view to identifying potential 'hazards' to the mental or physical wellbeing of the occupants. The types of hazard identified by the Act include matters that could be defined as disrepair but extend much further than this. The Act is concerned with any feature of residential premises that might cause harm: from unsafe staircases to overcrowding and security against intruders. The Act then provides for the local housing authority to take remedial action against the owner or manager of the property, either by serving notice compelling them to undertake works or by ordering them to cease using the property for a particular purpose. The Act also allows the local housing authority to enter into premises and carry out emergency works if the state of the premises poses an immediate threat of harm to the occupants. These provisions are considered in detail in Chapter 20.

Houses in multiple occupation

8.40   The Management of Houses in Multiple Occupation Regulations 2006, SI 2006/372 and 2007, SI 2007/1903 (WSI 2007/3229) impose a statutory duty on the managers of houses in multiple occupation (HMOs) to maintain the premises in a clean and safe condition. These Regulations are considered in Chapter 20 (20.102).

Secure tenants' right to repairs

8.41   Secure tenants of local authorities have a statutory right to compel their landlord to carry out minor repairs within a prescribed period (Secure Tenants of Local Housing Authorities (Right to Repair) Regulations 1994, SI 1994/133 (see 17.88)). The right only applies if the landlord has at least 100 properties and if the estimated cost of the repair is less than £250.

8.42   Under the Regulations a secure tenant is entitled to have qualifying repairs carried out at the landlord's expense and is entitled to compensation if the repairs are not carried out within a prescribed period. A list of qualifying repairs is set out in a schedule to the Regulations. The list of repairs covers relatively inexpensive but essential matters such as loss of electric power, a blocked sink or drain, or a leaking roof. The schedule also sets out the prescribed number of working days allowed for carrying out the repairs.

8.43   The Regulations provide that where a tenant applies to the landlord for a repair to be carried out the landlord must take action within a prescribed period. If the landlord considers it necessary to carry out an inspection this must be done immediately; if no inspection is necessary the landlord must issue a repair notice to a contractor. If the landlord does not consider that the repair is a qualifying repair it must give the tenant reasons for this decision (reg 5).

The repair must be carried out within a prescribed period (which will be calculated by **8.44** reference to the schedule and will depend on whether an inspection was necessary before the repair notice could be issued (reg 2)). If the repair is not carried out within this period the tenant is entitled to claim compensation. The amount of compensation is calculated according to the number of days beyond the prescribed period the repairs took to complete, up to a maximum of £50 (reg 7).

Decent Homes Standard

Government guidance for social landlords on the minimum standards expected for social **8.45** housing is set out in the Decent Homes Standard. In order to meet the Decent Homes Standard a dwelling must comply with four criteria:

(a) It must meet the current minimum statutory standard for housing.
(b) It must be in a reasonable state of repair.
(c) It must have modern facilities and services.
(d) It must provide a reasonable degree of thermal comfort.

The Decent Homes Standard was originally intended to provide guidance and to create **8.46** a national target for the standard of social housing. As such it was of very limited assistance to a tenant living in sub-standard accommodation. In England, however, the Housing and Regeneration Act 2008 (as amended by the Localism Act 2011) has introduced the Homes and Communities Agency (HCA) with the power to set standards and monitor the provision and management of social housing. The HCA has adopted the Decent Homes Standard as the standard of housing to be expected of registered providers of social housing. The HCA has the authority to penalize registered providers who do not comply with the Standard, and to award compensation to the tenants of defaulting landlords. The provisions of the Decent Homes Standard and the enforcement powers of the HCA are considered in more detail in Chapter 21.

KEY DOCUMENTS

Occupiers' Liability Act 1957

Defective Premises Act 1972

Housing Act 2004

Housing and Regeneration Act 2008

Secure Tenants of Local Housing Authorities (Right to Repair) Regulations 1994, SI 1994/133

A Decent Home: Definition and guidance for implementation Department for Communities and Local Government (<http://www.communities.gov.uk>)

Printed copies of all legislation can be ordered from The Stationery Office at <http://www.tsoshop. co.uk>. All legislation from 1988 onwards and most pre-1988 primary legislation is available online at <http://www. legislation.gov.uk>.

The Civil Procedure Rules are available online from <http://www.justice.gov.uk/courts/ procedure-rules>.

Court forms are available online from the HM Courts and Tribunals Service at <http://www.justice. gov.uk/forms/hmcts>.

9

ASSIGNMENT AND SUB-LETTING—
CONTINUING OBLIGATIONS

A INTRODUCTION

When one person grants a tenancy to another, the parties to the tenancy agreement enter **9.01** into a contractual relationship. As with any contractual relationship, the terms of the contract can be enforced between the parties to that contract. This is the contractual principle of privity of contract. So far so good—provided that the landlord and tenant remain the same throughout the course of the term, both of them will be obliged to comply with the terms of the tenancy agreement.

A tenancy, however, is capable of outliving its creators. Once granted its existence is inde- **9.02** pendent of the parties that created it. It can endure beyond the death of either landlord or tenant. It will continue when either the landlord or the tenant disposes of his or her interest in the property to another person. In such cases, whether by the rules of succession or by contract, the tenancy will become vested in a person who was not a party to the original agreement.

Obviously there must be rules to determine what happens in such a situation: unfortu- **9.03** nately there are rather a lot of them. The Landlord and Tenant (Covenants) Act 1995 (the 1995 Act) effected a sweeping reform of this area of law. However, the majority of the Act does not apply retrospectively (despite the fact that this was recommended by the Law Commission). The result is that for the foreseeable future there will be two sets of rules running parallel: the old rules, which apply to tenancies granted prior to the introduction of the 1995 Act (old tenancies); and the new rules, which, with a few exceptions, apply to tenancies granted after the 1995 Act was introduced (new tenancies). A new tenancy is defined by s 1 of the 1995 Act as a tenancy granted after 1 January 1996. A tenancy granted after 1 January 1996 will not be a new tenancy if it was granted in pursuance of an agreement (including an option or a right of first refusal) or an order of the court made before that date (s 1(3), (6), and (7)).

9.04 This chapter will consider both sets of rules, but it is necessary first to look at the ways in which a tenancy can end up in the hands of a third party. Consider the following situation:

9.05 **Example** Bruce has a 10-year fixed-term tenancy of Flat C, 12 Cranley Gardens. This tenancy was granted to him by Simon. Bruce has lived there for three years and he now wants to go travelling for a year. He has saved up the money for his holiday, but he cannot afford to go if he has to continue paying rent while he is away. He does, however, want to ensure that he will have somewhere to live when he returns.

9.06 Tom likewise has a 10-year fixed-term tenancy of Flat B, 12 Cranley Gardens, also granted by Simon. Tom has recently acquired a new job in the West Country and he wants to move there permanently.

9.07 Bruce and Tom both wish to dispose of or sell some or all of the rights they have over their respective properties. As tenants, Bruce and Tom are faced with two options: either they can sub-let or they can assign. For the purposes of this example it is assumed that neither lease contains any provision restricting the right to assign or sub-let (for covenants against assigning and sub-letting see 6.81 to 6.112).

B SUB-LETTING

9.08 To create a sub-lease the tenant carves a smaller interest out of his or her interest in the property. The sub-lease granted by the tenant must therefore be for a lesser period of time than the tenant's term. The tenant retains an immediate reversion, so at the termination of the sub-lease he or she is again entitled to occupy the premises.

9.09 This arrangement is well suited to Bruce's situation. Unlike Tom and Simon, Bruce wants to be able to regain possession of his flat after a year when he returns from travelling. Bruce therefore decides to grant Andrew a sub-tenancy for a fixed term of 12 months.

9.10 This situation may be rendered diagrammatically as follows:

Figure 9.1 Granting a sub-tenancy

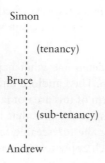

9.11 By granting a sub-tenancy to Andrew, Bruce has created a second relationship of landlord and tenant. The original relationship of landlord and tenant has not been altered by the creation of a second tenancy. For Bruce this has the disadvantage that his liability to pay rent to Simon will continue while he is away travelling; however, Bruce will be able to use the rent he receives from Andrew to help defray the cost of his rent to Simon.

If a tenant seeks to grant a sub-tenancy for a term longer than or equal to his or her **9.12** own remaining interest in the property, the sub-tenancy will operate as an assignment. If Simon granted Bruce his 10-year fixed-term tenancy on 1 October 2006, and then Bruce tries to grant Andrew an eight-year fixed-term tenancy on 1 November 2008, Andrew's sub-tenancy will expire on 1 November 2016, a month after Bruce's term has expired. Bruce has not therefore retained an interest in the land and his attempt to sub-let will in fact function as an assignment of the remainder of his tenancy.

The fact that a tenant may have a periodic tenancy rather than a fixed term does not pre- **9.13** clude that tenant from sub-letting. Say that Bruce does not have a 10-year fixed term, but instead holds a monthly tenancy. This does not mean that he can only grant a sub-tenancy of less than a month. In law, a periodic tenancy continues until it is determined. Thus, Bruce, as the holder of a monthly periodic tenancy, can grant to Andrew a perfectly valid fixed term for a year, or even for a longer period. Andrew, however, would be wise to be wary of such an arrangement, for if Simon decides to terminate Bruce's tenancy Andrew's sub-tenancy will also be ended at common law.

The formalities of creating a sub-tenancy

A sub-tenancy is created in the same way as any other tenancy and the same formalities **9.14** will apply. A sub-lease should normally be created by deed, unless it is granted for a term of less than three years (see 3.13 to 3.29).

C ASSIGNMENT

When a tenant assigns his or her lease, the tenant hands over his or her interest in the prop- **9.15** erty entirely. The original tenant (the assignor) retains no reversion and the new tenant (the assignee) steps into the shoes of the old tenant. The assignee becomes the tenant and the assignor drops out of the picture (although, as we shall see, this does not mean that all the obligations under the lease cease on assignment).

This arrangement suits Tom well: he does not want to retain any interest in the property **9.16** but wants to be free to move to his new job and set up home elsewhere. If Tom was granted his tenancy on 1 December 2006 and then assigns his interest to John, John acquires the whole of the remainder of Tom's term right up to 1 December 2016.

This situation may be rendered diagrammatically as follows: **9.17**

Figure 9.2 Assignment of a lease

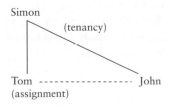

Simon

(tenancy)

Tom ----------------- John
(assignment)

9.18 An assignment does not create a new relationship of landlord and tenant. Prior to the assignment, Simon was Tom's landlord. On assignment Tom hands over his tenancy to John. There is still only one relationship of landlord and tenant.

9.19 Of course it is not only the tenant who may wish to dispose of his or her interest in land. A landlord too may decide to pass his or her interest on to a third party. In our example Simon could sell his freehold interest to Peter. Peter would become the new freeholder of 12 Cranley Gardens and also Tom's landlord.

9.20 This situation may be rendered diagrammatically as follows:

Figure 9.3 Disposal of the landlord's interest

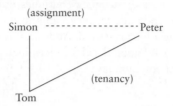

The formalities of assigning

9.21 To pass the legal estate all assignments must be made by deed by virtue of the LPA 1925, s 52(1). These provisions apply to all leases whether they are created orally, in writing, or by deed. It should be noted that while the LPA 1925 requires the strict observance of formalities in order to assign a lease, it does not impose such stringent requirements upon the creation of a lease (see *Crago v Julian* [1992] 1 All ER 744). This results in a curious inconsistency. A perfectly valid legal tenancy for a term of less than three years can be created orally by virtue of s 54(2) of the LPA 1925 (see 3.21); but an assignment of the very same tenancy must be made by deed in order to pass the legal estate.

9.22 If the assignment is not made by deed but there is an agreement to assign which satisfies either the LPA 1925, s 40 or the Law of Property (Miscellaneous Provisions) Act 1989, s 2(1), the assignee may acquire an equitable interest in the property under the principle in *Walsh v Londsdale* (see 3.58).

Involuntary assignment

9.23 Not all assignments will take place, as in our example, because the tenant wishes to get rid of an interest in the property. Sometimes an assignment may occur by force of circumstances. For example, if a tenant dies his or her tenancy does not vanish into thin air; rather, by the Administration of Estates Act 1925, the tenancy will vest in the deceased tenant's personal representatives. Likewise, if the tenant becomes bankrupt the lease will vest in the trustee in bankruptcy. However, detailed consideration of such involuntary assignments is beyond the scope of this book.

D LIABILITY AFTER SUB-LETTING OR ASSIGNMENT

In each of the three situations considered earlier, a person who was not party to the origi- **9.24** nal contract between landlord and tenant has acquired an interest in either a part or the whole of 12 Cranley Gardens: Andrew has acquired a sub-tenancy of Flat C; John has acquired the tenancy of Flat B by assignment; Peter has purchased the freehold of the whole building.

The original tenancy agreements entered into between Simon and Bruce and between **9.25** Simon and Tom contained, among others, the following terms:

(a) The tenant covenants:
    (i) that every third year he will decorate the interior with good quality paint;
    (ii) that he will use the flat for the purpose of a private dwelling-house only.
(b) The landlord covenants:
    (i)   that he will keep the structure and exterior of the building in good condition;
    (ii) that at the end of the term the landlord will return the deposit to the tenant;
    (iii) that on being given six months' notice by the tenant, the landlord will sell a
          99-year fixed-term lease of the flat to the tenant at a price to be fixed by an inde-
          pendent surveyor.

Two questions then arise: **9.26**

(a) To what extent do the original parties to the contract remain bound by the terms of
    that contract?
(b) To what extent are the people who were not party to the original contract but who
    have subsequently acquired an interest in the property bound under the terms of the
    original contract?

The continuing contractual liability between the original parties

Example A—liability of Bruce to Simon

As we saw earlier, the granting of a sub-tenancy brings into being a second relationship **9.27** of landlord and tenant. The original tenancy continues unaltered and Simon will remain bound by its terms. Bruce will also be liable for the actions or omissions of his sub-tenant (either because of an express term in the agreement or by virtue of s 79 of the LPA 1925, see below). Thus, if Andrew starts running a business from Flat C, Simon's remedy will be against Bruce. Bruce should therefore ensure that the sub-lease contains the same terms as his original contract with Simon so that he can prevent Andrew from doing anything which might amount to a breach of his own tenancy agreement.

Example B—liability of Tom to Simon

 The situation where a tenancy is assigned, rather than having a sub-tenancy carved out **9.28** of it, is very different. In such a case the person who assigns (the assignor) retains no interest in the land. However, the assignor was party to the original contract, and in that contract he or she undertook to abide by the covenants it contained for the full dura-tion of the term. The key question, therefore, is whether his or her liability under this contract continues after the assignment has been made: if the principle of privity of con-tract is adhered to strictly, liability will continue; if it is not, liability will end when the tenancy is assigned. However, as we have seen, an estate in land is a concept to which the principles of contract law are not always appropriate. For this reason the Landlord and Tenant (Covenants) Act 1995 has abrogated the principle of privity of contract with regard to leasehold covenants. Nevertheless, because the majority of the provisions of the new Act apply only to tenancies granted after 1 January 1996 it is necessary to consider the situation both before and after this date.

9.29 **Under the old rules—tenancies granted before 1 January 1996** Under the old rules contractual liability will not end simply because the person who entered into the contract has handed his interest in land on to a third party. If Tom was granted his tenancy before 1 January 1996 then, even after Tom has assigned his tenancy to John, his contractual liability to Simon will remain despite the fact that Tom retains no interest in the land. This will usually be because in entering into the contract with the landlord a tenant expressly covenants to be responsible for the acts and omissions of the tenant's successors in title (ie assignees) and persons deriving title under the tenant (ie sub-tenants). Even in the absence of express terms to this effect, they will be implied by s 79 of the LPA 1925 unless they have been expressly excluded by clear wording to the contrary.

9.30 As a result of this continuing contractual liability, Tom will remain liable to Simon for any breach of covenant by John throughout the whole term of the lease. If John falls into rent arrears Simon can sue Tom for the outstanding rent (see *Estates Gazette v Benjamin Restaurants* (1994) 26 EG 140, CA; *Warnford Investments Ltd v Duckworth* [1979] Ch 127, [1978] 2 All ER 517). If John fails to fulfil his decorating covenant Simon can sue Tom for damages (*Thames Manufacturing Co. Ltd v Perrotts (Nichol & Peyton) Ltd* (1984) 271 EG 284).

9.31 As we shall see later, Simon will also have the option of suing John directly, and in the majority of cases this will be the course of action that a landlord will take (after all it is much more convenient to sue the current occupier of the land). Simon might not even be able to trace Tom's whereabouts a few years after he has left the property. Nevertheless, in certain circumstances it may be worthwhile for a landlord to sue the original tenant, for example if the current tenant does not have sufficient money to compensate the landlord for the breach.

9.32 In such a case the original tenant can try to recover any loss by suing the assignee. Section 77 of the LPA 1925 will imply a covenant that an assignee will indemnify the assignor for any breach of covenant in the lease. However, if the landlord chose to sue the original tenant because the assignee was insolvent, the original tenant may find himself or herself in the unfortunate position of being liable to the landlord for a breach of covenant for which he or she was not responsible and yet unable to recover from the assignee.

9.33 This is precisely the sort of injustice that the 1995 Act is designed to remedy. Under the old rules the original tenant ends up effectively acting as a guarantor of the lease, and as a result a heavy responsibility is placed on tenants to pick reliable, solvent assignees. There may be a certain logic in this reasoning with regard to the first assignment, for the tenant will be able to choose who is to be the new occupier of the land. However, it is possible that the first assignee may later assign the lease to a second assignee, and then this second assignee may assign to a third. In such a case the original tenant will have little control over who is occupying the land. Nevertheless, if a landlord does decide to pursue the original tenant for breaches by an assignee, the 1995 Act now demands that he or she must do so within six months of the charge becoming due (see s 17, 9.35).

9.34 For a while it was even thought that an original tenant would be liable for covenants that had been varied by agreement between the original landlord and a subsequent assignee (see *Centrovincial Estates Plc v Bulk Storage Ltd* (1983) 46 P&CR 393). However, the position at common law is now that if an assignee and the original landlord vary the lease so that the assignee takes on some additional obligation that was not contemplated in the original contract, the original tenant will not find his or her liability increased (*Friends' Provident Life Office v British Railways Board* [1996] 1 All ER 336). This will not be the case if the original agreement included some provision for a future variation of the tenant's obligations, such as a rent review clause, notwithstanding the fact that the original tenant will not be party to the negotiations over revised rent (see *Selous Street Properties Ltd v Oronel Fabrics Ltd* (1984) 270 EG 643 at 650, as explained in *Friends' Provident Life Office v British Railways Board*).

Statutory restrictions on the common law principles Though the majority of provisions in the 1995 Act apply only to new tenancies, ss 17–20 apply to old tenancies as well and serve to temper the potentially harsh consequences of the common law for former tenants who have assigned their leases: **9.35**

(a) **Restriction on liability for rent and service charge** Section 17 is a particularly important provision that imposes a procedure upon a landlord who wishes to recover money from a former tenant (or from the guarantor of a former tenant in the case of a new tenant where there is an authorized guarantee agreement, see below). It provides that a former tenant will not be liable to the landlord to pay any fixed charge (which includes both rent and service charges (s 17(6)), unless, within six months of that charge becoming due, the landlord serves notice on the former tenant. This notice must inform the former tenant that the charge is due and also state that the landlord intends to recover such amount as is specified in the notice (s 17(2)). It should be made on Form 1 as prescribed by s 27 and the Landlord and Tenant (Covenants) Act 1995 (Notices) Regulations 1995, SI 1995/2964. Effectively, s 17 provides a cut-off point six months from the date of a charge becoming due, after which a landlord will not be able to pursue a claim against a former tenant. Where there is a rent review clause it is not necessary to serve a s 17 notice at the beginning of the review period for a debt that may subsequently become payable; rather, notice should be served when the debt actually becomes due (*Scottish and Newcastle Plc v Raguz* [2008] UKHL 650).

(b) **Restriction on liability where tenancy is subsequently varied** We saw earlier how, for a while, the common law permitted a former tenant to be liable to the original landlord under covenants that had been varied by agreement between the landlord and the subsequent lessee even where such variations in the agreement increased the original tenant's liability without his or her knowledge or consent. Section 18 was included in the 1995 Act to prevent this particular form of injustice. It provides that a former tenant will not be liable under a covenant to pay any amount in respect of the covenant to the extent that the amount is referable to any relevant variation of the tenant covenants in the tenancy effected after the assignment. The scope of s 18, however, is limited. It applies only to a variation of covenants that the landlord could have refused to allow (s 18(4)) for example where, by mutual agreement between the landlord and a subsequent assignee, the premises are improved and the rent correspondingly increased. It will not apply where a rent review clause was included in the original agreement but was exercised after the original tenant had assigned the tenancy. Thus, the effect of s 18 is similar to that under the common law as stated in *Friends' Provident Life Office v British Railways Board*.

(c) **Overriding leases** Once a tenancy has been assigned, the key problem that the original tenant encounters is the fact of his or her relative impotence with regard to control of subsequent assignees in comparison with his or her continuing liability to the original landlord. While the landlord can hold the original tenant responsible for a defaulting tenant, the original tenant has little recourse against that defaulting tenant other than under an indemnity covenant (which may well be of little use if that tenant is insolvent). The 1995 Act has provided an imaginative solution to this problem by providing a mechanism which enables a former tenant to put himself back into the picture by requiring the landlord to grant him or her an overriding lease. An overriding lease takes effect as a lease of the reversion which is granted for a term equal to the remainder of the term of the relevant tenancy plus three days (s 19(2)). It therefore restores a degree of power to the original tenant by making him or her the defaulting assignee's immediate landlord. The original tenant thereby acquires a landlord's remedies over the defaulting tenant, including the right to forfeit the lease, regain possession of the premises, and then sub-let or assign them to a new tenant and thereby recoup some or all of his or her losses. However, an original tenant will have the right to demand an overriding lease only where he or she has made full payment to the landlord for a fixed sum that has been demanded in accordance with s 17.

9.36   An original tenant who wishes to demand an overriding lease must do so in writing, either at the time of making the payment under s 17 or within 12 months of that payment being made (s 19(5)). The landlord is then under a duty to grant the original tenant the overriding lease within a reasonable time, but the original tenant will be liable for the landlord's reasonable costs in doing so (s 19(6)). An overriding lease should state that it is a lease granted under s 19, and also whether it is a lease to which the new or the old rules apply (s 20(2)). It will be a new tenancy only if the tenancy in respect of which it was granted was a new tenancy (s 20(1)).

9.37   **Under the new rules—statutory release of tenant**   If the tenancy is granted after 1 January 1996 the position is governed by statute and is very different from the situation under the common law. Section 5 of the 1995 Act gets rid of the principle of privity of contract. It provides that on assignment of the whole of the premises the tenant will automatically be released from the tenant covenants of the tenancy and will cease to be entitled to the benefit of the landlord covenants of the tenancy as from the assignment (s 5(2)). Under the 1995 Act a 'tenant covenant' means a covenant falling to be complied with by the tenant of the premises demised by the tenancy; a 'landlord covenant' correspondingly means a covenant falling to be complied with by the landlord of the premises demised by the tenancy (s 28(1)). A personal covenant by the landlord, which would not be binding on his or her successors, will not be a 'landlord covenant' (*BHP Petroleum Great Britain v Chesterfield Properties* [2001] EWCA Civ 1797, [2001] 1 All ER 821). Section 5 applies not only to the original tenant but also to any subsequent assignee of the tenancy if he or she makes a further assignment of the tenancy. The automatic release of the tenant (or subsequent assignee), however, will not affect any liability that arises from a breach of covenant occurring before the assignment (s 24(1)).

9.38   If the tenant assigns only part of the premises demised to him or her then the automatic release will apply only to the extent that the covenants in question fall to be complied with in relation to that part of the demised premises (s 5(3)). Clearly, where a tenant assigns only part of the premises there will be some covenants that can be attributed to that particular part of the premises and some that cannot, for example where the premises consist of a shop with a flat above it and the tenant assigns the shop but retains the flat as his or her own residential accommodation. In such a situation a covenant to use the shop only for a particular purpose applies only to the shop and the assignor will be released from the burden of that covenant. Other covenants, however, may not be so easy to attribute to a particular part of the premises, such as a covenant to pay rent or keep the structure in repair. In this case s 13 provides that both the assigning tenant and his or her assignee will be jointly and severally liable to the landlord. Under s 9 it is possible for the tenant and the assignee to agree to apportion liability between them. Where the tenant and assignee come to such an agreement they can apply, by following the procedure set out in s 10 and using Form 7 as prescribed by s 27 and the Landlord and Tenant (Covenants) Act 1995 (Notices) Regulations 1995 to make the proposed apportionment binding on the landlord.

It should be noted that the system of statutory release makes it unnecessary for a tenant to be deemed to covenant on behalf of himself or herself, his or her successors, and the persons deriving title under him or her, nor for an implied indemnity covenant to be inserted into the lease. Sections 79 and 77 of the LPA 1925 (see 9.29 to 9.32) do not, therefore, apply to new tenancies (s 30).   **9.39**

Guarantors   Section 24(2) extends the system of statutory release to any other person bound by a covenant of the tenancy imposing liability or a penalty in the event of a failure to comply with that tenant covenant. Thus, a guarantor of the tenant will be released to the same extent that the tenant is released. Any attempt by a landlord to require a tenant's guarantor to provide a guarantee for an assignee of that tenant as a condition of granting a licence to make that assignment will fall foul of the Act's anti-avoidance provisions contained in s 25 (see 9.52) and will be invalid. The only way in which liability can be continued beyond assignment is under an authorized guarantee agreement (see 9.41) and such an agreement is only intended to be made by the tenant (*Good Harvest Partnership LLP v Centaur Services Ltd* [2010] EWHC 330 (Ch)).   **9.40**

Authorized guarantee agreements   While the system of automatic release set out in s 5 benefits tenants, it is not, understandably, so popular with landlords. After all, where a tenant assigns the premises, the landlord will have no say in choosing the assignee. For this reason, the 1995 Act introduced a mechanism by which, despite the abrogation of the principle of privity of contract, the landlord can in certain circumstances require a tenant to remain contractually liable even after the lease has been assigned. The basis of this mechanism is the 'authorized guarantee agreement'.   **9.41**

Where, on an assignment, the assignor (be they the original tenant or a subsequent assignee) is released from his or her obligations by virtue of s 5, the landlord can require the assignor to guarantee the continuing performance of a particular covenant in the lease by the assignee by entering into an authorized guarantee agreement. However, the landlord may require such an agreement only in certain circumstances: **9.42**

(a) the agreement must be one under which the tenant guarantees the performance of the covenant by the assignee (s 16(2)(a));
(b) there must be a covenant against assignment in the lease which prevents the tenant from effecting the assignment in question without the consent of the landlord (s 16(3)(a));
(c) the landlord's consent to the assignment is subject to a condition (lawfully imposed) that requires the tenant to enter into an agreement guaranteeing the performance of the covenant by the assignee (s 16(3)(b)); and
(d) the agreement is entered into by the tenant under that condition (s 16(3)(c)).

Many landlords will include a provision in the tenancy agreement requiring the tenant to enter into an authorized guarantee agreement on assignment.   **9.43**

The scope of an authorized guarantee agreement is limited by statute. It must not impose on the tenant any requirement to guarantee in any way the performance of the relevant covenant by any person other than the assignee (s 16(4)(a)) and it must not impose on the tenant any liability, restriction, or other requirement (of whatever nature) in relation to any time after the assignee is released from that covenant by virtue of the 1995 Act. Thus,   **9.44** the original tenant will be required to guarantee only his or her immediate assignee. If that assignee then hands on his or her interest to a subsequent assignee the original tenant will not be responsible for the new assignee. These provisions make sense, because while the original tenant has some control over who is to take the first assignment he or she will have no control over assignees further down the line.

9.45 All the same, being the guarantor of the first assignee can impose considerable liabilities on the original tenant. By s 16(5)(a) an authorized guarantee agreement may impose on the tenant any liability as sole or principal debtor in respect of any obligation owed by the assignee under the relevant covenant. These liabilities, however, may not be more onerous than those to which he or she would be subject in the event of his or her being liable as sole or principal debtor (s 16(5)(b)). So, where a landlord, in agreement with the assignee, has increased the rent after the date of the assignment, the landlord cannot claim the additional amount from the original tenant under the authorized guarantee agreement.

9.46 In the event of the tenancy being disclaimed (eg where the assignee goes bankrupt), the authorized guarantee agreement may require the assigning tenant to enter into a new tenancy of the premises whose term expires no later than the term assigned by the tenant and whose covenants are no more onerous than those of that tenancy (s 16(5)(c)). Furthermore, while on disclaimer the bankrupt assignee's liability is extinguished, the liability of the guarantor is deemed to continue by virtue of s 178(4) of the Insolvency Act 1986 (*Shaw v Dolmen* [2009] EWCA Civ 279).

9.47 Where as the result of an excluded assignment (eg one made in breach of covenant, see 9.53) the tenancy becomes vested in an assignee who then seeks to make a further assignment, the original assignor may find that he or she will not be released from liability by virtue of s 11(2). If, on the second assignment, the landlord requires the second assignee to enter into an authorized guarantee agreement, he or she may also require the original assignor to enter into an authorized guarantee agreement (s 16(6)).

9.48 It should be noted, however, that where the worst comes to the worst and a tenant finds himself or herself having to pay damages to the landlord because of his or her immediate assignee's breach of covenant, or having to reimburse sums to the landlord because the assignee has not paid them, then provided the tenant has paid off the outstanding amounts in full he or she may demand an overriding lease from the landlord under s 19 (see 9.35, point (c)). Thus, the original tenant will become the defaulting assignee's landlord and will be able to take direct measures against that assignee either to recover the payment under s 17 or by forfeiting the defaulting assignee's lease (see 9.35, point (a)).

Example C—liability of Simon to Tom

9.49 **Under the old rules**   Where the landlord assigns his reversion to a third party, the original landlord will continue to remain liable to the tenant, either because there was an express term stating that the landlord would be liable for the acts or omissions of his successor in title, or because s 79 of the LPA 1925 will imply such a term. If Peter, as Tom's new landlord, breaches a covenant, Tom will be able to sue Simon for the breach.

9.50 **Under the new rules—statutory release of landlord**   If the landlord assigns the reversion of a tenancy that was granted after 1 January 1996, he or she may also be released from his or her obligations under the tenancy agreement by virtue of s 6 of the 1995 Act. However, unlike the tenant's release, this will not happen automatically on assignment. The reason for this difference is the fact that while landlords have some control over their tenant's ability to assign, a tenant has no similar control over the landlord.

Section 6 provides that where the landlord assigns the reversion in the whole of the premises **9.51**
of which he is the landlord, he may apply to be released from the landlord covenants of the
tenancy in accordance with the procedure set out in s 8 (s 6(2)(a)). If he is released from
the landlord covenants he ceases to be entitled to the benefit of the tenant covenants of
the tenancy as from the assignment (s 6(2)(b)). If the landlord assigns the reversion in part
only of the premises he may also apply to be released, but only with respect to the landlord
covenants of the tenancy to the extent that they fall to be complied with in relation to that
part of those premises (s 6(3)(a)); and if he is released from those covenants he will cease to
be entitled to the benefit of the tenant covenants to the extent that they fall to be complied
with in relation to that part of those premises (s 6(3)(b)). Section 7 similarly provides that
where a former landlord either failed to apply for release on an earlier assignment of the
reversion (or applied but failed to obtain a release) he or she may apply under s 8 if the
current landlord makes a further assignment.

Section 8 requires that a landlord who wishes to be released must serve notice on the ten- **9.52**
ant either before or within the period of four weeks beginning with the date of the assignment. This notice must be on Form 3 as prescribed by s 27 and the Landlord and Tenant
(Covenants) Act 1995 (Notices) Regulations 1995. It must inform the tenant of the proposed assignment (or the fact that an assignment has taken place) and request for the covenant to be released. If the tenant makes no objection the covenant is released to the extent
mentioned in the notice (s 8(2)(a)). If the tenant does wish to object he or she must serve
notice within four weeks and the landlord may apply to the county court for a declaration
that it is reasonable for the landlord to be so released (s 8(2)(b)). Section 25 of the 1995 Act
contains anti-avoidance provisions under which any clause in an agreement will be void
to the extent that it would 'have the effect to exclude, modify or otherwise frustrate the
operation of the Act'. However, this has been held not to apply to a clause in the lease that
provided that 'the landlord covenants with the tenant as follows (but not in the case of the
[former landlord] only, so as to be liable after the landlord has disposed of its interest in
the property)' (*Avonridge Property Company Ltd v Mashru* [2006] 01 EG 100, HL). The
effect of this clause is to allow the former landlord an instant release without the need for
notice under s 8. Such a clause had previously been held to be void under s 25. It is anticipated that landlords will now incorporate a clause of this type into tenancy agreements
as a matter of course, thus significantly reducing the importance of the statutory release
requirements.

Excluded assignments   The release of landlord and tenant covenants will not apply in the **9.53**
case of an excluded assignment. There are two types of excluded assignments:

(a) assignments in breach of a covenant in a tenancy (ie where the tenancy agreement
     contains a covenant forbidding assignment);
(b) assignments by operation of law (eg where on the death of a tenant the tenancy
     becomes vested in the deceased's personal representatives, or where the tenant goes
     bankrupt and the tenancy becomes vested in the trustee in bankruptcy) (s 11(1)).

Where a tenant remains bound because the assignment made was an excluded assignment, **9.54**
he or she will nevertheless be released if and when a further assignment of the tenancy
is made, provided, of course, that that further assignment is not an excluded assignment
(s 11(2)(b)). Similarly, a landlord who has not been released on the assignment of his or her
reversion (either because the assignment was an excluded assignment, or because the tenant successfully opposed the landlord's application for release) may apply again for release
on any future assignment of the reversion (s 11(3)(b)).

Liability between persons not party to the original agreement

9.55 We have already seen that when a tenant assigns his or her tenancy, that tenant will either remain liable under the original contract (in the case of an old tenancy) or will be automatically released from the obligations in the original contract (in the case of a new tenancy). Now we need to consider the position of a person who was not party to the original agreement but who later acquires an interest in the land.

9.56 Consider the example set out in Figure 9.2. Here Tom, the original tenant, has assigned his tenancy to John. It comes to Simon's attention that John is running a small mail order company from the flat; furthermore that he has failed to redecorate the interior. John on the other hand is concerned about patches of damp that appear to be caused by a leaking downpipe. John would also like to buy a long lease on the flat if he can.

9.57 John wants to know whether the terms of the original agreement 'run with the land' or whether they bind only Tom. He needs to know the answer to two questions:

(a) Has he acquired the burden of the covenants entered into between Tom and Simon, ie does Simon have the right to enforce the covenants against John? Can Simon prevent him from running a business and make him redecorate the interior?

(b) Has he acquired the benefit of the covenants entered into between Tom and Simon, ie can John enforce the covenants against Simon? Can he make Simon repair the leaking downpipe and can he exercise the option to purchase?

9.58 How the answer to these questions is determined will depend upon the date of the grant of the original tenancy. If John holds a new tenancy the 1995 Act will apply; if he holds an old tenancy the position will be governed by the old common law rules.

Under the old rules

9.59 In the case of the assignment of a tenancy the situation is governed by the rule in *Spencer's Case* [1583] 5 Co Rep 16a. The rule states that the assignee of a tenancy will acquire both the burden and the benefit of the covenants in a lease provided that:

(a) there is *privity of estate* between the person seeking to enforce the covenant and the person against whom he is seeking to enforce it;

(b) the covenant in question *touches and concerns the land*.

9.60 Both of these concepts need to be considered.

9.61 **Privity of estate**   Privity of estate arises when two parties are in a relationship of landlord and tenant (a relationship of tenure). There will be privity of estate between the parties regardless of whether or not the parties have contracted with each other. If we consider the original position, when Simon granted a tenancy to Tom, we can say that there is both privity of contract and privity of estate between Simon and Tom: privity of contract because they were both parties to the tenancy agreement; privity of estate because they were in a relationship of landlord and tenant. However, once Tom has assigned his tenancy to John the situation is somewhat different: there continues to be privity of contract between Simon and Tom (the assignment does not affect the fact that they were both parties to the agreement), but they are no longer in a relationship of landlord and tenant; thus there is no privity of estate between them. However, John is in a relationship of landlord and tenant with Simon. There is privity of estate (but not privity of contract) between Simon and John.

This situation can be rendered diagrammatically as follows: **9.62**

Figure 9.4 Liability following assignment

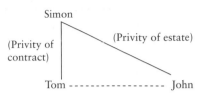

Covenants that touch and concern the land   A covenant will 'touch and concern the land'   **9.63**
if it affects landlord *qua* landlord and the tenant *qua* tenant (*Breams Property Investment
Co. Ltd v Stroulger* [1948] 2 KB 1), ie it must be a covenant which affects the parties to the
tenancy agreement in their capacities as landlord and as tenant.

Virtually all the common covenants we considered in previous chapters touch and concern   **9.64**
the land. Thus, covenants concerning rent, insurance, user, repair, and quiet enjoyment will
all run with the land. However, as we saw in Chapter 4, the variety of different covenants
is virtually unlimited. The following covenants have also been held to touch and concern
the land:

(a) A covenant requiring the tenant to sell only the landlord's brand of product on the
     premises (*Clegg v Hands* (1890) 44 ChD 503; *Regent Oil Co. Ltd v JA Gregory (Hatch
     End) Ltd* [1966] Ch 402).
(b) A covenant requiring the tenant not to permit a particular person to be involved with
     the running of the business on the premises (*Lewin v American & Colonial Distributors
     Ltd* [1945] Ch 255, [1945] 1 All ER 529).

A covenant will not touch and concern the land if it does not affect the parties in their   **9.65**
capacity as landlord and tenant, or if it does not have direct reference to the land. Thus,
a covenant giving the tenant an option to buy the premises does not touch and concern
the land because it affects the parties as vendor and purchaser, not as landlord and tenant
(*Woodall v Clifton* [1905] 2 Ch 257) (but an option to purchase is an equitable interest in
land and therefore may be able to run, see 9.67).

Further covenants which have been held *not* to touch and concern the land are: **9.66**

(a) A covenant entitling the tenant to put up advertising on land other than the demised
     premises (*Re No. 1 Albermarle Street* [1959] Ch 531).
(b) A covenant requiring the tenant to pay rates on a property other than the demised
     premises (*Gower v Postmaster General* (1887) 57 LT 527).
(c) A covenant requiring the tenant to pay a premium for the grant of a lease (*Hill v Booth*
     [1930] 1 KB 381, [1929] All ER 84, CA).
(d) A covenant requiring a tenant to repair premises other than the demised premises
     (*Dewar v Goodman* [1909] AC 72).
(e) A covenant requiring the landlord to repay a deposit at the end of the term (*Hua
     Chiad Commercial Bank Ltd v Chiaphua Industries Ltd* [1987] AC 99, [1987] 1 All
     ER 1110).

9.67 If we apply the rule in *Spencer's Case* to John, we find that he will have acquired the burden of the covenant to redecorate and of the covenant to use the flat only as a private residence. John is therefore currently in breach of covenant. He will also acquire the benefit of Simon's covenant to repair the structure and exterior of the flat and is entitled to enforce this right against Simon. The option to purchase, however, will not automatically run with the land. It is a personal right binding only between Tom and Simon. (However, an option to purchase may be made to bind a subsequent purchaser of the landlord's interest if it is registered, see 9.80 and 9.81.)

Liability after assignment of the tenancy under the new rules

9.68 For new tenancies the situation is governed by statute. Section 3 of the 1995 Act provides:

> (1) The benefit and burden of all landlord and tenant covenants of a tenancy—
>   (a) shall be annexed and incident to the whole, and to each and every part, of the premises demised by the tenancy and of the reversion in them, and
>   (b) shall in accordance with this section pass on assignment of the whole or any part of those premises or the reversion in them.

9.69 Thus, s 3 fixes the benefit and burden of all covenants to the land. There is no need to consider whether the covenant in question touches and concerns the land; in fact, s 2(1)(a) provides specifically that the 1995 Act applies to a landlord or tenant covenant whether or not the covenant has reference to the subject matter of the tenancy. However, by virtue of s 3(6)(a), covenants which are expressed to be personal are excluded from the operation of s 3. This is distinctly different from the position for old tenancies. Under the old law a personal covenant would not run on assignment because it did not touch and concern the land. What is important under the 1995 Act is not the nature of the covenant but the fact that is it expressed to be personal. Therefore, if a landlord wishes to enter into a covenant with a tenant which he or she wishes to be purely personal and not binding on subsequent assignees of the tenancy, that landlord should make sure that that covenant is expressed to be personal in the tenancy agreement, although the personal nature of the covenant may be implied from the language of the tenancy agreement (*First Penthouse Ltd v Channel Hotels & Properties (UK) Ltd* [2003] EWHC 2713 (Ch), [2004] 1 EGLR 16).

9.70 Section 3(2) goes on to provide that where a tenant assigns his or her tenancy the assignee will become bound by the tenant covenants in the tenancy and entitled to the benefit of the landlord covenants in the tenancy. However, the provisions do contain a number of exceptions. First, the assignee will not be bound by tenant covenants which, immediately before the assignment, did not bind the assignor (s 3(2)(a)(i)). Thus, if a landlord includes a tenant covenant in the original agreement but subsequently releases the tenant from the obligation (or waives his or her right to rely upon the covenant) this covenant will not run to bind a subsequent assignee, unless the release or waiver was expressed to be personal to the assignor (s 3(4)). Secondly, an assignee will not become bound by the tenant covenants or acquire the benefit of the landlord covenants where they fall to be complied with in relation to any demised premises not comprised in the assignment (s 3(2)(a)(ii) and (b)). This provision provides for the situation where part only of the premises is assigned. For example, where Andrew has a tenancy of premises that contain a shop on the ground floor and a flat on the first floor and he decides to assign the flat to David, David will not be bound by covenants in the original tenancy that relate only to the shop.

9.71 Thus, in our example all the covenants in the original tenancy will run on assignment to John, with the possible exception of the option to purchase. An option to purchase will not run if it is expressed to be personal between the original tenant and the original landlord.

Liability of the assignor to the assignee

Where an assignment was made before 1 July 1994, the LPA1925, s 76 implies a number **9.72** of covenants into the transaction on the part of the assignor for the benefit of the assignee. These are: a covenant for title; a covenant for quiet enjoyment; a covenant for further assurance; and a covenant that the lease is not liable to forfeiture and that the tenant's covenants have been performed by the assignor.

Where the assignment was made after 1 July 1994, Pt 1 of the Law of Property (Miscellaneous **9.73** Provisions) Act 1994 will apply to the transaction. Again these provisions imply covenants on the part of the assignor that he or she has good title, and, in the case of leasehold land, that the lease is subsisting at the date of the disposition, that there is no breach of the tenant's obligation, and that the lease is not liable to forfeiture.

Liability of the assignee to the assignor

Assignments made prior to the coming into force of the Landlord and Tenant (Covenants) **9.74** Act 1995 will contain an implied covenant on the part of the assignee that he or she would, at all times from the date of the assignment, pay the rent and perform the tenant's covenants, and indemnify the assignor against failure to do so (LPA 1925, s 77 and Sch 2, Pt IX). Where the assigned tenancy was granted after 1 January 1996 the exclusion of continuing liability afforded to the tenant by the 1995 Act means that this implied covenant is no longer necessary.

Liability after sale of the landlord's interest

If an assignee of the original tenant acquires the benefit of a covenant, it will be of little **9.75** use unless the landlord has to take the burden; a covenant can be enforced only if there is someone to enforce it against. Simon, as a party to the original tenancy agreement, is clearly bound by the terms of that agreement; but what if Simon assigns his reversion: do the burden and benefit pass in the same way as they do on an assignment of a tenancy?

If Simon sells his interest the situation may be rendered diagrammatically as follows: **9.76**

Figure 9.5 Relationship of the parties following assignment of the reversion

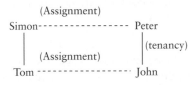

Peter will want answers to the following questions: **9.77**

(a) Has he acquired the benefit of the covenants entered into between Tom and Simon, ie can he enforce the covenants against John? Can he prevent him from running a business and make him redecorate the interior?

(b) Has he acquired the burden of the covenants entered into between Tom and Simon, ie can John enforce the covenants against him? Can John make Peter repair the leaking down-pipe and can John exercise the option to purchase?

9.78 **Under the old rules**   In the case of tenancies entered into before 1 January 1996, the question as to whether the benefit and the burden of the covenants in the original lease will run to bind an assignee of the reversion is determined by statute. Section 141 of the LPA 1925 states that the rent reserved by a lease and the benefit of all the covenants in a lease 'which refer to the subject matter of the lease' will run to benefit the assignee of the reversion. Section 142 likewise states that an obligation (ie the burden) under a condition or a covenant in a lease will run to bind an assignee provided, again, that it 'has reference to the subject matter of the lease'.

9.79 The requirement that covenants must have reference to the subject matter of the lease seems to be identical to the requirement in *Spencer's Case* that covenants must touch and concern the land. One difference, however, between the common law rule that applies to assignees of the tenancy and the statutory rules that apply to assignees of the reversion is that the statutory rules do not demand that there be privity of estate between the parties (*Arlesford Trading Co. Ltd v Servansingh* [1971] 1 WLR 1080). Section 141(2) also provides that rent may be recovered and the covenants enforced by 'the person from time to time entitled, subject to the term, to the income of the whole or any part, as the case may require, of the land leased'. This means that the assignee of the reversion may be entitled to sue the tenant for arrears that were incurred before the assignment took place. The tenant, however, is not entitled to sue the assignee of the reversion for breaches committed by the former landlord prior to the assignment (LPA 1925, s 142(2)). If, however, the assignee of the reversion sues the tenant for rent due to the original landlord, the tenant is entitled to set off against that sum any damages claimed by the tenant for breach of covenant by the original landlord (*Duncliffe v Caerfelin Properties* [1989] 2 EGLR 38).

9.80 Peter will therefore acquire the benefit of the covenant by the tenant to redecorate the interior of the premises and the covenant against business use (and any other covenants in the original lease which have reference to the subject matter of the lease, such as the covenant to pay rent). He will also acquire the burden of the landlord's covenant to repair the structure and exterior of the premises. However, he will not be bound by the option to purchase that was entered into between Simon and Tom. Such an option, as we saw previously, will not run to benefit an assignee of the tenancy. Nevertheless, in certain circumstances, the holder of an option to purchase may be able to enforce it against an assignee of the reversion. If Tom had not assigned his lease but remained the tenant of the property after Simon had assigned his reversion to Peter, he might be able to exercise his option against Peter. This, however, will be the case only if Tom has protected his option against a subsequent purchaser by registering it under the Land Registration Act 1925 or as a class C(iv) land charge under the Land Charges Act 1972.

9.81 **Liability after sale of the reversion under the new rules**   For new tenancies the rules which govern the transmission of the benefit and burden of the covenants contained in the original lease after the assignment of the reversion are virtually identical to those which govern transmission when there is an assignment of the tenancy. An assignee of the landlord's reversion will be bound by the landlord covenants in the tenancy and becomes entitled to the benefit of the tenant covenants (s 3(3)). There are similar exceptions in the case of covenants which did not bind the assignor immediately before the assignment (s 3(3)(a)(i)) and covenants which fall to be complied with in relation to any premises not comprised in the assignment (s 3(3)(a)(ii)). Section 4 also specifically provides that the benefit of the landlord's right of re-entry under a tenancy will pass on assignment of the whole or any part of the reversion. Such a right of re-entry may be used by the new landlord in relation to any breach of a covenant occurring before the assignment (s 23(3)). Section 3(6)(b) of the 1995 Act also specifically provides that nothing in s 3 will operate to make a covenant enforceable against any person if it would not have been enforceable by reason of its not having been registered under the Land Registration Act 1925 or the Land Charges Act 1972. Thus, if Tom has failed to register his option to purchase it will not be enforceable against Peter. These provisions supersede the old statutory rules and ss 141 and 142 of the LPA 1925 do not apply to new tenancies (s 30(4)(b)).

Liability of sub-lessees

Under the old rules

Consider our original example of a sub-lease (see 9.09). Here there is both privity of estate **9.82** and privity of contract between Simon and Bruce; they are in a contractual relationship and they are in a relationship of landlord and tenant. Likewise between Bruce and Andrew there is privity of estate and privity of contract. However, there is no privity of estate between Simon and Andrew (they are not in relationship of landlord and tenant), neither is there privity of contract (there is no contract between them). In fact there is no direct relationship between Simon and Andrew at all.

In general then, if Andrew breaches any terms of the original contract between Simon and **9.83** Bruce, Simon's course of action will be against Bruce. The covenants in the head tenancy will not run to bind a sub-lessee. There is, however, one important exception to this rule. A head landlord may be able to enforce a covenant contained in the head tenancy directly against a sub-lessee under the rule in *Tulk v Moxhay* [1848] 2 Ph 774 (a doctrine more commonly encountered in the context of freehold covenants).

The rule in *Tulk v Moxhay* permits the head landlord to enforce a restrictive covenant **9.84** against any occupier who takes possession of the premises with notice of the covenant. A restrictive covenant can be registered as a minor interest in registered land or as a class D(ii) land charge in unregistered land. If the restricted covenant is registered the occupier will be deemed to have notice of that covenant even if he or she has no actual knowledge of its existence. Thus, provided Andrew had actual notice of the covenant or the covenant was registered, Simon will be able to enforce the covenant against business use directly against Andrew. (The fact that the covenant is phrased as a covenant to use the premises only as a private dwelling-house is irrelevant; the substance of the covenant is restrictive. A covenant not to assign or sub-let has also been held to be a restrictive covenant (*Hemmingway Securities Ltd v Dunraven Ltd* [1995] 1 EGLR 61).) On the other hand, the rule in *Tulk v Moxhay* will not apply to the covenant to redecorate the interior every three years.

Under the new rules

The provisions of the 1995 Act that we have already considered apply only to the transmis- **9.85** sion of the burden and benefit of covenants on assignment: they do not function to make covenants enforceable between a head landlord and a sub-tenant. However, special rules apply in the case of restrictive covenants. Section 3(5) of the 1995 Act provides:

> Any landlord or tenant covenant of a tenancy which is restrictive of the user of land shall, as well as being capable of enforcement against an assignee, be capable of being enforced against any other person who is the owner or occupier of any demised premises to which the covenant relates, even though there is no express provision in the tenancy to that effect.

Thus, as under the old rules, a head landlord will be able to enforce a restrictive covenant **9.86** directly against a sub-lessee.

Where the sub-tenant is at fault and the landlord's remedy lies only against his immediate **9.87** tenant, the practical solution is for the landlord to sue the tenant, and for the tenant to join the sub-tenant in the action under the provisions of CPR Part 20.

Equitable leases

9.88 The question now arises as to what the situation would be in the example at 9.06 if Tom held on an equitable lease (because the formalities were not observed and the invalid lease is construed as an agreement for a lease) or under an agreement for a lease (Simon never having made the actual grant). Under the doctrine of *Walsh v Lonsdale* we have seen that an agreement for a lease will give the tenant very similar rights to those he or she would have had if he or she had been granted a lease (see 3.58). What will happen if a tenant seeks to assign such a lease?

9.89 For new tenancies the position is relatively clear. The 1995 Act defines a tenancy as including an agreement for a tenancy (s 28(1)). An assignee of an agreement for a lease will therefore take both the burden and the benefit of the covenants contained in the agreement. For old tenancies, however, the position is a little more complicated, though it seems that the outcome will be broadly the same. On assignment of the reversion, ss 141 and 142 of the LPA 1925 will apply to an agreement for a lease as they would to a lease by deed. This will be because s 154 of the LPA defines a 'lease' as including 'an under lease or other tenancy'. Where the tenant seeks to assign an agreement for a lease the key question is whether the rule in *Spencer's Case* (see 9.59) will apply. It was held in *Boyer v Warbey* [1953] 1 QB 234 that the rule could apply to a written lease of less than three years that created a legal estate by virtue of LPA 1925, s 54(2) (see 3.21). Furthermore, given the provisions of LPA 1925, s 54(2) and the wording of s 154, it seems likely that both ss 141 and 142 and the rule in *Spencer's Case* will also apply to oral leases created for a term of less than three years.

E REMEDIES

9.90 Remedies for breaches of covenants in leases are considered in Chapters 6 and 7. The same remedies will apply in actions to enforce continuing obligations against the appropriate party following assignment or sub-letting.

KEY DOCUMENTS

Law of Property Act 1925

Law of Property Act (Miscellaneous Provisions) Act 1994

Landlord and Tenant (Covenants) Act 1995

Landlord and Tenants (Covenants) Act 1995 (Notices) Regulations 1995, SI 1995/2965

Civil Procedure Rules 1998

Form N1—Part 7 Claim

Forms N9B and N9D Defence and counterclaim

Form N208—Part 8 Claim

Form N208A—Part 8 Claim (notes for claimant)

Form N208B—Part 8 Claim (notes for defendant)

Form N211—Part 20 Claim

Form N211A—Part 20 Claim (notes for claimant)

Form N211C—Part 20 Claim (notes for defendant)

Printed copies of all legislation can be ordered from The Stationery Office at <http://www.tsoshop. co.uk>. All legislation from 1988 onwards and most pre-1988 primary legislation is available online at <http://www. legislation.gov.uk>.

The Civil Procedure Rules are available online from <http://www.justice.gov.uk/courts/ procedure-rules>.

Court forms are available online from the HM Courts and Tribunals Service at <http://www.justice. gov.uk/forms/hmcts>.

10

TERMINATION OF TENANCIES:
AN OVERVIEW—THE COMMON LAW RULES

A INTRODUCTION

No lease can last forever. A term of years absolute is distinguished from the fee simple in **10.01** that it lasts for a definable period. It may last for a couple of days, it may last for 999 years; but at some point it will come to an end. It can come to an end voluntarily with the agreement of both parties (surrender, merger), unilaterally, where only one party wishes to end the relationship (notice to quit, forfeiture), or where it simply comes to an end of its own nature (effluxion of time).

The rules regarding the termination of tenancies may seem complex at first. This, as with so **10.02** much of the law of landlord and tenant, is because such reform as has taken place has been piecemeal. Common law rules co-exist with a variety of statutory provisions and both must be taken into account by the housing adviser. (These statutory provisions are considered in Part II of this book.) The whole area is in need of a comprehensive overhaul.

Nevertheless, it is possible to grasp the logic of the current system provided one bears **10.03** continually in mind that a tenancy is not simply one thing but a multifaceted relationship displaying a variety of different aspects. A tenancy is all of the following:

(a) It is a contractual relationship. In terminating a tenancy the requirements of the contract must be followed.
(b) It is an interest in land. As an interest in land a tenancy has qualities beyond the strictly contractual; any action taken to terminate a tenancy may affect third parties. The law therefore demands that strict formalities must be observed.
(c) It is a creature of statute. The termination of a tenancy will, in the majority of cases, trigger statutory provisions which will limit the ways in which the parties may act. Any relevant statutory provisions must therefore be taken into account.

10.04 To end the relationship of landlord and tenant effectively and finally, both parties will have to deal successfully with all three aspects of the tenancy in question.

10.05 **Example** In 1987, Harry granted Jane a monthly tenancy of Flat C, 7 Mount View Road. The tenancy attracts Rent Act protection. Harry has now decided to sell the flat. The flat will command a far higher price if he can sell it with vacant possession, so he decides to evict Jane. Harry therefore sets about terminating Jane's contractual periodic tenancy at common law. He follows all the correct procedures, satisfying both the provisions set out in the contract and the common law, and her contractual tenancy is successfully terminated on 1 February 1994. Harry has not yet achieved his goal of vacant possession though. The contractual tenancy is at an end but his relationship with Jane is as yet far from over. The termination of the contractual tenancy has triggered a statutory tenancy under the Rent Act, and Jane stays in occupation and continues to pay rent. (For a detailed discussion of the functioning of the Rent Act 1977, see Chapters 13 and 14.) In practical terms little has changed; to a large extent the same rights and obligations exist between Harry and Jane as did before the termination of the contractual tenancy. To finally end his relationship with Jane, Harry will have to satisfy one of the grounds of possession set out in the Rent Act 1977 and obtain a court order for possession. For the sake of argument we will assume that Harry is successful in his claim—the court makes a possession order and Harry re-enters the property. Only now is Jane's right to exclusive possession of the flat extinguished; no rights or obligations are outstanding on either side and the relationship between Harry and Jane is finally at an end. Harry will now be able to sell the flat with vacant possession.

10.06 From this example it can be seen that the termination of Jane's tenancy is in effect a two-stage process. Harry must end first the contractual tenancy and secondly the statutory tenancy before he can go on to regain possession. The exact procedure to be followed will of course depend upon the type of tenancy involved and the statutory protection, if any, that it attracts. It is vital to realize that the landlord cannot skip the first stage in the process: the statutory provisions do not replace but are superimposed upon the common law. If Harry attempted to seek possession of the flat without first terminating the contractual tenancy at common law then Jane would have a complete defence regardless of the fact that Harry may well be able to satisfy one or more of the statutory grounds. (The only major exception to this is the termination of a periodic assured tenancy under the Housing Act 1988, see 15.89 to 15.94.)

10.07 In this chapter we shall deal with the first stage in this process—the termination of contractual tenancies at common law. The various statutory codes will be considered in later chapters.

B FIXED-TERM TENANCIES

10.08 At common law a fixed-term tenancy terminates automatically when the term comes to an end. There is no need for either landlord or tenant to do anything in order to end the tenancy. It ends because its length was defined when it was created, it was contractually agreed that the tenancy should be for a certain period, and once this period has run the contractual tenancy comes to an end by what is normally called *effluxion* of time.

10.09 The fact that a fixed-term tenancy has run its course does not invariably mean that the contractual relationship between the landlord and the tenant is over. In entering into the tenancy agreement the parties are free to include terms which may extend the relationship beyond the expiry of the fixed term. Likewise the fact that a fixed term is granted does not

mean that the tenancy must last for the full term, for the parties may include provisions in
the agreement enabling the tenancy to be terminated early.

Contractual provision that tenancy may continue beyond expiry of fixed term

Sometimes the terms of the contract may provide that the tenancy should not simply   **10.10**
end once the term has expired. For example, the agreement may state that the tenancy is
granted 'for a term of five years and thereafter from month to month'. Once the fixed five-
year period has expired, this tenancy will continue as a monthly periodic tenancy and will
have to be terminated by notice (see 10.35).

Contractual provision that tenancy may be renewed at the end of the term

The terms of the contract may also provide that the tenant will have a right to renew his or   **10.11**
her fixed term when the original tenancy expires. Such a provision normally takes the form
of an option to renew (see 6.116). An option to renew will usually set out a procedure to
be followed by the tenant if he or she wants to renew the term. To exercise the option the
tenant will have to comply with these terms. Usually the tenant will have to serve notice on
the landlord stating that he or she wants to renew the tenancy and this notice will probably
have to be served at a prescribed time (eg six months before the expiry of the original term).
Furthermore, the right to renew is often made conditional on the tenant's performance of
the obligations under the lease, so if the tenant is in breach of covenant he or she may well
be unable to renew the tenancy. Options to renew apply only to tenants—after all, a landlord who wishes to offer a tenant a second term can do so if he or she wishes.

Contractual provision that tenancy may be terminated before the expiry of the fixed term

A fixed-term tenancy may also provide that the tenancy can be terminated before the term   **10.12**
has run its full course. Such a contractual term is known as a *break clause* or an option to
determine (see 6.122). Usually break clauses can be exercised only at specified periods in
the term (eg in a 21-year lease the agreement may give both parties the right to terminate
the lease at the end of every seventh year), or on the occurrence of a specified event (eg if the
landlord requires the land for redevelopment). In either case the party seeking to exercise
the break clause will have to comply strictly with the procedure set out in the contract.

Option to purchase

A fixed-term tenancy may also be terminated prematurely by means of an *option to pur-*   **10.13**
chase (see 6.128). As we saw, an option to purchase is regarded as collateral to the lease
and therefore as independent of the landlord and tenant relationship. Nevertheless, if it is
validly exercised in accordance with the contract it will terminate the tenancy. The tenant,
by purchasing the landlord's interest, will bring the relationship of landlord and tenant to
an end (see 10.28).

A condition

In drawing up the tenancy the parties may agree to make the continuation of the ten-   **10.14**
ancy conditional upon the tenant performing (or not performing) some act (see 4.14). For
example, the tenancy may be made conditional on the tenant remaining in occupation or
conditional on the tenant not becoming bankrupt (see *Halliard Property Co. Ltd v Jack*

Segal Ltd [1978] 1 WLR 377, [1978] 1 All ER 1219). With service tenancies it is common to make the tenancy conditional upon the tenant remaining in the landlord's employment. If the tenant breaches a condition, the tenancy will terminate automatically at common law. It is also possible for a condition to be implied into a tenancy that it will terminate if certain expectations cannot be met. Thus, where a tenancy was granted on the belief (held by both parties) that the rent would be paid by housing benefit, a term was implied into the tenancy that it would terminate if the tenant was actually unable to claim housing benefit (*Graves v Graves* [2007] EWCA Civ 660).

Repudiation

10.15   A tenancy agreement is first and foremost a contract. Where a party can establish that the other party has persistently refused to comply with an obligation under the lease, it may be possible for that party to repudiate the tenancy under common law contractual principles (*Hussein v Mehlman* [1992] 2 EGLR 87). The breach would have to be serious in order to justify repudiation, and it must be clear that the defaulting party has given notice that he or she does not intend to comply with the obligations. For example, under the terms of Jane's tenancy Harry is obliged to keep Flat C in repair. In fact the flat has fallen into a considerable state of disrepair, and for that reason Jane does not want to live there anymore. Jane asks Harry to carry out essential repairs and he flatly tells her that he has no intention of spending any money on the property. Jane could then treat the contract, and therefore the tenancy agreement, as being at an end and leave the flat.

Frustration

10.16   It has been held that the contractual doctrine of frustration can apply, in principle at least, to leases (see *National Carriers v Panalpina (Northern) Ltd* [1981] AC 675, [1981] 1 All ER 161, HL). Frustration occurs where the circumstances surrounding the contract change so radically that the whole basis of the contract is removed. In the context of leases the frustrating event must therefore be so severe that it goes to the foundation of the lease. If a lease is frustrated the parties will be released from their obligations under the lease. Where the introduction of wartime regulations prohibited building on land let under a building lease this was held not to amount to frustration because the regulations were temporary (*Cricklewood Property and Investment Trust Ltd v Leighton's Investment Trust Ltd* [1945] AC 221, [1945] 1 All ER 525, HL). Similarly, where a tenant rented a warehouse and the access road was closed by the local authority because a nearby building was derelict and dangerous, this was not frustration because the interruption lasted for only 20 months, while the lease itself was for 10 years (*National Carriers v Panalpina*).

Surrender

10.17   A periodic tenant who wishes to terminate his or her tenancy can do so by serving a notice to quit on the landlord (see 10.35). In comparison, a fixed-term tenancy is a relatively inflexible instrument. If there is no break clause or other provision in the lease providing for early termination, the tenancy will come to an end only when it has run its course and expires by effluxion of time.

10.18   **Example** James was granted a five-year fixed-term tenancy by Peter two years ago. James is now in some financial difficulty and is finding it hard to honour his obligations under the lease. Ideally he would like to move to a cheaper property, but the tenancy makes no provision for early termination. Peter is now threatening forfeiture proceedings. James does not want to contest forfeiture proceedings. His best option, he feels, is to enter into negotiations with Peter to see if he can surrender the lease.

Surrender, as its name implies, means giving back to the landlord the remainder of the tenant's interest. The tenant who surrenders a lease gives up his or her estate in land. Where there were formerly two estates in land there will be, from the date of surrender, only one: the tenant's interest is absorbed back into the landlord's larger interest. Once surrender has taken place all obligations and rights under the lease end (although it is possible that the tenant may remain liable for breaches of agreement that occurred before the date of surrender). **10.19**

The crucial feature of surrender is that it can occur only by mutual agreement. It has little in common with a notice to quit which operates unilaterally to terminate the tenancy. If there is no agreement (although this agreement can be implied) between landlord and tenant there can be no surrender. If only one of a number of joint tenants offers to surrender the lease the surrender will not be effective. **10.20**

Express surrender

If James's negotiations with Peter are successful and Peter agrees to let James surrender his tenancy, the required formalities will have to be complied with. In effect a surrender is a disposition of an estate in land. The express surrender of a lease for a term exceeding three years must therefore be made by deed (LPA 1925, s 52, see 3.16). A lease for less than three years which is at the best rent available without taking a fine can be surrendered in writing signed by the surrenderer (LPA 1925, ss 53(1), 54(2)). **10.21**

Surrender by operation of law

In some cases the law will imply a surrender. The key factor is that the parties must behave in an unequivocal way which is inconsistent with the continuation of the existing tenancy. The basis of surrender by operation of law is the doctrine of estoppel. If the tenant seeks to surrender the tenancy but fails to comply with the required formalities and there is some change in circumstances resulting from the purported surrender, the landlord will be estopped from claiming that the tenancy is still in existence (see *Foster v Robinson* [1950] 2 All ER 342 *per* Sir Raymond Evershed MR at 346). **10.22**

If James's negotiations with Peter fail and they are unable to agree to an express surrender, James might decide that the best thing he can do is simply to stop paying rent and move out of the property. If James leaves the property and Peter re-enters the property and rents it to Simon, the law will imply a surrender. By granting a tenancy to Simon, Peter is acting in a way inconsistent with the continuation of James's tenancy. The same would be the case if Peter moves into the property himself. In either case it would be inequitable for Peter to claim that the tenancy was continuing after he had taken such action. The law will regard the original tenancy as having been surrendered by operation of law (*Wallis v Hands* [1893] 2 Ch 75, [1893] All ER Rep 719; *Artworld Financial Corporation v Safaryan* [2009] EWCA Civ 303; *QFS Scaffolding Ltd v Sable* [2010] EWCA Civ 682). Likewise, if Peter agreed to grant James a new tenancy of the same premises for a shorter term, the creation of the new tenancy will lead to the implication that the old tenancy has been surrendered (*Lyon v Reed* [1844] 13 M&W 285, [1843–60] All ER Rep 178; *Phene v Popplewell* [1862] 12 CB NS 334). The new lease must be more than simply a variation of the terms of the old lease (*Smirk v Lyndale Developments* [1975] 1 All ER 690). If the new lease was for some reason invalid, there will be no surrender of the old lease unless the surrender was made by deed (*Rhyl UDC v Rhyl Amusements Ltd* [1959] 1 WLR 465, [1959] 1 All ER 257). **10.23**

10.24   James, however, should be wary of simply walking out on the tenancy. The fact that the tenant leaves the premises will not constitute an implied surrender if the landlord performs no action indicating that he too regards the tenancy as being at an end (*Preston BC v Fairclough* (1982) 8 HLR 70). If there is no implied surrender, Peter may still be entitled to sue James for rent arrears. However, if the tenant has been absent for a long time and there are substantial rent arrears, surrender may be implied (*Preston BC v Fairclough* at 73). In order for surrender to be implied there must, however, be an unambiguous act or series of acts on the part of the tenant that show an intention to give up possession of part of the property. In *Andre v Robinson* [2007] EWCA Civ 1449 it was held that the fact that the tenant had allowed another person to occupy a room in her flat, and allowed the landlord to collect rent from that person, was not sufficient to amount to a surrender of possession of that room.

10.25   Acceptance of rent by the landlord from an occupier who is not the tenant will not amount to an acceptance of surrender unless the landlord does so with intention of effecting a surrender (*Mattey Securities v Ervin* [1998] 2 EGLR 66; *Bhogal v Cheema* [1999] L&TR 59). The fact that the tenant has given the key to the premises back to the landlord and the landlord has accepted the key will amount to surrender in the right circumstances (*Furnivall v Grove* [1860] 8 CB (NS) 496; *Phene v Popplewell*). However, the act of giving back the key must be unequivocal; where the key was handed over so that the landlord could do repairs there was no surrender (*Boynton-Wood v Trueman* (1961) 177 EG 191). Similarly, where the key to a property was handed back on the understanding that a surrender would take place as soon as a new lease was granted to another party, the landlord's acceptance of the key was not sufficient to effect a surrender. The surrender of the old lease would take place only when the new lease was granted (*Proudreed Ltd v Microgen Holdings Plc* [1996] 1 EGLR 89, CA). It is also necessary that the tenant give back possession of the premises to the landlord. Where a husband tried to surrender a tenancy while his wife was still living in the premises this was not held to be a valid surrender (*Hoggett v Hoggett and Wallis* (1979) 39 P&CR 121).

10.26   If, at the time of surrender, there is a subsisting sub-tenancy, the sub-tenancy will not be terminated. By virtue of s 139 of the LPA 1925, the sub-tenancy will be preserved, the tenant will drop out of the picture, and the sub-tenant will become the direct tenant of the head landlord. This will be the case even if the sub-tenancy was created in breach of covenant.

10.27   If the tenant remains in occupation after surrendering the lease a statutory tenancy will arise, and the landlord will need to bring proceedings for possession despite the fact that when the two parties agreed to the surrender it was envisaged that the tenant was willing to leave (*Appleton v Aspin and Plane* (1987) 20 HLR 182, CA).

Merger

10.28   Merger occurs when one of the parties' interest in land is absorbed into the other party's interest with the result that there is no longer a relationship of landlord and tenant. Surrender is, in fact, just one type of merger. Merger will also occur when the tenant acquires the landlord's reversion (as opposed to surrender when the landlord acquires the tenant's interest), for example where a tenant exercises an option to purchase.

10.29   For merger to take place the tenant must hold both interests in the same legal capacity; if the tenant holds the tenancy in his or her own name and the reversion as a trustee there will be no merger. Furthermore, merger will not be implied by operation of law if it is against the interests of the parties. Section 185 of the LPA 1925 states that no merger will be implied if there would have been no merger in equity. As with surrender, s 139 of the Act will preserve any sub-tenancy subsisting at the time of merger.

Notice of increase of rent

This will affect only Rent Act-protected tenants. By virtue of the Rent Act 1977, s 49(4), a **10.30** notice of an increase of rent served by a landlord will operate to determine the contractual tenancy; a statutory tenancy will then arise (see 13.154).

Forfeiture

The only other way a landlord can terminate a fixed-term tenancy before the expiry of the **10.31** term is by forfeiture. This is covered in detail in Chapter 11.

C PERIODIC TENANCIES

In contrast to a fixed-term tenancy, a periodic tenancy will not end of its own accord by **10.32** effluxion of time. In a periodic tenancy the length of each rental period is defined in the agreement but no limit is placed upon the total length of the term. A periodic tenancy will continue renewing itself as each period expires and can, theoretically at least, go on *ad infinitum*. To terminate a periodic tenancy it is necessary for either the landlord or the tenant to take some positive step to end it.

It is essential to the nature of a tenancy that it should be for a definable period (see Chapter **10.33** 1). Periodic tenancies usually provide that both the landlord and the tenant can terminate the tenancy by giving notice to quit. If the tenancy is not capable of termination by both parties, or if a party's right to terminate will only arise in certain circumstances which may never come about, it could be argued that a periodic tenancy is not for a definable period and therefore cannot be a tenancy at all. This situation was considered in *Berrisford v Mexfield Housing Co-operative Ltd* [2011] UKSC 52. In this case the tenant occupied under a monthly periodic tenancy that could only be terminated by the landlord if the tenant breached a covenant in the lease (which the tenant might never do). This meant that on the face of the agreement there was no definable period. The landlord sought to argue that the lack of certainty in respect of the period meant that there was no tenancy and it could terminate the occupation agreement by giving common law notice to quit (see 10.35). The Supreme Court held that as the tenant was an individual such an agreement would have been treated as a common law tenancy for life prior to the Law of Property Act 1925 and therefore, by virtue of s 149(6) of the Act, was to be treated as being for a term of 90 years determinable on the death of the tenant. This construction would not be available if the tenant was not an individual. In such a case the agreement would create a contractual licence but not a tenancy. This would, however, mean that the terms of the licence would include the restriction on the landlord's right to serve notice to quit.

When a tenancy is successfully terminated it brings to an end a large number of rights and **10.34** obligations that were previously held by the parties to the lease. The consequences to both sides can be serious, in particular the consequences to the tenant, who may be rendered suddenly homeless. The methods by which a periodic tenancy can be ended are therefore controlled by various common law and statutory requirements. The requirements are particularly strict when the tenancy is not brought to an end by mutual agreement but unilaterally by the act of one party.

Notice to quit

10.35   One party to a periodic tenancy can bring that tenancy to an end by means of a *notice to quit*. A notice to quit is served by the party wishing to terminate the tenancy upon the other party to the tenancy and gives him or her advance warning that the tenancy is to be ended. Strictly speaking, at common law the notice to quit does not have to be in any particular prescribed form provided it sets out a clear intention to terminate the tenancy and specifies the date upon which this is to take place. In theory the notice to quit does not even have to be in writing (*Ahearn v Bellman* [1879] 4 Ex D 201, CA). In practice, however, the notice to quit will have to comply with any terms set out in the tenancy. The majority of tenancies include a term stating that notice must be given in writing and specifying what period of notice must be given. Furthermore, the notice to quit will also have to comply with any statutory provisions; in the case of residential leases this will be the Protection from Eviction Act 1977; for business leases the Landlord and Tenant Act 1954, Pt II.

Timing and length of notice

10.36   A notice to quit must fulfil two important common law requirements:

(a)   It must state with certainty when the notice expires, ie the day upon which it is stated that notice takes effect.

(b)   It must give sufficient notice, ie the time between the date of service of the notice and the date upon which it expires must be equal to or longer than the minimum periods as defined by the common law.

10.37   A periodic tenancy is strictly speaking terminable only at one point in time in each rental period—at midnight on the day before the anniversary of the start of the tenancy. Thus, a weekly tenancy that started on a Monday is terminable only at midnight on Sunday; a monthly tenancy starting on the first of the month is terminable only at midnight on the last day of the month. Usually the tenancy agreement will specify the date upon which the tenancy began. However, if it is not clear when the tenancy started, the timing will be calculated from the date on which the rent is paid. If a dispute arises over the commencement date of the tenancy it will be up to the party seeking to serve notice to establish the commencement date.

10.38   The common law, however, permits a little latitude with regard to the date upon which the notice is stated to expire. A notice to quit will be valid so long as it is expressed to expire either on the same day on which the tenancy commenced (or on which rent is payable), or upon the preceding day (*Newman v Slade* [1926] 2 KB 328; *Harley v Calder* (1989) 21 HLR 214, [1989] 1 EGLR 88, CA).

10.39   It is not necessary that the notice to quit should actually state the specific date so long as the correct date can be ascertained clearly. A notice to quit will be sufficient so long as the party receiving the notice is able to work out the day of expiry from information with which he or she will be familiar, such as the tenancy agreement (see *Addis v Burrows* [1948] 1 All ER 177 *per* Evershed LJ at 182). For example, a notice stating 'at the expiration of the present year's tenancy' was held to be valid in *Doe d Gorst v Timothy* [1847] 2 Car & Kir 351.

10.40   Thus, if Peter has a monthly tenancy that commenced on the 5th of the month, the notice to quit must be expressed to expire either on the 5th or the 4th of the month. The need for accuracy and the consequences of a mistake (namely that the notice will be invalid if the date is wrong) make it common for a saving clause to be added by landlords. If Peter's landlord gave notice to Peter expressing the notice to expire on the 3rd of the month, but added the phrase 'or at the end of the period of your tenancy which will end next after the expiration of one month from service upon you of this notice', the notice would still be valid (*Addis v Burrows*). Similarly, the need for accuracy could be avoided by including an express provision in the tenancy agreement permitting the tenancy to be terminated 'at any time' by giving a specified period of notice, in which case the notice would not need to be expressed to expire on an anniversary.

Notice, as well as expiring upon the correct date, must be of sufficient length. Generally **10.41** the length of notice should be at least one rental period. Thus, a weekly tenancy requires one week's notice, a monthly tenancy one month, a quarterly tenancy three months, and a six-monthly tenancy six months. A periodic tenancy for any period of over six months requires only six months' notice. These are the notice periods demanded by the common law and they can be overridden by an express provision in the lease as to the period of notice. A term in the lease may say that the notice period should be shorter or longer than the common law period. For example, if in a quarterly periodic tenancy a term states that the tenancy is terminable upon four weeks' notice then four weeks will be sufficient.

For residential tenancies s 5(1) of the Protection from Eviction Act 1977 lays down a **10.42** minimum period of four weeks' notice. By virtue of s 5(1A), these provisions also apply to licences but they will not apply to certain categories of tenancies and licences excluded by s 5(1B) (see 19.23). The minimum period cannot be overridden by an express term in the lease and applies to both landlords and tenants. Thus, if an express term states that only two weeks' notice is required to terminate a monthly tenancy, this term will not be effective and to terminate the tenancy validly the landlord will have to give four weeks' notice.

Prescribed information

The Protection from Eviction Act 1977 also provides that notice will not be valid unless **10.43** it is in writing and contains the prescribed information set out in the Notices to Quit (Prescribed Information) Regulations 1988, SI 1988/2201. The notice must inform the tenant (or licensee) that if he or she does not leave the dwelling the landlord must get an order for possession from the court before the tenant can be evicted, and that the landlord cannot apply for such an order until the period of notice has expired. It must also inform the tenant that advice can be obtained from a solicitor, Citizens' Advice Bureau, or housing centre if the tenant is unsure of his or her position and that financial assistance may be available under the Legal Aid Scheme.

This provision is designed to inform tenants of their legal rights on receipt of a notice to **10.44** quit. A tenant serving notice upon his or her landlord does not need to include the prescribed information. It seems that even if the exact wording of the statutory form is not followed, the notice will still be valid provided the information is clear.

Service

Obviously, to be valid the notice to quit must be served on or before the date from which **10.45** time starts to run. The time at which service takes place can therefore be of great importance in a dispute—if service is late the notice to quit will be invalid.

The tenant, the landlord, or an authorized agent of either party can serve a notice to quit. **10.46** If the notice to quit is served by an authorized agent it is usual for the notice to state that it is served on behalf of the party for whom the agent is acting. A notice to quit can be served only by the immediate landlord upon his or her tenant, or by the tenant upon his or her immediate landlord. A head landlord cannot serve a notice to quit upon a sub-tenant, nor can a sub-tenant serve a notice to quit upon a head landlord.

A tenancy agreement may specifically provide that s 196(4) of the LPA 1925 will apply to **10.47** notices served in respect of the tenancy. If this provision is included service will be regarded as sufficient whether or not the notice was actually received by the tenant if one of the following methods is used:

(a) service to the tenant's last known abode or business in the UK;
(b) affixing or leaving the notice on the land or building in the lease;
(c) sending the notice by registered or recorded delivery to the tenant at his or her last known place of abode or business.

10.48 In the case of (c), if the letter is not returned by post it will be deemed to have been served at the time at which the letter would arrive in the ordinary course of the post.

10.49 At common law the rules relating to service are not entirely clear. Service does not need to be personal; it can be by ordinary post, or by registered post or recorded delivery, or by any other means prescribed by the lease. A notice to quit left with a tenant's wife or servant with clear instructions to hand it on to the tenant has been held to be valid even though it was not actually received by the tenant until after time had started to run (*Tanham v Nicholson* [1872] LR 5 HL 561). A notice to quit need not be addressed by name; a description will be enough.

Joint landlords or joint tenants

10.50 In the case of joint tenancies it is important to remember that the four unities must exist (see 2.48). Thus, if one joint tenant serves a notice to quit on the landlord, this will determine the joint tenancy whether or not the other joint tenants have agreed to serve a notice to quit. Likewise if a landlord serves a notice to quit on one of a number of joint tenants, termination of one joint tenant's interest terminates the interests of all the other joint tenants (*Hammersmith and Fulham LBC v Monk* [1992] 1 AC 478, [1991] 3 WLR 1144).

10.51 Where there are joint landlords the common law position is the same: a tenancy will continue only for so long as *all* of the parties agree its continuation. Thus, it can be determined by notice to quit given by just one joint landlord even without the concurrence of another joint landlord (*Hammersmith v Monk*, 10.50).

10.52 The situation is different if the tenancy agreement expressly requires notice to be served by all of the tenants or all of the landlords. In *Fitzhugh v Fitzhugh* [2012] EWCA Civ 694 (a case concerning a licence but decided on principles applicable equally to tenancies) it was held that where two licensors were described in the licence agreement as 'the licensor' and the notice to quit was served under a clause in the agreement that required it to be served by 'the licensor', this meant that it had to be served by both of them (even though one of them was also a licensee under the agreement and therefore highly unlikely to want to serve notice to quit on himself).

10.53 It should also be noted that where joint tenants wish to terminate a tenancy by operating a break clause in the lease, notice must be given by all of them.

Waiver of notice

10.54 Once a valid notice to quit is given, the tenancy will automatically terminate when the notice period expires. It is possible for a valid notice to quit to be waived by the parties by either express or implied agreement. Express waiver of the notice to quit by both parties will give rise to a new tenancy on the expiry of the old tenancy. Waiver of notice may also be inferred by the actions of the parties. For example, waiver may be inferred by acceptance of rent by the landlord following the expiry of a notice to quit, although the intentions of the parties in offering and accepting rent in such circumstances must be considered (*Clark v Grant* [1950] 1 KB 104; *Land v Sykes* [1992] 1 EGLR 1).

Disclaimer

If one of the parties to a tenancy goes bankrupt, the tenancy will become vested in a trustee **10.55** in bankruptcy. If the bankrupt's interest cannot be sold or is likely to result in the bankrupt incurring further expense, the trustee in bankruptcy has the power under s 315 of the Insolvency Act 1986 to disclaim the tenancy. Likewise, in the case of company lets, a liquidator may disclaim a lease under s 178 of the Insolvency Act 1986. Disclaimer operates by terminating the lease and ending all obligations between landlord and tenant.

Possession proceedings

Most tenancy agreements are governed by one of the statutory codes discussed in Part II **10.56** of this book. It is important to note that although a landlord can terminate a tenancy by one of the methods discussed earlier, he or she will not be able to obtain possession of the property without an order of the court. Landlords wishing to obtain possession of property must first establish which, if any, of the statutory codes apply to the tenancy (see 12.12); they must then follow the procedure for possession set out in the relevant statutes and in the Civil Procedure Rules. Possession proceedings cannot be commenced until the relevant notice to quit has expired.

KEY DOCUMENTS

Protection From Eviction Act 1977

Notice to Quit (Prescribed Information) Regulations 1988, SI 1988/2201

Civil Procedure Rules 1988

Form N5—Claims for possession of property

Form N5B—Claims for possession of property (accelerated procedure)

Form N11B—Defence Form (accelerated procedure)

Form N11R—Defence Form (rented residential premises)

Printed copies of all legislation can be ordered from The Stationery Office at <http://www.tsoshop. co.uk>. All legislation from 1988 onwards and most pre-1988 primary legislation is available online at <http://www. legislation.gov.uk>.

The Civil Procedure Rules are available online from <http://www.justice.gov.uk/courts/ procedure-rules>.

Court forms are available online from the HM Courts and Tribunals Service at <http://www.justice. gov.uk/forms/hmcts>.

11

FORFEITURE

A INTRODUCTION

Example Jean owns the freehold of two terraced houses, 12 and 14 Guildford Street. On **11.01**
1 September 1992, she grants Dominic a monthly periodic tenancy of No 12 and Steven
a five-year fixed-term tenancy of No 14. Both tenancy agreements contain similar obligations, including covenants:

(a) to pay a monthly rent of £500;
(b) not to assign or sub-let;
(c) to use the premises for residential purposes only;
(d) to redecorate the interior of the premises every three years with good quality emulsion
    paint;
(e) not to affix window-boxes to the exterior of the building.

Steven's fixed-term tenancy does not contain a break clause or an option to determine (see **11.02**
6.122). It does, however, contain a provision permitting Jean to re-enter the premises in
certain circumstances. This clause reads:

> Provided that if the Rent or any part thereof shall be in arrear for fourteen days after the same
> shall have become due (whether legally demanded or not) or in the event of the breach of any
> of the agreements on the part of the Tenant herein contained the Landlord may re-enter upon
> the Property and immediately thereupon the tenancy shall absolutely determine but without
> prejudice to the other rights and remedies of the landlord.

11.03   A local property developer has already converted several of the houses in Guildford Street into luxury flats. He approaches Jean and makes her a very generous offer for Nos 12 and 14, but is only interested in purchasing the properties with vacant possession. Jean decides to try to regain possession of both houses.

11.04   As we saw in the last chapter, Jean can terminate Dominic's periodic tenancy by service of a notice to quit. In doing so she will have to comply with any terms set out in the tenancy agreement and abide by the common law rules as to timing and length of notice and any relevant statutory rules such as those under the Protection from Eviction Act 1977 (see 19.18 to 19.24). However, provided she follows the correct procedural requirements, she will be able to terminate Dominic's contractual tenancy unilaterally. It is in the nature of a periodic tenancy that it can be terminated (at common law at least) on the wishes of either party by service of a notice to quit at any time provided the notice requirements are satisfied. (For the purposes of this example we are assuming that Dominic has not acquired any further statutory protection under the Rent Act 1977 or the Housing Act 1988.)

11.05   With respect to Steven's tenancy the situation is somewhat different. Jean wants to regain possession but there are still over two years left to run of Steven's contractual term. A notice to quit has no application to a fixed-term tenancy unless the agreement contains an express provision that it should. Steven's tenancy contains no such provision. The only way in which Jean can unilaterally terminate Steven's tenancy is to forfeit the lease by relying upon the re-entry provision cited in 11.02. This provision, however, makes Jean's right of re-entry dependent upon Steven breaching an obligation in the tenancy.

11.06   Throughout the course of the tenancy Steven has always paid his rent on time and has generally been a very good tenant. However, recently Jean has noticed that he has placed two window-boxes on the sills of the ground-floor windows of No 14. When she knocks on the door to enquire about the window-boxes, Edward answers the door. Edward says that he has rented the house from Steven for three months while Steven is away on a training course. Jean wants to know whether she can forfeit Steven's lease for one or both of these breaches of obligation.

Forfeiture is a remedy

11.07   This leads us on to a most important point: forfeiture is not primarily a method of termination but a remedy. The purpose of the re-entry provision included in Steven's lease is not to enable Jean to terminate the fixed term in the pursuit of her own purposes, but rather to provide her with an effective sanction against a defaulting tenant. A landlord who feels there is a likelihood that he or she may wish to terminate a fixed term early should include a break clause in the tenancy agreement. In our example Jean may come to curse her lack of foresight, for unless Steven breaches a term of the agreement she will not be able to rely upon the re-entry proviso.

11.08   On the other hand, the end result of successful forfeiture proceedings can be the termination of the tenancy. Of all the remedies a landlord can employ against a defaulting tenant it is the most potent. The landlord will have other options available; he or she could pursue an action for damages for breach of covenant or seek an injunction, but neither of these remedies will be backed by the ultimate sanction of repossession. However, for this very reason, the law seeks to ensure that the landlord cannot use the right of forfeiture inappropriately or capriciously. In the words of Coke (*Duppa v Mayho* [1669] 1 Wms Saund 282 at 287, 85 ER 366 at 375), 'The law leans against forfeitures'.

The landlord's right to forfeit is limited in a variety of ways: **11.09**

(a) It can be used only in situations where the landlord has expressly reserved the right to forfeit in the tenancy agreement.
(b) The landlord must comply with strict procedural requirements.
(c) It is subject to strict rules of waiver.
(d) The tenant has extensive rights to apply to the court for relief from forfeiture.

Forfeiture of statutorily protected tenancies

Where a tenancy has acquired statutory protection under the Rent Act 1977, the Housing   **11.10**
Act 1988, or the Housing Act 1985 (see Part II), the effect of forfeiture proceedings will depend upon which code protects the tenancy. If the tenancy is a protected tenancy under the Rent Act 1977 the effect of successful forfeiture proceedings will be to convert the contractual tenancy into a statutory tenancy and the landlord will not be entitled to possession unless he can establish one of the statutory grounds for possession (see 14.25 to 14.69).

If the tenancy is an assured tenancy under the Housing Act 1988 the situation is very differ-   **11.11**
ent. An assured tenancy can only be brought to an end by relying on the statutory grounds of possession (see 16.30 to 16.71) and cannot be terminated by forfeiture (Housing Act 1988, s 45(4)). An assured tenant, therefore, has no right to claim relief from forfeiture. If the tenancy is a secure tenancy under the Housing Act 1985 special rules apply (see Housing Act 1985, s 82; and 17.100). Business tenancies protected by Part II of the Landlord and Tenant Act 1954 can be forfeited (see 26.73).

Who can forfeit?

It should be noted at the outset that, while a notice to quit can be served by either the   **11.12**
landlord or the tenant (see 10.35), proceedings to forfeit a lease can be brought only by the landlord. A tenant who wishes to end a fixed-term tenancy before the term has expired has very limited options. The only way the tenant can end the tenancy is to try to get the landlord to agree to surrender (see 10.17 to 10.21). For surrender, however, consent of both parties is required. If the landlord will not voluntarily agree to surrender, the tenant may well be compelled to fulfil his or her obligations under the fixed term.

The one-sidedness of the forfeiture procedure has already come in for considerable criti-   **11.13**
cism. It certainly seems unjust that while a landlord is able to forfeit a tenancy because a tenant fails to comply with the covenants in the lease, a tenant has no means by which to release himself or herself from the tenancy if the landlord breaches his or her obligations. As long ago as 1985 the Law Commission recommended that where a landlord breaches the covenants in the lease the tenant should be able to obtain a 'termination order' and should have the right to claim damages from the landlord for any losses incurred (Law Com No. 142: *Forfeiture of Tenancies* [1985]). Its latest report (Law Com No. 303: *Termination of Tenancies for Tenant Default* [2006]) states that the current system lacks transparency and 'is excessively technical and unnecessarily complicated'. It sets out a draft bill for a Landlord and Tenant (Termination of Tenancies) Act to abolish forfeiture and replace it with a statutory scheme.

However, as the law now stands, forfeiture is applicable only to landlords. The tenant may   **11.14**
be able to claim that he or she is entitled to repudiate the contract of letting because of the landlord's breach of covenant and thereby treat himself or herself as being discharged from the obligations under the tenancy agreement (see 10.15). What reform there has been of

the law of forfeiture so far has taken the form of protecting long leaseholders and tenants of dwellings by restricting a landlord's right to institute forfeiture proceedings (see 11.58 to 11.62 and 11.68 to 11.69).

B WHEN CAN A LANDLORD FORFEIT?

11.15 A landlord can acquire the right to forfeit a tenancy in only two situations. Both of these situations can be brought about only by some act or omission on the part of the tenant. If the tenant fulfils all the obligations in the lease, the landlord will not acquire any right to forfeit and will be unable to terminate the tenancy before the fixed term has expired.

11.16 The landlord will acquire the right to forfeit the lease if the tenant breaches either:

(a) a condition; or
(b) a covenant *and* the lease contains a proviso for re-entry.

11.17 The nature of conditions and covenants was considered in Chapter 4 (4.09 to 4.14). The basic difference between them is that if a tenant breaches a condition the landlord will automatically acquire the right to forfeit the lease; if the tenant breaches a covenant the landlord will acquire the right to forfeit only if he or she has expressly reserved a right of re-entry in the agreement. In practice virtually every modern lease will contain a re-entry clause (but see *Rainbow Estates Ltd v Tokenhold Ltd* [1999] Ch 64, [1998] 2 EGLR 38). Furthermore, if a tenant holds under an equitable lease a right of re-entry for non-payment of rent and for breach of covenant will be implied as a 'usual covenant' (see 4.24).

Proviso for re-entry

11.18 The proviso for re-entry will set out the circumstances in which the landlord may re-enter the property and terminate the tenancy. Normally the clause permits the landlord to forfeit for breach of covenant and for non-payment of rent (see the provision in Steven's lease at 11.02). A re-entry clause can be drafted to include other circumstances, for example the bankruptcy of the tenant (see *Cadogan Estates Ltd v McMahon* [2000] 3 WLR 1555, [2001] 1 EGLR 47).

11.19 The courts will construe any re-entry clause *contra proferentum* and apply it in favour of the tenant. For example, a clause that reserved the right to re-enter in respect of 'any act matter or thing contrary to and in breach of the covenants' was held not to extend to a breach of repairing covenant, because to fail to repair was an omission and not an act (*Doe d Abdy v Stevens* [1832] 3 B&Ad 299). A clause which referred to the covenants 'thereinafter contained', when they in fact preceded the clause in the lease, was also held to be ineffective (*Doe d Spencer v Goodwin* [1815] 4 M&S 264).

The landlord must choose to forfeit—an unequivocal act

11.20 If a tenant breaches one of the covenants in the lease, the landlord acquires the right to forfeit. The landlord does not *have* to do anything and if he or she wishes can treat the tenancy as continuing. If the landlord decides to forfeit the lease, he or she must perform some unequivocal act which demonstrates that he or she regards the relationship of landlord and tenant as being at an end.

Peaceable re-entry

In the past the landlord would commonly be able to make clear his or her intention to end   **11.21**
the tenancy by actually physically re-entering the premises and thereby recovering possession. Today, however, the landlord would be unwise to take the wording of the forfeiture
clause in the lease too literally; the situations in which the landlord can physically re-enter
are severely limited by statute (see 11.22 to 11.24) and arise rarely in practice. It is only in
the case of unoccupied business premises that peaceable re-entry can be a realistic option
for a landlord. Physical re-entry has the advantage that the landlord will not have to wait
for the outcome of a possession hearing.

Peaceable re-entry has no application with regard to residential tenancies. Section 2 of the   **11.22**
Protection from Eviction Act 1977 provides that:

> Where any premises are let as a dwelling on a lease which is subject to a right of re-entry or
> forfeiture it shall not be lawful to enforce that right otherwise than by proceedings in the court
> while any person is lawfully residing in the premises or part of them.

For the purposes of s 2, 'let as a dwelling' means let wholly or partly as a dwelling.
Accordingly, s 2 will apply where premises are let for mixed residential and business purposes (*Patel v Pirabakaran* [2006] EWCA Civ 685, [2006] 1 WLR 3112).

If the landlord tries physically to re-enter residential premises he or she may be liable to   **11.23**
criminal prosecution for unlawful eviction if 'any person' (it does not have to be the tenant)
is lawfully occupying the premises.

Furthermore, the Criminal Law Act 1977 prohibits anyone using force to re-enter premises.   **11.24**
Section 6(1) provides that:

> ... any person who, without lawful authority, uses or threatens violence for the purpose of
> securing entry into any premises for himself or for any other person is guilty of an offence,
> provided that—
> (a) there is someone present on those premises at the time who is opposed to the entry
>   which the violence is intended to secure; and
> (b) the person using or threatening the violence knows that that is the case.

The fact that a person has an interest in or right to possession of the premises does not   **11.25**
constitute lawful authority for the purpose of seeking possession (s 6(2)).

Service of court proceedings

The usual way in which the landlord indicates conclusively that he or she intends to treat   **11.26**
the breach as giving rise to forfeiture is by taking court proceedings, namely by issuing and
serving a claim for possession. (In the majority of cases the landlord will have to give the
tenant notice even before issuing proceedings under s 146 of the LPA 1925, see 11.44.)
Serving a claim form upon the tenant is equivalent to the landlord actually re-entering
the premises. If the tenant then voluntarily leaves the premises the landlord will be able
to regain possession. In practice, however, the service of a claim for possession upon the
tenant is rarely the end of the story. Once the claim form has been served it is by no means
a foregone conclusion that the court will make a possession order, and in any case the tenant's right of occupation will continue until a warrant for possession is executed.

If at the hearing the court decides to grant the landlord a possession order, the lease is actu-   **11.27**
ally regarded as being forfeited upon the date of the service of the proceedings. This leaves
the status of the tenant between service and possession somewhat unclear (see *Liverpool
Properties Ltd v Oldbridge Investments Ltd* [1985] 2 EGLR 111, CA). Certainly the tenant

possesses some sort of interest, for as we shall see the tenant is able to apply for relief from forfeiture; and if he or she is applying for relief the tenant can still enforce the landlord's covenants (*Peninsular Maritime Ltd v Padseal Ltd* (1981) 259 EG 860, CA).

11.28   On the other hand, once the landlord has made clear his or her intention to forfeit the lease by serving a claim form he or she ceases to be able to enforce any of the covenants in the lease. By forfeiting the lease the landlord treats the lease as being at an end and the notional date of forfeiture is the date of the service of the claim form. If the landlord issues proceedings that assume the continuation of the lease beyond this notional date of forfeiture—if, for example, the landlord seeks an injunction to restrain a future breach—these proceedings will not be regarded as an unequivocal act and will not give rise to forfeiture (*More v Ullcoats Mining Co. Ltd* [1908] 1 Ch 575).

11.29   If a claim has been made for relief against forfeiture the status of the tenancy will remain uncertain. Therefore, if the tenant is eventually granted relief, the landlord will be able to claim rent for the entire period up until the final hearing (*Maryland Estates Limited v Joseph* [1998] EWCA Civ 693, [1998] 3 All ER 193). Similarly, if the landlord discontinues the forfeiture claim he or she will be able to claim rent for the period during which the lease was forfeited (*Mount Cook Land v Media Business Centre* [2004] EWHC 346 (Ch), [2004] 2 P&CR 25). This point is of great importance when assessing the amount of arrears of rent that must be paid by a tenant in order to claim relief from forfeiture (see 11.91 to 11.97). If no application for relief is made the tenancy will terminate on the date of service of the claim form and the landlord will only be entitled to claim mesne profits for occupation from that date to the date he regains possession.

11.30   Mesne profits are a special form of damages payable to the landlord for losses incurred due to a tenant staying in possession after the tenancy has ended.

C WAIVER

11.31   We have seen that once a tenant had breached an obligation in the lease the landlord must choose whether or not to forfeit. It is often said that once the breach has occurred the landlord is 'put on his election'. The crucial date, however, is not when the breach itself occurs, but when the landlord first has knowledge of the breach. Once the landlord knows about the breach he or she must choose what to do. If the landlord chooses to issue proceedings straightaway he or she has made clear his intentions. If, however, the landlord does something to indicate that he or she regards the tenancy as still continuing then the landlord is deemed to have waived the breach. The doctrine of waiver has no application once the landlord has elected to forfeit, either by issuing proceedings or by peaceable re-entry.

11.32   The law, as we have said, 'leans against forfeiture', and as we shall see the rules of waiver are very strict. For waiver to operate the landlord must:

(a)   have knowledge of the breach;
(b)   do something which recognizes the continuation of the tenancy.

Knowledge of the breach

11.33   The landlord cannot waive the right to forfeit a lease if he or she does not know that the right has arisen. It is not always a straightforward question whether the landlord knows of the breach, particularly in situations where the landlord rarely visits the property or where the property is managed through an agent. The general rule, however, is that where a landlord's agent or other employee knows of a breach of obligation, this knowledge will be imputed to the landlord provided that the employee has had a reasonable amount of time to inform the landlord of the breach. This is based on the principle that an employee is under a duty to communicate information to his or her employer. For example, where a tenant sub-lets a flat in breach of covenant and the porters in the building are aware that someone else is living in the flat, the landlord is deemed to know of the breach (*Metropolitan Properties v Cordery* (1979) 251 EG 567, (1979) 39 P&CR 10). However, where a tenant sub-let his premises and the landlord became aware that there had been a change of occupation but accepted the tenant's untruthful explanation that the new tenant was a housekeeper, the landlord did not lose his right to forfeit (*Chrisdell Ltd v Johnson and Tickner* (1987) 19 HLR 406; see also *Cornillie v Saha* (1996) 28 HLR 561, (1996) 72 P&CR 147).

Recognizing the continuation of the tenancy

Once a landlord has knowledge of a breach he or she can of course expressly consent to it and thereby waive the right to forfeit. Waiver may also be implied from the landlord's actions, however. Waiver is judged objectively, without regard to the motive or intention of the landlord, or to the actual understanding or belief of the tenant (Buckley LJ in *Central Estates (Belgravia) Ltd v Woolgar (No. 2)* [1972] 1 WLR 1048, 1054; cited in *Expert Clothing Service & Sales Ltd v Hillgate House Ltd* [1986] Ch 340 at 360). **11.34**

Accepting rent

The most common way by which a landlord who has knowledge of a breach of obligation by the tenant can recognize the continuation of the tenancy is by accepting or demanding rent which falls due after the breach. To some extent this stands as a special category on its own; the law takes a very strict line and the implication of waiver will be virtually inevitable. To accept rent 'without prejudice' makes no difference: the landlord will still be deemed to have waived the right to forfeit (*Segal Securities Ltd v Thoseby* [1963] 1 QB 887), even if rent is accepted by mistake, for example where an employee sent out a demand for rent to the tenant (*Central Estates*). However, where a landlord banks a cheque stated to be made up of two sums, one discharging a bankruptcy debt and the other as part payment of arrears of rent, and promptly returns the sum relating to rent, the processing of the cheque does not amount to waiver (*Osibanjo v Seahive Investments Ltd* [2008] EWCA Civ 1282). The question as to whether an unqualified demand for rent has the same effect as accepting rent is not yet decided, but in *Greenwood Reversions Ltd v World Environment Foundation Ltd* [2008] EWCA Civ 47 the Court of Appeal assumed this to be the case. If, therefore, having discovered that Steven has sub-let 14 Guildford Street to Edward, Jean wishes to take forfeiture proceedings, she must be very careful not to demand or accept rent from Steven. **11.35**

Other acts of waiver

If a landlord gives a tenant notice of his or her intention to enter the property to carry out repairs, this will amount to waiver of the right to forfeit for breach of repairing covenant (*Doe d De Rutzen v Lewis* [1836] 5 Ad&E 277). If the landlord serves a notice to quit on the tenant requiring the tenant to give up the tenancy at a date in the future, this will also amount to an act affirming the existence of the tenancy (*Marche v Christodoulakis* (1948) 64 TLR 466). **11.36**

The effect of waiver

The effect of waiver depends upon the nature of the breach of covenant. In the case of a once-and-for-all breach, such as the breach of a covenant against sub-letting, once the **11.37** landlord has waived the breach he or she will lose any right to forfeit for that particular breach in the future. The breach of covenant consists of the act of granting the sub-lease. The fact that the sub-lease continues to exist after the act of waiver does not give rise to a fresh cause of action. Other examples of a once-and-for-all breach would be a breach of covenant against alterations or a failure to put premises in repair by a specified date. Failure to pay rent is also a once-and-for-all breach in respect of any one particular rent period.

11.38 So, with regard to 14 Guildford Street, if, after the date of the sub-letting and with knowledge that the sub-letting has taken place, Jean accepts rent from Steven, Jean will not be able to start new proceedings for forfeiture just because Edward is still in occupation. If, however, on the expiry of the first sub-tenancy, Steven sought to sub-let the property, she would again be able to take forfeiture proceedings. Steven would be committing a new breach of covenant and the fact that in the past Jean had waived a similar breach would not give him *carte blanche* to repeat the breach. Similarly with regard to rent: if Steven failed to pay his monthly rent in April, Jean would waive her right to forfeit by demanding that rent. If Steven then failed to pay the rent in May a new right to forfeit would arise in respect of that month's breach.

11.39 If the breach is a continuing breach, such as a failure to repair, the right to forfeit will arise again on the day after the waiver. If after three years Steven fails to redecorate the interior of 14 Guildford Street, he has breached a term of the tenancy agreement. If, after the date upon which he should have decorated, Jean accepts rent, this would amount to waiver. The breach, however, consists of Steven's failure to perform a positive act. Each day that he fails to redecorate the breach arises anew and Jean again acquires the right to forfeit. Other examples of a continuing breach would be a failure to keep the premises insured or a breach of covenant prohibiting a particular type of user.

D LIMITATION

11.40 By s 15(1) of the Limitation Act 1980, the limitation period for all proceedings relating to land is 12 years. Once the tenant has breached an obligation in the lease and a cause of action has accrued (namely that the landlord has knowledge of the breach), the landlord must therefore take action to pursue his or her right to forfeit within 12 years. In practice, because of the strict rules of waiver, it is most unlikely that a landlord will lose his right to forfeit through limitation.

E FURTHER RESTRICTIONS ON FORFEITURE

11.41 Even if a breach of obligation can be established and the landlord does nothing to waive his or her right, it is by no means a forgone conclusion that forfeiture will be the end result of the process. Two further restrictions come into play. First, the landlord must comply with *strict procedural rules* which give the tenant the opportunity to remedy the breach; and, secondly, the tenant in any case may be granted *relief from forfeiture*.

11.42 The procedural rules relating to forfeiture for non-payment of rent are different to those relating to breach of any other covenant.

Procedure for forfeiture for breaches of covenant other than non-payment of rent: LPA 1925, s 146

11.43 All breaches of covenant other than non-payment of rent are governed by s 146 of the LPA 1925 (apart from a few limited exceptions contained in s 146(8) and (9) regarding breaches that occurred before the commencement of the Act, mining, agricultural, and other special-ized leases). The landlord cannot exclude the operation of s 146 by any contrary provision contained in the lease (s 146(12)).

Section 146 demands that before a landlord can exercise a right of re-entry, whether it is **11.44** intended to issue a claim for possession or to re-enter peaceably, he or she must serve on the tenant a s 146 notice. A s 146 notice is thus the first step that must be taken by a landlord before he or she proceeds to forfeiture: it is a statutory condition precedent to forfeiture proceedings. If a landlord does not serve a valid s 146 notice, any further action that he or she takes will not be enforceable.

Section 146(1) provides: **11.45**

> A right of re-entry or forfeiture under any proviso or stipulation in a lease for a breach of any covenant or condition in the lease shall not be enforceable, by action or otherwise, unless and until the lessor serves on the lessee a notice—
> (a) specifying the particular breach complained of; and
> (b) if the breach is capable of remedy, requiring the lessee to remedy the breach; and
> (c) in any case, requiring the lessee to make compensation in money for the breach;
> and the lessee fails, within a reasonable time thereafter, to remedy the breach, if it is capable of remedy, and to make reasonable compensation in money, to the satisfaction of the lessor, for the breach.

The way in which s 146 functions is thus as follows. It requires the landlord formally to set **11.46** out the complaint by specifying the breach. For the notice to be valid it also requires the landlord to require the breach to be remedied within a reasonable time, if that breach is capable of remedy. The procedure demanded by statute thus gives the tenant a last chance to put his or her house in order once he or she has been given notice of the landlord's complaint. If the breach is capable of remedy the tenant can evade forfeiture proceedings altogether by remedying the breach within a reasonable time; the landlord is prevented from proceeding further until the tenant is given this final opportunity. The landlord can go on to forfeit only if:

(a) the breach is not capable of remedy within a reasonable time; or
(b) the breach is capable of remedy within a reasonable time and, having been given a reasonable time to do so, the tenant has failed to remedy the breach.

Remediable and irremediable breaches

When drafting the s 146 notice the landlord will have to decide whether the tenant's **11.47** breach is capable of remedy, for if the landlord fails to require the tenant to remedy a breach that is in fact capable of remedy the notice itself will be invalid. Unfortunately this question is not always easily determinable and the case law on this subject is not entirely consistent.

On one line of reasoning it can be said that no breach can ever truly be capable of remedy: **11.48** the act (or omission) which constituted the breach of covenant can never be undone so as to eradicate its occurrence altogether. However, such an interpretation would be inconsist-ent with s 146, which obviously regards at least some breaches of covenant as being capa-ble of remedy. The courts therefore have adopted a more pragmatic approach; the test is not whether the breach is capable of remedy, but whether the damage caused by the breach is capable of remedy.

Positive covenants A positive covenant places an obligation upon the tenant to do some- **11.49** thing. The nature of such covenants makes them easier to remedy than negative covenants. A failure by a tenant to repair, or (as in our example) to redecorate the interior of the premises every three years, can be resolved by requiring the tenant to do the work and to compensate the landlord for any loss caused by finishing the work late. The harm would be remedied and there would be no irretrievable damage to the landlord's interest (see *Expert Clothing Service v Hillgate House Ltd* [1986] Ch 340).

11.50 **Negative covenants** A negative covenant is a covenant that places an obligation upon the tenant not to do something. In many situations it seems that breaches of such covenants will be regarded by the courts as remediable breaches, particularly where they are continuing breaches. In *Savva and another v Houssein* [1996] EWCA Civ 1302, [1996] 2 EGLR 65 it was held that a breach is capable of remedy as long as the mischief caused by the breach is capable of remedy. A breach of covenant not to keep a pet can be remedied by getting rid of the pet without causing significant harm to the landlord; likewise, as in our example, the removal of window boxes and payment for any damage caused by them would remedy a breach of covenant not to have window boxes. Thus, when drafting a s 146 notice with regard to window boxes at 14 Guildford Street, Jean should require the breach to be remedied.

11.51 There is a line of authority suggesting that in certain cases the breach of a negative covenant will be viewed more severely by the courts (*Rugby School (Governors) v Tannahill* [1935] 1 KB 87; *Egerton v Esplanade Hotels London Ltd* [1947] 2 All ER 88; *Hoffman v Fineberg* [1949] 1 Ch 245). These cases all involved a breach of covenant not to cause or permit immoral use of the premises and the 'stigma' that would attach to the property once it had been used for prostitution or gambling. However, there is no reason to regard these cases as being completely at odds with the views expressed in *Savva v Houssein*. If the stigma is such as to irretrievably damage the landlord's interest, the breach may be irremediable, but if prompt action is taken by the tenant to stop the breach before the damaging stigma can become established the breach can be capable of remedy (*Glass v Kencakes Ltd* [1966] 1 QB 611; see also *Patel v K & J Restaurants Ltd* [2010] EWCA Civ 1211).

11.52 It used to be thought that once-and-for-all breaches of negative covenant are irremediable. This remains the case where there has been a breach of covenant not to assign without consent (*Scala House and District Property Co. Ltd v Forbes* [1974] 1 QB 575; *Savva v Houssein*). Following *Sava v Houssein* it now seems that breaches of other negative covenants will usually be held to be capable of remedy, even a covenant against parting with possession, provided it does not create a tenancy (see *Akici v L R Butlin Ltd* [2005] EWCA Civ 1296, [2006] 1 WLR 201). If the principle to be applied is whether the mischief resulting from the breach can be removed, it seems that the distinction between continuing and once-and-for-all breaches is no longer so significant and each case will be judged on its particular facts. If the damage caused to the landlord can be quantified and compensated for there is no reason to maintain that it is irremediable.

11.53 A landlord serving a s 146(1) notice should therefore, in the vast majority of cases, make sure that the notice requires the lessee to remedy the breach and require the lessee to make compensation in money for the breach.

11.54 If the tenant is unable or unwilling to remedy the breach complained of by the landlord within a reasonable time, or if the breach is of a type not capable of remedy, the statutory condition precedent set by s 146 will be satisfied and the landlord will be free to re-enter, either by service of a claim form upon the tenant or by peaceable re-entry. The tenant, however, is provided with a further opportunity to avoid forfeiture by applying to the court for relief (see 11.72 to 11.97).

Section 146 notice in the case of disrepair

Where a landlord seeks to serve notice under s 146(1) for a breach of covenant to keep **11.55**
or put premises in repair the Landlord and Tenant Act 1927, s 18(2) imposes additional
requirements upon the landlord. Section 18(2) provides that a right of re-entry or forfeiture
for a breach of covenant to repair shall not be enforceable by action or otherwise unless the
landlord proves that the fact the notice was served was known either:

(a) to the lessee; or
(b) to an under-lessee holding under an under-lease which reserved a nominal reversion
　　 only to the lessee; or
(c) to the person who last paid the rent due under the lease either on his or her own behalf
　　 or as an agent for the lessee or under-lessee,

and that a time reasonably sufficient to enable the repairs to be executed had elapsed since
the time when the fact of the service of the notice came to the knowledge of any such
person.

Where notice is sent by registered post to a person's last known place of abode in the UK **11.56**
then, unless the contrary is proved, that person will be deemed to have had knowledge of
the fact that the notice had been served.

Forfeiture of long leases for disrepair

The Leasehold Property (Repairs) Act 1938 imposes strict procedural requirements upon **11.57**
a landlord taking forfeiture proceedings (or seeking damages) for a breach of covenant to
repair against a tenant with a long lease (see 7.108 to 7.110).

Forfeiture of long leases of dwellings

In the past there was something of a tendency for unscrupulous freeholders to threaten **11.58**
leasehold owners with forfeiture in disputes involving relatively small sums. Section 168
of the Commonhold and Leasehold Reform Act 2002 (CLRA 2002) introduced important protection for long leaseholders against forfeiture proceedings being brought on ill-
founded or spurious grounds. Section 168 provides that a landlord under a long lease of
a dwelling may not serve a notice under the LPA 1925, s 146(1) in respect of a breach by
a tenant of a covenant or condition in the lease unless one of the following conditions is
satisfied:

(a) on an application by the landlord (under s 168(4)) it has been finally determined by
　　 a leasehold valuation tribunal that a breach of covenant or condition in the lease has
　　 occurred;
(b) the tenant has admitted the breach; or
(c) a court in any proceedings, or an arbitral tribunal in proceedings pursuant to a post-
　　 dispute arbitration agreement, has finally determined that the breach has occurred.

Even if a final determination has been made under (a) or (c) in 11.58, notice may not be **11.59**
served for 14 days (s 168(3)). A decision that a breach has occurred is finally determined
when that decision is not appealed against or otherwise challenged and the period for
bringing an appeal has expired (s 169(2)).

A long lease is defined by ss 76 and 77 of the CLRA 2002 (effectively the same definition **11.60**
as under s 7 of the Leasehold Reform, Housing and Urban Development Act 1993 for the
right to enfranchise, see 24.100), with the exception that a shared ownership lease is a
long lease regardless of the tenant's total share. This does not include business tenancies,
agricultural holdings, or business farm tenancies (s 169(4)).

11.61   A landlord may not apply to a leasehold valuation tribunal for a determination under s 168(4) in respect of any matter which:

(a)   has been, or is to be, referred to arbitration pursuant to a post-dispute arbitration agreement to which the tenant is party;

(b)   has been the subject of determination by the court; or

(c)   has been the subject of determination by an arbitral tribunal pursuant to a post-dispute arbitration agreement.

11.62   It is not possible to contract out of the provisions of s 168: any agreement by a tenant under a long lease of a dwelling (other than a post-dispute arbitration agreement) is void in so far as it purports to provide for a determination in a particular manner or on particular evidence of any question which may be the subject of an application under s 168(4) (s 169(1)).

Procedure for forfeiture for non-payment of rent

11.63   If the landlord is seeking to forfeit for non-payment of rent, the requirements of the LPA 1925, s 146 do not apply (s 146(11)). A s 146 notice will be required, however, if a landlord seeks to forfeit a lease for a breach of covenant to pay any sums to the landlord which are not reserved as rent, for example service charges. For this reason landlords will frequently describe service charges as 'rent arrears'.

11.64   Where a tenant is in breach of the covenant to pay rent, no issue arises as to whether or not the breach is capable of remedy; it is clear that here the object of the forfeiture clause is to secure payment. If the tenant pays the arrears, relief will almost certainly be granted (see 11.92). Forfeiture is only one of a number of remedies available to the landlord, who could also pursue an action for debt or distrain. Forfeiture, of course, will be available to the landlord only if a right of re-entry has been reserved in the lease; but modern leases will usually contain a proviso permitting re-entry if the rent remains unpaid for a specified period (generally 14 or 21 days).

The necessity for a formal demand

11.65   At common law the landlord is unable to enforce a right of re-entry for breach of covenant to pay rent until he or she has made a formal demand for the rent. Such a formal demand must be made by the landlord or the landlord's agent, at the demised premises or at the place specified in the lease for the payment of rent, and must require the exact sum due to be paid before sunset on the last date for due payment (*Duppa v Mayho* [1669] 1 Wms Saund 282 at 287). To obviate these inconvenient requirements, virtually all leases will now state that the landlord can re-enter once rent is in arrears for a certain period, whether or not the rent has been formally demanded (see the re-entry clause in our example at 11.02).

11.66   Even if there are no words in the lease dispensing with the landlord's need to give a formal demand for rent, a formal demand may not be required if the landlord is taking forfeiture proceedings where more than half a year's rent is in arrears. Section 210 of the Common Law Procedure Act 1852 (for proceedings in the High Court) and s 139(1) of the County Courts Act 1984 state that there is no need for a formal demand if at least half a year's rent is in arrears and the goods present on the premises that are available for the purposes of distress are insufficient in value to cover the arrears due.

11.67   Once the landlord has dealt with the requirements for a formal demand, either because he or she has dispensed with the necessity for such a demand in the lease or by making the formal demand, the landlord can go ahead and issue proceedings for possession.

Forfeiture for non-payment of service charges

Section 81 of the Housing Act 1996 provides particular protection for tenants of premises **11.68** that are let as a dwelling. Where premises are let as a dwelling, a landlord may not, in relation to those premises, exercise a right of re-entry or forfeiture (which includes serving a s 146(1) notice (s 81(4A)) for failure by a tenant to pay a service charge or an administration charge unless:

(a) it is finally determined by (or on appeal from) a leasehold valuation tribunal or by a court, or by an arbitral tribunal in proceedings pursuant to a post-dispute arbitration agreement, that the amount of the service charge or administration charge is payable by the tenant; or
(b) the tenant has admitted that it is so payable (s 81(1)).

Even if a final determination has been made under (a), notice may not be served for 14 days (s 81(3)). A decision on the amount of service/administration charge payable is finally determined when that decision is not appealed against or otherwise challenged and the period for bringing an appeal has expired (s 81(3)).

The term 'premises let as a dwelling' does not include premises let on business tenancies, **11.69** agricultural holdings, or business farm tenancies (s 81(4)). A 'service charge' has the same meaning as under s 18(1) of the Landlord and Tenant Act 1985 (see 23.12) and 'dwelling' has the same meaning as defined in s 38 of the 1985 Act (see 23.08).

Forfeiture for failure to pay a small amount for a short period

By s 167(1) of the CLRA 2002 a landlord under a long lease of a dwelling may not exercise **11.70** a right of re-entry or forfeiture for failure by a tenant to pay an amount consisting of rent, service charges, or administration charges (or a combination of them) unless the unpaid amount:

(a) exceeds a prescribed sum; or
(b) consists of or includes an amount which has been payable for more than a prescribed period.

The current prescribed sum is £350 and the prescribed period is three years (Rights of Re-entry and Forfeiture (Prescribed Sum and Period) Regulations 2004, SI 2004/3086, WSI 2005/1352).

A long lessee is not liable to pay rent unless the landlord has given notice in the pre- **11.71** scribed form demanding payment in accordance with s 166 of the CLRA 2002 and the Landlord and Tenant (Notice of Rent) Regulations 2004, SI 2004/3096, WSI 2005/1355. If the unpaid amount includes a default charge or penalty charge (ie a sum charged because of the tenant's failure to pay), this will not be included in calculating the unpaid amount (s 167(3)). A long lease of a dwelling does not include a business tenancy, agricultural holding, or farm business tenancy (s 167(4)).

F RELIEF FROM FORFEITURE

Relief from forfeiture for breaches of covenant other than non-payment of rent

Once the landlord has served a valid s 146 notice, avoided the potential pitfalls of the **11.72** doctrine of waiver, and successfully elected to forfeit, there still remains one last barrier between the tenant and forfeiture: the tenant can apply to the court for relief.

11.73 The LPA 1925, s 146(2) states:

> Where a lessor is proceeding, by action or otherwise, to enforce such a right of re-entry or
> forfeiture, the lessee may, in the lessor's action, if any, or in any action brought by himself,
> apply to the court for relief; and the court may grant or refuse relief, as the court, having regard
> to the proceedings and conduct of the parties under the foregoing provisions of this section,
> and to all the other circumstances, thinks fit; and in case of relief may grant it on such terms, if
> any, as to costs, expenses, damages, compensation, penalty, or otherwise, including the granting
> of an injunction to restrain any like breach in the future, as the court, in the circumstances of
> each case, thinks fit.

11.74 Generally the tenant's application will be made by counterclaiming in the landlord's forfeiture proceedings, but the tenant can also issue his or her own proceedings claiming relief
if he or she so wishes. If the landlord has not issued forfeiture proceedings and is seeking
instead to forfeit the tenancy by peaceable re-entry then the tenant will have to issue his or
her own proceedings to bring the matter before the court.

When can the tenant apply for relief?

11.75 A tenant can apply for relief at any time when the landlord 'is proceeding, by action or
otherwise' to enforce a right of re-entry or forfeiture. When the landlord seeks to enforce
his or her rights by taking court proceedings the tenant may therefore apply for relief from
the moment the landlord serves a s 146(1) notice (*Packwood Transport Ltd v Beauchamp
Place Limited* [1977] 3 P&CR 112). The tenant's right to apply for relief will continue
until the landlord, pursuant to the court's judgment, repossesses the premises (*Billson v
Residential Apartments Ltd* [1992] 1 All ER 141). Up until this point the landlord can be
said to be 'proceeding' within the meaning of s 146(2).

11.76 Where a landlord elects to proceed by peaceable re-entry the courts have chosen to adopt
a broad interpretation of the meaning of 'proceeding'. The tenant's right to apply for relief
does not end when the landlord re-enters the premises, for otherwise the tenant may be
deprived of the right to apply for relief at all. However, the tenant's right to apply for relief
does not continue indefinitely. The application must be made within a reasonable time
and in considering the application the courts will consider the circumstances of the case,
including whether the tenant has delayed in making the application (*Billson v Residential
Apartments Ltd*, 11.75).

Procedure for tenant's application

11.77 A tenant can apply for relief either by bringing a counterclaim or Part 20 claim within the
landlord's action; or by commencing his or her own claim under Part 7 or Part 8 of the
CPR. If the landlord is no longer 'proceeding' within the meaning of s 146(2) and the right
to apply for relief has been lost (see 11.75), the tenant's only available remedy is to apply
to have the judgment set aside (*Rexhaven v Nurse* (1996) 28 HLR 241).

When will the court grant relief?

11.78 The LPA 1925, s 146(2) gives the court a very wide discretion to grant relief. Relief may be
granted subject to terms as to costs, expenses, damages, and compensation. The court can
also grant an injunction to prevent a future breach of obligation.

11.79 When it comes to deciding whether or not to grant relief, each case will turn on its own
facts. The courts have generally been reluctant to set out anything more than very broad,
general principles. The courts will take into account all the circumstances of the case,
which will include:

(a) the nature of the breach;

(b) the seriousness of the breach;

(c) the conduct of the parties;

(d) the value of the property and the extent of the damage caused by the breach;

(e) the losses that will be suffered by the tenant if relief is not granted.

It should always be remembered that the purpose of a forfeiture clause is to act as security **11.80** for the landlord in the event of a tenant breaching an obligation in the lease. If compliance with the terms of the lease can be achieved without having to resort to forfeiture, the courts will be likely to grant relief.

Breaches of positive covenants are generally regarded as being remediable (*Expert* **11.81** *Clothing v Hillgate House* [1986] Ch 340, see 11.49). Thus, if a tenant is willing and able to remedy the breach within a reasonable time (the court may well impose a time limit), relief will almost certainly be granted. For example, if Jean sought to forfeit Steven's lease for a breach of the covenant to redecorate the interior, it is probable that Steven would be granted relief provided he undertook to perform the required work within, say, two weeks.

Where a breach is irremediable (see 11.47 to 11.54) the courts are less likely to grant **11.82** relief. In cases where the tenant has breached a covenant against immoral user and caused a stigma to become attached to the premises it is less likely that relief will be granted. However, this is not a hard-and-fast rule: the court will look at all of the circumstances, including the area in which the property is situated and the conduct of the parties both before and after the s 146 notice is served, and has a relatively unfettered discretion as to whether to grant relief (*Patel v K & J Restaurants Ltd* [2010] EWCA Civ 1211). If the damage is slight and the refusal of relief would cause a disproportionate loss to the tenant, relief may be granted. In *Ropemaker Properties Ltd v Noonhaven* [1989] 2 EGLR 50, the judge took into account a variety of factors, including the fact that forfeiture would result in substantial financial loss to the defendants, the fact that the immoral use had already been ended, and the fact that any stigma was likely to be short-lived. Relief was granted on condition that the defendants permitted the inclusion of a term in the lease which excluded 'hostesses' from the premises.

With regard to a breach of covenant not to assign or sub-let, the courts may grant relief. **11.83** If the sub-letting or assignment was one to which the landlord would not have been able reasonably to withhold consent had the tenant asked for such consent, it will be more likely that relief will be granted; likewise if the sub-letting was unintentional and has caused no damage to the lessor (*Scala House Ltd v Forbes* [1974] 1 QB 575, CA). If the sub-letting or assignment results in the sub-tenant or assignee acquiring statutory protection that the original tenant would not have had, relief is likely to be refused (*Leeward Securities v Lilyheath* (1983) 17 HLR 35, CA). In our example Steven would probably have a reasonable chance of being granted relief. The fact that the lease granted to Edward was only for three months would mean that the situation could be remedied reasonably rapidly, and in any case the sub-lease caused Jean no real damage.

The conduct of the landlord is also a factor to be taken into account (*Segal Securities v* **11.84** *Thoseby* [1963] 1 All ER 500). If the court felt that Jean was seeking forfeiture primarily in order to be able to gain vacant possession so that she could take advantage of the local property developer's offer, it would be likely to grant Steven relief.

Where the tenant's breach is wilful and deliberate it is also less likely that the court will **11.85** grant relief, although if the breach itself is trivial relief will probably be granted. Clearly, great injustice would result if a landlord was able to forfeit a lease for any minor breach of covenant. Long leases commonly contain many detailed but often minor covenants (see the example at 4.05). It would be absurd if the law permitted the freeholder to forfeit a

99-year lease because the tenant kept a goldfish, failed to clean the windows, or played a stereo after 11 pm.

Protection of sub-lessees

11.86 At common law the rule is that if a lease is successfully forfeited by the landlord any sub-tenancy is also destroyed. This leaves any sub-tenants in a particularly vulnerable position.

11.87 Sub-tenants are entitled to apply for relief under s 146(4) of the LPA 1925. The right of a sub-tenant to apply under this section is in fact broader than the right given to a tenant, for s 146(4) gives the right to apply when the landlord is seeking to enforce a right of forfeiture under *any* covenant in the lease, including non-payment of rent. A sub-tenant will also be able to apply in situations where a tenant may not be able to apply, for example where the tenant is bankrupt.

11.88 As with tenants, the court has a broad discretion to grant relief. The aim will be to put the landlord back in the position he or she would have been in prior to forfeiture. The means by which this is done is by use of a vesting order. The effect of a vesting order is not, as would be the case if the tenant was granted relief, to continue the original tenancy, but to create a new tenancy which makes the old sub-tenant the tenant of the landlord; the original tenant against whom forfeiture proceedings have successfully been taken drops out of the picture. However, the effect of a vesting order is to compel a landlord to enter into a landlord and tenant relationship with a person he or she has had no control over choosing and so the court's jurisdiction to grant relief should be used sparingly (*Fivecourts v JR Leisure Developments* (2001) 81 P&CR 292; *Ropac v Inntrepreneur* [2001] L&TR 10).

11.89 The new tenancy will not be for a term exceeding that of the old sub-tenancy and the length of the term granted is generally at the discretion of the court. Section 146(4) does not contain any guidelines as to the level of rent payable under the new tenancy, but the court does have power to vary the rent if it thinks it appropriate (*Ewart v Fryer* [1901] 1 Ch 499). The court can also impose any conditions it thinks fit upon the new tenant (see *Chatham Empire Theatre (1955) Ltd v Ultrans* [1961] 1 WLR 817 at 820). Relief may be granted in respect of part of the premises.

Protection of mortgagees

11.90 If the tenant has taken out a mortgage on his or her lease, and that lease subsequently is forfeited by the landlord, the mortgage will be destroyed. A mortgagee therefore is able to apply for relief under the LPA 1925, s 146(4) in the same way as a sub-tenant.

Relief from forfeiture for non-payment of rent

11.91 Two different sets of rules govern the operation of relief from forfeiture for non-payment of rent, depending upon whether the proceedings are being taken in the county court or in the High Court. In general, proceedings will be taken in the county court under s 138 of the County Courts Act 1984. The county court has unlimited jurisdiction regardless of the amount of rent arrears or the value of the premises (High Court and County Court Jurisdiction Order 1991, SI 1991/724, art 2(1)). The CPR r 55.3 and Practice Direction 55.3 provide that claims should only be brought in the High Court in exceptional circumstances.

In the county court

Section 138 of the County Courts Act 1984 gives the tenant three opportunities of relief **11.92** from forfeiture:

(a) Relief before the hearing. Under s 138(2), if the tenant pays into court or to the lessor all the rent in arrears and the costs of the action five clear days before the date of the hearing, the action will automatically cease and the tenancy will continue as it was.

(b) Relief after the hearing. If the tenant fails to pre-empt the hearing under s 138(2) and at the trial the court is satisfied that the landlord has grounds to enforce forfeiture, the court will order possession. The order for possession must be suspended for a period of at least four weeks, however (s 138(3)). If the tenant pays all the arrears and costs within the specified period then the tenant will automatically gain relief and the tenancy will continue as it was. The court may, at its discretion, extend the period of suspension at any time before possession is actually recovered by the landlord (s 138(4)). The court may also adjourn the hearing to enable enquiries to be made into the tenant's ability to pay, but unless the landlord consents there should not be more than two such adjournments (see *R v A Circuit Judge, ex parte Wathen* (1976) 33 P&CR 423).

(c) Relief after possession. Once the court has made an order for possession and the landlord has actually recovered possession, the tenant may still apply to the court for relief at any time within six months of the landlord recovering possession (s 138(9A)). The court will grant such relief as it thinks fit, subject to such terms and conditions as it thinks fit. If the landlord has sought to forfeit by peaceable re-entry, the tenant can apply for relief under s 139(2) at any time within six months from the date upon which the landlord re-entered. The court has a discretion to grant the tenant such relief as the High Court could have granted.

Summary

(a) Arrears paid five days before hearing—automatic relief.   **11.93**

(b) Arrears paid within four weeks (or other period specified by the court) of hearing— automatic relief.

(c) Application within six months of the landlord recovering possession—relief at the discretion of the court.

Protection for sub-lessees and mortgagees

Sub-lessees and mortgagees can apply under the LPA 1925, s 146(4) when the landlord is **11.94** seeking to forfeit both for a breach of covenant and for non-payment of rent (see above). Difficulties may arise where a mortgagee or sub-tenant finds out about the forfeiture proceedings only after an order for possession has been made. In such a case the landlord is no longer 'proceeding' within the meaning of s 146(4) and the third party will not be able to apply for relief. Similarly, s 38 of the Senior Courts Act 1981 does not give the court jurisdiction to grant relief to third parties when the landlord seeks to forfeit by peaceable re-entry.

In exceptional cases the court may grant relief by exercising its general equitable jurisdic- **11.95** tion (*Abbey National Building Society v Maybeech Ltd* [1984] 3 All ER 262; *Ladup Ltd v Williams and Glyn's Bank Plc* [1985] 1 WLR 851).

In the High Court

Under the Common Law Procedure Act 1852, special procedures apply if the tenant has **11.96** more than six months' rent arrears. We saw earlier that by s 210 of the Act the landlord does not need to give formal notice if six months' rent is outstanding. However, if an order for possession is made in such a case it will be stayed for six months to give the tenant time to apply for relief. By s 212, the tenant will be automatically entitled to relief if he or she pays off all the arrears and costs before the hearing.

11.97   If the tenant falls outside the operation of ss 210 and 212 of the 1852 Act, because there are less than six months' arrears or because the landlord has not begun an action by writ but has peaceably re-entered, the tenant can apply for relief under s 38 of the Senior Courts Act 1981 (formerly the Judicature Act 1925, s 46). The court's power to grant relief is governed by the old principles of equity, and if the tenant pays off all the arrears and costs before judgment is given, relief will almost invariably be granted. The fact that a tenant may have a bad past record of payment will be irrelevant to the question as to whether discretion should be exercised in the tenant's favour. Relief will even be granted after the landlord has re-entered provided the tenant applies within six months and it is equitable to grant such relief. Relief will be refused only in exceptional cases where it would be inequitable to grant it, for example where the landlord had, after judgment for possession, reasonably let the premises to a new tenant.

KEY DOCUMENTS

Law of Property Act 1925

County Courts Act 1984

Housing Act 1996

Commonhold and Leasehold Reform Act 2002

Civil Procedure Rules 1998

Form N5—Claims for possession of property

Form N5A—Relief against forfeiture

Form N11R—Defence form (rented residential premises)

N211—Part 20 claim form

N211A—Part 20 claim (notes for claimant)

N211C—Part 20 claim (notes for defendant)

Printed copies of all legislation can be ordered from The Stationery Office at <http://www.tsoshop.co.uk>. All legislation from 1988 onwards and most pre-1988 primary legislation is available online at <http://www. legislation.gov.uk>.

The Civil Procedure Rules are available online from <http://www.justice.gov.uk/courts/procedure-rules>.

Court forms are available online from the HM Courts and Tribunals Service at <http://www.justice.gov.uk/forms/hmcts>.

PART II
THE STATUTORY CODES

12

INTRODUCTION TO THE STATUTORY CODES

A INTRODUCTION

In the second half of this book we shall be considering the statutory codes which, on top of **12.01** the common law principles already covered, serve to regulate the relationship of landlord and tenant. Broadly speaking, all of these statutory codes function in roughly the same way—by restricting a landlord's common law right to terminate a tenancy. However, the means by and the extent to which they do this varies from statute to statute: some simply give a tenant the right to renew his or her tenancy when it expires; whereas others provide a tenant with a security of tenure so comprehensive that in the absence of a flagrant breach of covenant it can be virtually impossible for a landlord to regain possession. Some of the statutory codes even interfere with a landlord's rights to restrict the amount of rent he or she is able to charge.

Which code applies to a particular tenancy in question will depend upon a variety of fac- **12.02** tors: the purpose of the letting (business, agricultural, or residential use?); the length of the lease (is it a long lease at a low rent, a short fixed-term, or a periodic tenancy?); the nature of the landlord (public or private?); and the date upon which it was granted.

B FACTORS TO BE CONSIDERED

Is there a tenancy?

The first question to ask when confronted with a potential landlord and tenant problem **12.03** is whether there is a tenancy at all (see Chapter 2). The vast majority of the statutory provisions we are about to consider will apply only to tenancies, though there are a few exceptions: a licensee of a public sector landlord may be a 'secure licensee' and acquire protection equivalent to a secure tenant under the Housing Act 1985 (see 17.15 to 17.18); under the Rent Act 1977 a lodger or licensee may possibly have acquired limited protection under a 'restricted contract' (see 13.159 to 13.166); and agricultural workers who are licensees may be protected by the Rent (Agriculture) Act 1976 (see 29.05 to 29.20) or as assured agricultural occupiers under the Housing Act 1988 (see 29.21 to 29.32).

Business, agricultural, or residential use?

The second thing to consider is whether the premises are occupied for the purpose of a **12.04** business. If this is the case the tenancy will fall under Part II of the Landlord and Tenant

Act 1954 (see Chapter 26) and will consequently be excluded from claiming security under any of the codes applying to residential tenancies. Furthermore, all the residential statutory codes require the premises in question to be 'a dwelling-house', thereby excluding many commercial properties. Similarly, most of the residential codes require that the tenant be 'an individual', which prevents companies or other artificial persons from claiming protection. If the land that is the subject of the tenancy is agricultural land that is farmed for the purposes of a trade or business, it will not fall under Part II of the Landlord and Tenant Act 1954 but will be governed by one of the two codes that apply to agricultural tenancies. If the tenancy was granted on or after 1 September 1995 it will be a farm business tenancy under the Agricultural Tenancies Act 1995 (see Chapter 28). If it was granted before that date it will be an agricultural holding under the Agricultural Holdings Act 1986 (see Chapter 27).

Is it a long lease at a low rent?

12.05   If the tenancy in question is a residential long lease which was granted on the payment of a lump sum, and the tenant pays only a minimal 'ground rent' throughout the course of the term, then it will be excluded from the operation of the three main codes which apply to residential tenancies (the Housing Act 1985, the Rent Act 1977, and the Housing Act 1988). Instead, certain protection is available for the long leaseholder at the end of the term under Part I of the Landlord and Tenant Act 1954 or under Sch 10 to the Local Government and Housing Act 1989 (see Chapter 22).

Is the landlord public or private?

12.06   With regard to residential tenancies, the statutory code that applies will depend to a large extent upon the nature of the landlord. If the landlord is a local authority or other public body the tenancy will be a 'secure tenancy' under Part IV of the Housing Act 1985 (see Chapters 17 and 18). If the landlord is a private individual or other private sector landlord the tenancy will fall under Part I of the Housing Act 1988 or the Rent Act 1977. Unfortunately, however, the distinction between public sector and private sector landlords is not always clear-cut. Certain quasi-public bodies which were formerly regarded as belonging to the public sector are now considered to be part of the private sector, in particular registered social landlords (known as housing associations prior to the Housing Act 1996). Therefore, which code a particular tenant falls under may vary depending upon the date of the grant of the tenancy (see 17.10). If the tenancy was granted by a housing association (now registered social landlord) prior to 15 January 1989 it will be a secure tenancy under the Housing Act 1985. If it was granted after that date it will be an 'assured tenancy' under the Housing Act 1988 (subject to certain transitional provisions).

When was the tenancy granted?

12.07   The date of the grant of the tenancy is of particular importance in the private rented sector. Statutory protection for tenants of private landlords has a long history stretching back to the First World War and culminating in the Rent Act 1977 which consolidated the preceding legislation. For the next 12 years the Rent Act remained dominant, providing private sector tenants with both rent control and a high degree of security, until increasing governmental dissatisfaction with a regime that was regarded as being too 'tenant friendly' brought about the introduction of the Housing Act 1988. The 1988 Act removed the system of rent control and reduced the tenant's security of tenure. It also introduced a means by which landlords, if they so chose, could rent property on short fixed-term tenancies with only minimal security. This system of shorthold lettings was then extended further by the Housing Act 1996, to the extent that now, in the absence of any contrary agreement, a shorthold tenancy will be what a tenant acquires when he or she enters into a tenancy agreement with a private landlord.

A brief example can illustrate this legislative trend. Consider two identical periodic tenancies, both granted by private landlords and created using simple, standard-form tenancy agreements. The only difference between them is the date of the grant. The first tenancy was granted on 1 January 1989; the second was granted on 1 January 1998. The first tenant will acquire a protected tenancy with all its associated rights to security of tenure and rent control. Provided the tenant abides by the terms of the agreement, he or she will have a tenancy for life (and even beyond if he or she has a spouse or family member eligible to succeed to the tenancy). The second tenant will acquire only an assured shorthold tenancy; there is only minimal rent control, security of tenure is limited to the duration of the term (which may be as short as six months), and once the term has expired the landlord can regain possession by giving two months' notice. **12.08**

Therefore, when considering private sector residential tenancies, there are two dates that need continually to be borne in mind. The first of these dates is 15 January 1989. This is the date on which the Housing Act 1988 came into force. Broadly speaking, any tenancy granted before this date will fall under the Rent Act 1977 (see Chapters 13 and 14), while those granted after that date will fall under the Housing Act 1988 (see Chapters 15 and 16). However, the nature of the transitional provisions, the fact that there are rights of succession and the fact that security under the 1977 Act is so comprehensive mean that though the Rent Act 1977 is of dwindling importance there are still a considerable number of Rent Act tenancies in existence. Furthermore, the Rent Act 1977 is, in a sense, the direct ancestor of the more recent statutes; much of the terminology used in the subsequent statutes is taken from its provisions. **12.09**

The second important date is 28 February 1997. This is the date on which the Housing Act 1996 came into force. After this date the vast majority of tenancies granted will automatically be 'assured shorthold tenancies' (see 15.119 to 15.132) and will benefit from only minimal security of tenure. In practical terms this is an extremely significant amendment to the Housing Act 1988. Prior to this date, if a private sector landlord wanted to ensure that his or her tenant did not acquire significant security of tenure the onus was on the landlord to serve notice on the tenant stating that the tenancy was to be an assured shorthold tenancy. After 28 February 1997 a tenant will acquire significant security of tenure only if the landlord actively chooses to confer such security upon the tenant. **12.10**

C OTHER STATUTORY PROVISIONS

Part II of this book will also consider a number of other statutory provisions which endow certain tenants with rights that they would not have had under the common law. In particular we shall be looking at the right of long leaseholders to enfranchise or extend their leases under the Leasehold Reform Act 1967, Part I of the Landlord and Tenant Act 1987, and Part I of the Leasehold Reform, Housing and Urban Development Act 1993 (Chapter 24); the provisions of the Commonhold and Leasehold Reform Act 2002 (Chapter 25); the right to buy of secure tenants under Part V of the Housing Act 1985; the rights of long leaseholders with regard to service charges and management (Chapter 23); the right to compensation for improvements for business tenants under Part I of the Landlord and Tenant Act 1927 (see 26.205 to 26.226); and the right to compensation for agricultural tenants under the Agricultural Holdings Act 1986 (see 27.101 to 27.121) and Agricultural Tenancies Act 1995 (see 28.43 to 28.54). **12.11**

D WHICH STATUTORY CODE?

12.12 Figure 12.1 briefly illustrates under which statutory code a particular tenancy will fall. It is, of course, only an outline and in each case proper reference should be made to the statutory definitions and any relevant transitional provisions.

Figure 12.1 Outline of statutory codes

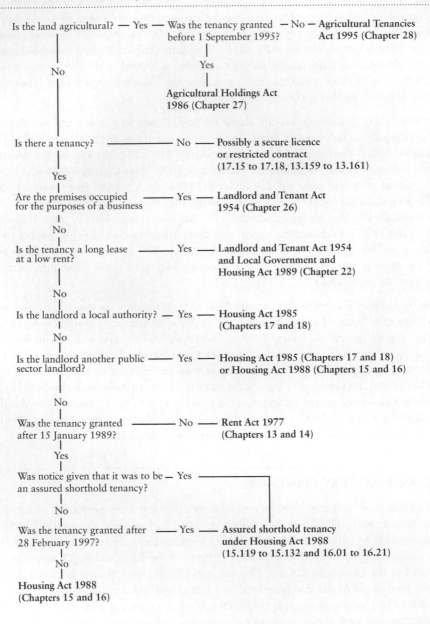

13

THE RENT ACT 1977–
1. PROTECTED TENANCIES

A INTRODUCTION

The Rent Act 1977 is the first of the two comprehensive statutory codes which apply to **13.01**
rented residential accommodation in the private sector. In this and the following chapter
we shall be dealing with the provisions of the Rent Act 1977. The second code, the Housing
Act 1988, will be dealt with in Chapters 15 and 16.

The first question to ask, when confronted with any residential private sector landlord **13.02**
and tenant problem, is which of these two codes applies to the tenancy in question. The
general rule is that any residential tenancy granted on or after 15 January 1989 will fall
under the Housing Act 1988 (15 January 1989 being the date on which the 1988 Act came
into force). Consequently, the Rent Act 1977 will generally only apply to tenancies created
before 15 January 1989.

13.03   Section 34 of the Housing Act 1988, however, contains a number of transitional rules which permit, in certain circumstances, the creation of a protected tenancy after 15 January 1989. A tenancy granted after 15 January 1989 may be a protected tenancy:

(a)   If it is entered into in pursuance of a contract made before 15 January 1989 (s 34(1)(a)).

(b)   If it is granted to a person who, immediately before the tenancy is granted, was a protected or statutory tenant (for the nature of protected and statutory tenants, see below and 13.92). The tenancy must be granted by the same landlord. If under the previous tenancy there were joint landlords it is sufficient if only one of the joint landlords was the tenant's landlord. Similarly, if there were joint tenants it is sufficient if only one of them was a protected or statutory tenant. It should be noted that this exception will apply even if the tenant or tenants are granted a tenancy of different premises (s 34(1)(b)).

(c)   Where, before the grant of the tenancy, an order for possession was made against the tenant on the ground of suitable alternative accommodation and the court has directed that the grant of an assured tenancy would not afford the required security (see 14.13) (s 34(1)(c)).

The words 'immediately before' in (b) mean that there should have been no break at all between the tenancies. The new tenancy must come into effect on the expiry of the old tenancy (see *Truro Diocesan Board of Finance Ltd v Foley* [2008] EWCA Civ 1162 in which the Court of Appeal also rejected the tenant's argument that the new tenancy had been granted at the time it was agreed upon, which was before the expiry of the old tenancy by surrender).

B   WHAT IS A PROTECTED TENANCY?

13.04   Subject to this Part of the Act, a tenancy under which a dwelling-house (which may be a house or part of a house) is let as a separate dwelling is a protected tenancy for the purposes of this Act (Rent Act 1977, s 1). This seemingly straightforward definition is deceptive. Virtually every word demands close scrutiny. Furthermore, the apparent breadth of the definition is subject to a considerable number of exceptions which are contained in the subsequent provisions of the Act.

'a tenancy'

13.05   Only a tenancy can attract full Rent Act protection. The tenancy may be periodic or fixed-term, it may be legal or equitable, and it may be granted by the freeholder or be a sub-tenancy. Both a tenant at will and a tenant at sufferance will fall within the Rent Act (*Chamberlain v Farr* [1942] 2 All ER 567, CA; *Artizans, Labourers and General Dwellings Co. v Witaker* [1919] 2 KB 301; for the definition of a tenancy at will and a tenancy at sufferance, see 3.28 to 3.31).

13.06   Any form of occupation that falls short of being a tenancy cannot be a protected tenancy. A licence therefore cannot attract full Rent Act protection. The difference between a tenancy and a licence, and the ways in which landlords have sought to circumvent the Rent Act by granting rights of occupation purporting to be licences rather than tenancies, has already been discussed at length in Chapter 2.

13.07   Certain occupiers who hold their property under a licence, or who have a tenancy but fall within one of the classes excluded from full Rent Act protection (eg because they are the tenants of a resident landlord), may enjoy a limited level of protection under the Rent Act. Such occupiers hold their premises under what is known as a 'restricted contract' and will be considered in detail in a later section (13.159 to 13.166).

'a dwelling-house'

There is no statutory definition of what constitutes 'a dwelling-house'. In each case it is a **13.08** question of fact whether the premises in question fall within s 1 of the Rent Act 1977. The courts have adopted a flexible approach, the key question being whether the premises in question are the 'home' of any person, a home being a place where a person 'moves and has his being', where he or she carries out the basic activities of living such as sleeping, eating, and cooking (see *Curl v Angelo* [1948] 2 All ER 189 *per* Lord Greene MR at 190). Thus, 'a dwelling-house' does not need to be a house at all; it can be a self-contained flat, a single bed-sittingroom, and in certain circumstances a hotel room (*Uratemp Ventures v Collins* [2001] 3 WLR 806, HL), or even a caravan (*Makins v Elson* [1977] 1 WLR 221) or houseboat provided the structure has been rendered immobile and is used as a permanent home (*R v Rent Officer of Nottingham Registration Area, ex parte Allen* [1985] 2 EGLR 153; and contrast *Chelsea Boat & Harbour Ltd v Pope* [2000] 1 WLR 1941, CA). It is even possible for two non-adjacent flats in the same block to be a dwelling-house if they are let together under one agreement and are used by the occupants as a single home (*Langford Property Co. Ltd v Goldrich* [1949] 1 KB 511, [1949] All ER 402).

'let'

We saw in Chapter 1 (1.25) how the payment of rent is not an essential element of a ten- **13.09** ancy. However, for a dwelling-house to be 'let' within the meaning of s 1 of the Rent Act 1977, it is necessary that a quantifiable rent should be paid. An essential aspect of the Rent Act 1977 is to provide a mechanism for regulation and control of the rent payable by the tenant; if the rent payable is not quantifiable in money terms this aspect of the Act would be inoperable (*Barnes v Barratt* [1970] 2 QB 657 *per* Sachs LJ at 667E). Thus, where an occupier is given a tenancy in return for the performance of services, this tenancy will not attract Rent Act protection. A service occupier may be a protected tenant, however, if a quantifiable amount is deducted from his or her wages in respect of his or her accommodation (*Montague v Browning* [1951] 1 WLR 1039 at 1044).

'as a separate dwelling'

This phrase has come in for considerable judicial scrutiny. Discussion has centred round **13.10** three issues which we will consider in turn:

(a) The word 'as' indicates that it is the purpose of the demise that should be considered, not the actual use to which the demised premises are put.
(b) The use of the word 'a' indicates that the phrase must be given a singular construction.
(c) The difficulty of interpreting the phrase 'separate dwelling'.

The purpose of the letting

The fact that a building is a dwelling-house does not necessarily mean that that building will **13.11** always be used as a dwelling-house. The user of a building can change; a residential house may be converted into office space, a warehouse or barn might be converted into flats. We saw earlier that it will be a question of fact whether a building is a 'dwelling-house', the key question being whether the premises are used as a home by any person. Section 1, however, demands not only that the tenancy be of a dwelling-house, but also that the dwelling-house must be '*let as* a separate dwelling'.

13.12 **Example** Paul decides to set up a small language school. He rents a house on the high street from James, under a lease that specifies that the house is to be used for business purposes. The language school is not a success and Paul find himself in financial difficulties. He sells his own flat and moves into the house. When James tries to regain possession of the house, Paul claims he is a protected tenant.

13.13 The house is a dwelling-house in that it was originally constructed as a residential building; it is also a dwelling-house in the sense that Paul is currently using the house as his home. However, when the house was let to Paul it was not let to him as a dwelling but for business purposes. Paul's tenancy therefore cannot be a protected tenancy.

13.14 The logic behind such reasoning is clear: a tenant cannot bring the tenancy of a particular building within the protection of the Rent Act 1977 simply by using that building as his or her home. If that were the case, the tenant of a shop, an office block, or a lock-up garage would be able to become a protected tenant by moving in and living in the building. The word 'as' in s 1 indicates that it is the original purpose of the letting that is important, not the subsequent use to which the tenant puts the premises (see 26.39 to 26.40 for a further discussion on change of use).

13.15 Usually (as in the case of Paul) it will be possible to ascertain the purpose of the letting from the lease itself. Where this is not clear from the tenancy agreement, the courts will look to the surrounding circumstances and, if still unable to discern the purpose of the letting, to the actual user of the premises. (See *Wolfe v Hogan* [1949] 2 KB 194, [1949] 1 All ER 570; *British Land Co. Ltd v Herbert Silver (Menswear) Ltd* [1958] 1 QB 530, [1958] 1 All ER 833, CA.)

13.16 In some cases, even where the terms of the lease state that the premises are to be used as a separate dwelling, practical considerations may override the terms of the lease. This will occur if it is obvious that at the time of the letting the intention of the parties could not be to use the premises as a separate dwelling. We mentioned earlier how two flats could together constitute a 'dwelling-house' within the meaning of the Act. In *Grosvenor (Mayfair) Estates v Amberton* (1983) 265 EG 693, two flats were let together under one agreement but one of the flats was still occupied by three licensees. It was held that it could not have been the intention of the parties at the time of the letting that the tenants were to use both flats as a separate dwelling, even though in the future, when the licensees left, the tenants would acquire use of both flats. The court held that the two flats together could not constitute a protected tenancy.

The singular construction of 'a separate dwelling'

13.17 Considering that the object of the Rent Act 1977 is to protect the residential occupier, it may seem somewhat strange that s 1 does not require the tenant actually to reside in the demised premises. The Act requires the dwelling-house initially to be let as a separate dwelling, but there is nothing to prevent the tenant immediately sub-letting either part or the whole of that dwelling once the tenancy has commenced. However, if the tenant is not resident on the premises at the end of the contractual term, no statutory tenancy will arise and the protection of the Act will cease.

13.18 **Example 1** Henry is an entrepreneur. He rents a large Victorian house from Peter. Immediately after acquiring the lease he converts the house into four flats and sub-lets each of them. In order to maximize his profit he claims to have a protected tenancy and seeks to have his rent registered as a fair rent.

Example 2 Steven is also an entrepreneur. He too rents a large Victorian dwelling-house **13.19** from Peter, but this house has already been converted into four flats which Steven promptly sub-lets to individual tenants. Steven also seeks to have his rent registered.

A case similar to Steven's was considered by the Court of Appeal in *Horford Investments* **13.20** *Ltd v Lambert* [1976] Ch 39. The court held that the phrase 'let as a separate dwelling' should be given a singular construction. Steven has rented a number of separate dwellings, not a separate dwelling, and therefore he will not be a protected tenant. Certainly there is some logic in this, as the aim of the Rent Act 1977 is not to protect an entrepreneur with a primarily commercial interest in the property.

The same rules will also apply where the tenant is not seeking to maximize profits, but **13.21** rather to pass on the benefit of rent registration to his or her sub-tenants. In *St. Catherine's College v Dorling* [1980] 1 WLR 66, the college rented a large house which it then sub-let as individual bed-sits to students, each student paying a proportion of the rent to the college. The terms of the lease made it clear that the house was intended to be let for multiple occupation use and therefore the court held that it was not let as *a* separate dwelling. In certain cases, however, such tenancies may count as business tenancies within Pt II of the Landlord and Tenant Act 1954 (see 26.45 and *Groveside Properties Ltd v Westminster Medical School* (1983) 9 HLR 118).

In Henry's case, where the house had been rented as a single dwelling prior to its conver- **13.22** sion into separate flats, it seems possible, at least in principle, that Henry can be a Rent Act protected tenant. However, it should always be borne in mind that Henry's tenancy might fall within the definition of a 'business tenancy' as given by Pt II of the Landlord and Tenant Act 1954. If this is the case, the tenancy will be excluded from Rent Act protection by s 24(3) of the 1977 Act (see 26.09 to 26.49).

Defining a 'separate dwelling'

To be a separate dwelling the accommodation must be sufficient for the tenant to carry out **13.23** the major activities of life, namely sleeping, cooking, and eating (*Wright v Howell* (1947) 92 Sol Jo 26, CA). The premises do not have to be completely self-contained as long as the tenant has exclusive use of the rooms he can be said to occupy. Therefore, the fact that the tenant shares basic cooking facilities with tenants of other rooms may not take his accommodation out of the ambit of s 1, but the shared occupation of a kitchen as a living space would do so (*Marsh v Cooper* [1969] 1 WLR 803; *Uratemp Ventures v Collins* [2001] UKHL 43, [2001] 3 WLR 806). Sharing the use of a bathroom or lavatory will not prevent the accommodation from being let as a separate dwelling (*Cole v Harris* [1945] KB 474). If the person sharing occupation with the tenant is a resident landlord, however, the tenancy may be exempt from Rent Act protection (see 13.70).

Sharing living accommodation Where there is no resident landlord and a house is let for **13.24** multiple occupation, it is common for the tenants to share the use of certain living rooms other than just the kitchen or bathroom.

Example Sarah, Jane, and Robin, by separate agreements, rent separate rooms in a **13.25** house from Brenda. The agreements provide that they each have exclusive possession of a bedroom in the house, but share use of a kitchen, bathroom, and sitting room with the other two tenants. The bedrooms are numbered and have locks fitted to the individual doors.

13.26 Strictly speaking, none of the tenants in such a situation could be said to have rented 'a separate dwelling', for none of them has exclusive possession of all of the rooms he or she occupies as a living space. However, the requirements of s 1 of the Rent Act 1977 are modified by s 22. Section 22 provides that where the tenant has exclusive occupation of *some* accommodation and shares other accommodation with persons other than the landlord, the tenant can have a protected tenancy of the separate accommodation (ie the accommodation of which the tenant has exclusive possession). Thus, Sarah, Jane, and Robin can each acquire Rent Act protection for their individual rooms. Section 22(5) further provides that a landlord cannot obtain a possession order for the shared accommodation unless an order is also made for the separate accommodation.

13.27 If the arrangement between the sharers is such that no individual can claim exclusive possession of any part of the shared premises then none of them will be able to claim protection. One possible exception to this will be where a number of people share a house as joint tenants (see 2.48), in which case, because joint tenants count as one person in law, they will be able to claim that together they have let the property as a separate dwelling. Surprisingly, however, the Rent Act 1977 makes no mention of joint tenancies.

13.28 **Sharing with a sub-tenant** If the tenant grants a sub-tenancy in respect of part of the dwelling-house, and therefore shares the property with the sub-tenant, this will not enable the landlord to claim that the tenant no longer has exclusive occupation of the property (Rent Act 1977, s 23).

13.29 Each case will turn upon its own facts and it is difficult to lay down any hard-and-fast principles. Where there is an argument as to whether any sharing arrangement would exclude the tenancy from protection, the burden is on the tenant to show that the arrangement does not prevent the tenant from having exclusive occupation (*Hall v Haskins* (1949) 153 EG 285). The living situation will be considered as at the date it was raised as an issue. This will usually be the date of the commencement of proceedings (*Baker v Turner* [1950] AC 401).

13.30 **Occupation of two premises** As we saw earlier, there is no reason why a tenant should not have a protected tenancy of two flats if, on the facts of the case, both flats together are used as the tenant's home and are treated as one living unit (*Langford Property Co. Ltd v Goldrich* [1949] 1 KB 511). However, if the tenant splits his or her living activities between the two properties, for example by sleeping in one and cooking and eating in the other, it is likely that neither property will be protected (see *Wimbush v Cibulia, Wimbush v Levinski* [1949] 2 KB 564, [1949] 2 All ER 432). *In Hampstead Way Investments v Lewis-Weare* [1985] 1 All ER 564, the tenant, who managed a night club and worked till 4.00 am, slept at one flat five nights a week but ate and performed all his other living activities at a house where his wife and step-daughter lived, which was about half a mile away. He was held not to have a protected tenancy of the flat.

C STATUTORY EXCLUSIONS FROM THE RENT ACT

Dwelling-houses with a high rateable value

13.31 The aim of the Rent Acts has always been to provide protection for the less privileged tenant, not for the wealthy tenant of luxury accommodation. The 1977 Act therefore provides a mechanism by which dwelling-houses with a high rateable value are excluded from protection. Section 4(1) provides that a tenancy cannot be a protected tenancy if it falls within one of the three classes set out in s 4(2). Each of these classes sets out the maximum rateable value limits on certain days. To determine whether the property in question exceeds any of these limits, it is first necessary to ascertain into which of the three classes the property falls. This is done by determining what the 'appropriate day' is for the property.

The appropriate day

If the rateable value of the dwelling-house was shown already in the valuation list on 23 **13.32** March 1965 then 23 March 1965 is the appropriate day. If the rateable value was not shown in the valuation list on 23 March 1965 then the appropriate day will be the date on which the dwelling-house first appears in the valuation list. The significance of 23 March 1965 is that this was the date on which the Rent Bill 1965 was first introduced in the House of Commons.

The rateable value limits if the tenancy was entered into before 1 April 1990 Once the **13.33** appropriate day has been determined, it is then necessary to see into which class the dwelling-house falls and to see whether, on each day specified, the rateable value was exceeded.

Class A The dwelling-house will fall into this class if the appropriate day is on or after **13.34** 1 April 1973. (This was the date on which a new valuation list came into effect.) The dwelling-house will be excluded from the Rent Act if, on the appropriate day, the rateable value exceeded £1,500 if it is in Greater London, or £750 if it is situated elsewhere.

Class B The dwelling-house will fall into this class if the appropriate day is on or after 22 **13.35** March 1973 but before 1 April 1973. (On 22 March 1973 the Counter-Inflation Act 1973 was passed, increasing the limits so as to take inflation into account.)

The dwelling-house will be excluded from the Rent Act if: **13.36**

(a) on the appropriate day the rateable value exceeded £600 in Greater London, or £300 if elsewhere; and
(b) on 1 April 1973 the rateable value exceeded £1,500 in Greater London, or £750 elsewhere.

Class C The dwelling-house will fall into this class if the appropriate day is before 22 **13.37** March 1973.

The dwelling-house will be excluded from the Rent Act if: **13.38**

(a) on the appropriate day the rateable value exceeded £400 in Greater London, or £200 elsewhere; and
(b) on 22 March 1973 the rateable value exceeded £600 in Greater London, or £300 elsewhere; and
(c) on 1 April 1973 the rateable value exceeded £1,500 in Greater London, or £750 elsewhere.

Rent limits for tenancies entered into on or after 1 April 1990 After 1 April 1990, no new **13.39** rateable values could be listed for domestic property. If the tenancy was entered into on or after 1 April 1990 (except where the tenancy was entered into in pursuance of a contract made before 1 April 1990 and had a rateable value on 31 March 1990), it cannot be a protected tenancy if the rent payable exceeds an amount initially set at £25,000 per year.

Example 1 John is granted a tenancy of a Georgian house in Islington in 1984. He wants **13.40** to know if he will be a protected tenant. The flat's rateable value according to the valuation list on 23 March 1965 was £500, on 22 March 1973 it was £900, and on 1 April 1973 it was £1,000.

13.41   John's house appeared on the valuation list at 23 March 1965, so that date is the appropriate day. The house therefore falls into class C. It is situated in Greater London so the higher limits apply. On 23 March 1965 and 22 March 1973, the rateable value was in excess of the pre-scribed limits, but on 1 April 1973 it was within the limit. John's house will therefore qualify for Rent Act protection provided John can satisfy the other requirements of eligibility.

13.42   **Example 2** Sarah is likewise granted a tenancy in 1984. Sarah's tenancy is of a new flat in Brighton. The flat was built in 1971 and first appears on the valuation list on 22 March 1973. The valuation list gives the rateable value as £400 at this date, and on 1 April 1973 it is given as £900.

13.43   For this flat the appropriate date is 22 March 1973, because this was when the flat first appeared in the valuation list. The flat falls within class B. The rateable value exceeds the prescribed limits both on 22 March 1973 and on 1 April 1973. Sarah's flat is therefore excluded from Rent Act protection. If the flat had been in London it would have been within the limits.

Apportionment

13.44   If the dwelling-house forms only part of the property that features in the valuation list, the rateable value of that property should be apportioned as appropriate. Similarly, if the dwelling-house is made up of two properties with separate rateable values then these rate-able values should be aggregated (Rent Act 1977, s 25(1)(b)).

Tenancies at a low rent

13.45   At first sight it may seem strange that tenancies at a low rent should be excluded from the protection of a statute designed to protect the less advantaged tenant. The purpose of this provision, however, is not to exclude those periodic tenants paying a very low rent, although it will function to do so, but to exclude long leaseholders who pay a nominal ground rent to their freeholder. The Rent Act 1977, s 5(1) provides that:

> A tenancy which was entered into before 1st April 1990 or (where the dwelling-house under the tenancy had a rateable value on 31st March 1990) is entered into on or after 1st April 1990 in pursuance of a contract made before that date, is not a protected tenancy if under the tenancy either no rent is payable or, the rent payable is less than two-thirds of the rateable value which is or was the rateable value of the dwelling-house on the appropriate day.

13.46   The appropriate day will be determined as described at 13.32 to 13.43, with the excep-tion that for properties rated on or before 22 March 1973 which have a rateable value of more than £400 in Greater London or £200 elsewhere, the appropriate day will be taken as 22 March 1973 (s 5(2)). In the case of long tenancies (those granted for a term of more than 21 years) a service charge is not to be included as part of the rent (s 5(4)).

13.47   If the tenancy was entered into on or after 1 April 1990 (except where the tenancy was entered into in pursuance of a contract made before 1 April 1990 and the dwelling-house had a rateable value on 31 March 1990), the tenancy will not be a protected tenancy if either no rent is payable or the rent payable is less than £1,000 per annum in London or £250 per annum elsewhere (s 5(2A)).

Shared ownership leases

13.48   A shared ownership lease (see 15.20) does not qualify for Rent Act protection (Rent Act 1977, s 5A).

Dwelling-houses let with other land

The Rent Act 1977, s 6 provides: **13.49**

> Subject to section 26 of this Act, a tenancy is not a protected tenancy if the dwelling-house which is subject to the tenancy is let together with land other than the site of the dwelling-house.

Section 26 provides: **13.50**

> (1) For the purposes of this Act, any land or premises let together with a dwelling-house shall, unless it consists of agricultural land exceeding 2 acres in extent, be treated as part of the dwelling-house.

To determine whether the dwelling-house is let with other land within the meaning of s 6,   **13.51** the question to be asked is whether the land is an adjunct to the dwelling-house or whether the dwelling-house is an adjunct to the land (*Pender v Reid* 1948 SC 381). In *Pender v Reid*, a dwelling-house was let along with land used as a coal merchants. The house occupied only a quarter of the total site, and it was held that the dominant purpose of the letting was as a coal merchants. The house was therefore excluded from Rent Act protection. Likewise in *Reyereisel v Turnidge* [1952] 2 QB 29, a bungalow was let along with a camp-site. The court held that the camp-site formed the dominant purpose of the letting; the bungalow was an adjunct to the land and was therefore not protected. A house let with land used merely as a garden, even if the garden is larger than two acres, would fall within the Rent Act for the land would be an adjunct to the dwelling-house. Section 26 provides that if the land let with the house is used for agricultural purposes, the house can still fall within the Rent Act provided that the agricultural land does not exceed two acres. If the agricultural land forms an area greater than two acres, the dwelling-house cannot be protected.

Payments for board and attendance

Under the Rent Act 1977, s 7(1):   **13.52**

> A tenancy is not a protected tenancy if under the tenancy a dwelling-house is bona fide let at a rent which includes payments in respect of board or attendance.

A tenancy will fall within s 7(1) if board or attendance is provided under the terms of   **13.53** the tenancy. It is irrelevant that the tenant may not in fact take advantage of the services provided. If the tenant is entitled to board or attendance and the landlord is contractually obliged to provide it then the tenancy will be excluded from Rent Act protection. The provision of board or attendance must however be 'bona fide' and not a sham designed to evade the consequences of the Act.

'board'

There is no statutory definition of 'board' but its accepted meaning is the provision of   **13.54** one or more daily meals. Unlike the provisions with regard to attendance, the Rent Act 1977 does not require the amount of rent attributable to the provision of board to be a substantial part of the whole rent. In theory, at least, the provision of any amount of board should be sufficient to bring the tenancy within this exception, thus enabling a landlord to avoid the Rent Act protection by providing a tenant with only minimal board. The courts, however, have attempted to restrict such exploitation of s 7(1) by application of the *de minimis* rule. Supplying a morning cup of tea, for example, is not enough to count as board (*Wilkes v Goodwin* [1923] 2 KB 86, CA). The meals do not have to be cooked, however; it has been held that the provision of a continental breakfast in a communal dining room on the premises is sufficient to amount to board (*Otter v Norman* [1988]

2 All ER 897, HL). If board is provided, the tenancy will be completely excluded from Rent Act protection.

'attendance'

13.55 'Attendance' likewise has no statutory definition. In *Palser v Grinling* [1948] AC 291 *per* Viscount Simon at 310f, attendance was said to be 'service personal to the tenant performed by an attendant provided by the landlord ... for the benefit or convenience of the individual tenant in his use or enjoyment of the demised premises'. Examples of attendance would be the delivery of coal and the removal of rubbish (*Palser v Grinling*), the delivery of letters and messages (*Wood v Carwardine* [1923] 2 KB 185), and cleaning the room and providing clean linen (*Marchant v Charters* [1977] 1 WLR 1181, [1977] 3 All ER 918, CA). If a landlord provides services to all the tenants of a block of flats, such as communal central heating, hot water, or cleaning of the common parts, these do not count as attendance for they are not services personal to the individual tenant. If an occupier is excluded from full Rent Act protection because attendance is provided, that occupier may still acquire limited protection under a restricted contract (see 13.159 to 13.166).

13.56 The Rent Act 1977, s 7(2) provides that:

> For the purposes of subsection (1) above, a dwelling-house shall not be taken to be bona fide let at a rent which includes payments in respect of attendance unless the amount of rent which is fairly attributable to attendance, having regard to the value of the attendance to the tenant, forms a substantial part of the whole rent.

13.57 In each case it will be a question of fact and degree whether the attendance provided is substantial in this sense. The court has a broad discretion. The judge should try to work out the cost to the landlord of providing the attendance, consider the value this attendance has for the tenant, and then compare the value of the attendance with the total rent. This can involve complex calculations, but whether or not the attendance is substantial should not be regarded as just a question of arithmetic (*Woodward v Docherty* [1974] 2 All ER 844). 'Substantial' should be given its everyday meaning, as when we speak of a 'substantial meal' or a 'substantial argument'; it cannot be put down to merely a question of percentages (*Palser v Grinling* at 317). For example, the provision of daily cleaning, laundry services, and the removal of rubbish has been held to amount to substantial attendance (*Nelson Developments Ltd v Taboda* (1992) 24 HLR 462). However, where the court ascertained the value of delivering coal and removing rubbish to be about £4 out of a total rent of £175, this was not regarded as substantial (*Palser v Grinling*).

Lettings to students

13.58 Under the Rent Act 1977, s 8(1):

> A tenancy is not a protected tenancy if it is granted to a person who is pursuing, or intends to pursue, a course of study provided by a specified educational institution and is so granted either by that institution or by another specified institution or body of persons.

13.59 A student is thus excluded from full Rent Act protection if his or her landlord is a specified educational institution. A specified educational institution is one specified by the Secretary of State by statutory instrument (s 8(2)) and includes universities and teacher training colleges.

13.60 The aim of this provision is to permit a college to retain control over the accommodation it provides for its students. If students were eligible for statutory protection, it would result in halls of residence soon becoming clogged with protected tenants (even after their courses had ended) and little space being available for new students. This provision only benefits an educational institution: a private landlord who rents directly to a student will not fall within s 8 and the student will acquire full Rent Act protection if the other conditions are satisfied.

A landlord may rent to an educational institution which may then sub-let to students. In **13.61** such a case neither the college nor the student sub-tenants will come within the Rent Act. The college will be excluded because it will not satisfy s 1, and the student will be excluded by s 8 because his or her direct landlord is an educational institution (see *St. Catherine's College v Dorling*, 13.21). (If a college rented a premises that came within the s 1 requirement of being 'a' separate dwelling, it might be eligible for protection. A student letting, however, may be a restricted contract if the premises are furnished or services are provided, but not if board is provided (see 13.159).) Certain bodies providing accommodation have been specified for exclusion by the Assured and Protected Tenancies (Lettings to Students) Regulations 1998, SI 1998/1967.

Holiday lettings

The Rent Act 1977, s 9 provides: **13.62**

> A tenancy is not a protected tenancy if the purpose of the tenancy is to confer on the tenant the right to occupy the dwelling-house for a holiday.

The policy of the Rent Act is to protect long-term residential property and not to endow **13.63** holiday-makers and tourists with extensive rights in respect of short-term accommodation. Section 9 was introduced by the Rent Act 1974. Before 1974, furnished lettings could be excluded from Rent Act protection. Because holiday lettings would invariably be furnished there was originally no need for a specific provision to exclude them from the Rent Acts. Whether the specific exemption of holiday lettings from the Rent Act was really necessary is open to question, for a person occupying a house or cottage for a holiday would be unlikely to be able to satisfy the residence requirement (see s 2, 13.97). It could be argued that s 9 served more to provide unscrupulous landlords with a ready-made device to avoid the provisions of the Act than to exclude the genuine holiday-maker from protection.

Where the tenant alleges that the letting is not truly a holiday letting but that s 9 is being **13.64** used by the landlord to evade the Rent Act, the onus is on the tenant to prove that the letting is a sham. The fact that the tenancy agreement describes the letting as a holiday letting is prima facie evidence that the letting is in fact a holiday letting, and in the absence of any evidence to the contrary this will be sufficient to bring the letting within s 9. Where, however, there is clear evidence that a holiday is not the true purpose of the letting and that any statement stating otherwise is a sham—as in *R v Rent Officer for LB of Camden, ex parte Plant* (1981) 257 EG 731, where the tenants were studying to be nurses—the tenancy will be held to be protected by the Rent Act.

As with many of the terms employed in the Rent Act 1977, there is no statutory defini **13.65** tion of 'holiday'. The courts instead adopted the dictionary definition of 'a period of cessation of work or period of recreation' (*Buchmann v May* [1978] 2 All ER 993 at 995, CA). However, when confronted with the problem of a 'working holiday' in *Franke v Hakmi* [1984] CLY 1906, this was adapted to include 'a temporary suspension of one's normal activity not necessarily implying a period of recreation' but where there must be an intention 'to resume one's normal activity at its conclusion'. A holiday letting cannot be a restricted contract (see 13.159).

Agricultural holdings

13.66 Under the Rent Act 1977, s 10:

> A tenancy is not a protected tenancy if the dwelling-house is comprised in an agricultural holding (within the meaning of the Agricultural Holdings Act 1986) and is occupied by the person responsible for the control (whether as tenant or as servant or agent of the tenant) of the farming of the holding.

13.67 Tenants of agricultural holdings have their own code of protection under the Agricultural Holdings Act 1986 (see Chapter 27) and are therefore excluded from Rent Act protection. Section 137(3) of the Rent Act 1977 does however provide that where part of a building which falls within s 10 is sub-let as a separate dwelling, the sub-tenant will acquire a protected tenancy as against both the tenant and the head landlord.

Licensed premises

13.68 Section 11 of the 1977 Act provides:

> A tenancy of a dwelling-house which consists of or comprises premises licensed for the sale of intoxicating liquors for consumption on the premises shall not be a protected tenancy, nor shall such a dwelling-house be the subject of a statutory tenancy.

13.69 Since the introduction of the Landlord and Tenant (Licensed Premises) Act 1990, a tenancy of licensed premises will probably be a business tenancy under Pt II of the Landlord and Tenant Act 1954 (see 26.53).

Resident landlords

13.70 We have seen how an occupier can acquire a protected tenancy within the meaning of s 1 of the Rent Act 1977 even where essential living facilities are shared with other occupiers (see 13.23 to 13.29). Sharing a bathroom or toilet with another person can often be a source of social conflict. Where that person is also the landlord, the potential for 'social embarrassment' is even greater (see *Bardrick v Haycock* (1976) 31 P&CR 420 *per* Scarman LJ at 424). For this reason the Rent Act 1977 excludes from protection tenants with resident landlords.

13.71 Section 12 of the Act sets out three conditions that must be satisfied if the tenancy is to fall within the resident landlord exclusion:

> (1) Subject to subsection (2) below, a tenancy of a dwelling-house granted on or after 14th August 1974 shall not be a protected tenancy at any time if—
>
> (a) the dwelling-house forms part only of a building and, except in a case where the dwelling-house also forms part of a flat, the building is not a purpose-built block of flats; and
>
> (b) the tenancy was granted by a person who, at the time when he granted it, occupied as his residence another dwelling-house which—
>
> (i)   in the case mentioned in paragraph (a) above, also forms part of the flat; or
>
> (ii) in any other case, also forms part of the building; and
>
> (c) subject to paragraph 1 of Schedule 2 to this Act, at all times since the tenancy was granted the interest of the landlord under the tenancy has belonged to a person who, at the time he owned that interest, occupied as his residence another dwelling-house which—
>
> (i)   in the case mentioned in paragraph (a) above, also formed part of the flat; or
>
> (ii) in any other case, also formed part of the building.

The somewhat tortuous wording of this section is designed to deal with the practical dif- **13.72**
ficulties raised by purpose-built blocks of flats. A purpose-built block of flats is one building, but each flat within that building is an independent unit. The aim of the statute is to
prevent a tenant from acquiring protection when that tenant lives in close proximity to his
or her landlord.

The first condition Section 12(1)(a) will be satisfied in only two situations: **13.73**

(a) Where the building is not a purpose-built block of flats and the tenant occupies one
part of the building.
(b) Where the building is a purpose-built block of flats and the tenant occupies one part
of a flat within that building.

The first condition will not be satisfied where the building is a purpose-built block of flats **13.74**
and the tenant occupies one flat within the building.

The second condition Section 12(1)(b) requires that if in accordance with the first condi- **13.75**
tion the tenant occupies part of a building, the landlord must be occupying another part of
the same building *as his residence* when the tenancy starts. A landlord can*not* move into
a part of the same building after the tenancy has started and thereby deprive the tenant of
Rent Act protection, but must have been resident in part of the building before the commencement of the tenancy. What counts as 'occupying as a residence' will be considered
later when we look at statutory tenancies (see 13.97 to 13.109). By Sch 2, para 5, the criteria used to assess 'residence' are the same for s 12 as for s 2(1). It should be noted that a
company cannot 'reside', and therefore a landlord company will not be able to rely upon
this exception (see 13.99).

The second condition will therefore be satisfied: **13.76**

(a) Where the building is not a purpose-built block of flats and the tenant occupies one
part of the building and the landlord occupies another part of the same building as his
or her residence.
(b) Where the building is a purpose-built block of flats and the tenant occupies one part
of a flat within that building and the landlord occupies another part of the same flat as
his or her residence.

It will *not* be satisfied where the building is a purpose-built block of flats and the tenant **13.77**
occupies one flat within the building and the landlord occupies another flat within the same
building as his or her residence.

Determining whether the landlord and tenant both occupy parts of the same building **13.78**
will in each case depend upon the particular layout of the premises themselves. The fact
that the premises are structurally linked to each other does not necessarily mean that
they count as one building if there is no internal means of access between the two buildings. For example, where the tenant occupied one premises and the landlord lived in an
extension built on the side of the tenant's premises but there was no inter-communicating
door between the two living units, the exception did not apply (*Bardrick v Haycock*).
However, where two adjoining premises had been converted by the removal of internal
walls and the construction of an inter-communicating door between the two premises,
the two dwelling-houses were held to be part of the same building (*Guppy v O'Donnell*
(1979) 129 NLJ 930). In *Bardrick v Haycock*, it was pointed out that an important factor is whether the two dwelling units have separate front doors. If both landlord and
tenant have separate, individual access to their dwelling units then the possibility of
constant and potentially embarrassing social encounters is considerably reduced.

13.79   **The third condition** Section 12(1)(c)) requires that for the tenancy to fall within s 12 the landlord must continue to occupy part of the building as his or her residence throughout the course of the tenancy. If a resident landlord moves out during the course of the tenancy, s 12 will cease to apply and the tenant will become a protected tenant. There are, however, two exceptions to this rule, known as statutory periods of disregard (Rent Act 1977, Sch 2, para 1):

(a) If the landlord sells his interest in the property, a 28-day period of non-residence is disregarded. This provision prevents a tenant gaining protected status if there is a brief gap in residence between the old landlord moving out and the new landlord moving in. This period runs from the date of the completion of the purchase and can be extended up to a period of six months by the incoming landlord within the 28-day period provided the new landlord gives the tenant written notice of his or her intention to occupy.

(b) If the landlord's interest becomes vested in trustees, or if the landlord dies and his or her interest becomes vested in personal representatives, there is a two-year period of disregard.

13.80   Section 12(2) provides a further important exception to the resident landlord rule:

> This section does not apply to a tenancy of a dwelling-house which forms part of a building if the tenancy is granted to a person who, immediately before it was granted, was a protected or statutory tenant of that dwelling-house or of any other dwelling-house in that building.

13.81   If a tenant is already a protected tenant of part of a building, the landlord cannot therefore deprive the tenant of this status by moving into the building and then granting him or her a new tenancy.

13.82   **Example 1** James owns two three-bedroom flats in a tower block, one on the fifteenth floor and one on the ground floor. James rents the flat on the fifteenth floor to Mary and lives in the ground floor flat. He also rents out a room in the ground floor flat to Peter. Peter's room has its own cooking facilities and counts as a separate dwelling within the meaning of s 1, but Peter shares use of the bathroom with James. Clearly Peter lives in very close proximity to James while Mary, although technically living in the same building, rarely ever encounters James except when she pays the rent. Six months after granting the tenancy to Peter, James purchases a nearby house and moves out of the ground floor flat.

13.83   **Example 2** Henry owns a terraced house. Both the upper floor and the ground floor have their own bathroom and kitchen; they do not, however, have separate front doors and access to the upper floor is through the ground floor hallway. Henry rents the upper floor to Jim. Several months later Henry moves into the ground floor of the house.

13.84   The question is now whether any of these tenants can acquire a protected tenancy, or whether they will be excluded by virtue of s 12.

(a) Mary will have a protected tenancy. She occupies a separate flat within a purpose-built block and does not fall within the exclusion.

(b) Peter does not have a protected tenancy while James continues living in the ground floor flat, for Peter occupies only a part of this flat. When James moves out Peter will acquire a protected tenancy unless James sells his interest in the flat and the new owner moves into the flat within 28 days of completion of the purchase (unless the landlord extends this period by giving Peter written notice).

(c) Jim does have a protected tenancy even though Henry occupies another part of the same building. He would not have a protected tenancy if Henry had already been occupying the ground floor as a residence when he was granted the tenancy.

If an occupier is excluded from being a protected tenant purely by virtue of s 12, he or she **13.85** will have a restricted contract (see 13.159). This should be contrasted with the situation under the Housing Act 1988 (see 15.92).

Landlord's interest belonging to the Crown

A tenancy cannot be a protected tenancy (or a statutory tenancy) at any time when the **13.86** landlord's interest belongs to Her Majesty in right of the Crown or to a government department, or is held on trust for Her Majesty for the purposes of a government department (Rent Act 1977, s 13(1)). The tenancy can be a protected tenancy if the interest is under the management of the Crown Estate Commissioners (s 13(2)).

Landlord's interest belonging to a local authority

A tenancy cannot be a protected tenancy (or a statutory tenancy) at any time when the **13.87** landlord's interest belongs to a local authority, including a county council, a district council, a London borough or the City of London, a joint authority, the Commission for the New Towns, a development corporation, the Development Board for Rural Wales, a National Park Authority, and an urban development corporation (Rent Act 1977, s 14). Local authority tenants may well be secure tenants, however, under the Housing Act 1985 (see Chapters 17 and 18).

Landlord's interest belonging to a housing association

A tenancy cannot be a protected tenancy (or a statutory tenancy) at any time when the **13.88** landlord's interest belongs to a housing corporation, Housing for Wales, a housing trust which is a charity, a registered social landlord, or a co-operative housing association (Rent Act 1977, s 15). Before 15 January 1989, many housing association tenancies will have been secure tenancies under the Housing Act 1985. After 15 January 1989, most housing association tenancies will be assured tenancies under the Housing Act 1988 (see Chapters 15 and 16).

Landlord's interest belonging to a housing co-operative

A tenancy cannot be a protected tenancy at any time when the landlord's interest belongs **13.89** to a housing co-operative (within the meaning of s 27B of the Housing Act 1985) and the dwelling-house is comprised in a housing co-operative agreement within the meaning of that section (Rent Act 1977, s 16).

Business tenancies

If the tenancy is a business tenancy, namely a tenancy to which Pt II of the Landlord **13.90** and Tenant Act 1954 applies, it cannot be a regulated tenancy (Rent Act 1977, s 24, see Chapter 26).

D SECURITY OF TENURE UNDER THE 1977 ACT

What is security of tenure?

'Security of tenure' is one of those expressions that is sometimes bandied about as if it **13.91** had some sort of magical meaning. There is, however, nothing mystical about security of tenure. It consists of nothing more than a number of rights that a tenant may acquire by virtue of statutory provisions. A tenant has security of tenure when he or she falls within the ambit of a statutory code which overrides the normal common law rules of termination. The exact nature of the security of tenure provided will depend upon the wording of the particular code. In the case of the Rent Act 1977, security of tenure is provided in two ways:

(a) by the mechanism of the statutory tenancy, which automatically continues the tenancy beyond the termination of the contractual term provided certain preconditions are met;
(b) by allowing the landlord to recover possession only in certain statutorily defined situations.

The statutory tenancy

The nature of a statutory tenancy

13.92 A statutory tenancy is not an easy thing to define in terms of landlord and tenant law. It is created by statute and not by a grant by the landlord, and consists of the right of the tenant to retain possession of the premises after the contractual term has come to an end. As such, a statutory tenancy is a personal right; it is not an estate in land (and therefore strictly speaking is not really a tenancy at all). Unlike an estate in land, a statutory tenancy cannot be assigned except in certain statutorily prescribed situations (in matrimonial proceedings or with the agreement of the landlord (see Rent Act 1977, Sch 1, Pt II, paras 13 and 14; also *Keeves v Dean* [1924] 1 KB 685)), it cannot be disposed of by will, and on bankruptcy it will not vest in the trustee in bankruptcy; nor can a statutory tenant sub-let the whole of the premises. On the other hand, a statutory tenancy exhibits certain features that are akin to the rights held by a contractual tenant. A statutory tenant can sue in trespass, can sub-let part of the premises, and, like an estate in land, a statutory tenancy will bind a successor to the landlord's title.

How does a tenant acquire a statutory tenancy?

13.93 No statutory tenancy can ever arise if the previous tenancy was not a protected tenancy. A statutory tenancy will arise in only two situations:

(a) by virtue of a previous protected tenancy within the terms of s 1 of the Rent Act 1977;
(b) by succession.

13.94 Both of these require the tenant claiming a statutory tenancy to satisfy the key requirement that he or she is occupying the premises as his or her residence.

A statutory tenancy by virtue of a previous protected tenancy

13.95 A protected tenancy lasts only as long as there is a contractual relationship between landlord and tenant. When this contractual relationship ends, be that by a notice to quit, effluxion of time, forfeiture, or any other of the common law methods of termination, the Rent Act 1977, s 2(1) provides that the relationship between landlord and tenant will continue as a statutory tenancy:

(a) after the termination of a protected tenancy of a dwelling-house the person who, immediately before that termination, was the protected tenant of the dwelling-house shall, if and so long as he occupies the dwelling-house as his residence, be the statutory tenant of it;

To become a statutory tenant by virtue of s 2(1), the following conditions have to be **13.96** satisfied:

(a) The tenant must have held a contractual tenancy that was a protected tenancy in accordance with s 1 of the Rent Act 1977.
(b) That tenancy must have ended.
(c) The tenant must have held a protected tenancy of the dwelling-house immediately before the contractual tenancy terminated.
(d) The tenant must continue to occupy the dwelling-house as his or her residence.

Occupation as a residence

Throughout the duration of the contractual term a tenant can be a protected tenant whether **13.97** or not he or she actually lives in the dwelling-house. The requirement that the tenant must occupy the dwelling-house arises only when the contractual term comes to an end. This means that certain tenants, despite having a protected tenancy immediately before the termination of the contractual tenancy, will not acquire a statutory tenancy.

For example, a tenant who has sub-let the whole of the premises will not become a statu- **13.98** tory tenant when the contractual tenancy ends. The tenant is not in occupation and fails to fulfil the residence requirement. Where a tenant has sub-let part of the premises and continues to occupy the other part as a residence, that tenant will acquire a statutory tenancy. Whether the statutory tenancy will apply to the whole premises or just to the part occupied by the tenant will depend upon whether the part sub-let forms a separate dwelling (see *Berkeley v Papadoyannis* [1954] 2 QB 149, [1954] 2 All ER 409, CA).

A further effect of s 2(1)(a) is that a company cannot acquire a statutory tenancy. A com- **13.99** pany is merely a legal personality: it has no physical presence and is therefore incapable of occupying a dwelling-house as a residence. As a result, landlords seeking to avoid the provisions of the Rent Act 1977 have been keen to rent residential properties to companies rather than to individuals. Frequently, artificial arrangements are made, such as where the prospective tenant buys an 'off-the-shelf' company, the landlord rents the property to the company, and the prospective tenant occupies the premises as a licensee of the company. The courts, however, have been surprisingly reluctant to declare such arrangements to be 'shams' (see *Hilton v Plustile* [1988] 3 All ER 1051, (1988) 132 SJ 1638; and *Kaye v Massbetter Ltd* (1991) 39 EG 129).

Continued residence

A statutory tenancy is dependent upon the tenant's continued occupation. If the tenant **13.100** ceases to occupy the dwelling-house as a residence the statutory tenancy ceases. Whether a tenant is occupying the dwelling-house as a residence will be a question of fact and degree. Clearly it does not mean that the tenant has to remain at home the whole time—it would be absurd if security of tenure could be lost by going to the shops or by taking a fortnight's holiday. If a tenant takes a job abroad for a year, though, the question is not so easy to answer.

Where there is a prolonged period of absence, such that the prima facie inference to be **13.101** drawn is that the tenant has ceased to occupy the premises, the onus is on the tenant to show that he or she has not ceased to occupy the premises. In determining the question of continued residence the court makes use of two old Roman law concepts:

(a) *animus possidendi*—an intention to return and reside in the dwelling-house; and
(b) *corpus possessionis*—visible evidence of an intention to return.

13.102   An intention to return must be more than a vague wish to return: 'It must be a real hope coupled with the practical possibility of its fulfilment within a reasonable time' (*Tickner v Hearn* [1960] 1 WLR 1406 *per* Ormerod LJ at 1410). Where such an intention can be established the absence can be for a considerable amount of time: in *Tickner v Hearn* the tenant had been in a mental hospital for six years; in *Gofor Investments Ltd v Roberts* (1975) 29 P&CR 366 the tenant was away for 10 years.

13.103   A mere intention, however, will not be sufficient; there must be some visible evidence of an intention to return. Examples of such visible evidence would be the occupation of the dwelling-house by members of the tenant's family or friends (provided that they are there to preserve the house as a residence for the tenant: see *Skinner v Geary* [1931] 2 KB 546), or the presence on the premises of furniture or other possessions of the tenant. In *Brown v Brash and Ambrose* [1948] 2 KB 247, the tenant went to prison; his common-law wife and children then left the property and the tenant was held to have ceased to occupy the premises. By contrast, in *Tickner v Hearn* the tenant did not lose her status as a statutory tenant because her furniture remained at the property and her daughter continued to occupy the premises.

Occupation by tenant's spouse

13.104   With regard to married couples, the requirement that a statutory tenant must occupy the dwelling-house as his or her residence was first modified by the Matrimonial Homes Act 1983. This has since been amended by the Family Law Act 1996 (s 30(4) as further amended by the Civil Partnership Act 2004). Where the tenant ceases to occupy a dwelling-house but his or her spouse or civil partner remains in occupation, the spouse's or civil partner's occupation will count as continued occupation by the absent tenant (Matrimonial Homes Act 1983, s 1(6)). This will apply only if at some point during the course of the tenancy the dwelling-house had been the matrimonial home of the couple. The right to occupy the dwelling-house vicariously through a spouse or civil partner will end if the couple divorce, or if the civil partnership is dissolved (see *Metropolitan Properties Co. v Cronan* (1982) 126 SJ 229, (1982) 262 EG 1077, CA).

Occupation of two homes

13.105   It is possible for the tenant of a rented property to fulfil the residence requirement even if the property in question is just one of the tenant's homes. We have already considered this question with reference to s 1 of the 1977 Act (namely, whether such a tenant can be said to be occupying the dwelling-house as a separate dwelling, see 13.30). For the purposes of s 1 the tenant's occupation is considered at the commencement of the tenancy. When, under s 2, it is necessary to decide whether the tenant is a statutory tenant, the residence requirement must be satisfied at and after the end of the contractual tenancy. It is possible then that even though s 1 was satisfied by the tenant at the start of the tenancy, subsequently the tenant may have ceased to occupy the dwelling-house as his or her residence within the meaning of s 2.

13.106   In all cases it will be a question of fact and degree whether the tenant is occupying the second premises as a residence. In *Hampstead Way Investments* (considered earlier at 13.30), merely sleeping at the premises five nights a week but not eating there was not considered sufficient. However, a tenant who has a house in the country and regularly uses a flat in London for two or three days a week can have statutory tenancy of the flat (*Bevington v Crawford* (1974) 232 EG 191). Likewise a person living in London can claim a statutory tenancy of a country cottage used at the weekend (*Regalian Securities Ltd v Scheur* (1982) 5 HLR 48 at 56). Even a tenant who works abroad most of the time but returns to the premises for two or three months each year can have a statutory tenancy (*Bevington v Crawford* at 193).

Where the tenant has sub-let the whole of a property under terms where he or she would **13.107** not be entitled to occupy it without a surrender by the sub-tenants he or she cannot be said to occupy that property: *Ujima Housing Association v Ansah* [1998] 30 HLR 831, CA.

A statutory tenancy by succession

The second way in which a statutory tenancy can arise is by succession. When a tenant **13.108** with security of tenure dies, whether a protected tenant or a statutory tenant, security of tenure does not die with the tenant but may be 'transmitted' to a member of the deceased tenant's family. The family member receiving this 'transmission' will acquire, except in a few cases, a statutory tenancy, regardless of whether the deceased tenant was a protected tenant at the time of death or whether the deceased tenant's contractual term had already expired and he or she had become a statutory tenant.

The Rent Act 1977 provides for two statutory successions in respect of the original tenancy. **13.109** When it is considered that the effect of these provisions can be to prevent a landlord from regaining possession of a property for three generations of the tenant's family, it is easy to understand why they are regarded as some of the most controversial aspects of the Rent Acts. New and more restrictive rules regarding the succession of Rent Act tenancies were introduced by the Housing Act 1988 and different rules apply when the original tenant dies after 15 January 1989. Different rules also apply depending upon whether the person succeeding to the tenancy is the original tenant's surviving spouse or civil partner (an addition made by the Civil Partnership Act 2004, Sch 8) or another member of the family.

Death before 15 January 1989

Surviving spouse When the original protected or statutory tenant dies, the surviving spouse **13.110** or surviving civil partner, if any, will become the statutory tenant by succession:

(a) if the surviving spouse or civil partner was residing in the dwelling-house immediately before the death of the original tenant; and
(b) if and so long as he or she occupies the dwelling-house as his or her residence (Rent Act 1977, Sch 1, para 2, as amended by the Housing Act 1980, s 76).

The requirement of continuing residence demanded of a tenant by succession is the same **13.111** as that demanded of a statutory tenant by s 2(1)(a) (see 13.97).

Other family members Where the original tenant has no surviving spouse or civil partner, **13.112** a person can become the statutory tenant by succession:

(a) if he or she is a member of the original tenant's family;
(b) if he or she was residing with the original tenant at the time of the original tenant's death and for the period of six months immediately before the death;
(c) if and so long as he or she occupies the dwelling-house as his or her residence (Rent Act 1977, Sch 1, para 3).

The Act provides that when one or more people are eligible under this definition, the par- **13.113** ties should agree between them who should succeed to the tenancy (Sch 1, para 6). If there is a dispute the question will be put into the hands of the court (Sch 1, para 7). For how the court will decide, see *Trayfoot v Lock* [1957] 1 WLR 351 (wishes of deceased tenant); *Williams v Williams* [1970] 1 WLR 1530 ('relative hardship').

13.114 **Second transmission** The spouse, civil partner, or member of the family who acquires the statutory tenancy immediately after the original tenant's death is known as the first successor. If the first successor continues living in the dwelling-house until his or her death and that death occurs before 15 January 1989, there can be a second transmission of the tenancy by Sch 1, para 5 to the 1977 Act. The provisions are the same as above for the first succession. The surviving spouse or civil partner of the first successor will become the statutory tenant if he or she was residing in the dwelling-house immediately before the death of the first successor, and if and so long as he or she occupies the dwelling-house as his or her residence. Likewise, a member of the first successor's family can succeed to the tenancy provided he or she resided with the first successor for at least six months immediately before the first successor's death. When the second successor dies, no further transmissions are possible.

Death on or after 15 January 1989

13.115 If the original tenant or the first successor dies after 15 January 1989, the rules regarding succession are a little different. The main changes implemented by the Housing Act 1988 are considered later, the most important difference being that where a family member succeeds to the tenancy he or she acquires not a statutory tenancy but an assured tenancy (see Chapter 15).

13.116 **Surviving spouse or civil partner** The position of the surviving spouse or civil partner of a deceased tenant is subject to the same rules as under the previous provisions of the 1977 Act, with the exception that under the amended provisions a person who was living with the tenant as his or her wife or husband or as his or her civil partner is treated as a surviving spouse or civil partner (Rent Act 1977, Sch 1, para 2(2), as amended by the Housing Act 1988, Sch 4, para 2 and the Civil Partnership Act 2004, Sch 8, para 13(3)). Where a surviving spouse succeeds to a statutory tenancy a second succession is possible (see below).

13.117 **Family members** If there is no surviving spouse, civil partner, or cohabitee, a family member can succeed to the tenancy only if he or she has resided in the dwelling-house for a minimum period of two years before the original tenant's death (Rent Act 1977, Sch 1, para 3, as amended by the Housing Act 1988, Sch 4, para 3). Furthermore, the family member will not acquire a Rent Act statutory tenancy but a Housing Act assured periodic tenancy (see Chapter 15). One important consequence of this is that an assured periodic tenancy will not be subject to the restrictions on rent imposed by the Rent Act (see *N & D (London) Ltd v Gadstone* [1992] 1 EGLR 112). Where a member of the original tenant's family succeeds to an assured tenancy there will be only one succession.

13.118 **Second transmission** A second transmission is possible after 15 January 1989 only if:

(a) the second successor was a member of the original tenant's family immediately before the death of the original tenant; and

(b) the second successor was also a member of the first successor's family immediately before the death of the first successor; and

(c) the second successor resided with the first successor in the dwelling-house for a period of at least two years before the death of the first successor.

Example of a statutory tenancy by succession

13.119 In 1975, Harry grants John a monthly periodic tenancy of Flat C, Tidy Street. John marries Noreen in 1986 and she moves in with him. In 1988 John dies. Noreen becomes the statutory tenant by succession and continues to live in the flat.

Noreen becomes ill, and in 1989 her sister Mabel moves in with her. Eight months later **13.120** Noreen dies. Mabel becomes the second successor as she has lived with Noreen for the six months before her death.

Julie, Mabel's daughter, moves in with her. When Mabel dies in 1994 Julie cannot keep the **13.121** flat as this would be the third succession.

If John died in 1990, Noreen would still become the statutory tenant by succession. On **13.122** Noreen's death, however, there would be no further succession. Mabel would not qualify to succeed either to a statutory or to an assured tenancy as she had not resided with Noreen for two or more years before Noreen's death.

Who is a family member?

The Rent Act 1977 provides no statutory definition of a 'family member'. Instead the courts **13.123** have adopted a common-sense way of determining the status of a given individual known as the 'family nexus test'. The word 'family' is to be given its ordinary, everyday meaning and whether a person is a member of that family is determined by asking whether an ordinary man in possession of the evidence before the judge would regard that person as a family member (*Brock v Wollams* [1949] 2 KB 388 at 395). As a result of this test the definition of 'family member' is quite broad. It includes brothers- and sisters-in-law, grandchildren, nieces by marriage, and adopted children. It does not seem, however, to extend to platonic relationships between unrelated individuals. In *Carega Properties SA v Sharratt* [1979] 1 WLR 928, a younger man who shared a property with a woman for 18 years failed in his claim to be a family member despite the fact that he called her 'auntie' and was clearly part of the household. Conversely, where the parties are actually related but their conduct does not indicate that they live together as family members, the court may not consider there to be the required 'family nexus'. In *Langdon v Horton* [1951] 1 KB 666 two elderly women lived for 30 years with their cousin, but the cohabitation was seen as being merely for mutual convenience. For an individual to succeed in a claim to be a family member of a tenant it seems that there must be both a relationship (either a blood relationship or a *de facto* relationship) and the family relationship must be demonstrated by conduct.

Cohabitees

Prior to the 1980s, courts were reluctant to find that cohabitees should be treated in the **13.124** same way as spouses for the purposes of Sch 1, para 2(1). That view changed with the case of *Watson v Lucas* [1980] 1 WLR 1493, in which the Court of Appeal felt that a negative attitude towards unmarried couples had lost its social relevance. The amendment made by the Housing Act 1988 regularized the position for couples of the opposite sex (see 13.116) but disputes still continued where the tenant was cohabiting with a person of the same sex. In *Fitzpatrick v Stirling Housing Association* [1999] 3 WLR 11 same-sex partners were held to be entitled to be regarded as members of the tenant's family, but it was not until *Ghaidan v Godin-Mendoza* [2004] UKHL 30, [2004] 2 WLR 113 that the courts ruled that a same-sex partner was capable of being treated as a tenant's spouse. The court's view was that to decide otherwise would amount to discrimination contrary to Article 14 of the European Convention on the Protection of Human Rights and the Human Rights Act 1988. The position has now been formally regularized by the Civil Partnership Act 2004 which inserts a new sub-para 2(2)(b) into the Rent Act 1977, Sch 1 to provide that: 'a person who was living with the original tenant as if they were civil partners shall be treated as the civil partner of the original tenant'. The distinction between a spouse or civil partner and a family member is obviously important in succession cases as the residence requirement for family members is more onerous than that for spouses or civil partners.

13.125 It should be noted that prior to 15 January 1989, a cohabitee could succeed to a statutory tenancy only as a member of the deceased tenant's family and therefore had to be capable of fulfilling the six months' residency requirement. After 15 January 1989, a cohabitee can succeed under the same rules that apply to a spouse or civil partner. This does not mean that legally married couples or civil partners and cohabitees are on the same footing: cohabitees must still establish that they are living together as man and wife, while a married couple or civil partners need only produce the relevant certificate.

'Residing with'

13.126 Whether the person claiming succession is residing with the original tenant is a question of fact. If that person has a permanent home elsewhere, his or her claim is unlikely to succeed, although, as we have seen earlier, it is possible for a person to reside in two separate homes. In *Swanbrae Ltd v Eliot* (1976) 131 SJ 410, CA, a daughter lived with her son about two miles away from her mother's house. When her mother fell ill the daughter slept at the mother's house three or four nights a week. She was held not to be residing with her mother. In *Hildebrand v Moon* (1989) 22 HLR 1, CA, a daughter moved in with her mother in order to nurse her. The daughter expressed an intention to continue living at her mother's and considered selling her own flat, but did not in fact do so. The court held that she was residing with her mother. The courts can be generous in their interpretation of 'residing with'. In *Hedgedale Ltd v Hards* [1991] 1 EGLR 118, a young man went to live with his grandmother. When he moved in the grandmother was not actually present in the flat because she was recovering from an accident. She moved back after four months and died five months later. The grandson was nevertheless held to have established the six months' qualifying period.

13.127 It should be noted that where succession is claimed by a surviving spouse or civil partner, the statute demands that the spouse or civil partner has been 'residing in the dwelling-house'. Where the original tenant died before 15 January 1989 and a member of the family is seeking succession, the statutory requirement is that the claimant was residing with the tenant for six months before the tenant's death. In this latter case it is not necessary that the original tenant and the claimant resided together in the dwelling-house to which succession is claimed provided that they lived together for the required six-month period. In *Waltham Forest LBC v Thomas* [1992] 2 AC 198 (a case about secure tenancies), two brothers lived together for two-and-a-half years; they moved house and 10 days later one of the brothers died. The remaining brother was entitled to succeed to the tenancy.

The terms of the statutory tenancy

13.128 In general the terms of the statutory tenancy will remain the same as those of the preceding contractual tenancy (Rent Act 1977, s 3(1)). For example, where the contractual agreement included a proviso for re-entry should the tenant go bankrupt, this clause translated into a condition in the statutory tenancy that the tenant would not go bankrupt (*Cadogan Estates Ltd v McMahon* [2000] 3 WLR 1555, HL).

13.129 Terms will not carry over if they are inconsistent with the provisions of the Rent Act 1977. For example, where the contractual tenancy contained a term that it was terminable on notice this will not be carried over, nor will terms agreeing a rental reduction or concession. In both cases the requirements of the Rent Act will supersede the original contractual terms.

13.130 In addition, certain terms setting out the landlord's right of access to carry out repairs are incorporated into the tenancy agreement by statute (Rent Act 1977, s 3(2)).

E RENT CONTROL

The most striking difference between the Rent Act 1977 and the Housing Act 1988 is the **13.131** absence of rent control in the latter statute. While, to a large degree, the Housing Act 1988 adopted a similar system to the Rent Acts when it came to providing security of tenure, it abandoned completely the system of rent registration developed in the Rent Acts.

Under the Rent Act 1977, the level of rent payable for a tenancy can be fixed by a pub **13.132** lic official known as a rent officer. This administratively determined rent is commonly described as a 'fair rent'. Once a fair rent has been fixed, the tenant need pay no more than the registered amount, thereby overriding both the contract between the landlord and tenant and the normal operation of market forces.

Application for rent registration

An application for the registration of a fair rent must be made to the rent officer in the pre- **13.133** scribed form (these forms should be available from the rent office and housing advice agencies). Both the landlord and the tenant can apply separately or, in certain circumstances, make a joint application (Rent Act 1977, s 67). The local authority can also apply (s 68) and is likely to do so when the tenant is in receipt of housing benefit. In such a situation the tenant will have no direct interest in restricting the rent payable under the tenancy, but the local authority will want to be able to ensure that public funds are not being wasted because the landlord is charging an excessive rent.

In making an application the applicant is required to state what he or she considers to be **13.134** a fair rent for the tenancy. When the application is made by one party, the rent officer will serve notice and details of the application upon the other party, who will then have the opportunity to put its side of the case. The rent officer will normally then hold a consultation and in the majority of cases will visit the premises. The consultation is informal. The parties may attend in person or may be represented. Once the rent officer has reached a decision he must inform the parties in writing, and is further under a duty to record the rent in the register of rents for that registration area. This register must be kept up to date and available for public inspection (s 66).

The registered rent attaches not to the parties but to the property and will bind any future **13.135** lettings, provided of course that the letting falls within the Rent Act 1977, regardless of whether there has been a change in landlord or tenant. In general, once the rent has been registered there can be no new application to the rent officer until a period of two years has elapsed (s 67) unless:

(a) the landlord and tenant make a joint application for a new rent to be registered;
(b) there has been a change in:
    (i) the condition of the premises,
    (ii) the terms of the tenancy,
    (iii) the furniture provided, or
    (iv) any other circumstances which were considered at the time the rent was registered so as to make the registered rent no longer a fair rent (s 67(3)).

The landlord may also apply in the last three months before the two-year period expires, **13.136** but any new rent registered will not take effect until the full two-year period has elapsed.

Appeals

13.137 If either party is dissatisfied with the rent registered by the rent officer it can make a written objection to a rent assessment committee within 28 days of receiving notice of the registered rent from the rent officer. The committee will either confirm the rent officer's decision or determine a fair rent itself. A rent assessment committee has no jurisdiction to determine points of law. If a party wishes to appeal against the rent officer's decision on a point of law, the appeal will be to the county court or the Divisional Court (s 141). The decision of a rent assessment committee can be appealed only on a point of law. Such an appeal should be made to the High Court.

Determining a fair rent

13.138 There is no definition of a 'fair rent' in the Rent Act 1977. Section 70 provides certain guidelines for the rent officer, in particular setting out the factors that the rent officer must consider, and those which must be disregarded:

(1) In determining, for the purposes of this Part of this Act, what rent is or would be a fair rent under a regulated tenancy of a dwelling-house, regard shall be had to all the circumstances (other than personal circumstances) and in particular to—

    (a) the age, character, locality, and state of repair of the dwelling-house; and

    (b) if any furniture is provided for use under the tenancy, the quantity, quality, and condition of the furniture; and

    (c) any premium, or sum in the nature of a premium, which has been or may be lawfully required or received on the grant, renewal, continuance or assignment of the tenancy.

(2) For the purposes of the determination it shall be assumed that the number of persons seeking to become tenants of similar dwelling-houses in the locality on the terms (other than those relating to rent) of the regulated tenancy is not substantially greater than the number of such dwelling-houses in the locality which are available for letting on such terms.

(3) There shall be disregarded—

    (a) any disrepair or other defect attributable to a failure by the tenant under the regulated tenancy or any predecessor in title of his to comply with any terms thereof;

    (b) any improvement carried out, otherwise than in pursuance of the terms of the tenancy, by the tenant under the regulated tenancy or any predecessor in title of his;

    (c) ...

    (d) ...

    (e) if any furniture is provided for use under the regulated tenancy, any improvement to the furniture by the tenant under the regulated tenancy or any predecessor in the title of his or, as the case may be, any deterioration in the condition of the furniture due to any ill-treatment by the tenant, any person residing or lodging with him, or any sub-tenant of his.

13.139 By way of illustration consider the following example:

13.140 **Example** Robert rents the basement flat of 16 Montpelier Road from Catherine. The flat is furnished. He has lived there for seven years and pays £120 per week rent. Robert has had to take a less-well-paid job recently and is struggling to pay the rent. The flat consists of one bedroom, a sitting room, kitchen, bathroom, and has a large garden. Robert suffers from back trouble: he finds it difficult to negotiate the steep steps down to the basement and he also is unable to maintain the garden. In the last year there have been recurring damp problems in the bedroom due to a faulty down- pipe. Furthermore, Robert has two badly behaved cats with a tendency to sharpen their claws on the sofa and armchairs in the sitting room, with the result that that furniture is now in a very bad state of repair. Two years ago Robert paid for and installed a new fitted kitchen and this year, in accordance with a term in the tenancy, he has repainted the interior of the flat.

Robert feels that his rent is too high and applies to the local rent officer suggesting a rent **13.141** of £70 per week. Catherine contends that, if anything, the rent is too low. The Montpelier area has become more up-market in the last five years and currently similar flats are being rented for between £150 and £200 per week. She also argues that the new kitchen and the fact that the flat has recently been decorated have raised the value of the flat. She feels that a rent of £170 would be more appropriate.

The rent officer must now try to assess what would be a fair rent for 16 Montpelier Road **13.142** having regard to the provisions of s 70. In performing this task the rent officer should seek to be fair to the landlord as well as fair to the tenant (*Mason v Skilling* [1974] 1 WLR 1437 *per* Lord Reid at 1440B). In reaching a valuation the courts have generally been happy to leave rent officers to rely upon their own expertise; this, after all, is their specialist area. In *Mason v Skilling*, Lord Reid said of s 70 (at 1439G):

> In my view this section leaves it open to the rent officer or committee to adopt any method or methods of ascertaining a fair rent provided that they do not use any method which is unlawful or unreasonable.

In general, however, it seems that a rent officer will use two main methods. First, he or she **13.143** will look at the registered rents of comparable properties in the area. This seems to be the preferred method of working. Secondly, however, in seeking to be equally fair to the landlord as to the tenant, he or she may consider whether the landlord is receiving a fair return upon the capital value of the property. If using the latter method the capital value of the property is the value with vacant possession, not the value of the property with the tenant still in occupation. The fact that, as a Rent Act protected tenant, the tenant will have security of tenure, is a personal circumstance and should be ignored by the rent officer (*Mason v Skilling*).

Scarcity value and comparison with assured tenancies

If the rent officer reaches his or her valuation on the basis of a consideration of compa- **13.144** rable properties in the area, the question arises as to what is a comparable property. This question is complicated considerably by the introduction of the Housing Act 1988. At the moment, and for some time to come, there will be two classes of tenants. One class will be subject to the Rent Act 1977 with its provisions for rent control: the other class will be subject to the Housing Act 1988. The rents of Housing Act tenants will largely be dependent upon the contracts they entered into with their landlords and therefore will be subject to market forces.

As a result of s 70(2), Rent Act tenancies have to a large degree remained immune from **13.145** market forces, so that in most areas fair rents determined by a rent officer have remained at a level significantly below that of properties let at a market rate. Section 70(2) demands that scarcity value should be ignored by the rent officer in assessing a fair rent. The valuation should be made on the assumption that the number of similar properties in the area is not significantly less than the number of people seeking accommodation. The aim of this provision is to prevent landlords from benefiting from the fact of a housing shortage in the area. The valuation should be based upon the inherent value of the property in question and should not reflect an increase in value brought about by a fluctuation in the market.

13.146   Section 70(2), however, will operate only where there is a scarcity of comparable property for rent. One of the main aims of the Housing Act 1988 was to encourage private sector lettings by removing the rent control that made the Rent Act 1977 so unpopular with landlords. To a large degree the Housing Act 1988 has succeeded in this aim. The question therefore arises as to whether, when assessing a fair rent for a Rent Act tenancy, a rent officer should have regard to comparable properties in the area which are let on assured tenancies. In *BTE Ltd v Merseyside and Cheshire RAC and Jones* (1991) 24 HLR 514 this question was answered in the affirmative. The landlord here produced evidence that there was no shortage of comparable properties to let at a market rent. The rent assessment committee accepted this evidence but did not consider these new lettings as appropriate comparables in assessing a fair rent for the tenancy in question. Instead, it assessed the rent having comparison only to similar properties let on regulated tenancies. This was held to be wrong. Where there is no scarcity of accommodation, lettings at market rents should be taken into account by the rent officer.

13.147   This decision is of considerable importance to regulated tenants. Fair rents can no longer be regarded as being immune to market forces and will presumably rise to a level comparable with the rents of assured tenancies.

13.148   If we consider our example it seems that the rent officer, in considering Robert's rent, will have to take into account the current market rent obtained for similar flats in the area let on assured tenancies.

Personal circumstances

13.149   In considering what a fair rent would be for the flat the rent officer must ignore 'personal circumstances'. The most common personal circumstance is the financial situation of the parties. The fact that Robert finds it difficult to pay the rent will be of no relevance to the assessment of a fair rent. The fact that Robert's back problem makes it difficult for him to get down the steps and to maintain the garden is likewise a personal circumstance. The garden is a feature that would generally make the flat more desirable for the average tenant, and it will be taken into account as such by the rent officer. The steps to the flat will be of relevance only if they are so steep as to cause inconvenience to an average tenant, in which case they may affect the value of the flat irrespective of the personal circumstances of the current tenant.

Improvements and deterioration

13.150   Catherine's contention that the value of the flat has been increased by the new kitchen will be ignored by the rent officer. Section 70(3)(b) specifically excludes improvements carried out by the tenant other than those carried out in pursuance of an obligation. The repainting of the interior was undertaken by Robert in pursuance of an obligation contained in the lease and will be taken into account by the rent officer. The damp in the bedroom will also be taken into account, for this is part of the general state of repair of the flat. (Under the lease Catherine will be responsible for the repair of the structure of the flat. If the damp was due to a failure by Robert to comply with his repairing obligations the damp would be ignored.) The deterioration of the furniture will be ignored because it was caused by Robert's cats and is excluded by s 70(3)(e).

Maximum fair rent

13.151   A maximum fair rent limit was introduced for the first time by the Rent Acts (Maximum Fair Rent) Order 1999, SI 1999/6. It applies in respect of applications made after 1 February 1999. The maximum rent is calculated as the current rent plus the difference between the current retail price index and the retail price index at the time the rent was last registered, plus 7.5 per cent (on the first application after 1 February 1999) or five per cent (on any subsequent application). The maximum limit only applies where the rent has previously been registered. In January 2000 the Court of Appeal held that this Order was *ultra vires*. This decision was overturned by the House of Lords in December 2000 (*R v Secretary of State for the Environment, Transport and the Regions, ex parte Spath Holme Ltd* [2001] 2 AC 349, [2001] 2 WLR 15, HL) but in the intervening period a number of landlords will have served notices of rent increases above the capped limit. Any such increase will be unlawful and is recoverable by the tenant.

The effect of rent registration

Once a fair rent is registered by the rent officer that rent is the maximum rent recoverable by the landlord. The registered sum will also include any amount charged by the landlord for the provision of services in addition to rent, even where such sums are recoverable under separate agreements (Rent Act 1977, s 71(1)). The fair rent is effective from the date of registration (Rent Act 1977, s 72, as amended by the Housing Act 1980, s 61(1); prior to the Housing Act 1980 the fair rent was back-dated to the date of application). The immediate effect upon the tenant varies, however, depending upon whether the tenant is currently holding under a protected or a statutory tenancy and whether the rent registered is higher or lower than the rent the tenant is currently paying. **13.152**

If the tenant is a protected tenant (ie the contractual tenancy has not been terminated) and the rent being paid under the contract is higher than the rent registered then the excess is not recoverable by the landlord (Rent Act 1977, s 44(2)). If the tenant has already paid rent in excess of the registered rent, he or she can recover this by taking county court proceedings or by deducting the amount from future payments of rent (Rent Act 1977, s 57). **13.153**

If the tenant is a protected tenant and the rent being paid under the contract is lower than the rent registered, the landlord and tenant will remain bound by the contract. The landlord can raise the rent only if he or she is entitled to do so by the contract, and in any case cannot raise it higher than the registered rent. If the lease provides for a rent increase the landlord will have to follow the requirements of the lease and also serve a valid notice of increase in the prescribed form (Rent Act 1977, s 49(2)). The effect of serving a notice of increase will be to terminate the contractual tenancy and replace it with a statutory tenancy (s 49(4)). **13.154**

If the contractual tenancy has already come to an end and the tenant is holding under a statutory tenancy, the landlord cannot recover any more than the registered rent (Rent Act 1977, s 45(2)). If the tenant is paying less than the registered rent, the landlord can increase the rent up to the amount registered by serving a notice of increase (s 45(2)(b)). **13.155**

If no rent is registered

If no fair rent has been registered there are still certain restrictions upon the amount of rent the landlord can charge. If the tenant is a new tenant, the rent will be whatever is contractually agreed between landlord and tenant. If the tenant was previously a regulated tenant and is granted a new tenancy of the same premises, the rent must not be any more than the rent payable at the end of the former tenancy. Likewise, if, when the contractual tenancy comes to an end, no rent has been registered then the rent will be limited to the rent payable during the last contractual period (Rent Act 1977, s 45). **13.156**

Provision is made by s 51 of the Rent Act 1977 to enable the rent to be increased by agreement. Any rent agreement, however, must be in writing and in the specified form. It must **13.157** state clearly that the tenant is not obliged to enter into the agreement and that his or her security of tenure will not be affected by a refusal to enter into the agreement. It must also advise the tenant of the right to apply to a rent officer at any time to have a fair rent registered.

Premiums

13.158 The Rent Act 1977 further imposes a variety of restrictions upon the charging of premiums by the landlord. Clearly it would be all too easy for an unscrupulous landlord to circumvent the consequences of rent control by demanding a lump sum from the tenant as a condition of the grant or the renewal of a tenancy. Section 119 therefore makes it illegal for any person to require or receive a premium or loan as a condition of, or in connection with, the grant, renewal, or continuance of a protected tenancy.

F RESTRICTED CONTRACTS

13.159 Certain classes of occupier who do not benefit from full Rent Act protection, either because they are not tenants but licensees, or because they are tenants but fall within an excluded category, may acquire limited protection if they have a restricted contract. Since the introduction of the Housing Act 1988 it has not been possible to create a restricted contract (unless the restricted contract was granted pursuant to a contract made before 15 January 1989) (Housing Act 1988, s 36). Furthermore, if the rent under a restricted contract has been varied by agreement (as opposed to being varied by a rent tribunal) after 15 January 1989, a new contract will be deemed to be created and this contract will not be a restricted contract. Given these rules, and the fact that the holders of restricted contracts are provided with only very limited security, the number of restricted contracts remaining must be very limited.

What is a restricted contract?

13.160 A restricted contract is defined generally by s 19 of the Rent Act 1977 as a contract whereby one person grants to another person, in consideration of a rent which includes payment for the use of furniture or for services, the right to occupy a dwelling as a residence. Sections 20 and 21 provide for two further specific situations where a restricted contract can arise. In all cases the occupier must have exclusive possession of at least part of the premises (s 19(6)). An occupier who has exclusive possession of one room in a house and shares further living accommodation with other occupiers can have a restricted contract (*Luganda v Service Hotels Ltd* [1969] 2 Ch 209; *R v South Middlesex Rent Tribunal, ex parte Beswick* (1976) 32 P&CR 67).

13.161 There are three situations in which an occupier will commonly acquire a restricted contract:

(a) Where the occupier is excluded from full Rent Act protection by s 7 because the landlord supplies board and attendance, but not if the value of the board supplied forms a substantial proportion of the whole rent (s 19(5)(c)).

(b) Where the occupier is excluded from full Rent Act protection by s 12 because the landlord is resident in a separate part of the same building (although not in the case of purpose-built flats), notwithstanding that the rent may not include payment for the use of furniture or services (s 20).

(c) Where the occupier is excluded from full Rent Act protection because he or she shares living accommodation with the landlord, notwithstanding that the rent may not include payment for the use of furniture or services (s 21).

Excluded categories

A contract cannot be a restricted contract if: **13.162**

(a) the rateable values are too high (£1,500 in London, £750 elsewhere) (s 19(4));
(b) it creates a regulated tenancy (ie has full Rent Act protection) (s 19(5)(a));
(c) the landlord's interest belongs to the Crown (s 19(5)(b));
(d) the rent includes payment for board and the value of the board to the lessee forms a substantial proportion of the whole rent (s 19(5)(c));
(e) it creates a qualified shared ownership lease (s 19(5)(cc));
(f) it is a protected occupancy as defined by the Rent (Agriculture) Act 1976 (s 19(5)(d));
(g) it creates a Housing Association tenancy to which Pt IV of the Rent Act 1977 applies (s 19(5)(e));
(h) it creates an assured tenancy within the meaning of s 56 of the Housing Act 1980;
(i) it is a holiday letting (s 19(7)).

Rent control

Both parties to a restricted contract can refer the contract to a rent tribunal and the **13.163** tibunal can register a 'reasonable' rent (Rent Act 1977, ss 77 and 78). Once a rent tribunal has determined the rent it cannot be made to hear a further application within two years unless there has been a change in the circumstances as to make the old rent no longer reasonable, or a joint application is made by both parties (s 80). If the landlord charges or seeks to charge more than the registered rent it is a criminal offence (s 81(4)).

Security

The very limited security granted to restricted contracts was reduced still further by the **13.164** Housing Act 1980. The rules therefore differ depending upon whether the restricted contract was entered into before or after 28 November 1980.

Restricted contracts entered into before 28 November 1980

An occupier can obtain security only if the restricted contract is referred to the rent tribunal. If, after the restricted contract has been referred to the rent tribunal, the landlord serves a notice to quit on the occupier, this notice to quit will not take effect until six months (or any lesser period the tribunal may substitute) after the decision of the tribunal (Rent Act 1977, s 103). Thereafter, if the occupier applies, the tribunal has the power to order further extensions of the notice to quit for periods of up to six months at a time (Rent Act 1977, s 104). The occupier can therefore prevent the landlord from terminating the tenancy by applying to the tribunal every six months for an extension. This can continue until the tribunal refuses to grant a further extension. The operation of s 104 is limited by s 106 which enables the tribunal to reduce the extension period on the landlord's application if the occupier is in breach of obligations in the contract. Section 105 contains special provisions preventing ss 103 and 104 from applying where the landlord was formerly an owner-occupier of the premises.

Restricted contracts entered into after 28 November 1980

13.166 Sections 102 to 106 of the Rent Act 1977 were repealed by the Housing Act 1980. The rent tribunal no longer has any jurisdiction to extend the notice to quit. Instead the county court has the power to suspend an order for possession for up to three months (Rent Act 1977, s 106A). Normally a possession order cannot be suspended for more than six weeks (Housing Act 1980, s 89).

14

THE RENT ACT 1977—
2. RECOVERY OF POSSESSION BY
THE LANDLORD

A INTRODUCTION

In this chapter we are concerned not simply with the termination of the tenancy (for, as **14.01** we have seen, terminating a contractual tenancy does not necessarily mean the end of the relationship between landlord and tenant), but with the ways in which the landlord can recover possession. To regain possession successfully of a property let on a protected tenancy, the landlord must first terminate the contractual tenancy. The contractual tenancy may be terminated by any of the common law methods considered in Chapter 10: a periodic tenancy will need to be terminated by a notice to quit; a fixed-term tenancy may come to an end by effluxion of time, in which case the landlord need take no action to terminate it. If a landlord wishes to regain possession of a fixed-term tenancy during the currency of the contractual term, he or she will first have to forfeit the tenancy according to the rules set out in Chapter 11 before he or she can make a claim for possession under the Rent Act 1977 (although both matters may be heard at the same hearing).

14.02   If the landlord fails to terminate the contractual tenancy, for example because the notice to quit is invalid or because the tenant is granted relief from forfeiture, the tenant will have a complete defence against possession proceedings. If the landlord successfully terminates the tenancy at common law and then satisfies the requirements of the Rent Act 1977, the court will make an order for possession. Once the landlord has recovered possession there are no outstanding rights and obligations between the parties and the relationship between landlord and tenant is finally at an end.

14.03   There are only two ways in which a landlord can recover possession of a property subject to a Rent Act protected tenancy:

(a)   if the tenant voluntarily leaves the dwelling-house;
(b)   if the landlord obtains a court order for possession.

B   VOLUNTARY DEPARTURE BY THE TENANT

14.04   A statutory tenancy will end, as we saw, when the tenant fails to satisfy the residency requirement. If a statutory tenant moves out of the premises, provided he or she removes all his or her belongings and does not exhibit an intention to return (see 13.100 to 13.103 on temporary absences), the landlord will be free to regain possession. If the tenant's contractual protected tenancy has not yet expired or been terminated, the tenant will have to surrender the tenancy (usually by a deed of surrender, but surrender can also be implied in certain circumstances, see 10.17 to 10.27) before the landlord will be entitled to possession. In neither case can the landlord compel the tenant to leave; however, if vacant possession of the premises is of sufficient value to the landlord he or she may well be prepared to offer the tenant a considerable financial inducement to give up the tenancy. This was a situation frequently encountered in the late 1980s when high property prices enabled developers to make large profits by renovating and converting older houses into flats to be sold. Even if a tenant is not offered any financial inducement to give up the tenancy, he or she may regard surrender as a better option than going to court, particularly if the tenant owes a considerable amount of rent arrears and feels that at the end of the court process he or she would end up not only having to give up his or her home but also liable to pay back the debt, as well as possibly having to pay legal costs.

C   OBTAINING A POSSESSION ORDER

14.05   If the tenant will not voluntarily leave the premises, the landlord's only option is to go to court and seek an order for possession. Under the Rent Act 1977, s 98, the situations in which the court will grant a possession order are severely limited:

(1)   Subject to this Part of this Act, a court shall not make an order for possession of a dwelling-house which is for the time being let on a protected tenancy or subject to a statutory tenancy unless the court considers it reasonable to make such an order and either—
(a)   the court is satisfied that suitable alternative accommodation is available for the tenant or will be available for him when the order in question takes effect, or
(b)   the circumstances are as specified in any of the Cases in Part I of Schedule 15 to this Act.
(2)   If, apart from subsection (1) above, the landlord would be entitled to recover possession of a dwelling-house which is for the time being let on or subject to a regulated tenancy, the

court shall make an order for possession if the circumstances of the case are as specified in any of the Cases in Part II of Schedule 15.

Part I of Sch 15 sets out a list of Cases (Nos 1 to 10) known as 'discretionary Cases'. Part II of Sch 15 contains a further 10 Cases (Nos 11 to 20) which are known as 'mandatory Cases'. The mandatory Cases all share the common factor that on commencing the tenancy the tenant should have been given warning that the landlord may require possession of the premises at some point in the future. Both the discretionary and the mandatory Cases are discussed in detail later. **14.06**

A landlord will be able to obtain an order for possession only if: **14.07**

(a) he or she can satisfy the court that suitable alternative accommodation is available for the tenant and the court considers it reasonable to make an order for possession;
(b) he or she can satisfy one or more of the discretionary Cases listed in Part I of Sch 15 and the court considers it reasonable to make an order for possession;
(c) he or she can satisfy one or more of the mandatory Cases listed in Part II of Sch 15.

Suitable alternative accommodation

If the landlord can show the court that suitable alternative accommodation will be available for occupation by the tenant, the court will make an order for possession provided it considers it reasonable to do so. The alternative accommodation does not have to be owned by the existing landlord; the requirements will be satisfied if the landlord obtains a certificate from the local authority saying that it will provide the tenant with alternative accommodation, or if the existing landlord arranges for alternative accommodation to be made available for the tenant from another private landlord. **14.08**

Obviously, a tenant will not want to move to premises which are significantly inferior or less suitable than the tenant's current home. Schedule 15, Pt IV to the 1977 Act therefore provides further guidance as to what is to be regarded as 'suitable alternative accommodation' for the purposes of s 98(1). **14.09**

Local authority certificate

The Rent Act 1977, Sch 15, Pt IV, para 3 provides that a certificate from the local authority certifying that it will provide suitable alternative accommodation for the tenant by a date specified in the certificate will be conclusive evidence that suitable alternative accommodation will be available for the tenant by that date. In practice, however, it is very rare for local authorities to issue such certificates. **14.10**

Security of tenure

Clearly, a tenant will not want to move into new accommodation to find that his or her rights under the new tenancy are significantly less extensive than his or her rights were under the old tenancy. As a Rent Act protected tenant or a statutory tenant, the tenant had extensive security of tenure; by offering the tenant alternative accommodation the landlord cannot reduce this security of tenure. The Rent Act 1977, Sch 15, Pt IV, para 4 provides that the accommodation provided will be deemed suitable only if it consists of: **14.11**

(a) premises which are to be let as a separate dwelling such that they will then be let on a protected tenancy (other than one under which the landlord might recover possession of the dwelling-house under one of the Cases in Part II of this Schedule), or
(b) premises to be let as a separate dwelling on terms which will, in the opinion of the court, afford to the tenant security of tenure reasonably equivalent to the security afforded by

Part VII of this Act in the case of a protected tenancy of a kind mentioned in paragraph (a) above.

14.12   In other words, the alternative accommodation will only be suitable provided it offers:

(a)   full Rent Act protection; or
(b)   security of tenure reasonably equivalent to full Rent Act protection.

14.13   Whether the security of tenure offered is 'reasonably equivalent' will depend upon the facts of the case. We have seen that, generally speaking, after 15 January 1989 no new Rent Act protected tenancies can be created. However, the security of tenure provided by an assured tenancy is not as extensive as that provided by a protected tenancy—there are wider grounds of possession and only minimal rent control. Section 34(1)(c)(iii) of the Housing Act 1988 therefore provides that the court may direct that the alternative accommodation should be held on a protected tenancy if 'in the circumstances, the grant of an assured tenancy would not afford the required security'. This is one of the few ways in which a protected tenancy can be created after 15 January 1989.

Proximity to workplace

14.14   The tenant will not want to find that, having moved to a new home, he or she is now expending considerably more time and money travelling to work. The Rent Act 1977, Sch 15, Pt IV, para 5(1) therefore requires that the accommodation must be 'reasonably suitable to the needs of the tenant and his family as regards proximity to place of work'.

14.15   This provision includes not only the tenant, but also any members of the tenant's family who reside with the tenant and have to travel to work. In each case what is 'reasonably suitable' will be a question of fact, and the court should consider not simply the distance from the place of work but also the time it takes to travel there and the means of transport available. (See *Yewbright Properties Ltd v Stone* (1980) 40 P&CR 402.)

Rental and extent

14.16   The tenant will not want to end up in a property which is much more expensive, smaller, or otherwise inferior to his or her present accommodation. As well as being suitable with regards to the proximity to the place of work, the Rent Act 1977, Sch 15, Pt IV, para 5 requires that the accommodation must also be:

(a)   similar as regards rental and extent to the accommodation afforded by dwelling-houses provided in the neighbourhood by any local housing authority for persons whose needs as regards extent are, in the opinion of the court, similar to those of the tenant and of his family; or
(b)   reasonably suitable to the means of the tenant and to the needs of the tenant and his family as regards extent and character;...

14.17   The landlord can satisfy these requirements in two ways. First, he may obtain a certificate from the local authority stating what sort of accommodation the local authority would provide for persons of similar needs to the tenant and his or her family. It is not that common for the local authority to issue such certificates, and even if it does the court should not blindly follow the certificate but should decide on the facts, having considered the certificate, whether the accommodation offered by the landlord is similar to that which would be provided by the local authority (*Jones v Cook* (1990) 22 HLR 319, CA).

14.18   More commonly, the landlord will have to persuade the court under the second requirement set out in para 5 that the alternative accommodation is reasonably suitable to the needs and means of the tenant and his or her family. The tenant's 'needs' in this context are his or her 'housing needs'. This is illustrated best by the case of *Hill v Rochard* [1983] 1 WLR 478. The tenants here lived in a large isolated country house, with a paddock and outbuildings which enabled them to keep a number of domestic animals. The alternative accommodation offered was a modern four-bedroom house on an up-market housing estate in the area. The tenants had lived in the country house for 16 years and objected that the move to the new house would entail a change of lifestyle. The court held that the alternative accommodation was suitable. The Rent Acts, said Lord Justice Dunn (at 485), were not intended to protect 'incidental advantages' relating to the tenant's own 'particular taste for amenities'.

The fact that the alternative accommodation offered is smaller than the tenant's current accommodation does not necessarily mean that it will not be suitable. In *Mykolyshyn v Noah* [1970] 1 WLR 1271, it was held that part of the present premises can be suitable alternative accommodation. The court, however, should take into account the tenant's professional needs, for example an artist who uses a room as a studio (*MacDonnell v Daly* [1969] 1 WLR 1482), the need to entertain business associates (*De Markozoff v Craig* (1949) 93 SJ 693), or the need to have sufficient room to take in lodgers (*Warren v Austen* [1947] 2 All ER 185). **14.19**

Environmental factors will also be taken into account. Where a landlord was seeking possession of a flat with a garden in a quiet residential road, a flat with no garden on a busy thoroughfare, next to a fish and chip shop and near a pub, was held not to be suitable even though the new flat was larger than the old flat (*Redspring Ltd v Francis* [1973] 1 WLR 134). However, where a tenant who lived in London but worked in Luton objected to alternative accommodation because it would take him away from his friends, mosque, and cultural interests, the court held that the alternative accommodation was suitable (*Siddiqui v Rashid* [1980] 1 WLR 1018). Environmental factors are relevant only in so far as they relate to the character of the property itself (but environmental factors can be taken into account when it comes to considering reasonableness, see 14.20 to 14.24). **14.20**

Furniture

A tenant occupying a furnished flat will not want new accommodation which is either unfurnished or furnished to a lesser standard than the tenant's old accommodation. The Rent Act 1977, Sch 15, Pt IV, para 5 further provides: **14.21**

> that if any furniture was provided for use under the protected or statutory tenancy in question, furniture is provided for use in the accommodation which is either similar to that so provided or is reasonably suitable to the needs of the tenant and his family.

Reasonableness

Wherever a landlord is seeking an order of possession by establishing that suitable alternative accommodation is available for the tenant or by establishing one of the discretionary grounds of possession, he or she must not only demonstrate to the court that the suitable alternative accommodation is available or that the discretionary ground is satisfied, but also satisfy the court that it is reasonable to make the order. When a landlord has clearly made out a case under one of the discretionary grounds, the court can refuse to grant a possession order if it does not consider it reasonable. The requirement of reasonableness is an 'overriding requirement'. If the court fails to consider the question of reasonableness before granting an order for possession, the judgment will be a nullity (*Minchburn v Fernandez (No. 2)* (1986) 19 HLR 29, CA; *Verrilli v Idigoras* [1990] EGCS 3, CA; *R v* **14.22**

Bloomsbury and Marylebone County Court, ex parte Blackburne (1985) 275 EG 1273, CA). If a landlord establishes a mandatory ground of possession, the question of reasonableness does not arise.

14.23 The court has a very wide discretion: it must take into account 'all relevant circumstances as they exist at the date of the hearing' (*Cumming v Danson* [1942] 2 All ER 653 *per* Lord Greene MR at 655). Thus, virtually any factor which might affect either the landlord or the tenant if the order for possession is made can be considered by the court, and it is the task of the judge to consider these factors 'in a broad common-sense way' and to give them such weight as he or she sees fit. However, reasonableness is a question of fact based upon the particular circumstances of the individual case and it is difficult for any party dissatisfied with the court's exercise of discretion to appeal the court's decision unless it is possible to show that the judge misdirected himself or herself in law (*Darnell v Millwood* [1951] 1 All ER 88 at 90).

14.24 Some factors that have been found to be relevant include:

(a) emotional attachment to premises in which the tenant had lived for many years (*Battlespring Ltd v Gates* (1983) 11 HLR 6; *Whitehouse v Lee* [2009] EWCA Civ 375, [2010] HLR 11);

(b) health of the parties (*Briddon v George* [1948] 1 All ER 609; *Williamson v Pallant* [1924] 2 KB 173);

(c) age of the parties (*Battlespring v Gates*);

(d) the financial position of the parties, in particular whether an immediate sale of the property with vacant possession is a financially necessity for the landlord (*Whitehouse v Lee*);

(e) the purpose of the Act (*Redspring Ltd v Francis*, 14.20);

(f) the public interest (*Cresswell v Hodgson* [1951] 1 All ER 710; *Wallasey v Pritchard* [1936] 3 LJNCCR 35);

(g) loss of amenities (*Siddiqui v Rashid*, 14.20);

(h) the landlord's reasons for wanting possession (*Minchburn v Fernandez*, 14.22);

(i) the conduct of the parties including previous breaches of covenant.

D DISCRETIONARY GROUNDS FOR POSSESSION

14.25 The Rent Act 1977, Sch 15, Pt I lists the following Cases in which the court may order possession under s 98(1) of the Act.

Case 1—breach of obligation of the tenancy or rent arrears

Where any rent lawfully due from the tenant has not been paid, or any obligation of the protected or statutory tenancy which arises under this Act, or—

(a) in the case of a protected tenancy, any other obligation of the tenancy, in so far as is consistent with the provisions of Part VII of this Act, or

(b) in the case of a statutory tenancy, any other obligation of the previous protected tenancy which is applicable to the statutory tenancy, has been broken or not performed.

14.26 Case 1 includes two grounds of possession and is probably the most commonly used of all the discretionary grounds for possession. It permits a landlord to obtain an order for possession either when the tenant fails to pay rent or when the tenant breaches any other obligation in the tenancy.

Rent

The crucial date with regard to a claim under Case 1 for arrears of rent is the date of **14.27** the commencement of legal proceedings (*Bird v Hillage* [1948] 1 KB 91). The landlord must establish not only that rent is lawfully due (ie that it has not been paid by midnight on the day upon which it is payable), but also that some rent is outstanding at the time proceedings are issued. If no rent is outstanding at the date of issue the court cannot make an order for possession. If some rent is outstanding at the date of issue the court may make an order for possession but will first consider whether such an order is reasonable. If the amount of arrears is small, or where there are special circumstances (eg the tenant may be withholding rent because of a landlord's failure to comply with a covenant to repair), it is most unlikely that the court will consider it reasonable to make an absolute order. The court will, however, take into account all the surrounding circumstances and might consider an order as reasonable where a tenant has a bad past record of non- and late payment of rent (*Dellenty v Pellow* [1951] 2 KB 91, [1951] 2 All ER 716). For this reason a landlord seeking to rely on this ground should send a 'letter before action' to the tenant warning him or her that legal proceedings will be commenced if the tenant does not pay before a certain date. Failure to give the tenant due warning of proceedings and an opportunity to make good the arrears will make it unlikely that the court will consider the making of a possession order reasonable.

If the occupier has acquired a statutory tenancy by succession, he or she is not liable to the **14.28** landlord for rent owed by the previous tenant at the time of that tenant's death.

It should be noted that Case 1 under the Rent Act 1977 is merely a discretionary ground, **14.29** in contrast with the Housing Act 1988 where serious rent arrears are a mandatory ground of possession (see 16.46).

Breach of tenancy obligation

A landlord may seek possession under Case 1 for any breach of tenancy obligation. The **14.30** obligation may be express or implied, but it must be an obligation of the tenancy. Case 1 cannot be used in respect of a collateral agreement, for a collateral agreement does not form part of the tenancy (see 4.15). If the contractual tenancy had come to an end and the tenant occupies now under a statutory tenancy, the tenant will continue to be bound by the obligations contained in the original contractual tenancy so long as they are compatible with the provisions of the Rent Act 1977 (see 13.129).

Case 1 can be used in respect of both continuing and once-and-for-all breaches of obli- **14.31** gation. There is no requirement that the breach must actually be subsisting at the time of the issue of proceedings or at the time of the hearing, but if the tenant has in fact remedied the breach at the time of the hearing it is unlikely that the court will consider it reasonable to make a possession order. A landlord cannot rely upon a breach that he has waived (see 11.31 to 11.39). In determining whether or not a breach has been waived, there is a difference depending upon whether the tenant holds under a contractual tenancy or under a statutory tenancy. If the tenant still holds under a contractual tenancy the strict common law rules will apply (see 11.35); thus, even a qualified acceptance of rent by a landlord with knowledge of the breach will amount to waiver. However, if the tenant holds under a statutory tenancy the common law rules do not apply and it will be a question of fact as to whether the landlord had waived the breach; thus, a qualified acceptance of rent may not, on the facts, constitute a waiver by the landlord (*Oak Property Co. Ltd v Chapman* [1947] 2 All ER 1; *Trustees of Smith's (Henry) Charity v Wilson* [1983] 1 All ER 73).

Case 2—nuisance, annoyance, use for immoral or illegal purposes

Where the tenant or any person residing or lodging with him or any sub-tenant of his has been guilty of conduct which is a nuisance or annoyance to adjoining occupiers, or has been convicted of using the dwelling-house or allowing the dwelling-house to be used for immoral or illegal purposes.

14.32   Like Case 1, Case 2 also contains two separate grounds of possession. Possession may be granted where the landlord can show that the tenant has been guilty of conduct which is a nuisance or an annoyance to adjoining occupiers, or where the tenant has been convicted of using the dwelling-house for immoral or illegal purposes.

Nuisance or annoyance

14.33   The inclusion of the word 'annoyance' gives Case 2 a far wider ambit than that which would be connoted by the single word 'nuisance'. 'Nuisance' generally requires some act of physical interference, but the combined words 'nuisance or annoyance' are, for the purposes of Case 2, to be given a common-sense, non-technical meaning. Thus, the keeping of dogs can amount to a nuisance or annoyance, as can loud music (*Crowder v Mercer*, unreported, 6 March 1981, CA) or the use of abusive and obscene language (*Cobstone Investments Ltd v Maxim* [1985] QB 140 at 143C). The 'nuisance or annoyance' does not even have to take place on the demised premises. In *Whitbread v Ward* (1952) 159 EG 494, the fact that a married tenant exercised 'undue familiarity' with the landlord's 16-year-old daughter in an alley some 200 yards away from the premises was held to be an annoyance to the landlord who lived in the flat above the tenant. Furthermore, a person will be an 'adjoining occupier' provided he or she lives in sufficient proximity to be affected by the tenant's conduct; he or she does not have to occupy a flat directly next to the tenant's premises (*Cobstone v Maxim*).

14.34   This ground can be relied upon even where the nuisance or annoyance complained of has ceased (*Florent v Horez* (1983) 12 HLR 1).

Immoral or illegal purposes

14.35   The landlord may be able to get a possession order if the tenant had been convicted of using the dwelling-house, or of allowing the dwelling-house to be used, for immoral or illegal purposes. The landlord, however, must show that the premises themselves had a connection with the crime; it is 'not enough that the tenant has been convicted of a crime with which the premises have nothing to do beyond merely being the scene of its commission' (*Schneiders & Sons v Abrahams* [1925] 1 KB 301 *per* Scrutton LJ at 311). For example, if a person is convicted of possession of an unlawful drug and the drug was found in his or her pocket while he or she was on the premises, it could not be said that that person was *using* the premises for illegal purposes. If, however, the person convicted had concealed a stash somewhere in the premises then the landlord may be able to rely on Case 2 (*Abrahams v Wilson* [1971] 2 QB 88). Typical examples of using premises for an illegal purpose would be using them as a store for stolen goods or as a brothel.

14.36   Complaints against, or the conviction of, a sub-tenant or any other person occupying the property can provide a ground of possession against the tenant even if the tenant has done nothing wrong. In such a case the tenant could only remedy the breach by taking steps to remove the wrongdoer from the premises.

Case 3—waste or neglect

Where the condition of the dwelling-house has, in the opinion of the court, deteriorated owing to acts of waste by, or the neglect or default of, the tenant or any person residing or lodging with him or any sub-tenant of his and, in the case of any act of waste by, or the neglect or default of, a person lodging with the tenant or a sub-tenant of his, where the court is satisfied that the tenant has not, before the making of the order in question, taken such steps as he ought reasonably to have taken for the removal of the lodger or sub-tenant as the case may be.

The landlord may be entitled to possession under Case 3 where the condition of the **14.37** premises has deteriorated as a result of neglect by the tenant or the tenant's sub-tenants or lodgers. He or she may be entitled to possession where the tenant, sub-tenant, or lodger has made unauthorized alterations or improvements to the property (*Marsden v Edward Heyes Ltd* [1927] 2 KB 1, CA) (see 7.77). However, the court will take into account the fact that the deterioration occurred before the occupier became tenant of the property. In *Holloway v Povey* (1984) 15 HLR 104, a possession order was suspended in order to give a tenant who had succeeded to his father's tenancy the opportunity to tidy up the garden, which had been neglected by his father. It should be noted that a landlord may be able to succeed under Case 3 despite the fact that the tenant has not breached the terms of the tenancy or any implied common law duty (*Lowe v Lendrum* (1950) 159 EG 423). A tenant may rely on Case 3 against a sub-tenant or lodger and may indeed be obliged to do so in order to avoid this ground being used against the tenant.

Case 4—furniture

Where the condition of any furniture provided for use under the tenancy has, in the opinion of the court, deteriorated owing to ill-treatment by the tenant or any person residing or lodging with him or any sub-tenant of his and, in the case of any ill-treatment by a person lodging with the tenant or a sub-tenant of his, where the court is satisfied that the tenant has not, before the making of the order in question, taken such steps as he ought reasonably to have taken for the removal of the lodger or sub-tenant, as the case may be.

As for Case 3, but referring to deterioration or damage to furniture. **14.38**

Case 5—notice to quit by tenant

Where the tenant has given notice to quit and, in consequence of that notice, the landlord has contracted to sell or let the dwelling-house or has taken any other steps as the result of which he would, in the opinion of the court, be seriously prejudiced if he could not obtain possession.

Case 5 is specifically designed to deal with the situation where a tenant serves a notice **14.39** to quit upon the landlord and then changes his or her mind. If the landlord has already entered into a contract to sell or to rent the property to a third party, he or she may be liable to this third party if unable to gain vacant possession of the premises because the tenant has decided not to move out (and is now a statutory tenant). This ground may also enable the landlord to gain possession against a lawful sub-tenant even though it was the head tenant who gave notice (*Lord Hylton v Heal* [1921] 2 KB 438). For the position of sub-tenants generally, see 14.70.

Case 6—sub-letting

Where, without the consent of the landlord, the tenant has, at any time after—
- (b) 22nd March 1973, in the case of a tenancy which became a regulated tenancy by virtue of section 14 of the Counter-Inflation Act 1973;
- (bb) the commencement of section 73 of the Housing Act 1980, in the case of a tenancy which became a regulated tenancy by virtue of that section;

(c)   14th August 1974, in the case of a regulated furnished tenancy; or

(d)   8th December 1965, in the case of any other tenancy,

assigned or sub-let the whole of the dwelling-house or sub-let part of the dwelling-house, the remainder being already sub-let.

14.40 Given that the Rent Act 1977 can endow a tenant with a status of virtual irremovability, a landlord will not want to find a new and unknown tenant occupying his or her premises. Case 6 therefore may entitle the landlord to possession if a tenant assigns or sub-lets the property without consent, even when there is no prohibition against sub-letting or assigning in the tenancy agreement. Case 6 applies only when the tenant has assigned or sub-let the whole of the premises or, where part of the premises is already sub-let, the tenant sub-lets the remainder. In practice Case 6 is of relevance only to contractual tenants, for a statutory tenant cannot assign a tenancy (see 13.92) and if a statutory tenant sub-lets the whole of the premises he or she will cease to occupy the premises as his or her residence.

14.41 Case 6 does not demand that the sub-tenancy be subsisting at the time of the issue of proceedings, but if the sub-tenancy has already expired the court may well regard it as unreasonable to make an order for possession. However, if the court regards it as reasonable, a landlord can obtain possession under Case 6 against both the tenant and the sub-tenant notwithstanding the effect of s 137 of the 1977 Act (effect on sub-tenancy of determination of superior tenancy).

Case 7—off-licences

14.42 Repealed by the Housing Act 1980, s 152 and Sch 26.

Case 8—former employees

Where the dwelling-house is reasonably required by the landlord for occupation as a residence for some person engaged in his whole-time employment, or in the whole-time employment of some tenant from him or with whom, conditional on housing being provided, a contract for such employment has been entered into, and the tenant was in the employment of the landlord or former landlord, and the dwelling-house was let to him in consequence of that employment and he has ceased to be in that employment.

14.43 Case 8 applies only to service tenants. Its aim is to provide that where a flat or house 'goes with the job' and the current tenant/employee stops working for his or her landlord, the landlord will be able to regain possession of the flat or house so that it may be offered to the new tenant/employee. To rely on Case 8 the landlord will have to show that:

(a)   the current tenant was engaged in full-time employment by the landlord or by a former landlord;

(b)   the dwelling-house was originally let to the current tenant in consequence of that employment;

(c)   that employment has now ceased;

(d)   the dwelling-house is reasonably required for a prospective tenant;

(e)   the prospective tenant is engaged in full-time employment by the landlord or by one of the landlord's tenants, or the prospective tenant has entered into a contract of employment which is conditional on the provision of housing.

Case 9—dwelling required for member of landlord's family

Where the dwelling-house is reasonably required by the landlord for occupation as a residence for—

(a) himself, or

(b) any son or daughter of his over 18 years of age, or

(c) his father or mother, or

(d) if the dwelling-house is let on or subject to a regulated tenancy, the father or mother of his spouse or civil partner;

and the landlord did not become landlord by purchasing the dwelling-house or any interest therein after—

(i) 7th November 1956, in the case of a tenancy which was then a controlled tenancy;

(ii) 8th March 1973, in the case of a tenancy which became a regulated tenancy by virtue of section 14 of the Counter-Inflation Act 1973;

(iii) 24th May 1974, in the case of a regulated furnished tenancy; or

(iv) 23rd March 1965, in the case of any other tenancy.

Under the Rent Act 1977, Sch 15, Pt III, para 1:   **14.44**

A court shall not make an order for possession of a dwelling-house by reason only that the circumstances of the case fall within Case 9 in Part I of this Schedule if the court is satisfied that, having regard to all the circumstances of the case, including the question whether other accommodation is available for the landlord or the tenant, greater hardship would be caused by granting the order than by refusing to grant it.

Case 9 may be used by the landlord to recover possession when the dwelling-house is **14.45**
reasonably required for occupation as a residence by the landlord, by one of his or her children over 18, a parent, or a parent in law. The aim of this provision is to allow a landlord to gain possession for use by the landlord or his or her family, not to benefit the speculator. Case 9 cannot be used if the landlord purchased the property when the tenant was already in occupation, or when he or she wants to gain possession in order to sell the property (*Rowe v Truelove* (1976) 241 EG 533).

Whether the property is reasonably required by the landlord is a question of fact. The **14.46**
court will take into account such factors as the proximity of the property to the landlord's place of work (*Jackson v Harbour* [1924] EGD 99), whether the landlord already has a place to live (*Dennealy v Dunne* [1977] QB 837, [1977] 2 All ER 696, CA), the size of the landlord's family, the health of the landlord and his or her family, and any other relevant circumstances. The landlord's requirement of possession need not be immediate; the court may order possession when that requirement will arise in the ascertainable but not too distant future (*Kidder v Birch* (1983) 265 EG 773). The tenant's interests are not relevant in determining whether the premises are reasonably required, but they will be considered under the overall question of reasonableness.

If a landlord seeks possession under Case 9, Sch 15, Pt III, para 1 requires that the court **14.47**
considers the question of greater hardship. Possession will not be granted to the landlord if the tenant is able to show that greater hardship would be caused to him or her if the possession was granted than would be caused to the landlord if the possession order was not granted. The court has very wide discretion and should take into account all relevant considerations, eg the financial means of both parties, the availability of other accommodation for both parties, the health of both parties, and future as well as present hardships that may arise for either party.

Case 10—overcharging sub-tenant

Where the court is satisfied that the rent charged by the tenant—

(a) for any sub-let part of the dwelling-house which is a dwelling-house let on a protected tenancy or subject to a statutory tenancy is or was in excess of the maximum rent for the time being recoverable for that part, having regard to ... Part III of this Act, or

(b) for any sub-let part of the dwelling-house which is subject to a restricted contract or was in excess of the maximum (if any) which it is lawful for the lessor, within the meaning of Part V of this Act to require or receive having regard to the provisions of that Part.

14.48   Where the sub-tenant who rents part of the premises falls within the Rent Act 1977, either as a protected tenant, a statutory tenant, or a under a restricted contract, and the rent payable for the sub-tenancy has been registered or fixed by a rent tribunal, the landlord may recover possession under Case 10 if the tenant is charging the sub-tenant more than the designated rent.

E MANDATORY GROUNDS FOR POSSESSION

14.49   If a landlord can establish one of the mandatory Cases for possession set out in the Rent Act 1977, Sch 15, Pt II, the court will make an order for possession under s 98(2) of the Act: there is no element of discretion and the court will not consider whether or not it is reasonable to make such an order. However, any attempt by a landlord to seek possession under a mandatory Case should not come as a complete surprise to the tenant. All of the mandatory Cases require the landlord to serve written notice upon the tenant not later than 'the relevant date' stating that possession may be recovered under the Case in question. The relevant date is defined by Sch 15, Pt III, para 2 and in the vast majority of cases it will be the start of the tenancy. Nevertheless, under Cases 11, 12, 19, and 20 the court may dispense with the requirement of notice if it is of the opinion that it is just and equitable to do so.

Case 11—returning owner-occupier

14.50   The aim of this case is to enable an owner-occupier who has let out his or her house to regain possession if he or she wishes to move back into that house. For example, it allows a person who goes to work abroad to let out his or her home but to retain the possibility of moving back in if he or she wants to return.

14.51   To be able to rely on this Case a variety of conditions must be satisfied:

(a) The landlord must have served notice on the tenant as described earlier (although this requirement may be dispensed with by the court if it considers it just and equitable to do so). Where there has been a chain of lettings the landlord should have served notice on each successive tenant, although, again, the court has power to dispense with this requirement (Sch 15, Pt II, Case 11, condition (b)).

(b) The landlord must have occupied the dwelling-house as his or her residence at some time before the letting. The requirement of residence is the same as that which applies to statutory tenants (see 13.97 to 13.107).

(c) The dwelling-house has not since:

(i) 22 March 1973, in the case of a tenancy which became a regulated tenancy by virtue of s 14 of the Counter-Inflation Act 1973;

(ii) 14 August 1974, in the case of a regulated furnished tenancy; or

(iii) 8 December 1965, in the case of any other tenancy,

been let by the owner-occupier on a protected tenancy, unless that protected tenancy was subject to notice served by the landlord as in (a) (ie that possession might be required under Case 11).

(d) One of the conditions set out in Sch 15, Pt V, paras (a) and (c) to (f) is satisfied (see 14.52).

The conditions contained in Sch 15, Pt V, para 2 are that: **14.52**

(a) the dwelling-house is required as a residence for the owner or any member of his family who resided with the owner when he last occupied the dwelling-house as a residence; [In contrast to Case 9, there is no necessity under Case 11 for the landlord's requirement to be reasonable.]

(b) the owner has retired from regular employment and requires the dwelling house as a residence;

(c) the owner has died and the dwelling-house is required as a residence for a member of his family who was residing with him at the time of his death;

(d) the owner has died and the dwelling-house is required by a successor in title as his residence or for the purpose of disposing of it with vacant possession;

(e) the dwelling-house is subject to a mortgage, made by deed and granted before the tenancy, and the mortgagee—

(i) is entitled to exercise a power of sale conferred on him by the mortgage or by section 101 of the Law of Property Act 1925; and

(ii) requires the dwelling-house for the purpose of disposing of it with vacant possession in exercise of that power; and

(f) the dwelling-house is not reasonably suitable to the needs of the owner, having regard to his place of work, and he requires it for the purpose of disposing of it with vacant possession and of using the proceeds of that disposal in acquiring, as his residence, a dwelling-house which is more suitable to those needs.

Case 12—retirement homes

Case 12 is useful to a person who has purchased a property with the intention of moving   **14.53**
into it when he or she retires. It allows the owner to rent out the property while he or she continues in full-time work, but to regain possession on retirement. This Case is broadly similar to Case 11, but there is no requirement that the owner must previously have occupied the premises as his or her residence. For the landlord to be able to rely upon this Case, the following conditions must be satisfied:

(a) The landlord must have served notice on the tenant as described earlier (although this requirement may be dispensed with by the court if it considers it just and equitable to do so).

(b) Since 14 August 1974, the dwelling-house must not have been let by the owner on a protected tenancy, unless that protected tenancy was subject to notice served by the landlord as in (a).

(c) One of the conditions set out in Sch 15, Pt V, paras (b) to (e) is satisfied (see 14.52).

Case 13—off-season holiday lets

The aim of this case was to allow a landlord who normally rented out a property as holi-   **14.54**
day accommodation during the summer to grant a longer tenancy out of season that may not fall within the definition of a holiday letting and may therefore be eligible for Rent Act

protection. The aim of this Case was to provide the landlord with a means of regaining possession of the property so that it could again be used as holiday accommodation. As any such existing letting would realistically have had to have been made well after 15 January 1989 it would be an assured tenancy and could not attract Rent Act protected status (see 13.02). Case 13 is, therefore, no longer of any real relevance.

Case 14—educational institutions

14.55 Case 14 is similar to Case 13. Like holiday accommodation, lettings to students by educational institutions are also excluded from Rent Act protection (see s 8 at 13.58). An educational institution may wish to grant a tenancy which does not fall within the exclusion, for example during a college holiday. This ground was intended to enable the institution to regain possession at the end of such a letting. As with Case 13 any existing letting would, by its nature, have had to be relatively recent and would no longer attract Rent Act protected status.

Case 15—ministers of religion

14.56 This Case may be used by the owner of a dwelling-house which is normally used to provide accommodation for a minister of religion, to gain possession of that dwelling-house so that it can be used for this purpose.

14.57 To rely upon this Case:

(a) The dwelling-house must be held for the purpose of being available for occupation by a minister of religion as a residence from which to perform the duties of his or her office.

(b) The landlord must have given notice that possession might be recovered under this Case.

(c) The court must be satisfied that the dwelling-house is required for occupation by a minister of religion as a residence from which to perform his or her duties.

Case 16—agricultural employees

14.58 This Case enables a landlord to gain possession of a property so that it can be occupied by an agricultural employee of the landlord.

14.59 To rely on this Case:

(a) The dwelling-house must, at any time, have been occupied by a person under the terms of his employment as a person employed in agriculture.

(b) The tenant must not be, nor at any time have been, employed in agriculture by the landlord and must not be the widow of a person who was so employed.

(c) The landlord must have given notice that possession might be recovered under this Case.

(d) The court must be satisfied that the dwelling-house is required for occupation by a person employed, or to be employed, by the landlord in agriculture.

Case 17—farmhouses made redundant by amalgamation

14.60 Where a dwelling-house was originally occupied by a person responsible for farming land, and where that dwelling-house has been made redundant under a scheme of amalgamation under the Agriculture Act 1967, the landlord can gain possession of the property if it is again required for the occupation of a person employed in agriculture.

In order to rely on Case 17 the landlord must have given the tenant written notice, not later **14.61** than the relevant date (usually the commencement of the tenancy) that possession might be recovered under this case.

Proceedings for possession must be commenced within five years of the date on which pro- **14.62** posals for the amalgamation were approved. If, however, the person farming the land (or his widow) continued to occupy the dwelling-house at the time of amalgamation, proceedings must be commenced within three years of the date the dwelling-house next became unoccupied. Case 17 cannot be used against a tenant if his or her tenancy is regulated by s 99 of the 1977 Act.

Case 18—farmhouses made redundant without amalgamation

Case 18 applies where a dwelling-house was formerly occupied by a person responsible for **14.63** farming the land within which the dwelling is situated. The dwelling must then have been let on a regulated tenancy (but not after the implementation of a scheme of amalgamation under the Agriculture Act 1967), and the tenant given written notice not later than the relevant date (usually the date of the commencement of the tenancy) that possession might be recovered under this case.

Possession will be ordered if the court is satisfied that the dwelling-house is now required **14.64** for occupation by a person responsible for farming any part of the land, or a person employed by the landlord in agriculture.

Where the relevant date was before 9 August 1972 possession proceedings must have been **14.65** commenced within five years of the end of occupation of the tenant who was formerly responsible for farming the land. Like Case 17, Case 18 cannot be used against a tenant if his or her tenancy is regulated by s 99 of the 1977 Act.

Case 19—protected shorthold tenancies

The protected shorthold tenancy was the forerunner of the assured shorthold tenancy. **14.66** It was created by the Housing Act 1980 and permitted a landlord to grant a short fixed-term tenancy (of between one and five years) without conferring security of tenure upon the tenant. No more protected shorthold tenancies could be created after 15 January 1989 (unless created pursuant to a contract made before that date) and so there are now very few protected shorthold tenancies in existence. New tenancies granted to former protected shorthold tenants will be assured shorthold tenancies (Housing Act 1980, s 34(3)).

When a protected shorthold tenancy comes to an end and the tenant continues in occupa- **14.67** tion as a statutory tenant, Case 19 gives the landlord the right to a possession order provided the following two conditions are satisfied:

(a) there has been no grant of a further tenancy of the dwelling-house since the end of the protected shorthold tenancy or, if there was such a grant, it was to a person who immediately before the grant was in possession of the dwelling-house as a protected or statutory tenant; and

(b) the proceedings for possession were commenced after appropriate notice by the landlord to the tenant and not later than three months after the expiry of the notice.

Case 20—armed forces personnel

14.68 Case 20 has a similar aim to Cases 11 and 12 (returning owner-occupier and retirement homes). It enables a member of the armed forces who purchases a property intending to occupy it at some time in the future (eg when he or she retires or leaves the armed forces) to rent the property out and still regain possession when it is needed. To rely on this Case the landlord must fulfil the following requirements:

(a) At the time when the dwelling-house was acquired the owner must have been a member of the armed forces.

(b) At the start of the tenancy the owner must have been a member of the armed forces.

(c) The owner must have given the tenant notice that possession might be recovered under this ground. (This requirement may be dispensed with by the court if it considers it just and equitable to do so.)

(d) Since the commencement of the Housing Act 1980, the dwelling-house must not have been let on a protected tenancy in respect of which notice (as in (c)) had not been given. (This requirement may be dispensed with by the court if it considers it just and equitable to do so.)

(e) The court must be satisfied that:

    (i) the dwelling-house is required as a residence for the owner; or

    (ii) one of the conditions set out in Sch 15, Pt V, paras (c) to (f) is satisfied (for the conditions in Pt V, see Cases 11 and 12).

Overcrowding

14.69 There is one other ground for possession which is not listed in Sch 15 to the 1977 Act and which, in effect, provides a further mandatory ground of possession. Section 101 provides that if at any time a dwelling-house is overcrowded, within the meaning of Pt X of the Housing Act 1985, in such circumstances as to render the occupier guilty of an offence, nothing in Pt VII of the Act shall prevent the immediate landlord of the occupier from obtaining possession of the dwelling-house.

The position of sub-tenants

14.70 Where a Rent Act protected tenant has lawfully sub-let his or her property a landlord wishing to obtain possession must also consider the position of the sub-tenant. The common law rule is that a sub-tenant has no right to remain in occupation following the termination of the superior tenancy. Thus, if the possession order is granted against the superior tenant the sub-tenant would have to leave the property. The Rent Act 1977, s 137, however, provides some sub-tenants with protection against this situation.

14.71 The protection of the 1977 Act will only be afforded to a lawful sub-tenant who was in possession before the commencement of the possession proceedings. If the sub-tenancy was granted in breach of a covenant in the superior tenancy it will not be lawful. It is however possible for a sub-tenancy which was initially unlawful to become lawful if the landlord waives the breach.

14.72 If the sub-tenant can establish that the premises have been lawfully sub-let, he or she will not be affected by a possession order made on discretionary grounds against the superior tenant (s 173(1)). Instead, he or she will in effect take that tenant's place and a direct relationship of landlord and tenant will exist between the sub-tenant and the head landlord (s 173(2)). The terms of this tenancy will be the same as for the old head tenancy. If the landlord wishes to obtain possession against the sub-tenant he will have to join him or her in the proceedings for possession and obtain a possession order against the sub-tenant separately.

Possession proceedings

Landlords seeking to obtain possession of a property held under a Rent Act protected or statutory tenancy must follow the same strict procedural rules as landlords of assured tenants. These rules are discussed at 16.74 to 16.77. **14.73**

Dispensing with the need for service of notices

The statutory codes often provide that, where a landlord is obliged to serve notice on a tenant, the court may dispense with this requirement if it is just and equitable to do so. The court will have to consider all of the circumstances of the case including the hardship caused to each party (*R J Dunnell Property Investments Ltd v Thorpe* (1989) 21 HLR 559). **14.74**

If notice should have been given in writing but instead was given orally it may be just and equitable to dispense with the requirement (*Davies v Peterson* (1988) 21 HLR 63, CA). If the tenants were aware of the landlord's circumstances and intentions and there was no possibility of a misunderstanding the court may consider it just to dispense with the need for service (see *Fernandes v Parvardin* (1982) 264 EG 49; and *Bradshaw v Baldwin-Wiseman* (1985) 49 P&CR 382, CA). **14.75**

KEY DOCUMENTS

Rent Act 1977

Form N5—Claims for possession of property

Form N11R—Defence (rented residential premises)

Printed copies of all legislation can be ordered from The Stationery Office at <http://www.tsoshop. co.uk>. All legislation from 1988 onwards and most pre-1988 primary legislation is available online at <http://www. legislation.gov.uk>.

Court forms are available online from the HM Courts and Tribunals Service at <http://www.justice. gov.uk/forms/hmcts>.

The Civil Procedure Rules are available online from <http://www.justice.gov.uk/courts/procedure-rules>.

15

THE HOUSING ACT 1988— 1. ASSURED TENANCIES

A INTRODUCTION

15.01 The majority of tenancies created after 15 January 1989 will be either assured or assured shorthold tenancies. The main difference between the two is the level of security given to the tenant. Where a tenant is in occupation under an assured tenancy the landlord can obtain possession only by proving one of the grounds under Sch 2 to the 1988 Act. Where the tenancy is an assured shorthold the landlord needs only to show that the tenancy has come to an end and that he or she has given the tenant proper notice requiring possession before possession will be ordered.

B ASSURED TENANCIES

15.02 Most assured tenancies granted after 28 February 1997 will be assured shorthold tenancies. It is important to remember, however, that an assured shorthold tenancy is a form of assured tenancy and all of the most important general provisions concerning the creation, terms, continuation, and termination of assured tenancies apply equally to assured shorthold tenancies.

C WHAT IS AN ASSURED TENANCY?

15.03 Under the Housing Act 1988, s 1, an assured tenancy is defined as follows:

> (1) A tenancy under which a dwelling-house is let as a separate dwelling is for the purposes of this Act an assured tenancy if and so long as—
>   (a) the tenant or, as the case may be, each of the joint tenants is an individual; and
>   (b) the tenant or, as the case may be, at least one of the joint tenants occupies the dwelling-house as his only or principal home; and
>   (c) the tenancy is not one which, by virtue of subsection (2) or subsection (6) below, cannot be an assured tenancy.

15.04 The initial part of s 1(1) of the Housing Act 1988 should already be familiar. It reiterates, almost word for word, the phrasing of s 1 of the Rent Act 1977. The Housing Act 1988, however, has added two further requirements to the Rent Act definition (paras (a) and (b)) and therefore draws significantly stricter parameters around the type of tenancy that will qualify for statutory protection.

15.05 What follows is a brief overview of the phrase 'a tenancy under which a dwelling-house is let as a separate dwelling'. For detailed consideration of these words reference should be made to the first part of Chapter 13 on the Rent Act 1977 (13.04 to 13.30). The case law on the Rent Act with regard to these words remains, in the absence of contrary authority, applicable to the Housing Act 1988.

'a tenancy'

15.06 To fall within the Housing Act 1988 there must first be a tenancy. This tenancy can be for a fixed term or periodic, it may be a sub-tenancy or an agreement for a tenancy (Housing Act 1988, s 45(1)). It can be assumed that, as under the Rent Act 1977, a tenancy at will and a tenancy at sufferance are capable of attracting assured tenancy status, but this will be the case only if rent is payable under the tenancy (see Housing Act 1988, Sch 1, Pt I, para 3).

A licence will not be eligible for protection under the 1988 Act. The difference between a   **15.07**
licence and a tenancy has already been considered in Chapter 3. However, the introduction
of the assured shorthold tenancy by the Housing Act 1988 means that, since 15 January
1989, landlords have been able to grant short fixed-term tenancies with no security of
tenure. Consequently, landlords who wish to ensure that they can regain possession of the
premises at short notice no longer need to seek to evade statutory protection by granting a
licence rather than a tenancy.

'a dwelling-house'

A dwelling-house includes a house or part of a house (Housing Act 1988, s 45(1)). It can   **15.08**
be a flat, a single room within a house, or even a caravan provided it has been rendered
immobile (see 13.08).

'let as a separate dwelling'

The dwelling-house must be let at a quantifiable rent. If no rent is payable, the tenancy   **15.09**
will be excluded by Sch 1, para 3 to the 1988 Act. The dwelling-house must also be let *as*
a separate dwelling, and therefore the purpose for which the premises are let at the time of
the original letting will be considered rather than the purposes to which the premises are
later put (see 13.11). To be a separate dwelling the accommodation must be sufficient for
the tenant to carry out the major activities of life (see 13.23).

Special provisions are made with regard to tenants who share accommodation. If the ten-   **15.10**
ant has exclusive occupation of some accommodation (the separate accommodation) and
shares other accommodation in common with a person or persons other than the landlord,
the separate accommodation will be deemed to be a dwelling-house let on an assured
tenancy regardless of the fact that the separate accommodation alone may not form a
separate dwelling (Housing Act 1988, s 3). In *Uratemp Ventures Limited v Collins* [2001]
3 WLR 806, HL, the House of Lords held that the fact that the tenant's room did not have
any cooking facilities did not prevent it from being a 'separate dwelling'. In such a case the
tenant does not hold the shared accommodation under an assured tenancy, but the court is
prevented from making a possession order in respect of the shared accommodation unless
it has already made, or makes at the same time, a possession order in respect of the separate
accommodation (s 10). These provisions are very similar to those found under s 22 of the
Rent Act 1977 (see 13.26).

The tenant is an individual

This requirement excludes companies and other artificial persons from Housing Act 1988   **15.11**
protection. Under the Rent Act 1977, a company or other artificial person could acquire a
protected tenancy under s 1 of that Act (although once the contractual tenancy came to a
end a company would not be able to fulfil the residency requirement and therefore would
be unable to acquire the benefits of a statutory tenancy (see 13.97)). If a tenancy is granted
to a number of joint tenants and one of these tenants is a company, the tenancy will be
excluded from the Housing Act 1988 since s 1(1)(a) requires each of the joint tenants to
be an individual.

The fact that company lets are excluded from Housing Act 1988 protection has enabled   **15.12**
landlords to avoid the consequences of the statute by granting tenancies to companies
rather than to individuals. This can be achieved, even where the premises are intended for

residential occupation, by requiring the prospective occupier to purchase an 'off-the-shelf' company. The landlord then grants the tenancy to the company and the company (which is really just the *alter ego* of the occupier) permits the occupier to live in the premises. Such arrangements are obviously artificial but the courts have been reluctant to declare them to be 'shams'. The view taken by the courts is that provided the agreement between the land-lord and prospective occupier does reflect the common intention of the parties, that agree-ment will be effective, even if its purpose is to avoid the statutory provisions. If an occupier wishes to argue that the agreement is a sham, the onus is upon him or her to establish that the agreement does not reflect the common intention of the parties (see *Hilton v Plustile* [1988] 3 All ER 1051; and *Kaye v Massbetter Ltd* (1991) 39 EG 129).

Occupy as only or principal home

15.13   The requirement that a tenant must occupy the dwelling-house as his or her only or prin-cipal home is significantly stricter than the requirement under s 2 of the Rent Act 1977 (that the tenant must occupy the dwelling-house as his or her residence in order to become a statutory tenant). The Housing Act 1988 restricts assured tenancy status to the tenant's main residence. A tenant with a house in town and a cottage in the country, which he or she uses at weekends, might be able to establish that the cottage is occupied as a residence but would probably fail if he or she sought to claim that the cottage was his or her only or principal home.

15.14   Whether a tenant is occupying a dwelling-house as his or her only or principal home will in each case be a question of fact. Because of the difference in wording, Rent Act 1977 authorities should only be used with care. The Housing Act 1985, however, employs the same wording (see 17.13) and secure tenancy cases may therefore be helpful.

15.15   The requirement that the dwelling-house is occupied as the tenant's only or principal home does not mean that the tenant cannot absent himself or herself from the premises for even quite lengthy periods. Such an absence may create a presumption that the tenant has ceased to reside but it is open to the tenant to rebut that presumption by showing that he or she has an intention to return by a specific date or within a finite period. In order to do this the tenant must be able to demonstrate a 'practical possibility' or a 'real possibility' that he or she will be able to return within a reasonable time. There must also be some visible sign of the intention to return, for example furniture or personal possessions left at the property. (See *Islington LBC v Boyle and Collier* [2011] EWCA Civ 1450 for a comprehensive sum-mary of the principles to be applied.)

15.16   In *Crawley BC v Sawyer* (1987) 20 HLR 98, CA (a case on secure tenancies) the tenant left the property for over a year to live with his girlfriend; the electricity and gas were discon-nected but the tenant left furniture in the flat. He returned after being served a notice to quit. The court held that, despite staying with his girlfriend, the tenant's flat had remained his principal home.

15.17   In *Ujima Housing Association v Ansah* (1998) 30 HLR 831, CA, a tenant who sub-let the whole of the premises and went to live elsewhere was held no longer to occupy the prop-erty (despite the fact that he had left all of his furniture there). This was because he had no right to occupy the premises himself unless the sub-tenants surrendered it to him.

15.18   If an assured tenant leaves the dwelling-house but his or her spouse or civil partner remains in occupation, the absent tenant continues to occupy the dwelling-house through his or her spouse or civil partner by virtue of the Family Law Act 1996, s 30(4), as amended by the Civil Partnership Act 2004. This will apply only provided the dwelling-house was previously occupied as the couple's matrimonial home and as long as the couple remain married or civil partners (see 13.104).

If an assured tenant ceases to occupy the dwelling-house as his or her principal home the tenancy will cease to be assured. The contractual tenancy, however, will continue until it expires or is terminated in accordance with the provisions of the tenancy agreement and the Protection from Eviction Act 1977.   **15.19**

Shared ownership leases

Shared ownership leases are an increasingly popular scheme offered by housing associa-   **15.20**
tions to people who would not otherwise be able to purchase a property. Under the scheme the tenant pays a premium and then occupies at a reduced rent, retaining the option to buy the remainder of the lease as and when he or she may be able to afford to do. The tenant, however, only has the status of an assured tenant and has no other rights of ownership over the property. In *Richardson v Midland Heart Ltd* [2007] L&TR 31 Mrs Richardson paid a premium of £29,500 for a 99-year shared ownership lease with a housing association and paid the association an annual rent of £1,456. Following threats of violence she left the property in order to live in a refuge and fell into arrears with her rent. The housing association sought possession of the property under Sch 2, Ground 8 to the Housing Act 1988 (see 16.46). Mrs Richardson's claims that she had an equitable interest in the property or that she held a long lease failed. It was held that her only interest in the property was that of a tenant under a 99-year fixed-term lease and, as the tenancy did not fall within any of the exclusions in Sch 1 to the 1988 Act (see 15.21 to 15.44), she was an assured tenant. The housing association was entitled to possession and once possession had been granted Mrs Richardson had no rights over the property and no legal right to recover the premium she had paid.

D STATUTORY EXCLUSIONS FROM THE HOUSING ACT 1988

Even if a tenancy satisfies s 1 of the 1988 Act, it will not be an assured tenancy if it falls   **15.21**
within any of the exceptions listed in Sch 1. Many of these exceptions are similar to the exceptions in the Rent Act 1977, but there are some notable differences.

Tenancies entered into before commencement

Under Sch 1, para 1, no tenancy created before 15 January 1989, or a tenancy entered into   **15.22**
pursuant to a contract made before 15 January 1989, can be an assured tenancy. The general rule is therefore that tenancies entered into before 15 January 1989 will be Rent Act protected tenancies, while those entered into after that date will fall under the Housing Act 1988. There are, however, certain transitional rules set out in s 34 of the Housing Act 1988 which allow the creation of a Rent Act protected tenancy after 15 January 1989 in certain limited circumstances (see 13.03).

Tenancies of dwelling-houses with high rateable values

The Housing Act 1988 is not intended to protect the tenants of very high value properties.   **15.23**
Under Sch 1, para 2 a tenancy will not be an assured tenancy if:

(a) the tenancy was entered into on or after 1 April 1990 (otherwise than, where the dwelling-house had a rateable value on 31 March 1990, in pursuance of a contract made before 1 April 1990) and the rent payable is more than £100,000 per annum (increased from £25,000 as from October 2010 in England and December 2011 in Wales);

(b) the tenancy was entered into before 1 April 1990 (or in pursuance of an agreement made before that date) and the rateable value of the premises on 31 March 1990 was over £1,500 in Greater London or £750 elsewhere (Sch 1, para 2A).

15.24 'Rent' for the purposes of Sch 1, para 2(1) does not include any sum payable by the tenant which is expressed to be payable in respect of rates, services, management, repairs, maintenance, or insurance (Sch 1, para 2(2)).

15.25 A rent review clause in an assured tenancy agreement which allowed the landlord rapidly to increase the rent to above the prescribed limit was held to be unenforceable as it was designed purely to deprive the tenant of the protection of the 1988 Act (*Bankway Properties Ltd v Penfold Dunsford* [2001] WLR 1369, CA).

Tenancies at a low rent

15.26 The aim of Sch 1, paras 3 to 3C is to exclude long tenancies at low rents from the protection of the 1988 Act. A tenancy will not be an assured tenancy if:

(a) for the time being no rent is payable; or

(b) the tenancy was entered into before 1 April 1990 (or in pursuance of an agreement made before that date) and the rent payable for the time being is less than two-thirds of the rateable value of the dwelling-house on 31 March 1990; or

(c) the tenancy was entered into on or after 1 April 1990 and the rent payable for the time being is less than £1,000 per annum in Greater London or £250 per annum elsewhere.

15.27 As with Sch 1, para 2, sums expressed to be payable in respect of rates, services, management, etc will not be regarded as rent.

Business tenancies

15.28 A tenancy to which Pt II of the Landlord and Tenant Act 1954 applies cannot be an assured tenancy (Sch 1, para 4). Where there is mixed residential and business use, the tenancy will normally fall under the 1954 Act unless the business use is merely incidental to the residential use (see 26.33).

Licensed premises

15.29 A tenancy under which the dwelling-house consists of or comprises premises licensed for the sale of intoxicating liquors for consumption on the premises cannot be an assured tenancy (Sch 1, para 5). Since the introduction of the Landlord and Tenant (Licensed Premises) Act 1990, a tenancy of licensed premises will probably be a business tenancy under Pt II of the Landlord and Tenant Act 1954.

Tenancies of agricultural land

15.30 Under Sch 1, para 6, if the dwelling-house is let with more than two acres of agricultural land it cannot be an assured tenancy. 'Agricultural land' here has the meaning set out in s 26(3)(a) of the General Rate Act 1967.

Where a dwelling-house is let together with other land, s 2(1) of the 1988 Act provides that **15.31** the tenancy can be an assured tenancy if and so long as the main purpose of the letting is the provision of a home for the tenant (or where there are joint tenants, at least one of the joint tenants). If the main purpose of the letting is not the provision of a home for the tenant the tenancy will not be assured (s 2(1)(b)).

The combined effect of these two sections may be summarized as follows: **15.32**

(a) If the dwelling-house is let together with more than two acres of agricultural land, the tenancy cannot in any event be an assured tenancy.
(b) If the dwelling-house is let together with less than two acres of agricultural land and the main purpose of the letting is not to provide the tenant with a home, the tenancy will not be an assured tenancy.
(c) If the dwelling-house is let together with other non-agricultural land, whether more or less than two acres, it can be an assured tenancy provided the main purpose of the letting is to provide a home for the tenant.

Tenancies of agricultural holdings

A tenancy under which the dwelling-house is comprised in an agricultural holding (within **15.33** the meaning of the Agricultural Holdings Act 1986) cannot be an assured tenancy where the dwelling-house is occupied by the person responsible for the control (whether as tenant or as servant or agent of the tenant) of the farming of the holding (Sch 1, para 7). A tenancy of an agricultural holding will fall under the protection of the Agricultural Holdings Act 1986 (see Chapter 27).

Lettings to students

This exception (Sch 1, para 8) is the same as under s 8 of the Rent Act 1977 (see 13.58). **15.34**

Holiday lettings

This exception (Sch 1, para 9) is the same as under s 9 of the Rent Act 1977 (see 13.62). **15.35**

Resident landlords

Like the Rent Act 1977, the Housing Act 1988 seeks to exclude tenants from protection **15.36** when they live in close proximity to their landlord. The provisions of Sch 1, para 10 are largely similar to those of s 12 of the Rent Act 1977 (see 13.70 to 13.85). As with s 12, the landlord must have occupied part of the dwelling at the date of the grant and at all times subsequently. One key difference is that under the 1988 Act the resident landlord must be 'an individual' and must occupy a part of the building or flat as his or her 'only or principal home'. A further important difference is that, while under the Rent Act 1977 a tenant with a resident landlord could hold under a restricted contract, under the Housing Act 1988 such a tenant will have no protection at all except that available under the Protection from Eviction Act 1977, ss 3 and 5 (see 19.18 to 19.24). If the tenant shares accommodation with the landlord or a member of the landlord's family, even this minimal protection may not be available (see Protection from Eviction Act 1977, s 3A).

To summarize, an occupier will not acquire an assured tenancy where either: **15.37**

(a) the building is a purpose-built block of flats; and
(b) the tenant occupies a dwelling-house which forms part of one of the flats; and

(c) the landlord is an individual who occupies a dwelling-house which forms another part of the same flat as his or her only or principal home. As in the Rent Act 1977, Sch 2, para 1 (see 13.79), certain periods of non-residence by the landlord are to be disregarded (Housing Act 1988, Sch 1, para 17);

OR:

(d) the building is not a purpose-built block of flats; and
(e) the tenant occupies a dwelling-house within the building; and
(f) the landlord is an individual who occupies a dwelling-house which forms part of the same building as his or her only or principal home.

15.38   The exception will not apply where the building is a purpose-built block of flats and the tenant occupies a flat within the building and the landlord occupies another flat within the building.

Crown tenancies

15.39   A tenancy under which the interest of the landlord belongs to Her Majesty in the right of the Crown or to a government department, or which is held in trust for Her Majesty for the purposes of a government department cannot be an assured tenancy. A tenancy may be an assured tenancy if the interest of the Crown is managed by the Crown Estate Commissioners (Sch 1, para 11).

Local authority tenancies

15.40   A tenancy under which the interest of the landlord belongs to a local authority, including a county council, a district or London borough, the City of London, the Inner London Education Authority, a joint authority, or to various other bodies, including the Commission for the New Towns, the Development Board for Rural Wales, an urban development corporation, a development corporation, a residuary body, a fully mutual housing association, or a housing action trust, cannot be an assured tenancy (Sch 1, para 12).

Family intervention tenancies

15.41   Family intervention tenancies were introduced into Sch 1 at para 12ZA by the Housing and Regeneration Act 2008, s 297 to address the behavioural problems of persistently anti-social tenants. Social landlords are often faced with the problem of finding accommodation for households which have lost their previous accommodation because of the behaviour of one or more members of the household. Rather than simply evicting the whole household, registered providers and registered social landlords are now able to offer non-secure tenancies to tenants who have lost or are in danger of losing their secure or assured tenancy because of anti-social behaviour. The tenancy will allow the tenant or a member of the household to access behavioural support services under the terms of a behavioural support agreement entered into between the tenant, the landlord, and the local housing authority.

Notice

15.42   For a tenancy to be a family intervention tenancy the landlord must serve notice on the tenant before the tenancy is entered into (Sch 1, para 12ZA(5)). This notice must inform the tenant of the reason the tenancy is being granted, the dwelling-house in respect of which the tenancy is to be granted, and the main terms of the new tenancy (including any require-ments on the new tenant in respect of behavioural support services). The notice must also inform the tenant of the security of tenure granted under the tenancy. It must inform the tenant that he or she is not obliged to enter into the tenancy, but must also set out the likely action taken by the landlord if the tenant does not enter into the tenancy (usually possession proceedings or eviction). Compliance with the review procedures in s 298 of the Housing and Regeneration Act 2008 is currently only mandatory for local authority landlords (see 17.56) and not for registered providers (who make up the majority of social landlords of assured tenants).

A family intervention tenancy can become an assured tenancy if the landlord notifies the **15.43** tenant that it is to be regarded as an assured tenancy (Sch 1, para 12ZA(2)). However, where a registered provider of social housing in England (see 21.04) has granted a family intervention tenancy to a former assured *shorthold* tenant after 1 April 2012, that landlord may serve notice on the tenant stating that the family intervention tenancy will become an assured shorthold tenancy (Housing Act 1988, s 20D, inserted by the Localism Act 2011, s 163(3)).

Housing asylum seekers

A tenancy granted to asylum seekers or their dependants by a local housing authority **15.44** under its Housing Act 1985 duties is also exempted. Such a tenancy will not become an assured tenancy until 12 months after the landlord has been officially informed by the Secretary of State that the tenant has ceased to be an asylum seeker. It is however possible for the landlord to agree to grant the tenant an assured tenancy before this date (Asylum and Immigration Appeals Act 1993, s 4(5) and Sch 1, para 6(1)).

E SECURITY OF TENURE UNDER THE 1988 ACT

Like the Rent Act 1977, the Housing Act 1988 gives the tenant security of tenure by pre- **15.45** venting the landlord from exercising his or her common law right to end the tenancy. How the Act operates depends upon whether the tenant holds under a fixed-term or periodic tenancy, but in both cases the system is fundamentally the same; the landlord cannot regain possession of the premises without executing a court order for possession, and a court order will be granted only if the landlord can make out one or more of the grounds con-tained in Sch 2 to the Act.

Security of tenure is provided for assured tenants by ss 5 and 7. Section 5 states: **15.46**

(1)   An assured tenancy cannot be brought to an end by the landlord except by:
    (a)   obtaining—
        (i)   an order of the court for possession of the dwelling -house under section 7 or 21, and
        (ii)   the execution of the order,
    (b)   obtaining an order of the court under section 6A (demotion order), or
    (c)   in the case of a fixed-term tenancy which contains power for the landlord to deter-mine the tenancy in certain circumstances, by the exercise of that power,

and, accordingly, the service by the landlord of a notice to quit shall be of no effect in relation to a periodic assured tenancy.

(2)   If an assured tenancy which is a fixed-term tenancy comes to an end otherwise than by
virtue of—

(a)   an order of the court of the kind mentioned in subsection (1)(a) or (b) or any other
order of the court, or

(b)   a surrender or other action on the part of the tenant,

then, subject to section 7 and Chapter II below, the tenant shall be entitled to remain in possession of the dwelling-house let under that tenancy and, subject to subsection (4) below, his right
to possession shall depend upon a periodic tenancy arising by virtue of this section.

(Housing Act 1988, s 5, as amended by Sch 11, Pt I, para 5 to the Housing and Regeneration
Act 2008.)

Section 7 states:

(1)   The court shall not make an order for possession of a dwelling-house let on an assured
tenancy except on one or more of the grounds set out in Schedule 2 to this Act; ...

15.47   The grounds of possession available under the Housing Act 1988 are considered at 16.30
to 16.70. An additional ground for possession applies to assured shorthold tenancies
(s 21); however, in the case of fixed-term shorthold tenancies this ground can only be used
to regain possession at the end of the fixed term. If a landlord wants to regain possession
of an assured shorthold tenancy during the fixed term he or she will need to rely on one of
the Sch 2 grounds.

Periodic tenancies

15.48   At common law a landlord wishing to regain possession of premises let under a periodic
tenancy would normally terminate the tenancy by serving a notice to quit upon the tenant. The Housing Act 1988 provides that the service of a notice to quit shall be of no
effect. A periodic assured tenancy, therefore, will continue on its original terms even after
the landlord serves a notice to quit; it can be terminated only by the execution of a court
order for possession. (This way of providing security of tenure resembles the Housing
Act 1985 rather than the Rent Act 1977.) There is no distinction between a contractual
tenancy and the statutory tenancy which arises when the contractual tenancy is brought
to an end; the original tenancy simply continues regardless of any attempt at common
law to terminate it. A notice to quit served by a tenant upon a landlord, however, will
still be effective to end the tenancy (see 10.35), as will an agreement by the tenant to
surrender the tenancy (see 15.88 and *Truro Diocesan Board of Finance v Foley* [2008]
EWCA Civ 1162).

Fixed-term tenancies

15.49   The position with regard to fixed-term tenancies is a little more complicated. Unlike a
periodic tenancy, a fixed-term tenancy will come to an end of its own accord by effluxion
of time rather than by an action of the parties, and so the 1988 Act cannot prevent it from
coming to an end simply by preventing the parties from taking action. The Act therefore
provides that if the tenancy comes to an end in any way other than by an order of the
court, or by surrender or other action, a periodic tenancy will arise and thereby continue
the tenancy. This statutory periodic tenancy, as with an original periodic tenancy, can be
terminated only by the execution of an order of the court.

Consider the following three examples:

(a) Harry grants Andrew a five-year fixed-term tenancy on 1 January 1997. Andrew his rent monthly.

(b) Harry grants Beryl a 20-year fixed-term tenancy on 1 January 1997. The tenancy agreement contains a general re-entry clause allowing Harry to re-enter if Beryl breaches any term or condition of the tenancy. The agreement also contains a break clause permitting Harry to terminate the tenancy on six months' notice after five years of the tenancy have expired. Beryl is currently two months behind with her rent.

(c) Harry grants Charlie a 20-year fixed-term tenancy on 1 January 1997. The tenancy agreement contains a specific re-entry clause allowing Harry to re-enter if Charlie is more than three months' rent in arrears. Charlie is currently six months behind with his rent.

It is now 2013 and in each of these cases Harry wants to regain possession. **15.51**

Tenancy expires by effluxion of time

Andrew's tenancy has already expired by effluxion of time (not by an order of the court, or **15.52** by a surrender or other action on Andrew's part) and therefore, by virtue of the Housing Act 1988, s 5(2), a statutory periodic tenancy has arisen. Harry can terminate Andrew's tenancy only by obtaining an order of the court and executing a warrant for possession (ie by evicting Andrew). Harry will be able to obtain an order of the court only if he can establish one or more of the grounds set out in Sch 2 to the Act.

Tenancy has not yet expired by effluxion of time

The vast majority of fixed-term tenancies will contain provisions permitting the landlord **15.53** to bring the tenancy to an end before it has expired. A landlord will nearly always reserve a right of re-entry for breach of covenant (see 11.18). The aim of such a clause is to enable the landlord to forfeit the lease if the tenant breaches an obligation under the lease. A lease may also contain a break clause entitling the landlord (or the tenant) to terminate the tenancy by notice at specific intervals during the term.

In Beryl's case, her fixed term has not yet expired. Harry, however, wishes to terminate the **15.54** tenancy. Two questions therefore arise:

(a) Can he terminate the tenancy by exercising his right of re-entry?
(b) Can he terminate the tenancy by exercising the break clause?

When looking at s 5, it appears at first sight that the answer to both of these questions will **15.55** be 'Yes'. Both a right of re-entry and a break clause seem to be 'a power for the landlord to determine the tenancy in certain circumstances' under s 5(1). The wording of s 5 is misleading, however. Section 5 must be read in conjunction with s 45(4), which provides that:

> For the avoidance of doubt, it is hereby declared that any reference in this Part of this Act (however expressed) to a power for a landlord to determine a tenancy does not include a reference to a power of re-entry or forfeiture for breach of any term or condition of the tenancy.

The Act therefore does not permit Harry to forfeit Beryl's tenancy under the re-entry clause **15.56** for her breach of covenant. However, provided he does so in accordance with the terms of the tenancy, Harry will be able to terminate the tenancy by exercising the break clause. This does not mean that he will be able to regain possession immediately. By virtue of s 5(2), a statutory periodic tenancy will arise on the termination of Beryl's fixed term. If Harry wishes to regain possession he will first have to obtain an order of the court by satisfying one or more of the grounds in Sch 2 to the 1988 Act.

15.57 If this were the end of the story it would leave the landlord in the awkward position of never being able to forfeit a tenancy no matter how seriously the tenant was in breach of the terms of that tenancy. In fact there would be no point in even including a re-entry clause in any tenancy agreement that was going to give rise to an assured tenancy. Section 7(6) and (6A) of the Act, however, provide that a landlord can seek a court order for possession before a fixed-term tenancy has expired in certain limited circumstances. The court can make an order for possession only where:

(a) the landlord is seeking possession under Grounds 2 or 8, or 10 to 15 of Sch 2 or Ground 7 of Sch 2 where the premises are in England; and

(b) the terms of the tenancy make provision for it to be brought to an end on the ground in question.

15.58 Thus, a landlord does have recourse against a defaulting tenant in certain situations, most notably where a tenant is in serious rent arrears (Ground 8, a mandatory ground), but also where there are persistent rent arrears or breaches of repairing obligations, although in these cases the court will make an order for possession only if it considers it reasonable to do so.

15.59 The landlord will be able to seek possession only where he or she has reserved the right to re-enter for a breach of the ground in question. Thus, while Harry will be able to terminate Beryl's tenancy by exercising the break clause, he will not be able to seek possession under s 7(6) because he has not made provision in the tenancy agreement to permit him to terminate on the ground of rent arrears (the general re-entry clause is not sufficient). Harry will be able to seek possession of Charlie's flat because the tenancy agreement specifically permits him to bring the tenancy to an end on the ground of serious rent arrears (Ground 8). Although this procedure is similar to forfeiture it is not treated as such. Charlie would not be entitled to apply to the court for relief against forfeiture (see 11.11).

15.60 The grounds for possession listed in Sch 2 to the Housing Act 1988 are discussed in detail in Chapter 16.

Statutory periodic tenancy

15.61 As we saw earlier, when a fixed-term tenancy comes to an end, either by effluxion of time or by the valid exercise of a power to determine the tenancy (a break clause but not a right of re-entry), a statutory periodic tenancy will automatically arise. The terms of this statutory periodic tenancy will be determined by s 5(3) of the Housing Act 1988:

(3) The periodic tenancy referred to in subsection (2) above is one—

(a) taking effect in possession immediately on the coming to an end of the fixed-term tenancy;

(b) deemed to have been granted by the person who was the landlord under the fixed-term tenancy immediately before it came to an end to the person who was then the tenant under that tenancy;

(c) under which the premises which are let are the same dwelling-house as was let under the fixed-term tenancy;

(d) under which the periods of the tenancy are the same as those for which rent was last payable under the fixed-term tenancy; and

(e)   under which, subject to the following provisions of this Part of this Act, the other
       terms are the same as those of the fixed-term tenancy immediately before it came
       to an end, except that any term which makes provision for determination by the
       landlord or the tenant shall not have effect while the tenancy remains an assured
       tenancy.

It should also be noted that any provision in the fixed-term tenancy setting out a mecha-   **15.62**
nism for rent review will not apply to the statutory periodic tenancy as such a provision will automatically be superseded by the rent assessment provisions contained in the
Housing Act 1988, s 6(4) (see 15.67 and *London District Properties Management Ltd v
Goolamy* [2009] EWHC 1367 (Admin), [2010] 1 WLR 307).

Therefore, when Andrew's tenancy expired on 1 January 2002, he will automatically have   **15.63**
acquired a statutory periodic tenancy on the same terms as the previous fixed-term tenancy.
This will be a monthly periodic tenancy because the periods of the tenancy are to be the
same as those for which rent was payable under the previous tenancy.

A statutory periodic tenancy will not have arisen, however, if on 1 January 2002 Harry   **15.64**
offered Andrew a further tenancy of the flat. By s 5(4) of the 1988 Act, a statutory periodic
tenancy:

   shall not arise if, on the coming to an end of the fixed-term tenancy, the tenant is entitled, by
   virtue of the grant of another tenancy, to possession of the same or substantially the same
   dwelling-house as was let to him under the fixed-term tenancy.

Altering the terms of a statutory periodic tenancy

If either the landlord or the tenant wishes to change the terms of the statutory periodic   **15.65**
tenancy, he or she may do so by following the procedure set out in the Housing Act 1988,
s 6. Section 6 applies only to a statutory periodic tenancy arising following a fixed-term
tenancy by virtue of s 5 and cannot be used to alter the terms of a periodic tenancy or a
fixed-term tenancy.

The party wishing to alter the terms must serve notice on the other party in the prescribed   **15.66**
form within one year of the date on which the former tenancy came to an end (s 6(2)). The
proposed terms can also include an adjustment in the amount of rent to take account of
the proposed terms; but if a party wishes to vary only the rent, a separate procedure must
be followed (see below).

The party receiving the notice has three months from the date of service to refer the notice   **15.67**
to a rent assessment committee (s 6(3)(a)). If a referral is not made within three months
of service of the notice, 'the terms proposed in the notice shall become terms of the tenancy in substitution for any of the implied terms dealing with the same subject matter and
the amount of the rent shall be varied in accordance with any adjustment so proposed'
(s 6(3)(b)).

If a referral is made to a rent assessment committee, the committee must consider the pro-   **15.68**
posed terms in accordance with s 6(4):

   … the committee shall consider the terms proposed in the notice and shall determine whether
   those terms, or some other terms (dealing with the same subject matter as the proposed terms),
   are such as, in the committee's opinion, might reasonably be expected to be found in an assured
   periodic tenancy of the dwelling-house concerned, being a tenancy—
   (a) which begins on the coming to an end of the former tenancy; and
   (b) which is granted by a willing landlord on terms which, except in so far as they relate to
        the subject matter of the proposed terms, are those of the statutory periodic tenancy at
        the time of the committee's consideration.

15.69   The rent assessment committee can therefore:

(a)   accept the proposed terms; or

(b)   reject the proposed terms and refuse the variation; or

(c)   substitute its own terms for some or all of the proposed terms, provided the substituted terms deal with the same subject matter as the proposed terms.

15.70   Once the terms have been determined the rent assessment committee can, if it considers it appropriate, adjust the rent to take account of the new terms. It may do this regardless of whether a variation in rent was proposed in the notice (s 6(5)). The new terms (and new rent if appropriate) will take effect in substitution for the implied terms from a date determined by the rent assessment committee. This date should not be any earlier than the date specified in the notice (s 6(7)).

15.71   If neither the landlord nor the tenant serves notice proposing terms different from those implied by s 5 within one year of the end of the fixed-term tenancy, the terms of the implied statutory periodic tenancy will stay the same until that tenancy is brought to an end, although the rent may be increased by the landlord under s 13 of the 1988 Act (see below).

F   THE TERMS OF AN ASSURED TENANCY

15.72   Generally speaking, it is the contractual terms agreed between the parties which govern an assured tenancy. This accords with the basic philosophy of the Housing Act 1988 that the parties should be free to negotiate and enter into a tenancy on whatever terms they can agree (although the tenant may be able to seek the protection of the Unfair Terms in Consumer Contracts Regulations 1999, SI 1999/2083 to prevent a landlord seeking to rely on oppressive terms, see 6.05). In a limited number of situations, however, the 1988 Act will imply terms into an assured tenancy. It also permits the landlord to apply to a rent assessment committee to increase the rent.

Access for repairs

15.73   The Housing Act 1988, s 16 implies into every assured tenancy a term that the tenant will give the landlord access to the dwelling-house let on the tenancy and all reasonable facilities for executing any repairs which the landlord is entitled to execute.

Assignment and sub-letting

15.74   The Housing Act 1988, s 15(1) implies into every periodic assured tenancy (including statutory periodic tenancies) a term that the tenant shall not without the consent of the landlord:

(a)   assign the tenancy (in whole or in part); or

(b)   sub-let or part with possession of the whole or any part of the dwelling-house let on the tenancy.

15.75   This implied term is not subject to the provisions of s 19 of the Landlord and Tenant Act 1927 (which provides that a landlord may not unreasonably refuse consent, see 6.92) (s 15(2)). A landlord therefore is fully entitled to refuse consent to an assignment or a sub-letting of a periodic assured tenancy even where the refusal of consent is unreasonable. The exception to this is where the refusal amounts to statutory discrimination (for example if the landlord refuses consent because of the sex or race of the potential assignee or sub-tenant, see 6.105). In such a case the landlord would have to justify the refusal of consent.

The aim of this provision is to maintain the landlord's ability to choose the tenant who is **15.76** occupying his or her property. Even where the tenant seeks to assign or sub-let the tenancy to a seemingly acceptable tenant, the landlord will have the right to refuse (however unreasonably) the assignment or sub-letting. If the tenant goes ahead and sub-lets or assigns without consent, he or she will be in breach of an obligation in the tenancy (Ground 12, see 16.60) and the landlord will be entitled to seek a possession order.

Where the tenancy is a contractual (as opposed to a statutory) assured periodic tenancy, the **15.77** Housing Act 1988 will not interfere if the parties have already agreed terms dealing with assignment and sub-letting. Where the parties have agreed a provision either:

(a) prohibiting or permitting assignment, sub-letting, or parting with possession (whether absolutely or conditionally); or
(b) requiring a premium to be paid on the grant or renewal of the tenancy,

s 15(1) will not apply (s 15(3)).

In the case of fixed-term tenancies, no term against assigning and sub-letting will be implied **15.78** and it will be up to the landlord expressly to include such a term in the tenancy agreement. However, once the fixed term has expired and a statutory periodic tenancy has arisen, s 15 will apply.

Rent

The philosophy behind the Housing Act 1988 is that the market should determine the **15.79** amount of rent payable by the tenant. Housing Act 1988 tenancies are not regulated tenancies. There is no equivalent to the notion of a 'fair rent' as under the Rent Act 1977 and no mechanism of registration by which either the tenant or the landlord can override the amount of rent agreed between them in the tenancy agreement. Even the rent officer ceases to play any role under the 1988 Act; instead, in certain circumstances, the parties can refer to a rent assessment committee under s 6 or 13 of the Act. The basic premise is that the rent payable under an assured tenancy is the rent that the parties have agreed upon.

Fixed-term tenancies

Under a fixed-term tenancy the rent upon which the parties have agreed stands for the **15.80** whole of the term. The provisions of the Housing Act 1988, s 13, which enable the landlord to increase the rent, apply only to periodic and statutory periodic tenancies. The only way in which a landlord can increase the rent during the term of a fixed-term tenancy is by including a regular rent review clause in the agreement (see 6.22 to 6.30), in which case the rent may be increased by following the mechanism set out in the terms of the contract. The rent review clause may however be unenforceable if it can be seen as a device designed to enable the landlord to obtain possession of the property because he or she knows that the tenant could not possibly afford the increased rent. Such a clause would allow the parties to contract out of the provisions of the 1988 Act which are intended to provide security of tenure and therefore would not be upheld by the court (*Bankway Properties Ltd v Penfold Dunsford* [2001] 1 WLR 1369, CA). If there is no rent review provision in the agreement, the landlord will simply have to wait until the fixed-term tenancy has come to an end and a statutory periodic tenancy arises automatically.

Periodic tenancies

15.81 If a tenant holds an assured periodic tenancy, the landlord can increase the rent by following the procedure set out in the Housing Act 1988, s 13. Section 13, however, is not available to the landlord if the periodic tenancy contains a rent review provision. If this is the case it will be the terms of the contractual provision which govern the rent increase and s 13 will be excluded (s 13(1)(b)).

15.82 If the landlord wishes to increase the rent, he or she must first serve a notice in the prescribed form on the tenant (s 13(2)). This notice must propose the new rent and state the date upon which the new rent is to take effect. The new rent can take effect only from the beginning of a new period of the tenancy and the landlord must leave a minimum period of time between the service of the notice and the date upon which the new rent is to take effect. The minimum period must be:

(a) in the case of a yearly tenancy, six months;
(b) in the case of a tenancy where the period is less than a month, one month; and
(c) in any other case, a period equal to the period of the tenancy (s 13(3)).

15.83 Section 13(2), as amended by the Regulatory Reform (Assured Periodic Tenancies) (Rent Increases) Order 2003, SI 2003/259, provides that (apart from assured agricultural occupancies) a rent increase can take effect no earlier than 52 weeks after either the commencement of the tenancy or a previous rent increase.

15.84 If the tenant disagrees with the proposed rent set out in the notice, he or she can either enter into negotiations with the landlord with a view to agreeing upon an alternative figure, or refer the notice to a rent assessment committee (s 13(4)). If the landlord and the tenant are able to reach agreement on an alternative amount of rent, it will be the agreed rather than the proposed rent which takes effect when the notice expires. If the tenant chooses to refer the notice to a rent assessment committee, this must be done in the prescribed form and before the date on which the new rent is to take effect. If the tenant takes no action the new rent will take effect when the notice expires (provided of course that the landlord has specified the correct date in the notice and drafted the notice in the prescribed form). Once the notice has expired it is too late for the tenant to raise any objection and he or she will have to pay the rent proposed in the notice.

Referral to a rent assessment committee

15.85 Where a referral is made to a rent assessment committee, the committee will determine the rent at which it considers that the dwelling-house concerned might reasonably be expected to be let in the open market by a willing landlord under an assured tenancy:

(a) which is a periodic tenancy having the same periods as those of the tenancy to which the notice relates;
(b) which begins at the beginning of the new period specified in the notice;
(c) the terms of which (other than relating to the amount of rent) are the same as those of the tenancy to which the notice relates; and
(d) in respect of which the same notices, if any, have been given under any of Grounds 1 to 5 of Sch 2 to the 1988 Act (see 16.31 to 16.38), as have been given (or have effect as if given) in relation to the tenancy to which the notice relates (Housing Act 1988, s 14(1)).

15.86 The committee will disregard:

(a) any effect on the rent attributable to the granting of a tenancy to a sitting tenant;
(b) any increase in the value of the dwelling-house attributable to certain improvements carried out by a person who at the time they were carried out was the assured tenant

(however, where an assured periodic tenancy follows the expiry of a long lease, improvements carried out by the tenant whilst he or she was a long lessee will not be disregarded (*Hughes v Borodex Ltd* [2010] EWCA Civ 425, see 22.34)). The disregard will also not include improvements that were carried out in pursuance of an obligation to the immediate landlord and it is subject to the provisions of s 14(3)); and

(c) any reduction in the value of the dwelling-house attributable to a failure by the tenant to comply with any terms of the tenancy (s 14(2)).

15.87 The way in which a rent assessment committee determines assured tenancy rents is very different from the way in which a 'fair rent' is determined under the Rent Act 1977. Under the Rent Act the 'scarcity value' of a tenancy was to be disregarded (see 13.144); under the Housing Act 1988 full regard is to be had to the market value of other similar tenancies in the area.

15.88 Once the rent has been determined by the rent assessment committee, it will take effect from the beginning of the new period of the tenancy specified in the landlord's notice unless the landlord and tenant agree otherwise. If the committee considers that to give effect to the new rent at this date would cause undue hardship to the tenant (eg because the length of time between the landlord giving notice and the determination by the committee means that the tenant must pay off a large amount of back rent), it may specify a later date, but this date cannot be later than the date of the determination (Housing Act 1988, s 14(7)).

G ENDING AN ASSURED TENANCY

Termination by the tenant

15.89 The aim of the Housing Act 1988 is to protect the residential tenant from premature termination by the landlord, not to trap a tenant in a tenancy he or she no longer wants. Section 5(2) of the Act specifically retains the right for the tenant to end a fixed-term tenancy by 'surrender or other action on the part of the tenant'. A tenant may, for example, agree a surrender with the landlord (surrender can also be implied) or exercise a break clause contained in the lease. Likewise, with regard to periodic assured tenancies, s 5(1) restricts only the landlord's right to serve a notice to quit.

15.90 A tenant can serve a notice to quit whenever he or she likes, provided the tenant complies with the terms of the tenancy and the Protection from Eviction Act 1977. In contrast to the position at common law (see 10.50) the 1988 Act provides that where there are joint tenants notice must be served by all of them (s 45(3)). The required form and content of the notice to quit may be set out in the tenancy agreement. A mistake in the tenant's notice to quit will not necessarily make it invalid if the landlord is not misled by the mistake. In *Hussain v Bradford Community Housing* [2009] EWCA Civ 763, the tenant's notice gave two possible dates for termination, one of which was wrong. It was held that the mistake did not invalidate the notice as the landlord was able to calculate the correct date and was not misled (see also 6.130 for validity of notices generally).

15.91 Where the tenant terminates a tenancy, be that by surrender, exercise of a break clause, or a notice to quit, the tenant ceases to be an assured tenant and the landlord will be entitled to repossess.

15.92 A tenant may also lose his or her assured status if he or she ceases to qualify as an assured tenant under the provisions of s 1 of the Act or if the tenancy is demoted (see 15.95 to 15.99), or he or she changes the use of the premises so as to fall into any of the excluded categories in Sch 1, Pt I. For example, a tenant may cease to occupy the premises as his or her only or principal home, or he or she may start to use the premises for business purposes. However, the fact that a tenant ceases to be an assured tenant does not mean that the contractual tenancy is at an end. Before the landlord can seek possession he or she will have to terminate the contractual tenancy validly (complying with the provisions of the Protection from Eviction Act 1977).

Possession by the landlord

15.93 The landlord can terminate the contractual tenancy during the fixed term by any method provided for in the tenancy agreement. However, as we saw at 15.49, the tenancy will then continue as a statutory periodic tenancy. A landlord can only bring a statutory periodic tenancy to an end by obtaining a possession order from the court (Housing Act 1988, s 5). Even then the tenancy will not actually come to an end until the possession order is executed (s 5(1A), as amended by the Housing and Regeneration Act 2008, see 15.46).

15.94 The recovery of possession of an assured tenancy will be considered in Chapter 16 (see 16.22 to 16.77).

H DEMOTION OF AN ASSURED TENANCY

15.95 The Anti-social Behaviour Act 2003, s 14(4) inserted a new s 6A into the Housing Act 1988. This section provides that if the landlord of an assured tenant is a registered social landlord or registered provider (see 21.04), the landlord can apply to the court for a demotion of the assured tenancy on the grounds that the tenant (or a person visiting or residing in the property) has engaged in, or threatened to engage in, conduct:

(a) which is capable of causing a nuisance or annoyance to any person; and

(b) which directly or indirectly relates to or affects the housing management functions of a relevant landlord (Housing Act 1996 s 153A); or

(c) which consists of or involves using or threatening to use housing accommodation owned or managed by a relevant landlord for an unlawful purpose (Housing Act 1996, s 153B).

15.96 The effect of a demotion order is that the assured tenancy will only attract the security of tenure of an assured shorthold tenancy. The period of demotion will normally be one year. If the landlord does not give notice of intention to bring proceedings for possession within the year, the tenancy will then revert back to being an assured tenancy. The tenancy will also revert to its original assured status if such notice is withdrawn by the landlord, if possession proceedings are not brought within six months of the notice, or if the tenant successfully defends the possession proceedings (Housing Act 1988, s 20B, amended by the Anti-social Behaviour Act 2003, s 15). The Localism Act 2011 has also inserted a new s 20C into the 1988 Act which deals with the position where the original tenancy was already an assured shorthold tenancy. If the original tenancy was an assured shorthold tenancy for a fixed term of more than two years and the landlord is a registered provider of social housing in England (see 21.04) then (providing the tenancy was demoted after 1 April 2012) it will revert to being an assured shorthold tenancy of a fixed term of more than two years if the landlord serves notice to this effect during the demotion period (Localism Act 2011, s 163(2)).

15.97 The purpose of the demotion order is to allow certain landlords of anti-social tenants an alternative route to seeking an outright possession order. If the demoted tenant behaves for one year, he or she will regain his or her original status. If the tenant does not, the landlord has a relatively easy route to possession of the tenancy under the Housing Act 1988, s 21(4) (see 16.07 to 16.17). The Housing Act 1988, s 21(5A) provides that demoted tenancies are excluded from the rule that possession may not be granted under s 21 within six months of the commencement of the tenancy.

Under s 153A the behaviour complained of must only be 'capable' of causing nuisance, **15.98** etc, rather than 'likely to' as is the case under Ground 14 of Sch 2, Pt II to the Housing Act 1988 (see 16.62). In contrast to Ground 14(b) the landlord can rely on s 153B without the tenant having been convicted of a relevant offence. The nuisance allegation under the new ss 153A and 153B is, therefore, easier for the landlord to prove; however, a demotion order will only be made in cases where the court is satisfied that it is reasonable to do so.

The registered social landlord or registered provider must give the assured tenant two **15.99** weeks' notice of its intention to apply for demotion before proceedings can be issued. This is in contrast to a claim under Ground 14 which can be issued immediately. The notice must contain particulars of the alleged conduct and state that proceedings cannot be begun before a specified date (ie a date not less than two weeks from service of the notice). It must also state that proceedings will not begin later than 12 months from the date of service of the notice.

I SUCCESSION

Section 17 of the Housing Act 1988 provides a limited system of statutory succession. The **15.100** rules allowing succession differ according to whether the landlord is an ordinary private landlord or a registered provider of social housing in England (for example a Housing Association, see Chapter 21)

Succession where the landlord is a private landlord

The provisions for succession do not apply to assured fixed-term tenancies. If a fixed-term **15.101** tenant of a private landlord dies the tenancy forms part of the deceased tenant's estate and will pass according to his or her will or, if there is no will, the rules of intestacy. If a periodic assured tenant of a private landlord dies (whether the tenancy is a statutory periodic tenancy or a contractual periodic tenancy) that tenancy will also pass under the deceased tenant's will or the rules of intestacy unless it falls within s 17. It should be noted that where a person inherits a periodic assured tenancy under the deceased tenant's will or the rules of intestacy and occupies the dwelling-house in question as his or her only or principal home, the landlord will have the right to recover possession under Ground 7 (see 16.43).

Where the landlord is a private landlord only the tenant's spouse or civil partner is capable **15.102** of succeeding to the tenancy under s 17, but a person who was living with the tenant as his or her wife or husband or civil partner is treated as a spouse for the purposes of this section (s 17(4)).

For private landlords, therefore, s 17 will apply only where: **15.103**

(a) the sole tenant under an assured periodic tenancy dies; and
(b) immediately before the tenant's death, the tenant's spouse or civil partner was occupying the dwelling-house as his or her only or principal home; and
(c) the tenant was not a successor.

Succession where the landlord is a private registered provider of social housing in England

15.104　Section 17 has been amended by the Localism Act 2011 to extend the right to succeed in cases where the landlord is a private sector registered provider of social housing. These provisions apply to landlords of dwellings in England only. Unlike the provisions for private landlords, under s 17 the new provisions apply to both periodic tenancies and fixed-term tenancies for a term of not less than two years (s 17(1A), (1B) and (1C)).

15.105　The amended s 17 also allows for a person other than a spouse or civil partner to succeed to an assured tenancy if the landlord is a private registered provider of social housing in England (s 17(1A) and (1C)). If the sole tenant of such a landlord has died after 1 April 2012 and there is no spouse or civil partner living at the property at the time of the tenant's death the tenancy may pass to another person by succession. This will, however, only be the case if the tenancy agreement contains an express provision that such a person may succeed to the tenancy.

Only one succession

15.106　The Housing Act 1988 provides for only one succession. If the deceased tenant was already a successor, s 17 will not apply. The deceased tenant will be regarded as a successor if:

(a)　the tenancy became vested in the deceased tenant by virtue of s 17;

(b)　the tenancy became vested in the deceased tenant under the will or intestacy of a previous tenant;

(c)　the deceased tenant was a joint tenant and had, on the death of the other joint tenant (or tenants), become the sole tenant by the right of survivorship;

(d)　the deceased tenant succeeded to an assured tenancy by virtue of the Rent Act 1977 (see 13.115).

15.107　Even where the tenant, having succeeded to a previous tenancy, has been granted a further tenancy of the same or substantially the same dwelling-house, that tenant will still be regarded as a successor (s 17(3)).

J ASSURED SHORTHOLD TENANCIES

15.108　Landlords have long complained that the provisions of the Rent Act 1977 undermine their rights to control the use of their own property, their main concern being that the grant of even a short-term tenancy can result in their being unable to regain possession of the property for many years. As we saw in Chapter 2, one consequence of this was that landlords frequently sought to grant rights of occupation that did not fall within the ambit of the statutory codes. Another consequence was that some property owners were reluctant to release otherwise vacant property for rent.

15.109　The assured shorthold tenancy created by the Housing Act 1988 has proved to be very popular with landlords. Under an assured shorthold tenancy a tenant can still apply for a rent reduction, but will acquire no security of tenure after the fixed term and the landlord is able, under a relatively straightforward system, to regain possession of the premises at short notice. The landlord is of course still obliged to obtain a court order for possession before evicting the tenant where the tenancy is an assured shorthold.

15.110　The Housing Act 1996 introduced new rules governing the creation of an assured shorthold tenancy. Prior to the commencement of the 1996 Act (28 February 1997) a new tenancy could be a shorthold tenancy only if notice to that effect was given in accordance with the strict guidelines contained in s 20 of the Housing Act 1988. The fact that many landlords were unfamiliar with the procedure, and the rigid application by the courts of the notice provisions, meant that landlords who intended to create shorthold tenancies found that they had in fact granted an assured tenancy, with the resultant security of tenure. In order to address this problem a new s 19A was added to the 1988 Act, meaning that most tenancies created after 28 February 1997 will automatically be assured shorthold tenancies. There will, however, still be landlords, particularly in the social sector, who will wish to convey full assured status on their tenants by giving notice that the tenancy is not to be an assured shorthold tenancy. There will also continue to be a large number of assured tenancies which are not assured shortholds because they were created before 28 February 1997 and the landlord failed to give proper s 20 notice.

K ASSURED SHORTHOLD TENANCIES CREATED BEFORE 28 FEBRUARY 1997

Creating an assured shorthold tenancy

To be an assured shorthold tenancy the tenancy must first qualify as an assured tenancy. It **15.111** must therefore satisfy the provisions of s 1 of the 1988 Act and must not fall into any of the excluded categories in Sch 1 (see 15.03 to 15.44). In addition, any tenancy created prior to 28 February 1997 which is to be an assured shorthold tenancy must satisfy the requirements set out in the Housing Act 1988, s 20(1). It must be a tenancy:

(a) which is a fixed-term tenancy granted for a term certain of not less than six months; and
(b) in respect of which there is no power for the landlord to determine the tenancy at any time earlier than six months from the beginning of the tenancy; and
(c) in respect of which a notice is served as mentioned in s 20(2).

A fixed-term tenancy of not less than six months

If it is created prior to 28 February 1997 only a fixed-term tenancy can be an assured short- **15.112** hold tenancy. The term must be for six months or more, but there is no upper limit on the duration of the term. So despite the name, there is no actual requirement that a shorthold assured tenancy should actually be 'short'; however, given the purpose of the provisions, landlords are unlikely to grant lengthy terms.

No power to determine earlier than six months

A 'power to determine the tenancy' does not include a power of re-entry or forfeiture for **15.113** a breach of any term or condition of the tenancy (Housing Act 1988, s 45(4); see 15.55). Thus, the inclusion of a re-entry clause does not prevent a tenancy from being an assured shorthold tenancy; in fact, if the landlord wishes to retain the right to regain possession in the event of the tenant breaching a term of the lease, it is essential that the landlord should include such a clause in the agreement. However, if the landlord includes a break clause which can be exercised in the first six months of the tenancy, the tenancy cannot be an assured shorthold tenancy and will take effect as an assured tenancy.

Notice

Prior to 28 February 1997, if a landlord wanted to grant an assured shorthold tenancy he **15.114** or she must have ensured that the tenant knew, before entering into the agreement, that the tenancy he or she was being offered was an assured shorthold tenancy. In order to do this the landlord must have served notice in accordance with the Housing Act 1988, s 20(2). Section 20(2) contains the following requirements:

(a) The notice must be in the prescribed form (s 20(2)(a)). The prescribed form gives details of the tenancy, states clearly that the proposed tenancy is to be an assured shorthold tenancy, warns the tenant of the nature of the tenancy, informs the tenant of his or her right to apply to a rent assessment committee, and tells the tenant where to seek advice if he or she does not understand the notice.

(b) The notice must be served before the assured tenancy is entered into (s 20(2)(b)).

(c) The notice must be served by the person who is to be the landlord under the assured tenancy on the person who is to be the tenant under that tenancy (s 20(2)(c)).

(d) The notice must state that the assured tenancy to which it relates is to be a shorthold tenancy (s 20(2)(d)).

15.115 The court has no discretion to dispense with the requirement of notice. However, if the notice contains an error so obvious that no one is misled, the court may overlook the defect. For example, in *R v London Borough of Newham, ex parte Ugbo* (1993) 26 HLR 263, where a mistake was made in the address of the property but it was clear that all parties knew to which property the notice referred, the court held the notice to be valid. In *Stevens v Lamb* (*Legal Action*, March 1996, 12) it was held that the failure to include the landlord's name, address, and telephone number by the landlord's agent meant that the notice was invalid. In *Manel v Memon* [2000] 2 EG 74, (2001) 33 HLR 235, a notice was held to be invalid because it neglected to include a paragraph informing the tenant of the desirability of seeking legal advice. A s 20 notice can be validly served on a tenant's authorized agent (*Yenula Properties Limited v Naidu* [2003] L & TR 9).

15.116 A tenant facing a claim for possession of an old assured shorthold tenancy would be well advised to take a thorough look at the contents of the landlord's s 20 notice. If the notice is invalid the tenancy will in fact be an assured tenancy and it may be more difficult for the landlord to obtain possession.

Previous assured tenancy

15.117 Prior to 28 February 1997, if an assured tenant of a tenancy (which was not an assured shorthold tenancy) was granted a new tenancy by the same landlord, the new tenancy could not be an assured shorthold tenancy (Housing Act 1988, s 20(3)). This provision prevented a landlord from depriving an existing tenant of security of tenure by granting the tenant an assured shorthold tenancy when the original tenancy expired. Where the tenancy expires after 28 February 1997, the situation is somewhat different: the landlord may grant a previous assured tenant an assured shorthold tenancy, but only if the tenant gives notice that it is to be an assured shorthold tenancy (see 15.124).

Previous assured shorthold tenancy

15.118 Prior to 28 February 1997, if an assured shorthold tenancy came to an end and a new tenancy of the same (or substantially the same) premises was granted by the same landlord then the new tenancy would also be an assured shorthold tenancy regardless of the fact that no s 20 notice was given (s 20(4)). (In *Lower Street Properties v Jones* (1996) 48 EG 154, (1996) 28 HLR 877, CA, it was held that a number of tenancies which all succeeded a shorthold tenancy remained shorthold.) Similarly, if an assured shorthold tenancy came to an end and no new tenancy was granted but instead a statutory periodic tenancy arose by virtue of s 5(2) (since an assured shorthold tenancy is an assured tenancy like any other and will be continued by statute, see 15.61), this statutory tenancy would be an assured shorthold tenancy.

L ASSURED SHORTHOLD TENANCIES CREATED AFTER 28 FEBRUARY 1997

Any tenancy entered into on or after 28 February 1997 (otherwise than pursuant to a con-   **15.119**
tract made before that date) which qualifies as an assured tenancy under the provisions of s 1
(see 15.03) will be an assured shorthold tenancy unless it falls within the exceptions set out in
Sch 2A to the 1988 Act (s 19A). Thus, subject to the exceptions considered later, virtually all
new tenancies granted by private sector landlords will be assured shorthold tenancies.

Notice by landlord

It is, of course, still possible for a landlord to grant an assured tenancy which is not a   **15.120**
shorthold, but to do so he or she will have to serve notice on the tenant stating that the
tenancy to which it relates is not to be an assured shorthold tenancy. Such notice can be
served either before the tenancy is granted (Sch 2A, para 1) or during the course of the tenancy (in which case the notice will function to convert an assured shorthold tenancy into
an assured tenancy: Sch 2A, para 2). An assured tenancy can also be created if the tenancy
contains a provision stating that the tenancy is not to be an assured shorthold tenancy (Sch
2A, para 3). Effectively these provisions reverse the situation prior to the 1996 Act. Prior
to 28 February 1997 a tenancy would not be an assured shorthold tenancy unless notice
was served stating that it was to be an assured shorthold tenancy. After 28 February 1997
it will be an assured tenancy only if notice is served saying that it is not to be an assured
shorthold tenancy.

Assured tenancies by succession

Section 39 of the Housing Act 1988 amended the Rent Act 1977 to provide that where a   **15.121**
family member (but not a spouse) succeeds to a Rent Act tenancy on the first succession,
or anyone succeeds on the second succession, that person will acquire an assured tenancy
rather than a Rent Act statutory tenancy (see 13.115). Schedule 2A, para 4 to the 1988 Act
provides that such assured tenancies by succession will take effect as assured tenancies, not
as assured shorthold tenancies.

Former secure tenancies

Where a former secure tenant acquires an assured tenancy (for example, because a local   **15.122**
authority landlord transfers part of its housing stock into the private sector) that tenant
will acquire an assured tenancy and not an assured shorthold tenancy (Sch 2A, para 5).
This rule does not apply where a former secure tenancy has become an assured shorthold
tenancy by reason of demotion (Sch 2A, para 5A) (see 17.114 to 17.123).

Assured tenancies on the expiry of a long residential lease

Under the provisions of Sch 10 to the Local Government and Housing Act 1989, a long   **15.123**
leaseholder acquires the right to an assured tenancy at the expiry of his or her leasehold
term (see Chapter 22). Where this occurs the leaseholder will acquire an assured tenancy
and not an assured shorthold tenancy (Sch 2A, para 6).

Former assured tenancies

Where an assured tenancy is granted to a tenant who, immediately before the grant, held an   **15.124**
assured tenancy which was not an assured shorthold tenancy from the same landlord, that

tenant will acquire an assured tenancy even if the new tenancy is of a different property. This provision prevents a landlord from depriving an assured tenant of security of tenure by simply granting him or her a new tenancy. However, the landlord may grant a former assured tenant an assured shorthold tenancy if the tenant serves notice on the landlord that the tenancy is to be an assured shorthold (Sch 2A, para 7). The notice must be in the prescribed form (Form 8 of the Assured Tenancies and Agricultural Occupancies (Forms) Regulations 1997, SI 1997/194). Any material deviation from the prescribed form will be fatal to the landlord's claim that an assured shorthold tenancy has been granted, even if the landlord can assert that the tenant was well aware of the consequences of signing the notice (*Kahlon v Isherwood* [2011] EWCA Civ 602).

15.125   Where a tenant has a fixed-term assured tenancy which is not an assured shorthold tenancy and this tenancy comes to an end, on the expiry of the term a statutory periodic tenancy arises by virtue of s 5. This statutory periodic tenancy will be an assured tenancy and not an assured shorthold tenancy (Sch 2A, para 8). This provision will not apply where the former assured tenancy has been demoted (see 15.95 to 15.99).

Duty of landlord to provide statement as to terms of tenancy

15.126   Prior to 28 February 1997, the strict requirements as to notice and the fact that an assured shorthold tenancy had to be granted for a fixed term meant that virtually all assured shorthold tenancies were entered into by written tenancy agreement. After 28 February 1997, it is possible to create an assured shorthold tenancy much more informally. Consequently, a tenant may not always be fully apprised of the terms of the tenancy. Section 20A of the 1988 Act therefore gives a tenant who has been granted an assured shorthold tenancy under s 19A the right to give written notice to the landlord requiring the landlord to provide him or her with a written statement of certain essential terms of the tenancy that have not been evidenced in writing. The landlord must provide information on any of the following matters:

(a)   the date on which the tenancy began;
(b)   the rent payable under the tenancy and the dates on which that rent is payable;
(c)   any term providing for a review of the rent;
(d)   in the case of a fixed-term tenancy, the length of the fixed term.

Six-month minimum period

15.127   It should be noted that in the case of assured shorthold tenancies granted after 28 February 1997 there is no requirement that the tenancy be granted for a fixed term of more than six months. A new shorthold assured tenancy can therefore be a periodic tenancy or a fixed-term tenancy granted for less than six months. However, as we shall see, the six-month minimum period still effectively applies to assured shorthold tenancies, not because it is included in the terms of the tenancy but because the provisions with regard to possession of an assured shorthold tenancy prevent a landlord from obtaining a court order for possession until six months after the beginning of that tenancy (s 21(5), see 16.04). Thus, even if a landlord grants a two-month fixed-term tenancy, the tenant will be able to remain in occupation after the expiry of this term because a statutory periodic tenancy will arise under s 5 of the 1988 Act (see 15.46); and though the landlord may start proceedings for possession, no order for possession can be made that will take effect earlier than six months after the beginning of the original fixed-term tenancy.

Recovering possession of an assured shorthold tenancy

The recovery of possession of an assured shorthold tenancy will be considered in Chapter 16 **15.128** (16.01 to 16.21).

Rent

Assured shorthold tenants do benefit from one right that is not available to ordinary assured **15.129** tenants; they can apply under the Housing Act 1988, s 22 to a rent assessment committee to have their rent reduced. In the case of assured shorthold tenancies granted prior to 28 February 1997, such an application can be made only during the currency of the original fixed term. Thus, if a tenant is holding over after the expiry of the original fixed term by virtue of an assured shorthold periodic tenancy, he or she cannot make an application. In the case of assured shorthold tenancies granted after 28 February 1997, an application can be made only during the first six months of that tenancy. The application must be made in the prescribed form.

Where the tenant makes an application the rent assessment committee will not make any **15.130** determination unless it considers:

(a) that there is a sufficient number of similar dwelling-houses in the locality let on assured tenancies (whether or not shorthold); and
(b) that the rent payable under the assured shorthold tenancy in question is significantly higher than the rent which the landlord might reasonably be expected to obtain under the tenancy, having regard to the levels of rents payable under assured tenancies or assured shorthold tenancies of similar dwelling-houses in the locality (s 22(3)).

If a determination is made the new rent will take effect from such a date as the committee may **15.131** direct, but this date cannot be earlier than the date of the tenant's application (s 22(4)(a)).

Once the rent had been determined the tenant cannot make a further application (s 22(2)(a)). **15.132**

M DEPOSITS

Tenancy deposit schemes

If a landlord receives a deposit on behalf of an assured shorthold tenant after 6 April **15.133** 2007 the landlord must safeguard the deposit in accordance with a government-approved deposit protection scheme. It has been held in the county court that this will include situations where a landlord grants a new tenancy to an existing tenant after 6 April 2007 if the tenant had paid a deposit under the old tenancy and that deposit is retained as security for the new tenancy. In such a case the original deposit will be deemed to have been notionally received by the landlord on the granting of the new tenancy and must be safeguarded under a scheme (*Saad v Hogan*, Brentford County Court, 16 February 2009 (*Legal Action*, June 2009)). Landlords who grant replacement tenancies after 6 April 2007 would be best advised to ensure that any deposit they hold is safeguarded within a scheme no matter when the original tenancy was granted.

Two forms of scheme are offered: a custodial scheme and an insurance-based scheme. **15.134**

The custodial scheme

This scheme is most suitable for landlords who only have a small number of rental proper- **15.135** ties. Under this scheme the deposit is paid to the scheme provider who holds it on behalf of the landlord and tenant. Neither the landlord nor the tenant has to pay a fee to use the scheme, which is funded by a portion of the interest earned on the deposit whilst it is held by the scheme provider.

15.136   At the end of the tenancy the landlord and tenant jointly ask for the deposit to be repaid. If they agree to the proportion of the deposit that each (and/or any third party) should receive, the scheme provider will pay out the agreed amounts (plus any surplus interest) to the parties. If there is a dispute between the landlord and the tenant as to who should receive the deposit (or a proportion of it) the scheme provider offers an ADR (alternative dispute resolution) service to assist the parties in reaching an agreement. Complex disputes, or disputes already before the court at the date the deposit is to be repaid, will be decided by the court. The scheme provider will then pay out the deposit in accordance with the decision of the arbitrator or the court.

The insurance-based scheme

15.137   This scheme is more suited to 'professional' landlords with a large number of properties, and letting agents (who may be responsible for dealing with deposits under the Act, see 15.146). In order to participate, the landlord must be resident in the UK. Under this scheme the landlord retains the deposit but pays a fixed premium to the scheme provider. In the event of a dispute between the landlord and the tenant over repayment of the deposit at the end of the tenancy, the scheme provider will, again, offer an ADR service. The landlord should then deposit the disputed amount with the scheme provider until the dispute is resolved (either by ADR or by court proceedings).

15.138   If the landlord fails to return a deposit to the tenant, or pay any disputed sum into the scheme, the scheme provider will pay any amount found to be owing to the tenant. It is then up to the scheme provider to pursue the landlord for the outstanding deposit money. This scheme allows the landlord to retain control of the deposit, whilst satisfying the statutory requirement to safeguard the tenant's interest in the money. Insurance-based schemes place a greater administrative burden on the landlord or agent in terms of meeting the duty to supply relevant information to the tenant.

15.139   Details of the current approved scheme providers are given at the end of this chapter.

The statutory requirements

15.140   The Localism Act 2011, s 184 has made substantial amendments to the statutory requiremants under the Housing Act 2004. Prior to the coming into force of s 184 any deposit paid to a person in connection with a shorthold tenancy had to be safeguarded by a scheme within 14 days of its receipt and the landlord must also have provided the tenant with prescribed information relating to the deposit and the scheme within that 14-day period. Failure to comply with this requirement meant that the landlord would have to repay the deposit and pay the tenant a sum amounting to three times the deposit. The harsh consequences of non-compliance meant that landlords vigorously tested the exact wording of the Act (often with a sympathetic hearing from the courts). The courts finally concluded that the correct interpretation of the Housing Act as originally drafted would allow the landlord to avoid sanctions by securing the deposit and providing the information at any time before the tenant's application for compensation was heard. It was also held that a tenant could not make an application for compensation once the tenancy had been determined (even though this would often be the first time the tenant was aware that the deposit had not been properly safeguarded). (See *Tiensia v Vision Enterprises Ltd* [2010] EWCA Civ 1244; *Gladehurst Properties Ltd v Hashemi* [2011] EWCA Civ 604.)

In order to redress this situation s 184 of the Localism Act 2011 was brought into force. **15.141** The new provisions allow a longer period for compliance (30 days rather than 14) and give the court some discretion as to how much compensation a defaulting landlord should pay. The amendments also provide that a tenant may make an application for the return of the deposit and for compensation after the tenancy has ended. The new provisions apply to any deposit received after 5 April 2012 but the Act also provided an 'amnesty period' for landlords who took a deposit between 6 April 2007 and 6 April 2012. In these cases the landlord was required to secure the deposit and supply the tenant with the prescribed information before 6 May 2012 in order to avoid sanctions.

Prescribed information

This information is set out in the Housing (Tenancy Deposits) (Prescribed Information) **15.142** Order 2007, SI 2007/797. The information to be sent is as follows:

(1) The contact details of the tenancy deposit scheme provider.
(2) Any information supplied by the scheme provider explaining the scheme.
(3) The procedure for repayment of the deposit.
(4) The procedure to be followed if either the landlord or the tenant cannot be traced.
(5) Details of the procedure to be followed if there is a dispute.
(6) The information should also include:
    (i) The amount of the deposit.
    (ii) The address of the property to which the tenancy relates.
    (iii) The contact details of the landlord or agent and the tenant.
    (iv) The contact details of any relevant person (any third party with an interest in the deposit).
    (v) Details of the circumstances in which the landlord can retain any or all of the deposit (ie the relevant terms of the tenancy agreement).

The landlord should then certify that this information is correct and that he or she has **15.143** given the tenant the opportunity of confirming that the information is correct.

Under the terms of the custodial scheme the majority of this information will be provided **15.144** directly to the landlord and the tenant by the scheme provider immediately upon receipt of the deposit. The landlord will, however, need to ensure that the tenant has received the information, and will have to provide the further information regarding the reasons for withholding part or all of the deposit (ie the relevant terms of the tenancy agreement) and supply the necessary confirmation. The landlord must provide this information to the tenant him- or herself and cannot rely on the assumption that the information has been provided to the tenant by the scheme provider (*Suurpere v Nice and another* [2011] EWHC 2003 (QB)).

The lead tenant

Under the terms of the custodial scheme, where there is more than one tenant the landlord **15.145** can decide whether to register separate deposits in the names of each individual tenant or nominate a 'lead tenant' in whose name the deposit will be registered (even if it has been paid jointly by all of the tenants, or by someone else). The nomination of a lead tenant may make matters simpler for the landlord. However, if each tenant's share of the deposit is separately registered this may make it easier for the tenants when it comes to dividing up the repaid deposit at the end of the term. It should be noted that the fact that one joint tenant leaves the property before the end of the tenancy will not necessarily entitle him or her to the return of his or her deposit at that stage. Unless the landlord releases them from their obligations (usually by granting a fresh tenancy to the remaining or replacement tenants) they will remain liable under the terms of the tenancy until the landlord regains possession of the property and the landlord may be entitled to retain all deposits until then (see 15.145). The landlord may, however, choose to repay them their deposit and accept a deposit from a replacement tenant instead. If a premises has more than one occupier but each has exclusive possession of a particular room under an individual agreement, then each occupier may have a separate tenancy (see 2.45). In this case a deposit should be taken from each individual tenant and should be protected in that tenant's name.

The third party

15.146 The deposit must be protected no matter by whom it is paid (for example, it may be paid by a tenant's parent or a local authority). The landlord must also forward a copy of the prescribed information to any third party who has paid the deposit *to the landlord* on behalf of the tenants (under the custodial scheme the money cannot be held in the third party's name—it must be in the name of one of the tenants).

Notification of changes

15.147 The information held by the scheme provider must be kept up to date. It is the landlord's responsibility to ensure that the scheme provider is notified of any change in the identity of the landlord or the tenant or any changes to the tenancy or the deposit. The tenants should notify the scheme provider of any changes in the tenants' contact details. If the landlord transfers his or her interest to another person, the original landlord will have to notify the scheme provider of the change and the identity of the new landlord, since the new landlord will not yet be authorized to make changes to the data held by the scheme provider. If the identity of a deposit-paying or lead tenant changes the landlord must notify the scheme provider (the landlord should also obtain written confirmation from all tenants, including the exiting tenant, and any third party that this is to be the case). The scheme provider will have set out the mandatory details of the tenancy that it requires in the original deposit submission form. The landlord must ensure that the scheme provider is notified of any changes to these details. Other tenancy details may form part of the prescribed information and the landlord should ensure that this is kept up to date and that the tenant and any third party has received any updated information.

The date for repayment

15.148 The tenancy agreement may contain specific provisions concerning the date on which and the circumstances in which the deposit is to be repaid. Usually the deposit only falls to be repaid when the tenant has vacated the property and the landlord has had a reasonable opportunity to inspect the premises (or later if the agreement provides that the tenant must provide confirmation that bills etc have been paid). It is possible that the agreement will specifically provide for repayment at the end of the fixed term. If the tenancy continues after this date as a periodic tenancy, the landlord and tenant will have to agree between themselves whether the initial deposit should be retained until the end of the periodic tenancy, or whether it should be returned. The scheme provider should be notified of any material changes to the agreement. If the tenant demands return of the deposit, and the landlord does not agree, the tenant can argue the matter in court, or by submitting a joint repayment form and following the scheme's ADR process.

Absent or uncooperative landlords or tenants

15.149 If, at the end of the tenancy, either the landlord or the tenant cannot be traced, or will not complete the joint repayment form, the remaining party can apply for a release of the deposit by submitting a claim together with a statutory declaration setting out the reasons why a single claim is being made (Housing Act 2004, Sch 10, para 4A). A copy of the claim and declaration is sent to the last known address of the non-cooperating party. If they agree, or do not respond within 14 days, the deposit is paid out to the applicant. If they reply, disputing the claim, the dispute must be resolved before payment is made.

Penalties for non-compliance

[handwritten annotation: — 14? Gp Gov. oh says 30 days legislation. sav oh 14 days]

If the deposit has not been properly secured by the landlord and/or the required infor- **15.150**
mation has not been provided within the 30-day period the tenant may make an application to the court under s 214 of the 2004 Act. The remedies available differ slightly depending on whether or not the tenancy has come to an end at the time the application is made.

If the tenancy is still continuing the court must:

(a) order that the deposit be repaid to the tenant within 14 days; *and*
(b) order the landlord within 14 days to pay to the tenant an amount not less than the amount of the deposit and not more than three times the deposit (Housing Act 2004, s 214(3) and (4), as amended by Localism Act 2011, s 184).

If the tenancy has come to an end, the court may order the return of the deposit (depending **15.151**
on whether the landlord has a proper reason for withholding some or all of the deposit at the end of the tenancy) and must order the landlord to pay an amount of money to the tenant not less than the amount of the deposit and not more than three times the deposit (Housing Act 2004, s 214(1A), (3A), and (4)).

It should be noted that the sanctions in s 214(a) will be imposed against the person who **15.152**
it appears to the court is holding the deposit (s 214(3)(a)) and 'landlord' for the purposes of the Act includes a person acting on the landlord's behalf (s 212(9)). This means that the court may make an order under both parts of s 214 against the landlord's agent if the agent took the deposit on behalf of the landlord and continues to hold it (*Draycott v Hannells Lettings Limited* [2010] EWHC 217 (QB)).

The tenant may, therefore, make an application for the return of the deposit and for com- **15.153**
pensation at any time, including after the end of the tenancy. If there is more than one tenant the application should be made by all of them jointly (*Gladehurst Properties Ltd v Hashemi* [2011] EWCA Civ 604).

The tenant can apply to the court for such an order at any stage, although tenants might **15.154**
be well advised not to raise the matter until they need to: either at the end of the tenancy or when the landlord attempts to issue possession proceedings. An application made at the beginning of the tenancy, and the resultant fine, would probably guarantee that the landlord would seek possession promptly at the end of the fixed term. It is anticipated that, even if a tenant is unaware of his or her rights, the matter of compliance with a deposit scheme will be raised by the court as a matter of course when dealing with an application in respect of an assured shorthold tenancy.

Notice seeking possession

A landlord who has not safeguarded the deposit and provided the prescribed information **15.155**
will not be able to serve notice under the Housing Act 1988, s 21 (see 16.03 to 16.21) in respect of the tenancy (Housing Act 2004, s 215). As s 21 provides the easiest method of obtaining possession from a shorthold tenant, this sanction will cause considerable difficulties for the non-complying landlord. The Housing Act 2004, s 215(2A) does, however, allow

the landlord to serve a s 21 notice if he or she returns the deposit in full to the tenant (or returns any lesser amount agreed with the tenant as being due). The landlord may also go on to serve s 21 notice after the tenant's application under s 214(1) has been determined or settled.

15.156 Any landlord who has complied with the requirements of the 2004 Act and who wishes to serve a s 21 notice should ensure that he or she is able to supply proof that the deposit has been safeguarded and that the prescribed information has been given to the relevant parties. This is an important consideration for landlords who normally choose to serve a s 21 notice at the same time the tenancy agreement is entered into and the deposit taken. As they will not have complied with the requirements of the deposit scheme at that stage, the notice will not be valid. If the deposit is received by the landlord at a date after the commencement of the tenancy and the service of a s 21 notice, that s 21 notice will, however, remain valid.

15.157 Provided that a landlord has complied with the initial statutory requirements, any ongoing dispute concerning the repayment of the deposit will not normally affect his or her ability to obtain possession of the property or re-let the property.

15.158 If a landlord of an assured shorthold tenant has taken a deposit but has missed the 30-day deadline he or she will have to return the deposit to the tenant before serving a s 21 notice. Even if the landlord does not want to serve notice he or she would be best advised to return the deposit, or comply with the necessary requirements, at the earliest opportunity. If the tenant makes an application for compensation at some stage, late compliance by the landlord will not allow him or her to avoid paying compensation but it may mean that a lower amount would be ordered to be paid.

15.159 If the landlord has taken a deposit from any person that consists of property other than money the court will order that deposit to be repaid (Housing Act 2004, s 215(3)).

Scheme providers

15.160 At the date of writing the contact details of the three approved scheme providers are as follows:

Custodial scheme provider

The Deposit Protection Service Tel: 0844 4727 000 <http://www.depositprotection.com>

Insurance-based scheme providers

Tenancy Deposit Solutions Ltd Tel: 0844 980 0290 <http://www.mydeposits.co.uk>

The Dispute Service Limited Tel: 0845 226 7837 <http://www.thedisputeservice.co.uk>

16

THE HOUSING ACT 1988—
2. RECOVERY OF POSSESSION
BY THE LANDLORD

A POSSESSION OF AN ASSURED SHORTHOLD TENANCY

16.01   The main advantage from the landlord's point of view of an assured shorthold tenancy is that once the fixed term has expired possession can be recovered without having to establish any of the grounds set out in the Housing Act 1988, Sch 2.

Examples

16.02   (a) Simon is offered a temporary job in New York for the summer. He wants to rent out his flat while he is away, but is anxious to be able to recover possession when he returns in October. He therefore grants Peter a six-month shorthold assured tenancy of his flat starting on 1 April 2011.

   (b) Henry bought the freehold of his flat in 2005. In 2011 he decided to move. The value of the flat had dropped significantly since he bought it and rather than try to sell the flat he decided to rent it out for the time being. He granted Ann a one-year assured shorthold tenancy commencing on 15 June 2011. He has recently received a good offer for the flat and wishes to recover possession.

Possession at the end of the fixed term

16.03   Simon wants to recover possession of his flat when the six-month term comes to an end. He must therefore serve notice in accordance with the Housing Act 1988, s 21(1). Section 21(1) provides that on or after the coming to an end of a fixed-term assured shorthold tenancy the court will make an order for possession provided it is satisfied that:

   (a) the assured shorthold tenancy has come to an end and no further assured tenancy, other than an assured shorthold periodic tenancy, is in existence; and

   (b) the landlord (or at least one of a number of joint landlords) has given to the tenant not less than two months' notice in writing stating that he or she requires possession of the dwelling-house.

16.04   The requirement that the notice be in writing was added by the Housing Act 1996 to correct a strange omission on the part of the original draftsmen. The Housing Act 1996 has also amended s 21 to provide that an order for possession of an assured shorthold tenancy granted after 28 February 1997 may not be made earlier than six months after the beginning of the tenancy (s 21(5)(a)). If the shorthold tenancy is a replacement tenancy, possession may be granted after six months from the commencement of the original tenancy (s 21(5)(b)). (A replacement tenancy is a tenancy which comes into being at the end of an assured shorthold tenancy under which the landlord and tenant are the same as under the earlier tenancy and the premises let are the same or substantially the same as those let under the earlier tenancy (s 21(7)).) These provisions are intended to ensure that shorthold tenancies are to be granted for a minimum period of six months, since the requirement that an assured shorthold tenancy be granted for a term of not less than six months does not apply to tenancies granted after 28 February 1997.

16.05   Thus, to recover possession on 1 October, Simon must give Peter written notice before 31 July. If he fails to give notice before 31 July Simon may still recover possession under s 21(1) by giving notice at any time before the fixed term expires, but he will have to wait for two months to elapse from the giving of the notice until he can recover possession. In the meantime Peter's tenancy will continue as an assured periodic shorthold tenancy. If Simon does not serve notice by 30 September (the last day of the fixed term) he cannot rely on s 21(1) and will have to serve notice under s 21(4).

Slightly different requirements apply to fixed-term assured shorthold tenancies granted **16.06** by registered providers of social housing in England. If such a tenancy was granted after 1 April 2012 for a fixed term of more than two years and the landlord wants to gain possession at the end of the fixed term, the landlord must give the tenant at least six months' notice in writing stating that it does not intend to renew the tenancy at the end of the fixed term and informing the tenant of how to obtain help and advice about the notice (Housing Act, s 21(1A) and (1B) (inserted by the Localism Act 2011, s 164)).

Possession of a periodic assured shorthold tenancy

Henry has not served notice on Ann. Her fixed-term tenancy expired on 14 June 2012 **16.07** and since then she has been holding as an assured periodic shorthold tenant. Henry must therefore serve notice in accordance with the Housing Act 1988, s 21(4).

Section 21(4) provides: **16.08**

> A court shall make an order for possession of a dwelling house let on an assured shorthold tenancy which is a periodic tenancy if the Court is satisfied—
> (a) that the landlord or, in the case of joint landlords, at least one of them, has given to the tenant a notice in writing stating that, after a date specified in the notice, being the last day of a period of the tenancy and not earlier than 2 months after the date the notice was given, possession of the dwelling house is required by virtue of this section; and
> (b) that the date specified in the notice under paragraph (a) above is not earlier than the earliest day on which, apart from section 5(1) above, the tenancy could be brought to an end by a notice to quit given by the landlord on the same date as the notice under paragraph (a) above.

It is important to remember that a notice under s 21(4) is not a notice to quit. It is the **16.09** means by which a landlord can trigger the court's statutory power to grant possession. The requirements of s 21(4) must be followed to the letter (*Fernandez v McDonald* [2003] EWCA Civ 1219, [2004] 1 WLR 1027).

The last day of Ann's fixed-term tenancy was 14 June 2012. If she paid rent monthly, she **16.10** will have been occupying the flat since then under a monthly periodic tenancy. The first day of the periodic tenancy will have been 15 June 2012. The last day of each monthly period will be the 14th of the month.

If Henry gives notice on 11 May 2013, he will have to give at least two months' notice **16.11** (taking him to 11 July 2013). The earliest date that can be specified in the notice will be the end of a period of the tenancy after that date. This will be 14 July 2013.

To avoid any danger of invalidating a notice by calculating the wrong date for the last day **16.12** of a period of the tenancy, it is perfectly acceptable to add the catch-all phrase '*or at the end of the period of your tenancy which will end next after the expiry of two months from the service upon you of this notice*' after, or even instead of, the actual date (*Lower Street Properties Ltd v Jones* (1996) 48 EG 154, (1996) 28 HLR 877, CA). The Court of Appeal in *Notting Hill Housing Trust v Roomus* [2006] EWCA Civ 407 held that 'at the end of' meant the same as 'after' and so satisfied the requirements of s 21(4). Even if a landlord is confident in his or her calculation it does no harm to add this phrase in case there are any delays in service of the notice—in which case the notice would be valid to take effect after the end of the next period.

16.13   Henry's s 21(4) notice could take the following form:

Notice Requiring Possession of a Periodic Assured Shorthold Tenancy

HOUSING ACT 1988
Section 21(4)

To: Ann Johnson
      of Flat 4, 18 High Street, Nottingham

From: Henry Harris
         of Harris Towers, Hampshire

I give you notice that I require possession of the dwelling house known as Flat 4, 18 High Street, Nottingham after 14 July 2013 or at the end of the period of your tenancy which will end next after the expiry of two months from the service upon you of this notice.

Dated 11 May 2013

Signed: *Henry Harris*
             Landlord

16.14   If the notice says that Henry requires possession *on* 14 July, rather than *after*, it will be invalid as it does not conform with the exact requirements of s 21(4) (*Fernandez v McDonald*, 16.09); for the same reason it must be clear on the face of the notice that it is given under s 21 of the Housing Act 1988.

A period of a tenancy

16.15   The relevant period of the tenancy will be defined by the period agreed for the payment for rent under the original tenancy: usually weekly, monthly, quarterly, or yearly. Thus, even a yearly tenancy can be described as a monthly periodic tenancy after the end of the fixed term if the rent under the original tenancy was payable monthly (Housing Act 1988, s 5(3)(d); *Church Commissioners for England v Meya* [2006] EWCA Civ 821).

Additional notice

16.16   Section 21(4)(b) provides that additional notice must be given if it would be required for a notice to quit in respect of the tenancy. This will not affect the position for a weekly or monthly tenancy; but extra notice must be given in respect of quarterly or yearly tenancies. If Ann was holding over on a quarterly periodic tenancy (because rent was paid quarterly) s 21(4)(b) would require Henry to give three months' notice, this being the period required by the common law if Henry had served a notice to quit (see 10.41). In that case, the last day of a period of the tenancy would be the last day of a quarter. In Ann's case this would be 14 June, 14 September, 14 December, or 14 March. If Henry served notice on 11 May he would therefore require possession after 14 September (the first end day after three months) and the catch-all phrase should be amended to provide for a three-month notice period.

The order for possession

16.17   If the court is satisfied that proper notice has been give under either s 21(1) or 21(4) it has no discretion but to make an order for possession. The court cannot postpone the date of possession for more than 14 days unless exceptional hardship would be caused to the tenant (in which case the possession date can be postponed for up to six weeks) (Housing Act 1980, s 89), or unless the landlord consents. The court may, however, postpone the

date of possession under its own inherent jurisdiction if the tenant intends to appeal the
possession order (*Admiral Taverns (Cygnet Ltd) v Daly* [2008] EWCA Civ 1501, [2009]
1 WLR 2192).

Houses in multiple occupation

The Housing Act 2004 introduced new provisions concerning the licensing of certain types   **16.18**
of residential accommodation (see 20.41 to 20.136). Section 75 of the 2004 Act effectively
imposes a sanction on landlords or managers of houses in multiple occupation (HMOs)
who have not complied with licensing requirements by preventing them from using s 21
to recover possession. Section 75 provides that as 21 notice cannot be given in respect of a
tenancy in an unlicensed HMO which is subject to mandatory licensing; or, under s 98, a
property which is subject to selective licensing but is not licensed.

Tenancy deposit schemes—non-compliance by the landlord

If a landlord of a shorthold tenant has taken a deposit from that tenant after 6 April 2007   **16.19**
the landlord must safeguard the deposit under the terms of an approved tenancy deposit
scheme (Housing Act 2004, s 212). One of the penalties for failing to comply with this
requirement is that the defaulting landlord will not be able to serve a s 21 notice on the
tenant until the deposit is being held in accordance with an authorized scheme and the tenant has been provided with the prescribed information relating to the scheme (Housing Act
2004, s 215(1) and (2)). If the landlord has taken a deposit that consists of property, rather
than money, the landlord cannot serve a s 21 notice until that deposit has been returned to
the person who provided it (Housing Act 2004, s 215(3)).

Tenancy deposit schemes are considered in more detail in Chapter 15 (see 15.133 to   **16.20**
15.160).

During the fixed term

It is a common misconception to believe that a shorthold assured tenancy cannot be ter-   **16.21**
minated until the fixed term has expired. This is not the case; an assured shorthold tenancy is like any other fixed-term assured tenancy in that it is subject to the provisions of
the Housing Act 1988, s 7(6) and (6A). Thus, provided that the landlord has specifically
reserved the right to do so, he or she may seek possession on Grounds 2, 7 (in England), 8,
or 10 to 15 (see 16.32, 16.46, and 16.57 to 16.68) at any time during the course of the tenancy, even in the first six months. The landlord therefore will still have a powerful weapon
against a shorthold assured tenant who is in serious breach of covenant.

B POSSESSION OF AN ASSURED TENANCY

If a landlord wishes to start possession proceedings, the first step is to serve a notice seek-   **16.22**
ing possession upon the tenant in accordance with the Housing Act 1988, s 8. If there are
two or more joint landlords, it is sufficient that the notice is served by one of the landlords
(s 8(1)(a)).

A notice seeking possession must comply with certain requirements: **16.23**

(a) It must be in the prescribed form (Form 3 of the Assured Tenancies and Agricultural
     Occupancies (Forms) Regulations 1997, SI 1997/194) although minor deviations from

the prescribed form may not be fatal to the notice provided the notice gives the tenant all the information required by statute (see *Mountain v Hastings* (1993) 25 HLR 427).

(b) It must inform the tenant that the landlord intends to bring possession proceedings.

(c) It must state on which of the grounds set out in Housing Act 1988, Sch 2 the landlord intends to rely and also give particulars of the ground or grounds. The grounds specified in the notice may be altered or added to with the leave of the court (s 8(2)); however, they must initially be sufficient to enable the tenant to know what the alleged breach is in order that he or she can establish exactly what to do to remedy the breach (*Torridge DC v Jones* (1985) 18 HLR 107; *Marath v MacGillivray* (1996) 28 HLR 484, CA).

(d) The notice must also inform the tenant that proceedings will not be begun earlier than a date specified in the notice (s 8(3)(b)). In the majority of cases this date should be at least two weeks from the date of the service of the notice. If the landlord specifies that he or she wishes to rely upon any of Grounds 1, 2, 5 to 7, 9, and 16, this date should be at least two months from the date of service of the notice or, if it is longer, the earliest date on which the tenancy could be brought to an end by a notice to quit given by the landlord on the same date as the date of service of the notice (ie the contractual period of the tenancy) (s 8(4A)). For example, if John has a weekly periodic tenancy and his landlord wishes to regain possession on Ground 9 (that suitable alternative accommodation is available, see 16.54), the landlord will have to give John two months' notice. If John holds a quarterly periodic tenancy the landlord will have to give him three months' notice.

(e) Where the landlord seeks to rely on grounds which include Ground 14 (nuisance, see 16.62), the date specified in the notice can be any time on or after the date of service of the notice (s 8(4)). Thus, proceedings which include an allegation under Ground 14 may be commenced on the same day that notice is served thereby speeding up the process of recovery of the property and allowing the landlord to apply for an injunction if necessary. It should be noted, however, that the court cannot order the tenant to give up possession of the property until the earliest day on which the tenancy could be bought to an end by notice to quit. By virtue of s 5 of the Protection from Eviction Act 1977, the minimum period for a notice to quit is four weeks. For example, if John's landlord wishes to regain possession on Ground 14, alleging that John's brother has been visiting John's flat regularly and shouting racist comments at John's next-door neighbour, the landlord can issue proceedings on the same day that he gives notice. If the landlord succeeds in establishing the ground, the court cannot order John to quit the flat until four weeks from service of the notice or until the last day of the contractual notice period, whichever is the longer.

(f) If the landlord is a registered social landlord seeking possession under Ground 14A (domestic violence, see 16.67) there is an additional notice requirement: the landlord must serve a copy of the s 8 notice on the partner who has left the dwelling-house or satisfy the court that all reasonable steps have been taken to do so (s 8A(1)).

(g) The notice must inform the tenant that those proceedings will not begin later than 12 months from the date of service of the notice (s 8(3)(c)).

16.24 If proceedings are not issued within 12 months a fresh s 8 notice must be served.

16.25 The landlord must serve a s 8 notice stating that he or she seeks possession on Ground 8 of the Housing Act 1988, Sch 2, Pt 1 (serious rent arrears). The court has no discretion to dispense with the requirement of notice where Ground 8 is relied on. The landlord is strongly advised to serve notice where any of the other grounds in Sch 2 are relied on, but if he or she does not, or if the notice is defective, the court has discretion to dispense with the requirement of service of notice if it considers it 'just and equitable' to do so (s 8(1)(b); and *Knowsley Housing Trust v Revell*; *Helena Housing Ltd v Curtis* [2003] EWCA Civ 496, [2003] HLR 63).

Service of notices

At the possession hearing the court will need to be satisfied that the tenant has been served with the notice on the date claimed in the particulars of claim. The required method of service of notices is sometimes set out in the tenancy agreement and this must be adhered to. **16.26**

Notices under s 8 of the Housing Act 1988 (see below) must be 'served' on the tenant (s 8(1)(a)), rather than 'given', as is the case with notices under s 21. In the case of s 8 notices, delivery to the premises will only suffice if the tenancy agreement specifically provides that notices can be served this way. If there is no such provision, the notice should be personally served on the tenant or tenants. **16.27**

In all cases, unless the tenant has admitted receiving the notice, the landlord should be in a position to provide evidence at the hearing that notice has been given or served, either in the form of live evidence from the person who sent or delivered the notice, or in the form of a certificate of service. **16.28**

Once the landlord has successfully served a notice of intention to bring possession proceedings (or the court has used its discretion to dispose with the requirement of notice), the landlord must further establish one or more of the grounds for possession set out in the Housing Act 1988, Sch 2, before the court will grant an order for possession. If the landlord can establish a mandatory ground (Grounds 1 to 8) the court must grant a possession order (s 7(3)). If he or she can establish a discretionary ground (Grounds 9 to 17) the court will grant a possession order only if it considers it reasonable to do so (s 7(4)). **16.29**

C MANDATORY GROUNDS FOR POSSESSION OF DWELLING-HOUSES LET ON ASSURED TENANCIES

The Housing Act 1988, Sch 2, Pt I lists the following grounds on which the court must order possession under s 7 of the Act. **16.30**

Ground 1—returning owner-occupier

Not later than the beginning of the tenancy the landlord gave notice in writing to the tenant that possession might be recovered on this ground or the court is of the opinion that it is just and equitable to dispense with the requirement of notice and (in either case)—

(a) at some time before the beginning of the tenancy, the landlord who is seeking possession or, in the case of joint landlords seeking possession, at least one of them occupied the dwelling-house as his only or principal home; or

(b) the landlord who is seeking possession or, in the case of joint landlords seeking possession, at least one of them requires the dwelling-house as his or his spouse's only or principal home and neither the landlord (or in the case of joint landlords, any one of them) nor any person who, as landlord, derived title under the landlord who gave the notice mentioned above acquired the reversion on the tenancy for money or money's worth.

16.31   To be able to rely upon Ground 1, a landlord must have given written notice to the tenant at the beginning of the tenancy or before that possession might be recovered under this ground. (The court can, if it considers it just and equitable to do so, dispense with the requirement of notice.) If such notice has been given, the landlord can then recover possession in two situations:

(a)   If the landlord occupied the dwelling-house as his or her only or principal residence at some time before the grant of the tenancy he or she can recover possession of the premises. The landlord does not have to give any reasons for wanting to recover possession (in contrast to the Rent Act 1977, Sch 15, Case 11, where the landlord would have to show that he or she required the premises for his or her own personal occupation, see 14.52). Neither is it necessary that the landlord occupied the dwelling immediately before the letting to the tenant. In the case of joint landlords, it is sufficient that one of them previously occupied the dwelling-house as his or her only or principal home.

(b)   Where the landlord (or in the case of joint landlords, at least one of them) wants to regain possession of the premises for his or her own occupation, or for occupation by his or her spouse. There is no requirement that either the landlord or his or her spouse previously occupied the premises However, a landlord who bought the reversion from the tenant's original landlord cannot use this ground. (Unlike Case 9 under the Rent Act 1977, Sch 15, this is a mandatory ground, but the class of potential occupiers is narrower under Ground 1, see 14.44.)

Ground 2—mortgagees

The dwelling-house is subject to a mortgage granted before the beginning of the tenancy and—

(a)   the mortgagee is entitled to exercise a power of sale conferred on him by the mortgage or by section 101 of the Law of Property Act 1925; and

(b)   the mortgagee requires possession of the dwelling-house for the purpose of disposing of it with vacant possession in exercise of that power; and

(c)   either notice was given as mentioned in Ground 1 above or the court is satisfied that it is just and equitable to dispense with the requirement of notice; and for the purposes of this ground 'mortgage' includes a charge and 'mortgagee' shall be construed accordingly.

16.32   The aim of this ground is to enable a landlord to regain possession from the tenant when the bank or building society which lent the landlord the money to purchase the property wants to repossess the property in order to sell it. This will usually be because the landlord has defaulted on the mortgage repayments.

16.33   Ground 2 will apply only where:

(a)   the mortgage was granted before the beginning of the tenancy; and

(b)   the landlord has served notice in accordance with the requirements of Ground 1 (ie that the landlord may want possession at a future date because he or she intends to occupy the dwelling-house himself or herself).

16.34   This ground is intended to cover the situation where a landlord is unable to regain possession under Ground 1 because he or she cannot claim to require the dwelling-house as his or her only or principal home because the mortgagee intends to sell it. Notice may be dispensed with by the court if it feels that it is just and equitable to do so.

16.35   The majority of mortgages prohibit the renting out of the property without the mortgagee's consent. If a property is let without consent the tenant will have no protection (see 16.78).

It should be noted that this ground can also apply to a fixed-term tenancy before the expiry of the term (see 15.57).

Ground 3—holiday lets

The aim of this provision is to assist a landlord who habitually lets out property on holiday   **16.36**
lets during the summer. Holiday lets are, of course, excluded from being assured tenancies (Housing Act 1988, Sch 1, Pt I, para 9). A landlord who lets out property as a holiday home in season may wish to let it out for a longer period out of season. Such a letting might well not fall within the definition of a holiday letting and be an assured tenancy. Ground 3 enables the landlord to regain possession of the property for use as a holiday home in season. To rely upon this ground:

(a) the tenancy in question must be a fixed-term tenancy for a term not exceeding eight months; and

(b) the landlord must have given written notice to the tenant that possession might be recovered on this ground before the beginning of the tenancy (it should be noted that the court has no discretion under this ground to dispense with this notice requirement); and

(c) at some time within the period of 12 months ending with the beginning of the tenancy the dwelling-house must have been occupied under a right to occupy it for a holiday.

Ground 4—student lets

Ground 4 is similar to Ground 3. Like holiday lettings, lettings to students are precluded   **16.37**
from being assured tenancies (Housing Act 1988, Sch 1, Pt I, para 8). A letting of premises normally used to provide accommodation for students during a vacation period, however, might be capable of being an assured tenancy. Ground 4 therefore enables a landlord to recover possession when the term of the vacation let is over. To rely upon this ground:

(a) the tenancy must be a fixed-term tenancy for a term not exceeding 12 months; and

(b) the landlord must have given written notice to the tenant that possession might be recovered on this ground before the beginning of the tenancy (as with Ground 3 the court has no discretion to dispense with the notice requirement); and

(c) at some time within the period of 12 months ending with the beginning of the tenancy, the dwelling-house was let on a tenancy falling within Sch 1, para 8 to the 1988 Act.

Ground 5—ministers of religion

This ground is designed to enable the owner of a dwelling-house which is normally used to   **16.38**
provide accommodation for a minister of religion, to keep that accommodation available for those purposes. It permits a landlord to gain possession of such a dwelling-house, both when the dwelling-house is occupied by a minister of religion and when it is occupied by another tenant. To rely upon this ground:

(a) the dwelling-house must be held for the purpose of being available for occupation by a minister of religion as a residence from which to perform the duties of his or her office;

(b) the landlord must have given written notice to the tenant that possession might be recovered on this ground before the beginning of the tenancy (the court has no discretion to dispense with the notice requirement);

(c) the court must be satisfied that the dwelling-house is required for occupation by a minister of religion as a residence from which to perform his or her duties.

Ground 6—demolition, reconstruction, or substantial works

16.39 In relation to private residential tenancies this was an entirely new ground. Similar provisions may be found in s 30(1)(f) of the Landlord and Tenant Act 1954 with regard to business tenancies, and for public sector tenancies under the Housing Act 1985 (Ground 10). The inclusion of this ground in the Housing Act 1988 is no doubt partially due to the fact that the tenants of registered housing associations now derive their protection from the 1988 Act rather than as secure tenants under the 1985 Act.

16.40 To rely on this ground the landlord must show the following:

(a) That the landlord intends to demolish or reconstruct the whole or a substantial part of the dwelling-house, or carry out substantial works on the dwelling-house or any part thereof or any building of which it forms part. There must be a genuine desire to undertake the work and also a reasonable prospect that the work will actually go ahead. Where a landlord had not found a developer to undertake the projected work at the time of the hearing, the landlord was regarded as not having established the necessary intention (*Edwards v Thompson* (1990) 29 EG 41; see also *Wansbeck DC v Marley, The Times*, 30 November 1987).

(b) That the work could not reasonably be carried out without the tenant giving up possession of the premises. If the tenant is prepared to agree to a variation of the terms of the tenancy so as to enable the landlord access to undertake the work, possession will not be granted under this ground. Likewise, if the tenant is willing to take a tenancy of a part of the premises so that the landlord can work on the other parts, possession will not be granted under Ground 6. The landlord must show either that the tenant is not willing to agree to such an arrangement (be that a variation of terms or the grant of the tenancy of a part of the premises) or that the nature of the intended work is such that such an arrangement is not possible.

(c) That the landlord acquired his or her interest in the property before the tenancy was granted, or, if he or she acquired the interest after the grant of the tenancy, the landlord must not have acquired the interest for money or money's worth (ie the landlord could have acquired the interest under a will but must not have purchased the interest). The aim of this provision is to prevent speculators from exploiting Ground 6 for commercial gain by purchasing the landlord's reversion with the intention of evicting the tenants and redeveloping the property.

16.41 If a landlord is successful under this ground, s 11 of the 1988 Act requires the landlord to pay to the tenant a sum equal to the reasonable expenses likely to be incurred by the tenant in removing from the dwelling-house. If the landlord and tenant cannot agree on an appropriate sum the amount will be determined by the court.

Demolition orders

16.42 The position is different if a demolition order has been made in respect of the premises. In this case the protection of the Housing Act 1988 and the Rent Act 1977 will not apply to the tenancy (National Health and Community Care Act 1990, s 60(6)) although the landlord must terminate the tenancy, either by any specified contractual method or by service of notice to quit. The relevant local authority does, however, have a statutory duty to re-house a tenant who is dispossessed as a result of the making of a demolition order (Land Compensation Act 1973 s 39(1)).

Ground 7—inherited periodic tenancy

Under the Rent Act 1977, a statutory tenancy came to an end on the death of the tenant **16.43** unless a person succeeded to that tenancy under the provisions of the Act (see 13.108). Under the Housing Act 1988, there is no distinction between the original contractual tenancy and a statutory tenancy. It is therefore possible for an assured tenancy (even a statutorily implied periodic tenancy) to be passed to a third party by the will of the tenant. As a result a landlord may find, after the death of an assured tenant, that a third party has inherited the tenant's tenancy and is now occupying the dwelling-house. The landlord has had no say in choosing this new tenant and may possibly consider him or her undesirable. This ground therefore provides the landlord with a means of regaining possession in this situation.

Ground 7 applies to all periodic tenancies and statutory periodic tenancies. It also applies **16.44** to fixed-term tenancies where the dwelling-house is in England, but not to fixed-term tenancies in Wales (Localism Act 2011, s 162(5)). It applies only when a tenant has died and the tenancy has been passed to another person by virtue of the deceased tenant's will or intestacy. It does not apply when the deceased tenant's spouse or cohabitee has succeeded to the tenancy under s 17 of the 1988 Act (see 15.100). The landlord has one year from the date of the death of the original tenant, or the date upon which he or she became aware of the death of the tenant, to issue a claim for possession.

This ground also specifically provides that if, after the death of the original tenant, the **16.45** landlord accepts rent from a new tenant, this will not amount to an implied grant of a new tenancy. (Under common law rules the acceptance of rent by the landlord could well imply the creation of a new tenancy, see 3.26.) A new tenancy will be created only if there is a written agreement to vary the terms of the tenancy.

Ground 8—serious rent arrears

Ground 8 gives the landlord a mandatory ground for possession for rent arrears (there **16.46** are two further discretionary grounds also dealing with rent arrears, see 16.57 to 16.59). Under the Rent Act 1977, a landlord could only pursue possession proceedings for rent arrears under a discretionary ground. Furthermore, Ground 8 is one of the two exceptional mandatory grounds (along with Ground 2) that can apply to a fixed-term tenancy before the expiry of the contractual term (see 15.57).

To be able to rely upon this ground, the landlord must show that both at the date of service **16.47** of a s 8 notice (see 16.22 to 16.29) and also at the date of the hearing:

(a) if rent is payable weekly or fortnightly, at least eight weeks' rent is unpaid;
(b) if rent is payable monthly, at least two months' rent is unpaid;
(c) if rent is payable quarterly, at least one-quarter's rent is more than three months in arrears; and
(d) if rent is payable yearly, at least three months' rent is more than three months in arrears.

'Rent' here means rent lawfully due from the tenant. It may be possible for the tenant to **16.48** argue that rent is not lawfully due if the landlord has failed to provide him or her with details of a name and address at which notices may be served. This omission would allow the tenant to rely on the Landlord and Tenant Act 1987, s 48, which provides that rent is not to be treated as being due until these details have been provided. Such an argument could only buy the tenant more time, but it would give him or her the opportunity to pay off at least some of the arrears and thus avoid a mandatory possession order.

16.49   A tenant who receives a s 8 notice specifying that the landlord seeks to rely on Ground 8 therefore has a last chance to avoid repossession by paying off some or all of the arrears before the hearing date. An uncleared cheque accepted by the landlord at the hearing has been held to be sufficient to avoid repossession on Ground 8, provided it cleared on first presentation (*Day v Coltrane* [2003] EWCA Civ 342, [2003] 1 WLR 1379). Most landlords, however, are likely to combine a claim under Ground 8 with a claim under either or both of the discretionary grounds. A tenant may also be able to avoid possession under Ground 8 if he or she is able to counterclaim for breach of the landlord's covenant to repair. Any damages awarded on the counterclaim will be set off against the rent arrears and may thereby reduce the outstanding amount below the specified level.

D DISCRETIONARY GROUNDS FOR POSSESSION OF DWELLING-HOUSES LET ON ASSURED TENANCIES

16.50   The Housing Act 1988, Sch 2, Pt II lists the following grounds on which the court may order possession if it considers it reasonable to do so. In considering reasonableness the court should take into account all relevant circumstances as at the date of the hearing and apply a broad, common-sense view (*Cumming v Danson* [1942] 2 All ER 635 *per* Lord Greene MR at 655). In considering certain possession claims brought by social landlords (local authorities, housing action trusts, and registered social landlords) the court will have regard to additional considerations such as whether the landlord has complied with the requirements of the pre-action protocol for rent arrears claims (see 16.72 to 16.73), and the requirements of the Housing Act 1988, s 9A in the case of anti-social behaviour claims (see 16.65).

16.51   Under s 9 of the Housing Act 1988 the court also has wide powers to:

(a)   adjourn the proceedings for such period or periods as it thinks fit (s 9(1));

(b)   if a possession order is made, stay or suspend the execution of that order, or postpone the date of possession for such period or periods as it thinks fit (s 9(2));

(c)   impose other conditions as it thinks fit, provided it considers that such conditions would not cause exceptional hardship to the tenant or be otherwise unreasonable.

16.52   Section 5(1A) of the 1988 Act (as amended by Sch 11 to the Housing and Regeneration Act 2008) provides that where an order of the court for possession of the dwelling-house is obtained, the tenancy ends when the order is executed, ie when the tenant is evicted (see 15.45). The fact that the court makes a possession order will not, therefore, affect the status of the tenancy. An assured tenancy will not end until the tenant actually gives up possession of the property (see also *Knowsley Housing Trust v White* [2008] UKHL 70, [2009] 2 WLR 78).

16.53   Possession orders are discussed in more detail in Chapter 18 (18.36 to 18.65). It should be noted that the tolerated trespasser scenario discussed in that chapter will not have arisen in relation to assured tenancies.

Ground 9—suitable alternative accommodation

Suitable alternative accommodation is available for the tenant or will be available for him when the order for possession takes effect.

16.54   Part III of Sch 2 defines what will be regarded as suitable alternative accommodation. Two possibilities are open to the landlord:

(a)   The landlord can produce a certificate of the local housing authority certifying that the authority will provide suitable alternative accommodation for the tenant by a date specified in the certificate (Sch 2, Pt III, para 1).

(b) The landlord can seek to establish that suitable alternative accommodation is or will be available. This accommodation may be supplied by the current landlord or by some other landlord.

If the landlord takes the second option, the court will consider the proposed accommodation. It will be deemed suitable for the purposes of Ground 9 if it fulfils two requirements: **16.55**

(a) The proposed accommodation must, in the opinion of the court, afford to the tenant security of tenure reasonably equivalent to an assured tenancy (eg a secure tenancy under the Housing Act 1985). An assured shorthold tenancy or an assured tenancy in respect of which notice has been given that possession might be recovered under Grounds 1 to 5 will not be sufficient (Sch 2, Pt III, para 2(a)).
(b) The proposed accommodation must be reasonably suitable to the needs of the tenant and his or her family as regards proximity to place of work, and either:
  (i)   similar as regards rental and extent to accommodation provided in the neighbourhood by the local housing authority to persons whose needs are similar to those of the tenant and his or her family; or
  (ii) reasonably suitable to the means of the tenant and to the needs of the tenant and his or her family as regards extent and character.

If furniture was provided under the original assured tenancy, the alternative accommodation should provide furniture which is either similar to that provided under the original tenancy or suitable to the needs of the tenant and his or her family (Sch 2, Pt III, para 3).

These provisions are almost identical to those contained in the Rent Act 1977, and reference should be made to Chapter 14 for further consideration of how these provisions will be applied (see 14.08 to 14.24). As with Ground 2, s 11(1) of the 1988 Act provides that the landlord shall pay to the tenant a sum equal to the reasonable expenses likely to be incurred by the tenant in removing from the dwelling-house.   **16.56**

Ground 10—some rent arrears

> Some rent lawfully due from the tenant—
>   (a) is unpaid on the date on which proceedings for possession are begun; and
>   (b) except where subsection (1)(b) of section 8 of this Act applies, was in arrears at the date of service of the notice under that section relating to those proceedings.

Ground 10 is notably different from Ground 8 (serious rent arrears). First, all that is required is that the landlord shows that some rent is outstanding; no minimum amount is specified. Secondly, the landlord need show only that rent was outstanding at the date upon which proceedings were issued and at the date of service of the s 8 notice (unless the requirement of notice has been dispensed with by the court). The landlord does not have to show that any rent is outstanding at the date of the hearing. However, this is a discretionary ground and it is unlikely that a court would consider it reasonable to make an order for possession if the tenant has paid off all the arrears by the date of the hearing. Ground 10 is similar to Case 1 under the Rent Act 1977, Sch 15 (see 14.26).   **16.57**

As with a Ground 8 claim, a tenant facing a claim for possession under this ground or Ground 11 should check to make sure that the landlord has served the tenant with sufficient details of his or her name and address, as a failure to do so will mean that the rent is not yet due (see 16.48).   **16.58**

Ground 11—persistent rent arrears

> Whether or not any rent is in arrears on the date on which proceedings for possession are begun, the tenant has persistently delayed paying rent which has become lawfully due.

16.59 Even when there are no current rent arrears the landlord can rely upon this ground. There is no equivalent to Ground 11 in the Rent Act 1977, but a parallel provision can be found for business tenancies under s 30(1)(b) of the Landlord and Tenant Act 1954 (see 26.152). The aim of this provision is to provide the landlord with a means of regaining possession when a tenant persistently falls into rent arrears but avoids the consequences of Ground 8 by paying off some or all of the outstanding rent after the issue of proceedings but before the date of the hearing.

Ground 12—breach of obligation

> Any obligation of the tenancy (other than one related to the payment of rent) has been broken or not performed.

16.60 This ground is basically the same as Case 1 under the Rent Act 1977, Sch 15, and reference should be made to Chapter 14 (see 14.26). The landlord can seek to rely upon this ground even where there is only a trivial breach, but it is most unlikely that the court will regard it as reasonable to make a possession order unless the breach is serious. In determining the seriousness of the breach an important factor will be whether the breach is remediable and whether it is continuing. If the landlord has waived the breach (see 11.31 to 11.39) he will not be able to rely upon this ground.

Ground 13—deterioration of the dwelling-house

> The condition of the dwelling-house or any of the common parts has deteriorated owing to acts of waste by, or the neglect or default of, the tenant or any other person residing in the dwelling-house and, in the case of an act of waste by, or the neglect or default of, a person lodging with the tenant or a sub-tenant of his, the tenant has not taken such steps as he ought reasonably to have taken for the removal of the lodger or sub-tenant.
>
> For the purposes of this ground, 'common parts' means any part of a building comprising the dwelling-house and any other premises which the tenant is entitled under the terms of the tenancy to use in common with the occupiers of other dwelling-houses in which the landlord has an estate or interest.

16.61 This ground is basically the same as Case 3 under the Rent Act 1977, Sch 15 (see 14.37), but in addition to damage to the dwelling-house occupied by the tenant it also covers damage to the common parts of the building in which the dwelling-house is situated, eg the stairways and corridors in a block of flats.

Ground 14—nuisance, annoyance, or conviction for illegal or immoral user

> The tenant or a person residing in or visiting the dwelling-house—
> (a) has been guilty of conduct causing or likely to cause a nuisance or annoyance to a person residing, visiting or otherwise engaging in lawful activity in the locality, or
> (b) has been convicted of—
> (i) using the dwelling-house or allowing it to be used for immoral or illegal purposes, or
> (ii) an arrestable offence committed in, or in the locality of the dwelling-house.

16.62 This ground was amended by the Housing Act 1996, s 148 and is identical to Ground 2 under the Housing Act 1985 (see 18.07). It gives the landlord a powerful sanction against anti-social behaviour, not only on the part of the tenant but also on the part of any person residing with or even visiting the tenant. The behaviour does not have to cause actual nuisance; it is sufficient for it merely to be *likely* to cause nuisance of annoyance. Furthermore, the person to whom the nuisance or annoyance is caused does not have to be a neighbour but can be anyone engaging in lawful activity in the locality. Thus, where local residents may be wary of complaining for fear of reprisals, a landlord will be able to rely on evidence from professional witnesses. Ground 14 will also enable a landlord to seek possession where the tenant, or a person residing with or visiting the tenant, has been convicted not only of using the dwelling-house for immoral or illegal purposes but also of any arrestable offence committed in the locality of the dwelling-house (see *Knowsley Housing Trust v Prescott* [2009] EWHC 924 (QB), [2009] L&TR 24).

The court is unlikely to make a possession order unless it considers the offence to be suf- **16.63** ficiently serious. In *Knowsley v Prescott* the court made a possession order because Mr Prescott had been convicted of manufacturing and selling a Class A drug on a large scale. In contrast, in *North Devon Homes v Batchelor* [2008] EWCA Civ 840 the court held that the tenant's offence of possession of a small quantity of a Class A drug was not sufficiently serious to warrant the making of a possession order. It should be noted that where a landlord wishes to rely on Ground 14, court proceedings may be started at the same time a notice seeking possession is served (s 8(4), see 16.23(e)).

There will be a large number of cases where a 'nuisance tenant' suffers from a mental **16.64** illness which causes anti-social behaviour. In such cases the landlord's decision to bring possession proceedings could amount to discrimination under the Equality Act 2010. The fact of the disability is also something the court can consider when deciding whether it is reasonable to make an order for possession. For a more detailed consideration of disability discrimination claims in possession proceedings, see 18.56 to 18.58.

Reasonableness *← Put in*

The Anti-social Behaviour Act 2003 introduced a new s 9A into the Housing Act 1988 **16.65** which provides that, where a court is considering whether it is reasonable to make a possession order on Ground 14, the court must consider:

(a) the effect that the nuisance or annoyance has had on persons other than the person against whom the order is sought;
(b) any continuing effect the nuisance or annoyance is likely to have on such persons;
(c) the effect that the nuisance or annoyance would be likely to have on such persons if the conduct were repeated.

Injunctions

Registered social landlords also have increased powers to obtain injunctions against anti- **16.66** social tenants under ss 153A to 153E of the Housing Act 1996 (amended by the Anti-social Behaviour Act 2003, s 13). The behaviour complained of can include, but is not limited to, behaviour which constitutes a breach of terms of the tenancy agreement. The injunction may contain an exclusion order and/or be backed by a power of arrest (s 153C). A registered social landlord may also apply to the court for the demotion of an assured tenancy on the grounds of anti-social behaviour (see 15.95 to 15.99).

Ground 14A—domestic violence

The dwelling-house was occupied (whether alone or with others) by a married couple or civil partners or a couple living together as husband and wife or civil partners and—
(a) one or both of the partners is a tenant of the dwelling-house,
(b) the landlord who is seeking possession is a registered social landlord or charitable housing trust,

(c) one partner has left the dwelling-house because of violence or threats of violence by the other towards—
  (i) that partner, or
  (ii) a member of the family of that partner who was residing with that partner immediately before that partner left, and
(d) the court is satisfied that the partner who has left is unlikely to return.

16.67   This ground was introduced by the Housing Act 1996 primarily to help charitable landlords to obtain possession of family housing from the remaining occupant after his or her partner and children left as a result of that occupant's violence. The alleged violence must have been the dominant, principal, and real cause of the partner's departure, rather than a subsidiary cause of the breakdown of a relationship (*Camden LBC v Mallett* (2001) 33 HLR 204, CA). To be able to rely on Ground 14A the landlord must be a registered social landlord, registered provider, or charitable housing trust. The landlord must also comply with the additional notice requirements set out in s 8A (see 16.23). Ground 14A is identical to Ground 2A under the Housing Act 1985 (see 18.11).

Ground 15—deterioration of furniture

The condition of any furniture provided for use under the tenancy has, in the opinion of the court, deteriorated owing to ill-treatment by the tenant or any other person residing in the dwelling-house and, in the case of ill-treatment by a person lodging with the tenant or by a sub-tenant of his, the tenant has not taken such steps as he ought reasonably to have taken for the removal of the lodger or sub-tenant.

16.68   This ground is basically the same as Case 4 under the Rent Act 1977, Sch 15 (see 14.38).

Ground 16—employees

The dwelling-house was let to the tenant in consequence of his employment by the landlord seeking possession or a previous landlord under the tenancy and the tenant has ceased to be in that employment …

16.69   This ground is a much shortened version of Case 8 under the Rent Act 1977, Sch 15 (see 14.43). The landlord need only prove that he or she, or a predecessor in title, granted the assured tenancy to the tenant in consequence of that tenant's employment by the landlord and that this employment has now ceased. The landlord does not have to prove that the dwelling-house is required for another employee.

Ground 17—grant induced by false statement

The tenant is the person, or was one of the persons, to whom the tenancy was granted and the landlord was induced to grant the tenancy by a false statement made knowingly or recklessly by—
  (a) the tenant, or
  (b) a person acting at the tenant's instigation.

16.70   This ground was introduced by the Housing Act 1996, s 102. It is identical to Ground 5 of Sch 2 to the Housing Act 1985 (see 18.15). Since 15 January 1989 an increasing proportion of housing for the less privileged has been provided on assured tenancies by charitable bodies and registered social landlords. Ground 17 is designed to prevent tenants from acquiring an assured tenancy by falsely representing their circumstances.

Misrepresentation and concealment

If it appears to the court that a landlord has obtained a possession order by misrepresenta- **16.71** tion or concealment (either at the hearing, or before) the court may order the landlord to pay compensation to the tenant (Housing Act 1988, s 12). The tenant may also be able to set aside the possession order.

Pre-action protocol for possession claims based on rent arrears

A pre-action protocol has been introduced for social landlords (local authorities, hous- **16.72** ing action trusts, and registered social landlords and registered providers) contemplating bringing possession proceedings solely on grounds of rent arrears. It applies to all tenancies except long leases. It does not apply to claims where there is no security of tenure.

The protocol encourages the landlord to provide the tenant with full and up-to-date **16.73** information regarding the arrears and encourages the parties to try to agree a schedule of repayment. The protocol also places a duty on the landlord to investigate the reasons the tenant may have for getting into arrears and to provide reasonable assistance if neces- sary. Particular emphasis is placed on the social landlord's duty to assist the tenant with any claim the tenant may have to receive housing benefit. Where the court has discretion as to whether to grant possession on the grounds of rent arrears (ie in claims other than under the Housing Act 1988, Sch 2, Ground 8) the court will take into account the social landlord's compliance with the protocol when deciding whether it is reasonable to order possession. The protocol can be downloaded from the Ministry of Justice website (<http:// www.justice.gov.uk>).

E POSSESSION PROCEDURE

The Civil Procedure (Amendment) Rules 2001, SI 2001/256 introduced CPR Part 55 and **16.74** its accompanying practice direction (PD 55) to the Civil Procedure Rules. Part 55 applies to all claims for possession issued after 15 October 2001. Landlords and their advisors should not attempt to issue and prosecute possession proceedings without following the rules set out in CPR Part 55.

CPR Part 55 provides that, other than in exceptional circumstances, claims for possession **16.75** must be issued in the county court (CPR r 55.3). The claim form must be in a prescribed form and contain specific information about the tenancy (CPR r 55.4). The form to be used for each type of claim is specified in the annex to PD 55. Use of the appropriate form is mandatory (CPR r 55.3(5)). The Rules then go on to set out the procedure governing the hearing of claims.

Claims for possession of assured shorthold tenancies may be brought under the accelerated **16.76** procedure set out in CPR rr 55.11 to 55.17. This procedure may only be adopted where the landlord seeks to recover possession on the expiry of the tenancy. It is not appropriate where any other claim is made, eg for arrears of rent. Under the accelerated procedure it is possible for the court to make an order for possession on reading the relevant documents without the need for the parties to attend for a hearing.

In the case of claims for possession for arrears of rent, certain courts now have facilities to **16.77** allow claimants to commence possession claims online (see CPR PD 55Bb). Details can be found at <http://www.possessionclaim.gov.uk/pcol>.

F MORTGAGE REPOSSESSIONS: RIGHTS OF TENANTS

16.78 Where a mortgage lender brings possession proceedings against a landlord the tenant occupying the property may have very little protection (*Britannia Building Society v Earl* [1990] 1 EGLR 133). If possession is granted to the mortgage lender the tenant can be required to leave the property without the need for a further court order. Prior to April 2009 tenants would not necessarily even be aware that proceedings had been brought against their landlord until the bailiffs arrived at the property to evict them. An amendment to the Civil Procedure Rules has remedied this by providing that from 6 April 2009 mortgage lenders are required to send notice of the possession hearing date to the occupiers of the mortgaged property within five days of the lender receiving notification of this date from the court (CPR r 55.10(2)). Once a tenant has been given notice of the hearing he or she can participate in the case. There are, however, only limited circumstances in which the tenant will be allowed to remain in the property if possession is granted to the lender. These will be either where the lender has consented to the tenancy, or where the tenant can claim an overriding interest in order to defeat the lender's entitlement to possession.

Consent to the tenancy

16.79 If the landlord obtained the lender's consent to the tenancy before it was granted the tenancy will be binding on the lender. The lender can only terminate the tenancy and recover possession by using the same statutory methods that would have been available to the landlord (for example, possession by court order on grounds of rent arrears). The lender's consent to the tenancy will not necessarily be implied simply because it was aware of the tenancy and did not take any action. If, however, the lender has knowingly received rent payments directly from the tenant it may be possible to argue that it has created a tenancy between itself and the tenant.

Overriding interest

16.80 If the lender did not consent to the tenancy the tenant may be able to claim to have an overriding interest as a person in actual occupation, but this would only be the case if the tenancy was granted before the mortgage charge was registered.

16.81 If neither of these options is available to the tenant, the most the new procedure will achieve for the tenant is to give notice of the impending eviction. The five-day requirement in CPR r 55.10(2) is designed to ensure that the tenant will have around seven weeks' notice before the possession order is made.

16.82 The full text of CPR Part 55 and PD 55 is available at <http://www.justice.gov.uk>.

Mortgage Repossessions (Protection of Tenants etc) Act 2010

16.83 The Mortgage Repossessions (Protection of Tenants etc) Act 2010 allows the courts to give unauthorized tenants (ie tenants whose tenancies were not consented to by the lender or who cannot claim an overriding interest) further time in the property in order to allow them to make alternative arrangements. The Act gives the tenant a right to apply to the court dealing with the mortgage possession proceedings for an order postponing possession for up to two months, or for a stay of execution of any warrant of possession (s 1). Section 2 of the Act and the Dwelling Houses (Execution of Possession Orders by Mortgagees) Regulations 2010, SI 2010/1809 also provide that the mortgage lender is required to give any occupier of the mortgaged premises notice before making an application for a warrant for posses-sion. The notice must be in the form set out in the Schedule to the Regulations and must be served on the tenant in the manner set out in reg 5. A warrant of possession cannot be executed until at least 14 days after such notice has been given (s 2(2) and reg 3).

G POSSESSION PROCEEDINGS AND THE HUMAN RIGHTS ACT 1998

Whilst assured tenancies may be granted by both private and public sector landlords, this **16.84** section considers the position where a possession order is sought by a private landlord. The position of a public sector landlord is considered at 18.59. It should be noted, however, that many registered social landlords, who were previously regarded as being private land-lords, may now be regarded as being quasi public bodies for the purposes of the Human Rights Act 1998 (*R (Weaver) v London & Quadrant Housing Trust* [2009] EWCA Civ 587). Not being a public body, a private landlord has no direct obligations to his or her tenants under the Act. The court, as a public body, is, however, under a duty to make deci-sions in accordance with the Act.

Where a landlord seeks to rely on a contractual term against a tenant the court, in exercis- **16.85** ing its duties as a forum for a private dispute, does not take over the individual landlord's responsibilities towards his or her tenant (see *App No 11949/86 v UK*—a case concerning the court's ability to allow a landlord to forfeit a lease). Where a landlord seeks to rely on a statutory ground for possession the court's duties extend only to interpreting the statutory provision in accordance with the Human Rights Act 1998.

Unless a particular statutory provision has been found to be contrary to the Act (which **16.86** has not yet been the case) the court is entitled to make an order for possession provided the claimant has fulfilled the necessary statutory requirements. Where the ground is dis-cretionary the court will have to have regard to the provisions of the Human Rights Act in deciding what is 'reasonable'.

H DISABILITY DISCRIMINATION

The provisions of the Equality Act 2010 in relation to the disposal and management of **16.87** premises (including the decision to evict a tenant) apply to both private landlords and pub-lic sector landlords. Disability discrimination in possession claims is considered in more detail at 18.56 to 18.58.

KEY DOCUMENTS

Assured Tenancies and Agricultural Occupancies (Forms) Regulations 1997, SI 1997/194

Housing Act 1988

Civil Procedure Rules 1998

Mortgage Repossessions (Protection of Tenants etc) Act 2010

Dwelling Houses (Execution of Possession Orders by Mortgagees) Regulations 2010, SI 2010/1809

Form N5—Claims for possession of property

Form N5B—Claims for possession of property (accelerated procedure)

Form N11B—Defence form (accelerated procedure)

Form N11R—Defence form (rented residential premises)

Form N119—Particulars of claim for possession of property

Printed copies of all legislation can be ordered from The Stationery Office at <http://www.tsoshop.co.uk>. All legislation from 1988 onwards and most pre-1988 primary legislation is available online at <http://www.legislation.gov.uk>.

Court forms are available from the HM Courts and Tribunals Service at <http://www.justice.gov.uk/forms/hmcts>.

The Civil Procedure Rules are available online from <http://www.justice.gov.uk/courts/procedure-rules>.

17

THE HOUSING ACT 1985—
1. SECURE TENANCIES

A INTRODUCTION

17.01 Given the relatively long history of statutory protection for residential occupiers in the private sector, it is surprising to note that similar statutory protection was introduced into the public sector only in 1980. Before 1980 a public sector tenant had no statutory security of tenure. While it was felt that a private sector tenant needed to be safeguarded against the possibility of exploitation at the hands of landlords renting property for commercial gain, it was generally believed that local authorities, as non-profit-making organizations providing housing for the less privileged, could be relied upon to exercise their powers fairly.

17.02 Part I of the Housing Act 1980 introduced two very important measures into the public sector. First, Chapter 1 introduced the 'right to buy'. For the first time tenants of public sector landlords were able to compel their landlords to sell them the properties in which the tenants were living. Secondly, Chapter 2 conferred upon public sector tenants a statutory security of tenure similar, although not identical, to that already available for tenants in the private sector. These measures are now contained in Pts V and IV of the Housing Act 1985.

17.03 In considering secure tenancies it is important to bear in mind that the aim of the legislation is not so much to protect tenants from unscrupulous landlords but to provide a regime within which the public sector can effectively perform the function of providing housing for the less privileged—hence the inclusion of provisions such as those enabling public landlords to keep control of specialized housing for the elderly or handicapped.

17.04 Over the years the Housing Act 1985 has been subject to amendment by a variety of statutes, notably the Housing Act 1988, which shifted housing associations from the public to the private sector, and by the Housing Act 1996, which introduced a new ground for possession and provided a procedure by which tenancies can be granted on a trial basis. The 1996 Act also contained a new right to acquire for tenants of registered social landlords. More recently the Anti-social Behaviour Act 2003 introduced a range of measures to assist landlords dealing with anti-social tenants, including new powers to obtain injunctions and demotion of secure tenancies. The Civil Partnership Act 2004 has introduced amendments to the 1985 Act which formally endorse the rights of tenants' partners in same-sex relationships. The Housing Act 2004 has abolished the right to acquire on rent-to-mortgage terms, effected some limited restrictions on the secure tenant's right to buy his or her home, and granted landlords the power to extend the trial period of an introductory tenancy. Finally, the Housing and Regeneration Act 2008 has closed the gap in the 1985 Act that allowed tenants to continue in occupation with no security following the making of a suspended possession order and has introduced a regulatory framework for the provision and management of social housing in England

B WHAT IS A SECURE TENANCY?

17.05 Security of tenure in the public sector is rooted in the notion of a 'secure tenancy'. The Housing Act 1985, s 79(1) defines a secure tenancy as follows:

> (1) A tenancy under which a dwelling-house is let as a separate dwelling is a secure tenancy at any time when the conditions described in ss 80 and 81 as the landlord condition and the tenant condition are satisfied.

17.06 The initial wording here is the same as that used in the Rent Act 1977 and also in the Housing Act 1988. As with those two statutes there must be 'a tenancy' of 'a dwelling-house' which is 'let as a separate dwelling'. These important phrases have already been considered in Chapter 13 (see 13.05 to 13.30). There are, however, several notable differences between the public sector legislation and that of the private sector. First, s 79(3) of the 1985 Act qualifies s 79(1) and does not exclude licences from statutory protection. Secondly, the requirement that the dwelling-house is 'let as a separate dwelling' has harsher consequences within the context of the Housing Act 1985 than it does under the Rent Act 1977 and the Housing Act 1988. Thirdly, the words 'at any time when' mean that it is quite possible for a tenant to move in and out of Housing Act 1985 protection. The tenant will be a secure tenant at any time when the landlord and tenant conditions (see 17.07 to 17.13) are satisfied. If one of the conditions ceases to be satisfied (eg because of non-occupation by the tenant), the tenant loses security, but if at a later date the condition becomes satisfied again (because the tenant moves back in), the tenant will regain security (see *Hussey v Camden LBC* (1995) 27 HLR 5, CA). Where possession proceedings have been brought, in deciding whether a tenant is a secure tenant the court will look at the situation at the date of expiry of the notice to quit (*Hammersmith and Fulham LBC v Clarke* (2001) 33 HLR 881) although evidence of the tenant's position both before and after service of the notice may be relevant in deciding this issue (*Islington LBC v Boyle and Collier* [2011] EWCA Civ 1450).

The landlord condition

The key factor that makes a tenancy a secure tenancy is the identity of the landlord. To satisfy the landlord condition the landlord must be one of the prescribed public bodies set out in the list in s 80(1) of the Housing Act 1985. The most common landlord that features on this list is, of course, a local authority. However, the landlord condition will also be satisfied if the landlord is a new town corporation, a housing action trust (a trust which acquires and manages local authority housing under powers contained in Pt III of the Housing Act 1988), an urban development corporation, the Development Board for Rural Wales, and certain housing co-operatives. One important exception to this rule is that a tenancy granted by a local housing authority acting under a management order (see Chapter 20) will not be a secure tenancy.

17.07

Registered social landlords and registered providers

A registered social landlord is what was formerly known as a housing association until the advent of the Housing Act 1996. For the past 25 years or so they have played an increasing role in the provision of affordable housing. Starting with the Housing Act 1974, various administrations have sought to encourage the development of the voluntary sector, the aim being to permit social landlords to take over from local authorities the responsibility of providing cheaper housing for the less privileged in the community. (This policy proved so successful that in some areas local authorities handed over their entire housing stock to registered social landlords.) The Housing and Regeneration Act 2008 has replaced the registered social landlord in England with an extended class of 'registered providers' of social housing, which will include social housing providers that would not have qualified as registered social landlords under the Housing Act 1996, for example profit-making organizations (ss 110 to 121).

17.08

Registered social landlords and registered providers, however, are not included in the list of prescribed public bodies set out in s 80(1) of the Housing Act 1985. This was not always the case. The list contained in s 80(1) was substantially amended by Pt I of the Housing Act 1988. Prior to 1988, the list of prescribed public bodies also included housing corporations, charitable housing trusts, and registered and unregistered housing associations.

17.09

However, since 15 January 1989, these bodies have been removed from the list, with the result that since this date registered social landlords have been regarded as belonging to the private rather than to the public sector. From 15 January 1989, therefore, all new tenancies granted by registered social landlords and registered providers will be assured rather than secure tenancies.

17.10   This has the somewhat confusing result that, depending upon the date of the grant of their tenancy, certain tenants of the same registered social landlord may have different types of tenancies. The tenancies granted before 15 January 1989 will be secure tenancies under the Housing Act 1985, while those granted after 15 January 1989 will be assured tenancies under the Housing Act 1988. Anyone seeking to advise a tenant of a registered social land-lord should first check to see under which code the tenant falls. In doing so, regard must be had to the transitional provisions contained in the Housing Act 1988, s 35. This section provides that in certain circumstances a tenancy entered into after 15 January 1989 can still be a secure tenancy. The most important of the provisions of the Housing Act 1988, s 35 are the following:

(a)   if the tenancy was granted pursuant to a contract made before 15 January 1989 (s 35(4)(c));

(b)   if the tenancy was granted to a person who, immediately before the tenancy was entered into, was a secure tenant and the new tenancy was granted by the secure ten-ant's landlord (s 35(4)(d));

(c)   if the tenancy is granted to a person as 'suitable alternative accommodation' as a result of an order of the court and the court considers that an assured tenancy would not provide sufficient security of tenure (s 35(4)(e));

(d)   if the tenant was previously a private sector protected tenant or statutory tenant and the landlord's interest is transferred to a housing association (s 35(5)).

17.11   If, however, a secure tenancy to which the landlord is a registered social landlord is demoted (see 17.114) the tenancy will become an assured tenancy at the end of the demotion period, rather than reverting to its original secure tenancy status.

17.12   For most tenants of registered social landlords and registered providers, therefore, the general principles applying to assured tenancies (see Chapters 15 and 16) will apply. There are, however, are a number of situations in which their rights are more akin to those of public sector tenants; for example they may have the right to acquire their home (see 17.172), they may be able to access the services of the Homes and Communities Agency (see Chapter 21), and their landlord may be able to apply for demotion of the tenancy (see 15.95). In addition registered social landlords can in certain circumstances be regarded as quasi public bodies for the purposes of judicial review proceedings and the Human Rights Act 1998, s 6 (*R (Weaver) v London & Quadrant Housing Trust* [2009] EWCA Civ 587, [2010]1 WLR 713, [2009] 4 All ER 865).

The tenant condition

17.13   Under the Housing Act 1985, s 81, the tenant condition mentioned in s 79(1) will be satis-fied at any time where:

(a)   the tenant is an individual and occupies the dwelling-house as his or her only or prin-cipal home; or

(b)   the tenancy is a joint tenancy, and each of the joint tenants is an individual and at least one of them occupies the dwelling-house as his or her only or principal home.

This requirement is exactly the same as that demanded for eligibility as an assured tenant under the Housing Act 1988 (see 15.11 to 15.19).

Shared accommodation

We saw in Chapter 13 (13.10) that a 'separate dwelling' needs to be sufficient for the **17.14** occupier to carry out the major activities of life, namely cooking, eating, and sleeping. However, under the Rent Act 1977, s 22, and under the Housing Act 1988, ss 3 and 10, special allowance is made for tenants who share essential common parts of the premises with others. The Housing Act 1985 contains no similar provisions with regard to the sharing of accommodation.

Secure licences

The Housing Act 1985, s 79(3) to (4) provide that a licensee may be a secure tenant: **17.15**

> (3) The provisions of this Part apply in relation to a licence to occupy a dwelling-house (whether or not granted for a consideration) as they apply in relation to a tenancy.
> (4) Subsection (3) does not apply to a licence granted as a temporary expedient to a person who entered the dwelling-house or any other land as a trespasser (whether or not, before the grant of that licence, another licence to occupy that or another dwelling-house had been granted to him).

At first sight this provision seems to extend statutory protection to a whole class of occupi- **17.16** ers (licensees) who previously had no, or very limited, security of tenure. Section 79(4) prevents a squatter, who, having entered as a trespasser, is granted the temporary measure of a licence, from acquiring a secure tenancy, but s 79(3) appears to give security of tenure to any other person occupying a dwelling-house on a licence from his or her local authority.

The significance of s 79(3), however, was considerably restricted by the decision of the **17.17** House of Lords in *Westminster City Council v Clarke* [1992] 2 AC 288. Here it was held that a licensee could be a secure tenant only if he or she had exclusive possession of a separate dwelling-house. Mr Clarke, who occupied a room in a hostel run by the council, was held not to have exclusive possession of any particular room in the hostel and therefore was not a secure tenant. If this decision is considered in the light of the judgment in *Street v Mountford* (see 2.10), where it was held that in the majority of circumstances the presence of exclusive possession would lead to the existence of a tenancy, it becomes clear that the circumstances in which a licensee will be a secure tenant are very limited. Either the occupier will have exclusive possession and will be a tenant (and therefore a secure tenant under s 79(1)), or the occupier will not have exclusive possession and will be a licensee, but the absence of exclusive possession will prevent him or her from falling within s 79(3) of the 1985 Act. One possible example of a secure licence would be where a licence is granted to a person who is under 18 (and therefore unable to enter into a tenancy agreement).

It should be noted that where a licensee is capable of being a secure tenant, he or she will **17.18** not be able to take advantage of the right to buy. Section 79(3) states that it is only the provisions of this Part of the Act (Pt IV) that apply to licensees: the provisions regarding the right to buy are contained in Pt V.

Introductory tenancies

It should be remembered that public sector landlords are usually in control of a large hous- **17.19** ing stock and that a large part of their function is to keep existing tenants happy by means of good management. Frequently, owing to the nature of much public sector housing stock, it is necessary for tenants to live in close proximity. Public sector landlords, therefore, do not want to find themselves landed with a disruptive, undesirable, or anti-social tenant who has security of tenure and cannot easily be removed. As a practical measure the Housing Act 1996 has introduced a regime whereby it is possible for tenants to be granted a tenancy on a trial basis: a sort of probationary tenancy that, at its end, and provided the conduct of the tenant is satisfactory, will be converted automatically into a secure tenancy.

17.20   The provisions with regard to introductory tenancies are not mandatory. In order to make use of these provisions a local housing authority or housing action trust must first elect to operate an introductory tenancy regime. If they do choose to operate such a scheme then while it is in force every new periodic tenancy entered into or adopted by the authority or trust will be an introductory tenancy and not a secure tenancy. There are only three exceptions to this rule. A new periodic tenancy will not be an introductory tenancy in the following circumstances:

(a)   Immediately before the tenancy was entered into the tenant was a secure tenant of the same or another dwelling-house (s 124(2)(a)). Thus, if a new tenancy is granted to an existing secure tenant (for example, where he or she is rehoused by the local authority), that tenant will remain a secure tenant and will not lose security of tenure.

(b)   Immediately before the tenancy was entered into the tenant was an assured tenant (but not an assured shorthold tenant) of a registered social landlord in respect of the same or another dwelling-house (s 124(2)(b)). Thus, even if the new tenant was not formerly a local authority tenant but the tenant of a registered social landlord under an assured tenancy, he or she will not lose security of tenure and will become a secure tenant of the local authority without having to go through a trial period.

(c)   The tenancy was entered into or adopted in pursuance of a contract made before the election was made (s 124(3)).

17.21   If there are joint tenants and any one of them satisfies one of these conditions the tenancy cannot be an introductory tenancy.

What is an introductory tenancy?

17.22   An introductory tenancy is one which would have been a secure tenancy but for the local housing authority's having elected to operate an introductory tenancy regime. Thus it must fulfil the criteria set out earlier in this chapter (ie it must be a tenancy under which a dwelling is let as a separate dwelling, and both the landlord condition and the tenant condition must be satisfied). A secure licence may also be an introductory tenancy (s 126).

17.23   Where an introductory tenancy is granted or adopted it will remain 'introductory' until the end of the trial period. The trial period is the period of one year beginning with the date on which the tenancy was entered into or, if later, the date on which the tenant was first entitled to possession under the tenancy (s 125(2)(a)). If the tenancy was adopted by the local authority the trial period begins with the date of adoption (s 125(2)(b)).

17.24   However, where the tenant previously held another introductory tenancy, or held an assured shorthold tenancy from a registered social landlord, any period or periods during which he or she was such a tenant will count towards the trial period, provided:

(a)   if there was one such period, it ended immediately before the second introductory tenancy started; and

(b)   if there was more than one such period, the most recent period ended immediately before the start of the second tenancy and each period succeeded the other without interruption (s 125(3)).

Extension of the trial period

In the case of introductory tenancies commencing after 6 June 2006 the landlord has the power to extend the trial period by a further six months (Housing Act 1996, s 125A, inserted by the Housing Act 2004, s 179). The landlord can do this by serving notice of extension on the tenant at least eight weeks before the original one-year expiry date. The landlord must give reasons for the decision (which will normally be that the tenant has breached some of the tenancy obligations). The notice must also inform the tenant of his or her right to a review of the decision to extend the period. The request for a review must be made within 14 days of the service of the landlord's notice. The procedure for the review is similar to the procedure for a review of a decision to bring possession proceedings against an introductory tenant (see 17.30). **17.25**

During the course of the trial period a tenancy will cease to be an introductory tenancy if: **17.26**

(a) the circumstances are such that the tenancy would not otherwise be a secure tenancy (for example, if the landlord ceases to satisfy the landlord condition or the tenant ceases to occupy the dwelling as his or her only or principal home) (s 125(5)(a));

(b) a person or body other than a local housing authority or housing action trust becomes the landlord under the tenancy (for example, where housing stock is transferred to the private sector) (s 125(5)(b));

(c) the landlord revokes the election to operate an introductory tenancy regime (s 125(5)(c)): such an election can be revoked at any time without prejudice to the making of a further election (s 124(5));

(d) the tenancy ceases to be an introductory tenancy because the tenant has died and there is no one qualified to succeed to the tenancy. Succession to an introductory tenancy is dealt with in s 133 of the Housing Act 1996 (see 17.38).

If the tenancy ceases to be an introductory tenancy it will not end merely because it ceases to be an introductory tenancy; it will continue until it is determined by the usual common law methods, ie by a notice to quit. But once an introductory tenancy has ceased to be introductory it cannot later become introductory again (s 125(6)). Thus, a tenant under an introductory tenancy cannot move out of the dwelling for a period of time and then rekindle the introductory tenancy by moving back into possession. **17.27**

Seeking possession of an introductory tenancy

If by the end of the trial period the tenant's behaviour has given the landlord no cause for objection then the tenancy will automatically become a secure tenancy. However, the landlord may bring the introductory tenancy to an end at any point during the currency of the trial period if the landlord regards the tenant as unsuitable. **17.28**

To bring the introductory tenancy to an end the landlord need only obtain an order of the court for possession (s 127). The landlord does not have to establish a ground of possession, nor that suitable alternative accommodation is available, nor that it is reasonable to make such an order (as the landlord would if the tenant held under a secure tenancy, see 18.01 to 18.32). The court, however, will not entertain proceedings for possession unless the landlord has served notice on the tenant in accordance with s 128. Such notice must include the landlord's reasons for seeking possession (s 128(3)). The landlord's reasons must be sufficient to enable the tenant to know exactly what he or she is alleged to have done wrong. The notice must specify the date after which possession proceedings may be begun (s 128(4)). This date must not be earlier than the date at which the tenancy could be brought to an end by notice to quit if it were not an introductory tenancy (see 10.41 to 10.42). The notice must also inform the tenant of his or her right to request a review of the decision (s 128(6)). The review referred to is carried out by the landlord, rather than by an **17.29** independent body. An appeal against the sufficiency of the review would have to be made by way of judicial review. Provided these notice requirements are complied with the court must make an order for possession. If a landlord has issued proceedings for possession towards the end of the trial period and the proceedings are not complete by the date on which the trial period is due to come to an end, the tenancy will not automatically become a secure tenancy; rather, by virtue of s 130, the tenancy will remain an introductory tenancy until the proceedings are concluded.

The review

17.30   The tenant is entitled to seek a review of the landlord's decision. This must be done within 14 days of being served notice (s 129). The procedures for such a review are set out in the Introductory Tenants (Review) Regulations 1997, SI 1997/72.

17.31   The review must be concluded, and the tenant informed of the result, before the date specified in the s 128 notice as the date on which proceedings can be commenced. If this time limit is not complied with the landlord will have to serve a new notice. This may cause the landlord significant problems if the trial period was nearing its end at the date the original notice was served, as the landlord will not be able to serve a fresh notice once the trial period is over. By then the tenancy will have become secure.

17.32   Following the review, if the landlord confirms its decision to take possession proceedings, the landlord must give the tenant reasons for that decision.

17.33   Another possible outcome of the review is that the landlord decides not to issue possession proceedings on condition that the tenant remedies any breach of obligation. If the tenant does not remedy the breach, the landlord can then serve possession proceedings without the need to serve further notice (*Cardiff City Council v Stone* [2002] EWCA Civ 298, [2003] HLR 47). If the tenant commits further or different breaches, however, the landlord will need to serve a further s 128 notice.

Possession proceedings

17.34   A landlord can only bring an introductory tenancy to an end by obtaining a court order (Housing Act 1996, s 127(1)). The procedure for possession is as set out in CPR Part 55 (see 16.74 to 16.76).

17.35   The court will make an order for possession if it is satisfied that the tenancy was an introductory tenancy at the date at which proceedings were begun and:

(a)   notice has been served in accordance with the Housing Act 1996, s 128; and
(b)   the proceedings were begun after the date specified in the notice.

17.36   The landlord's adherence to the review procedure is a factor that may be considered by the court making the possession order (*Manchester City Council v Pinnock* [2010] UKSC 45, [2010] 3 WLR 1441).

The possession order

17.37   Other than by consent of the landlord, the court has no power to postpone the date for possession for more than 14 days unless exceptional hardship would be caused. In that case it may postpone the date for up to six weeks (Housing Act 1980, s 89). The court can, however, postpone the date of possession under its inherent jurisdiction pending the tenant's appeal of the possession order (*Admiral Taverns (Cygnet Ltd) v Daly* [2008] EWCA Civ 1501, [2009] 1 WLR 2192).

An introductory tenant may not have security of tenure but, because an introductory ten- **17.38**
ancy has the potential to become a secure tenancy at the end of the trial period, he or she
will acquire many of the rights that apply to a secure tenant. Sections 131 to 133 of the
Housing Act 1996 provide an introductory tenant with a similar right to succession as that
for a secure tenant under the Housing Act 1985. Section 134 gives an introductory tenant
a limited right to assign, and s 135 extends the secure tenant's repair scheme to introductory tenancies.

Human Rights Act 1998

Introductory tenancies have been challenged as being contrary to the Human Rights Act **17.39**
1998, ss 6 and 8. The Court of Appeal has held that they are not incompatible with the
Act (*R v Bracknell Forest BC, ex parte McLellan* (2001) 33 HLR 989, CA; *R (Gilboy) v
Liverpool City Council* [2008] EWCA Civ 751, [2009] 3 WLR 300). It is, however, possible for the tenant to raise a human rights defence to challenge the proportionality of the
landlord's decision to bring possession proceedings against an introductory tenant (see
Manchester City Council v Pinnock [2010] UKSC 45, [2010] 3 WLR 1441; *Hounslow
LBC v Powell; Leeds City Council v Hall; Birmingham City Council v Frisby* [2011] UKSC
8; and see 18.62 for a discussion on human rights defences).

Flexible tenancies

Section 154 of the Localism Act 2011 amended the Housing Act 1985 to allow social **17.40**
landlords to create a new type of secure tenancy known as a *flexible tenancy* (Housing
Act 1985, ss 107A to 107E). As with the introductory tenancy, the purpose of the flexible tenancy was to allow social landlords much greater control of their housing stock,
in this case by allowing them to let property to tenants for a fixed term while maintaining the ability to regain possession at the end without having to show fault on the part
of the tenant. The flexible tenancy operates in the same way as a normal fixed-term
secure tenancy with one important exception: when the fixed term is coming to an end
the landlord has the ability to serve notice on the tenant informing him or her that the
landlord does not intend to grant a new tenancy at the end of the term. If the landlord
follows the notice and review procedure properly it will have a mandatory ground for
possession.

Flexible tenancies must be granted for a term of at least two years (although it is expected **17.41**
that most will be for a term of at least five years). The tenant will enjoy the same rights
as any other secure tenant (for example, the right to buy and rights of succession) with
the exception that they will not be entitled to compensation for improvements to the
property.

Unlike the position under a private sector fixed-term tenancy, the tenant under a flexible **17.42**
fixed-term tenancy is allowed to terminate the tenancy by giving four weeks' notice to quit
at any time (Housing Act 1985, s 107C). Unless the tenant is in arrears of rent or in breach
of any other term of the tenancy the landlord will have no choice but to accept this notice
even if the fixed term has not expired.

Possession of a flexible tenancy

17.43 **During the fixed term** The landlord has the same ability to recover possession under one of the grounds set out in Sch 2 to the Housing Act 1985 (see Chapter 18).

17.44 **At the end of the fixed term** If the landlord decides that it wishes to recover possession of the premises at the end of the fixed term (for example if it considers that the current tenant's need for social housing is not as pressing as the needs of other people on its waiting list) the landlord can serve notice on the tenant informing him or her that the landlord does not intend to renew the tenancy. The landlord must give the tenant at least six months' notice (s 107D). The statute is silent on the point but it seems logical that this notice should be given at least six months before the end of the fixed term. The notice must inform the tenant of the reasons why the landlord has decided not to renew the tenancy and must notify the tenant of his or her right to seek a review of this decision within 21 days.

The review

17.45 The provisions governing the conduct of the review are set out in s 107E and in the Flexible Tenancies (Review Procedures) Regulations 2012, SI 2012/695. The main purpose of the review will be to consider whether the decision was legitimately made in accordance with the social landlord's tenancy strategy. There is no right of appeal from the review decision but it may be challenged by judicial review. It may also be open to the tenant to bring a Human Rights Act challenge against the proportionality of the decision to evict at any subsequent possession proceedings (see18.62).

Possession proceedings

17.46 At the end of the fixed term the landlord can apply for possession of the property. Before doing so it must give the tenant at least two months' notice that it requires possession of the premises. Before it will grant possession the court must, therefore, be satisfied that the following three conditions have been met (s 107D):

(1) that the fixed term has come to an end and no further secure tenancy is in existence (other than a periodic tenancy); and
(2) that the landlord has given the tenant six months' notice in writing of its decision not to grant another tenancy at the end of the fixed term, its reasons for the decision, and the tenant's right to request a review (17.44); and
(3) that the landlord has given the tenant two months' notice in writing stating that the landlord requires possession of the dwelling-house.

If these conditions have been met the court must grant possession. The only means by which the tenant could avoid a possession order being made are by demonstrating that he or she had asked for a review and that this was not carried out, or that the final review decision was wrong in law, or by successfully raising a public law or human rights defence.

C STATUTORY EXCLUSIONS FROM THE HOUSING ACT 1985

17.47 Schedule 1 to the Housing Act 1985 lists the types of tenancies that cannot be secure tenancies.

Long leases

17.48 Under the Housing Act 1985, Sch 1, para 1, a fixed-term tenancy granted for a term certain exceeding 21 years (as defined by s 115) cannot be a secure tenancy.

Introductory tenancies

Introductory tenancies (see 17.19 to 17.38) are excluded from being secure tenancies by **17.49** virtue of Sch 1, para 1A (inserted by the Housing Act 1996 (Consequential Provisions) Order 1996, SI 1996/2325).

Premises occupied in connection with employment

Under Sch 1, para 2 to the 1985 Act, if a tenant is either an employee of the landlord or an **17.50** employee of one of the public bodies listed in para 2 (eg a local authority), and the tenant's contract of employment requires the tenant to occupy the dwelling-house for the better performance of his or her duties, there cannot be a secure tenancy.

It is not necessary that the contract of employment expressly states that the employee must **17.51** occupy the dwelling-house for the better performance of his or her duties. Such a term will be implied by the court if the landlord can show that, in the particular circumstances of the case, it is essential for the employee to occupy the dwelling-house in order to do the job properly (see *South Glamorgan County Council v Griffiths* (1992) 24 HLR 334, but contrast with *Hughes v Greenwich LBC* [1994] 1 AC 170). If the nature of the occupier's employment changes the occupier may lose secure status. In *Elvidge v Coventry City Council* [1993] 3 WLR 976, an employee was originally a secure tenant. He was promoted and his change in duties made it necessary for him to occupy the particular dwelling-house to do his job. The court held that he was no longer a secure tenant. However, if an employee occupying a premises for the better performance of his or her duties retires, this does not mean that he or she becomes a secure tenant just because the employment has ceased (see *South Glamorgan County Council v Griffiths*). The purpose of this exception is to enable an employer/landlord to keep control of accommodation that 'goes with the job'. An employee is excluded from protection precisely so that if the employment is ended the landlord/employer will be free to allow a new employee into occupation. If an employee acquired security the moment his or her employment ended, this exception would be rendered ineffective.

It is also open to a landlord, by virtue of Sch 1, para 4, to exclude a tenant from acquiring **17.52** a secure tenancy by giving the tenant notice that the tenancy in question falls within this exception. Such notice can be given only if, for the three years immediately prior to the grant, the premises in question had been occupied by a tenant in connection with his or her employment (ie the previous tenancy or tenancies must have fallen within this exception). If such notice is given and the landlord is a local housing authority the tenancy will not become a secure tenancy unless the landlord notifies the tenant that it is to be a secure tenancy (Sch 1, para 4B). If the landlord is not a local authority the tenancy will automatically become a secure tenancy if it ceases to be occupied in connection with the tenant's employment for a period of more than three years in total (Sch 1, para 4A). This somewhat strange distinction, introduced by the Housing Act 1996, is presumably intended to give local housing authorities a slightly greater degree of control over their housing stock than other public sector landlords. Quite why a local housing authority should be treated differently from, say, a housing action trust or an urban development corporation is not clear.

Land acquired for development

A tenancy cannot be a secure tenancy if the dwelling-house is on land which has been **17.53** acquired for development and the dwelling-house is used by the landlord, pending development of the land, as temporary housing accommodation (Housing Act 1985, Sch 1, para 3(1)). This exception will apply even if the land was acquired for development by the landlord's predecessor in title (*Hyde Housing Association v Harrison* [1991] 1 EGLR 51; *Attley v Cherwell District Council* (1989) 21 HLR 613). However, if the development is no longer in prospect, the exception will not apply (for example, where the local planning authority has rejected the plans: *Lillieshall Road Housing Co-operative v Brennan* (1992) 24 HLR 195).

Homeless persons

17.54 Part VII of the Housing Act 1996 contains certain provisions that place a duty upon a local authority landlord to provide accommodation for homeless persons. Where a landlord provides accommodation in pursuance of these provisions, namely ss 63, 65(3), and 68(1), any tenancy granted will not be able to become a secure tenancy until a period of 12 months has expired, unless the landlord gives the tenant notice that the tenancy is to be secure (Housing Act 1985, Sch 1, para 4). The 12-month period runs from the date the tenant receives notice under the provisions of Pt VII (*Swansea City Council v Hearn* (1990) 23 HLR 284).

Family intervention tenancies

17.55 Family intervention tenancies were introduced into Sch 1 at para 4ZA by the Housing and Regeneration Act 2008, s 297(2). The general provisions for family intervention tenancies granted by local authorities under Sch 1, para 4ZA are the same as for tenancies granted by registered providers or registered social landlords under the Housing Act 1988, Sch 1, para 12ZA (see 15.41 to 15.42).

17.56 One additional requirement placed on local authority landlords is that no notice to quit can be served on a tenant of a family intervention tenancy unless the tenant has first been given written notice stating the reason for the decision to serve notice to quit and the date the authority intends to serve notice to quit (Housing and Regeneration Act 2008, s 298(2)). The notice must also inform the tenant of the right to request a review of the authority's decision and the notice (and any notice to quit) must contain advice to the tenant on how to obtain assistance in relation to the notice (s 298(7)). If the tenant requests a review within 14 days of service of the notice, the authority must conduct a review and inform the tenant of the decision and the reasons for it.

17.57 A family intervention tenancy may become a secure tenancy if the landlord notifies the tenant that it is to be regarded as a secure tenancy (Sch 1, para 4ZA(2)).

Temporary accommodation for persons taking up employment

17.58 When a person moves into the area in order to take up employment and rents accommodation from a public landlord, that landlord can prevent the tenant from acquiring a secure tenancy (Housing Act 1985, Sch 1, para 5). To do this the landlord must serve notice in writing on the tenant that this exception applies (Sch 1, para 5(1)(d)). This exclusion will apply only where:

(a) immediately before the grant of the tenancy the person was not resident in the district in which the dwelling-house is situated;

(b) before the grant of the tenancy, the person obtained employment, or an offer of employment, in the district or its surrounding area;

(c) the tenancy was granted to him for the purposes of meeting his or her need for temporary accommodation in the district or its surrounding area in order to work there, and of enabling him or her to find permanent accommodation there.

If the landlord is a local housing authority, the tenancy will remain excluded until the **17.59** authority notifies the tenant that the tenancy is to be regarded as a secure tenancy (Sch 1, para 5(1B)). If the landlord is not a local housing authority, the tenancy will become secure after one year from the date of grant, or earlier if the landlord decides to notify the tenant that the tenancy is to be regarded as a secure tenancy before that date (Sch 1, para 5(1A)).

Short-term arrangements

The aim of this exclusion under Sch 1, para 6 to the 1985 Act is to encourage pri- **17.60** vate landlords to help public sector landlords to provide accommodation. Sub-leasing schemes have been around for a long time. Before the introduction of statutory protection for public sector tenants, it was common for private landlords to let buildings to a local authority, which would in turn sub-let to residential tenants. Because the local authority was the direct landlord of the tenant, the tenant would not be able to claim Rent Act protection. Schedule 1, para 6 has enabled this practice to continue even after the introduction of statutory security for public sector tenants by preventing the tenant of a dwelling-house, let on a sub-letting scheme via a local authority landlord, from being a secure tenant.

This exclusion will apply only if: **17.61**

(a) the dwelling-house had been leased to the landlord with vacant possession for use as temporary housing accommodation;
(b) the terms on which it has been leased include provision for the lessor to obtain vacant possession from the landlord on the expiry of a specified period or when required by the lessor;
(c) the lessor is not a body which is capable of granting secure tenancies; and
(d) the landlord has no interest in the dwelling-house other than under the lease in question or as a mortgagee.

This exclusion will also operate if the private landlord grants a licence to the local author- **17.62** ity to use the dwelling-house as temporary housing accommodation (*Tower Hamlets LBC v Miah* (1991) 24 HLR 199).

Temporary accommodation during works

Under the Housing Act 1985, Sch 1, para 7, a tenancy is not a secure tenancy if: **17.63**

(a) the dwelling-house has been made available for occupation by the tenant (or a predecessor in title of the tenant) while works are carried out on the dwelling-house which he or she previously occupied as his or her home; and
(b) the tenant or predecessor was not a secure tenant of that other dwelling-house at the time when he or she ceased to occupy it as his or her home.

Thus, if a public landlord provides temporary accommodation for a tenant while works **17.64** are carried out on his or her home, the tenant will not acquire a secure tenancy of the temporary accommodation.

Agricultural holdings

A tenancy is not a secure tenancy if the dwelling-house is comprised in an agricultural **17.65** holding (within the meaning of the Agricultural Holdings Act 1986, see Chapter 27) and is

...pied by the person responsible for the control (whether as tenant or as servant or agent
...he tenant) of the farming of the holding (Housing Act 1985, Sch 1, para 8).

...ensed premises

17.66 A tenancy is not a secure tenancy if the dwelling-house consists of or includes premises
licensed for the sale of intoxicating liquor for consumption on the premises (Housing Act
1985, Sch 1, para 9).

Student lettings

17.67 The provisions excluding student lettings from statutory protection are more detailed under
the Housing Act 1985 than under the Rent Act 1977 or the Housing Act 1988. Under Sch 1,
para 10 to the 1985 Act, a tenancy of a dwelling-house will not be a secure tenancy if:

(a) it is granted for the purpose of enabling the tenant to attend a designated course at an
educational establishment; and

(b) before the grant of the tenancy the landlord notifies the tenant in writing of the circumstances in which this exception applies and that in its opinion the proposed tenancy would fall within the exception.

17.68 A designated course is defined by the Secure Tenancies (Designated Courses) Regulations
1980, SI 1980/1407, as amended by the Secure Tenancies (Designated Courses) (Amendment)
Regulations 1993, SI 1993/931. In giving notice the landlord must also specify the educational establishment which the person concerned proposes to attend (Sch 1, para 10(2)). If
the landlord is a local housing authority, the exclusion will operate until the authority notifies the tenant that the tenancy is to be regarded as a secure tenancy. If the landlord is not
a local housing authority, the exclusion will continue to operate until six months after the
tenant ceases to attend a designated course at the educational establishment, or, if the tenant
leaves the course earlier, until six months after the grant of the tenancy (Sch 1, para 10(3)).

Business tenancies

17.69 A tenancy is not a secure tenancy if it is one to which Pt II of the Landlord and Tenant
Act 1954 applies (tenancies of premises occupied for business purpose, see Chapter 26)
(Housing Act 1985, Sch 1, para 11).

Almshouses

17.70 A licence to occupy an almshouse cannot be a secure tenancy if certain conditions are satisfied (Housing Act 1985, Sch 1, para 12).

Demoted tenancies

17.71 In addition, if a demotion order is made in respect of a secure tenancy, it ceases to be a
secure tenancy for a period of one year (provided that possession proceedings are not commenced within that period) (see 17.114 to 17.124).

D THE TERMS OF A SECURE TENANCY

17.72 In general the terms of a secure tenancy will be those agreed between the parties, but certain terms will be implied by statute. These implied terms are dealt with in this section.

Clearly, a secure tenant should be apprised of the terms of his or her secure tenancy. The **17.73**
Housing Act 1985, s 104 therefore places a public sector landlord under a duty to publish
information about its secure tenancies. This information should explain 'in simple terms'
the express terms of the secure tenancies, the provisions of Pts IV and V (the right to buy,
see 17.137 to 17.170) of the Housing Act 1985, and the provisions of ss 11 to 16 of the
Landlord and Tenant Act 1985 (the landlord's repairing obligations, see 7.87). Each tenant
should be supplied with a copy of this information when the secure tenancy arises or as
soon as practical afterwards, and the landlord must keep it updated.

Section 105 further requires a landlord to maintain appropriate arrangements for consulta- **17.74**
tion with tenants over matters of housing management (housing management in this context does not include matters relating to rent or charges for services or facilities provided
by the landlord).

Assignment

The underlying philosophy behind the provision of housing by the public sector has always **17.75**
been to provide housing for the less privileged. To this extent at least, the grant of a secure
tenancy confers an essentially personal right upon the tenant. Whether or not a secure tenancy will be granted depends frequently upon the personal circumstances of the applicant.
If there was freedom to assign, a local authority or other public sector landlord would
be unable to control who was occupying its housing. The Housing Act 1985, therefore,
generally prohibits assignment of a secure tenancy except in three specified circumstances.
Section 91 provides that:

(1)   A secure tenancy which is—
    (a)   a periodic tenancy, or
    (b)   a tenancy for a term certain granted on or after 5th November 1982,
    is not capable of being assigned except in the cases mentioned in subsection (3).
(2)   If a secure tenancy for a term certain granted before 5th November 1982 is assigned, then,
except in the cases mentioned in subsection (3), it ceases to be a secure tenancy and cannot
subsequently become a secure tenancy.
(3)   The exceptions are—
    (a)   an assignment in accordance with section 92 (assignment by way of exchange);
    (b)   an assignment in pursuance of an order made under—
      (i)   sections 23A and 24 of the Matrimonial Causes Act 1973 (property adjustment
        orders in connection with matrimonial proceedings),
      (ii)   section 17(1) of the Matrimonial and Family Proceedings Act 1984 (property
        adjustment orders after overseas divorce, etc),
      (iii)   paragraph 1 of Schedule 1 to the Children Act 1989 (orders for financial relief
        against parents), or
      (iv)   Part 2 of Schedule 5 or paragraph 9(2) or (3) of Schedule 7 to the Civil Partnership
        Act 2004 (property adjustment orders in connection with civil partnership
        proceedings or after the overseas dissolution of a civil partnership).
    (c) an assignment to a person who would be qualified to succeed the tenant if the tenant
      died immediately before the assignment.

Assignment includes a deed of release from one joint tenant to another (*Burton v Camden
LBC* [2000] 2 AC 399).

Assignment by way of exchange

Section 92 of the Housing Act 1985 implies a term into every secure tenancy that the **17.76**
secure tenant may, with the written consent of the landlord, assign the tenancy to another

secure tenant who has also obtained written consent from his or her landlord to assign (either to the first-mentioned secure tenant or to another secure tenant, thus permitting three-way exchanges). Assignment by way of exchange is also permitted with an assured tenant, provided that that assured tenant's landlord is either the Housing Corporation, Housing for Wales, a registered social landlord, or a housing trust which is a charity (s 92(2A)). So, while the Housing Act 1985 generally prohibits assignment, it does allow an existing secure tenant to transfer his or her tenancy to another existing secure tenant or to an assured tenant who satisfies the conditions.

17.77 A landlord is not permitted to withhold consent to an assignment by way of exchange except on one or more of the grounds set out in Sch 3 to the Act. If the landlord wishes to object to the assignment by relying upon one or more of the grounds in Sch 3, he or she must serve notice on the tenant specifying and giving particulars of the ground within 42 days of receiving the tenant's application for consent (s 92(4)).

17.78 The grounds on which a landlord can withhold consent are:

(a) the tenant or the proposed assignee has already been obliged to give up possession by order of the court (Ground 1);

(b) notice of possession proceedings has been given, or possession proceedings have been begun against the tenant or the assignee on one or more of Grounds 1 to 6 in Pt 1 of Sch 2 to the Housing Act 1985 (see 18.03 to 18.16) (Ground 2);

(c) either:

   (i)   an injunction order against anti-social behaviour is in force against the tenant, the assignee, or any person residing with him or her or an application for such an order is pending before any court. This refers to orders for injunctions under s 152, s 153, s 153A, B or D of the Housing Act 1996, s 1 of the Crime and Disorder Act 1998, or s 91 of the Anti-social Behaviour Act 2003; or

   (ii) a suspended possession order under Ground 2 or 14 is in force in respect of the tenant, assignee, or any person residing with him or her, or an application is pending before any court for an order on Ground 2 or 14 or for a demotion order. Grounds 2 and 14 are the nuisance grounds under the Housing Acts 1985 and 1988 (Ground 2A; inserted by the Housing Act 2004);

(d) the dwelling-house is larger than that reasonably required by the assignee or is not reasonably suitable for his or her needs (Grounds 3 and 4);

(e) the property was let to the tenant as a consequence of his or her employment (Ground 5);

(f) the charitable purposes of the landlord, or the features of the dwelling-house, are intended to meet the needs of a certain category of person and the proposed assignee does not fit into this category (Grounds 6 to 10).

17.79 If consent is withheld for any reason other than for one of the grounds set out in Sch 3, the tenant may treat the consent as having been given (s 92(3)). The landlord can also make his or her consent conditional upon the tenant paying any outstanding rent or remedying a breach of obligation (s 92(5) and (6)).

17.80 The right to transfer a tenancy by way of exchange also applies in some circumstances to flexible tenants and assured shorthold tenants of registered providers of social housing in England (Localism Act 2011, s 158). The right will only apply where at least one of the other tenancies being exchanged is either:

(a) a secure tenancy that was not a flexible tenancy; or

(b) an assured tenancy that was not an assured shorthold tenancy

Section 158(9) of the Act provides that the new tenancy granted to that former secure or assured tenant will not be a flexible or shorthold tenancy but will instead have the same status as his or her old tenancy.

Matrimonial and civil partnership proceedings

The general prohibition on assignment does not apply to property adjustment orders made under ss 23A and 24 of the Matrimonial Causes Act 1973 or under s 17(1) of the Matrimonial and Family Proceedings Act 1984 (Housing Act 1985, s 91(3)(b)) or Sch 5, Pt 2 or Sch 7, para 9(2) or 3 to the Civil Partnership Act 2004. Thus, where the parties divorce, or the civil partnership is dissolved, the court can order the tenancy to be transferred from one spouse or civil partner to the other. **17.81**

Assignment to a potential successor

A secure tenant may assign a tenancy during his or her lifetime provided that the person to whom the tenancy is assigned would be qualified to succeed to the tenancy if the tenant died immediately before the assignment (Housing Act 1985, s 91(3)(c)). This provision is particularly useful where two or more people are qualified to succeed to a secure tenancy. The tenant can resolve any future dispute that may arise upon his or her death by choosing one of the potential successors and making an *inter vivos* assignment. **17.82**

Sub-letting

Under the Housing Act 1985, s 93: **17.83**

(1) It is a term of every secure tenancy that the tenant—
   (a) may allow any persons to reside as lodgers in the dwelling-house, but
   (b) will not, without the written consent of the landlord, sub-let or part with possession of part of the dwelling-house.
(2) If the tenant under a secure tenancy parts with the possession of the dwelling-house or sub-lets the whole of it (or sub-lets first part of it and then the remainder), the tenancy ceases to be a secure tenancy and cannot subsequently become a secure tenancy.

It is an implied term of every secure tenancy that the secure tenant has the right to take in lodgers. It is important to remember that an occupier will be a lodger provided only that he or she has not been granted exclusive possession (see 2.28 to 2.30). **17.84**

A secure tenant also has the right to sub-let part of the premises provided that he or she has the written consent of the landlord. Section 94(2) provides that: **17.85**

Consent shall not be unreasonably withheld (and if unreasonably withheld shall be treated as given), and if a question arises whether the withholding of consent was unreasonable it is for the landlord to show that it was not.

Consent may be given after the sub-lease has been granted (s 94(4)), but a tenant must always seek consent before sub-letting. Consent cannot be given subject to a condition (s 94(5)). If consent is refused the landlord must give the tenant a written statement of the reasons for refusal (s 94(6)). Factors which should be taken into account by the court when determining whether the withholding of consent was reasonable are whether granting consent would lead to overcrowding, or whether the landlord proposes to perform any works on the premises which would affect the accommodation to be used by the sub-tenant. **17.86**

There is no statutory provision prohibiting a secure tenant sub-letting the whole of the dwelling-house. However, if a secure tenant sub-lets the whole of the premises, whether **17.87** or not consent to do so was obtained from the landlord, the tenancy will cease to be a secure tenancy and will not be capable subsequently of becoming a secure tenancy again (s 93(2)). This prevents a secure tenant from renting out the whole of the property for a limited period of time and then moving back in and claiming still to be a secure tenant.

Repairs

17.88 The repairing obligations contained in the Landlord and Tenant Act 1985, s 11 (see 7.87 to 7.102) apply to secure tenancies. The Housing Act 1985, s 96 (as substituted for the previous s 96 by the Leasehold Reform, Housing and Urban Development Act 1993, s 121) entitles the Secretary of State to introduce regulations to assist secure tenants whose landlords are local housing authorities to have 'qualifying repairs' carried out. A 'qualifying repair' is a repair which the landlord is obliged by a repairing covenant to carry out. The Secure Tenants of Local Housing Authorities (Right to Repair) Regulations 1994, SI 1994/133 entitle the secure tenant to apply to the landlord to have a qualifying repair carried out. The Regulations only apply to landlords who have more than 100 dwellings, and only in respect of repairs where the repair costs less than £250. The Regulations are considered in more detail in Chapter 8 (at 8.41).

Alterations

17.89 By s 97(1) of the 1985 Act, it is an implied term of every secure tenancy that the tenant shall not make improvements without the written consent of the landlord. Section 97(2) defines 'improvement', to include any alteration in, or addition to, the dwelling-house, any alteration or addition made to the fixtures and fittings or provision of services to the dwelling-house, the erection of a wireless or TV aerial, and the carrying out of external decoration. Alterations in this context do not include repairs (*Dickinson v Enfield LBC* (1996) 29 HLR 465).

17.90 Consent to improvements cannot be withheld unreasonably, and if it is withheld unreasonably it will be treated as given (s 97(3)). The burden of proof will be on the landlord to show that consent was not withheld unreasonably (s 98(1)). If the landlord refuses consent, it must give to the tenant a written statement of the reasons why consent was withheld (s 98(4)(a)). If the landlord neither gives nor refuses consent within a reasonable time, consent is taken to have been withheld. The principles to be considered in determining whether consent had been withheld unreasonably are set out in s 98(2) (see 6.74)

17.91 The Housing Act 1985, s 99 provides that consent to an improvement may be made subject to a condition, but any such condition must be reasonable. If the condition is not reasonable, consent will be taken to have been withheld unreasonably. Non-compliance with a condition will be a breach of an obligation of the tenancy (s 99(4)).

17.92 A tenant who has improved a property may be entitled to compensation if the improvements have added to the value of the property or the rent that the landlord can charge. If the improvements were begun before 1 February 1994, compensation will be governed by s 100 of the Housing Act 1985. These provisions were amended by s 122 of the Leasehold Reform, Housing and Urban Development Act 1993, so compensation for improvements begun after 1 February 1994 will be governed by s 99A and s 99B, which were inserted into the Housing Act 1985 by the 1993 Act.

Variation of terms

The terms of a secure tenancy may be varied in three ways: **17.93**

(a) by agreement between the landlord and tenant (Housing Act 1985, s 102(1)(a));
(b) in accordance with the provisions of the tenancy agreement, or in an agreement vary-
     ing it, provided that the variation relates to rent or to payments in respect of rates,
     council tax, or services (s 102(1)(b));
(c) in accordance with s 103 of the 1985 Act.

Terms which have been implied by statute cannot be varied (s 103(3)(a)).   **17.94**

Section 103 applies only to a secure periodic tenancy. It sets out the procedure to be fol-   **17.95**
lowed by a landlord who wishes to vary the terms of a secure tenancy. First, the landlord must serve a preliminary notice on the tenant. This notice should give details of the
variation and invite comments on the proposed variation from the tenant (s 103(2)). The
landlord should consider any comments made by the tenant but does not have to act upon
them. If the tenant is dissatisfied with the proposed variation, his or her only real option is
to serve a notice to quit (s 103(6)). Secondly, the landlord should serve a notice of variation specifying the variation in terms and the date upon which it is to come into effect. The
period between the service of notice and the date upon which it is to take effect must be at
least four weeks or the rental period, whichever is the longer (s 103(4)).

Rent

In marked contrast to the Rent Act 1977, the Housing Act 1985 contains no system of rent   **17.96**
control. There is no intermediate body, equivalent to a rent officer or a rent assessment
committee in the private sector, to which the parties can refer in the event of a dispute
over the amount of rent payable. Local authorities are entitled by s 24(1) of the 1985 Act
to 'make such reasonable charges as they may determine for the tenancy or occupation of
their houses'. Section 24(2) further requires that 'The authority shall from time to time
review rents and make such changes, either of rents generally or of particular rents, as
circumstances may require'.

From 16 January 1990, local authorities, in exercising their functions under s 24, must   **17.97**
'have regard in particular to the principle that the rents of houses of any class or description should bear broadly the same proportion to private sector rents as the rents of houses
of any other class or description' (s 24(3), as introduced by the Local Government and
Housing Act 1989, s 162). This rather confusing wording does not mean that public sector rents must be similar to private sector rents, but that the differential between the rents
charged for different types of housing in the public sector should be broadly the same
as the differential between the rents charged for similar types of accommodation in the
private sector. Thus, if in the private sector the rent charged for a three-bedroom flat is
roughly four times the rent charged for a bedsit, the local authority should seek to maintain
the same ratio between a bedsit and a three-bedroom flat in the public sector.

A tenant who is unhappy about the amount of rent payable has very limited courses of   **17.98**
action available. Either the tenant can quit the tenancy, or he or she can seek judicial review
of the local authority's exercise of its discretion. The latter course of action is unlikely to be
successful. The discretion given to a local authority is very wide and the court can interfere
only if the tenant can prove that this discretion has been exercised in a manner that no
reasonable person could consider justifiable (*Luby v Newcastle-under-Lyme Corpn* [1964]
2 QB 64 *per* Diplock LJ at 72).

E SECURITY OF TENURE UNDER THE 1985 ACT

Termination by the tenant

17.99   The Housing Act 1985 restricts only the landlord's rights to end a secure tenancy: a tenant can still terminate the tenancy if he or she so wishes by surrender, or by use of a notice to quit for periodic or flexible fixed-term tenancies, or by exercising a break clause in the case of other fixed-term tenancies. A tenant may also give up his or her security of tenure by going out of possession of the property, for example by sub-letting the whole of it. In such a case the landlord may end the tenancy by simple notice to quit.

Termination by the landlord

17.100   Like the Rent Act 1977 and the Housing Act 1988 (which largely adopted the system of security of tenure from the 1985 Act), the Housing Act 1985 provides security of tenure for a secure tenant by preventing the landlord from using the usual common law methods of termination (s 82(1)). How this system will operate will depend upon whether the secure tenancy in question is a periodic tenancy or a fixed-term tenancy. If the tenancy in question is a fixed-term tenancy, the procedure will vary depending upon whether the landlord is seeking to terminate the tenancy before the fixed term has expired or whether the term has already expired by effluxion of time. In any event, the landlord will not be able to regain possession of the dwelling-house unless he or she has obtained an order for possession from the court. The court will not make an order for possession unless one or more of the grounds set out in Sch 2 to the Act are satisfied (s 84(1)).

Fixed-term tenancies

17.101   At common law a fixed-term tenancy could come to an end either by effluxion of time or because the landlord had exercised a right of re-entry or forfeiture contained in the lease.

17.102   Where the tenancy is a secure tenancy for a term certain and contains a provision enabling the landlord to exercise a right of re-entry of forfeiture, the landlord cannot forfeit the tenancy before the expiry of the term by using the common law forfeiture procedure. Instead, the landlord must apply to the court under s 82(3) of the 1985 Act for an order terminating the tenancy (note that to do this the landlord will have to comply with the notice procedure set out in s 83, see below). If the landlord can show that, had the tenancy not been secure, the court would have made an order forfeiting the tenancy, the landlord will be entitled to an order terminating the tenancy. Thus, despite the fact that strictly speaking the common law rules of forfeiture do not apply to a secure tenancy, a landlord who wishes to terminate a fixed-term tenancy before the expiry of the term (for, say, a breach of covenant) may do so. Section 82(4) further provides that the normal rules with regard to relief from forfeiture will apply where a landlord seeks to terminate a tenancy under s 82(3).

17.103   At common law, where a fixed-term tenancy comes to end by effluxion of time it terminates of its own accord and the landlord does not need to apply for an order of the court in order to terminate the tenancy.

17.104   When a secure tenancy for a fixed term comes to an end, a statutory periodic tenancy of the same dwelling-house will arise by virtue of the Housing Act 1985, s 86(1). This statutory periodic tenancy will arise whether the tenancy expired by effluxion of time or was terminated by an order of the court under s 82(3). The only situation in which it will not arise is where the landlord chooses to grant the tenant a further secure tenancy of the same dwelling-house (whether for a term certain or periodic) to begin when the original tenancy comes to an end.

The terms of the statutory tenancy are determined by s 86(2) of the 1985 Act. The periods **17.105** of the tenancy will be the same as those for which rent was last payable under the first tenancy. The parties and the terms of the tenancy will be the same as those at the end of the first tenancy, except that the terms are confined to those which are compatible with a periodic tenancy and do not include any provision for re-entry or forfeiture.

Thus, the fact that a fixed-term tenancy has come to an end does not mean that a landlord **17.106** is entitled to possession. The tenant will now hold on a periodic tenancy and the landlord will have to apply for a court order using the procedure outlined below.

Periodic tenancies

A secure periodic tenancy, be it the original contractual tenancy or a statutory tenancy, can- **17.107** not be brought to an end by the landlord by service of a notice to quit. Instead, the landlord must follow the notice procedure set out in ss 83 and 83A of the Housing Act 1985.

Before proceedings for possession can be started the landlord must serve on the tenant a **17.108** 'notice seeking possession' in accordance with s 83. However, the court may, if it considers it just and equitable to do so, dispense with the requirement of such notice (s 83(1)(b)). This notice must specify a date after which proceedings for the possession of the dwelling-house may be begun (s 83(4)(a)). This date must not be earlier than the date on which the tenancy could be brought to an end by notice to quit given by the landlord on the same date as the notice under this section (s 83(5)). Thus, possession proceedings cannot be started any earlier than the date at which the tenancy could have been terminated at common law by a notice to quit. Furthermore, the notice will only remain in force for a period of 12 months after the date specified in the notice (s 83(4)(b)). If the landlord fails to bring proceedings within this time the notice will lapse and it will be necessary for the landlord to serve another notice before proceedings can be taken. For the purposes of this section the landlord will have 'brought' the proceedings only when the claim form has been issued by the court (*Shepping v Osada* (2001) 33 HLR 146, CA).

Section 83(2) further provides that a 'notice seeking possession' must: **17.109**

(a) be in a form prescribed by regulations made by the Secretary of State (currently found in the Secure Tenancies (Notices) Regulations 1987, SI 1987/755, as amended by the Secure Tenancies (Notices) (Amendment) Regulations 1997, SI 1997/71);
(b) specify the ground on which the court will be asked to make an order for possession of the dwelling-house or for the termination of the tenancy; and
(c) give particulars of that ground.

The aim of the notice procedure under the Housing Act 1985 is to give the tenant a chance **17.110** to avoid possession proceedings by putting right any breaches under the tenancy. The landlord must therefore give sufficient particulars of the ground on which he or she intends to seek possession to enable the tenant to correct the breach. For example, if the landlord is alleging a breach of repairing covenant, he or she must give details of the disrepair; if the landlord is alleging non-payment of rent, the arrears should be specified (see *Torridge DC v Jones* (1985) 18 HLR 107).

Minor errors in the prescribed form of the notice will not be fatal to the notice provided **17.111** the notice is substantially to the same effect to that demanded by s 83 (Secure Tenancies (Notices) Regulations 1997, reg 2(1) as amended). Similarly, a mistake in the particulars set out in the notice will not render the notice invalid provided the landlord had a bona fide intention to prove those particulars at the time the notice was served (see *Dudley MBC v Bailey* (1990) 22 HLR 424 and see 6.130).

17.112 The court cannot make an order for possession on a ground of possession unless that ground has been specified in the notice, but the landlord may alter or add to the grounds specified with the leave of the court (s 84(3)).

17.113 If the landlord is seeking to recover possession under Ground 2 in Sch 2 (nuisance or other anti-social behaviour, see below), or Ground 2 is one of the grounds specified by the landlord then s 83(3) provides that a slightly different notice is required. Such notice must state that proceedings for possession may be begun immediately and also specify the date sought by the landlord as the date on which the tenant is to give up possession. The reason for this distinction is that where a landlord is taking action against a tenant for anti-social behaviour it may be important to act quickly and not wait until the date specified in the notice. If Ground 2A (domestic violence, see 18.11) is the ground or one of the grounds specified in the notice and the partner who has left the dwelling-house was not a tenant then the landlord must take all reasonable steps to serve a copy of the notice on that partner (s 83A).

F DEMOTION OF A SECURE TENANCY

17.114 If the landlord of a secure tenant is a local housing authority, a housing action trust, or a registered social landlord, that landlord may apply to the county court for an order demoting the tenancy (Housing Act 1985, s 82A, inserted by the Anti-social Behaviour Act 2003, s 14). The grounds for an application are that the tenant (or a person visiting or residing in the property) has engaged in, or threatened to engage in, conduct:

(a) which is capable of causing a nuisance or annoyance to any person; and

(b) which directly or indirectly relates to or affects the housing management functions of a relevant landlord (Housing Act 1996, s 153A); or

(c) which consists of or involves using or threatening to use housing accommodation owned or managed by a relevant landlord for an unlawful purpose (Housing Act 1996, 153B).

17.115 The Housing Act 1985, s 83(2) provides that in order to apply for a demotion order the landlord must serve notice in a prescribed form. The requirements of the notice are set out in the Secure Tenancies (Notices) (Amendment) (England) Regulations 2004, SI 2004/1627 and the Secure Tenancies (Notices) (Amendment) (Wales) Regulations 2005, SI 2005/1226.

17.116 The notice must contain particulars of the conduct complained of and specify the date after which proceedings may be begun. This date cannot be earlier than the date on which a notice to quit in respect of the tenancy could take effect (this will be at least 28 days by virtue of the Protection from Eviction Act 1977, s 5). Proceedings in respect of the notice must be issued within 12 months, otherwise a fresh notice must be issued. The court may, however, dispense with the requirement of the notice if it considers it just and equitable to do so (Housing Act 1985, s 83(1)(b)).

17.117 The court will only make an order for demotion if it considers it reasonable to do so. An application for a demotion order may be made in conjunction with an application for possession (although separate notices must be given before proceedings are commenced). The purpose of the demotion order is to allow social landlords (and the courts) a greater range of options in dealing with anti-social tenants. Relevant landlords can also consider applying for an injunction against such tenants in appropriate circumstances (see 18.10).

The effect of the demotion

If the landlord is a local authority or a housing action trust the formerly secure tenancy will become a demoted tenancy under the Housing Act 1996, ss 143A to 143P. If the landlord is a registered social landlord it will become a demoted assured shorthold tenancy (see 15.95 to 15.99). **17.118**

A demoted tenancy governed by the Housing Act 1996, ss 143A to 143P is similar to an introductory tenancy in that it provides only limited security of tenure (see 17.19 to 17.38). The demoted tenancy will become secure again after a period of 12 months provided that the landlord does not give notice of its intention to bring possession proceedings within that period. The tenancy will also revert to its original secure status if: **17.119**

(a) the landlord withdraws the notice;
(b) possession proceedings are not brought within six months of the notice; or
(c) the tenant successfully defends the possession proceedings (Housing Act 1996, s 143B).

The former secure tenancy will be terminated from the date specified in the demotion order. The parties to and the term of the demoted tenancy, and the terms as to payment of rent, will be the same as under the previous secure tenancy. Any rent arrears or rent credit in respect of the former secure tenancy will be transferred to the new demoted tenancy. **17.120**

Possession of a demoted tenancy

Notice

There is no prescribed form of notice but the Housing Act 1996, s 143E sets out the information that should be included in the notice. The landlord may seek possession on any ground, not just the ground or grounds upon which the demotion order was made. The notice seeking possession must set out the ground relied upon and specify the date after which proceedings may be brought (again, this will be the earliest date the tenancy could be brought to an end by notice to quit). The notice must also inform the tenant that he or she has a right, within 14 days of service of the landlord's notice, to request the landlord to review its decision. The tenant must also be informed of the available sources of legal advice. **17.121**

The review

The review must be conducted in accordance with the Demoted Tenancies (Review of Decisions) (England) Regulations 2004, SI 2004/1679 or the Demoted Tenancies (Review of Decisions) (Wales) Regulations 2004, SI 2004/1228. It must be conducted by a person of appropriate seniority who was not involved in the original decision to serve notice. The landlord must allow an oral hearing if the tenant requests one. The review must have taken place, and the tenant notified of the decision, before the date specified in the notice as the date after which possession proceedings could be brought. **17.122**

If the court considers that the procedures and requirements concerning the notice and the review have been properly followed it must make an order for possession. The order cannot be postponed for more than 14 days unless exceptional hardship would be caused, in which case the postponement may be for up to six weeks (Housing Act 1980 s 89(1)). The court has no power to suspend the execution of a possession order unless the landlord consents. **17.123**

Human Rights Act 1998

The tenant may be able to challenge the landlord's decision to seek possession of a demoted tenancy on the grounds that it infringed his or her rights under Article 8 of the Human **17.124**

Rights Act 1998. In order to do so the tenant must be able to show that the decision was not a proportionate means of achieving a legitimate end. In determining this issue the court may have regard to whether the landlord has complied with the correct procedure. The court may also conduct a full investigation into the facts giving rise to the making of the initial demotion order, the history of events leading up to the possession hearing, and any representations made by the tenant concerning his or her personal circumstances and likely future conduct (see *Manchester City Council v Pinnock* [2010] UKSC 45, [2010] 3 WLR 1441; *Houndslow LBC v Powell; Leeds City Council v Hall; Birmingham City Council v Frisby* [2011] UKSC 8). For a fuller discussion of Article 8 challenges in possession claims, see 18.62.

G SUCCESSION TO SECURE TENANCIES

Who is qualified to succeed?

17.125 The Housing Act 1985 has been amended by s 160 of the Localism Act 2011 to provide two slightly different regimes for England and for Wales. The old s 87 remains in force for Wales and a new s 86A applies to succession in England.

Section 87 ('Persons qualified to succeed tenant: Wales') provides:

A person is qualified to succeed the tenant under a secure tenancy in Wales if he occupies the dwelling-house as his only or principal home at the time of the tenant's death and either—

(a) he is the tenant's spouse or civil partner; or
(b) he is a member of the tenant's family and has resided with the tenant throughout the period of twelve months ending with the tenant's death;
unless in either case, the tenant was himself a successor, as defined in s 88.

Section 86A ('Persons qualified to succeed tenant: England') provides:

A person ('P') is qualified to succeed the tenant under a secure tenancy in England if P occupies the dwelling-house as his or her only or principal home at the time of the tenant's death and either—

(1) P is the tenant's spouse or civil partner; or
(2) at the time of the tenant's death the dwelling house is not occupied by a spouse or civil partner of the tenant as his or her only or principle home and
(a) an express term of the tenancy makes provision for a person other than such a spouse or civil partner of the tenancy to succeed to the term and
(b) P's succession is in accordance with that term.

As with s 87, this provision will not apply if the tenant who has died was himself or herself a successor.

17.126 The main difference between the two sections is that the position in England does not allow for the automatic right of succession for a member of the tenant's family (other than the spouse or civil partner) but provides that 'another person' (who need not even be a family member) may succeed to the tenancy but only if the tenancy agreement makes express provision for this to happen.

17.127 A tenant's spouse or civil partner will therefore be qualified to succeed (under s 86A or 87) provided he or she was occupying the dwelling-house as his or her only or principal home when the tenant died.

In Wales a member of the tenant's family will be qualified to succeed only if he or she has **17.128** resided with the tenant for a period of 12 months ending with the tenant's death. Section 113 (as amended by the Civil Partnership Act 2004) defines a member of the family as: a spouse or civil partner; a person who lives with the tenant as man and wife; or a civil partner's parent, grandparent, child, grandchild, brother, sister, uncle, aunt, nephew, and niece. It also provides that 'half-blood' relationships are to be regarded as 'whole-blood' relationships, stepchildren are to be treated as children, and illegitimate children are to be treated as legitimate. Under the amended s 113, relationships by marriage or civil partnership are to be treated as relationships by blood.

The residence requirement for family members does not demand that the person living **17.129** with the tenant lived with the tenant in the property to which that person is seeking to succeed. Where two brothers lived together for more than two-and-a-half years and then moved to a new house, one brother was entitled to succeed to the secure tenancy when the other brother died 10 days after the move (*Waltham Forest LBC v Thomas* [1992] 2 AC 198). In order to be said to be residing at the property, however, it is not enough for the family member to show that he or she simply stayed at the property (in order to provide full-time care to the tenant for example). He or she must show that he or she had made a home with the tenant (see *Islington LBC v Freeman* [2009] EWCA Civ 536, [2010] HLR 6).

Joint tenancies

Where the tenant who dies was a joint tenant the tenancy will carry on in the name of the **17.130** other joint tenant and no other person living at the property at the time of the tenant's death can claim the right to succeed. This will be the case even if the other joint tenant was not living in the property at the date of the tenant's death. In *Solihull MBC v Hickin* [2012] UKSC 39 Mr and Mrs Hickin were joint secure tenants. Mr Hickin left the property permanently when the marriage broke down but the tenancy remained in joint names. Mrs Hickin continued to live at the property with her daughter until her death. Mrs Hickin's daughter attempted to claim that she was qualified to succeed under s 87 but the Supreme Court held that on Mrs Hickin's death the joint tenancy continued in Mr Hickin's name and no one was entitled to override his interest in it by claiming a right to succession. As Mr Hickin was not residing at the property and had no intention to return the tenancy also ceased to be secure. The council, having served notice to quit on him, was entitled to possession. It should also be noted that Mr Hickin, as the surviving joint tenant, would also have been deemed to be a successor to the tenancy for the purposes of s 88(1) (17.131). If he had remained at the property his daughter would not have been able to succeed to the tenancy on his death either.

Only one succession

The Housing Act 1985 permits only one succession. If the deceased tenant was already **17.131** a successor, no one will be entitled to succeed to the tenancy. Section 88(1) gives a fairly broad definition to 'a successor':

(1) The tenant is himself a successor if—
    (a) the tenancy vested in him by virtue of s 89 (succession to a periodic tenancy), or
    (b) he was a joint tenant and has become a sole tenant, or
    (c) the tenancy arose by virtue of s 86 (periodic tenancy arising on the ending of a term certain) and the first tenancy there mentioned was granted to another person or jointly to him and another person, or

    (d) he became the tenant on the tenancy being assigned to him (but subject to subsections (2) and (3)), or

    (e) he became the tenant on the tenancy being vested in him on the death of the previous tenant, or

    (f) the tenancy was previously an introductory tenancy and he was a successor to the introductory tenancy.

17.132 Succession to a periodic tenancy under s 89 is discussed at 17.133 to 17.134. Where a joint tenant becomes the sole tenant of the dwelling-house by virtue of the right of survivorship, the remaining tenant will be deemed to be a successor already and no further succession will be possible. This will also be the case where the tenant has acquired the tenancy by assignment, unless the assignment was by virtue of s 23A or 24 of the Matrimonial Causes Act 1973 (s 88(2); or Pt 2 of Sch 5, or para 9(2) or (3) of Sch 7 to the Civil Partnership Act 2004 (property adjustment orders following overseas divorce or dissolution)) or if the assignment was by way of exchange and the tenant was not a successor in relation to the tenancy which he or she assigned (s 88(3) as amended). However, if the tenant is a successor who has been granted a new tenancy of the same dwelling-house within six months of the end of the previous periodic tenancy, he or she will cease to be regarded as a successor: the new tenancy will 'wipe the slate clean'.

Periodic tenancies

17.133 The succession of periodic tenancies is governed by the Housing Act 1985, s 89. If more than one person is qualified to succeed it is the deceased tenant's spouse or civil partner who takes priority (s 89(2)(a)). If the deceased tenant had no spouse or civil partner, or the spouse or civil partner is not qualified to succeed, and there is more than one other potential successor (either family member under s 87(b) in Wales or qualifying other person under s 86A(2) in England) it is for the potential successors to agree between them who is to succeed. If no agreement can be reached it is for the landlord to select which of the potential successors is to succeed (s 89(1A) and (2)(b)); however, it is not possible for the potential successors to succeed jointly (*Newham LBC v Phillips* (1997) 96 LGR 788).

17.134 Where there is no person qualified to succeed, the tenancy will be disposed of according either to the will of the tenant or to the intestacy rules. If this is the case the tenancy will cease to be a secure tenancy unless the vesting or disposal of the tenancy is in pursuance of an order made under s 23A or 24 of the Matrimonial Causes Act 1973 (s 89(3); or Pt 2 of Sch 5, or para 9(2) or (3) of Sch 7 to the Civil Partnership Act 2004). Once a tenancy has ceased to be secure by virtue of this section it cannot subsequently become a secure tenancy (s 89(4)).

Terms certain

17.135 If the tenancy is for a fixed term it will be disposed of according to the tenant's will or the intestacy rules. The tenancy will cease, on being vested or disposed of, to be a secure tenancy unless either:

    (a) the vesting or other disposal is in pursuance of an order made under s 23A or 24 of the Matrimonial Causes Act 1973, Pt 2 of Sch 5, or para 9(2) or (3) of Sch 7 to the Civil Partnership Act 2004, s 17(1) of the Matrimonial and Family Proceedings Act 1984, or para 1 of Sch 1 to the Children Act 1989; or

    (b) the vesting or other disposal is to a person qualified to succeed the tenant (Housing Act 1985, s 90(3)).

Once a tenancy has ceased to be secure by virtue of this section it cannot subsequently become a secure tenancy (s 90(4)). The landlord may apply for a mandatory possession order under s 90(6) (inserted by the Localism Act 2011, s 162) if it serves notice on the tenant that it requires possession of the dwelling-house, specifying a date not less than four weeks after service of the notice on which possession proceedings may be begun (s 90(7), (8)). **17.136**

H THE RIGHT TO BUY

The right to buy for local authority tenants was introduced by the Housing Act 1980 and is now to be found in Pt V of the Housing Act 1985. The right was extended to tenants of some housing associations and registered social landlords by the Housing Act 1996, s 16. The right to buy entitles secure tenants to purchase their homes from their local authority landlords at heavily discounted prices. Provided that the requirements laid down by the Act are satisfied the secure tenant can compel the landlord to make the sale. Not surprisingly, the right to buy has proved very popular among secure tenants and, as intended, has resulted in a considerable decrease in the amount of housing held by local authorities. The Housing Act 2004, however, introduced amendments to the 1985 Act that have made it more difficult to exercise the right to buy, most notably by extending the minimum qualifying period from two to five years, and increasing the time from three to five years before the right to buy purchaser can sell the property without repaying any of the discount. The 2004 Act also provides that if a right to buy purchaser wishes to resell the property within 10 years, he or she must offer the right of first refusal to a social landlord. The right to buy is in itself a complex area of law and what follows provides only an overview of the main provisions. **17.137**

The right to buy what?

Part V of the Housing Act 1985 confers upon the secure tenant the right either to buy the freehold or to be granted a long lease of the dwelling-house in which he or she is living. Whether the tenant can acquire the freehold or a long lease will depend upon the nature of the property and the nature of the landlord's interest (Housing Act 1985, s 118): **17.138**

(a) If the dwelling-house is a house and the landlord owns the freehold, the tenant will acquire the right to purchase the freehold.
(b) If the dwelling-house is a house and the landlord does not own the freehold, the tenant will acquire the right to be granted a long lease.
(c) If the dwelling-house is a flat, the tenant will acquire the right to be granted a long lease regardless of whether the landlord owns the freehold.

If the secure tenant has the right to be granted a lease this will usually be a lease for 125 years at a rent not exceeding £10 per annum. The terms of both a grant of a lease or the conveyance of the freehold are governed by detailed provisions set out in Sch 6 to the 1985 Act. **17.139**

Whether a dwelling-house is a 'house' or a 'flat' is defined in s 183: **17.140**

(a) Where the building is divided horizontally, the flats or other units into which it is divided are not houses.
(b) Where the building is divided vertically, the units into which it is divided may be houses.

(c)   Where a building is not structurally detached, it is not a house if a material part of it lies above or below the remainder of the structure.

17.141   Thus, while a terraced house will be a 'house' within this definition, a dwelling-house within a purpose-built block or within a converted house where the building has been divided horizontally will be regarded as a 'flat'.

Who can exercise the right to buy?

17.142   Usually the right to buy can belong only to a secure tenant or to a person closely connected to a secure tenant (for example, a member of the secure tenant's family, see 17.144). In certain circumstances the right to buy is available to assured tenants of housing associations and registered social landlords where the interest of the landlord has been transferred from the public to the private sector (Housing Act 1996, s 17) (see 17.172). A licensee who has acquired statutory protection under the Housing Act 1985 by virtue of s 79(3) (see 17.15 to 17.18) will not acquire the right to buy.

17.143   If the secure tenancy is a joint tenancy, the right to buy belongs jointly to all of the tenants, or to such one or more of them as may be agreed between them, provided that the person or at least one of the persons to whom the right to buy is to belong occupies the dwelling-house as his or her only or principal home (s 118(2)).

17.144   Where there is only one secure tenant, that tenant may choose to share the right to buy with not more than three members of his or her family regardless of the fact that the family members are not joint tenants. To be eligible to share the right to buy such a family member must be:

(a)   the tenant's spouse or civil partner, or a person living with the tenant as if he or she was the tenant's spouse or civil partner;
(b)   a family member who has been residing with the tenant throughout the period of 12 months ending with the giving of notice; or
(c)   a family member who does not satisfy the residence requirement, provided the landlord consents (s 123).

17.145   If the tenant chooses to share the right to buy with members of his or her family, the tenant must inform the landlord in his or her notice claiming to exercise the right to buy (under s 122). Provided that the family members are entitled to share the right to buy they will then be treated as joint tenants for the purposes of the right to buy (s 123(3)). In *Harrow LBC v Tonge* (1992) 25 HLR 99, [1993] 1 EGLR 49, CA, a daughter was not entitled to succeed to her late mother's secure tenancy because her mother was herself a tenant by succession. However, before her death the mother had served notice on her landlord claiming the right to buy and she had included her daughter in the notice. The daughter was therefore entitled to require the landlord to complete the sale.

The qualifying period

17.146   No secure tenant will be able to exercise the right to buy unless he or she can satisfy the 'qualifying period'. The qualifying period is defined by the Housing Act 1985, Sch 4. For tenancies created before 18 January 2005 the qualifying period is two years (Housing Act 1985, s 119). For tenancies created after 18 January 2005 the qualifying period is five years (s 119(1), as amended by the Housing Act 2004, s 180(1)). The amount of discount for which the applicant may be eligible is calculated with reference to the length of the qualifying period.

Basically, the qualifying period is the length of time that the tenant (or his or her spouse **17.147**
or civil partner if they were living together at the relevant time) has held a public sector
tenancy, a public sector tenancy being one where the 'landlord condition' and the 'tenant
condition' are satisfied (see 17.07 to 17.13). The period does not have to be a continuous
period (Sch 4, para 1), nor does it need to be a period immediately preceding the tenant's
exercise of the right to buy (Sch 4, para 2(a)). The tenant does not have to have had the
same landlord for the whole of the period, nor is it necessary that the tenancy was of
one particular dwelling-house. Where the secure tenancy is a joint tenancy, the qualifying
period only needs to be satisfied with respect to one of the joint tenants (s 119(2)).

The qualifying period may be extended where a person occupied a property as the child of **17.148**
a former public sector tenant, and later acquires a public sector tenancy. In that case, subject to the new tenant meeting the relevant residence qualifications, any period in which he
or she occupied his or her parent's property since reaching the age of 16 will count towards
the qualifying period (Housing Act 1985, Sch 4, para 4(1)).

Exclusions from the right to buy

The Housing Act 1985, s 120 provides that the right to buy *will not arise* in the cases speci- **17.149**
fied in Sch 5 to the Act. The most important of these exceptions are as follows:

(a) The landlord is a charitable housing trust or association.
(b) The landlord is a co-operative housing association.
(c) The landlord is a housing association which has never received a grant of public funds.
(d) The landlord does not own the freehold or an interest sufficient to grant a lease (21
     years in the case of a house or 50 years for a flat).
(e) The dwelling-house forms part of a building which is held mainly for purposes other
     than housing and was let to the tenant in consequence of the tenant's employment by
     the landlord.
(f) The dwelling-house was designed or altered to make it suitable for occupation by
     physically disabled persons.
(g) The dwelling-house is one of a group of dwelling-houses which it is the practice of
     the landlord to let for occupation by persons who suffer a mental disorder and social
     services or special facilities are provided.
(h) The dwelling-house is one of a group of dwelling-houses particularly suitable for
     elderly persons and special facilities are provided.
(i) The dwelling-house is due to be demolished within 24 months (inserted by the Housing
     Act 2004, s 182 and amended by the Housing and Regeneration Act 2008, Sch 13).

Disqualified secure tenants

The right to buy *cannot be exercised* where: **17.150**

(a) the tenant is subject to an order of the court for possession of the dwelling (s 121(1),
     as amended by Housing and Regeneration Act 2008, s 304(1)). Section 304(2) of the
     2008 Act qualifies this to provide that it will not apply if the tenant has given notice
     claiming to exercise the right to buy before 22 September 2009 (the date s 304 came
     into force) and that notice has not been withdrawn.
(b) the person, or one of the persons, to whom the right to buy belongs is an undischarged
     bankrupt or has a bankruptcy petition pending against him or her, or has made a com-
     position or an arrangement with his or her creditors, the terms of which remain to be
     fulfilled (s 121(2)).

In addition a tenant may not exercise the right to buy where the tenancy has been made the subject of a demotion order (Housing Act 1985, s 82A) (see 17.114 to 17.124).

17.151 The tenant must be qualified to exercise the right to buy at all stages of the process. If a tenant who is initially qualified loses his or her right to buy for one of the reasons set out before the contract for sale has been concluded (and the landlord has a duty to complete, see 17.167), he or she cannot proceed further unless and until that right is restored (for example where a possession order is discharged, see *Islington LBC v Honeygan-Green* [2008] UKHL 70, [2009] 2 WLR 78). Where a tenant is subject to a possession order but has been given suitable alternative accommodation as a condition of possession being granted he or she will retain the right to buy the alternative accommodation (*Manchester City Council v Benjamin* [2008] EWCA Civ 189, [2009] 1 WLR 2202).

Preserved right to buy

17.152 If, after 15 January 1989, a secure tenant's public sector landlord sells its interest in the dwelling-house to a private sector landlord (such as a registered social landlord), the tenant will cease to be a secure tenant and will become an assured tenant. This effectively means that the tenant loses the right to buy as from the date of the sale. Section 171(B) of the 1985 Act provides that in such cases the right to buy will be preserved, with certain modifications, so long as the tenant continues to occupy the dwelling-house as his or her only or principal home.

Procedure

Tenant's notice

17.153 If a tenant wishes to exercise the right to buy, he or she must set the ball rolling by serving written notice on the landlord (Housing Act 1985, s 122). This notice should be in Form RTB 1, as prescribed under reg 176 in the Housing (Right to Buy) (Prescribed Forms) Regulations 1986, SI 1986/2194, as amended by SI 1993/2246. This notice can be withdrawn at any time up to completion (s 122(3)).

Change of tenant or landlord after initial notice

17.154 If, after notice has been given, there is a change of tenant, the new tenant will be treated as if he or she had given the notice (s 136). This could happen where, for example, the original tenant dies and a family member succeeds to the tenancy (see 17.125 to 17.129), or where, prior to the original tenant's death, he or she has assigned the tenancy to a person who is entitled to succeed to the tenancy (see 17.82). The new tenant will also be eligible for the discount claimed in the notice by the former tenant (*McIntyre v Merthyr Tydfil BC* (1989) 88 LGR 1, (1989) 21 HLR 320, CA). Likewise, if there is a change of landlord, the new landlord is placed in the position the original landlord would have been in (s 137).

Landlord's reply

17.155 Once notice has been served by the tenant the landlord usually has four weeks in which to serve a written notice in reply (eight weeks in cases where the qualifying period was satisfied by a period or periods of residence with a different landlord). This notice must either:

(a) admit the tenant's right to buy; or

(b) deny the tenant's right to buy and state the reasons why, in the opinion of the landlord, the tenant does not have the right to buy (s 124).

The landlord's notice must be in Form RTB 2, as prescribed (see 17.153).

Landlord's second notice

If the right to buy is established, the next stage in the procedure is for the landlord to serve a **17.156** second notice upon the tenant in accordance with s 125 of the 1985 Act. This notice should be served within eight weeks of the right to buy being established if the tenant has the right to acquire the freehold, or within 12 weeks of the right to buy being established if the tenant has acquired the right to be granted a lease (s 125(1)). The notice should contain all the information the tenant will need to decide whether to go ahead with the purchase. In particular, it must describe the dwelling-house, state the price (including the discount) at which, in the opinion of the landlord, the tenant is entitled to acquire the freehold or to be granted a lease, and state the provisions which, in the opinion of the landlord, should be contained in the conveyance or grant. It must also apprise the tenant of the effects of the various notices that can be given, inform him or her of the various rights that he or she has (eg the right to acquire on rent to mortgage terms or to have the dwelling valued by the district valuer), and, if the tenant is to be granted a lease, it should include information about the service charges which will be payable (s 125A), and details of any known structural defects.

Disputing the landlord's decision

If the landlord denies the tenant's right to exercise the right to buy and the tenant wishes **17.157** to dispute the landlord's decision, the tenant can apply to the county court for a declaration (s 181). If the landlord admits the tenant's claim but the tenant disagrees with the price stated by the landlord, the tenant can apply under s 128 to the district valuer for a determination.

Tenant's second notice

The tenant must serve a further notice on the landlord within 12 weeks of receiving the **17.158** landlord's s 125 notice. This notice must state whether the tenant intends to pursue his or her claim to exercise the right to buy, or whether the tenant intends to withdraw the claim (s 125D).

If the tenant fails to serve notice in time the landlord may serve a default notice requir- **17.159** ing him or her to do so within 28 days. If the tenant does not comply, his or her claim for the right to buy will be deemed to have been withdrawn at the end of the default notice period.

The terms of the purchase

The price

The price payable for the dwelling-house is the value of the dwelling-house less the dis- **17.160** count to which the purchaser is entitled (Housing Act 1985, s 126).

The value

The value of the dwelling-house is the price it would realize if sold on the open mar- **17.161** ket by a willing vendor. The value should be calculated in accordance with s 127 of the 1985 Act, which sets out the assumptions that should be made in reaching a valuation. Improvements made by the tenant will be disregarded, as will a failure by the tenant to keep the dwelling-house in good internal repair (s 127(1)(b)). Service charges or improvement contributions will be assumed not to be less than the amounts specified in the landlord's notice under s 125 (s 127(1)(c)).

If the freehold is to be conveyed the assumptions are: **17.162**

(a) that the vendor was selling for an estate in fee simple with vacant possession;

(b) that neither the tenant nor a member of his or her family residing with him or her wanted to buy; and

(c) that the dwelling-house was to be conveyed with the same rights and subject to the same burdens as it would be in pursuance of Pt V of the Housing Act 1985 (s 127(2)).

17.163 If a lease is to be granted the assumptions are:

(a) that the vendor was granting a lease with vacant possession for a term of 125 years (or, if the landlord's interest is less than 125 years, for a term of five days less than the length of the landlord's term);

(b) that neither the tenant nor a member of his or her family residing with him or her wanted to take the lease;

(c) that the ground rent would not exceed £10 per annum; and

(d) that the grant was to be made with the same rights and subject to the same burdens as it would be in pursuance of Pt V of the Housing Act 1985 (s 127(3)).

17.164 If a dispute arises as to the value of the dwelling-house, this can be referred to the district valuer for determination under s 128. The landlord or the tenant may request a review of the determination under s 128A (as inserted by the Housing and Regeneration Act 2008, s 306).

The discount

17.165 The discount available to a tenant seeking to exercise the right to buy is dependent upon the 'qualifying period', ie the amount of time the tenant has been a public sector tenant (see 17.146). If the tenant is seeking to acquire a house the discount will be 32 per cent plus one per cent for each complete year by which the qualifying period exceeds the minimum period (two years if the tenancy was created before 18 January 2005 or five years if created after that date), up to a maximum of 60 per cent; if the tenant is seeking to acquire a flat the discount will be 44 per cent plus two per cent for each complete year by which the qualifying period exceeds the minimum period up to a maximum of 70 per cent (s 129(2)). The Housing Act 1985, s 131 allows regulations to be made to fix the maximum amount of the discount. This will vary between regions. The current maximum discounts are £16,000 in Wales and £75,000 in England.

17.166 Where joint tenants are seeking to exercise the right to buy the discount is calculated by taking the joint tenant who satisfies the longest qualifying period (s 129(3)). A full discount will not be available where the tenant has previously exercised the right to buy (s 130).

Duty to complete

17.167 Once all the matters relating to the purchase of the freehold or the grant of the lease have been agreed or determined, the landlord is under a duty to complete the purchase or grant the lease (s 138(1)). This duty can be enforced by an injunction (s 138(3)).

Removal or suspension of the right to buy

17.168 The duty will be suspended if the tenant fails to pay the rent (or any other payments due) for a period of four weeks or more (s 138(2)) and will not be revived until the arrears have been paid in full. The landlord has no duty to complete where a demolition notice is in force in respect of the premises or where the tenant has ceased to be a secure tenant. The duty to complete will be suspended where relevant proceedings are pending (Housing Act 1985, s 138, as amended by the Housing Act 2004, s 193). Relevant proceedings include possession proceedings under the Housing Act 1985, Sch 2, Ground 2 (see 18.07) and applications for demotion orders (Housing Act 1985, s 82A).

Under the Housing Act 1985, s 121A(1) and (2) (inserted by the Housing Act 2004, s 192) **17.169** the landlord may also apply to the county court for an order suspending the right to buy for a specific period on the grounds of anti-social behaviour as set out in the Housing Act 1996, s 153A or 153B (see 18.10).

The tenant can withdraw from the process at any time up to the completion or grant; this **17.170** should be done by serving notice on the landlord in writing (s 122(3)). If the tenant fails to continue with the process the landlord can serve a notice on the tenant requiring him or her to complete within a specified period of not less than 56 days (s 140). If the tenant fails to respond the landlord may serve a second notice (s 141). If the tenant fails to comply with the second notice within the specified time the right to buy will be deemed to be withdrawn (s 141(4)). The landlord cannot, however, use this provision to defeat the tenant's right to buy where completion is delayed because the parties have entered into negotiations regarding outstanding matters that need to be resolved before completion can sensibly take place (*Scinto v Newham LBC* [2009] EWCA Civ 837).

I THE RIGHT TO ACQUIRE ON RENT TO MORTGAGE TERMS

Notwithstanding the various restrictions that are placed on the right to buy by the Housing **17.171** Act 1985, the largest single factor that will prevent a secure tenant from exercising his or her right will be the problem of raising sufficient money to make the purchase. The original legislation, therefore, contained three measures intended to make it easier for a tenant to exercise the right to buy: the right to a mortgage, the right to defer completion, and the right to be granted a shared ownership lease. These measures were withdrawn by the Leasehold Reform, Housing and Urban Development Act 1993 and were replaced by the right to acquire on rent to mortgage terms. The right to acquire on rent to mortgage terms was not widely taken up and was abolished with effect from 18 January 2005 by the Housing Act 2004, s 190.

J THE RIGHT TO ACQUIRE FOR TENANTS OF REGISTERED SOCIAL LANDLORDS OR REGISTERED PROVIDERS

Prior to the introduction of the Housing Act 1996, very few tenants of registered social **17.172** landlords had the right to buy. For a start, the vast majority of tenancies granted by registered social landlords after 15 January 1989 will be held on an assured tenancy and the right to buy contained in the Housing Act 1985 does not extend to assured tenancies. Furthermore, even if the tenancy was granted prior to 15 January 1989 and was held on a secure tenancy, it would be likely to be excluded from the right to buy provisions under the exceptions contained in Sch 1 to the Housing Act 1985, most probably because the registered social landlord would be a charity. In fact, the only tenants of registered social landlords who might be able to acquire the right to buy under the 1985 Act would be those who were secure tenants of a non-charitable landlord and those who held under an assured tenancy but had a preserved right to buy under s 171 of the Housing Act 1985. The Housing Act 1996 significantly changed this situation, giving certain tenants (including assured tenants) of registered social landlords the right to acquire their homes provided that their homes were built or acquired using certain categories of public funds and that the tenants were able to fulfil the requirements of the Housing Act 1985. The Housing and Regeneration Act 2008, which replaced the registered social landlord in England with a new extended class of social landlord known as registered providers, has preserved the right to acquire for qualifying tenants of registered providers (s 180).

Which tenants have the right to buy?

17.173   The provisions of Pt V of the Housing Act 1985 are extended to apply to the tenant of a registered social landlord or registered provider by s 180 of the Housing and Regeneration Act 2008 (as amended by Localism Act 2011, s 165 and the Transfer of Tenancies and Right to Acquire (Exclusion) Regulations 2012, SI 2012/696). A tenant of a registered social landlord or registered provider will have the right to acquire the dwelling of which he or she is tenant if:

(a)   he or she is a tenant under an assured tenancy (but not an assured shorthold tenancy in Wales, or a periodic assured shorthold tenancy or fixed-term assured shorthold tenancy granted for a term of less than two years in England), a long tenancy, or a secure tenancy; and

(b)   he or she can fulfil the qualifying conditions applicable to a secure tenant's right to buy under Pt V of the Housing Act 1985 as it applies in relation to this section (the main one being that he or she must have been a tenant of a registered social landlord for at least two years).

17.174   The exceptions contained in paras 1 to 3 of Sch 5 excluding various registered social landlords do not apply (s 17(2)(b) of the Housing Act 1996, preserved by s 184 of the Housing and Regeneration Act 2008). However, the preserved right to buy provisions will not apply to the tenant of a registered social landlord or registered provider (s 17(2)(e)).

What dwellings can they buy?

17.175   A tenant will only be able to buy his or her home where that home was provided with public money and has remained within the social rented sector (ss 180(1) and 185(1)). For tenants in England s 181 provides that the property will be regarded as having been publicly funded if:

(a)   it was provided by a person in fulfilment of a condition imposed by the Homes and Communities Agency when giving assistance to that person, and that person was notified that the dwelling would be regarded as publicly funded;

(b)   it was funded from the disposal proceeds fund of a registered provider or registered social landlord;

(c)   it was acquired by the registered provider or registered social landlord on a disposal made by a public sector landlord on or after 1 April 1997; or

(d)   it was provided wholly or partly by means of a grant under s 18 or 27A of the Housing Act 1996.

17.176   For tenants in Wales s 16(2) of the Housing Act 1996 continues to apply. A property will have been provided with public money if it was built or acquired:

(a)   by means of a 'social housing grant' made under s 18 of the Housing Act 1996;

(b)   where the social landlord has used money from its disposal proceeds fund; or

(c)   where the social landlord has acquired housing from a public sector landlord after the commencement of the Housing Act 1996.

17.177   These provisions mean that the right to acquire for all tenants is limited to dwellings that were built or acquired after the commencement of the Housing Act 1996. Tenants of a dwelling that was built or acquired before the commencement of the Housing Act 1996 (1 April 1997) will not benefit from the extension of the right to buy, though they may be able to purchase their homes through a voluntary purchase scheme. To be regarded as remaining in the social rented sector the landlord's interest must have been held by a registered social landlord, a registered provider, or a public sector landlord since the dwelling was provided or acquired (Housing Act 1996, s 16(3) and Housing and Regeneration Act 2008, s 182).

K DISPOSALS AND REPAYMENT OF DISCOUNTS

A tenant who purchases a property under the right to buy will have to enter into a covenant (which is also binding on his or her successors) to the effect that, if there is a relevant disposal of the property within five years of the date the tenant purchased it, the tenant will repay to the landlord such sum (if any) as the landlord considers to be appropriate up to 'the maximum amount' (Housing Act 1985, s 155). The five-year period was introduced into s 155 by the Housing Act 2004, s 185. The period was previously three years and this limit will still apply to tenants who purchased their properties before 18 January 2005. **17.178**

Relevant disposal

A relevant disposal includes a conveyance of the freehold or the granting of a lease for a term of more than 21 years (Housing Act 1985, s 159). It also includes a 'deferred resale agreement' under which the tenant agrees to sell the property to a third party after the five-year period. This new provision was introduced by the Housing Act 2004, s 187. It is designed to prevent sham right to buy purchases under which the purchase price is paid by way of a loan from a third party in return for a promise by the secure tenant to give the third party the option to purchase the property at the end of the discount period, both parties sharing the profit. **17.179**

Exempt disposals

Certain disposals within the five-year period will be exempted. These are: **17.180**

(a) a disposal by way of the further conveyance of the freehold to the original tenant or his or her (qualifying) partners or family members (Housing Act 1985 s 160(2));
(b) the vesting of the property by will or intestacy;
(c) a disposal in pursuance of a court order under the Matrimonial Causes Act 1973, s 24 or a property adjustment order under the Civil Partnership Act 2004;
(d) a compulsory disposal (as defined by s 161);
(e) a disposal of land let together with the dwelling-house and treated as included in it (s 160(1)).

Amount to be repaid

The old system

The maximum amount repayable is initially a sum up to the amount of the entire discount. So if a tenant qualifies for a 50 per cent discount on a house valued at £50,000, the tenant will get a £25,000 discount on the purchase price. This is the maximum amount that could have to be repaid. The maximum amount will decrease by one-fifth for every complete year after the original conveyance to the tenant. **17.181**

The new system

17.182 The Housing Act 2004, s 185 introduced a new system of calculating the repayable discount based on the value of the property at the date of resale. This will apply to all purchasers who exercise the right to buy after 18 January 2005. Under this system the maximum amount is initially calculated by taking the percentage discount the tenant initially received when he or she purchased the home, and multiplying that by the sale price at the date of the disposal (Housing Act 1985, s 155A, as amended by the Housing Act 2004, s 185). For example: Steve qualified for a discount of 50 per cent when he bought his home from the council. The house was valued at £50,000 so Steve paid £25,000. Steve immediately resold his house for £60,000. He could be liable to repay £30,000 to the council (being 50 per cent of the sale price).

17.183 The maximum amount will decrease by one-fifth for every complete year after the original conveyance to the tenant. So if Steve sold his house for £60,000 two years after he bought it from the council, the amount he might have to pay would decrease to 30 per cent of the sale proceeds. No repayment would be required if Steve sold the property more than five years after he bought it.

17.184 **Home improvements** If Steve can argue that the increase in the value of his house was as a result of any improvements he made to it after he bought it, the value added by these improvements will be disregarded in calculating the value of the property at the date of the resale (s 155C). So if he can show that the entire £10,000 increase in value was as a result of his having put in a new bathroom, he will only have to repay 50 per cent of £50,000. If Steve and the council cannot agree the sum to be disregarded as a result of improvements it can be decided by the district valuer (s 155C(2)).

Deferred resale

17.185 If a relevant disposal takes the form of a deferred resale, the date of the disposal will either be the date the agreement was entered into or, if this occurred before the beginning of the discount repayment period, immediately after the beginning of that period (s 163A). So, if Ann entered into a deferred resale agreement with Loanshark Ltd two months before she bought her property, she will have to repay the full discount percentage of the sale price when she sells the property to Loanshark, even if this sale takes place more than five years later.

Landlord's discretion

17.186 In order to alleviate hardship in certain cases, amendments have been made to the Housing Act, s 155 to allow landlords discretion in deciding whether to demand repayment in the case of tenants who make a relevant disposal before the end of the discount repayment period (Housing Act 2004, s 185). Such discretion might be exercised, for example, where the buyer needs to resell because of illness or relationship breakdown.

Right of first refusal

17.187 The Housing Act 2004, s 188 also inserted a new s 156A into the 1985 Act. This section applies to all purchasers exercising the right to buy after 18 January 2005. It contains provisions requiring the tenant purchaser (or his or her successor) who wishes to resell the property within a 10-year period to offer first refusal to his or her former landlord (or such other body as the Secretary of State prescribes). A covenant to this effect will be inserted into all right to buy conveyances and grants.

The covenant will not apply to exempt disposals. It will take effect as a local land charge **17.188** and so the tenant will not be able to avoid it.

The aim of the provision is to allow as much housing stock as possible to be retained **17.189** within the public sector. The Act recognizes that the local authority will not always be the body that wishes to purchase such stock, and so allows the Secretary of State to afford the right of first refusal to other social landlords if this would be more appropriate.

18

THE HOUSING ACT 1985—
2. RECOVERY OF POSSESSION
BY THE LANDLORD

A GROUNDS FOR POSSESSION

Provided that a notice seeking possession has been served according to the provisions of **18.01** s 83 of the Housing Act 1985 (see 17.101 to 17.113) the landlord may then go to court and seek a possession order. A possession order will be granted only if the landlord can make out one or more of the grounds contained in Sch 2. In contrast to the Rent Act 1977 and the Housing Act 1988, there are no mandatory grounds as such in the Housing Act 1985. Instead, the grounds of possession are divided into three categories:

(a) Part I (Grounds 1 to 8)—an order for possession will be made only if the court considers it reasonable to make the order.
(b) Part II (Grounds 9 to 11)—the court will make an order for possession only if it is satisfied that suitable accommodation will be available for the tenant when the order takes effect.
(c) Part III (Grounds 12 to 16)—the court will make an order for possession only if it both considers it reasonable to make the order and is satisfied that suitable accommodation will be available for the tenant when the order takes effect.

Many of the grounds contained in Sch 2 to the 1985 Act are identical, or similar, to grounds **18.02** and cases already considered under the Rent Act 1977 and the Housing Act 1988, and where possible cross-references have been made.

Grounds on which the court may order possession if it thinks it reasonable

Ground 1—rent arrears or breach of obligation

Rent lawfully due from the tenant has not been paid or an obligation of the tenancy has been broken or not performed.

18.03 This ground is virtually identical to Case 1 under the Rent Act 1977 (see 14.26). It is a composite ground, permitting the landlord to seek possession for a breach of covenant to pay rent, or for a breach of any other covenant in the tenancy agreement.

18.04 With regard to a breach of covenant to pay rent, the landlord must show that some rent is outstanding at the date of the issue of proceedings. If the tenant pays off the arrears by the date of the hearing the court may still make an order for possession, but unless there are special circumstances (eg the tenant has a history of non- and late payment of rent) it will generally not be reasonable to make such an order (*Bird v Hillage* [1948] 1 KB 91).

18.05 If rent arrears seem to have occurred because of a difficulty in obtaining housing benefit the court should take this into account in deciding whether it is reasonable to make an order. Where the tenant is in receipt of benefits, the court may consider the possibility of enlisting the assistance of the relevant benefit authority to ensure that the tenant pays his future rent and the arrears (eg by authorizing direct payments of housing benefit to the landlord, or by deductions from social security benefits to pay off arrears) (*Second WRVS Housing Society v Blair* (1986) 19 HLR 104, CA).

18.06 In the case of a breach of an obligation of the tenancy, the court will take into account all the circumstances in determining whether it is reasonable to make the order. Important factors will include, among others, the seriousness of the breach, whether it is capable of remedy, whether there is likelihood of repetition, and whether alternative remedies may be available (eg an injunction). In *Wandsworth LBC v Hargraves* [1994] EGCS 115, CA, the tenancy contained a covenant 'not to permit to be done anything which may increase the risk of fire'. A visitor made petrol bombs in the flat and started a fire which caused considerable damage. Nevertheless, the Court of Appeal upheld the county court judge's decision that it was not reasonable to make an order for possession. The tenant had not actually participated in the making of the petrol bombs and there had been no repetition of the breach. On the other hand, where a tenant kept a dog in breach of covenant, the Court of Appeal overturned a county court judge's decision that it could not be reasonable to make an order for possession because the breach was deliberate and persistent (*Sheffield City Council v Jepson* (1993) 25 HLR 299).

Ground 2—nuisance, annoyance, or conviction

The tenant or a person residing in or visiting the dwelling-house—

(a) has been guilty of conduct causing or likely to cause a nuisance or annoyance to a person residing, visiting or otherwise engaging in a lawful activity in the locality, or

(b) has been convicted of—

    (i) using the dwelling-house or allowing it to be used for immoral or illegal purposes, or

    (ii) an arrestable offence committed in, or in the locality of, the dwelling-house.

18.07 This ground of possession was amended by the Housing Act 1996 and, more recently, by the Anti-social Behaviour Act 2003. It is one of a number of provisions in that Act intended to make it easier for public sector landlords to deal with anti-social behaviour. The ground now has a very wide application. It covers not just the conduct of the tenant and other people residing in the dwelling-house, but also the behaviour of visitors. The conduct itself does not have to amount to actual nuisance or annoyance; it merely has to be *likely* to cause a nuisance or annoyance; and this nuisance or annoyance may be caused not only to neighbours but to anyone visiting or carrying out a lawful activity in the locality. This has the advantage of enabling somebody other than the victim of the anti-social behaviour to give evidence—something which might be of considerable practical significance in sensitive cases where an actual neighbour might be wary of giving evidence for fear of reprisals (eg evidence could be given by a local authority employee or other professional).

The second limb of Ground 2 also has an extremely broad scope. It similarly applies to **18.08** visitors as well as to persons actually resident in the dwelling-house, and entitles a landlord to seek possession where such a person has been convicted not just of an offence involving the use of the dwelling-house but also of any arrestable offence that has been committed in the locality of the dwelling-house. Thus, a tenant could find himself or herself faced with possession proceedings under Ground 2 where a visitor to the dwelling-house has been convicted of an arrestable offence committed somewhere in the area.

In any case brought under Ground 2 the court must consider whether it is reasonable to **18.09** make an order for possession. The Anti-social Behaviour Act 2003, s 16 introduced a new s 85A into the Housing Act 1985, which provides that where a court is considering whether it is reasonable to make a possession order on Ground 2 the court must consider:

(a) the effect that the nuisance or annoyance has had on persons other than the person against whom the order is sought;
(b) any continuing effect the nuisance or annoyance is likely to have on such persons;
(c) the effect that the nuisance or annoyance would be likely to have on such persons if the conduct were repeated.

Ground 2 may be invoked where the person complained of has little connection to the dwelling-house and is not someone over whom the tenant is able to exercise control, although the court would take into account the lack of culpability on the part of the tenant in deciding whether it was reasonable to make an order for possession (*Portsmouth City Council v Bryant* (2000) 32 HLR 906, CA). However, if there is evidence that the anti-social behaviour is likely to continue it is more probable that a possession order will be awarded (*Woking BC v Bistram* (1993) 27 HLR, CA). In *Manchester City Council v Higgins* [2005] EWCA Civ 1423, [2006] 1 All ER 841, CA the Court of Appeal upheld the local authority's appeal against the making of a suspended possession order in a case where a tenant's son had terrorized her neighbours. The court found that the mother's lack of remorse for her son's actions and the likelihood that the behaviour would continue justified the making of an immediate possession order despite the fact that the mother and her three children would lose their home.

It should also be noted that seeking possession is not the only weapon in a social landlord's **18.10** armoury. Under ss 153A and 153B of the Housing Act 1996 (amended by the Anti-social Behaviour Act 2003, s 13) the court has an express power to grant a relevant landlord an injunction against anti-social behaviour and unlawful use of premises. The behaviour complained of can include, but is not limited to, behaviour that constitutes a breach of terms of the tenancy agreement. The injunction may include an exclusion order and a power of arrest (s 153C) and may be made *ex parte* (s 153E). A social landlord may also apply for the demotion of a secure tenancy on the grounds of anti-social behaviour (see 17.114 to 17.124).

Ground 2A—domestic violence

The dwelling-house was occupied (whether alone or with others) by a married couple or civil partners or a couple living together as husband and wife or civil partners and—

> (a) one or both of the partners is a tenant of the dwelling-house,
> (b) one partner has left because of violence or threats of violence by the other towards—
>   (i)   that partner, or
>   (ii) a member of the family of that partner who was residing with that partner immediately before the partner left, and
> (c) the court is satisfied that the partner who has left is unlikely to return.

18.11   This ground, introduced by the Housing Act 1996 (and amended by the Civil Partnership Act 2004 to include civil partners), is designed to counter a specific situation, namely where a couple separates due to domestic violence and one partner leaves while the other remains in occupation of the dwelling-house. In such a situation the landlord is often left with a single person occupying family-size accommodation. Ground 2A therefore gives the landlord a ground of possession against such a person. The usefulness of this ground is, however, tempered by the inevitable difficulties faced by the landlord in establishing both that the partner left because of domestic violence *and* that that partner is unlikely to return, particularly because that partner may well be reluctant to give evidence in open court. The landlord must also be able to show that the violence was the main, substantive, or significant reason why the partner left, rather than just a contributory factor (*Fitzpatrick v Sterling Housing Association Ltd* [2000] AC 27, HL).

18.12   If a landlord seeks to rely on Ground 2A, and the partner who has left is not the tenant, the landlord must serve a copy of the notice seeking possession on the departed partner. If this proves to be impossible the landlord must show that he or she has taken all reasonable steps to attempt to serve the notice (Housing Act 1985, s 83A).

Ground 3—deterioration in condition of dwelling-house

> The condition of the dwelling-house or of any of the common parts has deteriorated owing to acts of waste by, or the neglect or default of, the tenant or a person residing in the dwelling-house and, in the case of an act of waste by, or the neglect or default of, a person lodging with the tenant or a sub-tenant of his, the tenant has not taken such steps as he ought reasonably to have taken for the removal of the lodger or sub-tenant.

18.13   This ground is virtually identical to Case 3 under the Rent Act 1977 (see 14.37). However, its application is not restricted to the dwelling-house itself but extends to the common parts of the building as well. Thus, a landlord is able to take action when a tenant residing in a block of flats causes damage to the lifts, hallways, stairwells, or other common areas.

Ground 4—deterioration in condition of furniture

> The condition of furniture provided by the landlord for use under the tenancy, or for use in the common parts, has deteriorated owing to ill-treatment by the tenant or a person residing in the dwelling-house and, in the case of ill-treatment by such a person lodging with the tenant or a sub-tenant of his, the tenant has not taken such steps as he ought reasonably to have taken for the removal of the lodger or sub-tenant.

18.14   This ground is virtually identical to Case 4 under the Rent Act 1977 (see 14.38). As with Ground 3 its scope extends to furniture provided by the landlord for use in the common parts of the building. Under both of these grounds a tenant will be able to resist a landlord's claim for possession if the damage was caused by a person living with the tenant and the tenant can show that he or she has taken such steps as he or she ought reasonably to have taken to remove the person causing the damage. In contrast to Ground 2, Ground 4 will not apply to acts done by a visitor to the premises.

Ground 5—false statement by tenant

> The tenant is the person, or one of the persons, to whom the tenancy was granted and the landlord was induced to grant the tenancy by a false statement made knowingly or recklessly by—
> (a) the tenant, or
> (b) a person acting at the tenant's instigation.

Demand for public sector housing is invariably far higher than the amount of accommodation available. Local authorities, housing associations, and other bodies try to award housing to the candidates with the greatest need. The purpose of this provision is to prevent people from jumping the queue by falsely representing their circumstances, for example where a person who was already a secure tenant of a housing association obtained local authority housing by stating in her application form that she was currently living with family and friends (*Rushcliffe BC v Watson* (1991) 24 HLR 124). **18.15**

To establish this ground the landlord will have to prove not only that a false statement was made, but also that this false statement induced the grant of the tenancy. Depending on the nature of the misrepresentation its influence on the decision may be something that can easily be inferred by the court without the need for the decision-maker to give evidence to this effect (*Waltham Forest LBC v Roberts* [2004] EWCA Civ 940, [2005] HLR 2). The false statement must be made either by a person to whom the tenancy was granted, or by a person acting at that person's instigation (*Merton LBC v Richards* [2005] EWCA Civ 639, [2005] HLR 44). **18.16**

Ground 6—premium paid on assignment by virtue of exchange

> The tenancy was assigned to the tenant, or a predecessor in title of his who is a member of his family and is residing in the dwelling-house, by an assignment made by virtue of section 92 (assignments by virtue of exchange) and a premium was paid either in connection with that assignment or the assignment which the tenant or predecessor himself made by virtue of that section.
>
> In this paragraph 'premium' means any fine or other sum and any other pecuniary consideration in addition to rent.

This provision has no counterpart in the private sector. It is designed to prevent tenants exploiting s 92 of the 1985 Act. Section 92 permits public sector tenants to exchange tenancies (see 17.76). If a tenant (or a predecessor in title who is a member of the tenant's family and still lives in the dwelling-house) obtains a lump sum for exchanging the tenancy, the landlord will be entitled to seek possession under Ground 6. **18.17**

Ground 7—misconduct by employee tenant in certain accommodation

> The dwelling-house forms part of, or is within the curtilage of, a building which, or so much of it as is held by the landlord, is held mainly for purposes other than housing purposes and consists mainly of accommodation other than housing accommodation, and—
> (a) the dwelling-house was let to the tenant or a predecessor in title of his in consequence of the tenant or predecessor being in the employment of the landlord, or of—
> a local authority
> a new town corporation
> a housing action trust
> an urban development corporation
> the development Board for Rural Wales, or
> the governors of an aided school,
> and

(b) the tenant or a person residing in the dwelling-house has been guilty of conduct such that, having regard to the purpose for which the building is used, it would not be right for him to continue in occupation of the dwelling-house.

18.18   This rather complex ground is again peculiar to the Housing Act 1985. It is designed to enable a landlord to regain possession in a specific situation, ie where an employee of the landlord (or other body specified in para (b)) who lives within some non-housing building (a good example would be a caretaker of a school or hospital) is guilty of misconduct.

Ground 8—temporary accommodation while works carried out

The dwelling-house was made available for occupation by the tenant (or a predecessor in title of his) while works were carried out on the dwelling-house which he previously occupied as his only or principal home and—

(a) the tenant (or predecessor) was a secure tenant of the other dwelling-house at the time when he ceased to occupy it as his home,

(b) the tenant (or predecessor) accepted the tenancy of the dwelling-house of which possession is sought on the understanding that he would give up occupation when, on completion of the works, the other dwelling-house was again available for occupation by him under a secure tenancy, and

(c) the works have been completed and the other dwelling-house is so available.

18.19   This ground again enables the landlord to regain possession in a specific situation, namely where a secure tenant is temporarily rehoused by the landlord while works are carried out on the tenant's original dwelling-house, and after completion of the works the tenant refuses to move back to the original dwelling-house. It should be noted that to rely upon Ground 8 the landlord will have to show that when the arrangements for temporary accommodation were made the tenant agreed to move back into the original dwelling-house once the works were completed. As with all of the grounds in Pt I, Ground 8 is subject to the requirement of reasonableness. Thus, if the scheduled works take much longer than expected and the tenant has settled into the alternative accommodation, it may not be reasonable for the landlord to seek possession.

Grounds on which the court may order possession if suitable alternative accommodation is available

Suitable alternative accommodation

18.20   The requirements regarding suitable accommodation under the Housing Act 1985, Sch 2, Pt IV are very similar to those contained in the Rent Act 1977 (see 14.08 to 14.24). Accommodation will be suitable if it consists of premises:

(a) which are to be let as a separate dwelling under a secure tenancy; or

(b) which are to be let as a separate dwelling under a protected tenancy, not being a tenancy under which the landlord might recover possession under one of the Cases in Pt II of Sch 15 to the Rent Act 1977 (cases where the court must order possession); or

(c) which are to be let as a separate dwelling under an assured tenancy which is neither an assured shorthold tenancy within the meaning of Pt I of the Housing Act 1988, nor a tenancy under which the landlord might recover possession under any of the Grounds 1 to 5 in Sch 2 to that Act (this was added by the Housing Act 1988);

and, in the opinion of the court, the accommodation is reasonably suitable to the needs of the tenant and his family (Sch 2, Pt IV, para 1).

18.21   In determining whether the alternative accommodation is suitable, a certificate from the local authority stating that it will provide suitable accommodation for the tenant by the date specified in the certificate will be conclusive evidence that suitable accommodation will be available at that date (Housing Act 1985, Sch 2, Pt IV, para 4(1)). This will not apply when the landlord is itself a local authority (para 4(3)). If there is no local authority certificate, the court will determine whether the accommodation is suitable to the needs of the tenant having regard to the factors set out in Sch 2. These factors include:

(a) the nature of the accommodation which it is the practice of the landlord to allocate to persons with similar needs;

(b) the distance of the accommodation available from the place of work or education of the tenant and of any members of his family;

(c) its distance from the home of any members of the tenant's family if proximity to it is essential to that member's or the tenant's well-being;

(d) the needs (as regards extent of accommodation) and means of the tenant and his family;

(e) the terms on which the accommodation is available and the terms of the secure tenancy;

(f) if furniture was provided by the landlord for use under the secure tenancy, whether furniture is to be provided for use in the other accommodation, and, if so, the nature of the furniture to be provided (Sch 2, Pt IV, para 2).

18.22 The Pt II grounds are the closest thing there is to a mandatory ground of possession under the Housing Act 1985. If the landlord can establish the ground and prove that alternative accommodation is available, the court must order possession. The court will not consider whether or not it is reasonable to do so.

Ground 9—dwelling-house overcrowded

The dwelling-house is overcrowded, within the meaning of Part X of the Housing Act 1985, in such circumstances as to render the occupier guilty of an offence.

Ground 10—landlord intends to demolish or reconstruct dwelling-house

The landlord intends, within a reasonable time of obtaining possession of the dwelling house—

(a) to demolish or reconstruct the building or part of the building comprising the dwelling-house, or

(b) to carry out work on that building or on land let together with, and thus treated as part of, the dwelling-house,

and cannot reasonably do so without obtaining possession of the dwelling-house.

18.23 This ground is similar to the provisions for business tenancies contained in the Landlord and Tenant Act 1954, s 30(1)(f) (see 26.157 to 26.160). Like provisions, albeit with considerably lengthier wording, have also been included in the Housing Act 1988, Sch 2 (Ground 6, see 16.39).

Ground 10A—redevelopment scheme

The dwelling-house is in an area which is the subject of a redevelopment scheme approved by the Secretary of State or the Corporation in accordance with Part V of this Schedule and the landlord intends within a reasonable time of obtaining possession to dispose of the dwelling-house in accordance with the scheme.

or

Part of the dwelling-house is in such an area and the landlord intends within a reasonable time of obtaining possession to dispose of that part in accordance with the scheme and for that purpose reasonably requires possession of the dwelling-house.

18.24   These provisions were inserted into the Housing Act 1985 by the Housing and Planning Act 1986 to enable landlords to gain vacant possession of a property in order to sell it for redevelopment. It should be noted that Sch 2, Pt V requires the landlord to consult with tenants before entering into a redevelopment scheme.

Ground 11—charitable landlord

The landlord is a charity and the tenant's continued occupation of the dwelling-house would conflict with the objects of the charity.

Grounds on which the court may order possession if it considers it reasonable to do so and suitable alternative accommodation is available

Ground 12—certain accommodation required for new employee

18.25   This ground is similar to Ground 7 in that it applies to tenants who are employees of the landlord and are occupying accommodation in a building which is not primarily used for housing purposes (such as school caretakers). However, the aim of this provision is not to enable the landlord to remove the tenant for misconduct but to permit the landlord to release the accommodation for use by a new employee. (It is similar to the Rent Act 1977, Case 8, see 14.43.)

Ground 13—accommodation required for physically disabled person

The dwelling-house has features which are substantially different from those of ordinary dwelling-houses and which are designed to make it suitable for occupation by a physically disabled person who requires accommodation of a kind provided by the dwelling-house and—
(a) there is no longer such a person residing in the dwelling-house, and
(b) the landlord requires it for occupation (whether alone or with members of his family) by such a person.

18.26   This ground enables a landlord to release accommodation which has been specially adapted or designed for occupation by a physically disabled person when the current tenant does not need such special accommodation.

Ground 14—accommodation required for persons in especially difficult circumstances

18.27   Ground 14 contains similar provisions to Ground 13, but with regard to housing provided by a registered social landlord or housing trust which lets accommodation only for occupation by persons whose circumstances make it especially difficult for them to satisfy their need for housing.

Ground 15—accommodation required for persons with special needs

18.28   Ground 15 is again a similar provision to Ground 13, but this time dealing with groups of houses let for occupation by people with special needs where a social service or a special facility is provided in close proximity to the group of houses.

Ground 15A—accommodation in England too extensive for statutory occupier

18.29   The dwelling-house is in England and the accommodation afforded by it is more extensive than is reasonably required by the tenant and—
(a) the tenancy is vested in the tenant by virtue of s 89 (succession to periodic tenancy) or s 90 (devolution of a term certain) in a case where the tenant was not the previous tenant's spouse or civil partner, and

(b) notice of the proceedings for possession was served under s 83 (or, where no such notice was served, the proceedings for possession were begun) more than six months but less than twelve months after the relevant date.

For this purpose the 'relevant date' is—

(a) the date of the previous tenant's death, or
(b) if the court so directs, the date on which, in the opinion of the court, the landlord (or in the case of joint landlords, any one of them) became aware of the previous tenant's death.

The matters to be taken into account by the court in determining whether it is reasonable to make an order on this ground include—

(a) the age of the tenant,
(b) the period (if any) during which the tenant has occupied the dwelling-house as his only or principal home, and
(c) any financial or other support given by the tenant to the previous tenant.

Ground 16—accommodation in Wales too extensive for statutory successor

The dwelling-house is in Wales, the accommodation afforded by it is more extensive than is reasonably required by the tenant and—   **18.30**

(a) the tenancy is vested in the tenant by virtue of s 89 (succession to periodic tenancy) or s 90 (devolution of term certain), the tenant being qualified to succeed by virtue of s 87(b) (members of family other than spouse), and
(b) notice of the proceedings for possession was served under s 83 (or, where no such notice was served, the proceedings for possession were begun) more than six months but less than twelve months after the relevant date.

The relevant date and the factors to be taken into account by the court are the same as those under ground 15A.

Ground 15A was inserted by the Localism Act 2011, s 162, which also amended Ground 16. These grounds provide that in certain very limited circumstances the landlord may recover possession from a tenant who is 'under-occupying' a dwelling-house. The tenant must have succeeded to the tenancy as a member of the tenant's family, but not as the deceased tenant's spouse. The tenant must either have succeeded to a periodic tenancy or inherited a fixed-term secure tenancy under the Housing Act 1985 s 90 (see 17.135). The tenant must be under-occupying at the date of the hearing, not just at the date of succession (*Wandsworth LBC v Randall* [2007] EWCA Civ 1126). The most important effect of the amendment to the old ground 16 was to allow some flexibility in respect to the time limit for serving notice in cases where the landlord was not immediately aware of the tenant's death. Under the old ground the time limits for bringing proceedings applied even where the fact of the tenant's death was deliberately kept from the landlord by the succeeding tenant (see *Newport County Council v Charles* [2008] EWCA Civ 1541, (2008) *The Times*, 11 August. It should be noted that the old law will still apply where the tenant died before 1 April 2012).   **18.31**

Grounds 15A and 16 are distinctive in that they contain specific guidance for the court in deciding whether it would be reasonable to make an order and place a heavier onus on the court to consider the circumstances of the tenant than would be the case in respect of Grounds 12 to 15. Thus, in *Bracknell Forest Borough Council v Green* [2009] EWCA Civ 238, [2009] HLR 38 it was held that a tenant's personal circumstances may outweigh the availability of   **18.32** suitable alternative accommodation and the local authority's proven and pressing need for housing stock when the court is making a decision on reasonableness under this ground.

Extended discretion of court in certain proceedings for possession

18.33   In cases where the court must be satisfied that it is reasonable to make a possession order (ie where the claim is brought under Grounds 1 to 8 or Grounds 12 to 16), the court is given considerable discretion as to the terms of the order by virtue of s 85. Section 85(1) provides that the court may adjourn the proceedings for such period or periods as it thinks fit. If an order is made the court may stay or suspend the execution of the order or postpone the date of possession for such periods as it thinks fit (s 85(2)). This power can be exercised on the making of the order or at any time before the execution of the order.

18.34   If the court decides to exercise such powers it must impose conditions with respect to the payment of arrears of rent (if any) unless it considers that to do so would cause exceptional hardship to the tenant or would be otherwise unreasonable (s 85(3)(a)). It may also impose any other conditions as it thinks fit (s 85(3)(b)). If these conditions are complied with then the court may discharge or rescind the order for possession (s 85(4)).

18.35   Where a dwelling-house is occupied by the tenant's spouse or civil partner or former spouse or civil partner who has matrimonial home rights under Pt IV of the Family Law Act 1996 then as long as that spouse or former spouse remains in occupation he or she will have similar rights to an adjournment, stay, suspension, or postponement. These provisions are also extended to a cohabitant or former cohabitant, provided an order is in force under s 36 of the Family Law Act 1996 conferring rights on the cohabitant or former cohabitant, by virtue of s 85(5A) of the Civil Partnership Act 2004.

Postponement of the possession order, or suspension of execution

18.36   Under s 85(2) the court may make any of the following orders:

(a)   an order for possession that takes effect only (but automatically) in the event of a future breach;

(b)   an order for possession that takes effect immediately (or on a fixed date) but is only to be executed in the event of a future breach; or

(c)   an order that has no fixed date for possession but allows the landlord to apply for a date to be fixed in the event of a breach.

18.37   The type of order made can be of considerable importance. Prior to the commencement of Sch 11 to the Housing and Regeneration Act 2008 on 20 May 2009 a tenancy was deemed to come to an end on the date the tenant was ordered to give up possession even if he or she remained in occupation (Housing Act 1985, s 82(2)). This meant that if the court made an order for possession but suspended the order or postponed the date on which possession was to take effect for so long as the tenant complied with the terms of the order and the terms of the tenancy, the tenancy would continue unless and until the tenant breached a term. Once the tenant breached a term the possession order would take effect and the tenancy would automatically terminate. The tenant became what was known as a 'tolerated trespasser' and no longer had any of the rights of a tenant (eg the right to buy). This only applied where the tenancy was a secure tenancy. Assured tenancies do not terminate until the tenant delivers up possession of the property (*Knowsley Housing Trust v White* [2008] UKHL 70).

18.38   Prior to 20 May 2009, therefore, if an order was made in the terms set out in (a) or (b) (18.36) any breach of a term could or would result in the tenant losing all statutory protection and occupying the property only as a tolerated trespasser. An order in the terms set out in (c) would not have this result as there is no date given for possession.

This difficulty has been addressed to a large extent by Sch 11, para 2(3) to the Housing and **18.39** Regeneration Act 2008 which substituted a new s 82(2) into the 1985 Act. The new section provided that the tenancy will only end when the possession order is executed (ie where the tenant is evicted). The 2008 Act also provided that all former tolerated trespassers had their secure tenancies automatically reinstated as from 20 May 2009 (see 18.44). Nevertheless, care must still be taken with the form of order made, as there will be repercussions for both the landlord and the tenant if the intention of the court is not made clear.

Obtaining a warrant for possession

An order made in the terms set out in (a) or (b) above (18.36) gives the landlord the right **18.40** to apply for a warrant for possession as soon as the tenant breaches the terms of the order. The tenant has no right to defend the allegation that he or she has breached the order. In rent arrears cases, where non-payment is a matter of record, this may not be problematic. However, in cases where the alleged further breach may be disputed by the tenant (eg an allegation of nuisance) the tenant should normally be allowed to defend the allegations before a warrant is issued (*Wandsworth LBC v Whibley* [2008] EWCA Civ 1259). In such cases, therefore, the order made should be in the terms of order (c), requiring the landlord to apply to the court to fix a date for possession. As such an application is normally considered by a judge simply reviewing the evidence on paper, in complicated cases it may be desirable for the order also to contain the proviso that the application to fix a date should be considered at a full hearing so the court is able to test both parties' evidence.

If the order does not require the landlord to apply to fix a date for possession before apply- **18.41** ing for a warrant for possession the tenant will have no notice of the application for a warrant. The landlord must, however, give the tenant notice of eviction. This notice must inform the tenant that a warrant has been issued and give the date fixed for the eviction. The tenant's remedy is then to make an application to the court, before the date fixed for eviction, to postpone the date of possession or suspend the order under s 85(2).

Discharging the possession order

The order suspending or postponing possession may include a provision whereby the order **18.42** is automatically discharged once certain criteria have been met (for example, when the tenant has paid off all of the rent arrears). If the order itself does not make such a provision it is open to the tenant who feels that he or she has met all of his or her obligations under the order to apply to the court to have the order varied under s 84(2) or discharged under s 85(4) (*Porter v Shepherds Bush Housing Association*, as part of the judgment in *Knowsley Housing Trust v White* [2008] UKHL 70, [2009] 2 WLR 78).

Regaining tenant status

Prior to 20 May 2009

A former secure tenant who lost his or her status as a result of a possession order being **18.43** made was able to apply to the court to discharge the possession order (thereby reinstating the original tenancy) or may have been granted a new tenancy by his or her landlord. If the court discharged the possession order the reinstated tenancy was deemed to have been continuous with the original tenancy and the tenant retained all of his or her rights and obligations under that tenancy, including those accruing during the period when he or she was a tolerated trespasser (*Knowsley Housing Trust v White* [2008] UKHL 70 at [121]). If a new tenancy was granted by the landlord, however, these rights were lost (see 18.48).

After 20 May 2009

18.44   The Housing and Regeneration Act 2008, Sch 11, Pt 2 provided that from 20 May 2009 all remaining tolerated trespassers would be granted a new replacement tenancy, provided:

(a)   the tenant had occupied the property as his or her only or principal home at all times during the 'termination period' (the period where he or she was a tolerated trespasser);

(b)   the original landlord was still able to let the premises;

(c)   the tenant had not entered into a new tenancy agreement with the landlord in the meantime (Sch 11, para 16(1)).

18.45   The replacement tenancy was subject to the terms of any existing possession order unless and until it was varied or discharged (Sch 11, para 20).

18.46   The replacement tenancy would automatically come into effect on 20 May 2009 (the commencement date of this part of the Act). The terms and conditions of the original tenancy applied to the new tenancy (including any agreement for terms that were entered into during the termination period) (Sch 11, para 18).

18.47   It should be noted that the replacement tenancy was not a continuation of the original tenancy. There would have been a period between the termination of the old tenancy (on the date possession was ordered) and the commencement of the new tenancy, where the tenant occupied the property with no rights. In theory this meant that the tenant had no right to sue for any breach of obligation, for example disrepair, occurring during this period. This problem is addressed by Sch 11, para 21(3), which provides that in proceedings for a relevant claim the court can order that the new and original tenancies be treated as being the same, uninterrupted tenancy. Paragraph 21(2) provides that the two tenancies will be treated as being continuous for the purposes of succession rights and qualification periods for the right to buy.

18.48   The tenant who was granted a new tenancy by virtue of the Housing and Regeneration Act 2008 will, therefore, be in a much better position than a former tolerated trespasser who was granted a new tenancy by his or her landlord prior to 20 May 2009. Such a tenant will have lost any contractual or statutory rights during the period where he or she was a tolerated trespasser.

Successor landlords

18.49   The Housing and Regeneration Act 2008 provides for the automatic granting of a new tenancy only where the original landlord continues to let the premises, and does not allow for the situation where there has been a change of landlord during the termination period. In many cases the new landlord will have granted a new tenancy. Where this has not occurred, the Housing (Replacement of Terminated Tenancies) (Successor Landlords) (England) Order 2009, SI 2009/1262 and the Housing (Replacement of Terminated Tenancies) (Successor Landlords (Wales) Order 2009, WSI 2009/1260 provide for new replacement tenancies to be granted by the new landlord.

Type of tenancy to be granted

18.50   The type of tenancy granted under the Act will depend on the nature of the original tenancy and the status of the landlord at the date of the new grant:

(a) Where the original tenancy was a secure tenancy the new tenancy will also be secure unless the new landlord is a registered social landlord (who cannot grant secure tenancies), in which case the new tenancy will be assured.

(b) If the original tenancy was an introductory tenancy (see 17.19 to 17.39) the new tenancy will be an introductory tenancy unless the local authority landlord has revoked its introductory scheme, in which case it will be a secure tenancy, or the new landlord is a registered social landlord, in which case it will be an assured shorthold tenancy.

(c) If the original tenancy was a demoted tenancy (see 17.114 to 17.124) the new tenancy will be a demoted tenancy unless the new landlord is a registered social landlord or a housing association unable to apply for a demoted tenancy, in which case it will be an assured shorthold tenancy.

The duration provisions of the new demoted or introductory tenancy will apply in full **18.51** from the commencement of the replacement tenancy, rather than being the balance remaining from the original tenancy.

Possession procedure

CPR Part 55 and PD 55 apply equally to possession proceedings by public sector or private **18.52** sector landlords (see 16.74 to 16.76). Landlords must ensure that the procedure set out in Part 55 and the Practice Direction are followed.

Pre-action protocol for rent arrears

A pre-action protocol for possession claims based on rent arrears came into effect in **18.53** October 2006. It applies only to social landlords (local authorities, housing action trusts, and registered social landlords) contemplating bringing possession proceedings solely on grounds of rent arrears. The protocol applies to all tenancies except long leases. It does not apply to claims where there is no security of tenure. The protocol is discussed in more detail in Chapter 16 (see 16.72).

Bankruptcy of a secure tenant

A secure tenancy does not form part of the bankrupt tenant's estate and will not automati- **18.54** cally vest in the trustee in bankruptcy (Insolvency Act 1986, s 283(3A), inserted by the Housing Act 1988, s 117(1)). However, the trustee can reverse this position by serving notice in writing on the bankrupt tenant informing him or her that the tenancy will vest in the trustee as part of the estate (Insolvency Act 1986, s 308A, inserted by the Housing Act 1988, s 117(2)).

The making of a possession order against a bankrupt tenant on the ground of rent arrears **18.55** is not a remedy against the property of a bankrupt and is not precluded by the Insolvency Act 1986 (*Harlow DC v Hall* [2006] EWCA Civ 156).

Disability discrimination

The Equality Act 2010 imposes a duty on all landlords, both in the public and private **18.56** sector, not to discriminate against their tenants (or prospective tenants) on the grounds of a protected characteristic. Protected characteristics include sex, race, religion, and disability (Equality Act 2010, s 4). The full impact of the Equality Act on landlord and tenant relationships is beyond the scope of this book. Disability discrimination claims, however, are not uncommon in defences to possession proceedings and will become more important under the 2010 Act, which makes it easier for disabled tenants to show that the landlord's decision to bring proceedings is potentially discriminatory.

18.57 The Equality Act 2010 provides that it is unlawful for anyone who has the right to let or manage premises to discriminate against the occupier or potential occupier of those premises on the grounds that the occupier is a disabled person (ss 32 to 35). A disabled person is 'a person with a physical or mental impairment which has a substantial and long-term effect on his abilities to carry out day-to-day activities' (s 6).

18.58 Section 15 of the Act provides that:

(1) A person (A) discriminates against a disabled person (B) if—
  (a) A treats B differently because of something arising in consequence of B's disability, and
  (b) A cannot show that the treatment is a proportionate means of achieving a legitimate end.

(2) Subsection (1) does not apply if A did not know and could not reasonably have been expected to know, that B had the disability.

18.59 Discrimination may occur if a landlord takes the decision to evict a tenant for a reason arising as a consequence of the tenant's disability. Where the tenant suffers from a mental impairment it may be the case that this impairment has led to possession proceedings being brought, for example because the disability causes him or her to engage in anti-social behaviour, or because it makes it difficult for him or her to manage his or her finances and therefore pay the rent on time. It should be noted that s 15 presents a real change to disability discrimination legislation. Under the old law (Disability Discrimination Act 1995), in order to claim discrimination, a disabled person who had been evicted would have to show that the landlord would not have brought possession proceedings against a non-disabled person who had behaved in the same way. Obviously, in cases where the tenant had breached the terms of the tenancy it was extremely easy for the landlord to show that he would have treated the non-disabled tenant in exactly the same way and so escape liability (See *Lewisham LBC v Malcolm* [2008] UKHL 43, a case in which the tenant, who suffered from schizophrenia, unlawfully sub-let his flat because of his condition). By removing the need for a non-disabled comparator the 2010 Act has made it much more realistic for a disabled person to raise a claim of discrimination. It is, of course, open to the landlord to show that the decision to evict was legitimate and proportionate (for example to protect other tenants, or maintain the property). A landlord who did not know, and could not have known, of the disability will be provided with a defence. However, once the landlord does know of the disability (for example, if he or she is informed of it in a tenant's defence to a possession claim) the landlord may be said to be discriminating against the tenant if he or she continues with the possession claim.

18.60 Where proceedings have been brought against a tenant because he or she has breached a term of the tenancy it may also be possible to defend the claim for possession by arguing that the term itself was unduly onerous or unfair on the tenant because of the tenant's disability. In such a case a tenant could require the landlord to make a reasonable adjustment to the letting agreement by altering or removing the term (Equality Act 2010, Sch 4, para 2 and s 20). An obvious example would be where a term in a lease prohibits the tenant from keeping a dog. A tenant who loses his or her sight and is given a guide dog would be disadvantaged by such a term. Provided that the tenant had notified the landlord of the difficulty, and requested that the term be altered or modified, the tenant may be able to prevent the landlord from relying on the term in possession proceedings. It would of course be open to the landlord to argue that the refusal to alter the term was reasonable.

A person's disability will also be of relevance where the court is deciding whether to make **18.61** an order for possession (*Manchester City Council v Romano and Samari* [2004] EWCA Civ 834, [2005] 1 WLR 2775; *Lewisham LBC v Malcolm*, 18.59), for example where the court is deciding whether it would be reasonable to make an order where possession is sought under Ground 2 (see 18.07) against a tenant who has behavioural problems which arise as a result of a long-term mental impairment, or where the court is deciding the issue of proportionality in response to a claim under Sch 1, Article 8 of the Human Rights Act 1998 (see 18.62 to 18.68).

Possession proceedings and the Human Rights Act 1998

Since the Human Rights Act 1998 came into force a number of challenges under Sch 1, **18.62** article 8 have been made by secure tenants facing possession proceedings brought by local authorities or public sector landlords. Article 8 guarantees the right of respect for the home. Where they exercise their functions as 'public bodies', public sector landlords must have regard to their tenants' rights under this article. A registered social landlord may be considered to be a public body if its housing management and allocation functions are deemed to be public functions. Its actions when carrying out those functions can then be challenged under Article 8. Whether the social landlord's housing functions are deemed to be public functions will depend on factors such as the amount of public subsidy it receives and the degree of assistance it provides to local authorities in achieving the local authority's statutory duties and objectives (*R (Weaver) v London & Quadrant Housing Trust* [2009] EWCA Civ 587). The public sector landlord who wishes to remove a tenant, or any other occupier, from his or her home must be able to justify this action under Article 8(2).

Article 8(2) allows interference with an Article 8 right if it is: **18.63**

in accordance with the law and is necessary in a democratic society in the interests of national security, public safety or the economic well-being of the country, for the prevention of disorder or crime, for the protection of health or morals, or for the protection of the rights and freedom of others.

An occupier of land may invoke Article 8 as a defence in possession proceedings against a **18.64** public sector landlord if he or she can show either:

(a) that the law or procedure which allows the court to make a possession order is incompatible with Article 8; or
(b) that the decision to bring possession proceedings was not a proportionate means of achieving a legitimate aim.

In respect of the first ground the courts have so far taken the view that the law and pro- **18.65** cedure for possession set out in the statutory codes is sufficient to ensure that possession proceedings will satisfy the conditions of Article 8(2). (See *Lambeth LBC v Howard* (2001) 33 HLR 636; *Kay v Lambeth LBC, Leeds City Council v Price* [2006] UKHL 10, [2006] 2 WLR 570; *Doherty and others v Birmingham City Council* [2008] UKHL 57.)

The second ground has developed following a number of European Court of Human **18.66** Rights (ECtHR) decisions, culminating in *Kay v UK* (App No. 37341/06 (2010)). Prior to these decisions the UK courts had taken the view that an occupier could only challenge a decision to bring possession proceedings if it was a decision that no local authority could reasonably reach. The court was not required to take the personal circumstances of the occupier into account when assessing the reasonableness of the local authority's decision (see *Kay v Lambeth LBC*, 18.65 above). The ECtHR has, however, ruled that this was not sufficient to protect the occupier's rights under Article 8 of the European Convention. The ECtHR based its rulings on the principle that:

> ...the loss of one's home is the most extreme form of interference with the right to respect for the home. Any person at risk of an interference of this magnitude should in principle be able to have the proportionality of the measure determined by an independent tribunal in light of the relevant principles under article 8 of the convention, notwithstanding that, under domestic law, the right of occupation has come to an end. (*Kay v UK*, para 68)

18.67   Following these decisions the Supreme Court has provided further guidance on how courts are now to address Article 8 challenges brought by occupiers threatened with possession proceedings (see *Manchester City Council v Pinnock* [2010] UKSC 45, [2010] 3 WLR 1441; and *Hounslow LBC v Powell; Leeds City Council v Hall; Birmingham City Council v Frisby* [2011] UKSC 8). A tenant or occupier of land may now challenge the public sector landlord's decision to bring possession proceedings or execute a warrant for possession by arguing that, in the circumstances, the decision was not proportionate. The Supreme Court in *Powell* made it clear that it will be only in a small minority of cases that the court will be expected to look at the proportionality of the public sector landlord's actions: 'The court will only have to consider whether the making of a possession order is proportionate if the issue has been raised by the occupier and it has crossed the high threshold of being seriously arguable' (*per* Lord Hope at para 33). If the court then decides that the issue does need to be considered the landlord will be required to justify its reasons for seeking the possession order. It is expected that the courts will only interfere with the public sector landlord's decisions in connection with the legitimate management of its housing stock if the occupier is particularly vulnerable as a result of mental or physical illness or disability (*Manchester City Council v Pinnock*).

18.68   If the court is satisfied that the landlord's decision was not a proportionate means of achieving a legitimate aim (for example because its need to recover possession of a particular premises was not as pressing as a vulnerable tenant's need to remain in possession of premises in which he or she feels secure) the court may decide:

(a)   to grant an extended period before possession is ordered (although following *Manchester City Council v Pinnock* it seems that this must still be subject to the six weeks' maximum provided by s 89 of the Housing Act 1980 where this applies, see 16.17); or

(b)   to suspend the order for possession on terms; or

(c)   not to grant the order for possession at all.

KEY DOCUMENTS

Housing Act 1985

Civil Procedure Rules 1998

Form N5—Claims for possession of property

Form N11R—Defence form (rented residential premises)

Printed copies of all legislation can be ordered from The Stationery Office at <http://www.tsoshop.co.uk>. All legislation from 1988 onwards and most pre-1988 primary legislation is available online at <http://www.legislation.gov.uk>.

Court forms are available online from the HM Courts and Tribunals Service at <http://www.justice.gov.uk/forms/hmcts>.

The Civil Procedure Rules are available online from <http://www.justice.gov.uk/courts/procedure-rules>.

19

PROTECTION FROM EVICTION

A INTRODUCTION

Not every residential occupier will fall within the protection of one of the statutory codes **19.01** we have discussed in the preceding chapters. The occupier may be a licensee rather than a tenant, or, even if a tenant, he or she may fall within one of the categories excluded from statutory protection. The Protection from Eviction Act 1977 therefore provides a minimum standard of protection for the majority of residential occupiers. This protection is provided in a variety of ways. First, the 1977 Act defines the criminal offences of unlawful eviction and harassment. Secondly, it prevents a landlord from forfeiting a tenancy by peaceable re-entry. Thirdly, it prohibits a landlord or licensor from recovering possession from a residential occupier without taking court proceedings. Lastly, where a landlord or licensor seeks to terminate a tenancy or licence by means of a notice to quit, the Act provides that that notice to quit must be in the correct form and must give at least four weeks' notice.

B CRIMINAL LIABILITY

The Protection from Eviction Act 1977, s 1 creates two offences: one of unlawfully depriv- **19.02** ing the occupier of occupation of the premises and the second of harassment. These offences may be committed against a 'residential occupier', which term is defined by s 1(1):

> (1)   In this section 'residential occupier', in relation to any premises, means a person occupying the premises as a residence, whether under a contract or by virtue of any enactment or rule of law giving him the right to remain in occupation or restricting the right of any other person to recover possession of the premises.

This is a broad definition. It will include tenants and contractual licensees throughout the **19.03** currency of the contractual period because they are occupying 'under a contract'. It will include statutory tenants under the Rent Act 1977 because they are occupying 'by virtue of an enactment'. When read in conjunction with s 3 (see 19.18 to 19.21), it will also include certain tenants and licensees even after the contractual period has ended, because s 3 prevents a landlord or licensor from recovering possession otherwise than by an order of the court. Until such an order is obtained the former tenant or licensee will be occupying by virtue of an enactment 'restricting the right of any other person to recover possession of the premises'.

19.04   Section 1 will protect only persons who are occupying the premises as a residence. It will not protect a tenant who has sub-let the whole of the premises, nor will it protect a person who is occupying the premises for non-residential purposes. There is, however, no requirement that the premises should be occupied as the occupier's only or principal home. The phrase 'occupying as a residence' has already been discussed in the context of the Rent Act 1977 (see 13.97 to 13.99).

Unlawful deprivation of occupation

19.05   The Protection from Eviction Act 1977, s 1(2) provides that:

> (2)   If any person unlawfully deprives the residential occupier of any premises of his occupation of the premises or any part thereof, or attempts to do so, he shall be guilty of an offence unless he proves that he believed, and had reasonable cause to believe, that the residential occupier had ceased to reside in the premises.

19.06   The application of this offence is unrestricted; it can be committed by 'any person', whether or not that person is the occupier's landlord or licensor. To amount to a deprivation of occupation the act done must have 'the character of an eviction' (*R v Yuthiwattana* (1984) 128 SJ 661, CA). Where a person enters the occupier's house while the occupier is out, changes the locks, and puts the occupier's belongings on the street, this will almost certainly be a deprivation of occupation. However, where a tenant lost his key and the landlord refused to replace it, with the consequence that the tenant was unable to get back into his flat for a day and a night, the court held that this did not constitute an offence under s 1(2) (*R v Yuthiwattana*).

19.07   The act done must also be unlawful. This will virtually always be the case, because ss 2 and 3 of the Act (see below) prohibit a landlord or licensor from seeking to recover possession without a court order.

19.08   If the person accused of depriving the occupier of occupation can establish that he or she believed (with reasonable cause) that the residential occupier had ceased to reside in the premises then he or she will not be guilty of an offence; the burden of proof is on the defendant to establish this belief.

Harassment

19.09   Where the acts done by the landlord, licensor, or other person do not amount to an unlawful deprivation of occupation, they may still amount to harassment under s 1(3) or (3A) of the 1977 Act.

19.10   Section 1(3) provides that:

> (3)   If any person with intent to cause the residential occupier of any premises—
>   (a)   to give up the occupation of the premises or any part thereof; or
>   (b)   to refrain from exercising any right or pursuing any remedy in respect of the premises of part thereof;
> does acts likely to interfere with the peace or comfort of the residential occupier or members of his household, or persistently withdraws or withholds services reasonably required for the occupation of the premises as a residence he shall be guilty of an offence.

Section 1(3A) was added by s 29 of the Housing Act 1988 (which also substituted the word **19.11** 'likely' for 'calculated' in s 1(3)) and provides that:

> (3A) Subject to subsection (3B) below, the landlord of a residential occupier or an agent of the landlord shall be guilty of an offence if—
>   (a) he does acts likely to interfere with the peace or comfort of the residential occupier or members of his household, or
>   (b) he persistently withdraws or withholds services reasonably required for the occupation of the premises in question as a residence,
> and (in either case) he knows or has reasonable cause to believe, that that conduct is likely to cause the residential occupier to give up the occupation of the whole or part of the premises or to refrain from exercising any right or pursuing any remedy in respect of the whole or part of the premises.

Section 1(3B) provides: **19.12**

> (3B) A person shall not be guilty of an offence under subsection (3A) above if he proves he had reasonable grounds for doing the acts or withdrawing or withholding the services in question.

The two offences are broadly similar: both will be committed where a person seeks either **19.13** to get the occupier to give up occupation of the whole or part of the premises, or where a person seeks to prevent the occupier from exercising some right in respect of the property (for example, applying to a rent officer or a rent assessment committee) or pursuing a remedy. In both cases the acts done to achieve these aims can be either acts likely to interfere with the occupier's (or members of the occupier's household) peace or comfort, or persistent withdrawal of services (such as gas, water, and electricity). Neither section demands that the acts themselves have to be unlawful (*R v Burke* [1991] 1 AC 135).

The differences between the two subsections lie, first, in the identity of the person who can **19.14** commit the offence and, secondly, in the degree of intention required. Under s 1(3), 'any person' can commit the offence, while s 1(3A) applies only to the landlord of the residential occupier or his or her agent. Under s 1(3), the prosecution must show that the acts or the withdrawal of services were done with intent to cause the occupier to give up occupation or to refrain from exercising a right or pursuing a remedy. Under s 1(3A), it is necessary to show only that the landlord knew or had reasonable cause to believe that the conduct was likely to have this effect.

Penalties

If a person is found guilty of any of the three offences contained in s 1, he or she will be **19.15** liable on summary conviction to a fine, or to imprisonment for up to six months, or both. On conviction on indictment he or she will be liable to a fine, or to imprisonment for up to two years, or both (s 1(4)).

Civil remedies

The fact that criminal proceedings are taken under s 1 of the 1977 Act will not prejudice **19.16** the right of the occupier to seek a civil remedy (s 1(5)). Indeed, it will be necessary for the occupier to bring civil proceedings if he or she wishes to claim damages as this remedy is not available under the Protection from Eviction Act. It is not necessary for an act to be a breach of covenant or a tort for it to amount to an offence under s 1, but in many cases any attempt by a landlord to deprive a tenant of occupation or to harass a tenant will also be a breach of covenant for quiet enjoyment. In such a case the tenant will be able to obtain damages and possibly an injunction; in some cases he or she may even be able to claim exemplary or additional damages (see 5.23 to 5.31 on remedies for breach of covenant for quiet enjoyment). Where, as a result of harassment by the landlord, a tenant gives up occupation of the premises, the landlord will also be liable for the statutory tort of unlawful eviction under s 27 of the Housing Act 1988.

C FORFEITURE UNDER THE PROTECTION FROM EVICTION ACT 1977

19.17 The Protection from Eviction Act 1977, s 2 requires a landlord of residential premises who has reserved a right of re-entry or forfeiture in the lease to exercise that right by means of proceedings in the court. Section 2 will apply where any person (not necessarily the tenant) is lawfully residing in the premises or part of them. Thus, in the case of residential premises, the landlord is precluded from exercising a right of re-entry or forfeiture by means of peaceable re-entry (see 11.21 to 11.23).

D RECOVERY OF POSSESSION UNDER THE PROTECTION FROM EVICTION ACT 1977

19.18 At common law, when a tenancy or a licence comes to an end the landlord or licensor is entitled to re-enter and take possession of the premises. As we have seen in the preceding chapters, many occupiers will fall within the protection of a statutory code which will effectively prevent a landlord (and in some cases a licensor) from regaining possession after the original contractual term has come to an end. However, some occupiers, in particular licensees, may find themselves ineligible for statutory protection under one of the codes. In such a case s 3 of the 1977 Act provides a very important, if basic, level of protection. It will not permit the landlord or licensor to recover possession of the premises except by proceedings of the court.

19.19 Section 3 applies where a tenancy or licence has come to an end and the occupier continues to reside in the premises or part of them (s 3(1)). It will not apply to statutorily protected tenancies (as defined in s 8), or to tenancies or licences which fall into one of the excluded categories. These excluded categories are contained in s 3A, which was introduced into the 1977 Act by s 31 of the Housing Act 1988 which came into force on 15 January 1989.

19.20 Section 3 will therefore apply to:

(a) all tenancies entered into before 15 January 1989 (or pursuant to a contract made before that date);
(b) tenancies entered into after 15 January 1989 apart from excluded tenancies;
(c) licences, whenever created, apart from excluded licences.

19.21 A tenancy or licence will be excluded if:

(a) under its terms the occupier shares any accommodation with the landlord or licensor and immediately before the grant and also at the time it comes to an end the landlord or licensor occupied the shared accommodation as his or her only or principal home (s 3A(2));
(b) under its terms the occupier shares any accommodation with a member of the landlord's or licensor's family and immediately before the grant and also at the time it comes to an end the member of the landlord's or licensor's family occupied the shared

accommodation as his or her only or principal home and immediately before the grant and also at the time it comes to an end the landlord or licensor occupied as his or her only or principal home premises in the same building as the shared accommodation and that building is not a purpose-built block of flats (s 3A(3));

(c) it was granted as a temporary expedient to a person who entered the premises in question or any other premises as a trespasser (s 3A(6));

(d) it confers on the tenant or licensee the right to occupy the premises for a holiday only (s 3A(7)(a));

(e) it is not granted for money or money's worth (s 3A(7)(b));

(f) it confers rights of occupation in a hostel (as defined by s 622 of the Housing Act 1985) provided by certain public bodies (s 3A(8));

(g) it is granted in order to provide accommodation under Pt VI of the Immigration and Asylum Act 1999 (s 3A(7A)).

A licence will also be excluded if it is granted to a resident of an accommodation centre provided under the Nationality, Immigration and Asylum Act 2002, s 32.

E NOTICE TO QUIT

Section 5 of the Protection from Eviction Act 1977 provides that no notice to quit given by either a landlord or tenant will be valid unless: **19.22**

(a) it is in writing and contains such information as may be prescribed; and
(b) it is given not less than four weeks before the date on which it is to take effect.

These provisions will also apply to licensors and licencees (s 5(1A)). They will not, however, apply to excluded licences or to excluded tenancies made after 15 January 1989, unless entered into pursuant to a contract made before that date (s 5(1B)). **19.23**

These excluded categories are defined by s 3A (see 19.19 to 19.21). The nature of a notice to quit is dealt with in detail in Chapter 10 (10.35 to 10.53). **19.24**

KEY DOCUMENTS

Protection from Eviction Act 1977

Printed copies of all legislation can be ordered from The Stationery Office at <http://www.tsoshop. co.uk>. All legislation from 1988 onwards and most pre-1988 primary legislation is available online at <http://www.legislation.gov.uk>.

20

REGULATION OF RESIDENTIAL PREMISES— 1. THE PRIVATE SECTOR

A INTRODUCTION

Whilst the statutory codes we have considered in Chapters 12 to 18 provide a certain **20.01**
amount of protection to the tenant they are of very limited effect when it comes to ensuring that there is sufficient, good quality rented accommodation available to meet national

demand. Recent legislation has attempted to address this difficulty by establishing a more coherent framework to enable local authorities and government bodies to monitor and control the provision and quality of housing in both the public and private sectors.

20.02   This chapter considers the provisions contained in the Housing Act 2004 concerning the enforcement of housing standards in the private sector and the regulations concerning the management of houses in multiple occupation (HMOs).

20.03   The provisions of the 2004 Act impose an active duty on each local housing authority to monitor private sector housing conditions in its area. The local housing authority must develop an overall strategy to deal with problems such as: unsafe premises; bad management practices by landlords; a lack of available housing; and anti-social behaviour by tenants. The emphasis of the Act is on solving community problems, rather than simply addressing the individual rights of tenants. The Act provides the local housing authority with a new range of powers that it can use in order to implement its housing strategy. These include: the ability to enforce remedial action where premises fall below an acceptable standard; the power to require residential premises in certain areas to be licensed; the ability to make management orders in respect of unmanaged property; and the ability to facilitate the return of empty property to the rented housing market. The Act occasionally prescribes circumstances in which a local housing authority must take action (for example, it sets out conditions in which a house in multiple occupation must be licensed). Generally, however, the purpose of the Act is to allow the local housing authority a number of different options, each of which can be considered when deciding how to address a particular housing problem.

B   ENFORCEMENT OF HOUSING STANDARDS

20.04   The Housing Act 2004 introduced a new system under which local housing authorities (LHAs) must monitor the condition of residential premises in their area with a view to identifying hazards to the occupier or potential occupier. The Act then gives the LHA new powers to enforce remedial action where housing conditions are below an acceptable standard. The Act is extremely widely drafted. Its provisions refer to almost any type of property where a person could or does live, and address hazards caused by deficiencies in the property arising from almost any cause.

Residential premises

20.05   Residential premises for the purpose of the Act are defined as a dwelling, an HMO (see 20.41 to 20.47), or any common parts of a building containing one or more flats (s 1(4)).

Relevant hazards

20.06   A hazard is described as 'any risk of harm to the health or safety of an actual or potential occupier of a dwelling' (s 2). The risk may result from a deficiency in the premises themselves, or from the condition of a building or land in the vicinity of the dwelling. The cause of the deficiency may be 'the construction of the building, an absence of maintenance or repair, or otherwise' (s 2(1)).

Review of housing conditions

20.07   An LHA must keep the housing conditions in its area under review with a view to identifying any action that needs to be taken (s 3(1)). If an LHA becomes aware of any potential hazard, either through its own monitoring process or because it receives an 'official' complaint (this must be a complaint from a justice of the peace or parish or community council, s 4(3)), the LHA must carry out an inspection of the premises (s 4).

Inspection and assessment

The inspection is carried out by a proper officer of the LHA. The manner in which the **20.08** inspection is to be carried out and the method of identifying hazards is set out in the Housing Health and Safety Rating System (England) Regulations 2005, SI 2005/3208.

The inspector must first identify any matter that might cause a hazard. Schedule 1 to the **20.09** Regulations contains a list of 29 possible matters that might create such a risk. These cover a wide range and include: damp and mould growth, exposure to carbon monoxide, overcrowding, risk of entry by intruders, explosions, and structural collapse.

The Regulations provide a scoring system whereby the inspector can grade the hazard. The **20.10** seriousness of the hazard is assessed in relation to its possible effect on an occupier rather than in relation to the defect in the condition of the premises. The effect of a hazard may be physiological, psychological, a cause of infection, or a cause of accidents.

The inspector must identify the type of harm that might be a reasonably foreseeable result **20.11** of the hazard. Schedule 2 to the Regulations sets out four classes of harm. Class I, the most serious, includes risk of death from any cause, and permanent paralysis; class IV, the least serious, includes occasional severe discomfort, and regular serious coughs and colds.

Having identified the hazard and the possible class of harm it might cause, the inspector **20.12** must then assess the overall seriousness of the hazard. To do this the inspector must assess the likelihood of the hazard causing such harm to an occupier within the next 12 months. The inspector must consider the risk not only to the current occupier but also to a range of possible occupiers of different ages. The inspector chooses from a range of percentage likelihoods: the least likely being less than 1 in 4,200; the most likely being more than 1 in 1.5.

The inspector is then supplied with a mathematical formula with which to convert his or **20.13** her assessment into a final score. The score will fall into a band from A to J. A hazard falling within bands A, B, or C will be classed as a category 1 hazard; a hazard falling within bands D to J will be a category 2 hazard.

If, following the inspection, the inspector is of the opinion that a category 1 or 2 hazard **20.14** exists on the premises, he or she must submit a written report to the local authority without delay. The authority must consider the report as soon as possible.

Deciding on enforcement action

Category 1 hazards

If, on consideration of the inspector's report, the LHA considers that a category 1 hazard **20.15** exists on any residential premises, it must take appropriate enforcement action (s 5). The options open to it are to:

(a) serve an improvement notice (s 11) (see 20.19);
(b) make a prohibition order (s 28) (see 20.21);
(c) serve a hazard awareness notice (s 28) (see 20.29);
(d) take emergency remedial action (s 40) (see 20.30);
(e) make an emergency prohibition order (s 43) (see 20.34);

(f) make a demolition order under the Housing Act 1985, s 265 (see 20.36);

(g) declare the area in which the premises are situated a clearance area by virtue of the Housing Act 1985, s 289 (see 20.38).

Category 2 hazards

20.16 If a category 2 hazard exists the LHA has the power to act, but is not under a duty to do so. The options are those at (a), (b), (c), (f), or (g) above (20.15).

20.17 In the case of both categories of hazard, the LHA can only take up one option at one time. It cannot, therefore, serve an improvement notice and a prohibition notice at the same time. If, however, it has taken one course of action, and this has not had the desired result, it may subsequently choose another option or serve a further notice or order (s 5(4) and (5)).

Statement of reasons

20.18 Having decided on the course of action to be taken, the LHA must prepare a statement of its reasons. This should include an explanation of why a particular method of enforcement has been chosen.

Improvement notices

20.19 The improvement notice and the statement of reasons must be served on the person liable for the dwelling (the owner or manager of the property). The improvement notice must specify:

(a) the category and nature of the hazard or hazards complained of;

(b) the remedial action that is to be taken;

(c) the deficiency that gives rise to the hazard;

(d) the premises in which remedial action is to be taken and the nature of that action;

(e) the date the remedial action is to be started by (not less than 28 days from service of the notice);

(f) details of the right to appeal against the notice.

20.20 The remedial action specified must be such as to reduce the hazard to less than a category 1 hazard, but may extend further than this. The improvement notice becomes operative 21 days from the date on which it is served.

Prohibition orders

20.21 A prohibition order may prohibit the use of the whole of the residential premises, any flat or flats within the dwelling, and any common parts (s 20(3)). It may prohibit use for all purposes, or for specified purposes (s 22(4)). In particular it may prohibit its use by more than a particular number of people, or by a particular description of person (s 22(5)).

20.22 As with an improvement notice, the order, accompanied by the statement of reasons, must be served on the relevant parties. It must specify the nature of the hazard, the deficiency that causes it, and its location. The order must then specify the remedial action to be taken in order for the prohibition notice to be revoked (s 22(2)). It must also inform the recipient of his or her right to appeal. The prohibition order becomes operative 28 days from the date it was made.

Compliance with a notice or order

20.23 As we have seen, the Act makes provision for a date when the order or notice becomes operative (the 'operative time'). The relevance of this date is that it marks the point when, if the notice or order has not been suspended or appealed, sanctions for non-compliance will apply.

It is an offence to fail to comply with either an improvement notice or a prohibition order **20.24** without reasonable excuse. In both cases a person convicted of the offence is liable to a fine not exceeding level 5 on the standard scale (currently £5,000). A person convicted of failing to comply with a prohibition order is liable to a further fine of up to £20 per day for every day that he or she allows the prohibited use to continue.

Third parties

The Act also contains provisions to assist the owner of a property, or a person served with **20.25** a notice or order, to comply with requirements (or remove any excuse for non-compliance) when the action required would interfere with the legal rights of another person.

Recovery of possession If it is necessary for a person served with a prohibition order to **20.26** recover possession of the premises in order to comply with the order, the provisions of the Rent Act 1977 and Part 1 of the Housing Act 1988 (the statutory restrictions on the recovery of possession, see Chapters 14 and 16) will not operate to prevent this (s 33). The landlord can obtain possession simply by serving notice to quit.

Variation of leases Where compliance with a prohibition order would require either the **20.27** lessor or the lessee to determine or vary a lease, s 34 provides that the residential property tribunal has the power to make such an order if it is reasonable to do so.

Enforcement against uncooperative occupier or manager If the occupier of premises in **20.28** respect of which an improvement notice or prohibition order has been served refuses to allow remedial action to be taken on those premises, the magistrates' court has the power to order him or her to do so (s 35). The magistrates' court may also make an order allowing the owner of premises managed by another to enter onto those premises in order to undertake any action required by an improvement notice or prohibition order. The purpose of this provision is to allow the owner of a property to step in and take action where he or she believes that the person served with the notice will not do so (s 36).

Hazard awareness notices

The purpose of a hazard awareness notice is to advise the person responsible for the **20.29** premises of the existence of a hazard and to advise him or her of the steps it would be advisable to take to reduce or eliminate the hazard. The material difference between a hazard awareness notice and an improvement notice or prohibition order is that the former gives the owner or manager the opportunity to remedy the hazard; the latter demands that he or she does so. Failure to comply with a hazard awareness notice would generally result in an improvement notice being served.

Emergency remedial action

If an LHA believes that one or more category 1 hazard exists at any residential premises, it has **20.30** the power to take any remedial action it considers 'immediately necessary in order to remove the imminent risk of serious harm' (s 40(2)). Such action may be taken instead of serving an improvement notice, or where an improvement notice has not been complied with.

Recovery of expense of emergency action

Where an LHA has incurred expense in undertaking emergency remedial work it may **20.31** recover these expenses from the person on whom the relevant notice was served. If the person on whom notice was served receives rent as agent or trustee for another person (for example, if he or she is a managing agent) the LHA may recover the expense wholly or in part from that other person (Sch 3, Pt 3, para 8).

20.32   In order to recover expenses, the LHA must serve a demand on the person from whom it seeks to recover the money. An appeal against the making of such a demand may be made to the residential property tribunal within 21 days of the service of the demand. The most likely reason for such an appeal will be that the emergency action was not necessary because the person liable was making reasonable progress towards remedying the hazard.

20.33   Paragraph 12 of Sch 3, Pt 3 also allows the LHA to recover its expenses directly from the occupier of the property by requiring the occupier to pay all future rents to the LHA, rather than the landlord, until the debt is discharged.

Emergency prohibition orders

20.34   An emergency prohibition order will be justified where the LHA considers that a category 1 hazard exists and that the hazard involves imminent risk of serious harm to the health and safety of any of the occupiers of those or any other residential premises (s 43(1)). Unlike a normal prohibition order, the emergency order takes immediate effect and the prohibited use must cease forthwith (s 43(2)). The order is to be served on the day it is made. The provisions for revocation and enforcement are the same in the case of an emergency order as those concerning prohibition orders generally (s 43(3) to (6)).

Management orders

20.35   If a management order is in place in relation to premises (see 20.137) an improvement notice or prohibition order cannot be served, or, if previously served, will cease to have effect (s 39).

Demolition orders and slum clearance declarations

20.36   The Housing Act 2004, s 46 substitutes a new s 265 into the Housing Act 1985 and replaces the old subss (2) and (2A) of s 289 of the 1985 Act with new subss (2ZA) to (2ZE). The new provisions allow an LHA to make a demolition order or a slum clearance declaration in respect of residential premises where a category 1 or 2 hazard exists.

20.37   A demolition order would be appropriate where the hazard or hazards are contained in a single building or one or more flats within that building (Housing Act 1985, s 265). A demolition order may not be made where a management order is in place (s 265(5)), or in respect of a listed building (s 265(6)).

20.38   A slum clearance declaration would be appropriate where hazards exist in each of the residential buildings in an area, or where the buildings in the area are dangerous or harmful to the health and safety of the inhabitants of the area (Housing Act 1985 s 289(2), (2ZA), and (2ZB)).

Appeals

20.39   Appeals against the making of orders or notices must be made to the residential property tribunal. The general rules relating to appeals are set out in Schs 1 and 2. Appeals relating to emergency measures are covered by s 45.

Recovery of expenses—generally

As well as enabling the LHA to recover the cost of emergency remedial work, the 2004 **20.40**
Act also makes provision for the authority to recover expenses incurred in determining
whether to make a particular order and the service of notices and orders (s 49).

C LICENSING OF HOUSES IN MULTIPLE OCCUPATION

Under Pt 2 of the Housing Act 2004 certain houses in multiple occupation (HMOs) must **20.41**
be licensed by the LHA. Part 2 also provides that the LHA may impose licensing requirements on other HMOs within certain designated areas in its district if it feels that a significant proportion of HMOs in that area are being inefficiently managed.

Meaning of 'house in multiple occupation'

The Housing Act 2004, s 254 provides a new definition of a 'house in multiple occupa- **20.42**
tion'. In order to meet the definition a privately rented building must fall into one of three
categories. It must be:

(a) a building or part of a building that meets the conditions of one of the three statutory
tests; or
(b) a block of flats within the meaning of s 257; or
(c) a building or part of a building that is subject to an HMO declaration.

The statutory tests

The standard test

A building will meet the standard test if: **20.43**

(a) it consists of one or more units of living accommodation not consisting of self-contained
flats;
(b) the living accommodation is shared by persons who do not form a single household
and who occupy it as their main or only residence;
(c) their occupation of the living accommodation constitutes the only use of that
accommodation;
(d) at least one person pays rent; and
(e) two or more households share basic amenities (kitchen, personal washing facilities,
toilet) or the living accommodation lacks one or more basic amenity (s 254(2)).

For the purposes of the Act, people sharing accommodation will only be regarded as 'a **20.44**
single household' if they are members of the same family. Family members include whole
and half blood relatives, step-children, and couples living together as man and wife or civil
partners (s 258).

The self-contained flat test

A building will meet the self-contained flat test if it consists of a self-contained flat but **20.45**
otherwise the living accommodation (and basic facilities) are shared in the way described
in the standard test (s 254(3)).

The converted building test

A building meets this test if: **20.46**

(a) it is a converted building (a building in which separate units of accommodation have
been created since it was constructed);

(b) it consists of one or more units of living accommodation that do not consist of self-contained flats (whether or not it also contains any such flats);

(c) it is occupied by persons who do not form a single household as their only or main residence; and

(d) their occupation of the living accommodation constitutes the only use of that accommodation and at least one of them pays rent (s 254(4)).

Exceptions

20.47   Schedule 14 to the 2004 Act sets out a number of important exceptions whereby buildings that would otherwise satisfy one of the tests listed are excluded from HMO status for the purposes of the Act. These are:

(a) buildings controlled or managed by public sector bodies (para 2);

(b) any building specifically excluded by the appropriate national authority (para 3);

(c) buildings occupied by students where the building is managed by an educational establishment (eg halls of residence) (para 4);

(d) buildings occupied by religious communities (para 5);

(e) owner occupied buildings (para 6), eg a house that has been converted into flats, each of which is separately owned under a long lease (more than 21 years). The self-contained flat test may, however, apply to any one of the individual flats (para 6(2)).

Converted blocks of flats

20.48   Certain converted blocks of flats will be designated as HMOs. This will be the case where a building has been converted into flats but the building work does not comply with building standards, and less than two-thirds of the self-contained flats are owner-occupied (s 257). This provision prevents landlords from bringing properties outside the remit of the converted building test by carrying out substandard building work, and installing inadequate facilities in order to argue that all of the flats are self-contained. If a building containing several flats is classed as an HMO under the converted block of flats rule, it is also possible for any individual flat within the block to be an HMO if it is occupied by more than one household (s 257(5)). The provisions of Pt 2 of the 2004 Act in relation to s 257 HMOs have been modified by the Houses in Multiple Occupation (Certain Converted Blocks of Flats) (Modifications to the Housing Act 2004 and Transitional Provisions for section 257 HMOs) Regulations 2007, SI 2007/1904. These modifications provide for the identification of the 'person having control' of the s 257 HMO for licensing purposes (reg 3) (see 20.72) and impose an additional test for suitability of the house for licensing (reg 5) (see 20.79).

HMO declarations

20.49   In certain cases it may not be clear whether all of the occupants of a building are occupying it as their main or only home (so as to satisfy the standard test (see 20.43)). For example, a building may describe itself as a guest house offering short-term bed and breakfast accommodation when in reality the majority of the occupants are living there on a permanent basis. In such a situation the LHA has the discretion to declare the property to be an HMO even though there would otherwise be some doubt as to whether it falls within the definition of an HMO (s 255).

20.50   There follows a series of examples based on this scenario. John owns four buildings on Rackman Street: numbers 21, 22, 23, and 24. All of them are three storeys high. John has heard about the new licensing scheme and wants to know whether any of his properties are HMOs.

Example 1

Number 21 Rackman Street consists of nine bedsits: three on each floor. There is a bath-   **20.51** room and a toilet on each landing, and a shared kitchen on the ground floor. Most of the rooms are rented by single men. Several of them are heavy drinkers and can be somewhat argumentative. John has heard rumours that one of the residents deals drugs from the property. The neighbours complain but John minds his own business.

This property will be an HMO because it meets the requirements of the standard test. In   **20.52** particular, it is occupied by more than one 'household' as their only or main residence, the occupiers pay rent, and all share the basic facilities.

Example 2

Number 22 has a shop on the ground floor which John rents out to Pete. The first floor   **20.53** consists of two bedsits, a kitchen, and a bathroom. The second floor has been converted into a self-contained flat. The rent for all of the rooms is paid by Cynthia, who lives in the self-contained flat. She tells John she sub-lets the two bedsits to select young ladies. John suspects that the young ladies may be engaged in prostitution. The rooms seem to be occupied by different women at different times of the day. Again, he minds his own business.

If the women Cynthia sub-lets to: **20.54**

(a) are not members of the same household;
(b) occupy the bedsits as their only or main residence;
(c) only use them as living accommodation and share the kitchen and bathroom facilities;

number 22 will satisfy the converted building test and will be an HMO.

If Cynthia is in fact the only one who occupies the building as her main or only residence it   **20.55** will not be an HMO, but both she and John may have some explaining to do.

Example 3

At number 23, John has converted the building into three self-contained flats, one on each   **20.56** floor. Each flat is occupied by three students who have a bedroom each and share the kitchen and bathroom.

Number 23, in fact, consists of three HMOs. Each of the flats will meet the self-contained   **20.57** flat test (provided the students are not also family members) because the occupiers share basic facilities. The fact that they are occupied by students will not exempt the flats as they are not managed by an educational establishment.

Example 4

Number 24 has also been converted into self-contained flats. Mary lives on the top floor   **20.58** and has purchased a 99-year lease on the flat from John. The other two flats are each occu- pied by a family who pay rent monthly.

Number 24 will not be an HMO unless the conversion work carried out by John does   **20.59** not meet with building standards. For example, if John created each self-contained flat by placing a sink, shower, and toilet in a bedroom, installing a cooker in another room, and knocking through the dividing wall, he may well find that the conversion falls foul of s 257 and that the whole building is classed as an HMO. The fact that Mary's flat is owner occupied will not prevent this, as that flat comprises less than two-thirds of the number of flats in the building.

Which HMOs will require a licence?

Mandatory licensing

20.60   Prior to the coming into force of the 2004 Act, many LHAs had implemented licensing schemes in respect of HMOs. These HMOs will automatically have been transferred into the mandatory licensing scheme.

20.61   The Housing Act 2004, s 55 requires LHAs to license HMOs of such types as may be prescribed by the appropriate national authority.

20.62   Under the current provisions, an HMO must be licensed if it consists of a building of more than three storeys occupied by at least five persons who form more than one household. The number of storeys relates to the floors within the HMO, not the number of floors in the whole building. Therefore, a maisonette on two floors, which is situated above a ground floor shop, will not be subject to mandatory licensing.

20.63   In our example at 20.51, 21 Rackman Street would be subject to mandatory licensing as it is situated on three floors and has more than five occupiers. Number 22 would not qualify, even if it was occupied by five people or more, as the relevant premises are only on two storeys. Number 23 would not be subject to mandatory licensing as each flat would be considered separately: each self-contained flat has only three occupants and is situated on one floor. Number 24 might qualify if the standard of work brings it within the ambit of s 257 and if there are five occupiers or more.

Selective licensing of HMOs

20.64   As we have seen the provisions of the 2004 Act emphasize the LHAs' duty to monitor housing in their areas. The Act then provides LHAs with a broad range of options for tackling problems affecting whole communities, as well as those affecting individual tenants.

20.65   Selective licensing is an option that can be considered by an LHA where it has identified an area in which there are a large number of HMOs and it appears that the inefficient management of those HMOs is causing problems for the occupiers and for members of the local community (s 56). These problems may arise from poor quality buildings, or because of anti-social behaviour on the part of the occupants.

20.66   Returning to the example of Rackman Street, it may be the case that John's properties at number 21 and number 22 are typical of the houses in that area. The LHA may consider that one way of tackling anti-social behaviour is to impose a licensing scheme, in the hope that it could compel landlords like John to take greater responsibility for the behaviour of their tenants and the uses to which their property is put.

20.67   **Designating a licensing area**   Before designating any area as the subject of licensing, the LHA must consult those who are likely to be affected by the designation. This would include landlords, tenants, and local community groups. Before making its decision the LHA must consider any representations made during the consultation process. The LHA must also have regard to any relevant code of practice currently in place. Section 57 further provides that the decision to designate must be consistent with the LHA's overall housing strategy and be part of a co-ordinated approach to deal with wider social issues such as anti-social behaviour.

20.68   Any decision taken by an LHA to designate a licensing area must be approved by the appropriate national authority (s 58). A designation cannot come into force until at least three months after it has been made.

Once a designation has been made, the LHA must publish a notice containing details of the **20.69** designation and the date it is to come into force.

Duration of a designation A designation will remain in force for a period of not more **20.70** than five years. The LHA is under a duty to review the designation continually and may revoke it at any time it considers the designation is no longer effective or necessary (s 60).

Applying for a licence

Where an HMO is required to be licensed, either under the mandatory scheme or because **20.71** it is in a designated area, the person having control of or managing the HMO must apply to the LHA for a licence. Section 61(4) places an active duty on the LHA to take all reasonable steps to ensure that all those who are required to apply for a licence do so.

Where the HMO is a converted block of flats (a s 257 HMO) the person having control **20.72** will be either the person receiving the rack rent for the HMO (if no long lease has been granted) or the person holding a long lease of the HMO who falls first within the list of persons in reg 3(8) of the 2007 Modification Regulations (see 20.48)

The applicant must provide the landlord's personal details and basic information about **20.73** the property. Otherwise, the structure of the application form and the precise information required will be decided by each LHA according to its own licensing criteria.

A licence fee will be charged by the LHA. The amount of the fee will be decided by the **20.74** LHA and no upper limit has currently been set. The purpose of the fee is only to cover the cost to the LHA of administering the scheme. The licence fee will therefore vary according to the LHA's estimate of its costs but it should not exceed an amount that the LHA can reasonably justify.

The Act anticipates that a number of landlords will wish to take steps to take their proper **20.75** ties out of the category of properties requiring a licence. Section 62 allows LHAs to grant a temporary exemption of three months to such landlords to allow them to carry out any necessary adjustments. This exemption may be extended by a further three months in exceptional circumstances.

A licence may not relate to more than one HMO (s 68(1)), so a landlord or manager of **20.76** more than one HMO must apply for a separate licence in respect of each property. If the whole of Rackman Street was designated for licensing in our example at 20.51, John would need to apply for one licence for number 21, one licence for number 22, three licences for number 23 (one for each flat), and one licence for number 24 (if it qualified as an HMO). If John wanted to take all of his properties out of the licensing regime he would have to ensure that every flat within each building was completely self-contained (by making sure each had its own kitchen, bathroom etc). He would have to carry out any necessary conversion work in accordance with building regulations. Each flat could then only be let to a single household (an individual, a couple, or a family). Each letting agreement should stipulate that the occupants are not to share the flat with non-family members.

The licence holder does not have to be the owner. Many owners of large or numerous **20.77** properties will employ someone else to manage their property for them. This person usually applies for a licence. As the sanctions for non-compliance with the licensing provisions are severe (see 20.92) any such person would be well advised to consider the implications thoroughly before agreeing to assume control of the management of an HMO.

Grant or refusal of licence

20.78   A licence must be granted if:

(a)   the house is suitable;

(b)   the proposed licence holder and, where there is one, the proposed manager are fit and proper persons;

(c)   the proposed management arrangements are satisfactory.

Suitable house

20.79   The LHA must be satisfied that the house is suitable for occupation by the number of households, or people, it is intended that it be used by. A house that has been divided into flats will not be suitable if the common parts of the HMO or any flat within the HMO (other than a flat let on a long lease) fail to meet prescribed standards (s 65 as amended by the Houses in Multiple Occupation (Certain Converted Blocks of Flats) (Modifications to the Housing Act 2004 and Transitional Provisions for section 257 HMOs) Regulations 2007). If the LHA finds that a flat let on a long lease does not meet appropriate building standards it is entitled to disregard the long lease and the flat will need to meet prescribed standards (s 65(1A), as amended).

20.80   The LHA assesses the suitability of the house by reference to the 'prescribed standards'. These are standards as to the number, type, and quality of toilet and bathroom facilities, areas for food storage and cooking, laundry facilities, and other facilities or equipment that should be available in particular circumstances (s 65).

Fit and proper person

20.81   The guidance given by the Act as to what constitutes a fit and proper person for licensing purposes is concerned chiefly with any (unspent) criminal convictions the applicant may have (s 66(2)). Relevant convictions will be for offences involving fraud, dishonesty, violence, drugs, or sexual offences. The convictions of the applicant's associates or former associates (eg his or her spouse or business partner) are also to be taken into account. Evidence of unlawful discrimination in business, contravention of housing law, or any breach of an applicable code of practice will also be relevant (s 233). The Act provides that the LHA may additionally consider any other evidence it feels to be relevant (s 66(3)(b)).

20.82   The Act provides that the LHA must consider the fitness of not only the person applying for the licence, but also the person who, in reality, owns or manages the property (s 64(3)(b) and (c)). This provision is designed to prevent an unfit landlord using a 'front man' to obtain a licence.

Management arrangements

20.83   In deciding whether to grant a licence the LHA is also obliged to consider:

(a)   whether the proposed manager of the house has a sufficient level of competence and is a fit and proper person; and

(b)   whether any proposed management structures and funding arrangements are suitable (s 66(6)).

No suitable licence holder

20.84   Returning to the example of John's properties in Rackman Street (see 20.51). Even if the LHA has not imposed a selective licensing scheme, number 21 Rackman Street must be licensed. John, however, has a long string of convictions, mostly involving theft and violence. The LHA has indicated that it would not be prepared to grant him a licence. John has tried to convince the LHA that Cynthia will be looking after the property but the LHA knows that this is a sham. Closing down the house is not an attractive option for anyone. The house has nine occupants, all of whom would need to be rehoused, and John relies on the rent to support his large family. If John does not want to sell the property, he must find someone to manage it for him. He must, however, be able to show not only that this person is 'fit and proper', but also that he or she will genuinely be in control of the premises. In the short term, a possible solution would be for the LHA to take over the management of the property under the terms of an interim management order, until a suitable licence holder could be found (management orders are considered in detail later in this chapter, see 20.137).

Licensing conditions

A licence must include conditions requiring the licence holder: **20.85**

(a) to produce annually to the LHA an up-to-date gas safety certificate;
(b) to keep electrical appliances and furniture in a safe condition;
(c) to ensure that smoke alarms are installed in the house and to keep them working properly (s 67(3) and Sch 4, Pt 1).

In addition, the Act allows the LHA to impose such conditions in a licence as it feels to **20.86**
be necessary (s 67(1) and (2)). Those conditions may include restrictions on the use of the house, requirements to take steps to reduce anti-social behaviour, and requirements for installing and maintaining facilities and equipment within the house. They may also include a condition requiring the licence holder or manager to attend a relevant training course. A licence may not include a condition imposing restrictions or obligations on anyone other than the licence holder unless that person consents (s 67(5)); nor may it include conditions requiring the alteration of any tenancy or licence under which any person occupies the house (s 67(6)). All HMO managers are also required to comply with statutory management duties (see 20.102).

Duration of the licence

A licence cannot be granted for a period of more than five years (s 68(4)). It cannot be **20.87**
transferred to another person (s 68(6)). If the licence holder dies, a new licence holder must be found. The Act allows the HMO a three-month exemption period following the licence holder's death to enable the new licence to be obtained (s 68(8)).

Variation and revocation of licences

The LHA may vary a licence either on application by the licence holder or if it considers **20.88**
that there has been a change of circumstances since the licence was granted (s 69).

An LHA may revoke a licence in the circumstances set out in s 70. These include: **20.89**

(a) where the licence holder agrees;
(b) where the property ceases to be an HMO or where the structure of the property renders it unsuitable for the number of people occupying it;
(c) where there has been a serious breach of a condition of the licence or where the licence holder or manager ceases to be a fit and proper person.

The LHA may decide to revoke a licence on its own initiative or on application by the **20.90**
licence holder or a relevant person (s 70(9)). A relevant person is a person who has an

estate or interest in the property (but not a tenant under a lease with an unexpired term of three years or less), a person managing or having control of the property, or a person on whom any restriction or obligation is imposed by the licence (s 70(10)).

20.91   If an LHA is considering varying or revoking a licence it must serve notice of its intention and its reasons on the licence holder and consider any representations that person might make (Sch 5, Pt 2).

Offences in relation to licensing of HMOs

20.92   It is an offence punishable by a fine of up to £20,000 to control or manage an HMO without a licence if the HMO is required to be licensed (s 72(1)). The defendant in such proceedings may rely on the defence that he had a reasonable excuse. No offence is committed where there is an outstanding relevant application or a temporary exemption.

20.93   An offence is also committed if a licence holder knowingly and without reasonable excuse permits the HMO to be occupied by more persons than are permitted under the terms of the licence (s 72(2)). This offence is also punishable by a fine of up to £20,000.

20.94   It is an offence to breach a condition of a licence without reasonable excuse (s 72(3)). This offence is punishable by a fine not exceeding level 5 on the standard scale (currently £5,000).

Other consequences of operation of unlicensed HMOs

Rent repayment orders

20.95   If an HMO is required to be licensed and there is no licence in place, any tenancy or licence remains enforceable (s 73). This is an express exception to the common law rule that unlawful contracts are not enforceable (s 73(3)).

20.96   This provision means that the occupiers must continue to pay rent under the terms of any occupation agreement. However, a landlord receiving rent in respect of a property that should be licensed but is not could be liable to repay the rent received during the unlicensed period, up to a maximum of 12 months.

20.97   **Application by the LHA**   If housing benefit was being paid during the unlicensed period, the LHA is entitled to make an application to the residential property tribunal (RPT) for a repayment order where an offence has been committed under s 72(1) (whether or not there has been a prosecution, s 73(5)).

20.98   **Application by an occupier**   If the occupier of an HMO has made periodical payments in respect of his or her occupation during the unlicensed period, he or she may apply to the RPT for a repayment order. The RPT may make a repayment order if it is satisfied that the appropriate person has been convicted of an offence under s 72(1), or that a repayment order has been made in respect of housing benefit under s 73(5). Such an application must be made within 12 months of the conviction or order (s 73(8)).

20.99   **Subsequent licence or management order**   If a licence is subsequently granted in respect of the HMO, the LHA may make it a condition of the licence that any outstanding sum that the tribunal has ordered to be paid to the LHA is paid by the new licence holder (s 74(12)).

20.100   If a management order (see 20.137) is subsequently made in respect of the HMO, the order may contain provision for the recovery of any sum owed to the LHA (s 74(13)).

Restriction on terminating tenancies

The landlord of an HMO that should be licensed but is not may not serve notice seeking **20.101** possession under the Housing Act 1988, s 21 on any occupier of the HMO at any time the property remains an unlicensed HMO. Section 21 notices and possession proceedings are considered in detail in Chapter 16.

D REGULATIONS APPLYING TO HOUSES IN MULTIPLE OCCUPATION

All HMOs, whether or not they require to be licensed, are subject to Management **20.102** Regulations. Section 257 HMOs (see 20.48) are subject to the provisions of the Licensing and Management of Houses in Multiple Occupation (Additional Provisions) Regulations 2007, SI 2007/1903, WSI 2007/3229. All other HMO are governed by the Management of Houses in Multiple Occupation Regulations 2006, SI 2006/372, WSI 2006/1713. These Regulations impose a number of duties on the manager of an HMO to manage and maintain the property. The following is an outline of the Management Regulations. Any person directly involved with the management of an HMO should refer to the applicable regulations in full.

The HMO manager's duties

The HMO manager will be the licence holder if the HMO is licensed, otherwise he or she **20.103** will be the person having control of the premises. This is one of the reasons why s 257 HMOs are dealt with separately under the Regulations. In many cases it will not be possible to say that any one person has control over the entire block. If that is the case the manager's duties are confined to that part of the premises over which it would be reasonable to expect him or her to exercise control (reg 3 of the 2007 Regulations).

Duty to provide information

The manager of an HMO must ensure that his name, address, and telephone contact **20.104** number are available to each household in the HMO and are displayed in a prominent position in the HMO.

Duty to take safety measures

The manager must ensure that all means of escape from fire are in good repair, free from **20.105** obstruction, and clearly indicated and that fire-fighting equipment and alarms are in good working order. He or she must also make sure that all roofs, balconies, and windows are safe.

Duty to maintain water supply and drainage

The water supply to the building must be kept in a clean and working condition. **20.106**

Duty to supply and maintain gas and electricity

The manager has a duty to supply a copy of the latest annual gas appliance certificate (see **20.107** 7.104) to the LHA within seven days of a written request. The gas appliances in the property must be inspected by an engineer approved under reg 3 of the Gas Safety Installation and Use Regulations 1998, SI 1998/2451 (as amended by the Houses in Multiple Occupation (Management) Regulations 2009, SI 2009/724).

The manager must also ensure that all fixed electrical installation is inspected by a quali- **20.108** fied person at intervals not exceeding five years and be able to produce a certificate to that effect on request. He or she must also not cause the supply of gas or electricity used by any occupier to be interrupted unreasonably.

Duty to maintain common parts, fixtures, fittings, and appliances

20.109   The manager must ensure that all common parts are maintained in good and clean decorative repair, maintained in a safe and working condition, and kept reasonably clear from obstruction. Particular care must be taken to ensure that stairs and banisters are safe and that the common parts are adequately lit and ventilated.

20.110   Any fixtures, fittings, or appliances used in common by two or more households must be properly maintained.

20.111   Any garden or yard and any outbuildings must be kept safe and tidy and any boundary walls or fences kept in repair.

Duty to maintain living accommodation

20.112   Each unit of living accommodation must be in a clean condition at the beginning of a person's occupation of it. The internal structure and the landlord's fixtures and fittings must be maintained in good repair. This duty does not impose an obligation to repair where any disrepair is caused by the tenant's misuse of the accommodation.

Duty to provide waste disposal facilities

20.113   The manager must ensure that there are sufficient bins provided and that proper arrangements are made for the disposal of refuse by the local authority.

Duties of occupiers

20.114   The Regulations also impose a duty on the occupiers of HMOs not to frustrate or hinder the manager in the performance of his or her duties under the Regulations, to provide any information that may reasonably be requested, and to take care to avoid causing damage to the property.

Penalties for non-compliance

20.115   Failure to comply with the Regulations is an offence under s 234 of the Housing Act 2004 punishable with a fine not exceeding level 5 on the standard scale (currently £5,000).

E SELECTIVE LICENSING OF OTHER RESIDENTIAL ACCOMMODATION

20.116   Part 3 of the Housing Act 2004 contains further provisions allowing an LHA to introduce licensing schemes in certain areas in respect of houses that are not HMOs. The type of area targeted by Pt 3 is a run down area where low demand for property means that there are a large number of empty houses. The stagnant housing market in the area means that landlords have little incentive to improve or develop the properties. In such areas anti-social behaviour can become a persistent problem and landlords frequently have little interest in taking measures to prevent it. These problems are likely to get worse as the area becomes an increasingly undesirable place to live. The Act provides that if a Pt 3 licensing scheme is to be implemented this must be done in conjunction with other community development projects. The objective is to turn these housing areas around by ensuring that residential properties are properly maintained and managed and that the problem of anti-social behaviour is adequately addressed.

Designation of the licensing area

The designation of an area for licensing is to be considered in conjunction with other plans **20.117** that the LHA or any other body has for the general improvement of such an area, rather than simply as a measure to tackle poor housing conditions.

The considerations of the LHA are slightly different for this part of the Act from when **20.118** considering areas for the licensing of HMOs (see 20.64). The area designated for licensing under the Pt 3 scheme must satisfy two sets of general conditions (s 80(3)).

The general conditions

The first set of conditions is: **20.119**

(a) that the area is, or is likely to become, an area of low housing demand; and
(b) that making a designation will, when combined with other measures taken in the area, contribute to the improvement of the social or economic conditions in the area.

In order to determine whether an area is, or is likely to become, an area of low housing **20.120** demand, the LHA must consider: the value of properties in that area when compared with other areas, the turnover of occupants of residential premises, the amount of residential property available to buy or let, and the length of time properties remain unoccupied.

The second set of general conditions concerns anti-social behaviour in the relevant area **20.121** (s 80(6)). For this set of conditions to be satisfied, the LHA must consider:

(a) that the area is experiencing a significant and persistent problem caused by anti-social behaviour;
(b) that the private sector landlords who let premises in the area are failing to take appropriate action to combat the problem; and
(c) that making the designation will, when combined with other measures, reduce or eliminate the problem.

Duration of a designation

A designation will remain in force for a period of not more than five years. The LHA is **20.122** under a duty continually to review the designation and may revoke it at any time it considers that the designation is no longer effective or necessary (s 84).

Houses to be licensed under Pt 3

Section 85 provides that every qualifying house (houses let by private sector landlords) in **20.123** a licensing area is to be licensed under the provisions of Pt 3 unless:

(a) it is an HMO to which Pt 2 applies (where it will be licensed according to Pt 2 provisions, see 20.41);
(b) a temporary exemption notice is in force in relation to it under s 86 (see 20.126); or
(c) a management order is in force in relation to it (see 20.137).

Qualifying house

A 'house' is a building or part of a building consisting of one or more separate dwellings **20.124** (s 99). It may, therefore, be a single house occupied by one household or a building containing a number of self-contained flats, each occupied by one household. The sharing of essential facilities by members of different households will bring a house or flat within the definition of an HMO, and into the Pt 2 licensing regime. In order to qualify for licensing the house must be occupied either under a single tenancy or licence, or under two or more tenancies or licences as long as the whole of it is occupied this way. Part 3 will therefore not apply to houses that are wholly or partly owner occupied.

Exempt tenancies and licences

20.125 A house will not qualify for licensing if the landlord is a social landlord (a housing authority, housing trust, or registered social landlord: Housing Act 1996, Pt 1). The Act also allows the appropriate national authority to provide further categories of exempted tenancies.

Temporary exemptions

20.126 Section 86 sets out the provisions under which a temporary exemption from licensing requirements will be granted. These provisions are the same as the HMO provisions under s 62 (see 20.75).

20.127 Section 85 imposes a duty on the LHA to take all reasonable steps to ensure that licensing applications are made in respect of all houses that should be licensed. This may include taking steps to ensure that the owners or managers of qualifying houses are aware that a licensing scheme is in place.

Applications for licences

20.128 A licence must be granted for every qualifying Pt 3 house. A landlord who has more than one house must apply for a separate licence in respect of each of them (s 91(a)). The procedure for applying for a licence is the same as the HMO procedure under s 63 (see 20.71).

Grant or refusal of the licence

20.129 A licence must be granted if:

(a) the proposed licence holder is a fit and proper person and is the most appropriate person to be the licence holder (ie he or she is the person who actually owns or controls the house, rather than a 'front man');

(b) the proposed manager of the house is a fit and proper person;

(c) the proposed management arrangements for the house are satisfactory (s 88).

20.130 The tests to be applied in assessing fitness and satisfactory management arrangements under s 89 are the same as those in s 66 (see 20.81 to 20.83).

Licence conditions

20.131 Section 90 sets out guidance for the conditions that the LHA should consider including in a licence. These are broadly the same as those set out in s 67 with respect to the licensing of HMOs (see 20.85). As under s 67, s 90 provides that the mandatory conditions set out in Sch 4 must be imposed (production of a gas safety certificate, safety of furniture and electrical equipment, and installation of smoke alarms). Section 90 emphasizes the need for the LHA to consider imposing conditions requiring the licence holder to take 'all reasonable and practicable steps to prevent or reduce anti-social behaviour by persons occupying or visiting the house' (s 90(2)(b)).

Duration and variation of the licence

20.132 The provisions of ss 91 and 92 for Pt 3 houses are the same as those for HMOs under ss 68 and 69 (see 20.87 and 20.88).

Revocation of licences

Section 93 provides that the LHA may revoke a licence: **20.133**

(a) where the licence holder agrees;
(b) where the property ceases to be a Pt 3 house;
(c) where the property becomes an HMO and is subject to Pt 2 licensing;
(d) where the structure of the property renders it unsuitable for the number of people occupying it;
(e) where there has been a serious breach of a condition of the licence, or where the licence holder or manager ceases to be a fit and proper person.

The LHA may decide to revoke a licence on its own initiative or on application by the **20.134**
licence holder or a relevant person (s 93(7)). The definition of a relevant person in s 98(3)
is the same as that in s 70(10) (see 20.90).

If an LHA is considering varying or revoking a licence it must serve notice of its intention **20.135**
and reasons on the licence holder and consider any representations that person might make
(Sch 5, Pt 2).

Enforcement

The offences, penalties, and other sanctions in connection with licensed houses under ss 95 **20.136**
to 98 of Pt 3 are the same as under Pt 2 (see 20.92).

F MANAGEMENT ORDERS

There will inevitably be cases where an HMO or a house requires a licence but the owner **20.137**
or manager is either not a fit and proper person or declines to apply for a licence or act in
accordance with its conditions. Obviously in such a situation it would not be acceptable
simply to evict the residents and close down the building. Part 4 of the 2004 Act addresses
this problem by allowing LHAs the power to take over the management of residential
property, either on a short-term or long-term basis.

Interim management orders

An interim management order can be made for a period of up to 12 months. Its purpose **20.138**
is to allow the LHA to take immediate steps to protect the health, safety, or welfare of the
occupants or their neighbours and to give the LHA time to find a long-term management
solution (either by ensuring the grant of a licence to a suitable manager or, if that is not possible, by the making of a final management order) (s 101). An interim management order
can be made in respect of an HMO or a house to which Pt 3 licensing could apply.

Making of an interim management order

Where an order must be made   Section 102(2) provides that the LHA must make an **20.139**
interim management order where a house requiring a licence (either as an HMO or under
Pt 3) is not licensed and either:

(a) there is no reasonable prospect of it being licensed in the near future; or
(b) the health and safety condition is satisfied.

The health and safety condition   This condition is set out in s 104. It applies where an **20.140**
order is necessary to protect the health, safety, or welfare of the occupants of the house

or persons occupying or having an interest in property in the vicinity (s 104(2)). Section 104(3) provides that threatening to evict a tenant in order to avoid the need for a Pt 2 (HMO) licence constitutes a threat to the welfare of that person.

20.141 **Revoked licences** An interim management order must also be made in circumstances where the LHA has revoked a licence and it considers that, when the revocation comes into force, there will either be no reasonable prospect of a new licence being granted in the near future or that the health and safety condition will be satisfied (s 102(3)).

20.142 **Where an order may be made**   If a house is not required to be licensed the LHA has the discretion as to whether to make an interim management order. The rules relating to the LHA's discretionary powers to make an interim management order differ according to whether or not the property is an HMO.

20.143 **HMOs**   Section 102(4) allows the LHA to apply to the residential property tribunal for authorization to make an interim management order in respect of an HMO that does not require a licence under Pt 2 (that is, an HMO that is not subject to mandatory licensing and is not within a designated licensing area). Such an authorization can only be given where the tribunal considers that the health and safety condition is satisfied. In considering whether to authorize the making of an interim management order the tribunal must also have regard to the extent to which an applicable code of conduct has been complied with in respect to the HMO in the past. The national authority's power to approve a code of practice with regard to the management of HMOs is set out in s 233 of the Act.

20.144 **Non-HMOs—special interim management orders**   An LHA may also apply to the residential property tribunal for authorization to make an interim management order in respect of a property that is not an HMO and is not subject to licensing under Pt 3. The tribunal can make such an authorization where it is satisfied that an order is necessary to protect the health, safety, or welfare of the occupant of the house or persons occupying, visiting, or otherwise engaging in lawful activities in the vicinity of the house or having an interest in property in the vicinity (s 103(4)).

LHA duties under interim management orders

20.145 Section 106 sets out the steps that the LHA must take once an interim management order has been made. The steps must be taken 'as soon as is practicable after the order has come into force' (s 106(1)). The relevant duties are:

(a) to take such immediate steps as it considers necessary to protect the health, safety, or welfare of the occupants of the house or their neighbours (s 106(2)). This would include taking action against anti-social behaviour on the part of any occupant;

(b) to take appropriate steps to secure proper long-term management of the property (s 106(3)). In the case of a house that must be licensed these steps may be to make a final management order or to grant a licence to a suitable person. If the house is not subject to licensing, the LHA may make a final management order or, if the initial reasons for making the order have been resolved, the LHA may choose to revoke the interim management order.

20.146 The LHA's duties under s 106(3) expressly include a duty to make sure that the building is insured (s 106(7)).

The effect of interim management orders

20.147 **Powers of the LHA**   Whilst an interim management order is in force in respect of a house, the LHA has the right to possession of the house. This right is subject to the rights of any person already occupying the house under the terms of a lease or licence (s 107(3) and s 124(3)). The LHA does not, however, become the legal owner of the property (s 107(5)) and cannot sell it or dispose of any interest in it (s 107(5)).

The LHA may exercise any rights in respect of the property that a landlord may have (s 107(3)). It can, for example, evict tenants, carry out repairs, and enforce the tenants' covenants under the lease. The LHA cannot, however, grant new leases or licences without the consent of the person who holds the legal interest in the house (s 107(4)). **20.148**

Liability of LHA to owner Section 107(7) provides that, unless the LHA carries out its management functions negligently, it will not be liable to the owner or leaseholder of the property for any losses he or she may suffer whilst the LHA is managing the property. **20.149**

Leases and licences granted by the LHA A tenancy or licence granted by an LHA whilst an interim management order is in force takes effect as if it had been granted by the legal owner of the property (s 108). This is, of course, subject to the provision that it must have been granted with the consent of the legal owner. The normal common law and statutory rules will apply to the tenancy or licence, with the LHA assuming all of the rights and obligations of the landlord for the duration of the interim management order (s 108(3)). **20.150**

Effect on immediate landlords The immediate landlord is the owner or lessee of the property who, but for the management order, would have been entitled to receive the rents from the property. Where an interim management order has been made, the immediate landlord is no longer entitled to exercise any management functions in respect of the property. He or she is no longer entitled to grant leases or licences or receive rent directly from the occupiers (s 109(2)). The order will not, however, prevent any person from disposing of any legal interest in the property, for example by selling the freehold (s 109(3)). **20.151**

Rights of mortgagees and superior landlords The rights of any mortgagee or superior landlord are unaffected by the interim management order, save that the mortgagee or superior landlord cannot exercise any rights he or she may have to prevent the LHA from granting leases or licences (s 109(4)). This term is necessary as many mortgage agreements and long leases include terms that limit the ability of the owner or lessee to grant further leasehold interests (usually by requiring the permission of the mortgagee or the superior landlord). **20.152**

Financial arrangements

The LHA will inevitably incur expenses in managing the property under the interim management order. Section 110 provides the means by which the LHA can recover these expenses. **20.153**

During the life of the interim management order the LHA is entitled to receive the rents or occupation fees from the occupants of the property. The LHA can use all or part of this money to pay: **20.154**

(a) the expenditure reasonably incurred by the LHA in exercising its management functions in accordance with s 106(1); and

(b) any compensation payable to a third party in respect of any interference with that person's rights as a result of the making of the interim management order (s 128).

The LHA then pays any sums that are left over to the immediate landlord. The LHA will decide at what intervals these payments are to be made.

Duty to provide an account

The LHA must keep full accounts of its income and expenditure in respect of each house, and must provide copies of these to the relevant landlord (s 110(6)). If the landlord feels **20.155** that any expenditure included in the accounts was not reasonably incurred, he or she may apply to the residential property tribunal for the accounts to be adjusted (s 110(7)).

Variation or revocation of interim management orders

20.156   An interim management order may be varied or revoked either on the LHA's own initiative, or on the application by a relevant person

Final management orders

20.157   As we have seen, one of the options that must be considered by an LHA in its management duties under an interim management order is whether the property should be managed in the long term by the making of a final management order.

Making a final management order

20.158   Section 113 sets out the circumstances in which an LHA either may, or must, make a final management order.

20.159   **Where a final order *must* be made**   A final management order must be made to replace an interim management order on its expiry date if, on the expiry of the interim management order, the house would require a licence under Pt 2 or 3 and the LHA does not consider that it will be able to grant a licence (s 113(2)). The LHA also has a duty to make a final management order in respect of such a house where a final order is already in place but is due to expire and the LHA feels unable to grant a licence (s 113(5)).

20.160   **Where a final order *may* be made**   The LHA has the power, but not a duty, to make a final management order on the expiry of an interim management order if the house does not require a licence but the LHA considers that making a final management order is necessary to protect the health, safety, and welfare of the occupants and their neighbours on a long-term basis (s 113(3)). The LHA may also make a further final management order in respect of this type of house where an existing final order is due to expire and a further final order is needed to protect health, safety, and welfare (s 113(6)).

20.161   Section 113(7) allows part of a house to be excluded from the final management order if it is occupied by the owner or long leaseholder of the house.

LHA duties under final management orders

20.162   **The management scheme**   The LHA must implement a management scheme in respect of the property. The details of this scheme are to be contained in the final management order (s 119). The management scheme is to be divided into two parts.

20.163   **Part 1**   The first part contains details of the way the LHA intends to manage the house (s 119(4)). It must include such matters as:

(a) any works the LHA intends to carry out in connection with the house;
(b) an estimate of the capital expenditure to be incurred by the LHA during the time the order is in force;
(c) the amount of rental income expected from the property;
(d) how much compensation is likely to be payable to any third party and how this is to be paid;
(e) the procedure to be adopted for making payments of rent to the relevant landlord (after deductions), both during the term of the order and at its end.

Part 1 may also include matters such as payment of interest to the landlord, and final provisions for the recovery of the LHA's expenses (s 119(5)).

Part 2 The second part of the scheme is to describe, in general terms, any steps the LHA **20.164** intends to make to address the matters that caused it to make the final management order (s 119(6)). These may, for example, include measures to combat anti-social behaviour by occupants or measures to deal with disrepair.

Duty to manage Section 115 imposes a general duty on the LHA properly to manage the **20.165** property in accordance with the management scheme and to review both the order and the scheme from time to time. If at any time it appears to the LHA that a preferable course would be to grant a licence in respect of the property or to revoke the final management order, then the LHA must do this (s 115(5)).

The effect of final management orders

The effect of a final management order is largely the same as for an interim management **20.166** order (see 20.147 to 20.152). The principle difference where a final management order is in force is in the LHA's powers to grant occupation rights.

As we have seen, under an interim management order the LHA needs the permission of the **20.167** person who held the legal interest in the property before it can grant any type of lease or licence (s 107(4)).

Once a final management order has been made the LHA will still need permission: **20.168**

(a) if it intends to create a fixed-term lease or licence that will expire after the end of the final management order; or
(b) if the lease or licence is terminable by more than four weeks' notice.

This second provision would generally prohibit the granting of leases as the minimum **20.169** notice period under the statutory codes is in excess of four weeks. However, as an exception to the four weeks' notice rule, s 116(4) allows the LHA to grant an interest in the nature of an assured shorthold tenancy in respect of the property, without permission, as long as it is created at least six months before the final management order is due to expire. This ensures that the LHA can, if necessary, obtain possession against the occupant before the property is handed back to the landlord. The reasoning behind this is that the original landlord should not have to take the property back subject to tenancies he did not create or approve.

Financial arrangements

The details of the proposed financial arrangements for the implementation of the manage- **20.170** ment scheme will be contained in the final management order. As with an interim management order, the general structure will allow the LHA to deduct its expenses from the rents received. Again, the LHA will be under a duty to keep full accounts of its full income and expenditure in respect of the house and must provide details of these accounts to the relevant landlord (s 119(8)).

Enforcement of management scheme by relevant landlord

During the existence of a final management order the relevant landlord will remain inter- **20.171** ested in the running of the property, not least because he or she will be entitled to receive whatever portion of the rent remains after the deduction of the LHA's expenses. The relevant landlord has the right to appeal any of the details of the management scheme that seem excessive or inappropriate (s 119(9)). In addition, if the relevant landlord believes that the LHA is not managing the whole or part of the house in accordance with the management scheme, he or she may apply to the residential property tribunal. If the landlord's complaint is upheld, the tribunal may make an order requiring the LHA to adhere to the scheme, varying the scheme or revoking the final management order (s 120). The right to apply to a tribunal for an order under s 120 is also available to a person whose rights have been affected because of the imposition of a management order and who is therefore entitled to compensation.

Variation and revocation of a final management order

20.172   The provisions for variation of final management orders are contained in s 121 and are the same as for interim management orders.

Provisions relating to interim and final management orders

Effect of management orders on occupiers

20.173   The occupiers of a house subject to an interim or final management order have the same legal status they had before the management order was made. If the LHA grants a new tenancy this will be a private sector tenancy and cannot be a secure tenancy (s 124).

Agreements and legal proceedings

20.174   If the LHA serves written notice to this effect, it can take the place of the landlord in all legal proceedings affecting the house and in all agreements relating to the management of the house (s 125). The LHA can, however, pass on to the landlord any damages that are incurred as a result of the landlord's actions.

Furnished accommodation

20.175   Whilst a management order is in force the LHA has the right of possession over any furniture that has been provided for the use of the occupiers of furnished accommodation (s 126). This provision is designed to prevent the landlord removing furniture from the premises whilst an order is in force. In addition, where an LHA considers that furniture is needed in a property, s 127 permits the LHA to provide such furniture and charge its cost as an item of relevant expenditure.

Power of entry to carry out works

20.176   Section 131 provides that representatives of an LHA have the power to enter premises that are subject to a management order in order to carry out works. Provided the LHA has given the occupier sufficient notice of the works, the occupier will commit an offence if he obstructs them. This offence is punishable by a fine of up to £5,000.

Provisions on termination of management orders

Financial arrangements

20.177   When a management order comes to an end the LHA will do a final calculation to determine whether the rent it has received has been sufficient to meet its expenditure.

20.178   If the rent it has collected exceeds the amount of its expenditure (including any compensation payable to a third party) the LHA must pay the balance to the relevant landlord as soon as is practicable after the termination of the order (s 129(2)). If there is more than one relevant landlord, the balance will be paid in such proportions as the LHA thinks appropriate.

20.179   If, on the other hand, the LHA has spent more than it has received, s 129(3) allows it to recover the difference from the landlord or landlords.

20.180   Any amount recoverable by the LHA from the landlord will be secured as a charge against the property until it is recovered (s 129(7)).

Leases, agreements, and proceedings

By the time the management order comes to an end it is possible that the property will be **20.181** occupied by a number of occupants who were granted tenancies or licences by the LHA, as well as some of the original tenants or licensees. Section 130(2) provides that, when a management order comes to an end (and no further management order is made), the relevant landlord will take over from the LHA as the landlord of all of these occupants.

During the course of the management agreement it is also likely that the LHA will have **20.182** entered into a number of agreements with third parties (for example, for the provision of services) and possibly commenced legal proceedings (for example, for the recovery of rent arrears). It is possible for the returning landlord to take the place of the LHA in respect of these agreements and proceedings, but only if the LHA serves written notice to this effect on all of the other parties to the agreement or the proceedings (s 130(4) to (7)).

If a returning landlord is ordered to pay damages as a result of any action on the part of **20.183** the LHA whilst it was managing the property, the landlord must be reimbursed by the LHA (s 130(8)). For example, the LHA has instigated proceedings against a tenant for breach of covenant during the term of the management order. The proceedings are still ongoing at the date of termination of the order and the LHA gives notice substituting the landlord into the proceedings. If the court then finds that the tenant has not breached a covenant and the landlord is ordered to pay damages, he or she can recover those damages from the LHA.

Where two or more people would qualify as the relevant landlord under these provisions, **20.184** they can either agree amongst themselves who will take over these rights and liabilities, or they can apply to the residential property tribunal for a determination (s 130(10)).

Empty dwelling management orders

The purpose of an empty dwelling management order is to allow the LHA to assume the **20.185** management of a property that has been empty for some time with a view to making that property available as rented residential accommodation. The LHA might consider such action as part of its overall housing strategy if it appears that there is a shortage of residential accommodation in an area, yet houses are sitting empty. An order may be made in cases where the owner of the property will not, or cannot, let it out (possibly because he or she cannot afford to put it into a habitable state). An empty dwelling management order may also be made in respect of properties where the owner cannot be traced.

The provisions for the making of an empty dwelling management order are set out in Ch **20.186** 2, Pt 4 of the Housing Act 2004. The first stage in the process is for the LHA to apply to the residential property tribunal for authorization to make an interim empty dwelling management order. If appropriate, this is followed by the making of a final empty dwelling management order. The important difference between an interim and a final order is that under an interim order the LHA needs the permission of the proprietor before it can allow anyone to occupy the property; under a final order the LHA can grant leases and licenses without the proprietor's permission (s 132(2) and (3)).

Relevant dwelling

An empty dwelling management order can only be made in respect of certain premises. To **20.187** qualify:

(a) the premises must be a building, or a part of a building, intended to be occupied as a separate dwelling. If it is part of a building, it must be possible to enter the dwelling other than by going through non-residential premises (s 132(4)). For example, a flat above a shop would qualify if it had its own separate entrance. If the occupier had to go through the shop to enter the flat, the premises would not qualify;

(b) the premises must be wholly unoccupied (s 133(2)(a)). This means that no part must be occupied, even if the occupation is unlawful (eg by squatters);

(c) the relevant proprietor must not be a public sector body (s 133(2)(b)). The term 'public sector body' is defined in Sch 14 to the Act. It includes local housing authorities, social landlords, and certain police, fire and rescue, and health service authorities.

20.188 **Exempt dwellings** The Housing (Empty Dwelling Management Orders) (Prescribed Exceptions and Requirements) (England) Order 2006, SI 2006/367, WSI 2006/2823 sets out a number of situations in which an unoccupied dwelling will not be considered a relevant empty dwelling for the purposes of s 134. These are:

(a) where the dwelling has been occupied solely or principally by the relevant proprietor and is wholly unoccupied because:
   (i) he is temporarily resident elsewhere;
   (ii) he is absent whilst receiving personal care (for example by reason of old age);
   (iii) he is absent in order to provide personal care for another;
   (iv) he is serving as a member of the armed forces;

(b) the dwelling is a holiday home, or is otherwise occupied on a temporary basis;

(c) it is genuinely on the market for sale or letting;

(d) it is comprised in an agricultural holding or farm business tenancy;

(e) it is usually occupied by an employee;

(f) it is available for occupation by a minister of religion;

(g) it is subject to a court order freezing the property of the relevant proprietor;

(h) it is prevented from being occupied as a result of a criminal investigation or criminal proceedings;

(i) a mortgagee is in possession;

(j) the relevant proprietor has died and six months have not elapsed since the grant of representation was obtained.

Relevant proprietor

20.189 Where the building is not subject to a lease, the relevant proprietor will be the freehold owner. Where there is a leasehold interest, the relevant proprietor will be the person with the shortest unexpired term under the lease, provided that term still has more than seven years to run. For example: Andy owns a house and has granted a 99-year lease to Brenda. She has granted a 10-year lease to Claude, who in turn has granted a five-year lease to Doug. Claude has the shortest unexpired term over seven years, and will be the relevant proprietor.

Interim empty dwelling management orders

20.190 Before making an application to the residential property tribunal for authorization to make an empty dwelling management order, the LHA must make reasonable efforts to notify the relevant proprietor of its intentions and ask what steps the proprietor is taking to ensure that the building is occupied (s 133(3)).

20.191 **Termination of a lease or licence** If it is necessary to terminate an existing lease or licence in order to make the interim empty dwelling management order, such an application may be made to the residential property tribunal at the same time as the application for authorization. Such an application would, of course, be necessary only if the person to whom the lease or licence had been granted had no immediate intention of occupying the property. This provision is intended to prevent a relevant proprietor from granting a 'sham' lease or licence in an attempt to prevent an empty dwelling management order being made.

The tribunal's decision to authorize the order   In deciding whether to authorize the mak-   **20.192**
ing of an interim empty dwelling management order the tribunal must take into account
the interests of the relevant proprietor, the interests of the dwelling, and the interests of the
wider community (s 133(4)).

Section 134(2) provides that in order to grant authorization the tribunal must be satisfied: **20.193**

(a)   that the dwelling has been wholly unoccupied for at least six months (and is not an
       exempt dwelling);
(b)   that there is no reasonable prospect that the dwelling will become occupied in the near
       future;
(c)   that if an interim order is made there is a reasonable prospect that the dwelling will
       become occupied;
(d)   that the LHA has attempted to consult with the relevant proprietor. The Housing
       (Empty Dwelling Management Orders) (Prescribed Exceptions and Requirements)
       (England) Order 2006 has added a requirement to s 134 under which the LHA must
       demonstrate to the tribunal that it has:
       (i)   made efforts to establish whether the dwelling falls into one of the exempt
              categories;
       (ii)   attempted to notify the proprietor of the decision to make the order;
       (iii) made enquiries as to the steps the proprietor intends to take in relation to the
              property;
       (iv)   offered advice and assistance to the proprietor with a view to securing the occupa-
              tion of the dwelling.
       If the occupier has undertaken or plans to undertake works to the property, the LHA
       must also explain to the tribunal why it thinks an empty dwelling management order
       is necessary.

The tribunal may also order the LHA to pay compensation to any third party whose rights   **20.194**
would be affected by the making of the empty dwelling management order (s 134(4)).

The lengthy set of regulations to be complied with by the LHA, and the need for authori-   **20.195**
zation by a tribunal, reflect the fact that the making of an empty property order might be
considered to be a rather draconian measure. In the case of an ordinary management order
there has usually been some fault on the part of the landlord; in the case of an empty property order the owner might simply not currently want to have tenants in his or her property, or may have tenants who are absent for good reason. This section of the Act therefore
emphasizes the need for LHAs (and tribunals) to balance the needs of the community with
the concerns of those having an immediate interest in the property.

LHA's duties under an interim empty dwelling management order   Once an interim order   **20.196**
has been made, s 135 provides that the LHA then has a duty to take such steps as it considers appropriate:

(a)   to secure that the dwelling becomes, and continues to be, occupied; and
(b)   to ensure the proper management of the building until a final order can be made or the
       interim order can be revoked. This duty includes an express obligation to ensure that
       the property is insured (s 135(5)).

Further provisions relating to interim orders   Schedule 7, Pt 1 to the Act sets out the   **20.197**
relevant further provisions relating to the effect of interim empty dwelling management
orders. These provisions concern such matters as the legal rights of the parties, the effect of
the interim order on tenants and mortgagees, the financial arrangements under the order,
and variation of an interim order. These provisions are almost identical to those concerning

the effect of ordinary interim management orders under ss 107 to 112 (see 20.147 to 20.152).

Final empty dwelling management orders

20.198 An interim empty dwelling management order will normally come to an end after one year. The LHA must then decide whether to revoke the interim order or make a final order in respect of the property. The obvious advantage to the LHA in making a final order is that this will give it the power to grant certain leases or licences without the permission of the proprietor.

20.199 Section 136 provides that the LHA may consider it appropriate to make a final empty dwelling management order if:

(a) it considers that, unless a final order is made, the building is likely to become or remain unoccupied (s 136(1)(a));

(b) the dwelling is unoccupied and the LHA has already taken such steps as was appropriate to secure occupation (s 136(1)(b)). This subsection will be most relevant where the LHA has ensured that the property is suitable for occupation but has been unable to obtain the consent of the proprietor to grant tenancies or licences to any potential occupiers.

20.200 In deciding whether to make a final order the LHA must take into account the interests of the community and the interests of the proprietor (s 136(3)). It must also consider whether compensation should be paid to any third party whose rights will be affected by the making of a final order (s 136(4)).

20.201 **LHA's duties under a final empty dwelling management order**   The LHA must first set out a management scheme in respect of the building according to the provisions of Sch 7, Pt 1, para 13. This will be similar to a management scheme in respect of an ordinary final management order (see 20.162 to 20.165).

20.202 Once a final order has been made, s 137 provides that the LHA then has a duty to take such steps as it considers appropriate:

(a) to secure that the dwelling becomes, and continues to be, occupied; and

(b) to ensure the proper management of the building in accordance with the management scheme.

The LHA also has a continuing duty to review the order and the management scheme and consider whether the order should be varied or revoked.

20.203 **The operation of the final order**   A final empty dwelling management order comes into force when the time for appealing the making of the order has expired or the appeal has been concluded (Sch 7, Pt 2, para 9). The order will cease to have effect after seven years unless an earlier end date is provided for or the order is revoked or replaced.

20.204 **Further provisions relating to final orders**   The further provisions relating to the effect of final empty dwelling management orders are contained in Sch 7, Pt 2. Again, these provisions concern such matters as the legal rights of the parties, the effect of the order on tenants and mortgagees, the financial arrangements under the order, and variation of the order. These provisions are virtually identical to those concerning final management orders under ss 116 to 122 (see 20.166 to 20.172).

Provisions relating to interim and final empty dwelling management orders

20.205 **Revocation of an empty dwelling management order**   The provisions for revocation of an interim order are contained in Sch 7, Pt 1, para 7, and for a final order in Sch 7, Pt 2, para 16. The provisions are the same for both types of order.

They provide that the LHA may revoke an interim order where: **20.206**

(a) the LHA concludes that it has taken all steps it could take to secure that the dwelling
     is occupied;
(b) the LHA is satisfied that the dwelling will become, or will continue to be, occupied
     despite the order being revoked; or
(c) the dwelling is to be sold.

An interesting difference between the procedure for revoking an empty dwelling order and   **20.207**
that for an ordinary order is that the consent of the owner is required before an empty
dwelling order can be revoked. This condition is provided to prevent the inequity of an
owner being compelled to become a landlord when he or she did not choose this position.
If the LHA wants to revoke the order and return the dwelling, the proprietor may require
the LHA to terminate any occupation agreements before the order is revoked.

General provisions   The general provisions relating to both interim and final empty dwell-   **20.208**
ing management orders (such as arrangements on termination and provision of furniture)
are set out in Sch 7, Pt 3. Again, these are virtually identical to those relating to management orders under ss 124 to 131.

G OVERCROWDING NOTICES

The Housing Act 2004 Ch 3, Pt 4 contains additional measures the LHA can consider tak-   **20.209**
ing as part of its overall objective to improve housing standards in its area. Overcrowding
notices are an alternative to the measures already discussed in this chapter. The use of
overcrowding notices will be appropriate where the overcrowding does not give rise to
a hazard that should be dealt with under Pt 1 of the Act and the HMO is not subject to
licensing controls or management orders under Pts 2 and 3 of the Act. The Housing Act
2004, s 139(1) specifically provides that overcrowding notices can only be served in respect
of an HMO which is not required to be licensed, and cannot be served if an interim or final
management order is in force in respect of the house.

Overcrowding

Overcrowding for the purposes of the Act relates to the provision of sleeping accommoda-   **20.210**
tion in a house. Overcrowding can occur either when there are too many people sleeping
in any one room or when people are sleeping in rooms not suitable to be occupied as
sleeping accommodation (hallways or kitchens for example). For the purposes of the Act,
overcrowding will occur:

(a) when the number of people sleeping in any room exceeds the number for which it is
     suitable;
(b) when the number of people occupying premises means that inappropriate rooms have
     to be used as sleeping accommodation; or
(c) when the number of people occupying premises is such that persons of the opposite
     sex, who are over 10 years old and are not living together as man and wife, are obliged
     to share sleeping accommodation.

Under the provisions of the 2004 Act, the LHA can serve an overcrowding notice where it   **20.211**
considers that, having regard to the number of rooms in an HMO, an excessive number of
people is currently living there. It can also serve notice where there is no immediate overcrowding but it considers that there is likely to be an excessive number of people living
there in the future (s 139(2)).

Contents of overcrowding notices

20.212   Under s 140 the overcrowding notice must first state in relation to each room in the HMO:

(a)   whether that room is considered to be suitable for sleeping accommodation; and if so

(b)   the maximum number of people by whom it is suitable to be used as sleeping accommodation. This can include a variation to take into account use of the sleeping accommodation by children.

20.213   The notice must also contain either a requirement not to allow an excessive number of persons to sleep in the house (a s 141 requirement) or a requirement not to allow an excessive number of new residents (a s 142 requirement).

The s 141 requirement

20.214   This requirement is that the person served with the notice must refrain from:

(a)   permitting a room to be used as sleeping accommodation otherwise than in accordance with the notice; or

(b)   permitting persons to occupy the HMO as sleeping accommodation in such numbers that it is not possible to avoid persons of opposite sexes who are not living together as husband and wife sleeping in the same room.

The s 142 requirement

20.215   This requirement is that the person served with the notice must refrain from:

(a)   permitting a room to be occupied by a new resident as sleeping accommodation otherwise than in accordance with the notice; or

(b)   permitting a new resident to occupy the HMO as sleeping accommodation in such numbers that it is not possible to avoid persons of opposite sexes who are not living together as husband and wife sleeping in the same room.

20.216   A new resident is a person who was not occupying the HMO immediately before notice was served (s 142(3)).

20.217   For the purpose of the second part of both requirements, children under the age of 10 are to be disregarded (s 141(2)(a) and s 142(3)(a)). In neither case can the landlord avoid the requirement by moving any of the occupants to another room if this would mean that the number of people in that room then exceeded the maximum allowed (s 141(2)(b) and s 142(3)(b)).

20.218   A s 141 and a s 142 requirement cannot both be specified in the same notice but the LHA may withdraw a notice containing a s 142 requirement and serve a notice containing a s 141 requirement instead.

20.219   **Example** John lets out a two-bedroom, self-contained flat at 24 Rackman Street. The flat does not qualify for mandatory licensing (it is on less than three storeys, see 20.62) and it is not in a licensing area. The flat is made up of a large kitchen/sitting room, a bathroom, and two bedrooms. John lets bedroom 1 to Mr and Mrs Johnson and bedroom 2 to four male students.

20.220   The LHA decides to investigate the property as it feels that it may be overcrowded. It decides that the bedrooms are each large enough for three people to sleep in, but that the kitchen/sitting room is not suitable to be used as sleeping accommodation. It serves an overcrowding notice on John.

The notice will set out the LHA's determination of the maximum number of people who can sleep in each room. As the house is currently overcrowded, the notice will also contain the s 141 requirement. **20.221**

Under the terms of the notice Mr and Mrs Johnson's accommodation does not need to be changed. John cannot, however, continue to allow the four students to sleep in one room (as this exceeds the maximum number for that room). John does not want to lose one of the students as they all pay rent; however, the effect of the s 141 requirement is that there is nothing else John can do. He cannot allow one of them to sleep in the sitting room; this would breach the first part of the s 141 requirement as this room has been declared unsuitable. He cannot move one of the students in with Mr and Mrs Johnson (even if they would agree) as, although there would only be three people in the room, it would breach the second part of the s 141 requirement. **20.222**

If, at the time of the LHA inspection, there had been three rather than four students in bedroom 2, the LHA would not have needed to serve an overcrowding notice (according to its own assessment of the maximum allowable number of occupants). If, however, the LHA was concerned that John would introduce more people into the flat, the LHA might have chosen to serve notice containing a s 142 requirement. Such a notice would effectively prevent John from letting any more people live in the flat, as letting a new resident sleep in any of the rooms would be a breach of either the first or the second part of the s 142 requirement. If John did then allow a new resident into the flat, he would have committed an offence by breaching the notice. The flat would now be overcrowded and the LHA could also serve a new notice containing a s 141 requirement. John would be in breach of that notice (and commit a further offence) if he allowed the overcrowding to continue. **20.223**

Penalties

A person who contravenes an overcrowding notice without reasonable excuse commits an offence punishable by a fine not exceeding level 4 on the standard scale (currently £2,500). **20.224**

KEY DOCUMENTS

Housing Act 2004

Housing Health and Safety Rating System (England) Regulations 2005, SI 2005/3208

Health and Safety Rating System (Wales) Regulations 2006, WSI 2006/1702

Housing (Empty Dwelling Management Orders) (Prescribed Exceptions and Requirements) (England) Order 2006, SI 2006/367, WSI 2006/2823

Management of Houses in Multiple Occupation Regulations 2006, SI 2006/372, WSI 2006/1713

Houses in Multiple Occupation (Certain Converted Blocks of Flats) (Modifications to the Housing Act 2004 and Transitional Provisions for section 257 HMOs) Regulations 2007, SI 2007/1904

Licensing and Management of Houses in Multiple Occupation (Additional Provisions) Regulations 2007, SI 2007/1903, WSI 2007/3229

Houses in Multiple Occupation (Management) Regulations 2009, SI 2009/724, WSI 2009/1915

Printed copies of all legislation can be ordered from The Stationary Office at <http://www.tsoshop.co.uk>. All legislation from 1988 onwards and most pre-1988 primary legislation is available online at <http://www.legislation.gov.uk>.

21

REGULATION OF RESIDENTIAL PREMISES—
2. SOCIAL HOUSING

A HOUSING AND REGENERATION ACT 2008

The primary objective of the Housing and Regeneration Act 2008 (H&RA) was to **21.01** improve the supply and quality of social housing in England. (The Act does not apply to social housing providers in Wales where responsibility remains with the ministers of the Welsh Government.) To this end the H&RA established the Homes and Communities Agency (HCA) (which replaced the Housing Corporation) to support and finance the development of increased housing provision in England. The H&RA was amended by the Localism Act 2011 to provide that the HCA also has the responsibility for monitoring and regulating the supply and quality of social housing and providing support and guidance to both landlords and tenants.

The most important part of the H&RA for the tenant is Pt 2, which creates a system for **21.02** the registration of social housing providers and gives the HCA the power to impose and enforce standards in relation to the provision and management of social housing.

B WHAT IS SOCIAL HOUSING?

Social housing is defined by s 69 of the H&RA as being low cost rental accommodation **21.03** or low cost home ownership accommodation. Accommodation will be low cost rental accommodation if:

(a) it is made available for rent;
(b) the rent is below the market rent; and
(c) the accommodation is made available in accordance with rules designed to ensure that it is made available to people whose needs are not adequately served by the commercial housing market.

C REGISTERED PROVIDERS OF SOCIAL HOUSING

21.04   The H&RA allows landlords who provide social housing in England to apply for registration as a 'registered provider'. Local housing authorities and county councils were initially excluded from registration (s 113); however, an amendment made by the Housing and Regeneration Act (Registration of Local Authorities) Order 2010, SI 2010/844 has removed this restriction. The HCA is now required automatically to register any local authority that is, or intends to become, a provider of social housing. Registered providers will also include bodies which were previously described as 'registered social landlords' (such as housing associations) and the Act has also opened up the category of social landlords to include profit-making organizations which were previously excluded from registered social landlord status.

D REGULATION

21.05   When it initially came into force the H&RA provided for the establishment of a body known as the Office for Tenants and Social Landlords to regulate the provision of social housing. This body was abolished by the Localism Act 2011 and its functions taken over by the HCA's Regulatory Committee.

21.06   Under the provisions of Ch 6 of Pt 2 of the H&RA the HCA is allowed to set standards for registered providers as to the nature, extent, and quality of accommodation, facilities, and services provided by them in connection with social housing ('standards relating to consumer matters': s 193) and in matters relating to the management of their financial and other affairs ('standards relating to economic matters': s 194).

E STANDARDS FOR THE PROVISION OF SOCIAL HOUSING

21.07   The HCA published its national standards in March 2012 (*The Regulatory Framework for Social Housing in England*). These standards came into force on 1 April 2012 and are divided into seven categories.

Tenant involvement and empowerment standard

21.08   This standard obliges the registered provider to offer customer service and choice and to involve tenants in the management of their housing. It also requires the provider to have a clear and accessible complaints policy and to deal with complaints promptly and fairly. Emphasis is placed on the provider's duty to consider equality issues and the diverse needs of its tenants when applying all of the standards.

Home standard

21.09   This standard covers both the quality of accommodation and the repairs and maintenance service.

Quality of accommodation

21.10   Registered providers are required to meet the Government's Decent Homes Standard (or the standard of quality that was required when the home was built, if that was higher). Provision is made, however, for the HCA to agree a period of non-compliance where it would be reasonable. The Decent Homes Standard sets four key requirements: the minimum statutory standard, repair, modern facilities, and thermal comfort.

Minimum statutory standard for housing In order to meet this requirement the dwelling must be free from serious hazards (assessed by the Housing Health and Safety Rating System (HHSRS) as category 1 hazards, see 20.06 to 20.13). **21.11**

Reasonable state of repair A dwelling will not meet this requirement if one or more key building components are old and, because of their condition, need replacing or major repair. Key building components include the external walls and roof of the building, doors and windows, boilers, gas fires and heaters, and plumbing and electrics. The building may also fail to meet the repair requirement if two or more other building components (that are not key components) are old and need repair or replacement. **21.12**

Modern facilities A dwelling will not meet this requirement if it lacks three or more of the following facilities: **21.13**

(a) a kitchen which is 20 years old or less;
(b) a kitchen with adequate space and layout;
(c) a bathroom which is 30 years old or less;
(d) an appropriately located bathroom and WC;
(e) adequate external noise insulation; and
(f) adequate size and layout of common entrance areas for blocks of flats.

Thermal comfort Landlords are expected to ensure not only that the dwelling has an efficient heating system but also that it has effective insulation. **21.14**

Repairs and maintenance

This part of the standard requires registered providers to provide an efficient and cost-effective service and also requires them to consult with tenants about the standard and timing of repairs. **21.15**

Tenancy standard

Allocations and mutual exchange

This part of the standard requires the registered provider to cooperate with local authorities in meeting local housing needs, most importantly by providing assistance with local authorities' homelessness duties. The registered provider is also obliged to make efficient use of its housing stock and allocate housing, fairly taking into account the specific needs of individual tenants. Registered providers are also required to enable tenants to gain access to opportunities to exchange their tenancy with that of another tenant. **21.16**

Tenure

Registered providers are obliged to meet all applicable statutory requirements in relation to the form and use of tenancy agreements. They are also obliged to provide tenants with the most secure form of tenancy possible in the given circumstances and to prevent unnecessary evictions. **21.17**

Neighbourhood and community standard

This standard requires registered providers to keep the common areas associated with their housing clean and safe according to a local standard to be agreed with the tenants. Providers are also expected to cooperate with other relevant authorities in promoting the **21.18** social and economic environment where their properties are situated and in preventing and tackling anti-social behaviour in these neighbourhoods

Value for money standard

21.19 Registered providers are obliged to publish annual information to their tenants setting out how they have allocated expenditure. They must be able to demonstrate that they have secured value for money in that expenditure and explain how they will allocate future resources.

Governance and financial viability standard

21.20 This standard requires all registered providers (other than local authorities) to adhere to all relevant legislation and to comply with regulatory requirements. It emphasizes the provider's duty to account to the tenants and the HCA and to safeguard the taxpayer's interest. Registered providers are also obliged to manage their resources effectively to ensure their own future viability.

Rent standard

21.21 Registered providers are restricted in the weekly amount of rent they can charge. A formula for calculating the maximum rent recoverable for different types of accommodation is set out in the *Rent Standard Guidance* annexed to the Regulatory Framework. Provision is, however, made for the HCA to allow registered providers an extension of time to comply with the rent standard if meeting the standard would mean that the provider was unable to meet other standards, particularly in respect of financial viability.

21.22 Further details of the standards and advice on how to access the services of the HCA are available on the agency's website <http://www.homesandcommunities.co.uk>.

F ENFORCEMENT

21.23 The HCA, as regulator under the H&RA, is required to monitor the performance of registered providers and is given the power to inspect premises and require registered providers to prepare an annual report (ss 198A to 205). The HCA may also conduct an inquiry if it believes that the registered provider may have mismanaged its affairs (ss 206 to 210). If the HCA finds that the registered provider has failed to meet a standard under s 193 or 194 or has mismanaged its affairs the HCA may serve the registered provider with an enforcement notice. The powers of the HCA are, however, limited by s 198A(2) (inserted by the Localism Act 2011, Sch 17, para 9) which provides that such powers may only be exercised if the regulator has reasonable grounds to suspect that the failure has resulted (or if no action is taken there is a serious risk that the failure will result) in a serious detriment to the registered provider's tenants or potential tenants.

21.24 Failure to comply with an enforcement notice may result in the imposition of a fine (s 226), an order for the appointment of a manager (s 246), or the transfer of land (s 253). Most importantly from the tenant's point of view the HCA also has the power to award compensation to tenants who have suffered as a result of a registered provider's failure to meet standards set under s 193 or 194 (s 236).

KEY DOCUMENTS

Housing and Regeneration Act 2008

Localism Act 2011

A Decent Home: Definition and guidance for implementation Department for Communities and Local Government <http://www.communities.gov.uk>

The Regulatory Framework for Social Housing in England from April 2012 Homes and Communities Agency <http://www.homesandcommunities.co.uk>

Printed copies of all legislation can be ordered from the Stationary Office at <http://www.tsoshop.co.uk>. All legislation from 1988 onwards and most pre-1988 primary legislation is available online at <http://www.opsi.gov.uk>.

22

LONG RESIDENTIAL LEASES AT LOW RENTS

A INTRODUCTION TO LONG LEASES

For many people the largest single purchase they will ever make will be the purchase of 22.01
their home. What do you get for your money when you become a property owner? The
traditional answer to this question would be to say that there are only two things you can
buy: you can acquire the fee simple absolute in the form of the freehold estate, or a term of
years in the form of a long leasehold estate in the property (see Chapter 1). However, while
this remains true in principle, such a view no longer really reflects the reality of the options
available; a property buyer may purchase the freehold or the leasehold estate in a house, or
purchase the leasehold of a flat. He or she may also purchase the leasehold estate in a flat
together with a share of the freehold of the block in which it is situated or a commonhold
unit within a freehold estate in commonhold land.

The nature of long leases

Before going on to consider these possibilities it is necessary to consider the nature of a 22.02
long lease. Certainly the holder of a long lease can be seen as having more in common
with a freehold owner than with a periodic or short-term tenant. On the open market a
long leasehold interest will usually command only a marginally lower price than a freehold
interest and in practical terms the long leaseholder's primary concern is more likely to be
whether he or she can pay the mortgage than whether the landlord is likely to repossess
the property. All the same, the fundamental difference between a freeholder and a long
leaseholder cannot be ignored. First, a leasehold is a wasting asset. A defining feature of a
leasehold estate is that it is granted for a limited period and as the term expires the value
of the interest will decrease. Secondly, unlike a freeholder, a leaseholder is a tenant. There
will always be a person above the leaseholder who owns a greater interest in the property
over whom the leaseholder has only limited control. Because the leaseholder is in a relationship of landlord and tenant there will be rights and obligations outstanding between
the leaseholder and the person with a greater interest. Particularly in the case of residential
buildings, this person may have relatively little financial investment in the property in comparison with the leaseholder (or leaseholders).

22.03   It may seem reasonable to ask that if a leasehold estate is so obviously inferior to a free-hold estate, why would any person consider purchasing a leasehold estate? The answer is simply that in many cases the freehold estate will not be for sale, either because the current owner wishes to retain the freehold estate or because the nature of the property in question makes it impossible to acquire the freehold. We stated at the beginning of this book that landlord and tenant law is concerned with the rights and obligations that arise between people when they enter into a relationship to do with land. These rights and obligations can be simple or they can be very complex depending on the nature of the land itself and the number of people involved. Where the land in question is a single free-standing house occupied in its entirety by one person, the situation can be relatively straightforward. Where the land is a flat on the fourth floor of a large block containing many other flats, hallways, stairs, bin storage, garaging, lifts, and a communal roof-terrace, many more complex relationships can arise. Not only is the individual flat structurally dependent for its existence upon the rest of the building but there is the whole question of the use, management, and maintenance of the extensive common areas and facilities that are shared with the other people occupying the block. Ownership of such a flat is no simple matter. There has to be a mechanism in place to allocate the various rights and obligations between the parties involved, and not only the current parties; the mechanism must also be able to ensure that if the flat is sold the obligations and rights will pass on to the new owner.

The problem of positive covenants

22.04   In freehold land, unlike leasehold land, the burden of positive covenants does not pass to bind successors in title. Thus, where the original owner makes a promise to do something (eg to repair the roof or contribute to maintenance costs) this promise will not bind a subsequent purchaser of the property (see *Rhone v Stephens* [1994] UKHL 3, [1994] 2 AC 310). Such a lacuna in the law of freehold ownership would be fatal to the proper functioning of a block of flats because the good management of the building is dependent upon positive obligations undertaken by the individual owners of the various interdependent properties that make up the block. For this reason, until recently, the lease has been the only available way to deal with the complex relationships that arise when a number of different people occupy separate parts of a single building.

22.05   This is not to say that a lease is necessarily a satisfactory solution to the multiple occupation of a building. In fact, a lease, precisely because it is a relationship of landlord and tenant, has one notable drawback, namely that the leaseholder's contractual relationship is with the landlord and not with the other leaseholders in the block. It is therefore not possible for a leaseholder to enforce his or her rights directly against another leaseholder except in certain exceptional cases where it may be possible to establish the existence of a letting scheme (see *Williams v Kiley* [2002] EWCA Civ 1645, [2003] 1 EGLR 46).

Legislative development

22.06   The legislature, however, has been aware of the drawbacks of the leasehold estate since the 1960s. The first step in a chain of legislation culminating with the Commonhold and Leasehold Reform Act 2002 was taken by the Leasehold Reform Act 1967 (see 24.03 to 24.62). This Act granted long leaseholders two very important rights: the right to enfranchise by purchasing the freehold reversion from the landlord, and the right to extend the lease by 50 years. However, for the reasons discussed earlier, the Leasehold Reform Act applies only to buildings where the freehold can be isolated and sold separately—namely houses. The long leaseholder of a flat or maisonette acquired no rights under the 1967 Act.

With regard to multiply occupied buildings the breakthrough occurred with the Landlord   **22.07** and Tenant Act 1987 (see 24.63 to 24.92). Under Pt I of the 1987 Act, the long leaseholders of the individual flats in a block acquired the right to buy out the landlord's interest. The key problem the Act had to overcome was who should acquire the freehold interest—after all, the freehold cannot simply be split and divided between the former leaseholders. The solution to this problem was to enable the leaseholders to act collectively by joining together to appoint a 'nominee purchaser' to acquire the freehold from the landlord. Part I of the 1987 Act, however, confers upon the leaseholders only a right of first refusal. The right to enfranchise under Pt I of the 1987 Act will only arise when the landlord intends to sell his or her interest in the property.

The right to collective enfranchisement was further extended by the Leasehold Reform   **22.08** Housing and Urban Development Act 1993 (see 24.93 to 24.169). The 1993 Act gave long leaseholders occupying flats the right either to buy out the landlord's freehold interest collectively (regardless of whether the landlord wished to sell) or to be granted a new lease of their individual flats. In effect the 1993 Act conferred upon long leaseholders of flats rights similar to those which had already been enjoyed by long leaseholders of houses since the introduction of the Leasehold Reform Act 1967. All three of these statutes will be considered in Chapter 24. The final stage in the process, commonhold, will be dealt with in Chapter 25.

Leasehold reform and the introduction of commonhold, however, are not the only statutory   **22.09** solution to the problems inherent in the leasehold system. A second strand of legislative development has sought to apply itself to some of the practical problems encountered by the leaseholders of flats with regard to the management and maintenance of the buildings in which they live. These statutory provisions, centring around the Landlord and Tenant Act 1985, Pts II and III of the Landlord and Tenant Act 1987, and new rights and amendments introduced in the Commonhold and Leasehold Reform Act 2002, are the subject of Chapter 23. First, however, it is necessary to consider what statutory protection is available to long leaseholders in the event of their tenancies expiring by effluxion of time.

B PROTECTION OF LONG LEASES ON EXPIRY OF TERM

By virtue of the Rent Act 1977 and the Housing Act 1988, a tenant holding under a periodic   **22.10** or short fixed-term tenancy (with the notable exception of assured shorthold tenancies) may acquire, on the termination of the tenancy, a right to remain in occupation of the premises. A tenant holding on a long fixed-term lease, on the other hand, generally is excluded from claiming the benefit of either of these statutes, not because long fixed-term leases are precluded from protection due to their length, but because a long fixed term will usually be granted at a premium and the rent payable throughout the course of the term will be so low as to fall foul of the provisions excluding tenancies at low rents from statutory protection (Rent Act 1977, s 5; Housing Act 1988, Sch 1, para 3). (In the public sector long leases are also excluded from protection by the Housing Act 1985, Sch 1, para 1.)

In practice, the reality of the situation is that many long fixed-term leases will never expire.   **22.11** The tenant may well negotiate a new lease with the landlord before the actual expiry date. Furthermore, the tenant may acquire statutory rights to have the term of the tenancy extended or to purchase the landlord's interest. The extension of long leaseholders' rights by the Leasehold Reform, Housing and Urban Development Act 1993 and the Commonhold and Leasehold

Reform Act 2002 has made it even less likely that long leases will expire of their own accord and has significantly narrowed the gap between the freeholder and the leaseholder.

22.12   Nevertheless, some long leases will expire. Prior to 1954 there was no statutory protection for long leaseholders on the termination of the lease; the situation was governed by the common law. Part I of the Landlord and Tenant Act 1954 (LTA 1954) introduced provisions giving long leaseholders similar protection on the termination of the tenancy to that already available for periodic and short fixed-term tenants under the Rent Acts. The Rent Acts, however, were subsequently superseded by the Housing Act 1988 and the introduction of the assured tenancy as the main form of protection in the private sector. Correspondingly, new provisions were introduced to govern long leases granted after the enactment of the Housing Act 1988. These provisions are contained in the Local Government and Housing Act 1989, s 186 and Sch 10.

C ELIGIBILITY

22.13   To qualify for protection under Sch 10 to the Local Government and Housing Act 1989 a tenancy must:

(a)   be a long tenancy;
(b)   be at a low rent; and
(c)   satisfy the 'qualifying condition'.

A long tenancy

22.14   For the purposes of Sch 10 a long tenancy means 'a tenancy granted for a term of years certain exceeding 21 years, whether or not subsequently extended by act of the parties or by any enactment'. This definition does not include 'any tenancy which is, or may become, terminable before the end of the term by notice given to the tenant' (para 2(3)). A tenancy containing a 'break clause' entitling the landlord to terminate the tenancy early will therefore not be a long tenancy. It is not possible to bring a tenancy within the definition of a long tenancy by backdating the commencement date of the tenancy (*Roberts v Church Commissioners for England* [1972] 1 QB 274).

22.15   Where a long tenancy comes to an end and the tenant is granted (or the law implies) a second tenancy of the same property or part of that property, the second tenancy will be deemed to be a long tenancy irrespective of its terms (para 16(1)). Thus, if John is granted a 21-year term of a house and then on the expiry of the 21-year term is granted a further five-year term, the second term will automatically be treated as a long tenancy regardless of the actual length of the term. A third or fourth term granted to John will also be deemed to be a long tenancy provided the tenancy preceding it was either a long tenancy or was deemed to be a long tenancy by virtue of para 16(1). If the subsequent tenancy is a periodic tenancy rather than for a fixed term, it will also be deemed to be a long tenancy but with certain modifications with regard to notice periods (para 16(2)).

At a low rent

22.16   A tenancy is a tenancy at a low rent where:

(a)   no rent is payable under the tenancy;
(b)   the tenancy was entered into on or after 1 April 1990 and the rent payable is less than £1,000 a year in Greater London or £250 elsewhere; or

(c) the tenancy was entered into before 1 April 1990 and the rent payable is less than two-thirds of the rateable value of the dwelling house on 31 March 1990 (Sch 10, para 2(4)).

If a tenancy is entered into after 1 April 1990 in pursuance of a contract made before that **22.17** date and it had a rateable value on 31 March 1990, it must be below the limit set out in (c). If it did not have a rateable value on 31 March 1990, it must be below the limit in (b).

In calculating whether the rent payable falls within these limits, sums expressed to be **22.18** payable by the tenant in respect of rates, council tax, services, management, repairs, maintenance, or insurance are to be disregarded (para 2(5)). The rent payable is the maximum rent payable at any time, so if a rent which was within the limits is increased at any point to a level in excess of the limits, the tenancy will not be at a low rent.

The qualifying condition

The qualifying condition will be fulfilled when (Sch 10, para 1(1)): **22.19**

> ... the circumstances (as respects the property let under the tenancy, the use of that property and all other relevant matters) are such that, if the tenancy were not at a low rent, it would at that time be an assured tenancy within the meaning of Part I of the Housing Act 1988.

Schedule 10 thus effectively rides on the back of the Housing Act 1988 (see Chapter 15). To **22.20** work out whether the qualifying condition is fulfilled, it is necessary to look at the tenancy, ignore the fact that it is granted at a low rent, and see whether it falls within the protection of the 1988 Act, namely, whether:

(a) the tenancy is of a dwelling-house let as a separate dwelling;
(b) the tenant is an individual (ie not a company or other artificial person);
(c) the tenant occupies the dwelling-house as his or her only or principle home; and
(d) the tenancy does not fall into one of the excluded categories (eg it is not a business tenancy, an agricultural holding, a holiday letting, a local authority or Crown tenancy and there is no resident landlord).

With regard to the excluded categories ((d) in 22.20) Sch 10 makes certain alterations to **22.21** the provisions in Sch 1 to the 1988 Act to make them applicable to long leases. Obviously, the low rent exclusions (Sch 10, paras 3 to 3C) do not apply, but neither does Sch 10, para 1 which excludes tenancies created before the 1988 Act came into force on 15 January 1989 (Sch 10, para 1(2)). Long leases frequently have terms of 99 years or more and clearly many of the leases Sch 10 is designed to protect will have been created before this date.

For tenancies entered into after 1 April 1990 the exclusion applying to dwelling-houses **22.22** with a high rateable value (para 2(1)(b) and (2) of Sch 1 to the 1988 Act) is replaced by an alternative calculation of rateable value set out in para 2A of Sch 10. For tenancies entered into before 1 April 1990, however, the rateable value on 31 March 1990 must be within the limits set out in para 2A of Sch 1 to the 1988 Act (£1,500 in Greater London and £750 elsewhere, see 15.23).

Similarly, when determining whether a property is 'let as a separate dwelling' certain **22.23** assumptions are to be made. In the case of a long lease, which may originally have been granted over a century ago, it may be difficult to determine the purpose of the original grant. Paragraph 1(7) of Sch 10 therefore provides that the original nature of the property and the original purpose for which it was let will be deemed to be the same as the nature of the property and the purpose for which it is let at the time at which the question arises (ie at the end of the term when the question of eligibility is being considered).

Declaration that Sch 10 does not apply

22.24   One consequence of this rule is that a tenant may be able to satisfy the qualifying condition by moving back into the dwelling shortly before the expiry of the term. Paragraph 1(3) and (4) of Sch 10 gives the landlord a limited right to prevent this eventuality by applying to the court for a declaration that the tenancy is not to be treated as a tenancy to which Sch 10 applies. Such an application can only be made within the last 12 months of the tenancy preceding the term date and where, at the time of the application, the tenancy does not fulfil the qualifying condition. The court will make a declaration if it is satisfied that the tenancy is not likely, immediately before the term date, to be a tenancy to which Sch 10 applies. In considering the circumstances at a future date the court shall, by virtue of para 18, have regard to all rights, interests, obligations, and relevant circumstances relating to the tenancy as they subsist at the time of the determination and assume, except in so far as the contrary is shown, that they will continue unchanged until the term date. The onus of proof is therefore on the tenant to establish that the qualifying condition will be satisfied at a future date (eg by producing evidence of an intention to resume occupation of the dwelling). Once a declaration has been ordered the tenancy cannot fall within Sch 10, even if the qualifying condition is satisfied at the term date.

D SECURITY OF TENURE

22.25   By virtue of Sch 10, para 3, a tenancy which, immediately before the term date, is a long residential tenancy, shall not come to an end on that date except by being terminated under the provisions of Sch 10. The tenancy is automatically continued until it is so terminated, and while it is being continued it is deemed to be a long residential tenancy (notwithstanding any change of circumstances) (para 3(1)). The tenancy continues after the term date at the same rent and in other respects on the same terms as before the term date (para 3(3)).

E TERMINATION

Termination before the term date

22.26   Prior to the expiry of the tenancy both sides will be bound by the terms of the contract. The landlord may be able to terminate the tenancy prior to the term date by forfeiting for breach of covenant, but only if he or she has expressly reserved the right to do so in the lease. The right to forfeit is heavily restricted by both the common law and by statute (LPA 1925, s 146; Commonhold and Leasehold Reform Act 2002, s 168; Housing Act 1996, s 81 (see Chapter 11)). The tenant, on the other hand, generally is unable to terminate a long lease unilaterally before the term date. The only option for a tenant who wishes to be released from a long tenancy is to seek to negotiate a surrender of the tenancy (see 10.17).

Termination by the tenant

22.27   A tenant may terminate the tenancy at the term date by giving not less than one month's written notice to his or her immediate landlord (Sch 10, para 8(1)). A tenancy continuing beyond the term date by virtue of para 3 can likewise be terminated by giving at least one month's written notice. Such notice can be given before the term date provided that the date given for terminating the tenancy is after the term date (para 8(2)). Where a landlord has already served a notice seeking possession and specified a date of termination (see 22.41) the tenant may terminate the tenancy earlier than the specified date by giving one month's written notice; such notice can be served even if the tenant had previously informed the landlord that he or she wished to remain in possession (para 8(3)). Parties may not contract out of Sch 10 but nothing in the Schedule should be construed as restricting the tenant's ability to surrender the tenancy (s 186(4)).

Termination by the landlord

A landlord may seek to terminate a long residential tenancy either on the term date or after **22.28** the term date while the tenancy is being continued by virtue of Sch 10, para 3. This can only be done by serving notice in accordance with the provisions of Sch 10. Under Sch 10 there are two types of notice that can be served:

(a) A notice proposing an assured tenancy (see 22.31). Such notice will terminate the long residential tenancy and replace it with an assured monthly periodic tenancy. The tenant will therefore remain in possession of the property but will hold it under very different terms from the original long lease. Most notably, instead of paying a low annual ground rent, the tenant will be paying a monthly rent at normal commercial levels. The tenant will also lose any rights as to enfranchisement or lease extension that he or she may have had under the original long tenancy.

(b) A notice to resume possession (see 22.41). Such notice may entitle the landlord to terminate the long residential tenancy and take possession of the property. Possession however will only be granted where the landlord can establish one of the specified grounds of possession and obtain an order of the court.

Who is the landlord?

Usually the landlord will be the freeholder. Sometimes however there may be one or more **22.29** intermediate interests between the freeholder and the long residential tenancy that is coming to an end. In such cases the tenant's immediate landlord is not necessarily the landlord for the purposes of Sch 10. Paragraph 19 of Sch 10 adopts the definition of a landlord set out in s 21 of the Landlord and Tenant Act 1954 which requires the landlord's interest to fulfil the following conditions. It must be:

(a) an interest in reversion expectant on the termination of the long residential tenancy (whether or not immediately); and

(b) either the fee simple (ie the freehold) or a tenancy the duration of which is at least five years longer than that of the long residential tenancy that is coming to an end, and is not itself in reversion expectant (whether or not immediately) on an interest which fulfils those conditions.

Thus, the relevant landlord for the purposes of Sch 10 will be the next landlord up the **22.30** chain who possesses a term that is at least five years longer than the term of the long residential tenancy that is coming to an end.

Notice proposing an assured tenancy

Notice must be given in the prescribed form, Form 1, as set out in the Schedule to the Long **22.31** Residential Tenancies (Principle Forms) Regulations 1997, SI 1997/3008. It must specify the date on which the tenancy is to come to an end; this can be either the term date or a later date, and it must be served not more than 12 nor less than six months before the date specified (para 4(1)). It must also:

(a) propose a monthly periodic tenancy;

(b) state the proposed monthly rent (this must be at a sufficient level so that the tenancy will qualify as an assured tenancy, ie not less than £1,000 a year in Greater London or £250 elsewhere (Housing Act 1988, Sch 1, para 3A));

(c) inform the tenant of the rights he or she may have to enfranchise or extend his or her lease and make the tenant aware of the consequences of the notice (see 22.38);

(d) give the names and addresses of any other persons known to have a superior interest;

(e) specify the terms of the proposed tenancy (these may be the same, except with regard to rent, as the original tenancy or new terms);

(f) invite the tenant to reply within two months stating whether or not he or she wishes to remain in possession; and

(g) if the tenant does wish to remain in possession but does not accept the terms proposed for the new tenancy, invite the tenant to propose different terms.

Tenant's reply

22.32 On being served with a landlord's notice proposing an assured tenancy the tenant has a number of options:

(a) If the tenant wishes to give up possession he or she should inform the landlord in writing within two months and arrange to surrender the tenancy; this will save the extra expense of the landlord having to obtain a court order.

(b) If the tenant wishes to remain in possession and accepts the rent and terms of the proposed assured tenancy he or she should inform the landlord in writing within two months. If the tenant does not respond and is in occupation of the property as his or her only or principle home, the assured tenancy proposed by the landlord will take effect on the date specified in the notice. If the tenant does not respond to the landlord's notice and is not in occupation, he or she may lose the right to protection under Sch 10.

(c) If the tenant wishes to remain in occupation but does not accept either the rent or the terms of the assured tenancy proposed by the landlord, he or she must serve notice on the landlord proposing a different rent and terms in the prescribed form: Form 4 as set out in the Schedule to the Long Residential Tenancies (Principle Forms) Regulations 1997.

(d) If the tenant fulfils the qualifying requirements he or she may seek to exercise the right to enfranchise or extend the lease (see 22.39).

Referral to rent assessment committee

22.33 If a tenant serves notice proposing different terms or rent for the assured tenancy the landlord may accept the proposed alternative terms or, if matters cannot be agreed with the tenant, refer him or her to a rent assessment committee using the prescribed form (Sch 10, para 10 and Form 5 as set out in the Schedule to the Long Residential Tenancies (Principle Forms) Regulations 1997). The rent assessment committee will determine a rent at which it considers the property might reasonably be expected to be let on the open market by a willing landlord under an assured monthly periodic tenancy ignoring the fact that it is granted to a sitting tenant, any increase in value due to improvements carried out by the tenant during the long residential tenancy, or any reduction in value due to the tenant's failure to comply with the terms of the long residential tenancy (para 11(5)).

22.34 The provisions of Sch 10 serve only to fix the initial terms and rent of the assured tenancy. Once the assured tenancy is in place, the landlord may, at a later date, wish to increase the rent, in which case notice must be served on the tenant under s 13 of the Housing Act 1988 (see 15.81 to 15.88). The tenant may then refer the notice to the rent assessment committee (s 13(4)). In contrast to the position under Sch 10, in determining the rent the committee may disregard only 'relevant improvements'; to be a 'relevant improvement' the improvement must have been carried out within the last 21 years and while the dwelling-house was let on an assured tenancy (s 14(3)). This has the unfortunate result that improvements made by the tenant during the preceding long lease will not be disregarded. As a consequence the landlord may be able to impose a considerable rent increase and in some cases, if the new rent exceeds the statutory limits, the tenancy may even lose statutory protection altogether (*Hughes v Borodex Ltd* [2010] EWCA Civ 425).

Interim rent

As well as serving a notice proposing an assured tenancy the landlord may serve notice pro-   **22.35**
posing an interim rent (Sch 10, para 6). Such notice must be in the prescribed form (Form 3 as set out In the Schedule to the Long Residential Tenancies (Principle Forms) Regulations 1997) and can be served at the same time as the notice proposing an assured tenancy or at any time between that date and the date of termination. The notice must propose an interim monthly rent and specify the date upon which this interim rent is to start. This date must be at least two months after the service of the notice and may not be earlier than the date of termination specified in the landlord's notice proposing an assured tenancy.

If such notice is served, it will enable the landlord to charge a monthly rent at market rates   **22.36**
(not just ground rent) from the date specified in the notice up until the date the tenancy is finally terminated and the proposed assured tenancy comes into effect (ie while the original long tenancy is being continued by para 3). Usually the original tenancy will terminate on the date specified in the notice proposing an assured tenancy (and an interim rent cannot in any case begin any earlier than this date) but where the rent or terms of the proposed assured tenancy are not accepted by the tenant and the matters are referred to the rent assessment committee, the termination date will be three months after the date on which the application is finally disposed of (para 4(2)). By proposing an interim rent the landlord will be able to charge the tenant a market rent while matters are being settled between them.

If the tenant agrees with the proposed interim rent, he or she need take no action and the   **22.37**
rent will take effect from the date specified. If the tenant does not agree with the rent, the landlord's notice proposing an interim rent can be referred to the rent assessment committee within two months and the committee will determine the rent. A notice proposing an interim rent cannot be served where the landlord has served notice seeking possession.

Rights to enfranchisement or lease extension

When the term of a long residential tenancy comes to an end, some tenants may have options   **22.38**
beyond being granted a monthly assured periodic tenancy: they may have the statutory right to purchase the freehold or to extend their lease under either the Leasehold Reform Act 1967 (for houses) or the Leasehold Reform Housing and Urban Development Act 1993 (for flats). These rights can be exercised either during the term of the lease or after the original term of the lease has expired and the tenancy is being continued by virtue of para 3. They cannot be exercised once the tenancy is terminated. Once a landlord serves notice to terminate the tenancy (either proposing an assured tenancy or seeking possession) a timetable begins to run.

A tenant who wishes to acquire the freehold of a house under the 1967 Act or to extend   **22.39**
his or her lease under either the 1967 or the 1993 Act must serve the appropriate notice (see 24.41 and 24.123) within two months of receiving the landlord's notice. A tenant of a flat who wishes to jointly acquire the freehold of the building along with the other tenants under the 1993 Act must, together with the other tenants, serve the appropriate notice within four months of receiving the landlord's notice. If such notice is served, the landlord's notice to terminate the tenancy will cease to have effect. A tenant (or tenants) however will only be able to exercise the right to enfranchise or extend the lease where he or she fulfils the appropriate qualifying criteria (for details of eligibility and procedure for the 1967 and 1993 Acts, see Chapter 24).

Where a tenant gives notice of his or her wish to enfranchise there are a few restricted   **22.40**
grounds on which a landlord may apply to the county court for possession: either because

the landlord requires possession to redevelop (ss 23 and 47 of the 1993 Act and s 17 of the 1967 Act: see 24.145, 24.163, and 24.52) or because the property is required for occupation as a main residence by the landlord or an adult member of the landlord's family (s 18 of the 1967 Act: see 24.54).

Notice seeking possession

22.41 As an alternative to proposing an assured tenancy, the landlord may seek possession of the property. Possession however will only be granted if an order is made by the county court, and an order will only be made where the landlord can make out one or more of a limited number of grounds of possession (see 22.45 to 22.52).

22.42 A landlord's notice seeking possession must be in the prescribed form (Sch 10, para 4 and Form 2 as set out in the Schedule to the Long Residential Tenancies (Principle Forms) Regulations 1997). It must specify the date at which the tenancy is to come to an end (this can be the term date or a later date) and it must be served not more than 12 nor less than six months before the date specified. It must also:

(a) invite the tenant, within two months, to inform the landlord in writing whether he or she is willing to give up possession;

(b) inform the tenant that, if he or she is not willing to give up possession, the landlord intends to apply to the county court for possession, and specify the ground or grounds on which the landlord proposes to rely;

(c) inform the tenant of the rights he or she may have to enfranchise or extend his or her lease and make the tenant aware of the consequences of the notice (see 22.38);

(d) give the names and addresses of any other persons known to have a superior interest.

Tenant's reply

22.43 Having received a landlord's notice seeking possession a tenant has the following options:

(a) the tenant may choose to give up possession, in which case the tenancy will come to an end on the date specified in the notice;

(b) the tenant may choose to remain in possession and should inform the landlord of his or her intention to do so in writing within two months of receiving the notice;

(c) if the tenant fulfils the qualifying requirements, he or she may seek to exercise the right to enfranchise or extend the lease (see 22.38).

Landlord's application for possession

22.44 Where the tenant gives notice of his or her intention to remain in possession or where the tenant fails to respond but, at the end of the two-month notice period, remains in possession of the premises (ie fulfils the qualifying condition), the landlord may then apply to the county court for a possession order. Such an application must be made within two months of receiving the tenant's reply or, if no such reply is received, within four months of the date of serving the landlord's notice seeking possession (Sch 10, para 13(2)). If an application is not made within these time limits, the landlord's notice ceases to have effect (para 15(2)). If the tenant does not reply to the landlord's notice and does not fulfil the qualifying condition at the end of the two-month notice period, then the tenancy will terminate on the date specified in the notice.

Grounds of possession

22.45 The grounds of possession available to the landlord are set out in para 5 of Sch 10. All but two of these grounds are contained in Sch 2 to the Housing Act 1988 and only one of them is mandatory.

The mandatory ground is Ground 6 from Sch 2 (omitting para (c)) and entitles the landlord **22.46** to possession where he or she intends to demolish or reconstruct the whole or a substantial part of the dwelling or carry out substantial works to it and the work cannot reasonably be carried out without the tenant giving up possession (see 16.39). The landlord may not use this ground where the tenancy is a former 1954 Act tenancy (see 22.12).

The discretionary grounds from Sch 2 to the Housing Act 1988 are as follows (Ground **22.47** 10, see 16.57):

(a) that suitable alternative accommodation is available for the tenant or will be available when the order for possession takes effect (Ground 9, see 16.54);

(b) that some rent arrears are outstanding both on the date when the possession proceedings are begun and on the date the landlord's notice to resume possession was served;

(c) whether or not any rent is in arrears on the date on which proceedings for possession are begun, the tenant has persistently delayed paying rent which has become lawfully due (Ground 11, see 16.59);

(d) that any obligation of the tenancy (other than one related to the payment of rent) has been broken or not performed (Ground 12, see 16.60);

(e) that the condition of the dwelling house or common parts has deteriorated owing to the neglect or default of the tenant or any other person residing in the dwelling and, where the deterioration is caused by the tenant's lodger or sub-tenant, the tenant has not taken such steps as he or she ought reasonably to have taken to remove that lodger or sub-tenant (Ground 13, see 16.61);

(f) that the tenant of a person residing in or visiting the dwelling has been guilty of conduct causing or likely to cause annoyance to a person residing in or visiting the locality or has been convicted of using the dwelling for immoral or illegal purposes or of an arrestable offence committed in or in the locality of the dwelling (Ground 14, see 16.62);

(g) where the landlord is a social landlord and the dwelling is occupied by a couple, and one partner has left because of violence or threats of violence to that partner or a member of the partners family residing with the partner (Ground 14A, see 16.67);

(h) that the condition of any furniture provided for use under the tenancy has deteriorated owing to ill treatment by the tenant, a person lodging with the tenant, or a sub-tenant (Ground 15, see 16.68);

(i) that the tenant or a person acting at the tenant's instigation induced the landlord to grant the tenancy by knowingly or recklessly making a false statement (Ground 17, see 16.70).

Two further grounds are contained in Sch 10.

Redevelopment by a public body   The first of these two grounds is that, for the purposes **22.48** of redevelopment after the termination of the tenancy, the landlord proposes to demolish or reconstruct the whole or a substantial part of the premises (Sch 10, para 5(1)(b)) and the landlord is a body with a public function to which s 28 of the Leasehold Reform Act 1967 applies (para 5(4)). Such bodies include local authorities, county, borough, and district councils, housing action trusts, police authorities, health authorities, development corporations, colleges, and universities.

Where a landlord seeks to rely on para 5(1)(b) the court must not only be satisfied that the **22.49** landlord has established the ground but also:

(a) that possession of the premises will be required by the landlord on the date of termination; and

(b) that the landlord has made such preparations for proceeding with the redevelopment as are reasonable in the circumstances (ie obtaining, or making reasonable preparations to obtain, the requisite permissions and consents such as planning permission and consent of mortgagees or superior landlords) (para 13(7)).

If the court is not satisfied that possession is required on the date of termination but would be satisfied at a later date, the court may postpone the date of termination and order the tenant to give up possession on the postponed termination date. The postponed termination date may not be more than one year later than the termination date originally specified (para 14(1) and (2)).

22.50   **Required for occupation by landlord or landlord's family**   The second of the two grounds is that the premises or part of them are reasonably required by the landlord for occupation as a residence for himself or herself or any son or daughter over 18 years of age or his or her spouse's father or mother and, if the landlord is not the immediate landlord, he will be at the specified date of termination (Sch 10, para 5(1)(c)). This ground may not be used where the landlord's interest was purchased or created after 18 February 1966 (para 5(5)). Where the landlord does rely upon this ground, the court will not make an order for possession if it is satisfied that, having regard to all the circumstances of the case, including the question whether other accommodation is available for the landlord or the tenant, greater hardship would be caused by making the order than by refusing to make it (para 13(6)).

22.51   With regard to Grounds 9 to 15 of Sch 2 to the 1988 Act and the ground that the premises are required for occupation by the landlord or a member of the landlord's family (see above), the court must be satisfied:

(a)   that the landlord has established the ground; and

(b)   that it is reasonable that the landlord should be granted possession (para 13(4)).

22.52   If the court is satisfied that the qualifying condition is not satisfied at the date of the hearing (regardless of whether the tenant has informed the landlord of his or her intention to remain in possession), the court will order the tenant to give up possession of the property on the date of termination.

Where possession is not ordered

22.53   If the landlord fails to obtain an order for possession, the notice will lapse and the tenancy will continue as a long residential tenancy (Sch 10, para 13(3)). Having failed to gain possession the landlord may seek to terminate the long residential tenancy and substitute an assured tenancy by serving notice proposing an assured tenancy on Form 1 (see 22.31). If the landlord serves a notice proposing an assured tenancy within one month of the date on which the application for possession is finally disposed of, the earliest date which may be specified in the notice as the date of termination shall be the day following the last day of the period of four months beginning on the date of service of the notice proposing an assured tenancy (para 15(4)). If notice proposing an assured tenancy is served later than one month after the application is finally disposed of, the normal rules (para 4(1)) will apply and the specified date of termination must be at least six months and not more than 12 months from the date of service.

Withdrawal of notice

22.54   A landlord may withdraw his or her notice to resume possession at any time by serving notice in writing on the tenant (para 15(6)). Where an application for a possession order has already been made to the county court, the court may order the landlord to pay the tenant's costs. Where the landlord serves a notice proposing an assured tenancy within one month of withdrawing his or her notice to resume possession, the date of termination specified in the notice proposing an assured tenancy must be at least four months after the date of service of the notice (Sch 10, para 15(7)).

KEY DOCUMENTS

Landlord and Tenant Act 1954

Housing Act 1988

Local Government and Housing Act 1989

Long Residential Tenancies (Principle Forms) Regulations 1997, SI 1997/3008

Printed copies of all legislation can be ordered from The Stationery Office at <http://www.tsoshop.co.uk>. All legislation from 1988 onwards and most pre-1988 primary legislation is available online at <http://www.legislation.gov.uk>.

23

MANAGEMENT AND SERVICE CHARGES IN LONG LEASES

A   INTRODUCTION

23.01   When a building contains two or more flats or units that are occupied by different people, somebody must be responsible for the parts that do not belong exclusively to each of the individual occupiers. Where the individual flats within the block are held on long leases those leases will, in virtually all cases, place the responsibility for carrying out the repair, maintenance, insurance, and management of the block on the freeholder. These tasks, however, must also be paid for, and that burden will be placed upon the leaseholders. The vast majority of long leases will therefore contain a mechanism entitling the freeholder to recover the cost of carrying out his or her obligations from the individual leaseholders of the flats in the block. This is done by making provision for the leaseholders to pay a service charge.

23.02   A service charge clause should set out what proportion of the costs the leaseholder is liable to pay and when and how it should be payable. In most cases service charges will be calculated annually and the leases will provide for the tenants to pay a regular periodic charge which will be augmented at the end of the yearly period by an excess charge covering any costs the freeholder may have incurred over and above those accounted for by the periodic charge. It may also provide for a reserve or sinking fund enabling the landlord to accumulate funds towards future repair or maintenance works.

23.03   The fundamental problem with this arrangement, from the leaseholders' point of view, is that somebody else is responsible for spending their money, and that somebody, be they the freeholder or a managing agent, has only a relatively small interest in the property that they are supposed to maintain. There is therefore something of an inevitable tendency in this arrangement towards either neglect or extortion: neglect, in that the freeholder is frequently disinclined to maintain the property properly because there is little money to be made; extortion, in that an unscrupulous freeholder or managing agent will conclude that the only way to extract some sort of financial gain from his or her interest in the property is by undertaking extensive and sometimes unnecessary works.

23.04   For this reason, in recent years, the law has been moving steadily to improve the position of the long residential leaseholder. This movement has taken two forms. First, increasing rights of enfranchisement (see Chapter 24) have enabled the leaseholders in a block, by acting together, to take over the freeholder's interest and thereby become responsible for the management and maintenance of their own building. Secondly, a variety of statutes have sought, by a variety of means, to make freeholders and managing agents much more accountable to the leaseholders. This chapter is concerned with the second of these movements, although in certain ways the two are not inseparable: the right to manage introduced by the Commonhold and Leasehold Reform Act 2002 (which gives leaseholders the right to take over the management of their own block) is a close relative of the right to collective enfranchisement under the Leasehold Reform, Housing and Urban Development Act 1993 and can be viewed as a stage on the route to acquiring the freehold.

23.05   Enfranchisement however is not necessarily a solution to the problems of poor management. For many long leaseholders it may not be an option: there may not be a sufficient number of qualifying tenants in the building, too large a proportion of the building may be used for business purposes, or there may be a resident landlord. For others enfranchisement may not prove attractive or practicable, requiring, as it does, a high degree of cooperation between the leaseholders, the investment of a significant amount of time and effort in setting up and running a company to acquire the freehold, not to mention the attendant responsibilities and the potential social difficulties that can occur when disagreements arise between neighbours. There is also no guarantee that a company made up of the leaseholders will necessarily manage a building any better than the freeholder or the freeholder's managing agent. Many of the provisions dealt with in this chapter will apply to a company made up of the leaseholders just as they apply to a freeholder. Their aim is to ensure transparency and accountability where one party is responsible for handling funds provided by another party.

The key requirements are the following: **23.06**

(a) that costs incurred as service charges are reasonably incurred and that works carried out are performed to a reasonable standard;
(b) that tenants are properly consulted before works are carried out;
(c) that tenants are provided with sufficient information to ensure that monies provided as service charges are being properly used;
(d) that monies provided as service charges are held on trust.

There are also further provisions regarding insurance and administration charges and the rights of tenants to take over the management of their own building or to have a different manager appointed where the current management is unsatisfactory.

B STATUTORY CONTROL OF SERVICE CHARGES

The majority of the statutory provisions relating to the control of service charges are cur-   **23.07**
rently to be found in the Landlord and Tenant Act 1985 (LTA 1985), ss 18–30. These provisions deal with the reasonableness of service charges and a leaseholder's right to refer service charges to a leasehold valuation tribunal (LVT) for determination. These provisions have been substantially amended by the Commonhold and Leasehold Reform Act 2002 (CLRA).

A 'dwelling'

The statutory restrictions contained in the LTA 1985, ss 18–30 apply only to dwellings. A   **23.08**
'dwelling' is defined by s 38 to mean a building or part of a building occupied or intended to be occupied as a separate dwelling, together with any yard, garden, outhouses, and appurtenances belonging to it or usually enjoyed with it.

It would be thought that this seemingly straightforward definition would restrict the ambit   **23.09**
of the 1985 Act to residential property. However, in the case of *Ruddy v Oakfern Properties Ltd* [2006] EWCA Civ 1389 Jonathan Parker LJ took the view, following the earlier county court case of *Heron Maple House v Central Estates* [2002] 1 EGLR 35 on consultation requirements under s 20 (see below), that a tenant should not be excluded from the Act 'merely because whilst he is the tenant of a dwelling which extends to part of the building he is also the tenant of other parts of the building, be such other parts dwellings or common parts or some other type of property altogether (eg commercial property)'. In this case the tenant in question was an intermediate landlord, a not-for-profit management company that stood between the freeholder and the lessees of the flats in the block; however, if taken to their logical conclusion, these comments do appear to suggest that any mixed use property which includes a dwelling (eg a caretaker's flat in a factory) could potentially fall within the statutory restrictions.

23.10 In *Buckley v Bowerbeck Properties Ltd* [2009] 01 EG 78, a case concerning mixed-use premises with medical consulting rooms on the ground floor and a residential flat in the basement, the residential part was held not to be 'separate' within the meaning of s 38; an internal staircase linked the two floors, the doorbell rang in both parts of the premises, and the lease did not permit the two parts to be occupied separately.

23.11 Whether a holiday home is a dwelling is another question that has fallen to be considered by the courts. In *King v Udlaw* [2008] 20 EG 138 the leases of bungalows on a holiday park contained a covenant not to use the premises for any purpose other than as a holiday bungalow. The Lands Tribunal took the view that such a bungalow was not occupied as a home and therefore could not fall within the protection of the Act. This view, however, has recently been rejected by the High Court in *Phillips and Goddard v Francis* (LTL 16/4/2010) where it was held that the word 'dwelling' is not limited to use of a main home as a private residence.

'Service charge' and 'relevant costs'

23.12 For the purposes of the LTA 1985 a service charge is an amount payable by a tenant of a dwelling as part of or in addition to the rent:

(a) which is payable, directly or indirectly, for services, repairs, maintenance, improvements, or insurance or the landlord's cost of management; and

(b) the whole or part of which varies or may vary according to the relevant costs (s 18(1)).

23.13 Relevant costs are the costs or estimated costs incurred or to be incurred by or on behalf of the landlord, or a superior landlord, in connection with the matters for which a service charge is payable (s 18(2)). 'Costs' includes overheads and are relevant costs whether they are incurred in the period for which the service charge is payable or in an earlier or later period (s 18(3)).

23.14 Whether a particular item of expenditure can be charged as a service charge will depend on the terms of the lease. Most leases, for example, impose a repairing obligation on the landlord and a correlative right for the landlord to recover the expenses incurred in carrying out those obligations as service charges. However, where the lease does not oblige or allow the landlord to incur a particular expense, the landlord will not be able to charge this expense to the tenants. For example, where a lease does not provide that the landlord is able to employ managing agents to manage the property, the cost of doing this cannot be recovered from the tenants (*Embassy Court Residents' Association Ltd v Lipman* [1984] 2 EGLR 60).

23.15 A key feature of a service charge is that it varies, or at least a part of it is capable of variation. These provisions will not apply to a fixed amount, whether billed separately or included in the rent. They will apply to a variable amount even if it is reserved as rent. However, it must be capable of varying according to the relevant costs. This is not always a straightforward issue. The fact that a service charge is included in the rent and that the tenancy agreement allows the rent to be altered each year (subject to the rent control provisions of the Housing Act 1988) does not mean that it will fall within the s 18 definition where 'there is nothing in the tenancy agreement indicating that the altered amount is to be calculated in any particular manner, or linking any alteration in rent (including service charge) with an alteration in the costs of providing any relevant services' (*Home Group v Lewis* LRX/176/2006). On the other hand, where there is a provision in the lease directly linking a variation in the service charge to the cost of providing those services (eg by apportioning a surplus or deficit if the estimated charge for the previous year did not accord with actual expenditure) s 18 will apply (*Southern Housing Group Ltd and another, Re Ada Lewis House & Prince of Wales Court* [2010] UKUT 237 (LC)).

Though the provisions apply to insurance, it is normally regarded as a separate matter **23.16** and dealt with by the specific provisions contained in the Schedule to the Act (see 23.203). Similarly, overheads will normally fall under the provisions regarding administration charges (see 23.90)

There is an important distinction between the liability of a tenant to a landlord under a **23.17** lease and the liability of a shareholder to a company. Thus, where a management company is owned by the leaseholders, each of whom own one share in the company, sums payable to a recovery fund under the articles of the company are not a service charge within the meaning of s 18 (*Morshead Mansions Ltd v Di Marco* [2008] EWCA Civ 1371).

'Landlord'

For the purposes of the Act 'landlord' includes any person who has the right to enforce pay- **23.18** ment of a service charge (s 30). Managing agents and management companies are therefore subject to the provisions of the Act (see *Cinnamon Ltd v Morgan* [2001] EWCA Civ 1616, [2002] 2 P&CR 10). There is no exemption for resident landlords. The provisions of the Act will also apply to a company set up to acquire the freehold (see 24.118) or a right to manage company (see 23.157) that belongs to the leaseholders.

'Tenant'

For the purposes of the Act 'tenant' includes a statutory tenant and, where the dwelling or **23.19** part of it is sub-let, the sub-tenant (s 30). Sections 18–25 do not apply to tenants of a local authority, a National Park authority or a new town corporation unless the tenancy is a long tenancy (s 26(1)). If the tenancy is a long tenancy, ss 18–24 apply but s 25 (making non-compliance a criminal offence, see 23.67) does not. A long tenancy is a tenancy granted for a term of more than 21 years, a perpetually renewable tenancy, or a tenancy granted in pursuance of Pt V of the Housing Act 1985 (the right to buy and right to acquire) (s 26(2)). A tenant may be an intermediate landlord (see *Ruddy v Oakfern*, 23.09).

The requirement of reasonableness

The key limitation on the amount recoverable by a landlord as a service charge is provided **23.20** by s 19. Section 19(1) provides that relevant costs shall be taken into account in determining the amount of service charge payable for a period:

(a) only to the extent that they are reasonably incurred; and
(b) where they are incurred on the provision of services or the carrying out of works, only if the services are of a reasonable standard;

and the amount payable shall be limited accordingly.

Where the lease provides that all or part of a service charge is payable before work is **23.21** undertaken and relevant costs are incurred then no greater amount than is reasonable is payable. Any necessary adjustment will be made by repayment, reduction, or subsequent charges after the relevant costs have been incurred (s 19(2)).

It is important to bear in mind that s 19(1)(a) does not say that costs should be reason- **23.22** able but that they should be reasonably incurred, and these two things are not identical.

For example, it does not mean that the amount payable by the tenants should necessarily be reduced where the tenants can show that the repair work could have been performed at a lower price, nor that the landlord should always accept the cheapest tender from a number of estimates (see *Forcelux v Sweetman* [2001] 2 EGLR 173). What is important is that the landlord should act in a reasonable way in managing the premises and incurring the costs. For example, incurring costs for damp proofing when the work could have been done under guarantee at no cost to the tenants would not be reasonable (*Continental Property Ventures Inc v White* [2006] 1 EGLR 85). Where costs are incurred because of a landlord's failure to keep the premises in repair by remedying a leaking pipe within a reasonable time, these costs will not necessarily be unreasonable. However, the tenants would have a claim for damages for breach of covenant to repair which can be set off against the service charges (*Continental Property Ventures Inc v White*). It may also be reasonable for the landlord to take into account the financial impact of the works on the lessees and consider spreading the impact of the costs by undertaking the work in stages, but this will only be one factor amongst many. Whether the works would cause a particular tenant financial hardship is not a factor that will carry any weight; liability cannot be avoided by pleading poverty (*Garside and another v RFYC Ltd and another* [2011] UKUT 367 (LC)).

23.23   Where the works or services provided are not performed to a reasonable standard this does not mean that the whole item will be disallowed; rather, a deduction may be made to reflect the poor quality of the work. There is no presumption for or against a finding of reasonableness of standard or of costs; it is therefore up to the party alleging unreasonableness to establish it to the satisfaction of the LVT (*Yorkbrook Investments Ltd v Batten* [1985] 2 EGLR 100).

Codes of practice

23.24   Section 87 of the Leasehold Reform, Housing and Urban Development Act 1993 entitled the Secretary of State to approve codes of practice in relation to the management of residential property. The relevant code with regard to service charges is the Royal Institution of Chartered Surveyors Service Charge Residential Management Code (approved by the Approval of Codes of Management Practice (Residential Property) Order 2009, SI 2009/512) which sets out best practice guidelines to be followed in managing residential property. Failure to abide by the code will not render a freeholder or managing agent liable to any proceedings, but the code is admissible as evidence and any provision of the code which appears to the tribunal to be relevant to any question arising in the proceedings shall be taken into account in determining that question (s 87(7)).

C THE ROLE OF THE LEASEHOLD VALUATION TRIBUNAL

23.25   In the event of a dispute, s 27A(1) provides that an application may be made to an LVT for a determination of whether a service charge is payable and, if it is, as to:

(a) the person by whom it is payable;
(b) the person to whom it is payable;
(c) the amount which is payable;
(d) the date at or by which it is payable; and
(e) the manner in which it is payable.

23.26   This section applies whether or not any payment has been made (s 27A(2)). There is no restriction on who may apply. In the majority of cases it will be either the landlord or the tenant but there is nothing in the provisions to prevent, say, a former tenant applying for a determination if the tenant believes that he or she was overcharged in the past or an under-lessee applying for a determination of the reasonableness of service charges payable by the head-lessee to the freeholder (see *Ruddy v Oakfern*, 23.09). However, no application may be made under s 27A(1) or (3) (see below) in respect of a matter which:

(a) has been agreed or admitted by the tenant;
(b) has been, or is to be, referred to arbitration pursuant to a post-dispute arbitration agreement to which the tenant is a party;
(c) has been the subject of determination by a court; or
(d) has been the subject of determination by an arbitral tribunal pursuant to a post-dispute arbitration agreement (s 27A(4)).

Nevertheless, a tenant will not be taken to have agreed or admitted any matter by reason only of having made any payment (s 27A(5)).

Section 27A(3) allows an application to be made to the LVT for a determination whether, **23.27** if costs were incurred for services, repairs, maintenance, improvements, insurance, or management of any specified description, a service charge would be payable for the costs and, if it would, as to the persons by and to whom it is payable, and the amount, date, and manner of payment. Thus, either a landlord or tenant (or other party) can obtain a determination before relevant costs are incurred.

In neither case is it possible to contract out of the provisions of s 27A. Section 27A(6) provides **23.28** that an agreement by the tenant of a dwelling (other than a post-dispute arbitration agreement) is void in so far as it purports to provide for a determination in a particular manner, or on particular evidence (eg a provision stating that the decision of the landlord's surveyor is final), of any question which may be the subject of an application under s 27A(1) or (3).

The procedures governing applications to the LVT are set out in Sch 12 to the CLRA **23.29** and the Leasehold Valuation Tribunals (Procedure) Regulations 2003, SI 2003/2099, WSI 2004/681, as amended by the Leasehold Valuation Tribunals (Procedure) (Amendment) Regulations 2004, SI 2004/3098, WSI 2005/1356. An application form (LTV4) is available from the Residential Property Tribunal Service. The form has a section enabling a tenant to make a s 20C application to limit costs (see 23.33 to 23.34) at the same time.

Appeals

Decisions of the LVT may only be appealed to the Lands Chamber of the Upper Tribunal **23.30** with the permission of either the LVT or the Upper Tribunal (CLRA, s 175). The procedure is governed by the Tribunal Procedure (Upper Tribunal) (Lands Chamber) Rules 2010, SI 2010/2600 and the Practice Directions—Lands Chamber of the Upper Tribunal (2010). Particular attention should be given to para 4.3 of the Practice Directions which sets out the tribunal's approach to granting permission to appeal. The Rules, Practice Directions, and application forms are available from <http://www.justice.gov.uk/tribunals/lands>. Where leave to appeal is refused the only way to challenge that decision is to apply to the administrative court for judicial review. Judicial review of the decision will only be granted in exceptional circumstances (see *R (Sinclair Gardens Investments (Kensington) Ltd) v Lands Tribunal* [2005] EWCA Civ 1305, [2006] 06 EG 172 and *Wellcome Trust Ltd v 19–22 Onslow Gardens Freehold* [2012] EWCA Civ 1024).

Court fees and costs of proceedings

The total court fees payable in relation to a determination by an LVT are limited to £500 **23.31** (CLRA, Sch 12, para 9(3)). The amounts payable are set out in the Leasehold Valuation

Tribunal (Fees) Regulations 2003, SI 2003/2098, WSI 2004/683. Normally, the parties must pay their own costs; however, an LVT may require a party to the proceedings to pay the costs incurred by another party (up to a limit of £500) where it dismisses the matter for being frivolous, vexatious, or an abuse of process or where it considers that a party has acted frivolously, vexatiously, abusively, disruptively, or otherwise unreasonably (Sch 12, para 10). Unlike the county court (which has the power to make a civil restraint order under CPR r 3.11), other than costs the LVT has no direct powers against a vexatious litigant, but in exceptional cases the Attorney General may apply for an order under s 42 of the Senior Courts Act 1981 that no civil proceedings or applications can be made by the litigant in question without leave of the High Court (*HM Attorney General v Singer* [2012] EWHC 326 (Admin)).

23.32 The fact that the LVT will only order one party to pay the other party's costs in exceptional circumstances does not prevent the landlord from seeking to recover the costs of the proceedings from the tenant by including them in the service charge. This of course will only be possible where the terms of the lease expressly permit the recovery of legal costs by way of service charge. Such clauses are common in long leases. The basic rule is that any such clause should be in clear and unambiguous terms (*Sella House v Mears* [1989] 1 EGLR 65) but whether this is the case is often a tricky matter of construction depending upon the exact wording of the lease. It is not necessary that the words 'legal costs' are expressly used. A clause permitting all costs incurred by the landlord in carrying out its obligations under the covenants and conditions in the lease can be sufficient (*Iperion Investments Corporation v Broadwalk House Residents Ltd* [1995] 2 EGLR 47 and *Plantation Wharf Mangment Co. Ltd v Jackson and another* [2011] UKUT 488 (LC)), though in *Sella House* a clause permitting the landlord to employ 'other professional persons as may be necessary or desirable for the proper maintenance and safety of the building' was held not to include legal advisors.

23.33 Where the lease does permit the recovery of costs it does not necessarily mean that the landlord will be able to do so. Section 20C permits the tenant to make an application for an order that all or any of the costs incurred, or to be incurred, by the landlord in connection with proceedings before a court, residential property tribunal, or LVT, or the Upper Tribunal, or in connection with arbitration proceedings, are not to be regarded as relevant costs to be taken into account in determining the amount of any service charge payable by the tenant or any other person specified in the application (s 20C(1)). The application should be made to the relevant court or tribunal in accordance with the rules set out in s 20C(2); the application can be made while the proceedings are taking place or after they have concluded.

23.34 In determining the application the court or tribunal may make such an order as it considers just and equitable in the circumstances (s 20C(3)). The principles by which this wide discretion should be exercised were considered by HH Judge Rich QC in *The Tenants of Langford Court v Doren Ltd* LRX/37/2000 and *Schilling v Canary Riverside Development* LRX/26/2005:

(1) The only principle upon which the discretion should be exercised is to have regard to what is just and equitable in all the circumstances. The circumstances include the conduct and circumstances of the parties as well as the outcome of the proceedings.

(2) Where a court has the power to award costs and exercises such power, it should also exercise its power under s 20C in order to ensure that its decision on costs is not subverted by the effect of the service charge.

(3) Where, as in the case of the LVT, there is no power to award costs there is no automatic expectation of an order under s 20C in favour of a successful tenant.

(4) The primary consideration that the LVT should keep in mind is that the power to make an order under s 20C should be used only in order to ensure that the right to claim costs as part of the service charge is not used in circumstances that make its use unjust. Its purpose is to give an opportunity to ensure fair treatment as between landlord and tenant, in circumstances where, even though costs have been reasonably and properly incurred by the landlord, it would be unjust that the tenants or some particular tenant should have to pay them.

D ESTIMATES AND CONSULTATION

Where a landlord, managing agent, or management company intends to undertake works **23.35** or provide services, the cost of which will be born by the tenants, he or she may well be required to consult with the tenants before going ahead with the works or providing the services. The provisions governing consultation are extensive and are set out in ss 20 and 20ZA of the Act and in the Service Charges (Consultation Requirements) Regulations 2003, SI 2003/1987, WSI 2004/684, as amended by the Service Charges (Consultation Requirements)(Amendment) (No 2) Regulations 2004, SI 2004/2939, WSI 2005/1357 ('the Regulations').These provisions were introduced by the CLRA and were brought into force on 31 October 2003 in England and on 31 March 2004 in Wales. Where qualifying works (see 23.39) were begun or notice was given under the old s 20 prior to these dates the provisions of the original s 20 will apply. It should be noted that where a lease contains an express provision regarding consultation this will not be overridden by the statutory provisions; the landlord will have to comply with both the contractual and statutory requirements.

The details of the statutory consultation procedures are set out in the Schedules to the **23.36** Regulations. These will apply in three main cases:

(a) where the landlord is proposing to undertake expensive works to the premises (Sch 4, Pt 2);
(b) where that landlord is proposing to enter into a long-term agreement (Sch 1); and
(c) where expensive works are to be undertaken under a long-term agreement (Sch 3).

Slightly different consultation procedures are necessary when public notice is required (see **23.37** Schs 2 and 4, Pt 1). Public notice is defined as notice published in the Official Journal of the European Union pursuant to the Public Contracts Regulations 2006, SI 2006/5. This occurs where the amount of money involved is so substantial that EU public procurement rules apply. In such cases, while the tenants may submit their observations, they do not have the right to nominate a contractor. This is only likely to affect public sector landlords.

When must a landlord consult?

A landlord is required to fulfil the consultation requirements when he or she intends **23.38** either:

(a) to undertake qualifying works on the premises; or
(b) to enter into a long-term agreement (s 20(1)),

and the cost to be incurred exceeds the financial limits set out in the Regulations.

Qualifying works

Qualifying works mean works on a building or any other premises (s 20ZA(2)) and will **23.39** include, for example, any one-off works undertaken by the landlord such as redecorating the exterior or common parts or repairing the structure of the building. However, window cleaning does not fall within the definition (*Paddington Walk Management Ltd v Governors of Peabody Trust* [2010] L&TR 6).

Qualifying long-term agreement

23.40   A qualifying long-term agreement, on the other hand, means an agreement entered into, by or on behalf of the landlord or a superior landlord, for a term of more than 12 months (s 2ZA(2)), for example where the landlord enters into a contract with a third party to provide ongoing maintenance or services for the building, such as a service contract for lifts or entry phones, a long-term cleaning contract for the common areas, or a long-term maintenance contract. The recent county court case of *Paddington Walk Management Ltd v Governors of Peabody Trust* [2010] L&TR 6 has suggested that an agreement for an initial term of one year and then from year to year subject to a right to terminate is not a term for more than 12 months within the meaning of s 2ZA(2).

23.41   Certain long-term agreements are exempted however from the consultation requirement by reg 3(1), and these are:

(a)   a contract of employment (so, for example, a landlord would not have to consult with the tenants before employing a caretaker);

(b)   a management agreement made by a local housing authority and (i) a tenant management organization or (ii) a body established under s 2 of the Local Government Act 2000;

(c)   an agreement between a holding company and one or more of its subsidiaries or two or more subsidiaries of the same holding company; and

(d)   an agreement entered into when there are no tenants of the building and the agreement is for a term not exceeding five years (it appears that a tenant not in actual occupation of the building, such as an intermediate landlord, is still a tenant for the purposes of reg 3(1): *Paddington Walk v Peabody*).

Financial limits

23.42   For qualifying works the current appropriate amount is an amount which results in the relevant contribution of any tenant being more than £250 (reg 6). In respect of a qualifying long-term agreement consultation is required if, under the agreement, the relevant contribution of any tenant exceeds £100 in any 12-month accounting period (reg 4). The relevant contribution is the amount a tenant may be required to contribute to the relevant costs by service charge under the lease (s 20(2)). Thus, to know whether the consultation requirements need to be fulfilled, a landlord will need to calculate the contributions of each tenant. If one of the tenants has to contribute more than the financial limits, consultation is necessary.

23.43   If a landlord fails to comply with the consultation requirements, the amount he or she will be able to recover from each tenant by way of service charge will be limited to the appropriate amount, namely to £250 for qualifying works and £100 for a qualifying long-term agreement (s 20(7)).

23.44   Where the landlord's direct tenant is in fact a intermediate landlord of a block containing a number of flats (as in *Oakfern v Ruddy*, see 23.09, and *Paddington Walk v Peabody*) a difficulty of construction arises. Should the limits be calculated by reference to the contribution of the single tenant or by reference to the number of flats? In *Paddington Walk* the building contained 79 dwelling units and it was held that the limit was the aggregate of the contribution of each individual unit. This is consistent with the general philosophy of the Act and keeps the consultation requirements at a sensible level. If the limit is calculated with reference to the single tenant it would mean that the landlord would have to fulfil the consultation requirements if the total cost of qualifying works exceeded £250 (as opposed to £19,750 on the per unit basis).

Dispensing with consultation

The LVT has the power to dispense with any or all of the consultation requirements where **23.45** an application is made under s 20ZA(1) and the LVT is satisfied that it is reasonable to do so. For example, this might be appropriate where emergency works need to be undertaken urgently and it is not practical to comply with the consultation requirements. The key question will be whether any significant prejudice has been suffered by the tenant as a result of the landlord's failure to comply with the consultation requirements, not, as under the old law, whether the landlord had acted reasonably (*Eltham Properties v Kenny* [2008] L&TR 14, LRX/161/2006 and *Daejan Investments Ltd v Benson and Others* [2011] EWCA Civ 38). Where a dispensation is refused with regard to major works the consequences can be serious for the landlord who may well only be able to recover £250 from each tenant. However, such financial consequences are irrelevant when the LVT is exercising its discretion (*Daejan Investments Ltd*).

The most obvious examples of what would amount to prejudice suffered by the tenants **23.46** would be where, had the landlord complied with the consultation requirements, the work could have been carried out more cheaply and better by another contractor, or the tenants would have been able to obtain legal or a surveyor's advice, or they would have had sufficient time to make representations. Where, however, there is a clear breach of the consultation process, it is not necessary for the tenants to establish prejudice; it is reasonable to assume that it has taken place even though the landlord may argue that the lack of consultation made no difference (*Stenau Properties Ltd v Leek and others* [2011] UKUT 478 (LC)). Participation in the decision-making process is of real value. 'The effect of a properly conducted consultation process should be to give the tenants confidence in the decisions that are reached …' (*Stenau Properties* at para 22). It will be different where the failure to comply is only a minor breach of procedure, in which case the tribunal will require evidence that the tenants were prejudiced (*Eltham Properties v Kenny* and *Stenau Properties*).

In the vast majority of cases an application under s 20ZA(1) will be made after the qualify- **23.47** ing works have been undertaken but it is also possible to apply for a dispensation before undertaking the works or entering into a qualifying long-term agreement (*Auger v Camden* LRX/81/2007). An application form (LVT6) is available from the Residential Property Tribunal Service.

Grants

Where the landlord receives a grant to assist with the carrying out of works under s 523 **23.48** of the Housing Act 1985, Pt I of the Housing Grants, Construction and Regeneration Act 1996, or art 3 of the Regulatory Reform (Housing Assistance) (England and Wales) Order 2002, SI 2002/1860, the amount of the grant should be deducted from the costs and the amount of the service charge payable should be reduced accordingly (s 20A(1)).

The consultation requirements

As mentioned earlier, the consultation procedures set out in the Schedules to the Regulations **23.49** are detailed and different procedures apply depending on whether the landlord is undertaking works or entering into a long-term agreement and whether public notice is required.

The most commonly used consultation requirements for qualifying works where no public notice is required are contained in Pt 2 of Sch 4 and the process is outlined below. This is the procedure a landlord needs to follow when he or she is proposing to undertake one-off works to the premises, such as redecorating the exterior or common parts. It should be noted that, though following a similar time frame and structure, the requirements are different when the landlord is proposing to enter into a qualifying long-term agreement or to undertake qualifying works under a long-term agreement. In these cases reference should be made to Sch 1 and Sch 3 to the Regulations.

Landlord's initial notice

23.50 The first stage is for the landlord to give notice of his or her intention to carry out qualifying works to each tenant and to any recognized tenants' association (RTA) representing some or all of the tenants. The notice must:

(a) describe, in general terms, the proposed works or specify the place and hours at which a description of the proposed works may be inspected (Sch 4, para 8(2)) (where the description is made available for inspection, the place and hours must be reasonable, and either there should be facilities to take copies or the landlord should provide any tenant, on request and free of charge, a copy of the description (Sch 4, para 9));

(b) state the landlord's reasons for considering it necessary to carry out the proposed works;

(c) invite the making, in writing, of observations in relation to the proposed works;

(d) specify the address to which such observations may be sent;

(e) specify the period within which observations should be made (30 days beginning with the date of the notice (reg 2(1)) and the date on which the period ends;

(f) invite each tenant and the RTA (if any) to propose, within 30 days, the name of a person from whom the landlord should try to obtain an estimate for the proposed works (Sch 4, para 8(3)).

If observations are made within the relevant period, the landlord shall have regard to those observations (Sch 4, para 10).

Obtaining estimates

23.51 The second stage, after the 30-day notice period has expired, is for the landlord to obtain estimates. Where a tenant or the RTA has made a nomination, the landlord must try to obtain an estimate from the nominated person. Obviously, the landlord cannot compel the nominated person to give an estimate; the requirement will be satisfied as long as the landlord requests an estimate. If both the RTA and a tenant make a nomination, the landlord must try to obtain an estimate from both nominated persons. Where there are multiple nominations, the landlord may choose, but there is a scale of preference. If there is more than one nomination from tenants, the landlord should approach the person with the most nominations. If two persons receive more nominations than the others, the landlord must approach one of them (Sch 4, para 11(3)). If both the RTA and the tenants make more than one nomination the landlord must seek to get an estimate from one person nominated by the RTA and also from one nominated by a tenant (Sch 4, para 11(4)).

23.52 Once the landlord has obtained estimates he or she must supply each tenant and the secretary of the RTA with a statement ('the paragraph b statement'). This statement must:

(a) set out, as regards at least two of the estimates, the amount specified in the estimate as the estimated cost of the proposed works; and

(b) where, following the invitation given in the notice, the landlord has received observations on the proposed works, a summary of the observations, and the landlord's
response to them (Sch 4, para 11(5)).

At least one of the estimates must be that of a person wholly unconnected with the land- **23.53**
lord (Sch 4, para 11(6)). Paragraph 11(7) of Sch 4 sets out the situations in which there
shall be assumed to be a connection between the person and the landlord, for example if
both landlord and the person giving the estimate are companies and they share a director or manager, or where the person giving the estimate is a close relative of a director or
manager of the landlord company.

The landlord must make all of the estimates available for inspection and give each tenant **23.54**
and the secretary of the RTA a second notice which, in similar terms to the initial notice,
specifies the place and hours they may be inspected, invites written observations to be made
within 30 days, and specifies the day on which this period ends (Sch 4, para 11(10)). As with
the initial notice, the landlord shall have regard to these observations (Sch 4, para 12).

Contracting

After the 30 days have expired and the landlord has considered the tenants' observations **23.55**
the landlord may enter into a contract for the works. If the person with whom the contract
is made was either nominated by the tenants or the RTA or submitted the lowest estimate,
the consultation process is at an end. If the person was not nominated or did not submit the
lowest estimate, the landlord must give each tenant and the RTA a further written notice
within 21 days of entering into the contract. This notice must:

(a) state the landlord's reasons for awarding the contract or (as with the initial and second
notice) specify the place and hours at which the statement of those reasons may be
inspected; and
(b) where observation were received following the second notice, summarize the observations and set out the landlord's responses to them.

E TENANTS' RIGHTS TO INFORMATION

A tenant will obviously want to know how the money he or she contributes to the land- **23.56**
lord as a service charge is being spent. The suspicion that monies paid to the landlord as
a service charge are not being properly used is one of the most common disputes between
long leaseholders and their landlords. To be able to determine whether the funds are being
applied correctly the tenant will need to be possessed of information that lies in the hands
of the landlord. Currently, however, there is no statutory requirement for landlords to supply the tenant with annual figures, though in the majority of long leases there will usually
be a provision requiring the landlord to do so.

Sections 152 to 154 of the CLRA, by substituting new ss 21 and 22 and adding new **23.57**
ss 21A and B to the 1985 Act, were to have introduced a number of measures designed
to improve transparency. Of these, so far only s 21B (requiring the landlord to provide a
summary of the tenant's rights and obligations with a service charge demand, see 23.72) is
actually in force. The other provisions, requiring the landlord to supply a regular statement
of account and entitling the tenant to withhold payment if the landlord fails to do so, were
felt, after consultation, to be unsatisfactory. It was thought that they would prove difficult
for landlords (in particular social landlords) to implement and would result in the landlords
incurring further costs which would then be passed on to the leaseholders. Schedule 12

to the Housing and Regeneration Act 2008 has therefore substituted the replacement s 21 proposed by the CLRA (see 23.68) and amended the provisions of the new s 21A (see 23.70) and s 22 (see 23.73). At the time of writing, except for provisions concerning the power to make regulations, Sch 12 is not yet in force.

Right to basic information

23.58 Where the premises consist of or include a dwelling and are not held under a tenancy to which Pt III of the Landlord and Tenant Act 1954 applies (ie are not a business tenancy), Pt VI of the Landlord and Tenant Act 1987 provides that where the landlord makes a written demand for rent or other sums payable under the terms of the tenancy, that demand must include the name and address of the landlord and, if that address is not in England and Wales, an address in England and Wales at which notices (including notices in proceedings) may be served (s 47(1)). It is the landlord's actual address that is required, either his or her residence or, if a company, place of business. An agent's address is not sufficient (*Beitov Properties Ltd v Elliston Martin* [2012] UKUT 133 (LC)). Where a demand does not fulfil this requirement any part of the amount demanded which consists of a service charge shall be treated for all purposes as not being due until the landlord has provided the required information (s 47(2)). Under Sch 11 to the CLRA this section now also applies to administration charges (see 23.90) as well as to service charges.

Request for summary of relevant costs

23.59 As the law currently stands the landlord is not obliged automatically to provide the tenant with information about service charges (unless, of course, the lease requires it); the onus, rather, is on the tenant, who has the right to demand certain accounting information from the landlord under s 21 of the LTA 1985. Tenants may not always be aware of this right, but as of 1 October 2007 the landlord has to send tenants a summary of the tenants' rights and obligations in relation to service charges with every service charge demand.

23.60 Section 21 provides that a tenant may require the landlord to supply him or her with a written summary of the costs incurred:

(a) if the relevant accounts are made up for periods of 12 months, in the last such period ending not later than the date of the request; or

(b) if the accounts are not so made up, in the period of 12 months ending with the date of the request and which are relevant costs in relation to the service charges payable or demanded as payable in that or any other period (s 21(1)).

23.61 The request may be made by the secretary of an RTA (if one exists) and then the summary will be supplied to the secretary (s 21(2)). The landlord should comply with the request within one month of the request or within six months of the end of the accounting period (whichever is the later) (s 21(4)).

23.62 The summary should set out the costs to show how they have been or will be reflected in service charges and summarize each of the following items, namely:

(a) any of the costs in respect of which no demand for payment was received by the landlord within the accounting period;

(b) any of the costs in respect of which a demand for payment was received but for which no payment was made within the accounting period;

(c) any of the costs in respect of which a demand for payment was received and payment was made by the landlord within the accounting period.

It must also specify any amount still standing to the credit of the tenants from the amounts **23.63** received on account of service charges for the accounting period and state whether any relevant grant has been received by the landlord (s 21(5)). If the relevant costs are payable by the tenants of more than four dwellings, the summary should be certified by a qualified accountant as being a fair summary complying with s 21(5) and being sufficiently supported by accounts, receipts, and other documents which have been produced to that accountant (s 21(6)).

Inspection of supporting documents

Where a tenant or the secretary of an RTA (see 23.77) has obtained a summary of relevant **23.64** costs (whether under s 21 or otherwise), the tenant or secretary may, within six months of receiving the summary, require the landlord in writing to afford him or her reasonable facilities for inspecting the accounts, receipts, and other documents supporting the summary and for taking copies or extracts of them (s 22(2)). The landlord shall make the facilities available for a period of two months beginning not later than one month after the request is made (s 22(4)). The facilities should be provided free of charge, but reasonable payment may be required for making copies (s 22(5)) and the landlord is entitled to treat the cost incurred in making the facilities available as part of the costs of management (s 22(6)).

Information held by superior landlord

Where a tenant (or the secretary of an RTA) has made a request under s 21 and the tenant's **23.65** landlord is not the freeholder, and there are one or more intermediate landlords between the tenant and the landlord in possession of the relevant information, then the intermediate landlord must in turn make a request to his or her landlord for the relevant information. The superior landlord must comply with the request within a reasonable time (or if necessary request the information from his or her landlord). Once the immediate landlord has the information he or she must pass it on to the tenant within the time limits allowed by s 21 (s 23).

Assignment

If the tenancy is assigned after a request is made under s 21, 22, or 23 the request remains **23.66** valid. However, the landlord is not obliged to provide a summary or make facilities available for inspection of supporting documents more than once for the same dwelling and for the same period (s 24).

Offence not to comply with request

If a person fails to comply, without reasonable excuse, to perform a duty imposed by s 21, **23.67** 22, or 23 it is an offence and that person will be liable, on conviction, to a fine not exceeding level 4 on the standard scale (£2,500) (s 25).

New requirement for service charge information

Section 303 of and Sch 12 to the Housing and Regeneration Act 2008, when it comes into **23.68** force, will introduce a new s 21. This is a very different creature from the s 21 currently in force; instead of giving the tenant the right to request information about service charges, the new regime will require the landlord to provide that information as a matter of course. It is also different from the replacement s 21 originally intended to be substituted by s 152 of the CLRA, which, following consultation, was never brought into force, in that the new s 21 provides scant particulars and merely provides broad parameters within which regulations can be made. It is the regulations themselves, which have yet to be made, which will contain the details of the scheme.

23.69   Under s 21, the regulations will, subject to exceptions, require the landlord to provide information about the service charges of the tenant, any associated charges (defined by s 21(10) as the service charges of other tenants where they relate to the same costs to which the tenant contributes), and any relevant costs (defined by s 18(2) and (3), see 23.13) relating to those service charges (s 21(2)). They will require the landlord to provide the tenant with a report on the information provided by a qualified person (s 21(3)). The regulations may also make provision regarding the information and reports to be provided, the periods in relation to which the information is to be provided, the times at which it is to be provided, the form and manner in which it is to be provided, and the definition of a qualified person (s 21(4)). Section 21(6) further provides that regulations may make different provision for different cases, descriptions of case, or for different purposes. It seems likely, therefore, that there will be differing provisions for private landlords, local authority landlords, and registered providers and registered social landlords.

Withholding payment of service charges

23.70   The new s 21A(1) provides that a tenant may withhold payment of a service charge if the landlord does not provide him or her with the information or a report required at the correct time or if the form or content of information or a report does not conform exactly or substantially with the requirements prescribed by regulation. The maximum amount a tenant may withhold is the sum of the service charges paid by the tenant in that period to which the information or report relates plus a sum equal to the sum standing to the tenant's credit at the beginning of that period (s 21A(2)).

23.71   The tenant may not withhold payment once the correct information or report has been supplied even if it is supplied late (s 21A(3)). Similarly, payment may not be withheld if the landlord applies to an LVT and the tribunal makes a determination that the landlord had a reasonable excuse for his failure (s 21A(4)). A landlord includes any person with a right to enforce payment of a service charge (s 30, see 23.18).

Summary of rights and obligations

23.72   From 1 October 2007 in England and 30 November 2007 in Wales, s 21B requires a demand for payment of a service charge to be accompanied by a summary of the rights and obligations of tenants of dwellings in relation to service charges. The form and content of this summary is set out in the Service Charges (Summary of Rights and Obligations, and Transitional Provision) Regulations 2007, SI 2007/1257, WSI 2007/3160 and takes the form of a prescribed statement briefly setting out a tenant's rights, including the right to ask an LVT to determine the amount payable as service charge, the right to be properly consulted, the right to apply to an LVT for a variation of the lease, and the right to request a summary of costs, to inspect the landlord's accounts, and to an audit. If a summary of rights and obligations is not sent with a demand for a service charge, the tenant may withhold payment of that service charge (s 21B(3)) (see *Tingdene Holiday Parks Ltd v Cox and others* [2011] UKUT 310 (LC)).

Inspection of documents

When the new provisions are brought into force, s 22 of the 1985 Act will be replaced by **23.73** a new s 22 (CLRA, s 154). By notice in writing a tenant (or the secretary of a recognized tenants' association) may require the landlord:

(a) to afford the tenant reasonable facilities for inspecting documents relevant to the information required to be provided to him or her by virtue of s 21 and for taking copies; or

(b) to take copies of the relevant documents and send them to the tenant (s 22(1)).

Such a notice may only be served in the six months following the date on which the tenant is required to be provided with the information concerned by virtue of s 21 (s 22(3)). However, if the information is late or does not conform to the prescribed requirements, the six months does not begin to run until the proper information is provided (s 22(4)). Once notice has been received the landlord has 21 days to comply (s 22(6)). The landlord must supply facilities for inspecting the documents free of charge (though costs incurred in doing so may be treated as part of the landlord's management costs) but may make a reasonable charge for doing anything else in order to comply with the notice, eg photocopying (s 22(7) and (8)).

Where the information required is held by a superior landlord, a new s 23 (substituted **23.74** by para 1 of Sch 10 to the CLRA and amended by para 5 of Sch 12 to the Housing and Regeneration Act 2008) will give the landlord the right to require the superior landlord to provide him or her with the relevant information within a reasonable time. A new s 23A (to be inserted by para 2 of Sch 10 and amended by para 6 of Sch 12) will apply where a landlord (or superior landlord) disposes of his or her interest and obliges a landlord who is still under a duty imposed by s 21, 22, or 23 (ie with regard to providing information, facilities for inspection, or obtaining information from a superior landlord) to continue to discharge that duty to the extent that he or she is still responsible to do so.

Time limits

Relevant costs must be included in the service charge within 18 months of those costs **23.75** being incurred. Costs will usually be 'incurred' on the presentation of an invoice or on payment but that may vary depending upon the facts of the particular case (see *OM Property Management Ltd v Burr* [2012] UKUT 2 (LC)). If relevant costs were incurred more than 18 months before a demand for payment of the service charge is served on the tenant, the tenant will not be liable for those costs (s 20B(1)) unless, within the period of 18 months following the costs being incurred, the tenant was notified that they had been incurred and that he would subsequently be required to contribute to them (s 20B(2)). The court or LVT has no discretion to dispense with notification. Such a notification must refer to costs that had been incurred; the provision of estimates is not sufficient. Similarly, a demand for payment under s 20B(1) must be a demand for the actual expenditure incurred, not an estimated amount (see *Paddington Walk Management Ltd v Governors of Peabody Trust* [2010] L&TR 6).

Where payments are made on account and the cost of the actual expenditure is covered by **23.76** these payments, the tenants cannot use s 20B to recover monies already paid, even though the accounts (which showed an overpayment by the tenants) were sent to the tenant more than 18 months after the work was carried out. Supplying the accounts did not amount to a demand for payment within the meaning of s 20B(1) because there was no outstanding sum to be demanded (*Gilje v Charlegrove Securities Ltd* [2003] EWHC 1284 (Ch), [2004] 1 All ER 91). Where the actual expenditure exceeds the amount paid on account and a balancing payment is demanded, the tenant will not be liable to pay the balancing payment (but only the balancing payment, not money already paid on account) in respect of any costs that were incurred more than 18 months before the demand (*Holding and Management (Solitaire) Ltd v Sherwin* [2010] UKUT 412 (LC)).

Recognized tenants' associations

23.77   A recognized tenants' association (RTA) is defined by s 29 of the 1985 Act as an association of qualifying tenants (whether with or without other tenants) which is recognized for the purposes of the provisions of this Act relating to service charges either:

(a)   by notice in writing given by the landlord to the secretary of the association; or

(b)   by a certificate of a member of the local rent assessment committee panel (s 29(1)).

Qualifying tenants here are simply tenants who are required under their leases to contribute to the same costs by payment of a service charge (s 29(4)).

23.78   The creation of an RTA is thus a relatively simple process which can usually be achieved by obtaining a letter of recognition from the landlord. The landlord may withdraw recognition on six months' notice (s 29(2)). If the landlord refuses to recognize the association, an application can be made to the rent assessment committee for a certificate. A certificate will normally be granted, usually for four years, if the association represents more that 60 per cent of the tenants.

23.79   Since the introduction of the CLRA many rights (particularly with regard to consultation) which were formerly only available to RTAs are also available to individual tenants. However, there are certain rights that can only be exercised by an RTA, in particular the right to appoint a surveyor (see 23.80) and the right to be consulted about managing agents (see 23.109).

Right of tenants' association to appoint a surveyor

23.80   Under the Housing Act 1996, s 84 an RTA may appoint a surveyor to advise on any matters in relation to, or which may give rise to, service charges payable to a landlord by one or more members of the association. The appointment takes effect on the association giving notice in writing to the landlord stating the name and address of the surveyor, the duration of his or her appointment, and the matters in respect of which he or she is appointed (s 84(3)). The surveyor must be a 'qualified surveyor' as defined by the Leasehold Reform, Housing and Urban Development Act 1993, s 78(4)(a). The rights exercisable by an appointed surveyor are set out in the Housing Act 1996, Sch 4. These include the right to appoint assistants (para 2), to inspect documents (para 3 and para 6), to inspect premises (para 4), and to enforce these rights against the landlord by application to the county court (para 5).

Tenants' right to a management audit

23.81   Under the Leasehold Reform, Housing and Urban Development Act 1993, Ch V, qualifying tenants (as defined by s 77) of dwellings held on long leases from the same landlord may have the right, by notice, to have a management audit carried out on their behalf (s 76). A management audit is carried out for the purpose of ascertaining:

(a)   the extent to which the obligations of the landlord which are owed to the qualifying tenants or the constituent dwellings and involve the discharge of management functions in relation to the premises, are being discharged in an efficient and effective manner; and

(b) the extent to which sums payable by those tenants by way of service charges are being applied in an efficient and effective manner (s 78(1)).

'Management functions' include functions with respect to the provisions of services or the repair, maintenance, improvement, or insurance of the property (s 84). **23.82**

The right may be exercised: **23.83**

(a) where there are three or more dwellings let to qualifying tenants, by not less than two-thirds of those tenants; and

(b) where there are two dwellings let to qualifying tenants, by either or both of those tenants (s 76(2)); and

(c) where there is only one dwelling let to a qualifying tenants, by that tenant (s 76(5)).

In determining whether a landlord's obligations are being discharged in an efficient and effective manner regard shall be had to any code of practice approved by the Secretary of State under s 87 (see 23.24). **23.84**

Currently, the auditor must be a qualified accountant within the meaning of s 28(1) of the 1985 Act (ie he or she is eligible for appointment as a statutory auditor under Pt 42 of the Companies Act 2006 and does not fall under any of the disqualifying categories by being an officer, employee, or agent of the landlord). When Sch 12 to the HRA 2008 comes into force s 28 will be omitted from the 1985 Act and a new definition of a qualified person will be inserted into s 78(4) (he or she must be a qualified surveyor, a member of a recognized supervisory body, and not belong to a disqualified category). **23.85**

To exercise the right the auditor must give notice to the landlord. The notice must be signed by each of the tenants on whose behalf it is given (s 80(2)). It should give the names and addresses of those tenants and the auditor, specify any documents the auditor wants to inspect, and, if an inspection of the premises is required, state the date on which it is proposed to carry it out (s 80(3)). This date should be at least one month and not more than two months after the date of notice (s 80(4)). **23.86**

The landlord should respond to the s 80 notice within one month by supplying the required documents or facilities for inspecting them (or giving notice with reasons stating why the landlord objects to producing the documents) and approving the date for inspection (or suggesting an alternative) (s 81(1)). If the landlord does not respond to the notice within two months, the auditor may apply to the court for an order requiring the landlord to do so. **23.87**

When the new provisions as to service charge information come into effect, Sch 12 to the Housing and Regeneration Act 2008 will make minor amendments to s 79 to permit the auditor to inspect documents relevant to the information required to be provided. **23.88**

Forfeiture

A landlord's right to forfeit for non-payment of service charges is restricted by statute. These provisions are dealt with in Chapter 11. **23.89**

F STATUTORY CONTROL OF ADMINISTRATION CHARGES

Schedule 11 to the CLRA introduced statutory restrictions on a landlord's right to charge an administration charge. An administration charge is not a service charge but rather a **23.90** charge levied on the leaseholders to cover costs incidental to the management of the building. In particular, the definition of an administration charge in Sch 11 (see 23.91) will cover penalty payments levied on leaseholders by landlords or management companies for failing to pay rent or service charges (or any other payment) by the due date.

What is an administration charge?

23.91   An administration charge is an amount payable by a tenant of a dwelling as part of or in addition to the rent which is payable, directly or indirectly:

(a)   for or in connection with the grant of approvals under the lease, or applications for such approvals;

(b)   for or in connection with the provision of information or documents by or on behalf of the landlord or a person who is party to the lease otherwise as landlord or tenant;

(c)   in respect of a failure by the tenant to make a payment by the due date to the landlord or a person who is party to the lease otherwise than as landlord or tenant; or

(d)   in connection with a breach (or alleged breach) of a covenant or condition in his or her lease (Sch 11, para 1(1)).

23.92   A 'variable administration charge' is an administration charge that is neither specified in the lease nor calculated in accordance with a formula specified in the lease (para 1(3)).

Reasonableness of administration charges

23.93   A variable administration charge is payable only to the extent that the amount of the charge is reasonable (Sch 11, para 2). Where there is a fixed administration charge (ie where the charge or a formula for calculating the charge is specified in the lease) any party to the lease may apply to an LVT for an order to vary the lease on the grounds that either any administration charge specified in the lease, or any formula specified in the lease and used to calculate an administration charge, is unreasonable (para 3).

Demands for payment of administration charges

23.94   Like a demand for payment of a service charge (see 23.72), a demand for the payment of an administration charge must be accompanied by a summary of a tenant's rights and obligations (Sch 11, para 4(1)). The form and content of this summary is set out in the Administration Charges (Summary of Rights and Obligations) Regulations 2007, SI 2007/1258, WSI 2007/3162 and takes the form of a prescribed statement briefly setting out a tenant's rights in relation to administration charges. If the required information is not provided the tenant may withhold payment of the administration charge (para 4(3)).

Liability to pay administration charges

23.95   An application may be made to an LVT for a determination as to whether an administration charge is payable and, if it is, as to the person by whom and to whom it is payable, the amount payable, the date on which it is payable, and the manner in which it is payable (Sch 11, para 5(1)). An application form (LTV2) is available from the Residential Property Tribunal Service. An application can be made whether or not any payment has been made (para 5(2)). However, an application may not be made in respect of a matter that has been agreed or admitted by the tenant, has been referred to arbitration pursuant to a post-dispute arbitration agreement to which the tenant is party, or has been determined by a court or arbitral tribunal (para 5(4)). The tenant is not to be taken to have agreed or admitted to any matter by reason only of having made any payment (para 5(5)). It is not possible to contract out of the provisions of Sch 11. Any agreement by the tenant (other than a post-dispute arbitration agreement) is void in so far as it purports to provide for a determination in a particular manner, or on particular evidence, of any question which may be the subject matter of an application under para 5 (para 5(6)).

G DEALING WITH SERVICE CHARGE FUNDS

Funds to be held on trust

Effectively, when a landlord accumulates money payable by the tenants in service charges, **23.96** the landlord is looking after somebody else's money. The sums involved can be substantial, particularly where there is a sinking fund or where major works are being undertaken. The Landlord and Tenant Act 1987, s 42 therefore provides that such money is held on trust. Section 42 will apply where the tenants of two or more dwellings may be required under the terms of their leases to contribute to the same costs by the payment of service charges or where a single tenant is required to contribute to costs to which no other tenant may be required to contribute (s 42(1)). Section 42 will not apply to the tenants of exempt landlords as defined by s 58(1) (this will include most local authority and social landlords, see 24.68). 'Service charges' here has the meaning given by s 18(1) of the LTA 1985 (see 23.12).

By s 42(2) any sums paid to the landlord by the contributing tenants (or tenant) by way **23.97** of service charges, and any investments representing those sums, shall (together with any income accruing thereon) be held by the landlord either as a single fund or, if the landlord thinks fit, in two or more separate funds (s 42(2)). This fund (or funds) is held:

(a) on trust to defray costs incurred in connection with the matters for which the relevant service charges were payable; and

(b) subject to that, on trust for the persons (or person) who are the contributing tenants (or tenant) for the time being (s 42(3)).

In the Act the landlord is referred to as the 'payee'; this term includes any other person to whom service charges are payable by the tenants (or tenant) under the terms of their leases.

The contributing tenants (or tenant) are treated as entitled to such shares in the residue **23.98** of the trust fund as are proportionate to their respective liabilities to pay service charges (s 42(4)). This, however, only applies when the leases (or lease) are continuing. If the lease of a contributing tenant comes to an end, he or she is not entitled to any part of the trust fund, and any part of the fund attributable to relevant service charges paid under the lease will continue to be held on trust for the purposes stated above (s 42(6)). Where there are no other tenants left and the lease of the last contributing tenant comes to an end, the trust fund will be dissolved when the lease terminates and any assets left in the fund are retained by the landlord (s 42(7)). These provisions (s 42(4), (6), and (7)) take effect subject to any express term in the lease relating to the distribution, either before or on termination of the lease, of amounts attributable to relevant service charges paid under the lease (s 42(8)).

Apart from the provisions with regard to termination (s 42(4), (6), and (7), see 23.98), it **23.99** is not possible to contract out of the statutory trust. The provisions of s 42 prevail over the terms of an express or implied trust created by a lease in so far as they are inconsistent with the provisions of s 42.

23.100   The types of account in which trust funds may be held are designated by the Service Charge Contributions (Authorised Investments) Order 1988, SI 1988/1284, as amended by the Financial Services and Markets Act 2000 (Consequential Amendments and Repeals) Order 2001, SI 2001/3649. These are interest-bearing UK accounts with institutions authorized by Pt 4 of the Financial Services and Markets Act 2000 such as banks, building societies, friendly societies, and credit unions.

Designated accounts

23.101   Along with the provisions regarding service charge information (see 23.68) the CLRA was to introduce new ss 42A and 42B containing stricter provisions requiring service charge funds to be held in designated accounts. These provisions have not yet been brought into force. In particular it was felt that the requirement that each fund should be held in a separate account would result in increased administrative costs. The provisions have therefore been amended by Sch 12, para 12 to the Housing and Regeneration Act 2008. It is likely that they will be brought into force along with the provisions as to service charge information.

23.102   Any money held on trust under s 42 must be held in a designated account, and at a relevant financial institution (s 42A(1)). What counts as a relevant financial institution will be specified in regulations (s 42A(11)).

23.103   An account is a designated account if the relevant financial institution has been notified in writing that sums standing to the credit of the trust fund or funds within the account are to be held in it (s 42A(2)(a)). Other sums may be held in the account but they must be sums standing to the credit of one or more other trust funds and the account must be of a description specified in regulations (s 42A(2)(b)). Regulations may also be made to restrict the movement of trust funds from one account to another (s 42A(2A)).

23.104   Section 42A(3) to (8) will entitle a contributing tenant or the secretary of an RTA by notice to inspect or receive copies of all statements and documents that explain the monies being held in the designated client account.

23.105   If a tenant has reasonable grounds for believing that the landlord (payee) has failed to comply with his or her duties under s 42A(1), the tenant may withhold payment of a service charge. Any provisions of his or her tenancy relating to non-payment or late payment of service charges (eg penalty clauses) will not have effect in relation to the period for which he withholds it (s 42A(9)). Regulations may make further provision regarding the circumstances in which a tenant may withhold payment, the period for which payment may be withheld, and the amount that may be withheld (s 42A(9A)).

23.106   Section 42B will make it a criminal offence not to comply with the duties imposed by s 42A punishable with a fine not exceeding level 4 on the standard scale (£2,500). Specific provision is made, where the offence is committed by a body corporate, for directors, managers, secretaries, and other persons purporting to act for the body corporate to be personally liable.

23.107   Where a right to manage (RTM) company has acquired the right to manage the property it too will be required to hold service charges on trust according to the provisions of s 42 but subject to the modifications made by Sch 7, para 11 to the CLRA. Most notably the tenants of exempt landlords are not excluded from the provisions where an RTM is managing the property.

23.108   The county court has jurisdiction to hear and determine any question arising under the provisions of s 42 (s 52(2)(b)).

H MANAGEMENT AND MANAGING AGENTS

Right to consult

By s 30B of the LTA 1985 a recognized tenants' association (see 23.77) may serve notice **23.109** on the landlord requesting the landlord to consult the association on matters relating to the appointment or employment of a managing agent. The landlord must then give the association details of any proposed or existing managing agent and the obligations that that managing agent will be required to discharge, and give the association the opportunity to make observations on the proposed (or existing) appointment (s 30B(2) and (3)). Once notice has been served the landlord is under a continuing duty to keep the association informed by serving a notice every five years (s 30B(4)). If the landlord sells his interest in the premises, the association's notice ceases to have effect and the association must serve a fresh notice on the new landlord (s 30B(5)).

Appointment of manager by leasehold valuation tribunal

Comparison with the right to manage

Tenants of flats in a building who think that the landlord is not managing the building **23.110** satisfactorily may apply to the LVT for an order appointing a manager under the provisions of Pt II of the Landlord and Tenant Act 1987. An alternative might be to exercise the right to manage introduced by the CLRA (see 23.149). There are significant differences between the two options, both in terms of procedure and eligibility. A manager will only be appointed under the 1987 Act where the tenants can establish mismanagement, whereas the right to manage may be exercised regardless of the landlord's or managing agent's conduct. There is also no requirement under the 1987 Act that the tenants hold long leases. Where an application under the 1987 Act is successful it will result in a court-appointed official taking over the management. Under the CLRA it is the tenants themselves, in the form of a right to manage company, who take over the management of the building. This gives the tenants control of their own building but it also imposes considerable number of responsibilities on them as members of the right to manage company.

Eligibility

An application to appoint a manager may be made by the tenant of a flat contained in **23.111** premises to which Pt II of the Act applies (s 21(1)). Part II applies to premises consisting of the whole or part of a building if the building or part contains two or more flats (s 21(2)). A flat is defined by s 60(1) of the 1987 Act (see 24.67). An application cannot be made where the landlord is an exempt landlord (eg local authorities, social landlords, and charities) or a resident landlord as defined by s 58(1) and (2) of the 1987 Act (s 21(3)) (see 24.68 and 24.69).

The resident landlord exception will not apply if at least half of the flats contained in **23.112** the premises are held on long leases (which are not business leases) (s 21(3A)). A joint application may be made by the tenants of two or more flats provided they are each eligible to apply (s 21(4)). If a flat is held on a joint tenancy, any one or more of the joint tenants may apply (s 21(5)). The 1987 Act does not apply to business tenancies (s 21(7)). Business tenants however may be able to apply to the High Court under its general jurisdiction to appoint a receiver or manager; such an application is not open to residential tenants eligible to apply for an order under Pt II of the 1987 Act (s 21(6)).

Preliminary notice by tenant

23.113   Before applying to the LVT a tenant must serve a preliminary notice upon the landlord and any person (other than the landlord) by whom obligations relating to the management of the premises are owed to the tenant under the tenancy (s 22(1)). The notice must:

(a)   specify the tenant's name, the address of his or her flat, and an address for service of notices;

(b)   state that the tenant intends to make an application for an order under s 24 to appoint a manager;

(c)   specify the grounds on which the tribunal would be asked to make the order and the matters which would be relied upon by the tenant to establish those grounds;

(d)   if those matters are capable of being remedied, require the person on whom the notice is served, within a reasonable period, to remedy them (s 22(2)).

If the notice requires matters to be remedied and the landlord or other relevant person fails to do so, the tenant may go on to make an application to the LVT. However, the application may not be made until the period specified has expired (s 23(1)(a)).

23.114   The requirement of a preliminary notice may be dispensed with if the tribunal is satisfied that it would not be reasonably practical to serve such notice (eg where an absentee landlord cannot be found) (s 22(3)). If the landlord's interest is subject to a mortgage the landlord must serve a copy of the notice on the mortgagee (s 22(4)).

Application to tribunal

23.115   The application should be made on the appropriate form (LVT 3, available from the Residential Property Tribunal Service at <http://www.gov.uk/tribunals/residential-property>). It should give details of the premises, the parties, the landlord (if a managing agent rather than the landlord is the respondent), any RTA, and the person the tenants wish to have appointed as a manager. The application should be accompanied by a list of other people who may be significantly affected by the application, such as other lessees in the building.

23.116   The tribunal may appoint a manager to carry out in relation to the premises:

(a)   such functions in connection with the management of the premises; or

(b)   such functions of a receiver,

or both, as it sees fit (s 24(1)).

23.117   A tribunal will make an order for the appointment of a manager where it is satisfied:

(a)   that any relevant person is in breach of any obligation owed by him to the tenant under his tenancy and relating to the management of the premises (or, if the obligation is dependent on notice, that the relevant person would be in breach if the tenant had been able to give the appropriate notice) (s 24(2)(a));

(b)   that unreasonable service charges have been made, or are proposed or likely to be made (s 24(2)(ab));

(c)   that unreasonable variable administration charges (see 23.90 to 23.95) have been made, or are proposed or likely to be made (s 24(2)(aba));

(d)   that any relevant person has failed to comply with the provisions of a code of practice approved by the Secretary of State under s 87 of the Leasehold Reform, Housing and Urban Development Act 1993 (s 24(2)(ac)) (see 23.24); and

(e)   that, in all of the above cases, it is just and convenient to make the order in all the circumstances of the case (s 24(2)).

23.118   A 'relevant person' is a person on whom notice has been served under s 22 (see 23.113), unless the requirement to serve notice has been dispensed with (s 24(2ZA)). This will include persons other than the landlord by whom management obligations are owed under the tenancy, such as a management company which is party to the lease or an RTM company.

For the purposes of (b) (23.117) a service charge shall be taken to be unreasonable: **23.119**

(a) if the amount is unreasonable having regard to the items for which it is payable;
(b) if the items for which it is payable are of an unnecessarily high standard; or
(c) if the items for which it is payable are of an insufficient standard with the result that additional service charges are or may be incurred (s 24(2A)).

'Management' in this section is to include references to the repair, maintenance, improve- **23.120** ment, or insurance of the premises (s 24(11)).

An order made under s 24 may make provision with respect to such matters relating to the **23.121** exercise by the manager of his functions under the order and such incidental or ancillary matters as the tribunal thinks fit (s 24(4)).

Where the LVT does appoint a manager, the manager acts independently as a court- **23.122** appointed official and does not enter into a contractual relationship with the tenants. A tenant cannot set off claims he or she has against the landlord against service charges demanded by the manager (see *Maunder Taylor v Blanquiere* [2002] EWCA Civ 1633, [2003] 1 WLR 379).

Discharge and variation of the order

Section 24(9) entitles any person interested to apply to the LVT to vary or discharge an order. **23.123**

Acquisition orders

As a final sanction, Pt III of the Landlord and Tenant Act 1987 gives tenants of flats the **23.124** right to compulsorily acquire their landlord's interest in the building if the landlord is in serious and continuing breach of his or her duties with regard to repair, maintenance, insurance, or management. This right, however, will only arise if one or either of the two conditions set out in s 29 can be established (see 23.130 and 23.131).

Premises

Part III of the Landlord and Tenant Act 1987 applies to premises if: **23.125**

(a) they consist of the whole or part of a building; and
(b) they contain two or more flats (as defined by s 60(1), see 24.67) held by tenants of the landlord who are qualifying tenants; and
(c) the total number of flats held by such tenants is not less than two-thirds of the total number of flats contained in the premises (s 25(2)).

Premises will not be eligible if: **23.126**

(a) the internal floor area of non-residential parts of the premises (excluding common parts) exceeds 50 per cent of the total internal floor area of the premises (s 25(4)) (see 24.107 for the parallel provisions under the Leasehold Reform, Housing and Urban Development Act 1993); or
(b) if the interest of the landlord belongs to an exempt landlord or a resident landlord as defined by s 58 of the 1987 Act (see 24.68 and 24.69) or are included in the functional land of a charity as defined by s 60(1) (s 25(5)).

23.127 A tenant is a qualifying tenant if he or she is the tenant of the flat under a long lease (s 26(1)). A long lease is defined by s 59 as a lease granted for a term certain exceeding 21 years, a lease for a term fixed by law with a covenant for perpetual renewal, or a lease granted in pursuance of the right to buy under Pt V of the Housing Act 1985. A business tenant cannot be a qualifying tenant nor can a tenant who also holds the long leases (but not business tenancies or short leases) of at least two other flats contained in the premises (s 26(2)). Where the tenant holds the tenancy under a long lease but his landlord is not the freeholder but an intermediate landlord who is also a qualifying tenant, it is the intermediate landlord who is to be regarded as the qualifying tenant (s 26(3)).

Preliminary notice

23.128 Before an application for an acquisition order can be made a requisite majority of qualifying tenants must serve notice on the landlord (s 27(1)). A requisite majority means not less than two-thirds of the qualifying tenants where there is one vote in respect of each flat held by a qualifying tenant and the total number of votes corresponds to the total number of flats let to qualifying tenants (s 27(4)). The notice must give the names and addresses of the qualifying tenants, state that they intend to apply for an acquisition order, specify the grounds on which the court will be asked to make the order and the matters that will be relied upon to establish those grounds, and request that, where possible, the landlord remedies those matters within a specified reasonable period (s 27(2)). If the court thinks that it would not be reasonably practical to serve a preliminary notice on the landlord, it may dispense with the requirement (s 27(3)).

Application

23.129 An application for an acquisition order must be made by qualifying tenants who, at the time it is made, constitute a requisite majority. The application is made to the county court. If the preliminary notice required the landlord to remedy matters, no application can be made until the period specified in the notice for remedy has expired (s 28(2)(a)). If notice was dispensed with by the court, no application may be made until the tenants have taken any steps the court ordered them to take (s 28(2)(b)). The content of the application is set out in CPR Part 56 PD, para 8.2, and it must be accompanied by a copy of the notice unless the requirement of notice was dispensed with by the court (para 8.3).

23.130 For an acquisition order to be made, either or both of two statutory conditions must be satisfied. The first condition requires that the court must be satisfied:

(a) that the landlord is in breach of any obligation owed by him to the applicants under their leases and relating to the repair, maintenance, improvement, insurance, or management of the premises; or

(b) in the case of an obligation dependent on notice, that the landlord would be in breach of any such obligation but for the fact that it has not been reasonably practical for the tenant to give him the appropriate notice; and

(c) that the circumstances by virtue of which the landlord is (or would be) in breach of any such obligation are likely to continue (s 29(2)).

23.131 The second condition requires that both at the date when the application was made and throughout a period of two years immediately preceding that date, there was in force an appointment under Pt II of the Landlord and Tenant Act 1987 of a person to act as manager in relation to the premises (see 23.110 to 23.123) (s 29(3)). The court must also be satisfied that, at the date of the preliminary notice and the application, the premises fell within the Act and that they have not ceased to be such premises since the application was made (s 29(1)(a)) and that it is appropriate to make the order in all the circumstances of the case (s 29(1)(c)).

If an acquisition order is made, it will provide for a person nominated by the tenants to be **23.132** entitled to acquire the landlord's interest in the premises on such terms as may be agreed between the landlord and the qualifying tenants or determined by an LVT under s 31 (s 30(1)). Special provisions will apply if it has not been possible to find the landlord (see s 33).

Variation of leases

Another problem that tenants may encounter with regard to the management and main- **23.133** tenance of the building in which they live is that the lease may not contain sufficient or satisfactory provisions to enable the landlord to carry out the management or maintenance properly or to enable the tenants to ensure that proper maintenance and management is carried out. Part IV of the 1987 Act provides a procedure whereby parties to a lease may apply to vary the lease.

Who may apply?

Any party to a long lease of a flat may apply to the LVT for an order varying the lease **23.134** (s 35(1)). A long lease has the same meaning as for an acquisition order (see 23.127). A lease will not be regarded as a long lease if the demised premises consist of three or more flats contained in the same building or if it is a business tenancy (s 35(6)). A flat is defined as for applications for appointment of a manager and acquisition orders by s 60(1) (see 24.67). It should be noted that there is no provision in Pt IV excluding resident and exempt landlords.

Grounds for the application

An eligible party to a long lease may apply for a variation on the grounds that the lease fails **23.135** to make satisfactory provision:

(a) for the repair and maintenance of the tenant's flat, the building containing the flat, or any land or building let to the tenant under the lease;
(b) for the insurance of the building containing the flat or any land or building let to the tenant under the lease;
(c) for the repair and maintenance of installations;
(d) for the provision of services;
(e) for the recovery of expenditure incurred by the other party to the lease;
(f) for the computation of a service charge payable under the lease (s 35(2)).

Whether or not the lease fails to make satisfactory provision should be judged in all the **23.136** circumstances of the case. 'A lease does not fail to make satisfactory provision … simply because it could have been better or more explicitly drafted. For instance the need to imply a term is not necessarily, or even probably, an indication that the lease fails to make satisfactory provision for the matter in question' (*Gianfrancesco v Haughton*, per Bartlet QC, LRX/10/2007).

Application

The application is made to the LVT. The provisions governing the application and the **23.137** hearing are set out in the Leasehold Valuation Tribunals (Procedure) Regulations 2003, SI 2003/2099, WSI 2004/681, as amended by SI 2004/3098 and WSI 2005/1356. An application form (LTV5) is available from the Residential Property Tribunal Service. Importantly, the applicant must give notice of the application to the respondent and any person who the applicant knows, or has reason to believe, is likely to be affected by the variation specified in the application. The notice must state that any person may make a request to the tribunal to be joined as a party to the proceedings.

23.138   If a person who should have been served with the application is not, in fact, served, and the LVT goes on to make a variation order, that person may bring an action for damages for breach of statutory duty against the person who should have served the notice or apply to the LVT for the cancellation or modification of the variation (s 39(3)).

Application by respondent for variation of other leases

23.139   Where one party to the lease has made an application to vary the lease any other party to the lease may make a further application to the court asking it, in the event of the court deciding to make an order effecting a variation to the lease, to make an order which effects a corresponding variation to one or more other leases as are specified in the application (s 36(1)). Each of these leases must be a long lease held under the same landlord as the lease in the original application (s 36(2)(a)). However, the lease or leases in question do not need to be of flats in the same building as the flat in the original application, nor do they have to be drafted in terms identical to the lease of that flat (s 36(2)(b)). The grounds on which such an application may be made are:

(a)   that each of the leases specified fails to make satisfactory provision with respect to the matters specified in the original application; and

(b)   that, if any variation is effected in pursuance of the original application, it would be in the interests of the person making the further application, or in the interests of the other persons who are parties to the leases specified in the further application, to have all the leases in question varied to the same effect (s 36(3)).

Such a further application should also be made to the LVT and the provisions of the Leasehold Valuation Tribunals (Procedure) Regulations 2003 will apply.

Application by majority of parties for variation of leases

23.140   An application may be made for an order varying two or more leases. Those leases must be long leases of flats held under the same landlord but they do not need to be leases of flats which are in the same building, or leases which are drafted in identical terms (s 37(2)). In contrast to applications under s 35 and 36 there is no requirement that the leases fail to make satisfactory provision. However, such an application may only be made if:

(a)   where the application is in respect of fewer than nine leases, all, or all but one, of the parties concerned (including the landlord) consent to it; or

(b)   where the application is in respect of more than eight leases, it is not opposed for any reason by more than 10 per cent of the total number of parties concerned (including the landlord) and at least 75 per cent of that number consent to it (s 37(5)).

23.141   The grounds on which such an application may be made are that the object to be achieved by the variation cannot be satisfactorily achieved unless all the leases are varied to the same effect (s 37(3)). The form of such an application will be the same as where there is one applicant (see 23.137).

Application to vary insurance provisions

23.142   The provisions we have considered apply only to the tenants and landlords of flats. In the case of insurance provisions, however, the right to apply to vary a lease is extended to houses. Section 40 provides that any party to the long lease of a dwelling may apply to the court (or now the LVT) on the grounds that the lease fails to make satisfactory provision with respect to any matter relating to the insurance of the dwelling, including the recovery of the costs of such insurance. A long lease will not be regarded as the long lease of a dwelling if it is a business tenancy or if the demised premises consist of three or more dwellings (s 40(4)), nor may an application be made by a person who is a tenant under a long lease of a dwelling if (by virtue of that lease and one or more other long leases) he or she is also a tenant of the same landlord of at least two other dwellings. Section 36 (see 23.139) and s 38 (see 23.143 to 23.148) will apply to an application under s 40 with the modifications contained in s 40(3).

Variation orders

Where an application is made under s 35 (see 23.137) and the grounds on which the application is made are established to the satisfaction of the LVT, the LVT may make an order varying the lease as specified in the application (s 38(1)) or an order making such other variation as the LVT thinks fit (s 38(4)). **23.143**

Where the respondent makes a cross-application to vary other leases under s 36 (see 23.139) and the grounds are established to the satisfaction of the LVT, the LVT may make an order varying each of those leases as specified in the application (s 38(2)) or an order making such other variation as the LVT thinks fit (s 38(4)). **23.144**

Where an application is made by a majority of parties under s 37 (see 23.140) and the grounds are established to the satisfaction of the LVT, the LVT may make an order varying each of those leases as specified in the application (s 38(3)) but does not have the power to make other variations. In the case of applications under s 36 or 37, where the grounds set out in the application are satisfied only with respect to some of the leases, the power to make an order extends only to those leases (s 38(5)). **23.145**

The LVT, however, may not make an order under s 38 if it appears to the court that: **23.146**

(a) the variation would be likely substantially to prejudice any respondent to the application; or
(b) the variation would be likely substantially to prejudice any person who is not a party to the application who cannot be satisfactorily compensated by a monetary award (the LVT has the power to order such a payment under s 38(10)); or
(c) for any other reason it would not be reasonable in the circumstances for the variation to be effected.

In making an order varying a lease the LVT may either: **23.147**

(a) make an order varying the lease in such a manner as is specified in the order; or
(b) make an order directing the parties to the lease to vary it in such a manner as is specified (s 38(8)).

The court may also direct that a memorandum of any variation by an order be endorsed on such documents as are specified in the order (s 38(9)). **23.148**

I THE RIGHT TO MANAGE

Chapter 1 of Pt 2 of the CLRA introduced a new right enabling the long leaseholders of flats to take over the management of their building by setting up a right to manage (RTM) company. The important difference between this right and the right to apply to have a manager appointed by an LVT under Pt II of the Landlord and Tenant Act 1987 (see 23.110 to 23.123) is that the leaseholder no longer has to establish that the current management is at fault. Before exercising the right to manage tenants should bear in mind the duties and **23.149** obligations it will involve. As members of the RTM company they will be responsible for budgeting, managing, appointing officers, holding regular meetings, organizing works, and making decisions; these tasks can be time consuming and demand a high level of cooperation between individuals who will often also be neighbours. There is, of course, nothing to prevent the RTM company employing a professional managing agent to undertake the practical management of the building; in fact, for all but the smallest blocks of flats this will usually be advisable.

Qualifying premises

23.150   The qualifying rules for premises are contained in CLRA, s 72. These rules are effectively the same as the rules for eligibility for the right to collective enfranchisement under the Leasehold Reform, Housing and Urban Development Act 1993 (see 24.101). Schedule 6, however, excludes the following premises from the right to manage.

Buildings with substantial non-residential parts

23.151   The right to manage will not apply where the internal floor area of any non-residential part (or parts) exceeds 25 per cent of the internal floor area of the premises taken as a whole (Sch 6, para 1(1)). These provisions are again effectively the same as the exclusion from the right to enfranchise under s 4(1) of the 1993 Act (see 24.107).

Buildings with self-contained parts in different ownership

23.152   The right to manage will not apply where a different freeholder owns different parts of the premises if any of those parts is a self-contained part of a building (Sch 6, para 2).

Premises with a resident landlord

23.153   The right to manage will not apply to premises which have a resident landlord and do not contain more than four units. This exclusion is again effectively the same as the resident landlord exclusion from the right to enfranchise under the 1993 Act (see 24.110) (Sch 6, para 3).

Premises owned by local housing authority

23.154   The right to manage will not apply if a local housing authority is the immediate landlord of any of the qualifying tenants of flats contained in the premises (Sch 6, para 4). (The tenants of local housing authorities have their own right to manage scheme, currently governed by the Housing (Right to Manage) (England) Regulations 2012, SI 2012/1821, which enables tenants to form a tenant management organization and take over housing management services from the housing authority.)

Premises in relation to which rights previously exercised

23.155   The right to manage will not apply if it has already been acquired and is currently exercisable by an RTM company (see 23.157) or if the right has already been acquired and has ceased to be exercisable but four years have not yet elapsed since the right ceased to be exercisable. In the latter case an application may be made by an RTM company to an LVT to waive the four-year period (Sch 6, para 5).

Appurtenant property

23.156   Section 72 provides that the right to manage will apply to premises with or without appurtenant property. Appurtenant property is defined by s 112 as any garage, outhouse, garden, yard, or appurtenances belonging to, or usually enjoyed with, the building or part or flat.

Right to manage companies

In order to exercise the right to manage, an RTM company must be in existence. A company is an RTM company in relation to premises if: **23.157**

(a) it is a private company limited by guarantee; and
(b) its memorandum of association states that its object, or one of its objects, is the acquisition and exercise of the right to manage the premises (s 73(2)).

The memorandum and articles of association of an RTM company must be in the form prescribed by law and contained in the schedule to the RTM Companies (Model Articles) (England) Regulations 2009, SI 2009/2767, WSI 2011/2680. These provisions replaced the previous prescribed form of articles (SI 2003/2120, WSI 2004/675) from 9 November 2009. The old articles could continue to be used for a transitional period until 30 September 2010. From that date the new articles automatically apply to all RTMs including those incorporated before 9 November 2009. Once the transitional period is over, existing RTM companies do not need to file the new articles at Companies House.

A company cannot be an RTM company if it is a commonhold association (see 25.18) (s 73(3)) or if another company is already an RTM company in relation to the premises (s 73(4)). If the RTM company is used to acquire the freehold it ceases to be an RTM company when the transfer is executed (s 73(5)). **23.158**

Membership

Only two classes of people are entitled to be members of an RTM company: **23.159**

(a) qualifying tenants of flats contained in the premises; and
(b) landlords under leases of the whole or any part of the premises (s 74(1)).

Landlords will only be entitled to become members of the RTM company (if they so wish) after the company has acquired the right to manage (see 23.181). A landlord (or landlords) is entitled to membership because, unlike the position where the tenants exercise the right to enfranchise, he or she retains an interest in the property and should therefore be entitled to a say in the management. Some landlords will have larger interests than others; for example the landlord might let a number of flats in the block on short leases or commercial units in the block on business leases. Landlords with greater interests will be given a larger number of votes in the RTM company. Complicated provisions for ascertaining the number of votes are set out in article 33(3) of the articles of association. Where no landlords are members, there is simply one vote per flat (article 33(2)). **23.160**

Qualifying tenants

A person is a qualifying tenant of a flat if he or she is a tenant of the flat under a long lease (s 75(2)). Sections 76 and 77 give a long lease effectively the same definition as under s 7 of the Leasehold Reform, Housing and Urban Development Act 1993 for the right to enfranchise (see 24.100). **23.161**

Claim to acquire right to manage

Notice of invitation to participate

Before making a claim to acquire the right to manage any premises, an RTM company must serve a 'notice of invitation to participate' on all qualifying tenants of flats in the premises who are not, or have not agreed to become, members of the RTM company. The **23.162** notice of invitation to participate should be in the prescribed form and must state that the RTM company intends to acquire the right to manage the premises, state the names of the members of the RTM company, invite the recipients of the notice to become members of the company, and give details of the RTM company and its functions and responsibilities. Notice must be in the form set out in Sch 1 to the Right to Manage (Prescribed Particulars and Forms) Regulations 2010, SI 2010/825, WSI 2011/2684. It should be accompanied by a copy of the articles of association of the RTM company or a statement saying where and when the documents can be inspected (s 78(4) and (5)).

23.163   A notice of invitation to participate is not invalidated by an inaccuracy in any of the particulars required by virtue of s 78 (s 78(7)). This saving provision is similar to those found in the Leasehold Reform Act 1967 (Sch 3, para 6(3)), and in the Leasehold Reform, Housing and Urban Development Act 1993 (Sch 3, para 15(1)) (see 24.42 and 24.129). A failure to serve one of two joint lessees who were a couple living together has been regarded as an oversight and held not to invalidate the subsequent claim (*Sinclair Gardens Investments (Kensington) Ltd v Oak Investments RTM Co Ltd*, LRX/52/2004).

Service of claim notice

23.164   A claim to acquire the right to manage any premises is made by giving a 'claim notice' (s 79(1)). The 'relevant date' for the purposes of Ch 1 is the date on which the claim notice is given (s 79(1)). A claim notice may not be given until 14 days have passed since the service of any notice of invitation to participate (s 79(2)). In smaller blocks it is likely that all the qualifying tenants will be members of the RTM company from the outset and so there will be no need to serve a notice of invitation to participate. If there are only two qualifying tenants of flats in the premises on the relevant date both must be members of the RTM company (s 79(4)). In all other cases, the membership of the RTM company must, on the relevant date, include a number of qualifying tenants of flats which is not less than half of the total number of flats contained in the premises (s 79(5)).

23.165   The claim notice must be served on each person who on the relevant date is:

(a)   a landlord under a lease of the whole or any part of the premises;
(b)   a party to such a lease otherwise as landlord or tenant (eg a management company); or
(c)   a manager appointed under Pt 2 of the Landlord and Tenant Act 1987 (see 23.110 to 23.123) to act in relation to the premises (s 79(6)).

23.166   A copy of the claim notice must also be given to each person who, on the relevant date, is the qualifying tenant of a flat contained in the premises (s 79(8)) and, if there is a manager who has been appointed by the LVT under the Landlord and Tenant Act 1987, a copy must be given to the LVT (or court) by which the manager was appointed (s 79(9)).

23.167   If, as in the case where the freeholder is untraceable or his or her identity cannot be ascertained, there is nobody on whom the claim notice can be served, the RTM company may apply to an LVT for an order that the company is to acquire the right to manage the premises (s 79(7) and s 85(2)). The RTM company must give notice of the application to each of the qualifying tenants (s 85(3)) and the tribunal may require the company to make further steps to trace the landlord (or other parties to the leases) before making an order (s 85(4)).

Contents of claim notice

23.168   The form of a claim notice is set out in Sch 2 to the Right to Manage (Prescribed Particulars and Forms) Regulations 2010 (2011 for Wales). The claim notice must specify the premises and contain a statement of the grounds on which it is claimed that they are eligible for the right to manage (s 80(2)). It must state the name of each person who is both a qualifying tenant of a flat contained in the premises and a member of the RTM company and give the address of his or her flat and particulars of his or her lease (s 80(3) and (4)). It must state the name and registered office of the RTM company (s 80(5)). It must also contain a statement informing the landlord that he or she may alert the RTM company of any inaccuracies in the claim notice, a reminder to the landlord to serve contract and contractor notices (see 23.185), and that the landlord has a right to join the RTM company. A date must be specified, at least one month after the relevant date, by which each person who was given a claim notice may respond by giving a counter-notice (see 23.173) and a further date must be specified, at least three months after the first date, on which the RTM company intends to acquire the right to manage the premises (s 80(7) and (8)).

Like a notice of invitation to participate (see 23.162), a claim notice is not to be invalidated **23.169** by any inaccuracy in any of the required particulars (s 81(1)). The use of a prescribed form from the previous regulations (which was not materially different from the current form) has been held to be an inaccuracy (*Assethold Ltd v 14 Stansfield Road RTM Company Ltd* [2012] UKUT 262 (LC)); on the other hand, to give a completely incorrect address for the RTM company would invalidate the notice (*Assethold Ltd v 15 Yonge Park RTM Company Ltd* [2011] UKUT 379 (LC)). If a landlord wishes to claim that the tenants have not complied with the provisions he or she must give good reasons why he or she thinks so, not merely state that it has not been proved: there is no presumption of non-compliance (*Assethold v Stansfield Road*). Similarly, if one or more of the members of the RTM company whose names are stated in the notice was not, in fact, the qualifying tenant of a flat on the relevant date, the claim will not be invalidated on that account provided a sufficient number (ie not less than half of the total number of flats) of qualifying tenants were members of the RTM company on that date (s 81(2)). Once a claim notice is served it is not possible to serve a subsequent notice regarding the premises or any premises containing or contained in the premises so long as the earlier claim remains in force (s 81(3)). A claim will remain in force until it is withdrawn or deemed to be withdrawn or ceases to have effect by reason of any other provision (eg because it is determined that the company is not entitled to exercise the right to manage) (s 81(4)).

Right to obtain information

An RTM company may give notice to any person requiring him or her to provide it, within **23.170** 28 days, with any information that the company reasonably requires for ascertaining the particulars required in a claim notice (s 82).

Right of access

Once a claim notice has been given, the RTM company or any of the persons on whom **23.171** the claim notice has been served (ie landlords, other people who are party to the lease, or a manager appointed by an LVT) or a person authorized to act on behalf of the company or any such person, are given a general right of access to any part of the premises if that access is reasonably required in connection with any matter arising out of the claim (s 83(1) and (2)). This right can be exercised at any reasonable time by giving not less than 10 days' notice to the occupier of the premises (s 83(3)).

Enforcement of rights

If a person fails to comply with a requirement imposed on him or her by the RTM provi- **23.172** sions (eg by failing to supply information under s 82 or 93 (see 23.186) or grant access under s 83), any person interested may apply to the county court for an order requiring the defaulter to comply within a specified period (s 107). Before making such an application, notice must be served on the defaulter requiring him or her to remedy the default and 14 days must have elapsed since service of the notice (s 107(2)).

Counter-notice

23.173 Any person who receives a claim notice from an RTM company may give counter-notice to the company (s 84(1)). The form of the counter-notice is set out in Sch 3 to the Right to Manage (Prescribed Particulars and Forms) Regulations 2010 and can either:

(a) admit that the RTM company is entitled to acquire the right to manage; or
(b) state that the RTM company is not entitled to acquire the right to manage and give particulars as to why it is not considered eligible (s 84(2)).

23.174 Any counter-notice must be served on the company no later than the date specified in the claim notice for serving counter-notice (s 84(1)). The grounds upon which the claim notice can be disputed are limited to questions of eligibility, ie that the building is not eligible, that the RTM company is not properly constituted, or that the membership of the RTM company does not include sufficient qualifying tenants. If no counter-notice is served the right to manage will be acquired on the date specified in the claim notice.

23.175 If the RTM company receives one or more notices stating that it is not entitled to acquire the right to manage, the company may then apply to the LVT for a determination that it is eligible (s 84(3)). Any such application must be made within two months of receiving the counter-notice (s 84(4)).

23.176 The RTM company will not then acquire the right to manage unless either it is finally determined by the LVT that the company was, on the relevant date, entitled to acquire the right to manage or the person or persons who disputed the company's eligibility by counter-notice agree in writing that the company was, in fact, so entitled (s 84(5)). If the LVT finally determines that the company is not entitled to acquire the right to manage, the claim notice ceases to have effect.

Withdrawal of claim

23.177 An RTM company which has given a claim notice may withdraw that claim notice at any time before it acquires the right to manage the premises by serving a 'notice of withdrawal'. A notice of withdrawal must be served on all the persons on whom the claim notice was served and on all the qualifying tenants of flats contained in the premises (s 86).

23.178 A claim notice will be deemed to be withdrawn if, having received a counter-notice disputing its eligibility, the RTM company fails to make an application to an LVT for a determination within the two-month period, or where such an application is made and subsequently withdrawn (s 87(1)). A claim notice will also be deemed to be withdrawn if the RTM company becomes insolvent or is struck off the register of companies (s 87(4)).

Costs

23.179 An RTM company is liable to any of the persons on whom it has served a claim notice for reasonable costs incurred in consequence of the claim notice. Where an application is made to an LVT for a determination whether the company is entitled to acquire the right to manage, the company is only liable for costs the other parties incur as parties to the proceedings if the LVT determines that the company is not entitled to acquire the right to manage (s 88).

Where a claim ceases because the RTM company has withdrawn the claim, the claim is **23.180** deemed to be withdrawn, or an LVT determines that the company is not entitled to acquire the right to manage, the RTM company is liable for costs incurred up until the time the claim ceases (s 89(1) and (2)). Each person who is (or has been) a member of the RTM company is also jointly and severally liable for those costs along with the company and the other members of the company (s 89(3)). Thus, the payment of other people's costs for an aborted claim cannot be evaded by dissolving the RTM company. The only exception to this will be where, during the course of the claim, one of the members of the RTM company has assigned his or her lease to another person and that person has become a member of the company (s 89(4)).

Date of acquisition

Where there is no dispute over the entitlement of the RTM company to acquire the right to **23.181** manage (either because no counter-notices are served or because the counter-notices admit that the company is entitled) the date on which the company acquires the right to manage the premises (the acquisition date) will be the date specified in the claim notice (s 90(2) and (3)).

Where there is a dispute over the entitlement of the RTM company and the LVT determines **23.182** that the company is entitled to acquire the right (see 23.175) then the acquisition date is three months after the determination becomes final (s 90(4)).

Where a counter-notice is served, but the person who serves it then withdraws his or her **23.183** objection by agreeing in writing that the company is entitled to acquire the right to manage, the acquisition date will be three months after the date of that agreement, or if more than one person have objected, three months after the date of the last agreement (s 90(5)).

Where the landlord is untraceable and an application for an order is made to an LVT under **23.184** s 85 (see 23.167) the acquisition date will be the date given in the order (s 90(6)).

Transfer of the right to manage

Management contract

In small blocks containing a small number of flats and limited common areas and facilities **23.185** the transfer of management functions to the RTM company will be relatively straightforward. In larger blocks, however, there may be certain practical complexities. For example, the current manager of the property may have entered into an ongoing contract with a third party contractor to provide services to the building. To assist the transfer of management functions to the RTM company ss 92 and 93 of the Act require an existing manager to serve notice both on the third party contractor (a 'contractor notice' giving particulars of the RTM company and stating that it is going to take over the management of the building) and on the RTM company (a 'contract notice' giving details of existing contracts). The notices should contain the information prescribed by s 92(3) and (7) and regs 6 and 7 of the Right to Manage (Prescribed Particulars and Forms) Regulations 2010. If there are sub-contracts in place the contractor must send a copy of the contractor notice to the sub-contractor and a contract notice in relation to the sub-contract to the RTM company (s 92(4)).

Duty to provide information

In order to take over the management of premises the RTM company will need to be in **23.186** possession of sufficient information to perform its duties effectively. Much of this information will be in the hands of the landlord or managing company or whoever was formerly responsible for the management. Section 93(1) of the Act therefore provides for the RTM company to give notice to the landlord, any other party to the lease (eg a management company), or a manager appointed by an LVT requiring him or her to provide the company with any information in his or her possession or control which the company reasonably requires in connection with the exercise of the right to manage. Such notice can require the other party, within 28 days, to permit inspection of the relevant documents or to provide copies of the documents (s 93(2) and (4)). However, such notice may not require a person to do anything before the acquisition date (s 93(3)).

Service charges

23.187 A landlord or manager of the premises may also be in possession of funds paid as service charges and held on behalf of the tenants. Section 94 provides that these funds must be paid over to the RTM company on the acquisition date or as soon after as is reasonably practical. In the event of a dispute as to the amount of funds an application may be made by either party to the LVT for a determination (s 94(3)).

Management functions of an RTM company

23.188 'Management functions' are defined by s 95(5) as functions with respect to services, repair, maintenance, improvement, insurance, and management. When an RTM company acquires the right to manage it will take over the management functions that were formerly exercised by a landlord under a lease (s 96(2)) or by a person who is party to a lease otherwise than as landlord and tenant (ie a management company) (s 96(3)). Once the right to manage has been acquired, any provisions in the lease dealing with the management functions of a landlord or other party will cease to have effect (s 96(4)).

23.189 However, the RTM company will not take over the management functions relating to flats or units in the premises not held under a lease by a qualifying tenant (s 96(6)(a)). The landlord therefore remains responsible for the management of flats in the building which he or she owns and lets on short leases and for commercial units. Nor does the RTM company acquire any functions relating to re-entry or forfeiture (s 96(6)(b)).

23.190 Once an RTM company has taken over the management of a premises any landlord, other party to the lease, or manager appointed by an LVT may not carry out any of the management functions conferred on the RTM company by s 96 without the agreement of the company (s 97(2)). However, this provision will not prevent any person from insuring the whole or any part of the premises at his or her own expense (s 97(3)).

23.191 Any obligations to do with management functions which were formerly owed by a tenant under the lease to the landlord or other party will, once the right to manage has been acquired, be owed to the RTM company (s 97(4)). The main obligation owed by a tenant to the landlord or management company will be the payment of service charges to cover the cost of the management and maintenance of the building. Once the right to manage has been exercised, service charges will be payable to the RTM company. However, the RTM company will not be able to recover service charges payable by a tenant to meet costs incurred before the right to manage was acquired (s 97(5)).

23.192 It is important to remember that it is only management functions that are transferred to the RTM company; the landlord remains the landlord. Other non-management-related obligations between landlord and tenant (such as the obligation to pay ground rent or provide quiet enjoyment) are unaffected by the transfer.

Approvals

One of the functions of a landlord or third party management company under a lease may **23.193** be the granting of permissions or approvals for something which a tenant wishes to do, for example assigning or sub-letting his or her flat or making improvements or alterations. When an RTM company acquires the right to manage, it will take over these functions (s 98(2)). However, with regard to the granting of approvals, the RTM company's choice of action is not unrestricted. The RTM company must not grant an approval without first having given notice to the landlord. In the case of an approval relating to assignment, underletting, charging, parting with possession, or the making of structural alterations or improvements, the RTM company must give 30 days' notice; in any other case it must give 14 days' notice (s 98(4)). Similarly, any obligation of the tenant under a lease to seek consent from his or her landlord or another party will, after an RTM company acquired the right to manage, become an obligation to seek the consent of the RTM company (s 98(6)).

If the landlord objects to the granting of the approval, the RTM company may not grant **23.194** it unless either the landlord subsequently agrees in writing to the granting of the approval or in accordance with the determination of an LVT (s 99(1)). However, the landlord may only object if the landlord would have been able to refuse consent were he or she still the person responsible for granting the approval (s 99(2)). In considering whether a landlord could have withheld consent regard should be had to s 19 of the Landlord and Tenant Act 1927 (see 6.69 and 6.92). The provisions of s 19 of the 1927 Act will also apply to the RTM company (Sch 7, para 1).

Where the landlord wishes to object to the grant of an approval he or she must do so by **23.195** giving notice to both the RTM company and the tenant (and the sub-tenant, if the approval is to a tenant approving the act of a sub-tenant) (s 99(4)). If agreement cannot be reached regarding the approval, an application to the LVT can be made by the RTM company, the tenant, a sub-tenant (if appropriate), and the landlord (s 99(5)).

Enforcement of tenant covenants

Once an RTM company has taken over management of the premises it may not exercise **23.196** any right to re-entry or forfeiture (s 100(3)), but it may employ any other powers granted under a lease to enforce a tenant's covenants (s 100(2)) including a right to enter the tenant's premises to check that the tenant is complying with a covenant (s 100(5)).

Reporting tenant's breaches

Section 101 puts the RTM company under a duty to: **23.197**

(a) keep under review whether tenant covenants of lease of the whole or any part of the premises are being complied with; and
(b) report to the landlord any failure to comply with any tenant covenant of the lease (s 101(2)).

A report must be made within three months of the breach coming to the attention of the **23.198** RTM company (s 101(3)). However, the RTM company does not need to report the breach to the landlord if it has been remedied, if compensation has been paid in respect of the breach, or if the landlord has notified that RTM company that it need not report breaches of the description concerned.

Registration

23.199 Once the right to manage has been acquired it should be registered under r 79A of the Land Registration Rules 2003, SI 2003/1417, as amended by Sch 1, para 27 to the Land Registration (Amendment) Rules 2008, SI 2008/1919.

Statutory rights

23.200 Once an RTM company has taken over the right to manage, the majority of the statutory rights that would have been exercisable against a landlord or a management company will be exercisable (with certain modifications) against the RTM company. Schedule 7 to the Act sets out which provisions will apply and makes the necessary amendments.

Ending the right to manage

23.201 The right to manage will cease to be exercisable by an RTM company if:

(a) an agreement to that effect is made between the company and the landlord (or all landlords where there is more than one) (s 105(2));

(b) the RTM company becomes insolvent and a winding-up order is passed, a receiver is appointed, a voluntary arrangement is approved, or the company is struck off the register (s 105(3));

(c) a manager is appointed under the Landlord and Tenant Act 1987 (s 105(4)); or

(d) the RTM company ceases to be an RTM company in relation to the premises (s 105(5)).

Contracting out

23.202 Any agreement relating to a lease is void in so far as it purports to exclude or restrict the right of a tenant to exercise the right to manage (s 106).

J INSURANCE

23.203 In the case of blocks of flats the landlord will usually be responsible for the insurance of the building and the cost of the insurance will be recovered from the tenants by way of the service charge. Tenants may well be concerned that insurance cover is not being properly maintained or that the landlord is incurring unreasonable costs in arranging the insurance. The Schedule to the LTA 1985 gives tenants the right to demand information about the insurance of the building from their landlord.

Request for a summary

23.204 Where a service charge payable by the tenant of a dwelling consists of or includes an amount payable directly or indirectly for insurance the tenant may by notice in writing require the landlord to supply him or her with a written summary of the insurance for the time being effected in relation to the dwelling (para 2(1) of the Schedule). If the tenant is represented by a recognized tenants' association, the request may be made by the secretary of the association (para 2(2)). A 'landlord' for the purposes of the Schedule includes any person who has a right to enforce payment of that service charge (para 1). The request may be served on an agent of the landlord or the person who receives rent on behalf of the landlord (para 2(3)). Within one month of the request the landlord must supply the tenant (or secretary of the tenants' association) with a summary, which should include the amounts insured under any relevant policy, the name of the insurer, and the risks in respect of which the building or the dwelling is insured (para 2(4)). The landlord will be taken to have complied with the request if he supplies the tenant (or secretary) with a copy of every relevant policy (para 2(6)).

If the landlord is not in possession of the relevant information because it is in the hands of a **23.205** superior landlord, the intermediate landlord should in turn make a request to the superior landlord and the superior landlord should supply the information within a reasonable time (para 4(1)).

Request to inspect documents

Rather than request a summary under para 2, para 3 entitles the tenant (or secretary of the **23.206** tenants' association), by notice in writing, to require the landlord either to make facilities available to the tenant to inspect and copy any relevant policy or associated documents or to make copies of the relevant policy or documents and supply them to the tenant. 'Associated documents' means accounts, receipts, or other documents which provide evidence of payment of the premiums due both for the current period and the one preceding it (para 3(7)). The landlord must supply facilities for inspecting the documents free of charge (though costs incurred in doing so may be treated as part of the landlord's management costs) (para 3(5)). If the relevant information is in the hands of a superior landlord, the intermediate landlord must supply the tenant with the superior landlord's name and address and the superior landlord should provide the tenant with facilities for inspecting the relevant documents (para 4(2)).

Effect of change of landlord or assignment

If the landlord (or superior landlord) disposes of his or her interest following a request **23.207** either for a summary or to inspect documents, that landlord must still discharge the duty to the extent that he or she is capable of doing so (para 4A(2)). The new landlord is also liable to discharge the duty to the extent that he or she is able to do so, but in this case the 21-day period runs from the date of the disposal. If the tenancy is assigned following a request for a summary or to inspect documents, the landlord must still discharge the duty. However, the landlord is not required to comply with more than a reasonable number of requirements imposed by any one person (para 5).

Failure to comply

It is a summary offence for the landlord to fail, without reasonable excuse, to supply a sum- **23.208** mary or provide facilities for inspection. On conviction, a person committing such an offence is liable to a fine not exceeding level 4 on the standard scale (currently £2,500) (para 6).

Right to notify insurers of possible claim

If it appears to the tenant that damage has been caused to the tenant's dwelling or to any **23.209** other part of the building containing it in respect of which a claim could be made under the terms of the policy of insurance, the tenant may (within any period specified in the policy) serve written notice on the insurer informing the insurer of the possible claim (para 7). This provision is designed to assist a tenant where a landlord is not making a claim or is delaying a claim and the tenant is concerned that the period in which a claim can be made may expire.

Right to challenge choice of insurers

23.210 Where a tenancy of a dwelling requires the tenant to insure the dwelling with an insurer nominated or approved by the landlord, both the tenant and the landlord may apply to a county court or LVT for a determination whether:

(a) the insurance which is available from the nominated insurer is unsatisfactory in any respect; or

(b) the premiums payable in respect of any such insurance are excessive (para 8(2)).

23.211 However, no such application may be made in respect of a matter which:

(a) has been agreed or admitted by the tenant;

(b) under an arbitration agreement to which the tenant is a party is to be referred to arbitration; or

(c) has been the subject of determination by a court or arbitral tribunal (para 8(3)).

23.212 On an application under this paragraph the court or tribunal may make an order requiring the landlord to nominate or approve an alternative insurer specified in the order or who satisfies such requirements as are specified in the order (para 8(4)).

23.213 It is not possible to contract out of these provisions. If the tenant enters into an agreement (other than an arbitration agreement) purporting to provide for a determination in a particular manner, or on particular evidence, of any question that may be the subject of an application under para 8, that agreement will be void (para 8(6)).

Insurance of houses

23.214 Section 164 of the CLRA introduced a new right for tenants who hold a long lease of a house. A house, for the purposes of s 164, has the same meaning as in Pt I of the Leasehold Reform Act 1967 (see 24.07). What counts as a long lease is set out in ss 76 and 77 of the CLRA, a lengthy definition that is effectively the same as under s 7 of the Leasehold Reform, Housing and Urban Development Act 1993 for the right to enfranchise (see 24.100). Where the lease requires such a tenant to insure the house with an insurer nominated or approved by the landlord, the tenant does not have to do so and may arrange his or her own insurance provided that:

(a) the policy is issued by an authorized insurer, it covers the interests of both landlord and tenant, it covers all the risks which the lease requires to be covered, and the amount of cover is not less than that required by the lease; and

(b) the tenant gives a notice of cover in the form set out in the Schedule to the Leasehold Houses (Notices of Insurance Cover) (England) Regulations 2004, SI 2004/3097 to the landlord within 14 days of the cover being renewed or taking effect.

KEY DOCUMENTS

Landlord and Tenant Act 1985

Landlord and Tenant Act 1987

Leasehold Reform, Housing and Urban Development Act 1993

Housing Act 1996

Commonhold and Leasehold Reform Act 2002

Housing and Regeneration Act 2008

Leasehold Valuation Tribunals (Procedure) Regulations 2003, SI 2003/2099, WSI 2004/683

Leasehold Houses (Notices of Insurance Cover) Regulations 2004, SI 2004/3097, as amended by SI 2005/177, WSI 2005/1354

Service Charge (Consultation Requirements) Regulations 2003, SI 2003/1987, WSI 2004/684, as amended by SI 2004/2939 and WSI 2005/1357

Administration Charges (Summary of Rights and Obligations) Regulations 2007, SI 2007/1258, WSI 2007/3162

Service Charges (Summary of Rights and Obligations, and Transitional Provision) (England) Regulations 2007, SI 2007/1257, WSI 2007/3160

Right to Manage Companies (Model Articles) (England) Regulations 2009, SI 2009/2767, WSI 2011/2680

Right to Manage (Prescribed Particulars and Forms) (England) Regulations 2010, SI 2010/825, WSI 2011/2684

Tribunal Proceedure (Upper Tribunal) (Lands Chamber) Rules 2010, S1 2010/2600

Practice Directions—Lands Chamber of the Upper Tribunal (2010)

Leasehold Valuation Tribunal application forms

RICS Service Charge Residential Management Code 2009

Printed copies of all legislation can be ordered from The Stationery Office at <http://www.tsoshop.co.uk>. All legislation from 1988 onwards and most pre-1988 primary legislation is available online at <http://www.legislation.gov.uk>. Leasehold valuation tribunal applications forms are available from the Residential Property Tribunal Service at <http://www.justice.gov.uk/tribunals/residential-property>. Part 8 claim forms are available from <http://www.justice.gov.uk/courts/proceedure-rules/civil>. Upper Tribunal Rules and Practice Directions are available from <http://www.justic.gov.uk/tribunals/lands>.

24

ENFRANCHISEMENT AND LEASEHOLD EXTENSION

A INTRODUCTION

In this chapter we will be considering the Leasehold Reform Act 1967, Pt I of the Landlord **24.01** and Tenant Act 1987, and the Leasehold Reform, Housing and Urban Development Act 1993 (LRHUDA). These are the three Acts which grant long leaseholders the right to enfranchise by acquiring their landlord's freehold interest or to extend their leases (as outlined in the introduction to Chapter 22 at 22.06). The 1967 and 1993 Acts were modified by the Commonhold and Leasehold Reform Act 2002 (CLRA), the most significant change being the abolition of the original residency requirement as of 26 July 2002.

Enfranchisement and human rights

Before going on to look at the Acts themselves it is worth considering the nature of enfran- **24.02** chisement in the context of human rights. Enfranchisement, after all, is an expropriatory right. If, under statute, a tenant is able to compel his or her landlord to transfer the freehold to the tenant, that landlord has been deprived of his or her property (particularly if, as under the 1967 Act, the price payable for the freehold would be significantly lower than the market value). Article 1 of Protocol 1 to the European Convention on Human Rights requires that every natural or legal person is entitled to the peaceful enjoyment of his or her possessions and that no one shall be deprived of his or her possessions except in the public interest. In *James v United Kingdom* (1968) 8 ECHR 123 the European Court of Human Rights considered whether the 1967 Act was in contravention of Article 1 of Protocol 1. It was held that the enfranchisement legislation was in the public interest because its goal was to remove social injustice, even though its effect was to transfer property from one individual to another.

B HOUSES—THE LEASEHOLD REFORM ACT 1967

Who is eligible?

The tenant

24.03 For a tenant to acquire the right to enfranchise or to be granted a lease extension under the 1967 Act, the following basic conditions must be satisfied:

(a) the property must be a house;
(b) the tenancy must be a long tenancy;
(c) the tenant must have been a tenant of the house for the last two years.

Personal representatives of deceased tenant

24.04 If the tenant of a house dies and immediately before his or her death that tenant had the right to acquire the freehold or to extend the lease, that right may also be exercised by the personal representatives of that tenant (s 6A(1)). This right may be exercised by the personal representatives for a period of two years from the grant of probate or letters of administration (s 6A(2)). (This provision, introduced by the CLRA, is designed to help people who inherit a leasehold house.)

Resident family members of deceased tenant

24.05 If the tenant of a house dies and a member of the tenant's family resident in the house takes over the tenancy, that family member shall be treated as having been the tenant during any period when he or she was resident in the house and it was his or her only or main place of residence (s 7(1)).

Assignees

24.06 If a tenant has the right to enfranchise or be granted a lease extension and has served notice of his desire to do so, those rights may be passed on to an assignee of the tenancy (s 5(1)). However, this will only happen if the tenancy is assigned with the benefit of the notice and if the assignment is of the whole house and premises (s 5(2)).

What is a house?

24.07 The Leasehold Reform Act 1967, s 2 provides that:

(1) For the purposes of this Part of this Act, 'house' includes any building designed or adapted for living in and reasonably so called, notwithstanding that the building is not structurally detached, or was or is not solely designed or adapted for living in, or is divided horizontally into flats or maisonettes; and
    (a) where a building is divided horizontally, the flats or other units into which it is so divided are not separate 'houses', though the building as a whole may be; and
    (b) where a building is divided vertically the building as a whole is not a 'house', though any of the units into which it is divided may be.
(2) References in this Part of this Act to a house do not apply to a house which is not structurally detached and of which a material part lies above or below a part of the structure not comprised in the house.

24.08 **Horizontal divisions** Consider a large Victorian house which has been divided horizontally so as to contain an individual flat on each floor. In this case the individual flats will not count as separate houses. However, the fact that the house has been converted into flats does not prevent the whole building from being a house within the 1967 Act. Thus, while a tenant of an individual flat within the building will not be eligible to claim the benefit of the Act, a person who holds a long lease of the whole building will be able to exercise the right to enfranchise or claim a lease extension (provided of course that he or she fulfils the other requirements of the Act).

However, a tenant of one of the flats within the house may hold that flat under a long lease **24.09** and have the right to enfranchise under the LRHUDA (see 24.94). If this is the case it is the tenant of the flat who takes precedence and the leaseholder of the whole house will acquire no rights under the 1967 Act unless that leaseholder has been occupying the house, or part of the house, as his or her only or main residence (whether or not used for other purposes) for the last two years, or for periods amounting to two years in the last 10 years (s 1(1ZB)).

Example Nicola owns the freehold of a large Victorian house. She lets the entire house to **24.10** Boris on a 999-year lease. Boris grants a 99-year tenancy to Steven. Steven has split the house into three flats, keeping the ground floor for his own use but granting 35-year terms of the other two flats to Peter and Britta. Steven wishes to exercise his right to enfranchise under the 1967 Act and compel Nicola to sell him the freehold of the house. However, Peter and Britta are also interested in exercising their rights under the LRHUDA to collectively acquire the freehold of the whole house (see 24.93). In this situation Steven will only acquire the right to enfranchise if he has been occupying the ground floor flat as his only or main residence for the last two years, or periods amounting to two years in the last 10 years.

Vertical divisions The situation is reversed where the building in question is divided vertically, as in the case of a row of terraced houses. Here each of the individual units will count as a 'house', while the building as a whole will not. The key question is whether the building can reasonably be described as a house. Two adjacent mews houses let as a single dwelling-house and occupied together can count as a house for the purposes of the Act (*Collins v Howard de Walden Estates Ltd* (2003) 37 EG 137, CA). But where two linked properties, despite being let together under the same head lease, are vertically divided so as to form two distinct residential premises, the two properties together cannot be described as a single house (*Malekshad v Howard de Walden Estates* [2002] UKHL 49, [2002] 3 WLR 1881).

Furthermore, in the case of such houses which are not structurally detached, s 2(2) of the **24.12** 1967 Act provides that they cannot be a 'house' within the meaning of the Act if a material part of the premises lies above or below a part of the structure which is not comprised in the house. Thus, for example, a property will be excluded from being a house within the meaning of the 1967 Act where a material part of that property lies above the garage of the neighbouring property (see *Parsons v Viscount Gage (Trustees of Henry Smith's Charity)* [1974] 1 WLR 435; also *Duke of Westminster v Birrane* [1995] 2 WLR 270, CA and *Malekshad v Howard de Walden*).

Designed or adapted for living in Under the 1967 Act, a building does not have to have **24.13** been solely designed for living in; thus, a building which consists of a flat or maisonette on the upper floors with a shop below will fall within the Act so long as it can reasonably be called a house (see *Tandon v Trustees of Spurgeons Homes* [1982] AC 755 and *Hareford Ltd v Barnet LBC* (2005) 28 EG 122). However, a larger building containing a number of residential flats above a number of commercial units cannot, in the absence of any very unusual factors, reasonably be called a house (*Magnohard Ltd v RH Cadogan and others* [2012] EWCA Civ 594).

24.14 The position of a building originally constructed as a house that has been adapted to commercial use has recently been considered by the Supreme Court. To decide whether that building can reasonably be called a house it is important to look at its current physical character, whether derived from its original design or from subsequent adaptation. That such a building may look externally like a house and may be described as a house for some purposes (eg by English Heritage) does not mean that it can reasonably be called a house for the purposes of the Act when the interior of the building has been converted into small self-contained units and is wholly used as a self-catering hotel (*Day v Hosebay Limited* [2012] UKSC 41). Similarly, where all but the top floor of a building, which was used as a flat for senior employees, was converted to office use, that building, though originally designed as a house, could no longer be a house reasonably so called for the purposes of the Act (*Prospect Estates Ltd v Grosvenor Estates Belgravia* [2008] EWCA Civ 1281).

24.15 Whether the building can actually be lived in at the moment is not the question. In *Boss Holdings Ltd v Grosvenor West End Properties* [2008] UKHL 5 the three lower floors of a large eighteenth-century house were later used for commercial purposes while the upper three remained residential. At the time of notice the upper floors had been largely stripped back to basic structure and were not capable of residential occupation without further work. Nevertheless, the floor plan of the whole house had not been substantially altered from its original construction and it was held that it was a house for the purposes of the Act.

24.16 **House and premises** If the premises amount to a house within the meaning of s 2, and the tenant fulfils the other requirements of the 1967 Act, the tenant will be entitled to claim under the Act for enfranchisement or a lease extension, not just of the 'house' itself but for the 'house and premises'. Similarly, when considering the rateable value (see 24.36) it is the rateable value of the house and premises which must be assessed. Section 2(3) provides:

> ... where in relation to a house let to a tenant reference is made in this Part of this Act to the house and premises, the reference to premises is to be taken as referring to any garage, outhouse, garden, yard and appurtenances which at the relevant time are let to him with the house.

24.17 In *Methuen-Campbell v Walters* [1979] QB 525 a paddock divided from the garden by a fence was regarded as not being part of the garden nor an appurtenance and was therefore not part of the 'house and premises'. (For flats, it should be noted that what counts as an appurtenance under the LRHUDA may be determined slightly differently, see 24.131 and 24.158.)

A long tenancy

24.18 A long tenancy means a tenancy granted for a term of years certain exceeding 21 years. It will be a long tenancy whether or not the tenancy is or may become terminable before the end of that term by notice given by or to the tenant, or by re-entry, forfeiture, or otherwise (s 3(1)).

24.19 Where a tenant previously held a long tenancy at a low rent, and when that tenancy expired the tenant was granted a further tenancy of the same property or part of it (whether by express grant or by operation of law), the second tenancy will be deemed to be a long tenancy irrespective of its terms (s 3(2)).

24.20 Where a tenant under a long tenancy takes, at the end of the first tenancy, another long tenancy of the same property or part of it, the two tenancies shall be treated as if there was a single long tenancy granted for a term beginning at the commencement of the first term and expiring at the end of the second (s 3(3)).

Where a tenant is granted a term of 21 years or less but with a covenant for renewal with- **24.21**
out payment of a premium, and the tenancy is renewed so as to bring the total of the terms
granted (including any interval between the end of a tenancy and the grant of a renewal) to
more than 21 years, the 1967 Act will apply as if the term originally granted had been one
exceeding 21 years (s 3(4)). However, this section will not apply where enfranchisement is
sought under s 1AA (see 24.31).

A tenancy being continued by virtue of s 3 of the Landlord and Tenant Act 1954, or under **24.22**
Sch 10 to the Local Government and Housing Act 1989, will be a long tenancy, but not
after it has been converted into a statutory tenancy (see 22.25) (s 3(5)).

Special provisions apply with regard to tenancies terminable by notice on death or mar- **24.23**
riage. Originally, provided certain conditions were fulfilled, such tenancies would not be
treated as long tenancies if they were granted prior to 18 April 1980. The Leasehold
Reform Act 1967, s 1B, inserted by the LRHUDA, s 64(1), now grants to such tenants,
who would formerly have been excluded by s 3(1), the right to enfranchise but not to
extend the lease.

Exclusions Certain other types of leases are excluded, either partially or completely, from **24.24**
the operation of the 1967 Act. These include: business tenancies (apart from the exception
considered below) (s 1(1ZC)), agricultural holdings and farm business tenancies (s 1(3)),
certain tenancies granted by charitable housing trusts (s 1(3) and (3A)), leases where the
National Trust holds an interest (s 32), and property which has been transferred for the
public benefit (s 32A). Certain shared ownership leases will also be excluded, in particular those granted by public authorities, housing associations, and some other landlords
(s 33 and Sch 4) and those of hard-to-replace houses in designated protected areas (Sch
4A): the Housing (Shared Ownership Leases) (Exclusion from the Leasehold Reform Act
1967) (England) Regulations 2009, SI 2009/2097, and the Housing (Right to Enfranchise)
(Designated Protected Areas) (England) Order 2009, SI 2009/2098).

Occupation as a residence

There is no longer a requirement that a tenant must occupy the house as a residence in order **24.25**
to acquire the right to enfranchise or extend the lease. Although it was almost certainly not
part of the original intention of the Act, this means that corporate tenants may be able to
acquire the freehold of buildings with significant commercial element (see 24.13). The fact
that a tenancy to which Pt II of the Landlord and Tenant Act 1954 applies is excluded from
the Act by virtue of s 1(1B) can easily be circumvented by the device of sub-letting to an
associated company (see *Day v Hosebay Ltd* [2010] EWCA Civ 748).

A residency requirement only remains of significance in two limited situations: **24.26**

(a) in the case of business tenancies granted for a term of more than 35 years (see
     24.27);
(b) where the house contains a flat which is let to a tenant who has the right to enfranchise
     under the LRHUDA (see 24.09).

Business tenancies Business tenancies (ie tenancies to which Pt 2 of the Landlord and **24.27**
Tenant Act 1954 apply) are excluded from the operation of the 1967 Act apart from one
narrow exception. A business tenant will only qualify under the 1967 Act if that tenant has
occupied the house, or part of it, as his or her only or main residence (whether or not used
for other purposes) for the last two years or for periods amounting to two years in the last
10 years (s 1(1B)). In any case, even if this residence test is satisfied, business tenancies will
be excluded from the 1967 Act unless they can satisfy the provisions of s 1(1ZC). Section
1(1ZC) requires that the business tenancy must have been granted for a term of more than

35 years or be a tenancy that contains a covenant for renewal without payment of a premium that has been exercised to bring the total term to over 35 years.

24.28   **More than one long tenancy** One result of the abolition of the residency requirement is that it is now possible for more than one tenant to satisfy the qualifying conditions, for example where the tenant of a house has sub-let the house on a tenancy that is itself a long tenancy. In such a situation, where there are two long leases of the house, it is the tenant with the shorter term who is able to enfranchise. The holder of the superior term does not acquire any rights under the Act (s 1ZA).

24.29   If we return to our example (at 24.10), ignoring, for the sake of argument, the position of Peter and Britta, we can see that both Boris and Steven satisfy the qualifying conditions under the 1967 Act. Both have long leases of the house, and both have been tenants for at least the last two years. In this situation it will be Steven who qualifies to enfranchise or extend his lease because he has the shorter term.

The low rent test and rateable value limits

24.30   Section 300 of the Housing and Regeneration Act 2008 has amended the 1967 Act so as to remove the low rent test for determining eligibility to enfranchise. The amendments, however, only apply to tenancies granted after 7 September 2009 or granted after that date but arising from a written agreement made before that date (Housing and Regeneration Act 2008 (Commencement No. 6 and Transitional and Savings Provisions) Order 2009, SI 2009/2096, art 3(1)). It will therefore be some time until the abolition has a significant effect, and, in any case, the low rent test continues to apply to tenants seeking to extend their leases.

24.31   The vast majority of tenancies will be granted before 7 September 2009 and very few of these will be disqualified from the right to enfranchise because they are not at a low rent. Prior to its abolition by the 2008 Act, the requirement had been slowly eroded, each subsequent statute adding a new section under which the tenancy could qualify rather than replacing the original. The result is that for most tenancies there are currently four sections of the Act under which a tenant can qualify for the right to enfranchisement:

(a)   under s 1, where the house passes the original low rent test (s 4) and is below the rateable value limits set out in s 1(1);

(b)   under s 1A, where the house exceeds the rateable value limits in s 1(1) or fails the original low rent test but passes the alternative low rent test set out in s 4A(1);

(c)   under s 1B, where the tenancy is a long tenancy granted before 18 April 1980 and terminable by notice on death or marriage (see 23.21) ((b) and (c) were added by the LRHUDA);

(d)   under s 1AA, where the house fails the original low rent test and the alternative low rent test (added by the Housing Act 1996).

Thus, of tenancies granted before 7 September 2009, the only ones that will be disqualified from the right to enfranchise on account of not being at a low rent will be those that belong to the narrow class of tenancies in designated rural areas which are excluded from s 1AA by s 1AA(3).

24.32   However, the low rent and rateable value limits remain significant because if a tenancy qualifies under s 1 ((a) in 24.31) and the rateable value is below a second limit, the purchase price will be calculated on the original valuation basis (s 9, see 24.56). If the tenancy qualifies under s 1A, 1B, or 1AA or the rateable value exceeds the second limit, the purchase price will be calculated on an additional valuation basis (s 9(1A)) and compensation may be payable to the landlord (s 9A) (see 24.59 and 24.60). The price payable for the freehold under the original valuation basis will be much lower than under the additional valuation basis. The majority of tenancies granted after 7 September 2009 will qualify under s 1.

The tenants' additional rights under s 1A, 1B, or 1AA are rights of enfranchisement only. **24.33** Tenants wishing to extend their leases will have to satisfy the original low rent test and the rateable value limits.

A low rent The provisions with regard to what makes a tenancy qualify as a tenancy at a **24.34** low rent are complicated, but the basic rules can be stated as follows:

(a) If the tenancy was entered into before 1 April 1990 the rent payable must not be more than two-thirds of the rateable value of the property on the appropriate day (generally 23 March 1965) (s 4(1)(i)). (If the property had a rateable value of nil on the appropriate day—eg because it was derelict at the time—the date to be chosen is the date on which it did have a rateable value.)

(b) If the tenancy was entered into after 1 April 1990 the rent payable must not be more than £1,000 per annum if the property is in Greater London and £250 per annum if the property is elsewhere (s 4(1)(ii)).

(c) For tenancies entered into between August 1939 and April 1963 there is also the proviso that the rent payable must not exceed two-thirds of the letting value (s 4(1)(ii)). The letting value is 'the best annual return obtainable in the open market for the grant of a long lease on the same terms whether this be achieved by letting at a rack rent or letting at a lower rent plus the payment of a premium' (*Johnston v Duke of Westminster* [1986] 3 WLR 18, *per* Lord Griffiths at 23).

In each of these cases any part of the rent expressed to be payable in consideration of serv- **24.35** ices to be provided, or for repairs, maintenance, or insurance to be effected by the landlord, is to be disregarded (s 4(1)(b)). The tenancy must satisfy the low rent condition throughout the qualifying period of two years (s 1(1)(b)).

Rateable value limits To calculate whether the rateable value of the house and premises **24.36** will fall within the value limits, regard must be had to two factors: the date the tenancy was created and the appropriate day. The appropriate day means 23 March 1965 or, if later, the first day the property appeared on the rating list. The provisions are complicated but the basic rules are stated in 24.37.

A property will fall within the value limits if: **24.37**

(a) the tenancy was created after 1 April 1990 and the rateable value does not exceed £25,000 as calculated by the formula set out in s 1(1)(a)(ii);

(b) the tenancy was created before 1 April 1990 and after 18 February 1966 and:
   (i) the appropriate day was before 1 April 1973 and the rateable value on the appropriate day was less than £400 in Greater London or £200 elsewhere (s 1(1)(a)(i)); or
   (ii) the appropriate day was after 1 April 1973 and the rateable value on the appropriate day was less than £1,000 in Greater London or £500 elsewhere (s 1(5)(b));

(c) the tenancy was created before 18 February 1966 and the rateable value on the appropriate day was less than £1,500 in Greater London or £750 elsewhere (s 1(5)(a)).

Procedure

If a tenant fulfils the qualifying conditions considered earlier, he or she may then proceed **24.38** to exercise the following rights under the 1967 Act:

(a) the right to be granted the house and premises for an estate in fee simple absolute (s 8(1)); or

(b)   the right to be granted a new tenancy of the house and premises for a term expiring 50
years after the expiry date of the existing tenancy (s 14(1)).

24.39   Both of these rights may be exercised at any time during the currency of the lease. It is up
to the tenant whether to enfranchise or extend the lease. In most cases enfranchisement
will be the most attractive option (in certain cases, eg where the right is exercised under
s 1A, 1B, or 1AA, it will be the only option, see 24.33), but it will also be more expensive.
If a tenant chooses to extend the lease, this will not preclude that tenant from exercising
the right to enfranchise at a later date. If a sub-tenant holds a long lease from a tenant who
has already extended his or her lease, that sub-tenant has no right to extend the sub-lease,
though he or she does have the right to enfranchise (s 16(4)).

24.40   Thus, in our example (see 24.10), if Boris has already exercised his right to extend his lease
before granting the sub-lease to Steven, Steven would have no right to seek an extension of
his sub-lease, though he would be entitled to enfranchise if he so wished.

Tenant's notice

24.41   If the tenant decides to exercise either of the rights granted under the 1967 Act, the first
step is for the tenant to serve upon the landlord notice of his or her desire to do so. Notice
must be given in accordance with the procedure set out in Sch 3 to the Act and must be in
the prescribed form (Form 1, Leasehold Reform (Notices) Regulations 1997, SI 1997/640,
as amended by SI 2002/1715, WSI 2002/3187). The notice must make it clear whether
the tenant is seeking to enfranchise or to acquire an extended lease. Once notice has been
served its effect is the same as if the landlord and tenant had freely entered into a contract
for a sale or lease (s 5(1)). Thus, if one of the parties fails to carry out his or her obligations
arising from the notice, the other party can seek a contractual remedy to enforce his or her
rights (eg an order for specific performance).

24.42   The notice shall not be invalidated by any inaccuracy in the particulars or a misdescription of the property, and if it fails to include property that should be included, or
includes property that should not be included, notice can be given with leave of the court
to amend the notice on such terms as the court may see fit to impose (Sch 3, para 6(3)).
Leave will normally be granted unless the landlord can establish relevant prejudice (see
Malekshad v Howard de Walden Estates Ltd (No. 2) [2003] EWHC 3106 (Ch), [2004]
1 WLR 862). However, this does not mean that the notice will be valid if there is a serious error or omission, for example if the notice fails to give the required particulars
(*Speedwell Estates Ltd v Dalziel* [2002] 02 EG 104) or does not disclose that the tenant
lived somewhere else for part of the qualifying period (*Cresswell v Duke of Westminster*
[1985] 2 EGLR 151, CA).

24.43   When the price payable for the freehold has been ascertained in accordance with the Act
(see 24.56), the tenant can withdraw his or her application by giving written notice to
the landlord stating that he or she is unwilling or unable to acquire the house at the price
determined (s 9(3)). The tenant will have to compensate the landlord for any interference
with the landlord's rights. The tenant will also be precluded from making another claim
for enfranchisement within three years of the first claim. The tenant may, however, decide
to claim a lease extension rather than seeking to acquire the freehold.

24.44   Once the tenant has served notice the landlord is not permitted, during the currency of the
term, to start proceedings to terminate the tenancy without leave from the court (Sch 3,
para 4(1)). The court may, however, grant leave if the tenant's claim was not made in good
faith, for example where a tenant is seeking to enfranchise simply to avoid forfeiture (see
Central Estates (Belgravia) Ltd v Woolgar [1972] 1 QB 48). Once notice has been given the

tenant may still assign the lease, and if the tenant does so the new tenant will acquire the benefit of the notice (s 5(2)).

If the tenant is prevented from giving notice because the landlord cannot be found, an **24.45** application can be made to the court under s 27. The court may then order, if it thinks fit, the house to be vested in the tenant as if the tenant had given notice (s 27(1)) but it may require the tenant to take further steps to trace the landlord (s 27(2)). Such an application should be made to the county court.

Landlord's notice in reply

Once the tenant has given notice, the landlord has two months within which to give notice **24.46** in reply (Sch 3, para 7). The landlord's notice in reply must be in the prescribed form (Form 3, Leasehold Reform (Notices) Regulations 1997) and should state whether the landlord admits or rejects the tenant's claim. If the landlord has not replied within two months, the tenant can take court proceedings to enforce his or her rights.

If the landlord accepts the claim he or she will be deemed to have accepted that the ten- **24.47** ant is eligible to make the claim, and cannot therefore subsequently raise questions as to whether the tenant fulfilled the qualifying conditions unless the landlord's admission of the notice was induced by misrepresentation.

If the landlord wishes to reject the claim he or she must set out the grounds for the rejec- **24.48** tion in the notice in reply. The tenant can then start proceedings in the county court. The grounds upon which a landlord can oppose a claim are very limited under the 1967 Act. The landlord's main line of defence is to argue that the tenant does not qualify to exercise the right to enfranchise or extend the lease. Other than this the landlord has two options:

(a) the landlord may object to the inclusion of or exclusion of particular parts of the prop- erty in the tenant's claim; and
(b) in limited circumstances, the landlord may seek possession of the property under s 17 or 18 of the 1967 Act.

Inclusion or exclusion of particular parts Where a tenant seeks to enfranchise or to be **24.49** granted a lease extension, there may be parts of the property which belong to the landlord but which are not occupied or used by the tenant, and which therefore do not fall within the definition of 'house and premises' set out in s 2(3) of the 1967 Act (see 24.16). When the tenant acquires the freehold of the property the landlord may have no interest in retain- ing such a part. For example, there might be an outhouse that the tenant does not use but which the landlord has no desire to retain after the freehold has been handed over to the tenant. In such a situation the landlord can require the tenant to take this property as well. The landlord must first serve notice, within two months of having received the tenant's notice, objecting to the severance of the part from the rest of the estate (s 2(4)(a)). The tenant must then either agree to having the part included with the house and premises, or the matter can be referred to the county court. The court, if it is satisfied that it would be unreasonable to require the landlord to retain the part, may then order that the part be included in the house and premises (s 2(4)(b)).

Conversely, the landlord may also object if the tenant is seeking to exercise his or her **24.50** rights under the 1967 Act over property that lies above or below property in which the landlord has an interest. As above, the landlord must serve notice on the tenant objecting to the severance of that part (s 2(5)(a)). Failing agreement the court may order the part to be excluded from the tenant's acquisition if the court is satisfied that any hardship or inconvenience likely to result to the tenant from the exclusion is outweighed by the difficulties which would be involved in the severance and the hardship or inconvenience likely to result from that severance to the landlord or other persons interested in that property (s 2(5)(b)).

24.51 **Landlord's overriding rights** The 1967 Act contains two provisions under which the landlord may seek to resume possession of the house. In neither case, however, can the landlord regain possession before the termination date of the tenancy. In both cases, if the landlord succeeds, the tenant will be entitled to compensation (see Sch 2).

24.52 Under s 17 of the Act, the landlord can apply to the court for an order that he or she may resume possession of the premises on the ground that for the purposes of *redevelopment* the landlord proposes to demolish or reconstruct the whole or a substantial part of the house and premises. The landlord can apply only if:

(a)   the tenant has given notice that he or she desires to be granted a lease extension; or
(b)   a lease extension has already been granted.

24.53 Furthermore, the landlord can apply only at a time not earlier than one year before the expiry date of the original lease. Section 17 has no application when the tenant is seeking enfranchisement.

24.54 Under s 18, the landlord can apply to resume possession on the ground that the property or a part of it will be reasonably *required for occupation* as the only or main residence of the landlord or an adult member of the landlord's family. The landlord can apply under s 18 after the tenant has given notice of his or her desire to enfranchise or to be granted a lease extension, and until effect is given to the tenant's notice. The landlord cannot apply under s 18 if his or her interest in the property was purchased or created after 18 February 1966. The court will not make an order for possession if, in all the circumstances of the case, the court is satisfied that greater hardship would be caused by making the order than by refusing it.

Estate management schemes

24.55 Originally, under s 19 of the 1967 Act (and subsequently under Ch IV of the LRHUDA) it was possible to have an estate management scheme approved. Such a scheme would be relevant where a large estate was originally under the control of one freeholder and it would be for the benefit of the area and the estate as a whole for the freeholder to retain powers of management over properties in the estate after the tenants had exercised their right to enfranchise. No new schemes can be created under the 1967 Act but leasehold valuation tribunals have the power to vary or terminate schemes that are currently in existence under s 75 of the 1993 Act.

Price on enfranchisement

24.56 Detailed provisions for calculating the price to be paid by the tenant for the freehold are set out in s 9 of the 1967 Act. There are two bases of assessment, the first being used if the rateable value of the house and premises is less than £1,000 in Greater London or £500 elsewhere, the second being used where the rateable value exceeds these limits. The LRHUDA also introduced a further basis of assessment for tenancies brought within the ambit of the 1967 Act by virtue of s 1A, 1B, or 1AA (see 24.31). The basic goal of these provisions is to try to ascertain a price that represents the value of the site excluding the value of the building.

24.57 **Rateable value below £1,000 or £500** Where the rateable value is below the specified limits, the price to be paid is the amount which at the relevant time (the date of notice) the house and premises might be expected to realize if sold on the open market by a willing seller. Section 9(1) of the 1967 Act provides that the following assumptions are to be made:

(a)   that the landlord is selling the freehold subject to the existing tenancy;

(b) that the current tenancy has been extended under the 1967 Act (ie by 50 years);

(c) that the current tenancy does not confer a right to acquire the freehold;

(d) that it is being sold subject to the same rent charges as in the sale to the tenant;

(e) that the landlord is selling the freehold subject to the same rights and burdens as in the sale to the tenant;

(f) that the tenant and members of the tenant's family who reside in the house are not seeking to buy it. This can be a relatively important element in the calculation, for frequently a tenant already in occupation of a property is likely to pay more for the freehold than a third party (who would of course take the property subject to the existing tenancy) would pay on the open market. An existing tenant will pay more because he or she is the only purchaser capable of merging the leasehold and the freehold estates. This extra value is sometimes referred to as the 'marriage value'. Under this first basis of assessment the marriage value is not taken into account. (Provisions to this effect were inserted into the 1967 Act by the Housing Act 1969, s 82.)

Under this basis of assessment the price payable by the tenant for the freehold can be very low. **24.58**

Rateable value above £1,000 or £500 This second basis of assessment (set out in s 9(1A)) **24.59** was introduced by the Housing Act 1974 and results generally in a higher price being paid by the tenant. If the rateable value is above the specified limits, the price payable is assessed in the same way as for lower value properties, but no assumption is made that the tenancy will be extended by the 1967 Act. Instead, it is assumed that when the term comes to an end the tenant will have the right to remain in possession of the premises under the provisions of Pt I of the Landlord and Tenant Act 1954 or Sch 10 to the Housing and Local Government Act 1989 (see 22.10 to 22.54). Furthermore, while under the first basis of assessment it is assumed that the tenant or members of the tenant's family are not seeking to buy, under this second basis of assessment the 'marriage value' to the tenant will be taken into account. Under this basis it will be assumed that the tenant has no liability to carry out repairs, maintenance, and decoration, and the price will also be reduced to take into account any increase in value resulting from improvements carried out by the tenant or the tenant's predecessors in title.

Where the tenant's right to enfranchise arises as a result of either s 1A, 1B, or 1AA of the **24.60** 1967 Act (the provisions introduced by the 1993 and 1996 Acts, see 24.31), or where the lease has already been extended and notice of the desire to enfranchise was given after the original term date of the tenancy, the price to be paid is to be calculated on the second basis of assessment. Certain further alterations are made to the second basis of assessment by s 9(1C). First, the tenant's share of the marriage value will be fixed at 50 per cent (s 9(1D)) except where the unexpired term of the tenant's tenancy exceeds 80 years, in which case the marriage value shall be taken to be nil (s 9(1E)). Secondly, the landlord may claim compensation for any diminution in the value of any interest he or she has in other property under s 9A.

Lease extension

Where a tenant exercises his or her right to acquire a 50-year extension, no price or premium is payable; the tenant must pay only the rent due under the lease. Up to the expiry **24.61** date of the original tenancy the rent payable is the same as the old rent. After the expiry date the rent payable is a modern ground rent representing the letting value of the site alone at the time the new tenancy commences (s 15(2)). The landlord may include provisions enabling the ground rent to be revised after 25 years. The terms of the tenancy will generally be the same as the terms of the existing tenancy, subject to any alterations that may be necessary to take into account changes in the property (eg where a part of the property included in the original lease is not included in the extended lease) (s 15(1)). Any terms in the original lease relating to the renewal of the tenancy or to an option to purchase will not be included in the new lease, and neither will any clause giving the landlord a right to terminate the tenancy earlier than the expiry date except for breach of covenant (s 15(5)).

24.62   When a tenancy extended under the 1967 Act comes to an end, the tenant will acquire security of tenure under Sch 10 to the Local Government and Housing Act 1989 (see 22.25) regardless of whether or not that tenancy is a long tenancy at a low rent for the purposes of that Schedule (s 16(1B)).

C FLATS—THE LANDLORD AND TENANT ACT 1987

24.63   Under Pt I of the Landlord and Tenant Act 1987, the tenants of individual flats within a block can acquire the right to purchase their landlord's interest collectively. This right takes the form of a right of first refusal. It will arise only when the landlord intends to sell an interest in the block. The right acquired under the 1987 Act is therefore different from the right of enfranchisement acquired by leaseholders under the Leasehold Reform Act 1967 (for houses, see 24.03 to 24.62) and under the LRHUDA (for flats, 24.93 to 24.169). Under those two enactments the tenant or tenants in question can compel the landlord to sell them the freehold of the property whenever they wish, provided, of course, that the requirements of the relevant statute are satisfied. Under the 1987 Act the right to purchase the landlord's interest will arise only when the landlord seeks to make a 'relevant disposal'.

24.64   The Landlord and Tenant Act 1987 therefore functions as a fetter upon the landlord's right to dispose of his or her interest to a third party. For example, if Jennifer owns the freehold interest in a block of four flats and decides that she wishes to sell this interest to Tom for £10,000, she cannot simply go ahead and make the sale. She must first offer the freehold of the block to the tenants of the flats within the block at the same price in accordance with the provisions of the Act; if she does not, she commits a criminal offence punishable by a fine.

24.65   For the right of first refusal to arise certain requirements must be fulfilled:

(a)   the premises themselves must qualify under s 1 of the 1987 Act;
(b)   a sufficient number of the tenancies of the flats within the premises must be held by 'qualifying tenants';
(c)   the disposal in question must be a relevant disposal.

The premises

24.66   The 1987 Act will apply to premises if:

(a)   they consist of the whole or part of a building; and
(b)   they contain two or more flats held by qualifying tenants; and
(c)   the number of flats held by qualifying tenants exceeds 50 per cent of the total number of flats contained in the premises (s 1(2)).

24.67   A flat is defined by s 60(1) as a separate set of premises, whether or not on the same floor, which:

(a)   forms part of a building; and

(b) is divided horizontally from some other part of the building; and

(c) is constructed or adapted for use for the purposes of a dwelling.

The premises will not fall within the Act if: **24.68**

(a) any part or parts of the premises is or are occupied or intended to be occupied otherwise than for residential purposes and the internal area of that part or those parts (taken together) exceeds 50 per cent of the internal area of the premises (taken as a whole) (the internal floor area of any common parts should be disregarded) (s 1(3)) (see 24.107 for the parallel provisions under the LRHUDA);

(b) the landlord's interest is held by a resident landlord (s 1(4));

(c) the landlord's interest is held by an exempt landlord (s 1(4)). A list of exempt landlords is set out in s 58(1) of the Act and includes local authorities, registered social landlords, fully mutual housing associations, charitable housing trusts, and most public sector landlords.

Resident landlords

A landlord of any premises consisting of the whole or part of a building is a resident land-   **24.69** lord of those premises at any time if:

(a) the premises are not, and do not form part of, a purpose-built block of flats; and

(b) at that time the landlord occupies a flat contained in the premises as his or her only or principal residence; and

(c) he has so occupied such a flat throughout a period of not less than 12 months ending with that time (s 58(2)).

A purpose-built block of flats means a building which contained as constructed, and con-   **24.70** tains, two or more flats (s 58(3)). In other words, the building must have contained at least two flats when it was built (ie not be a conversion of an existing building) and it must continue to contain at least two flats.

Qualifying tenants

The Landlord and Tenant Act 1987 adopts a negative definition of a qualifying tenant. A   **24.71** person will be a qualifying tenant if he or she is the tenant of a flat under a tenancy other than:

(a) a protected shorthold tenancy;

(b) a tenancy to which Pt II of the Landlord and Tenant Act 1954 applies (business tenancies);

(c) a tenancy terminable on the cessation of his or her employment;

(d) an assured tenancy or an assured agricultural occupancy within the meaning of Pt I of the Housing Act 1988 (s 3(1)).

A tenant will not be a qualifying tenant if he or she holds a tenancy of three or more flats   **24.72** in the same premises (s 3(2)).

Thus, the vast majority of long leaseholders will be qualifying tenants, as will Rent Act-   **24.73** protected or statutory tenants. Business tenants, service tenants, and assured tenants are excluded from the 1987 Act, however, as are secure tenants because public sector landlords are exempt under s 58(1) of the Act. The tenant does not have to be an individual and so a company may be a qualifying tenant (provided it does not hold the tenancy of three or more flats). It is important to note that the Act does not lay down any residence requirement. A tenant who has sub-let the whole of his or her flat will still acquire the right of first refusal. In such a situation the sub-tenant will not be regarded as a qualifying tenant (s 3(4)).

Relevant disposal

24.74   Not every disposal by the landlord will mean that the tenant acquires the right of first refusal under the 1987 Act. Section 4(1) defines a 'relevant disposal' as the disposal by the landlord of any estate or interest (whether legal or equitable) in any such premises, including the disposal of any such estate or interest in any common parts of any such premises. By s 4(3), a 'disposal' means a disposal whether by the creation or the transfer of an estate or interest and includes the surrender of a tenancy (see *Kensington Heights Commercial Co. Ltd v Campden Hill Developments Ltd* [2007] EWCA Civ 245) and the grant of an option or right of pre-emption. It will not include a disposal under the terms of a will or under the law relating to intestacy (s 4(3)(b)). However, by virtue of s 4A the right of first refusal will apply to a contract to create or transfer an estate or interest in land, whether conditional or unconditional and whether or not enforceable by specific performance.

24.75   Most significantly, a relevant disposal does not include the grant of any tenancy under which the demised premises consist of a single flat (s 4(1)(a)). Thus, the right of first refusal will not arise when a landlord seeks to grant a tenancy of one individual flat within the building. However, a disposal of part of relevant premises is a disposal affecting those premises within the meaning of s 4(1) (*Dartmouth Court Blackheath Ltd v Berisworth Ltd* [2008] EWHC 350 (Ch)). What are relevant premises should be ascertained in an objective way disregarding the disposal concerned. In *Dartmouth Court* the granting of a lease of the airspace above the roof and of a light-well was held to be a relevant disposal. The airspace and the light-well were both, if not parts of the building, at least appurtenant to it. 'Appurtenant premises' are defined by s 4(4) as any yard, garden, outhouse, or appurtenance (not being a common part of the building containing the flat) which belongs to, or is usually enjoyed with, the flat. On the other hand, a garage block where the garages were let to tenants of flats in the building but on independent leases and not to every flat in the block were not enjoyed in such a way as to be considered appurtenant to the building.

24.76   By s 4(2), various other disposals are excluded from the definition of a relevant disposal. These include:

(a)   certain involuntary disposals, such as to a trustee in bankruptcy, in pursuance of an order under the Matrimonial Causes Act 1973 or the Inheritance (Provision for Family and Dependents) Act 1975, in pursuance of a compulsory purchase order;

(b)   a disposal by way of security for a loan;

(c)   a disposal by way of gift to a member of the landlord's family or to a charity;

(d)   a disposal by one charity to another;

(e)   a disposal consisting of a transfer by two or more persons who are members of the same family, either to fewer of their number or to a different combination of members of the family;

(f)   a disposal consisting of the surrender of a tenancy in pursuance of any covenant, condition, or agreement contained in it;

(g)   a disposal to the Crown;

(h)   a disposal by a body corporate to a company which has been an associated company of that body for at least two years.

24.77   If the landlord's estate has been mortgaged, a disposal by the mortgagee in exercise of a power of sale or leasing will be treated as a relevant disposal (s 4(1A)).

Who is the landlord?

In straightforward cases the landlord for the purposes of the 1987 Act will be the free- **24.78**
holder. However, if there is a chain of landlords and the qualifying tenants are in fact sub-
tenants, the situation may be more complicated. In such cases the landlord for the purposes
of the Act will be the immediate landlord of the qualifying tenants (s 2(1)(a)), or, if any of
the qualifying tenants is a statutory tenant, the person who would be entitled to possession
but for the statutory tenancy (s 2(1)(b)). (This latter provision is necessary because strictly
speaking a statutory tenancy is merely a personal right to remain in possession.) However,
where the immediate landlord of the qualifying tenants possesses a term which is either for
less than seven years, or is for a longer term but is determinable within the first seven years
by the superior landlord, then the landlord for the purposes of the Act will be the landlord
next highest in the chain (s 2(2)).

Procedure

Landlord's notice

Before a landlord can make a relevant disposal affecting any premises to which the 1987 **24.79**
Act applies, that landlord must serve notice upon the qualifying tenants in accordance with
s 5 of the Act. The precise content of this notice will depend upon the nature of the disposal. The various requirements are set out in ss 5A to 5E. In the most usual case, where the
disposal consists of a contract to create or transfer an interest in land, the notice must:

(a) contain particulars of the principal terms of the disposal, including details of the property to which it relates, details of the estate or interest in that property which is to
be disposed of, and the consideration required by the landlord for the making of the
disposal;
(b) state that the notice constitutes an offer by the landlord to dispose of the property on
those terms which may be accepted by the requisite majority of qualifying tenants of
the constituent flats;
(c) specify a period within which that offer may be accepted, being a period of not less
than two months which is to begin with the date of service of the notice;
(d) specify a further period, of a minimum of two months from the end of the acceptance
period, within which the tenants must nominate a person to acquire the landlord's
interest.

Notice should be served upon all the qualifying tenants, but the landlord will be deemed to **24.80**
have satisfied the requirements of s 5 if notice is served on not less than 90 per cent of the
qualifying tenants or, if there are fewer than 10 qualifying tenants, on all but one of them
(s 5(4)). The landlord must also serve a copy of the notice on the right to manage (RTM)
company (see 23.149 to 23.202) if one is in existence (CLRA, Sch 7, para 7).

Tenant's response

Choosing to accept the landlord's offer is a collective enterprise; all the tenants may not be **24.81**
in agreement as to what action to take, so acceptance must be made by the 'requisite majority'. The requisite majority is defined in s 18A of the 1987 Act and means more than 50 per
cent of the qualifying tenants, each flat being regarded as having one vote. If the tenants
choose to accept the offer they should serve an acceptance notice upon the landlord within
the period set out in the landlord's notice. The tenants should then nominate a person to
acquire the landlord's interest (in most cases this 'person' will be a company set up by the
tenants specifically for this purpose).

24.82   Once the landlord has served an offer notice on the qualifying tenants the landlord may not, during the period specified in the notice as the period during which the offer may be accepted, dispose of the interest (the 'protected interest') to anyone other than the person nominated by the tenants (s 6(1)). If the tenants then accept the offer this 'protected period' is extended and lasts up until the end of the period specified in the landlord's offer notice during which the tenants may nominate a person to acquire the landlord's interest (s 6(2)). Once the tenants have nominated a person, the landlord may not sell to anyone other than the person nominated (s 8(2)).

24.83   Within one month of being given notice of the nomination the landlord must either notify the nominated person that he or she no longer intends to proceed (s 8(3)), or send the nominated person a form of contract for the acquisition of the protected interest (s 8A(2)). If the landlord decides not to proceed he or she may not dispose of the protected interest for a period of 12 months following the notice of withdrawal (s 9B(2)). If the landlord sends the nominated person a contract, the tenants have two months in which either to withdraw from the purchase or to exchange contracts (s 8A(4)).

24.84   If the landlord serves an offer notice on the qualifying tenants but the tenants either do not serve an acceptance notice or fail (during the protected period) to nominate a person to acquire the landlord's interest, the landlord may, during the 12 months following the protected period, sell the protected interest to a different purchaser but only subject to certain restrictions (s 7(1)). Such a sale must be on the same terms as those specified in the offer notice (s 7(4)).

Enforcing the right of first refusal

24.85   If the landlord makes a relevant disposal affecting premises to which the 1987 Act applies without first serving an offer notice upon the tenants in accordance with s 5, or without complying with the procedure set out in ss 6 to 10, the landlord commits an offence punishable by a fine not exceeding level five on the standard scale (currently £5,000) (s 10A). In addition to this criminal sanction the qualifying tenants acquire certain rights under ss 11 and 12 of the 1987 Act. Of course, to take advantage of these rights, the tenants will need to be aware of the fact that a disposal has taken place. Section 3A of the Landlord and Tenant Act 1985 therefore requires a new landlord to give the tenants notice of his or her purchase and to inform the tenants that they may have rights under the 1987 Act. If the new landlord fails to give such notice then he or she commits a criminal offence.

Right to information

24.86   Section 11A entitles the requisite majority of the qualifying tenants to serve a notice on the landlord requiring the landlord to furnish them with particulars of the terms on which the disposal was made. Such notice must be given within four months of the qualifying tenants receiving notice of the change of landlord under s 3A of the Landlord and Tenant Act 1985, or of the receipt of any other documents that indicate that the disposal has taken place (s 11A(3)). The landlord must comply with the notice within one month (s 11A(4)).

Right to take benefit of contract

24.87   If the landlord has entered into a contract to sell the property a requisite majority of the qualifying tenants may serve notice on the landlord under s 12A. Such notice requires that the contract shall have effect to transfer the interest to a person nominated by the tenants and not to the prospective purchaser. Such notice must be served on the landlord within six months either of receiving notice under s 11A, or receipt of any other documents alerting the tenants to their rights under this section.

Right to compel sale by purchaser

If the tenants fail to serve notice under s 12A or the landlord sells the interest without entering into a contract the tenants still have a right to acquire the interest under s 12B. Section 12B enables a requisite majority of the qualifying tenants to serve notice on the purchaser requiring the purchaser to sell the interest to a person nominated by the tenants on the same terms as the original sale. Such notice must be served on the purchaser within six months of receiving notice of the sale, either by notice under s 11A or by other documents indicating that the sale has taken place. **24.88**

Right to compel grant of new tenancy by superior landlord

Where the tenants' immediate landlord is not the freeholder of the block but an intermediate landlord with a leasehold interest, the immediate landlord might seek to dispose of his or her leasehold interest by surrendering it to a superior landlord. In such a case s 12C gives the tenants the right to be granted a new tenancy of the premises by the superior landlord on the same terms as their original tenancy. **24.89**

Rights against subsequent purchasers

If the tenants have sought to enforce their rights against a new landlord by serving notice under s 11A, 12A, 12B, or 12C, but find that the new landlord has already sold the interest to someone else, they can compel the subsequent landlord to transfer the interest to them by virtue of ss 16 and 17. **24.90**

Notice by prospective purchaser

The extensive nature of the rights available to qualifying tenants where a landlord disposes of his or her interest in a property in contravention of the provisions of the 1987 Act, can put a prospective purchaser of the landlord's interest in a difficult situation. Obviously, a purchaser does not want to buy the landlord's interest only to find that it must immediately be transferred to the tenants. Section 18 of the Act therefore provides a procedure by which a prospective purchaser can find out in advance whether the property is one to which the right of first refusal applies by serving notice directly on the tenants. Such notice must inform the tenants of the proposed sale and invite the tenants to reply. The tenants can then state whether the landlord has served notice upon them in accordance with s 5 and whether, if notice has not been served, they would wish to exercise the right of first refusal. Thus, even where a landlord has failed to inform the tenants of a prospective sale, the purchaser can bypass the landlord and check whether or not the sale is a relevant disposal. If the prospective purchaser serves notice on at least 80 per cent of the tenants in the flats and less than 50 per cent of the tenants respond to the prospective purchaser's invitation within 28 days of being given notice, or more than 50 per cent of the tenants reply indicating that they do not wish to exercise the right of first refusal, the prospective purchaser may proceed and the premises will be treated as though the Act does not apply. **24.91**

Resolving disputes

Generally, the county court is the correct forum for resolving disputes arising under any of the provisions in the 1987 Act (s 52). Certain more minor matters, however, such as questions arising under notices given under s 12A, 12B, or 12C (though not the validity of the notice), may be heard by a leasehold valuation tribunal. **24.92**

D LEASEHOLD REFORM, HOUSING AND URBAN DEVELOPMENT ACT 1993

24.93 Under the LRHUDA, the holder of a long leasehold of a flat in a block can acquire the right either:

(a) to acquire the freehold of the block collectively with the other leaseholders; or

(b) to be granted a new lease of the individual flat.

Who is eligible?

Qualifying tenants

24.94 A tenant is a qualifying tenant of a flat under the Act if he or she is a tenant of the flat under a long lease (s 5(1)). No flat can have more than one qualifying tenant at one time (s 5(3)), so where a flat is held on a joint tenancy the joint tenants together are regarded as constituting one single qualifying tenant (s 5(4)(b)). The Act does not require that a qualifying tenant should occupy the flat as a residence. It is therefore possible to sub-let the whole of the flat and still be a qualifying tenant. The tenancy does not have to be the tenancy of just the flat, it can also include other property such as common areas, commercial units, and other flats. Thus, in *Howard de Walden Estates Ltd v Aggio* [2008] UKHL 44 a property investor holding the head lease of a block of flats could be a qualifying tenant under the Act. This will only be the case if none of the flats in the block are let on long tenancies. If the sub-lease is also a long tenancy and the sub-tenant is therefore a qualifying tenant, it is the sub-tenant that takes precedence and the superior tenant cannot be a qualifying tenant (s 5(4)(a)).

24.95 **Exclusions** The holder of a long lease will not be a qualifying tenant where:

(a) the lease is a business lease (ie a tenancy to which Pt II of the Landlord and Tenant Act 1954 applies) (s 101(1)); or

(b) the immediate landlord under the lease is a charitable housing trust and the flat forms part of the housing accommodation provided by it in the pursuit of its charitable purpose; or

(c) the lease was granted by sub-demise out of a superior lease other than a long lease, the grant was made in breach of the term of the superior lease, and there has been no waiver of the breach by the superior landlord (s 5(2)).

24.96 Where a charitable housing trust owns a block containing some flats let on assured short-hold tenancies in pursuit of its charitable purposes and others held on long leases, the long leaseholders, provided there are enough of them, will not be excluded from the right to enfranchise by s 5(2)(b) (*Brick Farm Management v Richmond Housing Partnership Ltd* [2005] EWHC 1650 (QB), [2005] 1 WLR 3934). The trust, however, will have the right to be granted a leaseback of the flats provided for social purposes (see 24.134).

24.97 Where a tenant would be the qualifying tenant of a flat but would also be regarded as being the qualifying tenant of two or more other flats contained in the premises, there will be no qualifying tenant for any of those flats (s 5(5)).

24.98 If a flat is let to a body corporate, any flat let to an associated company of that body corporate will be regarded as being let to that body corporate (s 5(6)). A company that holds the leases of three or more flats in a block cannot therefore avoid this exclusion by holding the individual leases in the names of different subsidiary companies. If a flat is held under a joint tenancy and one of the joint tenants also holds the leases of two or more flats in the premises, there will be no qualifying tenant for any of those flats.

Furthermore, Sch 3 to the Act sets out a number of situations where a qualifying tenant may not exercise the right to enfranchise (eg where either the landlord or the tenant has already given notice terminating the lease, an order for possession or proceedings for forfeiture are pending, or where compulsory purchase procedures have already been instituted). **24.99**

What is a long lease? A long lease is defined by s 7 of the Act as a lease granted for a term of more than 21 years, whether or not it is (or may become) terminable before the end of that term by notice given to the tenant or by re-entry, forfeiture, or otherwise. By s 7(4), this will include a lease granted for a term of less than 21 years which has been renewed (without taking a premium) so as to bring the total length of the terms to a period of more than 21 years. Where a tenant previously held under a long lease and this lease has expired but the tenant has been granted a further tenancy of the property or part of it, the subsequent tenancy will be regarded as a long lease irrespective of its terms (s 7(3)). Perpetually renewable leases and most leases terminable on death or marriage are regarded as long leases (s 7(1)(b) and (2)), as are leases granted in pursuance of the right to buy or the right to acquire on rent to mortgage terms (s 7(1)(c)), shared ownership leases where the tenant's total share is 100 per cent (s 7(1)(d)), and leases granted under the right to acquire as it has effect by virtue of s 17 of the Housing Act 1996 (s 7(1)(e)). **24.100**

Premises

For the right to collective enfranchisement to arise, the premises in question must fall within the definition set out in s 3(1) of the 1993 Act: **24.101**

(a) The premises must consist of a self-contained building or part of a building.
(b) The premises must contain two or more flats held by qualifying tenants.
(c) The total number of flats held by such tenants must not be less than two-thirds of the total number of flats contained in the premises.

What is meant by a 'self-contained building' is set out in s 3(2). A building is a self-contained building if it is structurally detached. A part of a building is a self-contained part of a building if: **24.102**

(a) it constitutes a vertical division of the building and the structure of the building is such that that part could be redeveloped independently of the remainder of the building; and
(b) the services provided by pipes, cables, and other installations are provided independently to that part or are such that they could be provided independently without causing significant interruption to the provision of services to the other occupiers in the building.

What constitutes a vertical division will be construed strictly. Only a *de minimis* deviation will be ignored. In *Re Holding and Management (Solitaire) Ltd* [2008] 2 EG 152 part of a basement car park ran under the adjoining premises; it amounted to approximately two per cent of the total floor area under consideration. The part of the building was held not to be vertically severed and therefore was not self-contained. (This was a case on the very similar provisions of CLRA, s 72 regarding the eligibility for the right to manage, see 23.149; the provisions regarding the vertical division of houses under the 1967 Act are not so strict, see 24.11.) **24.103**

The fact that a self-contained part of a building can itself be further sub-divided into smaller self-contained parts does not prevent that part from acquiring the right to enfranchise (*Craftrule Limited v 41–60 Albert Place Mansions (Freehold) Ltd* [2011] EWCA Civ 185). **24.104**

24.105   The provision of services was considered in *Oakwood Court (Holland Park) Ltd v Daejan Properties* [2007] 1 EGLR 121. Here one half of a mansion block was seen as properly vertically divided from the other but both halves were served by a shared boiler room. The part was therefore not self-contained and the tenants did not acquire the right to enfranchise.

24.106   A flat is defined by s 101 as a separate set of premises (whether or not on the same floor):

(a)   which forms part of a building; and
(b)   which is constructed or adapted for use for the purposes of a dwelling; and
(c)   either the whole or a material part of which lies above or below some other part of the building. (A sensible approach should be taken to the interpretation of this section: in *Cadogan v McGirk* [1996] EWCA Civ 1340, [1996] 4 All ER 643, a box room on the sixth floor of a block of flats was held not to be part of a flat on the second floor; it was, however, an appurtenance usually enjoyed with the flat (see 24.131 and 24.160).)

Excluded premises

24.107   The aim of the 1993 Act is to provide residential tenants with the right to enfranchise. The Act will not apply where there is a significant non-residential use of the premises. Section 4(1) therefore provides that premises will be excluded from the right to collective enfranchisement if:

(a)   any part or parts of the premises is or are neither:
   (i)   occupied, or intended to be occupied, for residential purposes, nor
   (ii) comprised in any common parts of the premises; and
(b)   the internal floor area of that part or of those parts (taken together) exceeds 25 per cent of the internal floor area of the premises (taken as a whole).

The onus of proving that a building falls with this exception lies on the landlord (*Indiana Investments v Taylor* [2004] 3 EGLR 63).

24.108   However, where certain parts of the premises are used, or intended for use, in conjunction with a particular dwelling contained in the premises, for example a garage or storage area, these parts will be taken to be occupied for residential purposes (s 4(2)).

24.109   Where certain common parts of a mixed-use building are used exclusively by the commercial occupiers, those common parts are nevertheless common parts for the purposes of s 4(1) (*Marine Court (St Leonards on Sea) Freeholders Ltd v Rother District Investments Ltd* [2008] 02 EG 148).

Resident landlords

24.110   Premises will also be excluded from the right to enfranchise (but not to lease renewal) where there is a resident landlord. This exclusion, however, is restricted by statute and of relatively narrow application. It will only apply where:

(a)   the premises do not form part of a purpose-built block of flats (ie it must be a building that has been converted into flats) (s 10(1)(a));
(b)   the premises do not contain more than four units (s 4(4)). A unit is defined by s 38(1) as a flat, any other separate set of premises which is constructed or adapted for use for the purposes of a dwelling, or a separate set of premises let, or intended for letting, on a business lease;
(c)   the same person has owned the freehold of the premises since before the conversion into two or more flats or other units (s 10(1)(b));

(d) that person, or an adult member of his family, has occupied a flat or other unit contained in the premises as his or her only or principal home for at least the last 12 months (s 10(1)(c)).

If we apply these requirements to our earlier example (at 24.10) we can see that Peter and **24.111** Britta would not be prevented from acquiring the freehold. Even if Steven has been occupying a flat in the house as his principal home, he is not the freeholder. The situation would be different if Nicola had never granted a lease of the whole house and had carried out the conversion into flats herself. In that case, provided she (or a member of her family) had occupied one of the flats as her only or principle home for a sufficient length of time, the premises would fall within the exclusion.

Procedure for collective enfranchisement

We have already seen that for premises to be eligible for collective enfranchisement under **24.112** the 1993 Act at least two-thirds of the total number of flats contained in the premises must be held by qualifying tenants. However, in order actually to make a claim more is required. To set the ball rolling an initial notice must be served upon the reversioner (see 24.123). The initial notice must be given by a number of qualifying tenants of flats contained in the premises which is not less than one half of the total number of flats contained in the premises (s 13(2)).

Qualifying tenants who may not participate

Certain individual tenants, who would otherwise be eligible as qualifying tenants, are **24.113** precluded from participating in the exercise of the right to collective enfranchisement by s 13(13) and Sch 3. The precluded categories include:

(a) a tenant who has previously given notice to terminate the tenancy or has agreed to the grant of a future tenancy (which is not a long tenancy at a low rent) on the termination of the existing tenancy (Sch 3, para 1);

(b) a tenant on whom the landlord has already served notice under the Local Government and Housing Act 1989 proposing an assured tenancy or seeking possession and four months have expired since the service of that notice (Sch 3, para 2, see 22.31 and 22.41);

(c) a tenant against whom an order for possession has been made (Sch 3, para 3(1));

(d) a tenant against whom proceedings are pending to enforce a right of re-entry or forfeiture unless leave is granted by the court (Sch 3, para 3(2));

(e) a tenant against whom compulsory purchase procedures have been instituted (Sch 3, para 4).

The reversioner

When a group of tenants are seeking to enfranchise there will obviously need to be a person **24.114** with whom they deal (ie a person who can receive the initial notice, give counter-notice, negotiate the terms of the acquisition, and execute the conveyance). This person is known as the reversioner. In a straightforward situation where the tenants have been granted their leases directly by the freeholder and are seeking only to acquire interests that belong to the freeholder, that freeholder will be the reversioner (s 9(1)).

It is however possible that the tenants propose to acquire interests that belong to other **24.115** parties. The tenants' leases may not have been granted directly by the freeholder with the result that there are intermediate leasehold interests that need to be acquired (see 24.132). The tenants may also be seeking to acquire appurtenant property or common parts (see 24.131) which are held from the freeholder by another tenant.

24.116 In these cases the reversioner will be the person identified by the provisions of Sch 1. This will usually be the freeholder (Sch 1, para 1); however, where all parties (ie the freeholder and all holders of intermediate interests) can agree, they may apply to the court to have one of their number appointed as the reversioner instead of the freeholder (Sch 1, para 2). Alternatively, one of them may ask the court to appoint a reversioner but only when special circumstances apply (such as the absence, incapacity, or unwillingness of the freeholder) (Sch 1, para 2). The court may also remove the reversioner and appoint an alternative on the application of the holder of an intermediate interest or the nominee purchaser, if it appears to the court proper to do so (Sch 1, para 4). The person appointed must always be either the freeholder or the holder of an intermediate interest (Sch 1, para 5).

24.117 Where there are multiple freeholders the reversioner will be the person specified in the tenants' initial notice (s 2A and Sch 1, para 5A); however, similar provisions to those above enable an application to be made to the court to appoint an alternative reversioner. These provisions were introduced by the Housing Act 1996 to close a loophole in the law. As originally enacted the 1993 Act only permitted tenants to enfranchise when the freehold of the building was owned by one person and landlords were therefore able to evade the provisions of the Act by splitting the freehold.

The nominee purchaser

24.118 In the course of a claim to collective enfranchisement the reversioner cannot deal with all of the tenants individually. As the law currently stands, the tenants must nominate a 'person' to conduct the proceedings on their behalf and, if the claim is successful, to acquire the freehold. Such a person is known as the 'nominee purchaser' (see s 15 of the 1993 Act). The nominee purchaser can be an individual or a group of individuals, but in the majority of cases it will be a company set up by the tenants for the purpose of acquiring the freehold. The CLRA contains provisions (ss 121 to 124) designed to replace the nominee purchaser with a right to enfranchise (RTE) company and standardize the enfranchisement process by use of prescribed forms of notice and memoranda and articles of association. There are no current plans to implement these provisions.

24.119 **Setting up a company** Setting up such a company is a relatively simple procedure which involves filing the company memoranda of association and articles of association and Form IN01 with Companies House. Details are available from <http://www.companieshouse.gov.uk>; standard form memoranda and articles of association are available from legal stationers and many solicitors offer a company incorporation service geared to enfranchisement. The identity of the nominee purchaser must be specified in the initial notice so the company will need to be set up before initial notice is served.

24.120 **Changing the nominee purchaser** Section 15 contains provisions permitting the participating tenants to terminate the appointment of the nominee purchaser and to appoint a replacement by notice given to the current nominee purchaser, the reversioner, and any intermediate landlords. Section 16 further provides for replacement on the retirement or death of the nominee purchaser.

24.121 **Participation agreements** Collective enfranchisement, as the name implies, is a process that requires the tenants to act together and demands a high degree of cooperation and financial commitment. Although it is not a legal requirement, tenants may wish to establish a legal basis for their action before embarking on the process, particularly in a block with a large number of tenants. This can be done by requiring the tenants who are serious about enfranchisement to enter into a participation agreement. Details of a participation agreement and a sample agreement are available from the Leasehold Advisory Service at <http://www.lease-advice.org>.

Preliminary inquiries

Tenants who are considering whether to make a claim for collective enfranchisement may **24.122** find that they are not possessed of sufficient information to make an informed decision. Sections 11 and 12 of the 1993 Act therefore provide a procedure whereby any qualifying tenant may serve notice on his or her immediate landlord (or the person collecting rent on behalf of the immediate landlord), or on the freeholder (if the tenant knows who the freeholder is) requiring the relevant information to be provided.

The initial notice

Once the tenants have decided to proceed and have appointed a nominee purchaser, the **24.123** next step in the enfranchisement process is to serve an initial notice. This notice, as we have seen, must be given by a sufficient number of qualifying tenants. The notice must be served upon the reversioner and contain the information prescribed by s 13 of the 1993 Act (forms are available from legal stationers). The initial notice must:

(a) specify and provide a plan showing the premises (and any other 'appurtenant property' or common parts, see below) of which the freehold is proposed to be acquired;

(b) specify any leasehold interests (see 24.132) which are proposed to be acquired;

(c) specify any flats or other units in the premises which are subject to a mandatory lease-back (see 24.134);

(d) specify the proposed purchase price of:
    (i) the freehold of the specified premises (or, where there are multiple freeholds, of each of the freeholds in the premises);
    (ii) the freehold of any appurtenant property of which the freehold is proposed to be acquired;
    (iii) any leasehold interest which is proposed to be acquired;

(e) give details of all the qualifying tenants in the premises;

(f) state the identity of the nominee purchaser and give an address for service;

(g) specify the date by which the reversioner must respond by giving counternotice. This date should be at least two months from the date upon which the notice is given.

Section 99(5) requires the initial notice to be signed by each qualifying tenant. Attaching **24.124** a signature form (that the tenants had completed earlier) to the notice is not sufficient (*Cascades and Quayside Ltd v Cascades Freehold Ltd* [2007] EWCA Civ 1555, [2008] L&TR 23). Where the tenant is a company, s 36A of the Companies Act 1985 must be complied with and the notice requires the signature of two directors or the director and secretary or the company seal; the signature of one director is insufficient (*Hilmi & Associates Ltd v 20 Pembridge Villas Ltd* [2010] EWCA Civ 314).

Where there are intermediate leasehold interests (see 24.132), the intermediate landlords **24.125** must be sent copies of the initial notice by the qualifying tenants (Sch 3, para 12).

Ascertaining the proposed purchase price There is no longer any statutory requirement **24.126** to do so, but it is highly advisable to obtain an initial valuation by a qualified valuer: first, because it will give the tenants an idea of what the final price will be, which will help them in deciding whether or not to proceed; secondly, because the proposed purchase price stated in the initial notice must be realistic, not just a nominal figure, and the notice will be invalid if it states an unrealistic price (*Cadogan Estates v Morris* [1998] EWCA Civ 1671, [1999] 1 EGLR 59).

Landlord's costs In considering the final cost of enfranchisement tenants should also **24.127** bear in mind that once the initial notice is served the nominee purchaser is liable for the reasonable legal, valuation, and conveyancing costs incurred by the reversioner and any intermediate landlords (s 33(1) and (2)). If the notice ceases to have effect the nominee purchaser will be liable for cost up to that date (s 33(3)) except where the notice ceases to have effect because of the landlord's intention to redevelop (s 23(4)) or a compulsory acquisition (s 30(4)). However, the nominee purchaser will not be liable for costs incurred by other parties in connection with LVT proceedings (s 33(5)).

24.128 **Withdrawal of notice** Participating tenants may withdraw the initial notice by giving notice of withdrawal in accordance with s 28. Notice will also be deemed to be withdrawn in the cases set out in s 29. Where notice is withdrawn or deemed to be withdrawn no new notice specifying the whole or part of the same premises may be served within 12 months of the date of withdrawal (s 13(9)). Where a second notice is served it is not open to the reversioner to claim that it is an abuse of process or a breach of CPR r 38.7 (which provides that a claimant needs leave of the court to bring a second claim arising out of substantially the same facts as the first). The Act is a self-contained code and it is clearly within its contemplation that more than one notice may be served (*Westbrook Dolphin Square v Friends Life Ltd* [2012] EWCA Civ 666). However, where notice is withdrawn or deemed to be withdrawn the participating tenants will be liable to the reversioner for costs incurred in pursuance of the notice up to the date of withdrawal (s 28(4) and 29(6)).

24.129 **Errors in notice** A notice will not be invalidated by an inaccuracy in the particulars or a misdescription of the property (Sch 3, para 15(1)). A complete failure to give the required particulars goes beyond a mere inaccuracy (*Mutual Place Property Management v Blaquiere* [1996] 2 EGLR 78) and the key question will usually be whether or not the error prejudices the reversioner. If the notice specifies any property or interest which is not liable to acquisition or fails to specify any property or interest that is liable to acquisition the notice may be amended with the leave of the court (Sch 3, para 15(2)).

24.130 **Rights of access** Once the initial notice has been served, s 17(2) grants a right of access to the nominee purchaser and any person acting on his behalf (eg a surveyor or valuer) where such access is reasonably required in connection with any matter arising out of the notice. Such access may be to any part of the specified premises including appurtenant property and common parts and is exercisable on giving at least 10 days' notice to the occupier (s 17(3)). Section 17(1) grants a similar right of access to the reversioner and the holders of any intermediate interests.

24.131 **Appurtenant property and common parts** The qualifying tenants may also be able to acquire other property which is not comprised in the premises (see 24.101) but which is owned by the freehold owner (s 1(2) and (3)). Such property must be either:

(a) appurtenant property which is demised by the lease held by a tenant of a flat contained in the relevant premises ('appurtenant property' means any garage, out-house, garden, yard, or appurtenance belonging to or usually enjoyed with the flat: s 1(7)); or

(b) property which any such tenant is entitled under the terms of the lease of his flat to use in common with the occupiers of other premises (whether or not those premises are contained in the relevant premises).

24.132 **Intermediate leasehold interests** Where the qualifying tenant is a sub-tenant, he or she does not hold the lease directly from the freeholder but from an intermediate landlord. Where several leasehold interests have been carved out of the freehold estate, there may even be a number of intermediate landlords superior to the qualifying tenant. Obviously, these interests cannot persist after the tenants have acquired the freehold. Section 2(1) and (2) therefore provide that when the right to collective enfranchisement is exercised the qualifying tenants shall also acquire the interests of any tenants which are superior to the lease held by a qualifying tenant.

The qualifying tenants may also acquire the interest of a tenant under which the demised   **24.133**
premises consist of or include:

(a) any common parts of the relevant premises; or
(b) any appurtenant property and common parts as defined (but held on a lease rather
     than by the freeholder),

provided that the acquisition of the interest is reasonably necessary for the proper management or maintenance of those common parts or appurtenant property (s 2(3)). A caretaker's flat has been held to be a common part where it was essential to the provision of
caretaking facilities for the other flats (*Cadogan v Panagopoulos* [2010] EWCA Civ 1259).
It also appears that it may be possible for the qualifying tenants to acquire part only of a
leasehold interest (*Hemphurst Ltd v Durrels House Ltd* [2011] UKUT 6 (LC)).

Leaseback In certain situations, when the freehold is acquired the nominee purchaser can   **24.134**
be obliged to grant the former freeholder a leaseback of a flat or other unit contained in
the premises. This will occur where the flat in question is let under a secure tenancy or
an introductory tenancy and the freeholder is the secure tenant's immediate public sector
landlord (Sch 9, para 2), or where the tenancy is not secure but the freeholder is a housing association and the tenant is not a qualifying tenant (Sch 9, para 3). In these cases the
leaseback is mandatory.

Where immediately before the acquisition date a unit is not let to a qualifying tenant,   **24.135**
the former freeholder has the right to require the nominee purchaser to grant him or her
a leaseback of that unit (Sch 9, para 5). A unit can be a flat or separate premises either
adapted for use as a dwelling or intended to be let under a business lease (s 38(1)). This
may occur, for example, where the freeholder has let out a flat in the block on a short
tenancy or where there are commercial units on the ground floor let on business leases.
These are valuable assets for the freeholder which need to be preserved, either through
the leaseback mechanism (which puts the former freeholder back in place by granting a
999-year lease at a peppercorn rent (Sch 9, para 8)) or because their worth will be taken
into account in the valuation. There is also a right to a leaseback where there is a resident
landlord (ie the freeholder is both a qualifying tenant and is occupying the flat or unit)
(Sch 9, para 6).

Assignment or sale after initial notice The initial notice can be registered as a class C(iv)   **24.136**
land charge (in unregistered land) or as an estate contract in registered land (s 97). If the
notice is registered and the landlord sells the freehold, the purchaser will acquire the freehold
subject to the application for enfranchisement. Where a participating tenant assigns his or
her lease the new lessee should inform the nominee purchaser of the assignment and whether
he or she wishes to participate in the proposed purchase within 14 days (s 14(2)). Where a
non-participating tenant assigns his or her lease the new lessee may choose to participate in
the acquisition but only with the agreement of the other participating tenants (s 14(3)).

Reversioner's counter-notice Once the qualifying tenants have served an initial notice on   **24.137**
the reversioner, the reversioner should give counter-notice to the nominee purchaser by the
date specified in the initial notice (s 21(1)). This counter-notice must:

(a) admit that the participating tenants are entitled to collective enfranchisement in rela-
     tion to the specified premises; or
(b) deny that the participating tenants are entitled to collective enfranchisement and spec-
     ify reasons; or
(c) admit or deny the claim but state that an appropriate landlord intends to apply to the
     court under s 23 for an order that the right to collective enfranchisement shall not

be exercisable in relation to those premises by reason of that landlord's intention to redevelop the premises (s 21(2)).

24.138 If the counter-notice does not specify one of these options, it will be invalid (*Burman v Mount Cook Land* [2001] EWCA Civ 1712, (2001) 48 EGCS 128, CA). Interestingly, in contrast to the position with the tenants' initial notice, specifying an unrealistic purchase price will not invalidate a reversioners' counter-notice (see 9 *Cornwall Crescent London Ltd v Kensington and Chelsea Royal London Borough* [2005] EWCA Civ 324, and 24.126). If the reversioner fails to give counter-notice at all, the nominee purchaser will be entitled to apply to the court and acquire the freehold on the terms specified in the initial notice (s 25(1) and *Willingale v Globalgrange* [2000] EWCA Civ 520, (2000) 18 EG 152, CA).

24.139 **Admitting the claim** Where the reversioner admits the claim, the next stage is to settle the terms of the acquisition. In the counter-notice the reversioner must therefore set out which of the proposals contained in the initial notice are accepted and which (if any) are not accepted. If certain proposals are not accepted the counter-notice should specify the reversioner's counter proposals (s 21(3)(a)(i)). If the reversioner wishes to make any leaseback proposals (see above), he or she should be specified in the counter-notice (s 21(3)(a)(ii)). If they are not specified in the counter-notice the reversioner may not raise them at a later date (*Cawthorne and others v Hamdam* [2007] EWCA Civ 6, [2007] 2 WLR 185).

24.140 Under s 21(4), the reversioner can also require the nominee purchaser to acquire the interest in any property of the freeholder or of any other relevant landlord, if the property:

(a) would for all practical purposes cease to be of use and benefit to him or her; or
(b) would cease to be capable of being reasonably managed or maintained by him or her.

24.141 Thus, the reversioner can avoid being left responsible for, say, a garage which was not included in the tenants' claim but which would be of no use to the reversioner once enfranchisement has taken place. If the reversioner requires the nominee purchaser to acquire such an interest this should be stated in the counter-notice (s 21(3)(c)). Similarly, if the reversioner wishes to retain rights over any property comprised in the claim on the grounds that these rights are necessary for the proper management or maintenance of other property in which he or she is to retain an interest, this should also be stated in the counter-notice (s 21(3)(d)).

24.142 The counter-notice should also state whether or not the specified premises are within the area of a scheme approved as an estate management scheme (Leasehold Reform (Collective Enfranchisement) (Counter Notices) Regulations 2002, SI 2002/3208, WSI 2003/990 (see 24.55).

24.143 If, once counter-notice has been given admitting the claim, the parties fail to come to agreement as to the terms of the acquisition, either party may apply to a leasehold valuation tribunal to determine the matters in dispute (s 24). Such an application cannot be made until two months after the date of the counter-notice, but it must be made before six months have elapsed from that date.

24.144 **Denying the claim** Where the reversioner does not admit the tenants' claim the nominee purchaser may apply to the county court for a declaration that the participating tenants are entitled to exercise the right to collective enfranchisement (s 22). Such an application must be made within two months of the date of the counter-notice.

24.145 **Intention to redevelop** Where the reversioner states in the counter-notice that it is the intention of an appropriate landlord to apply to the court under s 23 for an order preventing the tenants from exercising their right to collective enfranchisement, the appropriate landlord must make his or her application within two months of the counter-notice being given (s 23(3)). The appropriate landlord does not have to be the reversioner but may be any other relevant landlord holding an intermediate interest, or two or more landlords acting together (s 23(10)):

> (2) The court shall not make an order under s 23(1) unless it is satisfied—
> (a) that not less than two-thirds of all the long leases on which flats contained in the specified premises are held are due to terminate within the period of five years beginning with the relevant date; and
> (b) that for the purposes of redevelopment the applicant intends, once the leases in question have so terminated—
> (i) to demolish or reconstruct, or
> (ii) to carry out substantial works of construction on,
> the whole or a substantial part of the specified premises; and
> (c) that he or she could not reasonably do so without obtaining possession of the flats demised by those leases.

If these three criteria are satisfied the court may make an order: but it does not have **24.146** to; the statute, though, provides no guidance as to how such discretion is to be exercised. If the court makes an order the initial notice shall cease to have effect (s 23(4)). If the court dismisses the application the court shall make an order declaring that the reversioner's counter-notice shall be of no effect, and requiring the reversioner to give a further counter-notice to the nominee purchaser by such date as is specified in the order (s 23(5)).

Failure to give counter-notice If the reversioner fails to give counter-notice within the **24.147** required period, the nominee purchaser may apply to the court under s 25 of the 1993 Act. Such an application must be made within six months of the date by which the reversioner was to give counter-notice (s 25(4)). When such an application is made the court has the power to make an order determining the terms on which the nominee purchaser is to acquire the freehold (s 25(1)).

The purchase price

The price payable for the freehold is determined by s 32 of and Sch 6 to the Act. The basic **24.148** principle is that purchase price will be the aggregate of:

(a) the value of the freeholder's interest;
(b) the freeholder's share of the marriage value;
(c) any amount of compensation payable to the freeholder for losses caused by enfranchisement (Sch 6, para 2).

Value of the freeholder's interest

The value of the freeholder's interest is the value the premises would be expected to realize **24.149** on the open market assuming that neither the nominee purchaser nor any tenant of the premises is seeking to buy. Further assumptions to be made are:

(a) that the vendor is selling an estate in fee simple subject to the flat owners' existing leases and any other intermediate leases;
(b) that there is no right to enfranchise or extend the lease;
(c) that any increase in value of any flat due to improvements made by the tenant at his or her own expense is disregarded;

(d)   that the vendor is selling with and subject to the rights and burdens with and subject to which the conveyance to the nominee purchaser is to be made (Sch 6, para 3).

Marriage value

24.150   The marriage value is the increase in value that results from the fact of the nominee purchaser acquiring (on behalf of the tenants) every intermediate leasehold interest in the premises in comparison with the value those interests would have if they remained in the hands of the tenants. An increase in value occurs because once the nominee purchaser has bought the freehold the tenants are effectively (through the nominee purchaser) their own landlord and therefore have the ability to grant themselves new leases without having to pay a premium or being restricted as to their length; whereas if those interests were being sold on the open market the purchaser would have to agree to share this value with the sellers. The freeholder is entitled to a share of this value. The freeholder's share of the marriage value is fixed at 50 per cent unless the tenant's lease still has over 80 years to run at the date of the initial notice, in which case the marriage value is ignored (Sch 6, para 4).

Hope value

24.151   While marriage value arises where the tenants take over the freehold interest, hope value is the value attributable to the possibility of selling a share in the freehold or a new lease to the tenant at a future date. This may be taken into account in calculating the price to be paid by the nominee purchaser under Sch 6, para 3 where there are some flats that have not participated and there is the possibility that in the future leaseholders of those flats may wish to obtain new leases of their flats (*Pitts v Earl Cadogan* [2008] UKHL 71).

Compensation

24.152   The freeholder is entitled to be paid a reasonable amount of compensation for losses which are attributable to the acquisition of his or her interest in the property. This will include a diminution in value of the freeholder's interest in another property or a loss of development value in another property (Sch 6, para 5). Compensation under para 5, however, applies only to losses affecting other property owned by the freeholder; it does not refer to any loss of development value in the property that has been acquired, because this will be something that will be taken into account in calculating the market value of the property to be acquired. Similarly, the price payable for the freehold may be adjusted to take into account losses that result from the fact that the freeholder may no longer earn commission on the insurance premiums (*Blackstone Investments Ltd v Middleton-Dell Management Co. Ltd* (1997) 14 EG 135: but also *Moore v Escalus Properties* [1979] 07 EG 149).

Intermediate leasehold interests

24.153   Where the nominee purchaser is to acquire one or more intermediate leasehold interests a separate price is payable for each of those interests (Sch 6, para 6). This price will be calculated in accordance with Sch 6, para 7. The holder of the intermediate interest will also be entitled to compensation and a share of the marriage value (Sch 6, paras 8 and 9). Similarly, where there are multiple freeholders the nominee purchaser must pay a separate price for each of these interests in accordance with Sch 6, para 5A.

Individual lease renewal

24.154   Under the 1993 Act, the tenant of a flat may acquire the right to renew the lease of that particular flat. The right conferred by the Act is an individual right—the tenant does not have to act communally with the other tenants in the block. The right to an individual lease renewal may therefore be particularly attractive to a tenant where there are insufficient qualifying tenants in a block to be eligible for collective enfranchisement, or where the administrative complexity of the collective enfranchisement procedure discourages the tenant from entering into dealings with the other tenants. The procedure for individual lease renewal is in many ways simpler than that for enfranchisement.

Who can exercise the right?

A qualifying tenant

A tenant will be eligible to acquire a new lease if that tenant has been a qualifying tenant **24.155** of the flat for the two years preceding the date on which notice of the claim is given to the landlord (s 39(2)). A qualifying tenant, for the purposes of lease renewal, is virtually the same as for enfranchisement. Section 5 (see 24.94) and s 7 (see 24.100) apply with the omission of s 5(5) and (6) (see 24.97). In contrast to the provisions on enfranchisement, a person can be the qualifying tenant of two or more flats at the same time (s 39(4)). It is also possible for the head lessee of a block of flats to be the qualifying tenant of a flat in that block (*Howard de Walden Estates Ltd v Aggio* [2008] UKHL 44, see 24.94).

Personal representatives

If the tenant of the flat dies, and that tenant was, for the period of two years preceding his **24.156** or her death, a qualifying tenant of the flat, the right to acquire a new lease may be exercised by the deceased tenant's personal representatives (s 39(3A)). However, if the personal representatives wish to exercise the right they must give notice under s 42 no later than two years after the grant of probate or letters of administration (s 42(4A)).

The right to acquire what?

Where the tenant can fulfil these conditions, he or she will acquire the right to be granted, **24.157** in substitution for the existing lease, a new lease of the flat at a peppercorn rent for a term expiring 90 years after the term date of the existing lease (s 56(1)). The tenant will have to pay a premium, though, calculated in accordance with Sch 13. The premium will be made up of the diminution in value of the landlord's interest (based on market values), the landlord's share of the marriage value, and compensation payable to the landlord for loss arising out of the grant of the new lease.

A flat, for the purposes of the Act, includes any garage, outhouse, garden, yard, and appur- **24.158** tenances belonging to, or usually enjoyed with, the flat and let to the tenant with the flat on the date on which notice of the claim is given to the landlord (s 62(2)). Thus, an attic box-room let to a tenant under a separate agreement but for the same term as the lease of the flat can be included in the new lease as an appurtenance (*Cadogan v McGirk* [1996] EWCA Civ 1340, [1996] 4 All ER 643).

Procedure for individual lease renewal

The initial notice

The procedure for exercising the right to a new lease is broadly similar to that for collective **24.159** enfranchisement. The tenant must start the process by giving an initial notice in accordance with s 42 of the 1993 Act. This notice must be given to the landlord and to any third party to the tenant's lease (s 42(2)). The notice must give details of the tenant's claim as specified in s 42(3). In particular, it must specify the premises, the premium which the tenant proposes to pay in respect of the new lease, and the terms of the new lease. Further provisions regarding the effect of notice being given on other notices and forfeiture are contained in

Sch 12. As with notice to enfranchise, it will not be invalidated by inaccuracies in the particulars (Sch 12, para 9).

Who is the landlord?

24.160 In seeking to acquire a new lease the tenant will want to be dealing with someone with sufficient interest to grant the new lease. Section 40(1) therefore defines 'the landlord' as the person who holds an interest in the flat which satisfies the following conditions:

(a) it is an interest in a reversion expectant (whether or not immediately) on the termination of the tenant's lease; and

(b) it is either a freehold interest or a leasehold interest whose duration is such as to enable that person to grant a new long lease.

24.161 If there are two or more landlords who satisfy these conditions, 'the landlord' will be the one who is lowest down in the chain of intermediate landlords.

Preliminary inquiries

24.162 If the qualifying tenant is not possessed of sufficient information to ascertain the identity of the relevant landlord, that qualifying tenant can require the immediate landlord or any person receiving rent on behalf of the immediate landlord to supply the relevant information (s 41).

Landlord's counter-notice

24.163 The procedure to be followed by the landlord on receipt of the tenant's initial notice is very similar to the counter-notice procedure when a claim is made to enfranchise (see 24.137). The landlord can either admit the tenant's right to a new lease, or deny that right (s 45(2)). The landlord can also state in the counter-notice that he or she intends to make an application to the court under s 47(1) for an order that the right to a new lease cannot be exercised because the landlord intends to redevelop the premises in which the flat is contained. The court, however, will make an order under s 47 only where it is satisfied that the tenant's lease is due to terminate within the next five years and that for the purposes of redevelopment the landlord intends, once the lease has terminated, to demolish or reconstruct or to carry out substantial works of construction on the whole or a substantial part of the premises containing the flat and that such works could not reasonably be carried out without obtaining possession of the flat (s 47(2)). 'Premises', for the purposes of s 47, in which the flat is contained must be an objectively recognizable physical space. In most cases this will be the block itself, not a notional space defined by the landlord, such as two adjacent flats within the block which the landlord intended to knock into one (*Majorstake Ltd v Curtis* [2008] UKHL 10).

24.164 If the landlord admits the claim, he or she must state in the counter-notice which (if any) of the proposals in the tenant's initial notice the landlord does not accept and specify counter proposals. If, within a period of two months from the date of the counter-notice, the parties cannot come to agreement, either party may apply under s 48 to a leasehold valuation tribunal to have the terms determined. Such an application must be made within six months of the date of the counter-notice.

24.165 If the landlord does not admit the tenant's right to a new lease, the landlord should then go on to apply to the court under s 46 for an order that the tenant has no right to acquire a new lease of the flat. Such an application must be made within two months of the counter-notice. If the court makes an order the tenant's notice will cease to have effect (s 46(3)). If the court dismisses the landlord's application, the court will make an order that the landlord's counter-notice shall be of no effect and requiring the landlord to give a further counter-notice to the tenant by such date as is specified in the order (s 46(4)).

Where a landlord does not reply to the tenant's notice, the tenant may apply to the court for **24.166**
an order determining the terms of acquisition in accordance with the proposals contained
in the tenant's notice (s 49(1)). The court will make such an order only if it is satisfied that
the tenant has the right to acquire a new lease and that the tenant's notice procedure set
out in Pt I of Sch 11 was properly complied with (s 49(2)).

The terms of the new lease

Once all the necessary procedures have been complied with, the landlord is bound to grant **24.167**
the tenant a new lease on payment by the tenant of the appropriate premium. However, if
the tenant has not paid the rent up to the date of the new lease, or there are outstanding
costs incurred in connection with the new lease for which the tenant is liable under s 60, or
there are other sums due under the existing lease, then the tenant is not entitled to require
the execution of the new lease (s 56(3)).

The new lease will be on the same terms as the existing lease as they applied at the date of **24.168**
the tenant's notice, but with such modifications as may be required to take account of:

(a) the omission from the new lease of property included in the existing lease but not
     comprised in the flat;
(b) alterations made to the property demised since the grant of the existing lease;
(c) where the existing lease derives from more than one separate lease, their combined
     effect and the differences (if any) in their terms (s 57(1)).

Section 57(2) further provides that where the existing lease does not make appropriate **24.169**
provisions with regard to service charges such provisions should be included. Similarly,
either party to the lease can require a term in the existing lease to be excluded or modified
if it is necessary to do so in order to remedy a defect in the existing lease or to take account
of changes which have occurred since the commencement of the existing lease (s 57(6)).
Terms providing for the renewal of the lease, conferring an option to purchase or a right
of pre-emption in relation to the flat demised by the existing lease, or providing for the
termination of the existing lease before its term date otherwise than in the event of a breach
of its terms, will be excluded from the new lease (s 57(4)).

KEY DOCUMENTS

Leasehold Reform Act 1967

Landlord and Tenant Act 1986

Leasehold Reform, Housing and Urban Development Act 1993

Leasehold Reform (Notices) Regulations 1997, SI 1997/640, as amended by SI 2002/1715, 2002/3209 and WSI 2002/3187, 2003/991

Leasehold Reform (Collective Enfranchisement) (Counter Notices) Regulations, SI 2002/3208, WSI 2003/990

Printed copies of all legislation can be ordered from The Stationery Office at <http://www.tsoshop.co.uk>. All legislation from 1988 onwards and most pre-1988 primary legislation is available online at <http://www.legislation.gov.uk>.

25

COMMONHOLD

A INTRODUCTION

In the previous three chapters we have seen how in the last 40 years or so steps have been **25.01** taken to try and ameliorate the worst of the problems associated with leasehold ownership. Provisions have been put in place to provide long leaseholders with some protection against exploitation and bad management by landlords and management companies by the Landlord and Tenant Acts 1985 and 1987 (see Chapter 23). The Leasehold Reform Act 1967 gave long leaseholders of houses the right to purchase the freehold from the landlord or to extend their lease. Part 1 of the Landlord and Tenant Act 1987 gave the leaseholders of flats a right of first refusal to collectively purchase the freehold from their landlord; and the Leasehold Reform, Housing and Urban Development Act 1993 gave flat owners the right to collective enfranchisement (see Chapter 24). The rights under all three statutes were extended by the Housing Act 1996.

25.02 The Commonhold and Leasehold Reform Act 2002 (CLRA) sought to take the final step and introduce a system of freehold ownership applicable to blocks of flats and other developments in multiple occupation. Commonhold effectively takes the landlord and tenant relationship out of multiply occupied buildings. Under commonhold there is no longer a person with a superior interest to the people who own the individual sections of a building. These sections—be they flats in a block, separate offices or shops, or even freestanding units in a business park—are known as units. The owners of these separate units are known as unit-holders. The common parts of the land—the stairwells, corridors, lifts, grounds, gardens, and any other shared facilities—are owned, managed, and maintained by a body known as the commonhold association, a limited company set up specifically for this purpose, whose membership is restricted to the unit-holders. The responsibilities and duties of the unit-holders and the commonhold association are governed by the articles of association of the commonhold association and by the commonhold community statement. These two documents effectively take the place of a lease in commonhold land. Thus, under the commonhold system, all individual unit-holders effectively have two interests in the commonhold property: a direct interest in their own unit and an indirect interest in the common parts through their membership of the commonhold association. Unlike under a lease, these interests are infinite in duration.

25.03 The specific advantages of commonhold are therefore relatively easy to enumerate. First, because the unit-holders own the freehold of their units, a commonhold is not a wasting asset (see 22.02). Secondly, because the unit-holders are the only members of the commonhold association, they are in control of the management and maintenance of the property. Thirdly, because all the unit-holders are subject to the articles of association and the commonhold community statement, there is a uniformity of interest among unit-holders and commonhold does not suffer from a common difficulty in leasehold blocks, namely that it is frequently not possible for a leaseholder to enforce his or her rights directly against another leaseholder. Fourthly, because there is no landlord, a unit-holder is under no obligation to pay ground rent, nor is the unit-holder subject to the threat of forfeiture. And finally, through the system of mutual rights contained in the commonhold community statement, commonhold resolves one of the perennial bugbears of freehold land, namely that the burden of positive covenants does not run with the land to bind successors in title (see 22.04).

25.04 Nevertheless, it can hardly be said that commonhold has taken the leaseholders' world by storm. Whether its popularity will increase remains to be seen, but it seems likely that its take-up will be gradual and dependent on market forces. Commonhold, it should be stressed, is a completely voluntary scheme. (It will, for example, be of no use to the leaseholder who, frustrated with the poor management of his block, wants to compel the landlord to hand over the freehold; such a leaseholder should rather try to enfranchise under the Leasehold Reform, Housing and Urban Development Act 1993 (see 24.93) or use the new right-to-manage provisions (see 23.149).) Commonhold is an alternative form of ownership rather than a replacement of leasehold, and it is likely that, as it is taken up in practice and particular problems come to light, it will undergo a gradual evolution. In fact, the flexibility to allow this is built into the CLRA which, rather than prescribing a fixed set of rules for every eventuality, provides that many of the details are to be dealt with by regulations which can be amended much more easily than the primary legislation.

25.05 Although, in many ways, the introduction of commonhold is a radical departure for English landlord and tenant law, the new legislation has sought to introduce these changes without having to make major changes to the established principles of land law. This has been achieved by basing the commonhold system on already existing systems of registration.

A commonhold association, for example, is created as a private company in the usual way and, like any other company, will be registered at Companies House. The commonhold itself is created by registering the land as commonhold land with the Chief Land Registrar. A further benefit of the new system is uniformity of documentation. The form and content of the commonhold community statement and the articles of association are prescribed and it is hoped that such standardization will simplify and reduce the cost of conveyancing in the future.

B WHAT IS COMMONHOLD?

CLRA, Pt I, s 1(1) defines commonhold in terms of the key elements required for its creation. Land is commonhold land if: **25.06**

(a) the freehold estate in the land is registered as a freehold estate in commonhold land;
(b) the land is specified in the articles of association of a commonhold association as the land in relation to which the association is to exercise functions; and
(c) a commonhold community statement makes provision for rights and duties of the commonhold association and unit-holders (whether or not the statement has come into force).

Land which may not be commonhold land

Leasehold land

Only the registered freehold owner can apply to register land as a freehold estate in commonhold land (s 2(1)(a), see 25.41). The holder of a leasehold estate cannot apply. Therefore, if the leaseholders in a block of flats wish to convert to commonhold, they will either have to acquire the freehold first or persuade the freeholder to apply for them. **25.07**

Land without the proper consents

It is not possible to register land as a freehold estate in commonhold land unless the required consents are obtained in accordance with s 3 (see 25.43). **25.08**

Agricultural land

Farm business tenancies, agricultural holdings, and agricultural land within the meaning of the Agriculture Act 1947 cannot become commonhold land (Sch 2, para 2). **25.09**

Contingent title

Commonhold land cannot be created out of land where the ownership of the land may change on the occurrence or non-occurrence of a future event (Sch 2, para 3). **25.10**

Flying freeholds

One of the problems that has always dogged proposals to permit the freehold of individual units within a building is the flying freehold. When a person occupies a unit on a higher floor of a building, that unit is dependent for its structural integrity upon the portions of the building below it. If these portions are owned by someone else the person occupying the upper floor may find himself or herself in the difficult situation of being unable to enforce covenants against the owner of the lower floors. For this reason Sch 2, para 1 prohibits applications to register land which is above ground level as commonhold land unless all the land between the ground and the raised land is the subject of the same application. This will exclude a significant number of developments from becoming commonhold, in **25.11** particular blocks where residential flats have been built on the upper floors above commercial shop units. Such developments will only be able to be commonhold where the commercial units are also part of the same application.

Commonhold unit

25.12 For land to be registered as commonhold land there must be at least two commonhold units (s 11(2)(a)). These units do not necessarily need to contain all or any part of a building (s 11(4)). The commonhold system is designed to be applicable to a wide variety of land, from blocks of flats or offices and commercial developments with freestanding industrial units, to parking spaces or gardens. A commonhold unit may even consist of two or more areas of land, whether or not contiguous (s 11(3)(d)). What is important, however, is that there is some degree of interdependence in the form of shared common parts or facilities.

25.13 Each commonhold unit within the commonhold must be specified in the commonhold community statement and be defined by a plan which complies with the prescribed requirements (s 11(1) and (3)).

Unit-holder

25.14 A unit-holder is defined by s 12 as the person who is entitled to be registered as the proprietor of the freehold estate in the unit whether or not he or she is actually registered. This definition is designed to deal with the inevitable delay that will occur between the sale of a unit and the registration of the new owner at the Land Registry. Until registration takes place it will be the former unit-holder's name that appears on the register; nevertheless, for the purposes of the Act it is the new owner that is the unit-holder.

C CREATING A COMMONHOLD

25.15 **Example 1** Michael and Alex are the freehold owners of a large house which has been divided into four flats. They live in flat 1. Several years ago they sold the other three flats to Anne, James, and Tony, each of whom purchased a 99-year lease. Ann and James both live in their flats but Tony has sub-let his to Carl on a monthly periodic tenancy. Under the terms of the leases Michael and Alex (as joint lessors) are responsible for repairing the structure and exterior of the property and maintaining the common parts (the stairway and garden); the lessees are each obliged to pay ground rent and service charges. Michael and Alex have found that they do not want the responsibility involved in being landlords. They would rather share the obligations of running the building equally with the others. In turn, Anne, James, and Tony would like more say in the running of the building.

25.16 **Example 2** Amy is a property developer. Recently she has purchased the freehold of a large, run-down property, with vacant possession, which she is converting into a block of luxury flats. Once the development is complete she wishes to sell all of the flats individually. She has no wish to retain any long-term interest in the property.

25.17 In both of these examples the parties have been advised that a possible solution would be for them to create a commonhold under the provisions of the CLRA. To do this, the first steps they must take are to create a commonhold association and to formulate a commonhold community statement.

Commonhold association

Constitution of commonhold association

A commonhold association (CA) is a private company limited by guarantee: **25.18**

(a) the articles of which state that an object of the company is to exercise the functions of the CA in relation to specified commonhold land; and

(b) the statement of guarantee of which specifies £1 as the amount of the contribution required from each member in the event of the company being wound up.

Creation

A CA is created in the same way as any other company by filing the required documents **25.19** with Companies House in accordance with the provisions of the Companies Act 2006. Details are available from <http://www.companies-house.gov.uk>.

What are the articles of association?

The articles of association are the documents which control the day-to-day internal run- **25.20** ning of the CA. They set out the rules with regard to membership, the holding of meetings, voting, and the appointment, retirement, and powers of directors. They also contain basic information such as the name of the company, its registered office, its objects, and the fact that the liability of members is limited.

Form and content

One of the intentions of the CLRA is to achieve substantial uniformity in the documenta- **25.21** tion relating to a commonhold. The articles of association are therefore required to be in the prescribed form set out in Sch 2 to the Commonhold Regulations 2004, SI 2004/1829 ('the Regulations'), as amended by the Commonhold (Amendment) Regulations 2009, SI 2009/2363. A provision of the articles which is inconsistent with the Regulations shall have no effect (CLRA, Sch 3, para 2). Any alteration of the articles shall have no effect unless it is registered in accordance with the provisions of Sch 3, para 3.

Membership of commonhold association

One of the key aims of the CLRA is to keep the control and management of a common- **25.22** hold in the hands of the owners of the units. Third parties, therefore, are not permitted to become members of the CA. Membership of the CA is restricted to the unit-holders of commonhold units in relation to which the association exercises functions. A person becomes entitled to be entered on the register of members either when the unit becomes commonhold land, when it is registered with unit-holders under s 9 (see 25.52), or on the transfer of the unit (Sch 3, para 7).

During the transitional period

As we shall see, the Act provides for land to be registered as commonhold land without **25.23** unit-holders (see 25.49). In this situation the period between registration and the sale of the first unit is known as the 'transitional period'. During this period the only member of the CA will be the person (or persons) who has applied under s 7 for the land to be reg- istered as a freehold estate in commonhold land. He or she will remain the sole member (or members) throughout the transitional period until the first unit is sold and the new member (or members) is entitled to be entered in the register of members of the CA (Sch 3, paras 5 and 6).

25.24 In our Example 2 (25.16), Amy will be the sole member of her CA until she has sold one or more of the flats. As each flat is sold the purchaser will be entitled to be registered as a member of the CA.

Joint unit-holders

25.25 If two or more persons become joint unit-holders they must nominate one of themselves to be entered in the register of members. If no nomination is made it is the first person to appear on the proprietorship register whose name will be entered in the register. If one of the other joint unit-holders is dissatisfied with this he or she may apply to the court for his or her name to be substituted for the one that appears in the register (Sch 3, para 8).

25.26 In our Example 1 (25.15), Michael and Alex, as joint owners of flat 1, must decide which one of them will be named on the register.

Where the commonhold association owns units

25.27 A CA may not be a member of itself (Sch 3, para 9). This means that if the CA owns one or more of the units in the commonhold development, it cannot use the votes that attach to that unit.

Transfer

25.28 When a person sells or transfers his or her unit and ceases to be a unit-holder he or she ceases to be a member of the CA. However, this will not extinguish any right or liability that was incurred before the transfer of the unit (Sch 3, para 12).

Resigning from a commonhold association

25.29 A member of a CA may not resign except where the commonhold has been registered without unit-holders and is still in the transitional period (Sch 3, para 13).

Commonhold community statement

What is the commonhold community statement?

25.30 The commonhold community statement (CCS) is defined generally by s 31(1) as a document which makes provision in relation to specified land for:

(a) the rights and duties of the CA, and
(b) the rights and duties of the unit-holders.

By virtue of s 31(3) it may:

(a) impose a duty on the CA;
(b) impose a duty on a unit-holder;
(c) make provision about the taking of decisions in connection with the management of the commonhold or any other matter concerning it.

25.31 In commonhold land, therefore, the CCS is the most essential of documents. Like the lease in leasehold land it allocates the rights and obligations between the parties involved with the land. However, there are important differences. First, unlike leasehold land, there is no landlord over and above the unit-holders. Instead, the CCS is concerned to allocate rights and responsibilities between the unit-holders and the CA, of which the unit-holders are the individual members. Secondly, unlike a lease, the CCS must be in the prescribed form (s 31(2)). There will be one single CCS for all of the individual unit-holders in a commonhold development. It is hoped that this standardization of documentation will make the acquisition of a commonhold unit a relatively simple and inexpensive process. This is in contrast to the situation in leasehold land where the vast range of different possible leases containing different rights and obligations (even in the same block of flats) can often make the acquisition of a lease complex and costly.

Form and contents

The prescribed form of the CCS is set out in Sch 3 to the Regulations. The CCS must con- **25.32** tain all the prescribed provisions. If it fails to do so, it will be treated as containing those provisions (reg 15(2)).

The issues covered by the CCS include the following. **25.33**

(a) A definition, including plans in the prescribed form, of the location and extent of the commonhold land and of the commonhold units.

(b) A definition of any limited use areas (see 25.74) and permitted uses of commonhold units.

(c) Details of the percentage allocated to each commonhold unit in respect of the commonhold assessment and the reserve fund levy, and the procedure for calculating and demanding the commonhold assessment and the reserve fund levy (see 25.83 and 25.85).

(d) Details of the number of votes allocated to each member of the CA.

(e) Details of the procedure to be followed in the event of non-payment of the commonhold assessment or the reserve fund levy.

(f) Details of the responsibilities with regard to insurance of the common parts and of the commonhold units.

(g) Details of the responsibilities with regard to repair and maintenance of the common parts and of the commonhold units.

(h) Details of the procedure for transferring a commonhold unit.

(i) Details of the restrictions on letting a commonhold unit and the procedure for letting.

(j) Details of the CA's right to divert rent from a tenant or sub-tenant in the event of non-payment of the commonhold assessment or reserve levy by the unit-holder.

(k) Details of the responsibilities and procedure with regard to amending the CCS.

(l) Details of the responsibilities and procedure with regard to notices.

(m) Details of the responsibilities and procedure for dispute resolution and enforcement of rights.

(n) Details of any development rights (see 25.37 to 25.38).

(o) Details of any further 'local rules', ie supplementary provisions specific to the particular commonhold which do not appear in the model CCS.

The powers contained in the CCS will be subject both to the provisions of the Act and any **25.34** provision of the articles of association of the CA (s 31(4)). Furthermore, a duty conferred by a CCS on a CA or a unit-holder shall not require any other formality (s 31(7)). This means that rights and duties (eg an easement or a right of way) can be created without the further requirement of executing a deed.

Amending a commonhold community statement

Standardization of documentation is central to the commonhold system. It is therefore not **25.35** possible to amend any of the prescribed provisions of the CCS. Provisions and details particular to a specific commonhold and not prescribed by the Regulations (generally defined as 'local rules') may be amended but only in accordance with the procedures set out in Part 4.8 of the CCS.

25.36 An amendment to a CCS will have no effect until it is registered (s 33(3)). In applying to amend a CCS the application must be accompanied by a certificate given by the directors of the CA that the amended CCS satisfies the requirements (s 33(5)) and, where the amendment redefines the size of a unit or of the common parts, it must be accompanied by the appropriate consents (s 33(6) and (7)).

Development rights

25.37 Where a developer has applied to register land as commonhold and he or she is commercially involved in creating the commonhold development the CCS may confer rights on the developer to permit him or her to undertake development business, or to facilitate his undertaking of development business (s 58(2)). What counts as development business is set out in Sch 4 and basically relates to the completion and execution of works, the selling and advertising of units, and the adding or removing of land from the commonhold. The CCS may include a provision requiring the CA or a unit-holder to cooperate with the developer for a specified purpose connected with development business (s 58(3)(a)) and reg 10(10) of the Regulations). The CCS may also contain provisions making the developer's rights subject to terms or conditions (s 58(3)(b)) and set out the consequences of a breach of such terms or conditions (s 58(3)(c)). It may also disapply s 41(2) and (3) (see 25.90) thereby permitting the developer to add land to the commonhold without a resolution of the CA. Any development rights conferred on the developer in the CCS must be in accordance with reg 18 which provides that the developer must not interfere unreasonably with the unit-holder's enjoyment of the freehold estate in his or her unit or rights under the CCS.

25.38 If, during the transitional period (see 25.51), the developer transfers his estate in the commonhold land to another person, that person shall be treated as the developer in relation to the estate transferred (s 59(1) and (2)). Thus, a purchaser of all or part of the land will succeed to the development rights. If there is no transitional period, or the transitional period has already ended, then a new owner will only acquire the development rights if they are expressly included in the transfer (s 51(3)). Except during the transitional period no person can be treated as the developer and therefore have development rights unless he or she has at one time been the registered proprietor of one or more of the units and is still the registered proprietor of at least one (s 59(4)).

D REGISTRATION OF THE COMMONHOLD

25.39 Assuming in our examples (see 25.15 and 25.16) the parties have successfully set up their CAs and formulated their CCSs they may now apply to register their properties as commonhold land.

25.40 Registration is at the heart of the commonhold system. What makes land commonhold land is the fact that it is registered as commonhold land. Land cannot become registered as commonhold land unless an application is made to the Chief Land Registrar. Commonhold is therefore a completely voluntary system of land ownership. How prevalent it will become in future depends entirely upon how popular it will be among property developers and existing home owners.

Who can apply to register?

25.41 Commonhold land can only be created out of land that is already registered as freehold land. The only person who can apply to register a freehold estate in land as a freehold estate in commonhold land is the registered freehold owner of that land (s 2(1)(a)). The registered freehold owner is the only person with the authority to change the land to commonhold. A person who is not actually registered as the freehold owner of the land may apply but only if he or she has applied to be registered and the Registrar is satisfied that he or she is entitled to be registered (s 2(3)(b)). Furthermore, the land can only be registered as commonhold land provided no part of it is already commonhold land (s 2(1)(b)). If some of the land is already commonhold land, it will not be a question of creating a new commonhold but rather of adding land to an existing commonhold which will be governed by the rules set out in s 41 (see 25.90).

Procedure for application

For an application to be made, a CA must already be in existence. The application must be made on the prescribed form (Form CM1, set out in Sch 1 to the Commonhold (Land Registration) Rules 2004, SI 2004/1830, as amended by the Commonhold (Land Registration) (Amendment) Rules 2009, SI 2009/2024) and must be accompanied by the following documents (CLRA, Sch 1): **25.42**

(a) the CA's certificate of incorporation under the Companies Act 2006, s 15 (and any altered certificate);
(b) the articles of association of the CA;
(c) the CCS;
(d) a certificate given by the directors of the CA stating that:
   (i) (b) and (c) satisfy the regulations;
   (ii) the application satisfies Sch 2;
   (iii) the CA has not traded, and has not incurred any liability which has not been discharged;
(e) if consent is required (see below), the consent itself (Form CON 1), an order dispensing with the requirement for consent, or evidence of deemed consent;
(f) if the commonhold is being registered with unit-holders, a statement on Form COV that s 9 should apply (see 25.52).

Consent

Where a property developer has built, or is building, a brand new development of flats or other units it is likely that the developer will hold the freehold estate in the land unencumbered by any other interests. In fact, as we shall see, the Act specifically provides for this situation by permitting the developer to set up a commonhold scheme by registration before purchasers have been found for the individual units. However, this will not always be the case. The Act envisages not only that new developments may be registered as commonhold but also that existing properties may convert to commonhold. In order to convert to commonhold the registered freeholder of the land will have to apply to the Registrar for the land to be registered as commonhold. **25.43**

The registered freeholder of the land may only apply for registration under s 2 if he or she has the consent of anyone who is: **25.44**

(a) the registered proprietor of the freehold estate or the estate owner of any unregistered freehold estate in the whole or part of the land (s 3(1)(a) and reg 3(1)(a) of the Regulations);
(b) the registered proprietor of a leasehold estate or the estate owner of any unregistered leasehold estate in the whole or part of the land granted for a term of more than 21 years (s 3(1)(b) and reg 3(1)(b));

(c) the registered proprietor of a charge over the whole or part of the land (s 3(1)(c));

(d) the owner of any mortgage, charge, or lien over the whole or part of any unregistered land included in the application (reg 3(1)(c));

(e) the holder of a lease granted for a term of not more than 21 years which will be extinguished by virtue of s 7(3)(d) or 9(3)(f) (see 25.50 and 25.52), unless that person is entitled to the grant of a fixed term tenancy of the same premises:

    (i)   on the same terms as the extinguished lease (except to the extent necessary to comply with the Act and Regulations);

    (ii)   at the same rent (including the same provisions for rent review);

    (iii) for a term equivalent to the unexpired term of the lease which will be extinguished;

    (iv)   to take effect immediately after the original lease is extinguished; and

    (v)   which will be protected by notice in the land register (in registered land) or by an entry in the land charges register (in unregistered land) in the name of the estate owner of the freehold title before the application is made (reg 3(2)).

Details of consent

25.45 Consent must be given on Form CON 1 (or, for an application under s 8(4) during the transitional period (see 25.51), Form CON 2). It may be given subject to conditions (reg 4(3)). It will lapse after 12 months if an application is not made within this period unless a condition imposing a shorter period is imposed (reg 4(4)). Consent will be deemed to have been given by a successor in title to a person who has given consent (reg 4(5)(b)). Consent for a previous application which has been withdrawn may be used for a subsequent application provided that application is made within 12 months of the consent being given (reg 4(6)). Consent may be withdrawn at any time up to the date the application is submitted (reg 4(7)). The person making the application is deemed to have given his or her consent; he or she does not need to give it expressly (reg 4(5)(a)).

Dispensing with consent

25.46 The court may dispense with the requirement for consent if a person whose consent is required:

(a) cannot be identified after all reasonable efforts have been made to ascertain his or her identity;

(b) has been identified but cannot be traced after all reasonable efforts have been made to trace him or her; or

(c) has been sent the request for consent and all reasonable efforts have been made to obtain a response but he or she has not responded.

25.47 The effect of the rules outlined is that the only way in which existing land can convert to commonhold is with the agreement of the freeholder and if consent is obtained from all the other parties that hold sufficient interests in the land. This requirement for unanimous consent will undoubtedly operate to restrict the number of blocks that will convert to commonhold. All it will take to prevent conversion will be for one leaseholder to withhold consent to the scheme.

25.48 Consider our example at 25.15. First, the application can only go ahead if Michael and Alex (the freeholders) wish it to go ahead. Secondly, Anne, James, and Tony (the leaseholders) must all give their consent. Thirdly, consent will also have to be obtained from anyone with a charge over a part of the property, so if Michael and Alex or any of the leaseholders have a mortgage, consent will also be needed from their bank or building society.

Finally, consent will also be required from Carl as a sub-tenant unless Tony grants him an equivalent tenancy to take effect on the conversion to commonhold.

Registration without unit-holders

As we have mentioned, the Act specifically provides for developers to register land as commonhold before they have found purchasers for the individual commonhold units. This is a practical measure designed to deal with the situation where a developer is building a new development from scratch or where existing buildings are being developed and the developer has acquired the freehold of the building unencumbered by any other interests. The application under s 2 in this case must be an application which is not accompanied by a statement under s 9(1)(b) (s 7(1)) (see 25.52). **25.49**

On registration, the applicant (the developer) will be registered as the proprietor of the freehold estate in the commonhold land (s 7(2)(a)). However, the rights and duties contained in the CCS will not come into force immediately. Only when one of the units is sold and a person other than the applicant becomes entitled to be registered as the proprietor of the freehold estate of one or more of the commonhold units will the CCS take effect according to s 7(3) as follows: **25.50**

(a) the CA shall be entitled to be registered as the proprietor of the common parts;
(b) the registrar shall register the CA without need for an application to be made;
(c) the rights and duties conferred and imposed by the CCS shall come into force; and
(d) any lease of the whole or part of the commonhold land shall be extinguished (a lease, for the purposes of this section, meaning a lease granted for any term and granted before the CA becomes entitled to be registered as proprietor of the common parts).

Transitional period

The period between the registration of the land as a freehold estate in commonhold land and the purchase of the first unit is known as the transitional period. The transitional period is regulated by s 8 of the Act. Section 8 provides a power for regulations to be made to modify the provisions of the Act during the transitional period (s 8(2) and (3)) and it permits the applicant to apply for the registration of commonhold to be undone (s 8(4)) provided he or she has the required consents from anyone else with an interest in the land (s 8(5)). During the transitional period references in the Act to a CA exercising functions in relation to commonhold land will apply to the land notwithstanding that the land is in a transitional period and the CA has not yet been registered (s 8(6)). **25.51**

Registration with unit-holders

Where a development is converting to commonhold and there are already people with interests in the property (all of whom, as we saw at 25.43, must have given their consent for the application to be made) the application should be accompanied by a statement under s 9(1)(b) requesting that s 9 should apply. The statement must be on Form COV, include a list of the commonhold units, and give details of the initial unit-holders (or joint unit-holders) (s 9(2)). Where there is such a statement there will be no transitional period and the commonhold will be set up immediately as follows. On registration: **25.52**

(a) the CA will be entitled to be registered as the proprietor of the freehold estate of the common parts (s 9(3)(a));

(b) the persons specified in the statement as the initial unit-holders (or joint unit-holders) will be entitled to be registered as the proprietors of the freehold estates in those units without need for an application to be made (s 9(3)(b) and (c));

(c) the rights and duties conferred and imposed by the CCS will come into force (s 9(3)(e)); and

(d) any lease of the whole or part of the commonhold will be extinguished (s 9(3)(f)).

Registration in error

25.53 Where a freehold estate in land is registered as a freehold estate in commonhold land and:

(a) the application was not made in accordance with s 2;

(b) the certificate given by the directors of the CA under Sch 1, para 7 was inaccurate; or

(c) the registration contravened another provision of Pt 1 of the Act,

the court may grant a declaration that the freehold estate should not have been registered as commonhold land (s 6(1) and (3)). Such a declaration will only be granted on the application of a person who claims to be adversely affected by the registration (s 6(4)). The court may then make any order which appears to it to be appropriate (s 6(5)). In particular, it may order that the land should cease to be commonhold land, or that the land should continue to be commonhold land and that specified steps should be taken to put right the defects (s 6(6)).

Multiple site commonholds

25.54 A commonhold may include two or more parcels of land, whether or not contiguous (s 57(1)). However, a single CCS must make provision for all the land (s 57(2)). Where a joint application is made by two (or more) persons, each of whom owns the freehold of part of the land, a commonhold unit must be wholly within the land belonging to one freeholder and may not straddle the boundary between the two (or more) sites (reg 7 of the Regulations).

E SELLING OR TRANSFERRING A COMMONHOLD

25.55 For most people, purchasing a commonhold unit, whether as their home or for commercial purposes, will be the most expensive purchase of their life. That unit will be in a development containing other units and common parts and so the purchaser of a unit will not be free to do what he or she wishes with the unit; as in a lease, the CCS will allocate the rights and duties of the various unit-holders and of the CA and may restrict the uses to which a unit can be put. Nevertheless, in purchasing a commonhold unit a person will probably have borrowed large sums under a mortgage or used a substantial portion of his or her capital. That commonhold unit will be a valuable asset and, as such, it is important that he or she is free to dispose of it as he or she wishes. Section 15(2) of the Act therefore makes it clear that a CCS may not prevent or restrict the transfer of a commonhold unit. A transfer is defined by s 15(1) as a transfer of a unit-holder's freehold estate in a unit to another person:

(a) whether or not for consideration (eg a gift);

(b) whether or not subject to any reservation or other terms; and

(c) whether or not by operation of law (eg on death or bankruptcy).

Once the transfer of a commonhold unit has taken place, the new unit-holder must notify **25.56** the CA of the transfer within 14 days using Form 10 (transfer of commonhold unit), Form 11 (transfer of part of a commonhold unit), or Form 12 (vesting of a commonhold unit by operation of law).

The effect of transfer

When a commonhold unit is transferred to a new unit-holder the new unit-holder steps **25.57** into the shoes of the former unit-holder. Any right or duty imposed by the CCS (or by any charge or interest created by the former unit-holder under s 20, see 25.67) shall affect the new unit-holder in the same way as it affected the former unit-holder (s 16(1)). Thus, in contrast to the rule in ordinary freehold land (see 22.04), the burden of positive covenants will pass to the new owner. On the transfer the former unit-holder is released from responsibility and cannot incur a liability or acquire a right under the CCS (or by anything done under s 20) (s 16(2)). These rules cannot be contracted out of by any agreement, though the former unit-holder will remain bound by rights and obligations arising before the date of transfer (s 16(3)). For the purposes of s 16 it does not matter whether the new unit-holder has yet been registered as the registered proprietor; what is important is the date of the actual transfer (s 16(4)).

Debts incurred before transfer

Before buying a commonhold unit any prospective purchaser will want the current unit- **25.58** holder to provide him or her with a commonhold unit information certificate. A unit-holder can request such a certificate from the CA and the CA must provide it within 14 days (CCS, Part 4.7.1). Form 9 must be used for the certificate and it should state the debts currently owed to the CA and that the CA may require a new unit-holder to pay these debts. If the transfer goes ahead, the new unit-holder should pay these debts within 14 days of giving notice of the transfer or he or she may be charged interest (CCS, Part 4.7.5 and 4.7.6). If an information certificate has been provided the amount charged may not exceed the amount stated in the certificate (CCS, Part 4.7.4).

F LETTING A COMMONHOLD

While a unit-holder is free to transfer ownership of his or her unit as he or she wishes the **25.59** right to let that unit is restricted by the Act in the case of residential commonholds. This may appear at first to be something of an infringement on the rights of an owner but such a restriction is, in fact, necessary to the successful functioning of the commonhold system. If the freehold estate in a commonhold unit could be treated as an ordinary freehold there would be nothing to prevent its owner from carving out very long terms from his or her freehold estate, in which case, all the problems of leasehold ownership would resurface with the additional complexity of the fact that the leases were taking effect within the commonhold scheme.

Letting a residential commonhold unit

A commonhold unit is residential if the CCS requires it to be used only: **25.60**

(a) for residential purposes; or
(b) for residential and other incidental purposes (s 17(5)).

25.61 Section 17(1) and reg 11 of the Regulations provide that a term of years absolute in a residential commonhold unit or part of a residential commonhold unit must not:

(a) be granted at a premium (reg 11(1)(a));

(b) be granted for a term longer than seven years (except where granted as a compensatory tenancy for a tenancy extinguished by virtue of s 7(3)(d) or 9(3)(f) (see 25.44); such tenancies may be granted for a period of up to 21 years) (reg 11(1)(b) and (2));

(c) contain an option or agreement to renew or extend the lease which will make the total term exceed seven years (reg 11(1)(c), (d), and (e)); or

(d) contain a provision requiring the tenant to make payments to the CA in discharge of payments which are due to be paid by the unit-holder (reg 11(1)(f)).

25.62 An instrument or agreement that seeks to create a lease in contravention of these conditions shall be of no effect (s 17(3)). Where an instrument or agreement seeks to create a lease but fails because it contravenes s 17 a party to the instrument or agreement can apply to the court:

(a) providing for the instrument or agreement to have effect as if it provided for the creation of a term of years of a specified kind (ie one that is not prohibited by s 17);

(b) providing for the return or payment of money;

(c) making such other provision as the court thinks appropriate (s 17(4)).

25.63 The CCS also provides that:

(a) before entering a tenancy agreement the unit-holder must provide the prospective tenant with a copy of the CCS and give notice that the tenant must comply with the CCS Form 13 (CCS, Part 4.7.12);

(b) within 14 days of the tenancy being granted the unit-holder or tenant who grants the tenancy must give notice of the grant on Form 14 and a copy of any written tenancy agreement (or details of the terms of any oral agreement) to the CA (CCS, Part 4.7.15);

(c) before assigning a tenancy the tenant must give the prospective tenant a copy of the CCS and notice on Form 15 that the new tenant must comply with the CCS (CCS, Part 4.7.16);

(d) within 14 days of the assignment the new tenant must give the CA notice of the assignment on From 16 (CCS, Part 4.7.19).

25.64 Returning to Example 2 (25.15), Amy's wish was to sell all of the flats in the block. If she manages to do this her involvement in the building will cease as soon as the last flat is sold. For her this would be far preferable to the situation arising if she had had to sell each flat on a long lease. If this had been the case she would have remained in the picture as the freeholder of the property with all the obligations that entails. Another potential scenario is that Amy has managed to sell all of the flats except one. She has a potential buyer but he does not want to get involved in a CA and is only interested in purchasing a 99-year lease of the property. The buyer is offering a good price but CLRA, s 17 means that Amy will not be able to complete such a transaction. The best she can do is to offer a lease for a term of seven years for which she will not be able to charge a premium.

Letting a commercial commonhold unit

25.65 There is no statutory restriction upon the letting of a non-residential commonhold unit; however, any letting that takes place will have to take effect subject to the provisions of the CCS (s 18).

Diversion of rent

25.66 If a unit-holder fails to pay the commonhold assessment or reserve fund levy (see 25.83 and 25.85), the CA may require, by notice on Form 6 to both the tenant and the unit-holder, that the unit-holder's tenant pay all or part of the rent directly to the CA until the debt is paid off (CCS, Part 4.2.18). Such a diverted payment will discharge both the liability of the unit-holder to the CA and the liability of the tenant for rent owed to the unit-holder and will be deemed to be a payment of rent for the purposes of the tenancy agreement (CCS, Part 4.2.24). Outstanding debts to the CA may also be recovered direct from a sub-tenant on service of Form 7 (CCS, Part 4.2.28).

G SELLING OR CHARGING PART OF A COMMONHOLD UNIT

25.67 We have seen that the Act takes care to preserve unit-holders' rights to sell, or, with certain restrictions, lease their unit. By s 20(1), a unit-holder is also free to create a charge over his or her unit. However, a unit will be part of a commonhold development made up of other units and common parts. All these units are interdependent and changes made to one unit may affect the owners of other units in the development. If, for example, one unit-holder was to divide his or her unit into three and sell these parts off separately to three different people, this would be a significant change which may well have a detrimental effect on the other unit-holders.

Interests in a part-unit

25.68 For this reason s 21(1) of the Act prohibits the creation of an interest in part only of a commonhold unit. This prohibition, however, has a number of exceptions. A unit-holder is permitted:

(a) to create a lease of part only of a residential commonhold unit provided that the term of the lease satisfies the prescribed conditions (ie is not granted for a premium and is of a term of less than seven years, see 25.61) (s 21(2)(a));

(b) to create a lease of part only of a non-residential commonhold unit (s 21(2)(b));

(c) to transfer the freehold estate in part only of a commonhold unit provided the CA consents in writing to the transfer (s 21(2)(c)). The CA may only consent where it has passed a resolution to consent to the transfer and at least 75 per cent of those who vote on the resolution vote in favour (s 21(8)). The transferred part will become a new commonhold unit (s 21(9)(a)) or, if it is specified in the request for consent, it may become part of another commonhold unit (eg where one of the existing unit-holders in the block buys part of another unit-holder's unit) (s 21(9)(b)).

25.69 Any instrument or agreement that purports to create an interest in contravention of the provisions of s 21 shall be of no effect. If land becomes commonhold land or is added to a commonhold unit and prior to the transfer there was an interest over the land which would now be prohibited by s 21, that interest will be extinguished (s 21(4) and (5)).

Charging a part-unit

25.70 Section 22 prohibits the charging of part only of a commonhold unit (s 22(1)) and provides that any instrument or agreement that seeks to create such a charge shall be of no effect (s 22(2)). This provision is a logical consequence of the fact that it is not possible to create an interest in part only of a unit. If a unit-holder wishes to create a charge over a unit, that charge must be created over his or her interest in the whole unit. In any case, lenders would be reluctant to lend money against a charge over only part of a unit; it would provide little security in the event of default because it could not be sold separately. If land becomes commonhold land or is added to a commonhold unit and, prior to the transfer, there was a charge over that land which could not have been created after the transfer, then that charge will be extinguished (s 22(3) and (4)).

H CHANGING THE SIZE OF A COMMONHOLD UNIT

25.71   Sometimes it may necessary or desirable, for practical reasons, to change the size of a commonhold unit. This could be an increase in size, for example, where the CA purchases some additional land and decides to put it to use by dividing it and making it into individual gardens for each of the units in the development. (A commonhold unit, as we have seen (25.12), may be made up of two or more areas of land that are not contiguous.) Similarly it could be a decrease in size, for example where a development is made up of flats, each of which has its own private gardens and the CA decides to reduce the size of the gardens and use the land for some communal purpose such as shared parking spaces or a tennis court or some other facility that would form part of the common parts. It is also possible that part (or all) of a commonhold unit might be purchased by a neighbouring unit-holder (with the consent of the CA) and added to his or her commonhold unit. In any of these cases s 23(1) requires that any amendment to a CCS which redefines the extent of a commonhold unit may not be made unless the unit-holder consents in writing before the amendment is made.

25.72   Where the size of a commonhold unit is changed and there is a charge over that unit, the change of size may not take place unless the registered proprietor of the charge consents in writing to the change before it is made (s 24(2)). Where land is removed from the unit the charge, so far as it relates to the land which is removed, shall be extinguished (s 24(4)). Where land is added to the unit the charge shall be extended so as to relate to the land that is added (s 24(5)). The unit-holder must give notice in Form COE to the Registrar of the amendment to the CCS redefining the extent of the commonhold unit over which there is a registered charge and the Registrar must alter the register to reflect the changes (reg 10 of the Regulations).

I COMMON PARTS

25.73   Common parts are defined for the purposes of the Act as every part of the commonhold which is not for the time being a commonhold unit in accordance with the CCS (s 25(1)). The CCS, as we saw at 25.33, is the document which defines the extent of each commonhold unit. Depending upon the nature of the development the common parts may be small, eg the hallways and stairwells, or they may be extensive and include gardens, parks, garaging, swimming pools, gyms, or other shared facilities.

Restricting the use of common parts

25.74   Section 25(2) specifically provides that the CCS may also make provision restricting the classes of person who may use a specified part of the common parts or restricting the kind of use to which it may be put (s 25(2)). Such a specified area will be known as a 'limited use area'. Limited use areas may be particularly useful when dealing with such things as gardens to which only certain unit-holders have access or parking spaces which are allocated to particular unit-holders but whose maintenance is the responsibility of the CA. Limited use areas and any other restrictions on the use of common parts should be included in Annex 4 to the CCS as 'local rules'.

Maintaining common parts

The CA must repair and maintain the common parts (CCS, Part 4.5.1) and provide for **25.75** their insurance (CCS, Part 4.4.1). The CA may not make alterations to the common parts unless the proposed alteration is approved by ordinary resolution (a simple majority vote) (CCS, Part 4.6.1).

Selling or buying common parts

Section 27, like s 15 with regard to commonhold units, prohibits the CCS from prevent- **25.76** ing or restricting the CA from transferring (ie selling) its freehold estate in any part of the common parts or from creating an interest (eg a right of way) in any part of the common parts. For the purposes of s 27 an interest does not include a charge or an interest which arises by virtue of a charge (s 27(2)).

Charging common parts

Section 28(1) prohibits the creation of a charge over the common parts. If, when the CA is **25.77** registered under s 7 or 9 as the proprietor of the common parts, there is a charge over part or all of those common parts, that charge shall be extinguished (s 28(3)); similarly if land is added to the common parts under s 30 (see 25.78). However, s 29 provides that a CA may raise money against the security of the common parts by way of a mortgage provided that the mortgage is approved by a resolution of the CA (s 29(1)) and the resolution is passed unanimously before the mortgage is created (s 29(2)).

Adding to common parts

The CA may add land to the common parts of a commonhold. To do so the CCS must be **25.78** amended to include the added land. If there is a charge over added land such an amendment may not be made unless the registered proprietor of that charge consents in writing before the amendment is made (s 30(2)). The amended CCS (and any necessary consent or order dispensing with consent) must then be submitted to the Registrar for registration under s 33 (s 30(4)).

J MANAGEMENT OF A COMMONHOLD

Duty to manage

Section 35 of the Act imposes a duty to manage upon the directors of a CA. The directors **25.79** will exercise their powers so as to permit or facilitate so far as possible:

(a) the exercise by each unit-holder (or tenant of a unit) of his or her rights; and
(b) the enjoyment by each unit-holder (or tenant) of the freehold estate in his or her unit.

Management, however, is not only about permitting the enjoyment of rights; it is also **25.80** about enforcing duties and obligations. Section 37, therefore, also requires the directors of the CA to use their powers to prevent, remedy, or curtail any failure on the part of a unit-holder (or tenant) to comply with a requirement or duty imposed on him or her by the CCS or the Act.

Directors

25.81 Detailed rules on the powers and appointment of the directors of a CA are to be found in the articles of association. The minimum number of directors for a CA is two (article 39). A director of a CA does not have to be a member of the CA (article 40). Thus, it is possible for the members of a CA to appoint a professional director to run the CA on their behalf. Such an option may well prove popular in large developments where the duties and tasks to be performed by a director may be extensive. In small commonholds it is more probable that the directors will be drawn from the members of the CA. In very small commonholds with less than six members the draft commonhold regulations provide that there need only be one director.

Voting

25.82 Where resolutions of the CA must be passed by vote every member of the CA must be given an opportunity to vote in accordance with the articles of association (s 36(2)). A vote should be cast in person or in accordance with provisions which provide for voting by proxy (articles 29 to 37). A resolution is passed unanimously if every member who casts a vote votes in favour (s 36(4)).

Commonhold assessment

25.83 The directors of the CA must make an annual estimate of the income required to be raised from the unit-holders to meet the expenses of the CA (the commonhold assessement). Notice of the proposed commonhold assessment must be served on the unit-holders in Form 1, stating the amount of the estimate, the percentage allocated to the unit-holder, the details and dates of the required payments, and inviting the unit-holder to make written representations to the CA within one month of receiving the notice (CCS, Part 4.2.2). The directors must consider any representations made before serving further notice on Form 2 specifying the payments and the dates on which they are to be made (CCS, Part 4.2.4).

25.84 For urgent works the directors may request payment of an emergency commonhold assessment on Form 3 without seeking representations from the unit-holders; such a request for payment must set out the reasons why an emergency assessment is necessary (CCS, Part 4.2.5).

Reserve fund

25.85 In the first year in which the commonhold is registered the directors may commission a qualified person to make a 'reserve study' to assess whether it is appropriate to establish a reserve fund to deal with future expenses. If it is felt necessary, notice must be served on the unit-holders on Form 4 inviting their representations (CCS, Part 4.2.12). Alternatively, the unit-holders themselves may request the directors to establish a reserve fund by ordinary resolution (CCS, Part 4.2.10). The directors must review the decision to set up a reserve fund at appropriate intervals and should try to ensure that unnecessary reserves are not accumulated (CCS, Part 4.2.11). They must also commission a reserve study at least once in every 10 years (CCS, Part 4.2.7).

The assets of such a fund must not be used for the purpose of enforcement of any debt except **25.86** a judgment debt referable to a reserve fund activity (s 39(4)). A 'reserve fund activity' means an activity which, in accordance with the CCS, can or may be financed from the reserve fund (s 39(5)(a)). The reserve fund is therefore protected if the CA is sued, unless the person suing the CA is taking action over a matter which should be funded by the reserve fund.

Dispute resolution

Part 4.11 of the CCS contains detailed provisions with regard to dispute resolution. These **25.87** procedures must be used when a unit-holder or tenant is seeking to enforce against a CA a right or duty contained in the CCS or a provision made by virtue of the Act (CCS, Part 4.11.2). Where a unit-holder or tenant is seeking to enforce against the CA a duty to pay money or a right or duty in an emergency he or she may also refer the dispute directly to the ombudsman (if the CA is a member of an approved ombudsman scheme) or bring legal proceedings (CCS, Part 4.11.3). The procedures are standardized and initiated by serving a 'complaint notice' in the forms prescribed (Form 17 for a complaint against the CA, Form 19 for a default notice by a CA against a unit-holder or tenant, Form 21 for a complaint by a unit-holder or tenant against another unit-holder or tenant). The other side must then reply on the prescribed form within 21 days. If matters cannot be resolved by negotiation or mediation they may then be referred to the ombudsman (if the CA is a member of an approved scheme) or legal proceedings may be brought.

Rectification of documents

A unit-holder may apply to the court for a declaration if: **25.88**

(a) the memorandum and articles of association of the CA do not comply with the regulations set out under Sch 3, para 2(1);
(b) the CCS does not comply with the requirements of the Act (s 40(1)).

Such an application must be made within three months of the applicant becoming a unit- **25.89** holder, within three months of the alleged failure to comply, or with the permission of the court (s 40(4)). On granting a declaration the court may make any order which appears to it to be appropriate (s 40(2)). In particular, an order may require a director or other specified officer of a CA to amend a document or to take other specified steps. It may also make an award of compensation to be paid by the CA for a specified purpose or even make provision for land to cease to be commonhold land (s 40(3)).

Enlarging commonhold land

Land may be added to an already existing commonhold by making an application under **25.90** s 2 (see 25.41). Such an application cannot be made unless it is approved beforehand by a unanimous resolution of the CA (s 41(3)). When land is added to an existing commonhold the application should be made on Form CM4 and accompanied by an application to register the amended CCS on Form CM3, a directors' certificate, and any required consents.

K TERMINATING A COMMONHOLD

A commonhold may come to an end either voluntarily where the CA passes a winding-up **25.91** resolution or by an order of the court following a creditors' petition to declare the CA insolvent. However, it is unlikely that either of these will be common occurrences for many years to come. The situations in which a CA will wish voluntarily to terminate the commonhold are very limited, perhaps because the building has outlived its useful life or has been destroyed or damaged and the unit-holders choose not to repair or rebuild, or where a developer wishes to purchase the entire site. Similarly, in the case of an insolvent CA it is probable that more traditional civil remedies, such as charging the common parts, would resolve the situation before there would be a need to petition the court for the winding-up of the CA.

Voluntary winding-up

25.92   A winding-up resolution in respect of a CA shall be of no effect unless:

(a)   it is preceded by a declaration of solvency in accordance with the Insolvency Act 1986, s 89;

(b)   the CA passes a termination statement resolution (a resolution approving the terms of a termination statement) before it passes the winding-up resolution; and

(c)   each resolution is passed with at least 80 per cent of the members of the association voting in favour (s 43(1)).

One hundred per cent agreement

25.93   If the resolution is passed with 100 per cent of the members of the CA voting in favour then the liquidator shall make a termination application within six months of the passing of the resolution (s 44(1) and (2)). If the liquidator fails to make an application within six months, a unit-holder or other prescribed person may do so (s 44(3)). A termination application is an application to the Registrar that all the land in relation to which a particular CA exercises functions should cease to be commonhold land (s 46(1)). A termination application must be made on Form CM5 and should be accompanied by a termination statement (s 46(2)).

Eighty per cent agreement

25.94   If the resolution is passed with at least 80 per cent of the members voting in favour then the procedure is slightly different. The liquidator should apply to the court within the prescribed period for an order determining:

(a)   the terms and conditions on which a termination application may be made; and

(b)   the terms of the termination statement to accompany a termination application (s 45(2)).

25.95   The liquidator must then make a termination application within three months of the order (s 45(3)). Again, a unit-holder or other prescribed person may apply if the liquidator fails to make a termination application (s 45(4)).

Termination statement

25.96   When a commonhold is terminated following a termination application the CA becomes entitled to be registered as the proprietor of the freehold estate in each commonhold unit (s 49(3)). A termination statement must specify:

(a)   the CA's proposals for the transfer of the commonhold land following acquisition of the freehold estate; and

(b)   how the assets of the CA will be distributed.

25.97   A CCS may contain provisions requiring any termination statement to make arrangements about the rights of unit-holders in the event of the land ceasing to be commonhold land

and, if it does, the termination statement must comply with these provisions, though they may be disapplied by an order of the court (s 47(2), (3) and (4)).

Winding-up by court

Where the termination of the commonhold is not brought about voluntarily by a resolution **25.98** of the CA but is the result of a petition presented under the Insolvency Act 1986, s 124 for the winding-up of a CA by the court, there are additional provisions that apply. By virtue of s 51 an application can be made for a succession order. A succession order enables the commonhold development to continue to exist once the insolvent CA has been wound up by the court. A commonhold cannot exist without a CA, so a succession order functions by creating a new CA (a successor CA) to take the place of the insolvent CA. A succession order will only be made on application to the court. The court will not grant a succession order if it thinks that the circumstances of the insolvent CA make a succession order inappropriate (s 51(4)). Presumably, these provisions will be of importance where a CA becomes insolvent due to the default of a minority, or even one, of its members. They will allow those members who have paid their liabilities to the creditors to keep the commonhold in existence.

An application for a succession order can only be made by: **25.99**

(a) the insolvent CA;
(b) one or more members of the insolvent CA; or
(c) a provisional liquidator for the insolvent CA (appointed under the Insolvency Act 1986, s 125) (s 51(2)).

The application must be accompanied by: **25.100**

(a) prescribed evidence of the formation of a successor CA; and
(b) a certificate given by the directors of the successor CA that its memorandum and articles of association comply with the prescribed form and content.

Where a succession order is made, the successor CA takes the place of the insolvent CA **25.101** and is entitled to be registered as the proprietor of the freehold estate in the common parts (s 52(2) and (3)). The order will also make provisions as to the treatment of any charge over all or any part of the common parts (s 52(4)(a)). It may also require the Registrar to take action of a specified kind and/or make supplemental or incidental provisions (s 52(4)(b)–(d)). Section 53 provides that on the winding-up of the insolvent CA, responsibility is transferred to the successor CA. If the court makes a winding-up order and does not make a succession order the land will cease to be commonhold land. The liquidator must inform the Registrar as soon as possible that s 54 applies (s 54(2)(a)) and provide the Registrar with any information that is required under s 54(2)(b)–(g). The Registrar must then make all appropriate arrangements to ensure that the land ceases to be registered as a freehold estate in commonhold land (s 54(4)(a)) and take appropriate action to give effect to the liquidator's determinations (s 54(4)(b)). It is anticipated that the court would only refuse to make a succession order in a case where all of the unit-holders are responsible for the CA's insolvency.

Aside from an insolvency petition there are two other ways in which a court may order **25.102** that land should cease to be commonhold land: first, under s 6(6)(c) where the land was registered in error and should not have been registered as commonhold land (see 25.53); and, secondly, under s 40(3) where there is such a serious flaw in the memorandum and articles of association or CCS that the court thinks it appropriate to order that the land should cease to be commonhold land (see 25.88). In both of these cases the court shall have the powers which it would have if it were making a winding-up order in respect of the CA (s 55(2)). Similarly, a person appointed as liquidator will have the same powers and duties of a liquidator making a winding-up order by the court in respect of a CA (s 55(3)), though the court order may vary the liquidator's right and duties or require him or her to exercise his or her functions in a particular way (s 55(4)).

25.103   Where land ceases to be commonhold as a result of a winding-up order by the court, a voluntary winding-up resolution, or as a result of an order under s 6(6)(c) or 40(3), the reserve fund will cease to be protected against creditors by s 39(4) (see 25.86).

L COMPULSORY PURCHASE

25.104   The general rule is that when land is transferred to a compulsory purchaser that land will cease to be commonhold land (s 60(1)). However, if the Registrar is satisfied that the compulsory purchaser wishes the land to remain commonhold land then it will continue to be commonhold land (s 60(2)). With regard to compulsory purchase s 21(2)(c) (see 25.68) is disapplied; it is therefore possible for a compulsory purchaser to purchase part of a unit (s 60(3)). Section 60(4) and (5) enable regulations to make further provisions regarding the transfer, notice requirements, court powers, compensation, and other relevant matters.

KEY DOCUMENTS

Commonhold and Leasehold Reform Act 2002

Commonhold Regulations 2004, SI 2004/1829

Commonhold (Land Registration) Rules 2004, SI 2004/1830

Commonhold (Amendment) Regulations 2009, SI 2009/2363

Commonhold (Land Registration) (Amendment) Rules 2009, SI 2009/2024

Companies Act (Consequential Amendments, Transitional Provisions and Savings) Order 2009, SI 2009/1941

Printed copies of all legislation can be ordered from The Stationery Office at <http://www.tsoshop.co.uk>. All legislation from 1988 onwards and most pre-1988 primary legislation is available online at <http://www.legislation.gov.uk>.

26

BUSINESS TENANCIES

A INTRODUCTION

The first thing to be clear about is that just because a tenancy may be classified as a 'business tenancy' this does not mean that it is any different from any other tenancy. A tenancy is a tenancy, the use to which the premises are put does not change the nature of that tenancy; all the common law principles we have discussed in the first part of this book will apply to a business tenancy just as they apply to residential tenancies.

26.01

26.02   **Example**   On 31 January 2006, Jim acquired a 10-year fixed-term lease of Western House from City Property Ltd at a rent of £35,000 per year. Western House is a medium-sized three-storey building situated on the edge of the town centre. On obtaining the tenancy of Western House Jim installed a sauna, weight-training equipment, and a gym on the ground floor, and set up a fitness centre known as Jim's Gym. The second and third floors consist of residential flats which Jim has also sub-let. The fitness centre does very good trade, particularly at lunchtimes and in the early evening when it is popular with office workers from the neighbouring banks.

26.03   As we can see from this example, a tenant who uses premises for business purposes may have certain concerns that do not necessarily arise in the case of residential tenancies. First, there is the question of what is usually called 'goodwill'. When a person has spent several years building up a clientele for his or her business, the location of that business acquires considerable importance for that person. If that person has to move the business he or she will be losing more than just the building in which the business was located—a lot of custom may also be lost. This will be of particular importance in a case such as Jim's, where he relies largely on local customers for the success of his business. Secondly, in setting up a business the tenant may well have expended money on adapting the building for the purposes of the business. Both of these factors mean that when a tenancy comes to an end the tenant is unlikely to be willing to move his or her business elsewhere. As a result a landlord may be in a position to charge a far higher rent from the existing tenant on the renewal of the tenancy than he or she would be able to do if he or she was to let the premises to a new tenant on the open market.

26.04   Parliament intervened to prevent this potential injustice by enacting the Landlord and Tenant Act 1927. Part I of the 1927 Act entitled a business tenant or a professional tenant to compensation for improvements made by the tenant or by the tenant's predecessor in title. It also entitled a business tenant (but not a professional tenant) to compensation for the loss of goodwill, and in certain circumstances the right to be granted a new lease. The provisions of the 1927 Act with regard to compensation for improvements remain in force today and we shall consider them later in this chapter. The provisions with regard to compensation for loss of goodwill and the right to a new lease were generally criticized for not offering adequate protection (in particular the fact that to be eligible for compensation or renewal a tenant would have to have traded from the premises for a period of more than five years). These provisions were therefore repealed by the Landlord and Tenant Act 1954 and replaced with a new procedure. Since the introduction of the 1954 Act (which has now been amended by the Regulatory Reform (Business Tenancies) (England and Wales) Order 2003, SI 2003/3096) business tenants have a general right to have their tenancies renewed.

26.05   The basic principle of the 1954 Act has been not to interfere directly with the parties' freedom to contract, the presumption being that where two business persons are entering into a commercial arrangement they should be free to arrange it on any terms they can agree between them. During the contractual period the Act does not interfere with the parties' rights or obligations at all; the Act becomes significant only towards the end of the term where the parties may be seeking a renewal of the tenancy or compensation. Even then the objective of the Act is not to push the parties into litigation, but rather to provide a structure within which negotiations can take place.

26.06   A business tenant that comes within the protection of the 1954 Act acquires two important rights:

(a)   the right to apply for a renewal of the tenancy;
(b)   the right to compensation for disturbance if the application for renewal is unsuccessful.

Under the 1927 Act, a business tenant will also acquire the right to compensation for **26.07** improvements.

These rights are very different to the rights available to a tenant who falls within one of the **26.08** statutory codes applying to residential tenancies. In fact, the key difference between a residential tenancy and a business tenancy is not in the nature of the tenancy itself but in the differences between the codes they fall under. This question can be of particular importance when a tenant lives and works in the same premises. The codes are mutually exclusive. If the tenant falls under, say, the Rent Act 1977, he or she will acquire far greater security of tenure than under the 1954 Act (and will also have a right to rent control).

B WHO IS A BUSINESS TENANT?

To be eligible for protection as a business tenant under the Landlord and Tenant Act 1954, **26.09** the occupier in question must fall within the definition set out in s 23 of that Act. Section 23 provides:

> (1) Subject to the provisions of this Act, this Part of this Act applies to any tenancy where the property comprised in the tenancy is or includes premises which are occupied by the tenant and are so occupied for the purposes of a business carried on by him or for those and other purposes.

A person will therefore be a business tenant if he or she: **26.10**

(a) has a tenancy of the premises; and
(b) occupies at least part of the premises; and
(c) the premises or that part of the premises are occupied for the purposes of carrying on a business.

Each of these aspects needs to be looked at in detail. **26.11**

A tenancy

To be eligible for protection under the 1954 Act there must be a tenancy (see Chapter 1 **26.12** on the essential elements of a tenancy). The tenancy may be either periodic or for a fixed term. A sub-tenancy is just as eligible for protection as a tenancy; in many cases the tenant in occupation will not be renting directly from the freeholder but from an intermediate landlord. Even an unlawful sub-tenancy may fall within the Act (*D'Silva v Lister House Developments Ltd* [1971] Ch 17, [1970] 1 All ER 858). An equitable interest will also be eligible for protection, for example where the parties have entered into an agreement for a lease but the actual lease itself was never created (see Chapter 3), but this should be contrasted with the position where the potential tenant is in occupation whilst negotiations for a lease take place and both parties understand that there is to be no tenancy unless and until the negotiations are satisfactorily concluded (*Cameron Ltd v Rolls Royce Plc* [2007] EWHC 546 (Ch), see 2.20).

A tenancy at will (see 3.30), whether created by implication or by a written agreement, has **26.13** been held to fall outside the Act (see *Wheeler v Mercer* [1957] AC 416; *Hagee (London) Ltd v AB Erikson and Larson* [1976] QB 209; *Fitzkriston LLP v Panayi* [2008] L&TR 26).

An occupier holding under a licence will not come within the 1954 Act. In Chapter 2 we **26.14** considered how, when a landlord purports to grant a licence to an occupier, that occupier will in fact acquire a tenancy where the effect of the licence agreement is to confer a tenancy upon the occupier (namely by granting exclusive possession for a term at a rent). This principle, as set out by Lord Templeman in *Street v Mountford*, applies equally to business tenancies and residential tenancies. A landlord therefore will not be able to prevent a business tenant from acquiring protection under the 1954 Act merely by drafting a tenancy agreement as a licence agreement. However, it was pointed out in *Dresden Estates Ltd v Collinson* [1987] 1 EGLR 45 (*per* Glidewell LJ at 47A–B) that 'the attributes of residential premises and business premises are often quite different' and that 'the indicia, which may make it more apparent in the case of a residential occupier that he is indeed a tenant, may be less applicable or be less likely to have that effect in the case of some business tenancies'. In the *Dresden Estates* case the landlord retained the right to move the occupier to other premises. This was held to be inconsistent with a right to exclusive possession and therefore inconsistent with the existence of a tenancy.

Premises

26.15   The word 'premises' is used in a broad sense. 'Premises' includes a building or part of a building and can also include land, even when the land has no buildings upon it. For example, a tenancy of land used for training horses has been held to be a business tenancy within the 1954 Act *(Bracey v Read* [1963] Ch 88). Even a tenancy of a parking space in a basement garage may constitute a business tenancy (*Harley Queen v Forsyte Kerman* [1983] CLY 2077). An incorporeal hereditament such as an easement (eg a right of way) or a profit à prendre (eg fishing rights) will not come within the definition of 'premises'. However, where the tenant of premises has acquired other rights under his lease (eg a right of way, or the right to park a car on adjoining land), these additional rights may be renewed along with the tenancy under s 32(3) or 35 of the 1954 Act (*Pointon York Group v Poulton* [2006] EWCA Civ 1001, (2006) 38 EG 192).

Occupation

26.16   In most cases it will be fairly easy to determine whether the tenant is occupying the premises. For example, in the case of Jim's Gym (see 26.02), Jim has fitted out the premises with his own equipment and is present in the gym most days. Even if he hands over the management of the gym to his aerobics teacher, Mandy, and does not visit the premises himself, he will still be occupying the premises through his employee. However, in some cases the question of occupation may not be so clear-cut.

26.17   Examples

(a) Holloway Investments Ltd are a property management agency. They have rented a block of one-bedroom flats which they have furnished and sub-let individually to residential occupiers on short leases. They employ a caretaker who lives in one of the flats, and provide regular cleaning services of the flats.

(b) Homes Ltd rent a block of flats and have sub-let all the individual flats in the block. Homes Ltd do not provide services or a caretaker.

(c) Geoff's Clothiers Ltd decide to change the image of their shop. They close the shop down, but there are substantial delays before alteration work is undertaken. Neither Geoff nor any of his employees are present during this period and it is nearly a year before the shop reopens.

26.18   First, can Holloway Investments be said to occupy the block of flats? In the case of the flat provided for the caretaker the answer seems clear; this part of the building is occupied by Holloway Investments through their employee. With regard to the rest of the flats in the building the answer is not so obvious; each case will depend upon its own facts. In

Lee-Verhulst (Investments) Ltd v Harwood Trust [1973] 1 QB 204, [1972] 3 All ER 619, the landlord serviced each flat daily and imposed restrictions on the activities of the occupants. It was held to occupy the flats notwithstanding the fact that the sub-tenants of the individual flats in the block had exclusive occupation of their flats. However, the services offered by the landlord must be extensive (*Graysim Holdings v P&P Property Holdings* [1994] 1 WLR 992). The landlord must also be able to show that the services are actually provided to the residents (*Bassari v London Borough of Camden* [1999] L&TR 45). Thus, provided Holloway Investments Ltd exercise a sufficient degree of control over the other parts of the building, they may be regarded as occupying the whole block.

In contrast Homes Ltd, although they are engaged in the business of renting out flats, do not provide a caretaker or provide any services. Homes Ltd do not occupy any part of the premises. Their tenancy will not fall within the 1954 Act. **26.19**

The question that arises in the third example is whether a tenant will still fall within the Act if occupation is not continuous. Again this will depend upon the facts of the case. The question to be asked is whether the 'thread of continuity' has been broken. In *I & H Caplan v Caplan (No. 2)* [1963] 1 WLR 1247, [1963] 2 All ER 930, it was held that where a tenant stopped trading from a shop for a period of seven months it still continued to occupy the premises within the meaning of the Act. Occupation has also been held to be continuous for the purposes of the Act when that occupation was in fact seasonal (*Teasdale v Walker* [1958] 1 WLR 1076, [1958] 3 All ER 307, CA). In the case of Geoff's Clothiers, it is likely that occupation will be regarded as continuous despite the absence; throughout the period of non-occupation Geoff intended to reopen the shop and start trading again. The outcome might well be different if Geoff had instead decided to open up another shop on different premises. The fact that the tenant has communicated his or her intention to reoccupy the property to the landlord will be a relevant factor but the intention to occupy must be genuine. In *Pointon York Group v Poulton* [2006] EWCA Civ 1001, (2006) 38 EG 192, the tenant had sub-let the whole of the premises for a number of years. The sub-tenancy expired three days before the end of the tenant's term and shortly before this the tenant informed his landlord that he intended to reoccupy the premises at the end of the sub-tenancy. It was held that he occupied the premises for the purposes of the 1954 Act. Even though he had not actually moved back in during that three-day period, he had been in the process of refitting the premises and this, together with his stated intention to occupy, was sufficient. **26.20**

The Landlord and Tenant Act 1954, ss 41 and 42 cover two special cases: where the tenancy is held on trust, and where the tenancy is held by a company within a group of companies. **26.21**

Section 41 provides that: **26.22**

> (1) Where a tenancy is held on trust, occupation by all or any of the beneficiaries under the trust, and the carrying on of a business by all or any of the beneficiaries, shall be treated for the purposes of section 23 of this Act as equivalent to occupation or the carrying on of a business by the tenant...

Section 42(2) provides that: **26.23**

> (2) Where a tenancy is held by a member of a group, occupation by another member of the group, and the carrying on of a business by another member of the group, shall be treated for the purposes of section 23 of this Act as equivalent to occupation or the carrying on of a business by the member of the group holding the tenancy.

By s 42(1), two companies are to be taken to be members of the same group if, and only if, one is the subsidiary of the other or both are subsidiaries of a third company. **26.24**

Occupation for the purposes of a business

26.25   To fall within the 1954 Act the tenant must not only occupy at least part of the premises, he or she must also occupy the premises for 'the purposes of a business'. 'Business' is given a broad definition under the Act by s 23(2):

> (2) In this Part of this Act the expression 'business' includes a trade, profession or employment and includes any activity carried on by a body of persons, whether corporate or unincorporate.

26.26   Section 23(2) creates a difference between a tenant who is an individual and a tenant which is a body of persons.

Tenant an individual

26.27   For an individual to be a business tenant, he or she will have to carry out an activity that can be classed as a trade, profession, or employment. In *Lewis v Weldcrest Ltd* [1978] 1 WLR 1107, [1978] 3 All ER 1226, Mrs Lewis took in a number of lodgers but gained no real commercial advantage from doing so. The court held that on the facts this did not amount to a trade. This does not mean that taking in lodgers can never amount to a trade. A common-sense approach should be taken. It will always be a question of degree. A person running a seaside boarding house might well be carrying on a trade; a person taking in a few lodgers and making little or no profit would not (see Ormrod LJ at 1119). It should of course be noted that even where the renting out of rooms or property for commercial gain does amount to a business, the tenancy will not fall within the 1954 Act if the tenant is not in occupation of the premises (see above).

26.28   In the example given at 26.17, if Holloway Investments cannot be said to occupy the flats they let out, their occupancy of the caretaker's flat will not be for the purpose of a business (*Bassari v London Borough of Camden*, 26.18). In *Lewis v Welcrest Ltd*, the landlord sought to support his contention that Mrs Lewis was occupying the premises for business purposes with cases where tenants had been held to be in breach of covenants against business user when they had taken in paying guests. The court rejected this approach; the purpose of a covenant is very different from the purpose of the Landlord and Tenant Act 1954 (see Stevenson LJ at 1117). The fact that the activity carried on by the individual might be capable of amounting to a breach of covenant against business user did not mean that that activity would amount to a trade, profession, or employment within the meaning of the 1954 Act.

26.29   In *Abernethie v A M & J Kleiman Ltd* [1970] 1 QB 10 the tenant voluntarily conducted a Sunday school on the premises. Running a Sunday school was an 'activity', but the tenant was an individual. The court held that conducting a Sunday school was well outside the definition of a 'trade, profession or employment'.

Tenant a company

26.30   A new s 23(1A) has been inserted into the Act to clarify the position where premises are occupied by a company. Under s 23A occupation or the carrying on of a business:

(a)   by a company in which the tenant has a controlling interest; or

(b)   where the tenant is a company, by a person with a controlling interest in the company,

shall be treated as equivalent to occupation or the carrying on of a business by the tenant.

Tenant a body of persons

26.31   Where the tenant is a body of persons the statute seems to indicate that any activity will count as business purposes. Thus, where the trustees of a tennis club took a tenancy of tennis courts and a club house, the activity of a tennis club was held to be a business purpose within the 1954 Act (*Addiscombe Garden Estates Ltd v Crabbe* [1958] 1 QB 513, [1957] 3 All ER 536). Likewise, the administration of a hospital by a board of governors, a non-profit-making body, has also been held to be a business within the Act (*Hills (Patents) Ltd v University College Hospital Board of Governors* [1956] 1 QB 90, [1955] 3 All ER 356). However, the scope of the word 'activity' should not be regarded as infinite. In *Hillil Property & Investment Co Ltd v Naraine Pharmacy Ltd* (1980) 39 P&CR 67, Megaw LJ stated (at 74):

> Though [an] activity is something that is not strictly a trade, a profession or an employment, nevertheless to be an 'activity' for this purpose it must be something that is correlative to the conceptions involved in those words.

In this case the use of premises for dumping waste during the renovation of other premises was held not to be an activity. **26.32**

Mixed business and residential user

The Landlord and Tenant Act 1954, s 23 provides that a tenancy will fall within the Act if the premises are occupied for the purposes of a business carried on by the tenant 'or for those and other purposes'. Where those 'other purposes' are residential an interesting conflict between two statutes can arise. **26.33**

As far as the law is concerned, the statutory codes applying to business tenancies and the codes applying to residential tenancies are mutually exclusive. If a tenancy falls within the 1954 Act it will be excluded from being a Rent Act tenancy by s 24(3) of the Rent Act 1977, from being an assured tenancy by the Housing Act 1988, Sch 1, Pt I, para 4, and from being a secure tenancy by the Housing Act 1985, Sch 1, para 11. Where there is mixed business and residential user the crucial question will therefore be which statutory code should apply. **26.34**

The first point to make is that for the 1954 Act to apply, the business use of a premises must be a significant purpose of the tenant's occupation of the premises. This, of course, is not always an easy question to determine. At one end of the scale is the tenant who works nine to five in an office and occasionally brings home work to do in the evenings. At the other end is the tenant who lives in the flat above the shop where he or she runs a business. In between these two extremes is a wide variety of less clearly definable situations, for example the doctor who has his surgery away from his home but who also sees patients in his flat and the businessman who conducts an import business from home. Both these situations were considered in two appeals which were heard together: *Cheryl Investments Ltd v Saldanha, Royal Life Saving Society v Page* [1978] 1 WLR 1329. **26.35**

The doctor in *Royal Life Saving Society v Page* had his consulting rooms in Harley Street, but in entering into the tenancy of the maisonette where he lived he had asked for, and had been granted by the landlord, permission to carry on his profession there. Both addresses featured in the medical directory and both phone numbers were put on his stationery, but in fact he only very rarely saw patients at the maisonette. The court held that his professional use of the maisonette was only incidental to his residential use. The doctor therefore had a Rent Act protected tenancy of the maisonette. **26.36**

The businessman, on the other hand (*Cheryl Investments Ltd v Saldanha*), had installed a telephone, typewriter, and files in his flat in Knightsbridge. The importation business he ran appeared to have no other premises, its notepaper gave the telephone number at the flat and the address as a PO Box in Knightsbridge. The court held that in this case the business **26.37** use was a significant purpose for which he was occupying the flat and he was a business tenant.

26.38   The fact that a tenant's main objective in taking the lease was to provide himself with living accommodation will not necessarily mean that the tenancy is not a business tenancy. In *Broadway Investments Hackney Ltd v Grant* [2006] EWCA Civ 1790 a tenant took a lease of premises comprising a flat and shop. The lease contained an obligation on the tenant to keep the shop open for retail trade. The Court of Appeal held that the fact that the tenant's main motive in taking the lease was to have residential rights was insufficient to create a residential tenancy; the terms of the lease meant that the premises were occupied for the purpose of a business.

Change of user

26.39   A further point to be taken into account is the fact that the use of premises can change. If the doctor in the situation in 26.36 gave up his consulting rooms in Harley Street and started seeing his patients at home, he would cease to have a Rent Act tenancy and would now fall under the 1954 Act. A different result occurs if things happen the other way round. If the tenant of a shop with a flat above it ceases to trade from the shop but continues to live in the flat, he or she can no longer be said to be occupying the premises for business purposes. The protection of the 1954 Act will therefore cease. This tenant will not then acquire protection under a residential statutory code. Both the Rent Act and the Housing Act apply only to 'a dwelling-house let as a separate dwelling' (see 13.10 to 13.30). When the premises were let they were let for business purposes; if the business use ceases the premises will not come within the residential code unless the landlord agrees to the change of user (see *Pulleng v Curran* (1980) 44 P&CR 58, CA; *Wagle and another v Trustees of Henry Smith's Charity Kensington Estate* [1990] 1 QB 42). In order to assert that the landlord has agreed to the change of use the tenant must show that the landlord has given positive consent. Mere knowledge of the change of use and acceptance of rent would not be sufficient (*Tan v Sitkowski* [2007] EWCA Civ 30, [2007] 1 WLR 1628).

26.40   Interestingly, the situation is different if the property was originally let as a dwelling and the tenant subsequently uses it for business purposes. During the time the property is let as a dwelling the tenant will have security under one of the residential codes, for example the Rent Act 1977. When business use starts the tenancy will be protected under the 1954 Act; if the use then reverts to residential use the property will regain its Rent Act protected status (*Tan v Sitkowski*, 26.39).

Providing residential accommodation for employees

26.41   We saw earlier how a tenant can occupy a premises through his or her employees, where, for example, a manager occupies a shop run by the tenant. Here the tenant is clearly occupying the shop, through the manager, for the purposes of a business. Consider, however, the following situation:

26.42   **Example** Returning to our initial example of Jim and his fitness centre. When he started the fitness centre Jim lived in a flat in the neighbouring block. When the business became more successful he moved to a house in Surrey and Mandy, the aerobics instructor, moved into the flat. The fact that Mandy lives so near the gym means she is able to open the centre in the morning before Jim has arrived, and also to lock up again when it is open late and to be on hand if any emergencies arise out of hours.

Jim now claims that he has a business tenancy of the flat. His reasoning is that he is **26.43** occupying the flat through his employee, Mandy, and that he is occupying the flat for the purposes of his business. Whether the tenancy of the flat falls within the 1954 Act depends upon whether it is *necessary* for Mandy to occupy the flat in order to perform her duties properly, or whether it is merely *convenient* for her to live there (see *Chapman v Freeman* [1978] 1 WLR 1288). This, of course, will be a question of fact, but in the present example it seems likely that Mandy's occupation of the flat is merely convenient to both Mandy and Jim. A fitness centre does not require a person to be available constantly.

In *Chapman v Freeman*, the tenant of a cottage used the cottage to provide accommoda- **26.44** tion for employees who worked at his hotel. The cottage was only 50 yards away from the hotel. It was held that while it was convenient for the employees to reside in the cottage, it was not necessary that they do so for the better performance of their duties. In *Methodist Secondary Schools Trust Deed Trustees v O'Leary* [1993] 1 EGLR 1105, a school caretaker occupied a house adjacent to the school buildings on a service occupancy. The trustees of the school installed a phone and an alarm system in the house connected to the school so that the caretaker would be able to deal with emergencies occurring after normal school hours. In this case the judge was satisfied that it was necessary for the caretaker to occupy the house in order to perform his duties.

In *Groveside Properties Ltd v Westminster Medical School* (1983) 267 EG 593, CA, the **26.45** medical school rented a flat which was used to provide residential accommodation for students. The medical school retained a degree of control over the premises; it furnished the flat, chose the students who were to live there, kept a set of keys, and the secretary of the medical school visited the flat about once a month to see how the students were getting on. It was held that the medical school was occupying the flat for the purposes of its busi- ness (in the broad sense of an 'activity'). The student occupation of the flat was 'not merely to provide a residence but to foster a corporate or collegiate spirit in furtherance of their medical education'.

Business user in breach of covenant

If the tenant is carrying on a business in the premises in breach of a general covenant **26.46** against business user, or in breach of a covenant against use for the purposes of a trade, profession, or employment, that tenancy will not normally fall within the 1954 Act. Section 23(4) provides:

> (4) Where the tenant is carrying on a business, in all or any part of the property comprised in a tenancy, in breach of a prohibition (however expressed) of use for business purposes which subsists under the terms of the tenancy and extends to the whole of that property, this Part of this Act shall not apply to the tenancy unless the immediate landlord or his predecessor in title has consented to the breach or the immediate landlord has acquiesced therein.
>
> In this subsection the reference to a prohibition of use for business purposes does not include a prohibition of use for the purposes of a specified business, or of use for purposes of any but a specified business, but save as aforesaid includes a prohibition of use for the purposes of some one or more only of the classes of business specified in the definition of that expression in subsection (2) of this section.

There are, therefore, a number of situations in which the tenancy will still come within the **26.47** Act even where the tenant's use of the premises is in breach of covenant:

(a) If the covenant extends only to part of the premises.
(b) If the covenant prohibits use only for a specified business (eg not to use as a betting shop).

(c) If the covenant prohibits use for any business except a specified business (eg not to use except as a betting shop).

26.48 A tenancy will also come within the Act if the tenant is in breach of a covenant against business use but either:

(a) the immediate landlord or his predecessor in title has consented to the breach; or
(b) the immediate landlord has acquiesced in the breach.

26.49 'Acquiescence' and 'consent' are two distinct concepts. In both cases, however, the landlord must have knowledge of the breach. If, with knowledge of the breach, an immediate landlord takes no action and stands passively by, this can amount to acquiescence. Consent, on the other hand, requires the landlord to take some positive action which indicates consent (see *Bell v Alfred Franks & Bartlett Co. Ltd* [1980] 1 WLR 340).

C THE HOLDING

26.50 It is most important to note that where a person takes a tenancy of a building, the provisions of the 1954 Act will not necessarily apply to the whole of the premises let under that tenancy. Many of the provisions in the 1954 Act relate only to 'the holding'. The holding is defined by s 23(3):

> (3) In the following provisions of this Part of this Act the expression 'the holding', in relation to a tenancy to which this Part of this Act applies, means the property comprised in the tenancy, there being excluded any part thereof which is occupied neither by the tenant nor by a person employed by the tenant and so employed for the purposes of a business by reason of which the tenancy is one to which this Part of this Act applies.

26.51 'The holding' is of crucial importance, because where a tenant applies for a renewal of the tenancy he or she will be entitled only to a renewal of the tenancy of the holding. Consider again the situation of Jim. Jim's tenancy of Western House is coming towards its end and he therefore wants to know which parts of the premises will be included in the holding. Western House consists of three storeys: the upper floors contain residential flats, while the ground floor contains the gym. In addition the tenancy includes a small car park at the rear of the building which is used by Jim's customers and employees. Flat 1 on the first floor is occupied by Greg, the caretaker, who is employed full time by Jim. Greg looks after the cleaning, maintenance, and security of the gym, as well as acting as caretaker for the residential flats, performing odd jobs and regular maintenance work both in the individual flats and other common areas of the building.

26.52 Jim's holding will consist only of the parts of the building occupied for the purposes of a business. This will include the gym itself and also the car park. Greg's flat will also fall within the holding, since Greg as a full-time caretaker is employed by Jim for the purposes of the business. The residential flats, however, will be excluded from the holding (unless the services provided by Greg are extensive enough to amount to occupation, see 26.18).

D EXCLUSIONS FROM THE 1954 ACT

26.53 Certain tenancies are expressly excluded from the Landlord and Tenant Act 1954:

(a) agricultural holdings (s 43(1)(a)) and farm business tenancies (s 43(1)(aa));
(b) mining leases (s 431(1)(b));

(c) tenancies of premises licensed to sell alcohol, not including hotels and restaurants and other premises where the sale of alcohol is not the main use of the premises, which were granted before 11 July 1989 (s 43(1)(d)). Tenancies of premises licensed to sell alcohol granted on or after 11 July 1989 do fall within the 1954 Act (Landlord and Tenant (Licensed Premises) Act 1990, s 1(1));

(d) service tenancies, ie a tenancy granted to a tenant who holds an office, appointment, or employment from the landlord and which continues only so long as that employment or appointment continues. If the tenancy was granted after 1 October 1954, the tenancy must have been granted in writing which expresses the purpose for which the tenancy was granted (s 43(2));

(e) short tenancies, ie tenancies granted for a term certain not exceeding six months unless:

   (i)   the tenancy contains provision for renewing the term or extending it beyond six months from its beginning; or

   (ii) the tenant, either alone or together with any predecessor in title, has been in occupation for more than 12 months (s 43(3)). If the tenant wishes to rely on occupation by a predecessor, that person must have carried on the same business as the tenant now does. This situation would usually arise where the tenant has acquired the tenancy along with a business as a going concern.

E CONTRACTING OUT OF THE 1954 ACT

The provisions of the 1954 Act can sometimes be awkward for a landlord. For example, Tom has plans to redevelop a factory block he owns. The plans are not finalized but the redevelopment is likely to take place in the next two to three years. Tom does not want to leave the factory empty—aside from losing rent this would also mean that the building might be prone to vandalism. On the other hand, Tom does not want to find himself lumbered with a tenant who has acquired the right to renew the tenancy. **26.54**

The general rule is that any attempt by Tom to contract out of the provisions of the 1954 Act would fall foul of s 38(1). Section 38(1) renders void any agreement relating to a tenancy to which the Act applies: **26.55**

> … in so far as it purports to preclude the tenant from making an application or request under this Part of this Act or provides for the termination or the surrender of the tenancy in the event of his making such an application or request or for the imposition of any penalty or disability on the tenant in that event.

However, these strict rules against contracting out have been tempered by s 38A of the 1954 Act (which was inserted by the Regulatory Reform (Business Tenancies) (England and Wales) Order 2003 in place of the old s 38(4)). Section 38A allows the landlord and tenant to enter into an agreement that the provisions of ss 24 to 28 (the provisions relating to security of tenure) will not apply to the tenancy. In order for such an agreement to be valid the landlord must have served on the tenant a notice in the form set out in Sch 1 to the Regulatory Reform (Business Tenancies) (England and Wales) Order 2003 and the requirements specified in Sch 2 to that Order must have been met. **26.56**

The landlord's notice should be served not less than 14 days before the tenant enters into the tenancy. If the tenant agrees to the exclusion of the provisions of ss 24 to 28, he or she must sign a declaration to that effect before entering into the tenancy. The form of the declaration is set out in Pt 7 of Sch 2. If notice is served late, it is still possible for the parties to contract out of the provisions provided the tenant makes a statutory declaration in the **26.57** form set out in Pt 8 of Sch 2. Draft forms of suitable notice, agreement, and declarations are available in Appendices A to C to the government publication *Business tenancies: new procedures under the Landlord and Tenant Act 1954*, see 26.204.

26.58   Thus, if Tom can find a tenant who is prepared to agree to his terms then, provided he serves the correct form of notice and provided the tenant signs the declaration, the tenancy will not be continued beyond the end of the contractual term and the tenant will have no right to apply for a new tenancy.

26.59   In order to qualify for exclusion under s 38A the lease must be for a fixed term. If the lease is periodic, or for a fixed term and thereafter periodic (for example a lease for a term of five years and thereafter from month to month), it cannot be excluded, even if both parties initially agreed to exclusion (*London Borough of Newham v Thomas-Van Standen* [2008] EWCA Civ 1414).

26.60   Section 38A also allows for the landlord and tenant to agree the date and the circumstances of the surrendering of the tenancy and any terms of the surrender. Again, any such agreement will be subject to the requirement of service of notice by the landlord and the signing of a tenant's declaration.

26.61   The provisions of s 38A will only apply to agreements entered into after 1 June 2004. If the parties to a tenancy entered into an agreement to exclude ss 24 to 28 before that date, they will have to make an application to the court asking the court to authorize the agreement. The court has retained the jurisdiction to make such an order in cases where the old rules still apply.

F SECURITY OF TENURE UNDER THE 1954 ACT

Automatic continuation

26.62   The Landlord and Tenant Act 1954, s 24 (as amended by the Regulatory Reform (Business Tenancies) (England and Wales) Order 2003) contains the core of the security offered by the Act. The basis of this security is automatic continuation. A tenancy which falls within the Act will not come to an end unless it is terminated in one of the ways set out in the Act. A tenancy will not come to an end by effluxion of time (in the case of a fixed-term tenancy), or by the landlord's service of a notice to quit (in the case of a periodic tenancy). These are the two main common law methods by which a landlord can bring a tenancy to an end.

26.63   Section 24(1) provides:

> (1) A tenancy to which this Part of this Act applies shall not come to an end unless terminated in accordance with the provisions of this Part of this Act; and, subject to the following provisions of this Act either the tenant or the landlord under such a tenancy may apply to the court for an order for the grant of a new tenancy—
>
> (a) if the landlord has given notice under section 25 of this Act to terminate the tenancy, or
>
> (b) if the tenant has made a request for a new tenancy in accordance with section 26 of this Act.

26.64   Prior to the amendment made by the Regulatory Reform (Business Tenancies) (England and Wales) Order 2003 only the tenant could make an application under s 24.

26.65   Thus, when Jim's contractual term expires at midnight on 31 January 2016, his tenancy will not end but will continue as before on the same terms as the original contractual tenancy (excluding any terms which might be inconsistent with the statutory continuation).

This method of providing security of tenure is very different from that provided by the **26.66** Rent Act 1977. Under the Rent Act, a statutory tenancy arises when the contractual tenancy is terminated. A Rent Act statutory tenancy, as we saw in Chapter 13, is a personal right (although it does exhibit some characteristics akin to an interest in land) and cannot be assigned. The method used by the 1954 Act functions by preventing the tenancy from being terminated in the first place. The tenancy continues as it did before and it therefore remains an interest in land. The tenant under a statutorily continued business tenancy is free to dispose of the tenancy as he or she wishes (eg by assigning or sub-letting), provided that such a disposal is not prohibited by the terms of the contract.

It may seem reasonable to ask whether, if the tenancy automatically continues beyond the **26.67** expiry date, the expiry date has any significance for a tenancy to which the 1954 Act applies. The answer is that the expiry date (or the serving of a notice to quit in the case of a periodic tenancy) is of considerable significance, for it is only after the contractual term has expired that the landlord or tenant acquires the right to apply to the court for a new tenancy.

G TERMINATION OF A BUSINESS TENANCY

The methods of termination available under the 1954 Act are listed in this section. They **26.68** can be divided into two categories: (i) those common law methods of termination which are preserved by the Act; and (ii) the statutory methods of termination which are provided for in the Act.

Common law methods of termination

The Landlord and Tenant Act 1954, s 24(2) provides: **26.69**

> (2) The last foregoing subsection shall not prevent the coming to an end of a tenancy by notice to quit given by the tenant, by surrender or forfeiture, or by the forfeiture of a superior tenancy, unless—
>
> (a) in the case of a notice to quit, the notice was given before the tenant had been in occupation in right of the tenancy for one month.

Tenant's notice to quit

The aim of the 1954 Act is to provide protection for business tenants by preventing the **26.70** landlord from terminating the tenancy. The tenant's ability to terminate the tenancy by serving a notice to quit on the landlord is unaffected.

Surrender

As with a notice to quit, the 1954 Act does not prevent a tenant surrendering the tenancy **26.71** before the expiry of the term.

Paragraphs (a) and (b) of s 24(2) (which were added by the Law of Property Act 1969) pre- **26.72** vent the tenant from giving a notice to quit or surrendering the tenancy before he or she has been in occupation for one month. The aim of this is to prevent landlords from attempting to exclude the operation of the Act by getting a tenant to give a notice to quit or to execute a deed of surrender when the tenant enters into the tenancy.

Forfeiture

The Act does not affect the landlord's right to forfeit the tenancy in the event of the tenant **26.73** breaching an obligation under the lease. Of course, the landlord will be able to forfeit only if he or she has reserved a right of re-entry in the lease (see 11.18). Likewise, if a landlord forfeits a head tenancy this may also bring a sub-tenancy to an end. Where the landlord seeks to forfeit the tenancy the tenant, or the sub-tenant, will be able to apply for relief against forfeiture under s 146 of the Law of Property Act 1925 (see 11.72 to 11.96). In the case of tenancies to which Pt II applies the court also has the power to grant relief from forfeiture after the fixed term has expired. Even where the landlord has commenced forfeiture proceedings, until those proceedings have been finally disposed of the tenant is still able to apply for, and pursue a claim for, the grant of a new tenancy.

Statutory methods of termination

26.74   Under the 1954 Act there are four ways in which a tenancy to which the Act applies can be brought to an end:

(a)   by the landlord giving notice to terminate the tenancy under s 25;
(b)   by the tenant making an application for a new tenancy under s 26;
(c)   by the tenant giving notice to terminate the tenancy under s 27(2);
(d)   by the landlord and tenant agreeing a new tenancy under s 28.

26.75   Each of these will be covered in detail in the following sections.

What happens if the business use ceases after the fixed term has expired?

26.76   If a tenant ceases to use the premises for business purposes after the contractual term has expired and while the tenancy is being continued by s 24(1), then the tenancy ceases to be one to which the 1954 Act applies. Such a tenancy will not simply come to an end when the business user ceases, however. Section 24(3)(a) provides that the landlord may terminate the tenancy by not less than three nor more than six months' notice given in writing to the tenant (without prejudice to any means of termination contained in the terms of the tenancy).

What happens if business user starts after the landlord has served a notice to quit?

26.77   If a tenancy does not fall within the 1954 Act and the landlord gives the tenant notice to quit, the fact that the tenant may bring the tenancy within the Act before the notice expires (ie by starting a business on the premises) will not affect the operation of that notice (s 24(3)(b)).

The 'competent landlord'?

26.78   A tenant who may acquire the right to a renewal of his or her tenancy will want to negotiate the new tenancy with a landlord who has a substantial interest in the property. If the tenant's immediate landlord is the freeholder this will present no problem. However, if the tenant is a sub-tenant it is possible that the landlord may hold a term that is only a few days longer than the tenant's interest.

26.79   The 1954 Act therefore provides a mechanism for identifying one landlord with whom the tenant should deal. This landlord is known as the 'competent landlord'. Only a competent landlord is entitled to serve a notice to terminate on the tenant under s 25 of the Act. If the tenant wishes to apply for a new tenancy, his or her request under s 26 should be served on the competent landlord. The competent landlord will not always be the tenant's immediate landlord.

26.80   Section 44(1) of the Act provides that the competent landlord will be either:

(a)   the owner of the fee simple; or
(b)   the landlord lowest in the chain of tenancies who has a tenancy which will not come to an end within 14 months by effluxion of time, and no notice has been given which will end the tenancy within 14 months.

Example The freeholder grants Jane a 21-year tenancy of a factory. Jane then grants a **26.81** 10-year tenancy to Henry. Henry in turn sub-lets the whole of the premises to Sandra for nine years. Sandra occupies the factory for business purposes. Her tenancy is about to come to an end and she wants to apply for a renewal. Henry is Sandra's immediate landlord, but for the purposes of the 1954 Act Jane is the competent landlord, for Henry's term will expire in 12 months.

The situation would be different if Henry, instead of sub-letting the whole of the premises, **26.82** granted Sandra a tenancy of half of the factory while he continued to occupy the other half for business purposes. Henry's tenancy falls within the Act; there is only 12 months to run of his contractual tenancy, but on its expiry it will be continued by s 24(1). Henry's tenancy will not therefore come to an end by effluxion of time. Henry is therefore Sandra's competent landlord.

Termination of sub-tenancies

If a landlord serves a s 25 notice on his immediate tenant, or if the immediate tenant serves **26.83** a s 26 notice on the landlord, the effect of either notice will be to terminate that tenancy. The landlord will then become the competent landlord of any of the intermediate landlord's sub-tenants. If he or she wants to terminate their tenancies he or she will have to serve a s 25 notice on them. If, in the example at 26.82, Jane wants to regain possession of the entire premises, she must serve a s 25 notice on Henry. At that point Sandra will become Jane's direct tenant and Jane will also need to serve a s 25 notice on Sandra.

Requests for information

Sometimes the tenant may find that he or she does not possess sufficient information to be **26.84** able to identify the competent landlord. If this is the case s 40 of the Act (as amended by the Regulatory Reform (Business Tenancies) (England and Wales) Order 2003) allows for the tenant to serve notice on any landlord above the tenant in the chain requiring that landlord to furnish him or her with the appropriate information by virtue of s 40(3). Similarly, a superior landlord will need to establish the identity of any sub-tenants in order that he or she can serve a s 25 notice on them after he has served notice on the tenant. The landlord can request this information from his or her immediate tenant by serving notice under s 40(1). The tenant's notice should be on Form 5 and the landlord's notice on Form 4 of the Landlord and Tenant Act 1954, Part 2 (Notices) Regulations 2004, SI 2004/1005.

If the landlord or tenant upon whom such a notice has been served has transferred his or **26.85** her interest to another person, he or she must provide details of the transfer and the person to whom it was transferred (s 40A). Section 40B allows for a claim for damages for breach of statutory duty to be brought against any person who fails to comply with an obligation under s 40.

Agreement for a new tenancy

Section 28 provides that where the competent landlord and the tenant enter into an agree- **26.86** ment for the grant of a future tenancy of the holding, or the holding plus other land, and the agreement specifies the terms of that tenancy and its commencement date:

(a) the current tenancy will continue until that date but no longer; and
(b) the current tenancy ceases to be one to which Pt II of the 1954 Act applies.

The agreement must be in writing and the subject matter of the tenancy must be at least **26.87** the whole of the holding.

Termination by the landlord

Service of notice on the tenant

26.88   In order to terminate a tenancy to which the 1954 Act applies, the landlord must serve a notice in accordance with s 25. By serving such a notice the landlord puts in motion the mechanism of the renewal procedure. This functions, in essence, by setting out a series of time limits within which both the landlord and tenant must serve their respective notices and replies, and thereby provides a framework for the negotiations.

The contents of the notice

26.89   The landlord's s 25 notice must be given in the prescribed form. Section 25 was amended by art 4 of the Regulatory Reform (Business Tenancies) (England and Wales) Order 2003 which came into force on 1 June 2004. Where a landlord's notice was given before that date there was a requirement that the tenant serve a counter-notice. The 2003 Order has removed this requirement.

26.90   Under the amended provisions the s 25 notice must:

(a)   state whether the landlord is opposed to the grant of the tenancy (s 25(6));

(b)   if the landlord does oppose the new tenancy, specify the ground or grounds of opposition (s 25(7)); or

(c)   if the landlord does not oppose the new tenancy, set out the landlord's proposals for the property to be comprised in the tenancy, the rent payable, and any other terms of the new tenancy (s 25(8)).

26.91   Notice should be given on Form 1 (if the landlord is not opposed to the grant of a new tenancy) or Form 2 (if the landlord is opposed) of the Landlord and Tenant Act 1954, Part 2 (Notices) Regulations 2004. If the landlord is not sure that the tenancy is one to which Pt II of the Act applies, it is acceptable for him to serve a s 25 notice 'without prejudice' to his contention that the tenancy is not protected.

26.92   A s 25 notice must be given by the competent landlord or, if there is more than one, jointly by the landlords in a single notice to the tenant. If there are joint tenants the notice must be served on all of them.

26.93   A s 25 notice must apply to the whole of the demised premises (*Southport Old Links Ltd v Naylor* [1985] 1 EGLR 66, CA). Thus, if in the case of Jim's Gym, Jim's landlord served a s 25 notice with respect only to the ground floor of the building, the notice would not be valid. Jim's landlord must serve a s 25 notice with respect to the whole of Western House. This may prove problematic if the landlord's interest has been severed after the grant of the tenancy, for example if Jim's landlord had retained his interest in the ground floor of Western House but had sold its interest in the upper floors. It may be that in such a situation it will not be possible for either of the landlords to serve a valid s 25 notice (see *Dodson Bull Carpet Co. Ltd v City of London Corpn* [1975] 1 WLR 781, [1975] 2 All ER 497; contrast *Skelton & Son v Harrison and Pinder Ltd* [1975] QB 361, [1975] 1 All ER 182). The only solution would be for both landlords to serve notice jointly.

26.94   Once a valid s 25 notice has been served the landlord has no power to amend it. A notice can only be withdrawn in the very limited circumstance where, within two months of the service of the notice, a superior landlord becomes the competent landlord. Great care should therefore be taken when considering the timing and contents of the s 25 notice.

The timing of the notice

The notice must be given not more than 12 or less than six months before the date of termi-   **26.95**
nation specified in the notice (s 25(2)). So, as we shall see, the earliest date that a landlord can
give notice, in the case of a fixed-term tenancy, is a year before the tenancy is due to expire.

The date of termination

Where a landlord wishes to terminate a business tenancy, he or she must specify the date   **26.96**
of termination. Calculating the date of termination must be done with care; if a premature
date is given the notice will not be valid. The basic principle behind the 1954 Act is that
the date of termination cannot be earlier than the date upon which the tenancy can be terminated at common law. How this date is to be calculated will depend upon whether the
tenancy is a periodic or a fixed-term tenancy.

Periodic tenancies At common law a periodic tenancy is normally brought to an end by   **26.97**
means of a notice to quit. Under the 1954 Act the date of termination given in the notice
must not be earlier than the earliest date upon which the tenancy could have been brought
to an end at common law by a notice to quit (s 25(3)). At common law it is necessary that
the notice to quit expires on the anniversary of the tenancy (see 10.37). Under the 1954 Act
the landlord does not have to be so precise, provided that the date of termination given by
the landlord is later than the date at which the tenancy could be terminated by a notice to
quit. The notice, however, must be given not more than 12 or less than six months before
the date of termination specified in the notice (s 25(2)).

Example Beryl rents a shop on a monthly periodic tenancy from Andrew. The periods of   **26.98**
the tenancy run from the 5th of the month. At common law a monthly tenancy requires
one month's notice, and this notice should be expressed to expire on either the 4th or the
5th of the month. Andrew could therefore terminate Beryl's tenancy by a notice to quit
served on 4 February and expressed to expire on 5 March. Under the 1954 Act, a s 25
notice must not be given less than six months before the date specified for termination.
Thus, a notice served on 4 February could specify any date from 5 August onwards as the
date of termination (so long as this date was before 4 February of the following year).

If Beryl had a yearly tenancy running from 5 February, the period of notice required by   **26.99**
the common law is six months, and such notice would have to be expressed to expire on
4 or 5 February (ie the anniversary of the tenancy). Thus, if on 12 June Andrew decides he
wants to terminate Beryl's tenancy, the earliest date at which he can do this at common law
is 4 February the following year. He would have to serve a notice to quit specifying 4 or 5
February as the expiry date. Under the 1954 Act he could serve a s 25 notice giving the termination date as any date between 4 February and 12 June of the following year.

It may be that the terms of the tenancy require a period of more than six months' notice. If   **26.100**
the tenancy demands more than 12 months' notice, a landlord would find himself or herself
in serious difficulty. The earliest the tenancy could be terminated at common law would be
after one year's notice, and yet s 25(2) requires that notice must be given not more than 12
months before the date of termination. Section 25(3)(b) avoids this dilemma by stating that
where the period of notice required to bring a tenancy to an end by a notice to quit is more
than six months, the 12-month limit no longer applies; instead, the limit will be a period
six months longer than the length of notice required under the tenancy agreement, so if 12
months' notice is required under the tenancy agreement the maximum notice period for the
s 25 notice would be 18 months.

Fixed-term tenancies With fixed-term tenancies it is easier to calculate the date of termina-   **26.101**
tion. The earliest date of termination is the date upon which the tenancy would have come

to an end by effluxion of time if it had not been continued by s 24 of the 1954 Act. Thus, the earliest point at which a landlord can serve notice under s 25 is one year before the tenancy is due to expire. In every case the landlord must give at least six months' notice, even once the contractual tenancy has expired and the tenancy is being continued by s 24.

26.102   A considerable number of business tenancies, however, permit termination before the expiry of the term by incorporating a break clause into the tenancy agreement (see 6.113). What happens then if the landlord wishes to exercise such a break clause? Should the landlord adopt the statutory procedure under s 25, or follow the contractual provisions set out in the break clause; or does the landlord need to serve two notices, one under the Act and one under the contract?

26.103   If a s 25 notice can be served which fulfils both the statutory requirements and the requirements of the contract then one notice will be sufficient (*Scholl Manufacturing Co. Ltd v Clifton (Slim-Line) Ltd* [1967] Ch 41, [1966] 3 All ER 16). To achieve this joint goal may not always be easy, and in practice a careful landlord will often serve two notices—one under the break clause and one under s 25.

26.104   If a landlord serves a notice that satisfies s 25 but does not fulfil the provisions of the break clause, the s 25 notice will be of no effect, for if the break clause is not effectively operated the tenancy will continue under the contract. The landlord will have to wait either until the tenancy expires by effluxion of time, or until the next opportunity at which a break clause can be operated.

26.105   If a landlord serves a notice that fulfils the provisions of the break clause but does not comply with s 25, the contractual tenancy will be brought to an end; however, the tenancy will continue under s 24 until the landlord complies with the provisions of the Act. Even if a landlord does not wish to terminate the tenancy immediately, it may still be of benefit to him or her to operate a break clause.

26.106   **Example** Jane is granted a 21-year tenancy of a shop by Harry. The tenancy contains provisions permitting Harry to terminate the tenancy at the end of the seventh and fourteenth years by giving six months' written notice. Harry has plans to redevelop the shop in several years' time, but these plans are not finalized. As a precautionary measure Harry can exercise the break clause at the end of the seventh year. By doing so he ends the contractual tenancy. The tenancy of course continues under s 24, but now Harry will be in a position to serve a s 25 notice whenever his plans come to fruition. If he does not exercise the first break clause he will have to wait until the fourteenth year to have another opportunity to terminate Jane's tenancy.

The effect of the notice

26.107   The s 25 notice will terminate the current tenancy on the date specified in the notice. Before this event occurs it is open to both the landlord and the tenant to apply to the court for a new tenancy. Alternatively, the landlord may apply to the court for an order terminating the tenancy without renewal before the s 25 notice expires. These options are considered in more detail at 26.132 to 26.139.

Termination by the tenant

26.108   The tenant cannot end the tenancy simply by giving up possession of the property on the last day of the fixed term. Notice must be served or his or her obligations will continue under the provisions of the 1954 Act. Of course, if the tenant has quit the property before the end of the term the tenancy will have ceased to be one to which Pt II of the Act applies

and so the statutory provisions will be irrelevant. In that case the tenancy will simply come
to an end on its last day.

There are two ways in which a tenant can bring a business tenancy to an end under the   **26.109**
1954 Act:

(a)   by requesting a new tenancy under s 26;
(b)   by giving notice under s 27.

The first of these options is applicable where the tenant does not wish to give up possession   **26.110**
and wants to apply for a new tenancy. The second is applicable where the tenant wants to
end the tenancy and give up possession.

In general it is rarer for a tenant to request a new tenancy under s 26 than it is for a land-   **26.111**
lord to apply to terminate the tenancy under s 25. Until the landlord indicates that he or
she wishes to terminate the tenancy, it will usually not be in the tenant's interest to request a
new one. The tenancy will be continued anyway under s 24, and will probably be on terms
more favourable to the tenant than those of a new tenancy.

On the other hand, it will often be in the interest of the landlord to terminate the tenancy   **26.112**
under s 25 even if the landlord does not want to regain possession of the premises, for the
landlord will gain an opportunity to renegotiate the terms of the lease and may well be able
to demand a higher rent.

Who can request a new tenancy?

Not every tenant can take advantage of s 26 of the 1954 Act. First, the tenant must hold a   **26.113**
tenancy which is either:

(a)   a tenancy granted for a term of years certain exceeding one year (whether or not continued by s 24); or
(b)   a tenancy granted for a term of years certain and thereafter from year to year
(s 26(1)).

Neither the holder of a periodic tenancy nor the holder of a fixed term of less than one   **26.114**
year can request a new tenancy under s 26. Periodic tenants and the holders of terms of
less than one year can still apply for a new tenancy if the landlord serves them with a s 25
notice. (Note that the holder of fixed terms of less than six months will be excluded from
the Act in any case by s 43(3).)

Secondly, there are provisions designed to prevent the operation of s 26 clashing with the   **26.115**
operation of s 25 and s 27. If the landlord has already served a s 25 notice, the tenant cannot
then request a new tenancy under s 26. Similarly, if the tenant has already served notice under
s 27 (see 26.125), he or she cannot subsequently request a new tenancy under s 26 (s 26(4)).

The content of a s 26 request

A tenant's request for a new tenancy should be served on the competent landlord (see 26.78   **26.116**
to 26.82) and must:

(a)   be made in the prescribed form (s 26(3));
(b)   set out the tenant's proposals as to:
    (i)   the property to be comprised in the new tenancy (being either the whole or part
of the property comprised in the current tenancy);
    (ii)   the rent payable under the new tenancy;
    (iii)   the terms of the new tenancy (s 26(3));
(c)   specify a date for the commencement of the new tenancy.

26.117 The prescribed form is Form 3 of the Landlord and Tenant Act 1954, Part 2 (Notices) Regulations 2004.

26.118 The date referred to in (c) must not be more than 12 months or less than six months after the making of the request. The date must not be earlier than:

(a) the date upon which the current tenancy would come to an end by effluxion of time; or

(b) the date upon which the tenancy could be brought to an end by notice to quit given by the tenant (s 26(2)).

26.119 The two dates are not to be considered as alternatives. If the tenancy is for a fixed term, the date for commencement of the new tenancy cannot be earlier than the date the full term ends. Thus, a tenant who terminates the tenancy by exercising a break clause in the lease (see 6.122) cannot then serve a s 26 notice requesting a new tenancy, claiming that the tenancy has been brought to an end by notice to quit (*Garston v Scottish Widows Fund & Life Assurance Society* [1998] 2 EGLR 73, CA).

26.120 **Example** On 31 January 2006 Jim is granted a 10-year lease of Western House. The lease gives him an option to terminate the tenancy at the end of the fifth year. After four years Jim realizes that market rents in the area have gone down and he would like to terminate his tenancy and request a new one at a lower rent. Jim however will have no statutory right to do this. The earliest point at which he could make a s 26 request for a new tenancy would be 31 January 2015, one year before the date on which the tenancy was due to expire by effluxion of time. The date specified for the commencement of the tenancy in the s 26 notice would be 30 January 2016. If Jim exercises the break clause, his tenancy will come to an end and will not continue as a statutory periodic tenancy (see 6.125). Jim will have no right to remain at the property.

26.121 If Jim had instead been granted a tenancy for three years and thereafter from year to year, the fixed term would have expired on 30 January 2009 and the tenancy would have carried on as a yearly periodic tenancy. In this case Jim's s 26 notice must request that the tenancy starts on the date the periodic tenancy could be brought to an end by notice to quit. Any notice to quit given by Jim would need to expire on 30 or 31 January (see 10.38). Jim could, therefore, serve a s 26 notice requesting a new tenancy commencing on 30 January of the next year, providing he gave at least six months' notice.

26.122 The effect of a s 26 request is to terminate the tenant's current tenancy immediately before the date specified in the request for the beginning of the new tenancy (s 26(5)). Section 64 provides for the interim continuation of the tenancy until the application for a new tenancy is disposed of. If the new tenancy is not taken up by the tenant s 26(2) allows for a short continuation of the interim tenancy which should allow the parties time to sort out their affairs. Once a tenant has served a request on the landlord, he or she should be careful to comply with the procedure which follows, for if the right to apply for a new tenancy is lost the tenancy will nevertheless terminate and the landlord will be able to regain possession.

26.123 A s 26 notice, unlike a s 25 notice, does not have to relate to the whole of the premises. Once a tenant has served a valid request under s 26 it is not possible to withdraw it and serve a second request (a tenant might want to do this, for example, in order to enable him or her to comply with the time limits) (*Polyviou v Seeley* [1980] 1 WLR 55, [1979] 3 All ER 853).

26.124 Once the landlord has received the tenant's request, he or she has two months to serve notice on the tenant that he or she will oppose the application to the court for the grant of a new tenancy (s 26(6)). There is no prescribed form for the landlord's notice in opposition, but it must state on which of the grounds set out in s 30 of the 1954 Act the landlord will oppose the application. The notice in opposition cannot subsequently be amended or withdrawn and will be binding on anyone who takes over the landlord's interest. If the landlord fails to serve notice in opposition, he or she will lose the right to oppose the tenant's application for a new tenancy. The landlord will, however, still be able to argue the terms of the new tenancy.

Termination by tenant's notice under s 27

This second statutory method of termination applies when the tenant does not wish to apply for a new tenancy. It is applicable only in the case of fixed-term tenancies; a tenant under a periodic tenancy can always terminate the tenancy by means of a notice to quit served on the landlord, this being one of the common law methods of termination preserved by s 24(2) of the Act. Section 27 can be used only after the tenant has been in occupation in right of the tenancy for one month. This extra provision was added by the Law of Property Act 1967, s 4(2) to prevent possible evasion of the 1954 Act. **26.125**

Where a fixed-term tenancy is nearing its end and the tenant does not want to continue in occupation after the term has expired, the tenant can give notice under s 27(1). The tenant must give notice in writing to the immediate landlord not later than three months before the date on which the tenancy would come to an end by effluxion of time. If such notice is given, s 24 will not apply to the tenancy and it will come to an end normally by effluxion of time. **26.126**

Where the tenancy has already passed the date at which it would expire by effluxion of time and is being continued by s 24, the tenant can give notice under s 27(2). Such notice must be given in writing to the immediate landlord; three months' notice must be given. The notice can expire on any day of the tenancy (s 27(2), as amended by art 25 of the Regulatory Reform (Business Tenancies) (England and Wales) Order 2003). **26.127**

Service of notices

Section 23 of the Landlord and Tenant Act 1927 sets out rules governing service of notices and requests which are applicable to the Act. Notices must be in writing and can be served personally or sent to the last known place of abode in England or Wales of the person to be served. 'Place of abode' includes place of business. A landlord will often employ an agent to act on his or her behalf and notices can effectively be served on such an authorized agent. **26.128**

It should also be noted that a notice which is invalid due to a deficiency in either form or service may be effective if it is accepted by the person receiving it as being valid, and that person then goes on to require the person who served the notice to act on its terms. In doing this he or she may have waived the right to claim that the notice was invalid (*Keepers and Governors of the Possessions Revenues and Goods of the Free Grammar School of John Lyon v Mayhew* [1997] 1 EGLR 88, CA). **26.129**

Joint tenants

Where premises to which the 1954 Act applies are let to joint tenants, landlord's notices under the Act must be served on all of them. Similarly, tenants' requests under s 26 or notices to quit under s 27 must be served by all of the joint tenants. **26.130**

Applications to the court

Following the service of a s 25 or 26 notice the parties may agree to the grant of a new tenancy or may be in agreement that no new tenancy will be granted. If the tenant wants a new tenancy but the landlord does not, or if the parties cannot agree the terms of a new **26.131** tenancy, an application will have to be made to the court. Either the landlord or the tenant may apply for an order for the grant of a new tenancy (s 24(1)) or the landlord may apply for an order for the termination of the tenancy (s 29(2)). If either application is opposed it will be dealt with as an application for a new tenancy (see 26.140).

Summary: options at the end of the fixed term

26.132   **Example** Tony rents a shop from Lucy. His tenancy fits all of the criteria for protection under the 1954 Act and his lease is due to expire in six months' time. The future of the tenancy will depend on whether Tony or Lucy want the landlord and tenant relationship to continue and on what terms. If neither Lucy nor Tony takes any action, the tenancy will automatically continue as a statutory periodic tenancy. This may suit them if they are happy with the terms of the old lease and neither wants to commit to a further fixed-term agreement. It may be, however, that one or both of them would like the security of a further fixed term or would like to renegotiate the terms of the lease or the extent of the holding. It is also possible that Lucy would like the shop back at the end of the fixed term or that Tony would like to leave.

(a) Landlord wants to regain possession

26.133   If Lucy wants to terminate the tenancy and does not want to grant Tony a new tenancy, she should serve notice under s 25 stating her opposition (see 26.88 to 26.107). If Tony does not want to stay, no further action need be taken by either of them and the tenancy will automatically terminate in accordance with the s 25 notice. If the s 25 notice will not expire for some time and Lucy wants to regain possession more quickly, she can apply to the court for the termination of the tenancy without the grant of a new tenancy under s 29(2).

26.134   If Tony does not want to leave, he can apply to the court for the grant of a new tenancy under s 24 (see 26.140). He can only do this if Lucy has not yet made an application under s 29(2). If Lucy has made a s 29(2) application, Tony can defend it. If he is successful the court will grant a new tenancy.

26.135   If Lucy makes an application under s 29(2) or Tony makes an application under s 24, Lucy will have to rely on one of the grounds under s 30(1) in order to oppose the granting of a new tenancy (see 26.149 to 26.168). These grounds must be contained in her s 25 notice.

(b) Tenant does not want a new tenancy

26.136   If Tony does not want a new tenancy, he can serve notice under s 27 (see 26.125 to 26.127) and Lucy cannot compel him to enter into a new agreement. Tony cannot, however, continue in occupation under the terms of a statutory periodic tenancy if Lucy does not want him to. If Lucy serves a s 25 notice on Tony, his only option, if he wants to stay, is to accept the terms of a new tenancy. If these terms cannot be agreed, Lucy can make an application to the court for a grant of a new tenancy under s 24.

26.137   A new tenancy will not be granted if Tony notifies the court that he does not want one (s 29(5)). Tony can also choose not to accept any new tenancy that is granted, but in both cases he will lose the right to occupy the premises (see 26.203).

(c) Tenant wants a new tenancy but landlord does not

26.138   Tony can start the process off himself by making a request under s 26 (see 26.113 to 26.124). If Lucy opposes the granting of a new tenancy, she will need to reply, relying on one of the s 30(1) grounds. It is then open to either of them to make an application to the court: Lucy under s 29(2) or Tony under s 24. The application must be made before the date specified in the s 26 request (see 26.143 to 26.147). It is obviously in Tony's interest to ensure that an application is made because if it is not his tenancy will terminate on that date (see 26.122).

(d) Landlord and tenant want a new tenancy

If Lucy and Tony are in complete agreement about the terms of the new tenancy, they can, of course, simply enter into a new tenancy agreement without activating the machinery of Pt II of the Act. If they cannot agree, it is open to either of them to force the other's hand: Tony by serving a request under s 26 or Lucy by serving a s 25 notice stating that she does not oppose the granting of a new tenancy. They can then try to negotiate the terms of the new lease. If they can do this within the relevant time periods (26.146), they will have a contract for a lease and do not need to apply to the court. If they cannot agree terms, one of them will have to apply to the court under s 24. If neither of them makes an application within the prescribed time period the old tenancy will terminate. **26.139**

H APPLICATION FOR A NEW TENANCY

A business tenant's right to apply to the court for a new tenancy lies at the core of the 1954 Act. A new tenancy can be granted only when the current tenancy has been terminated. The right to apply for a new tenancy will therefore arise in only two situations: **26.140**

(a)   where the landlord has terminated the current tenancy by serving a s 25 notice;
(b)   where the tenant has terminated the current tenancy by requesting a new tenancy under s 26.

Article 3(2) of the Regulatory Reform (Business Tenancies) (England and Wales) Order 2003 has added the following further provisions to s 24(2) to take account of the fact that it is now possible for either a landlord or a tenant to serve notice: **26.141**

(2A)   Neither the tenant nor the landlord may make an application under s 24(1) if the other has made such an application and the application has been served.
(2B)   Neither the tenant nor the landlord may make such an application if the landlord has made an application under s 29(2) (for termination without the grant of a new tenancy) of the Act and the application has been served.
(2C)   The landlord may not withdraw an application under s 24(1) unless the tenant consents to its withdrawal.

A business tenant will acquire no right to apply for a new tenancy where the tenant has chosen to give up possession by surrender or by serving notice under s 27. **26.142**

Much of the enduring success of the 1954 Act can be attributed to the way in which it encourages the parties to reach agreement. First, it provides space for the parties to negotiate by continuing a fixed-term tenancy beyond the date on which it would expire by effluxion of time (s 24). During this time the parties have the opportunity to come to agreement without resorting to the statutory provisions. If agreement is not forthcoming then either the landlord or the tenant can serve notice under the Act. By serving notice a statutory framework is brought into play. This framework requires the parties to set out their intentions and reasons within strict time limits. The framework itself, by compelling the parties to put their cards on the table, provides a further impetus towards agreement. If agreement is not reached within the specified time limits, the tenant may then apply to court for the matter to be settled. In the meantime the landlord can apply to the court for an interim rent to be fixed (see 26.182). **26.143**

26.144 By s 28 of the Act, if agreement is reached between the parties for the grant of a new tenancy, the current tenancy will continue until the date specified in the agreement for the commencement of the new tenancy and will cease to be a tenancy to which the Act applies (the tenant no longer needs the protection of the Act because he or she will now hold a contract for a lease).

Time limits for making an application

26.145 The court's powers to order the grant of a new tenancy or to terminate the tenancy are contained in ss 29 to 31 of the 1954 Act (as amended by the Regulatory Reform (Business Tenancies) (England and Wales) Order 2003).

26.146 Any application made by a tenant or landlord under s 24(1) or by a landlord under s 29(2) (for the termination of a tenancy without renewal) must be made before the end of the statutory period. Under s 29A the statutory period is the period ending:

(a) where the landlord gave notice under s 25 of the Act, on the date specified in his or her notice; and

(b) where the tenant made a request for a new tenancy under s 26 immediately before the date specified in his or her request.

This time limit may be extended by agreement between the parties (s 29B).

26.147 These time limits are particularly important for those advising tenants in lease negotiations. Whilst s 24 allows either a landlord or a tenant to apply for a new tenancy, it is usually the tenant who will need to make the application. Often the landlord would rather not renew the tenancy and is only doing so because he or she has no valid grounds of opposition. In such a situation a landlord might deliberately delay the negotiation process in the hope that the s 25 or 26 notice will expire (and the tenancy terminate) without the tenant having made an application to the court. The tenant will then have lost the right to renew. Care must also be taken if an agreement has been reached to extend the time limit under s 29B. If no application is made by the last day of the extended period (or any further agreed extended period) the tenancy will automatically terminate on that date (s 29B(4)).

Procedure

26.148 An application for a new tenancy under s 24, or for the landlord's application for termination of a tenancy under s 29(2), can be commenced in the county court or, in exceptional circumstances, the High Court. The procedure for making an application is set out in Part 56 and Practice Direction 56 of the Civil Procedure Rules (CPR). An opposed claim for a new tenancy must be started using the CPR Part 7 procedure, whilst an unopposed claim must be started using a modified CPR Part 8 procedure (Part 8 procedure does not require the service of a defence). A claim for a new tenancy by either a landlord or a tenant must include details of the premises that are the subject of the application and the proposed terms of the new tenancy. A landlord's claim for termination without renewal must include full details of the landlord's grounds of opposition and details of the proposed terms of the new tenancy (in case his or her application fails). A claim under s 24 or 29(2) should not be commenced without reference to the full text of CPR Part 56 and PD 56.

Landlord's grounds of opposition

26.149 The Landlord and Tenant Act 1954, s 30(1) provides seven grounds upon which the landlord may oppose a tenant's application for the grant of a new tenancy. If the landlord wishes to rely upon any of these grounds, he or she must state them either in the s 25 notice or in the landlord's counter-notice to the tenant's s 26 request. Once the landlord has specified a ground or grounds they cannot be changed. If a landlord specifies grounds of opposition and subsequently sells his or her interest, the new landlord may rely only on the grounds specified by the original landlord at the hearing (*Marks v British Waterways Board* [1963] 3 All ER 28, CA).

Under the 1954 Act, the various grounds of opposition are not grouped separately as manda- **26.150** tory and discretionary grounds as are the grounds of possession under the Rent Act 1977 and the Housing Act 1988. Nevertheless, a similar distinction can be made: grounds (a), (b), (c), and (e) are discretionary in the sense that even if the landlord can establish the ground the court still has to consider whether 'the tenant ought not to be granted a new tenancy'; in the other cases the court must refuse to order the grant if the landlord can establish the ground.

Ground (a)—tenant's failure to comply with repair obligations

(a) where under the current tenancy the tenant has any obligations as respects the repair and maintenance of the holding, that the tenant ought not to be granted a new tenancy in view of the state of repair of the holding, being a state resulting from the tenant's failure to comply with the said obligations;

The landlord must establish that the holding is in a state of disrepair as a result of the ten- **26.151** ant's failure to comply with the repairing obligations in the lease. However, merely to estab- lish a breach of repairing covenant is not enough; the landlord must also demonstrate that the breaches are such that the court ought not to order the grant of a new tenancy. The court will consider relevant factors such as the severity of the breach, whether the tenant is will- ing and able to remedy the breach, and the tenant's past conduct (see, for example, *Lyons v Central Commercial Properties Ltd* [1958] 1 WLR 869, [1958] 2 All ER 767, CA).

Ground (b)—tenant's persistent delay in paying rent

(b) that the tenant ought not to be granted a new tenancy in view of his persistent delay in paying rent which has become due;

The landlord must establish that the tenant has a history of late payment: an occasional **26.152** delay in payment will not be enough, neither will the fact that there are currently out- standing arrears unless they are longstanding enough to amount to 'persistent delay'. The court will then consider whether the tenant ought not to be granted a new tenancy on this ground. A large range of factors may be taken into account, including;

(a) whether the delay caused the landlord inconvenience and expense;
(b) whether the tenant can offer a good explanation for the delay and show that it was exceptional (*Hurstfell Ltd v Leicester Square Property Co Ltd* [1988] 2 EGLR 105, (1988) 37 EG 109);
(c) whether the tenant can ensure future payment, eg by providing a deposit or by offering to pay interest on any future arrears (*Rawashdeh v Land* [1988] 2 EGLR 109, CA).

Ground (c)—tenant's breaches of other obligations or use of the holding

(c) that the tenant ought not to be granted a new tenancy in view of other substantial breaches by him of his obligations under the current tenancy, or for any other reason connected with the tenant's use or management of the holding;

This ground covers breaches of obligation by the tenant other than non-payment of rent **26.153** and failure to repair. The landlord must show that there is a 'substantial breach'. Ground (c) is not limited to breaches of obligations contained in the lease. It was used, for example, where some of the tenant's business activities had been carried out in contravention of planning regulations (*Fowles v Heathrow Airport Limited* [2008] EWCA Civ 757). Again the court must consider whether the tenant ought not to be granted a tenancy and should take into account all relevant circumstances (see *Eichner v Midland Bank Executor and Trustee Co. Ltd* [1970] 1 WLR 1120, [1970] 2 All ER 597, CA). In *Fowles* the court based its decision to refuse the tenant's application for renewal on his previous bad record. It considered the tenant's assertion that he would use the premises lawfully in the future to be irrelevant.

Ground (d)—suitable alternative accommodation available

(d) that the landlord has offered and is willing to provide or secure the provision of alternative accommodation for the tenant, that the terms on which the alternative accommodation is available are reasonable having regard to the terms of the current tenancy and to all other relevant circumstances, and that the accommodation and the time at which it will be available are suitable for the tenant's requirements (including the requirement to preserve goodwill) having regard to the nature and class of his business and to the situation and extent of, and facilities afforded by, the holding;

26.154 The court has no discretion when considering this ground; if the landlord can establish it then the tenant's application must be dismissed. If the landlord is unable to satisfy the court that suitable alternative accommodation will be available at the date of termination specified in the landlord's s 25 notice or the tenant's request for a new tenancy, but can establish that it will be available at a later date, the landlord will still be able to succeed under s 31(2) (see 26.171).

Ground (e)—landlord requires whole property for subsequent letting

(e) where the current tenancy was created by the sub-letting of part only of the property comprised in a superior tenancy and the landlord is the owner of an interest in reversion expectant on the termination of that superior tenancy, that the aggregate of the rents reasonably obtainable on separate lettings of the holding and the remainder of that property would be substantially less than the rent reasonably obtainable on a letting of that property as a whole, that on the termination of the current tenancy the landlord requires possession of the holding for the purpose of letting or otherwise disposing of the said property as a whole, and that in view thereof the tenant ought not to be granted a new tenancy;

26.155 This ground arises only rarely in practice. It applies where a landlord has let premises and the tenant has in turn sub-let part of the premises, and the intermediate landlord has less than 14 months of his or her term to run so that the superior landlord is the competent landlord of the sub-tenant under s 44(1). The landlord has to show:

(a) that the rent obtainable on separate lettings of the two parts of the property would be substantially less than the rent obtainable if he or she let the property as a whole; and

(b) that on the termination of the current tenancy (ie the sub-tenancy) the landlord requires possession of the holding for the purposes of letting the property as a whole.

26.156 It will be difficult for the landlord to show that he or she requires possession unless the intermediate tenancy is due to come to an end before the sub-tenancy is terminated. It should also be noted that this ground is discretionary and that s 31(2) (see 26.171) applies to it.

Ground (f)—landlord intends to demolish or reconstruct the premises

(f) that on the termination of the current tenancy the landlord intends to demolish or reconstruct the premises comprised in the holding or a substantial part of those premises or to carry out substantial work of construction on the holding or part thereof and that he could not reasonably do so without obtaining possession of the holding;

Ground (f) is one of the more popular grounds of opposition employed by landlords. **26.157**

The landlord's intention To have the intention to do something involves more than simply **26.158** possessing the desire to bring that something about; there must also be a reasonable prospect of being able to bring that something about. A landlord seeking to rely on ground (f) must therefore be able to show more than just a vague desire to demolish and reconstruct the premises. In *Cunliffe v Goodman* [1950] 2 KB 237, Asquith LJ expressed this by saying that the project must have 'moved out of the zone of contemplation—out of the sphere of the tentative, the provisional, and the exploratory—into the valley of decision'. Whether or not the landlord has a reasonable prospect of bringing about the desired project will be a question of fact. The majority of such projects will require a variety of steps to be taken: planning, financing, planning permission, and the employment of a builder. The landlord does not need to show that everything has been arranged, but there should not be too many obstacles left to resolve before the project can be started (*Gregson v Cyril Lord* [1963] 1 WLR 41, [1962] 3 All ER 907, CA). Obviously the more a landlord has organized before the hearing, the better will be his or her chances of success.

The landlord's intention must be established at the time of the hearing (*Betty's Cafes Ltd v* **26.159** *Phillips Furnishing Stores Ltd* [1959] AC 20, [1958] 1 All ER 607). 'The hearing' for these purposes is the substantive trial of the landlord's ground of opposition not, for example, the hearing of a tenant's application for summary judgment (*Somerfield Stores Ltd v Spring (Sutton Coldfield) Ltd* [2010] EWHC 2084 (Ch)). If the landlord's notice was served by a predecessor in title, the subsequent landlord can rely upon that notice; the fact that the original landlord had no intention to reconstruct or demolish the premises when the notice was served does not matter (*Marks v British Waterways Board* [1963] 1 WLR 1008, [1963] 3 All ER 28, CA). As long as the landlord can establish his or her intention to demolish or reconstruct at the date of the hearing, it is irrelevant that the landlord may have some ulterior purpose for wanting possession, for example if, after reconstructing the premises, the landlord intends to occupy them himself or herself (*Fisher v Taylors Furnishing Stores* [1956] 2 QB 78, [1956] 2 All ER 78); or if, having demolished the premises, the landlord intends to incorporate them into an agricultural holding (*Craddock v Hampshire County Council* [1958] 1 All ER 449).

It should be noted that s 31(2) applies to this ground too. If the landlord can satisfy the **26.160** court that ground (f) would be satisfied at a future date (this must be a date within one year of the date of termination specified in the landlord's s 25 notice or the tenant's request for a new tenancy) then the landlord has a second chance to succeed under this ground (see 26.171).

Demolition, reconstruction, or substantial reconstruction As well as establishing that he **26.161** or she has the intention to carry out the proposed works to the holding, the landlord must also establish that these works fall within the definition provided by ground (f). This will be a question of fact and will depend upon the nature and extent of the proposed work. The work must involve a substantial interference with the structure of the building. In *Joel v Swaddle* [1957] 1 WLR 1094, an intention to convert a small shop with two storage rooms into part of a large amusement arcade was held to be within ground (f). On the other hand, where the intended work involved re-wiring, re-roofing, redecorating, installing a central heating system, and repositioning a staircase, this was not within the ground (*Barth v Pritchard* [1990] 1 EGLR 109). Likewise, an intention to convert three separate floors into one unit by putting in new staircases did not come within ground (f) (*Percy E Cadle & Co. Ltd v Jacmarch Properties Ltd* [1957] 1 QB 323).

Two, more recent, cases, *Marazzi v Global Grange Ltd* [2002] EWHC 3010 (Ch) and **26.162** *Ivorygrove Ltd v Global Grange Ltd* [2003] EWHC 1409 (Ch), illustrate that there may be a very fine line between works that will satisfy ground (f) and works that will not. In both cases major works were required to the properties. In *Marazzi* the court decided that whilst some of the works required demolition or reconstruction they did not fall within ground (f) as they did not affect a substantial part of the building. In *Ivorygrove* the court held that structural works to the floor, taken together with other substantial work to the property, brought the works within ground (f). The major difference between the two cases seems to be that the works in *Ivorygrove* went further in affecting the internal structure of the whole building. The cases do, however, demonstrate that it would be perfectly possible for two different courts to reach different decisions on similar facts without either decision being criticized on appeal.

26.163 **Work could not reasonably be done without obtaining possession** The landlord must establish that he or she needs to terminate the tenancy and gain legal, rather than just physical, possession of the holding in order to carry out the work. If the landlord is able to enter and perform the works under the terms of the lease (ie under a covenant that gives the landlord a right of entry to perform alterations and improvements), the landlord will not be able to succeed under this ground because there is no need to terminate the tenancy (see *Heath v Drown* [1973] AC 496, [1972] 2 All ER 561; *Leathwoods Ltd v Total Oil (GB) Ltd* (1984) 270 EG 1083).

26.164 Even where, under the terms of the current tenancy, the landlord is able to show that he or she requires possession of the holding, the landlord may still fail to succeed under ground (f). Section 31A of the Act, inserted by s 7(1) of the Law of Property Act 1969, provides that in two situations the court will order the tenant to be granted a new tenancy. The court will not hold that the landlord requires possession if:

(a) the tenant agrees to the inclusion in the terms of the new tenancy of terms giving the landlord access and other facilities for carrying out the work intended and, given that access and those facilities, the landlord could reasonably carry out the work without obtaining possession of the holding and without interfering to a substantial extent or for a substantial time with the use of the holding for the purposes of the business carried on by the tenant; or

(b) the tenant is willing to accept a tenancy of an economically separable part of the holding and either paragraph (a) of this section is satisfied with respect to that part or possession of the remainder of the holding would be reasonably sufficient to enable the landlord to carry out the intended work.

26.165 Thus, if a tenant is prepared to agree to a new tenancy of the holding on terms permitting the landlord to do the work, or to agree to give up part of the holding and take a tenancy of another part of the holding so that the landlord can perform work on the other part, the tenant will succeed in resisting possession under ground (f). All the same, the intended works must not involve interference with the tenant's use of the holding to a substantial extent or for a substantial time. This means interference with the actual use of the holding, not interference with the tenant's business. Thus, a tenant who is prepared to move temporarily to an alternative building while the works are carried out will not necessarily be saved by s 31A (even though the tenant's business may not be unduly affected) if the interference with the holding is to be substantial (see *Redfern v Reeves* (1979) 37 P&CR 364, CA; *Graysim Holdings Ltd v P&O Property Holdings Ltd* [1995] 3 WLR 854, HL).

Ground (g)—landlord intends to occupy the holding

(g) ... that on the termination of the current tenancy the landlord intends to occupy the holding for the purposes, or partly for the purposes, of a business to be carried on by him therein, or as his residence.

26.166 Section 30(2) provides that a landlord cannot rely upon ground (g) if the landlord's interest 'was purchased or created after the beginning of the period of five years which ends with the termination of the current tenancy'. In other words, the landlord must have owned the interest for five years. The aim of this provision is to prevent someone from buying the landlord's interest with the intention of terminating the tenancy and going into occupation himself or herself.

As with ground (f), the landlord will have to establish a real, fixed, and settled intention. It will be a question of fact. Where a landlord intended to change the use of the land in question from a street-cleaning depot to a marina, and the council indicated that planning permission for this change of use would be refused, this was regarded as a factor that should be taken into account by the court. Ironically, in this case, the council happened to be the tenant and the court held that the landlord had satisfied ground (g) because the council's ground for refusal of planning permission was invalid and a properly considered planning application would have had a reasonable chance of success (*Westminster City Council v Bristol Waterways Board* [1985] AC 676, [1984] 3 All ER 737, HL). The landlord must be able to show that, at the date of the hearing, he or she intends to occupy the premises for the purpose of conducting a business and that he or she has a reasonable prospect of doing this within a short or reasonable time after the termination of the tenancy (*Dolgellau Golf Club v Hett* [1998] EWCA Civ 621, [1998] L&TR 217, CA). The landlord must intend to occupy for more than the short term. What is short-term will depend on the facts of the case. In *Patel v Keles* [2009] EWCA Civ 1187, (2009) NPC 128, the landlord planned to sell the property in five years' time and intended to occupy it only until it was sold. It was held that this intended occupation was insufficient for the purposes of satisfying ground (g). **26.167**

The landlord does not need to show that he or she intends to occupy the premises personally; occupation through an agent or manager will be enough. In *Parkes v Westminster Roman Catholic Diocese Trustee* (1978) 36 P&CR 22 it was held that the trustees could occupy through the agency of a parish priest. Occupation through a management company is also sufficient (*Teeside Indoor Bowls Ltd v Stockton on Tees BC* (1990) 46 EG 116, CA). **26.168**

The effect of successful opposition

If the landlord successfully establishes any of the grounds in s 30(1) to the satisfaction of the court, the court cannot make an order for the grant of a new tenancy (s 31(1)). However, by the time the court has heard the matter, the termination date specified in the original s 25 notice or the tenant's request for a new tenancy may have long passed. The question therefore arises as to when the tenancy should actually come to an end. **26.169**

Section 64(1) provides that the tenancy will terminate three months after the date on which the application is finally disposed of. The application will be disposed of only once the court process is at an end. Because the tenant has a right to appeal within four weeks of the court's judgment, this means that the tenancy will continue until three months and four weeks after the court's judgment. **26.170**

Where ground can be satisfied at a future date

Where a landlord seeks to rely on ground (d), (e), or (f) (suitable alternative accommodation, uneconomic sub-tenancy, intention to demolish or reconstruct) but fails to establish the ground to the satisfaction of the court, s 31(2) offers a further chance of obtaining possession. Section 31(2) provides that: **26.171**

(2) ... if the court would have been satisfied of any of those grounds if the date of termination specified in the landlord's notice or, as the case may be, the date specified in the tenant's request for a new tenancy as the date from which the new tenancy is to begin, had been such later

date as the court may determine, being a date not more than one year later than the date so
specified—

   (a) the court shall make a declaration to that effect, stating on which of the said grounds the
        court would have been satisfied as aforesaid and specifying the date determined by the
        court as aforesaid, but shall not make an order for the grant of a new tenancy;

   (b) if, within fourteen days after the making of the declaration, the tenant so requires the court
        shall make an order substituting the said date for the date specified in the said landlord's notice
        or tenant's request, and thereupon that notice or request shall have effect accordingly.

26.172 **Example** Peter serves a s 25 notice upon Jane, specifying the termination date as 1 November
2012. Jane informs Peter that she is not willing to give up possession and applies for a new
tenancy. Peter opposes Jane's application on ground (d). However, the alternative premises
Peter has in mind are currently occupied and will not become vacant until 1 June 2013. At
the hearing Peter is unable to establish that the alternative accommodation will be available
at 1 November 2012 and therefore fails under ground (d). He is, however, able to satisfy the
court that the alternative accommodation will be available on 1 June 2013. The court therefore makes a declaration that ground (d) would be satisfied had the date of termination been
given as 1 June 2013 and does not make an order for the grant of a new tenancy. Within 14
days of the declaration Jane can then obtain an order from the court giving the date of termination as 1 June 2013, and the tenancy will terminate on this date. If she does not apply, the
tenancy will come to an end three months and four weeks after the court's judgment.

The tenant's right to compensation

26.173 Where a landlord opposes the tenant's application for the grant of a new tenancy under
grounds (a), (b), or (c), the basis of the opposition is that the tenant has breached some
obligation in the lease. In the case of ground (d) there is no loss to the tenant because suitable alternative accommodation is provided in exchange for the original tenancy. Grounds
(e), (f), and (g), however, are based not on the default of the tenant but on the needs of the
landlord. Under these grounds the tenant may have to give up the tenancy through no fault
of his or her own. Section 37 of the 1954 Act (as amended by Regulatory Reform (Business
Tenancies) (England and Wales) Order 2003) therefore gives the tenant a right to compensation where the landlord has served notice opposing the grant of a new tenancy under any
of these three grounds. Section 37 will apply where:

   (a) the tenant has applied for a new tenancy under s 24(1) and the landlord has success-
        fully opposed the application under ground (e), (f), or (g) (s 37(1A)); or

   (b) the landlord has specified ground (e), (f), or (g) in his or her application for the ter-
        mination of a tenancy under s 29(2) and the court has been unable to grant a new
        tenancy by reason of any of these grounds (s 37(1B)); or

   (c) the landlord has specified ground (e), (f), or (g) in his or her s 25 or 26(6) notice and
        the tenant has either not applied for a new tenancy or has made an application but has
        subsequently withdrawn it (s 37(1C)).

26.174 The amount of compensation is calculated by multiplying the rateable value of the holding by
the appropriate multiplier. The rateable value for these purposes is the rateable value appearing
in the valuation list at the date when the landlord served the s 25 notice or the tenant served a
request for a new tenancy. The appropriate multiplier is fixed by the Secretary of State.

26.175 Longer-standing business tenancies attract a higher rate of compensation by virtue of
s 37(3). Where s 37(3) applies, compensation is calculated by multiplying twice the rateable value by the appropriate multiplier. Section 37(3) will apply if:

   (a) during the whole of the 14 years immediately preceding the termination of the cur-
        rent tenancy, premises being or comprised in the holding have been occupied for the
        purposes of a business carried on by the occupier or for those and other purposes;

(b)   during those 14 years there was a change in the occupier of the premises, and the person who was the occupier immediately after the change was the successor to the business carried on by the person who was the occupier immediately before the change.

If the conditions specified in s 37(3) apply only to one part of the holding the two parts are to be assessed separately and the compensation payable will be the aggregate of the two calculations (s 37(3A)).   **26.176**

A claim for compensation can be made at the end of the unsuccessful hearing for the grant of a new tenancy, or separately under the provisions of CPR Part 23.   **26.177**

Currently, the appropriate multiplier is one, as prescribed by the Landlord and Tenant Act 1954 (Appropriate Multiplier) Order 1990, SI 1990/363.   **26.178**

Compensation for misrepresentation

Section 37A provides that a tenant may claim compensation from the landlord if the tenant has not applied for a new tenancy, or has not been granted a new tenancy because the landlord has misrepresented facts to the tenant or the court, or has concealed material facts. Misrepresentation may include the landlord's failure to inform the tenant that there has been a change in circumstances. In *Inclusive Technology v Williamson* [2009] EWCA Civ 718, [2009] L&TR 4, the landlord informed the tenant in a letter accompanying its s 25 notice that it intended to redevelop the property. The landlord then changed its mind but did not inform the tenant. The tenant did not pursue an application to renew his lease and instead took a lease on another property. The court held that the original representation had been made false by the change in circumstances and awarded compensation to the tenant.   **26.179**

The damages will be calculated to compensate the tenant for any loss or damage sustained because of the refusal of the grant of a new tenancy. If the tenant has left the property as a result of the landlord's misrepresentation that tenant will be entitled to compensation for any loss or damage he or she has sustained as a result of having to leave the property. The damages awarded in *Inclusive Technology v Williamson*, 26.179, were based on the difference between the assumed market rent for the original premises and the rent for the new premises.   **26.180**

Interim continuation

Where a s 25 notice or request has been served and an application has been made to the court under s 24 or 29(2), the tenancy will automatically continue until a date three months after the application has been finally disposed of (s 64(1)). This final disposal may be the conclusion of the court proceedings (including any appeal); or it may come about by the withdrawal of the tenant's application. If the tenant has given notice to the court under s 29(5) that it does not want to renew, the tenancy will terminate three months from the date this notice was received by the court (*NM Pensions Ltd v Lloyds TSB Bank Plc* [2009] PLSCS 297).   **26.181**

Interim rent

Between the time the landlord makes a s 25 notice, or the tenant requests a new tenancy under s 26, and the granting of the new tenancy there may be a considerable delay. Negotiations can take a lot of time, and if they do not result in agreement there will probably be a delay until a trial date can be obtained. Even once the issue is finally resolved by the court it will be three months before the new tenancy starts (s 64). Throughout this   **26.182** time, as we saw earlier, the tenancy will be continued by virtue of s 24 on the terms of the original tenancy. Depending on the current level of market rents, the tenant may feel that the rent payable under the terms of the original tenancy is too high or the landlord may believe that it is too low.

Application for a determination of interim rent

26.183 During this period the tenant or the landlord may apply to the court for the determination of an interim rent. The provisions governing the application and the determination of the interim rent are contained in ss 24A to 24D of the 1954 Act (as amended by art 18 of the Regulatory Reform (Business Tenancies) (England and Wales) Order 2003). The application must be made within six months of the termination of the old tenancy (s 24A(3)). The procedure for the making of an application is set out in PD 56.40 to the Civil Procedure Rules.

The amount of the interim rent

26.184 Usually, if the landlord and tenant have agreed that a new tenancy will be granted, the amount of rent payable under that new tenancy will also be the interim rent (s 24C). If the landlord or tenant can show that the interim rent should be different (for example because the new tenancy will be on different terms than the interim tenancy), the court can order the tenant to pay such interim rent as it determines is reasonable (s 24C(6)).

26.185 Similarly, if the landlord and tenant have not agreed that a new tenancy will be granted the court will be asked to determine the rent which it would be reasonable for the tenant to pay whilst the tenancy continues under s 24 (s 24D).

26.186 In making the determination the court shall have regard to the rent payable under the terms of the tenancy, and the rent payable under any sub-tenancy of part of the property, but otherwise the court should determine the rent as it would under s 34(1) and (2) as if a new periodic yearly tenancy were to be granted of the whole premises (ie not just the holding).

26.187 The rent will be determined with regard to the current state of repair of the premises, even where the poor state of repair is due to the breach of a repairing obligation by one of the parties (*Fawke v Viscount Chelsea* [1980] QB 441, [1979] 3 All ER 568). The court may determine a differential interim rent, so that if the premises are out of repair due to the landlord's failure to repair the rent will increase when the repairs are carried out (*Fawke v Viscount Chelsea*).

26.188 The fact that the court is to have regard to the rent under the current tenancy means that where there is a considerable difference between the current rent and the open market rent that would be determined under s 34, the court can determine the interim rent at a level below the current market rent in order to 'cushion the blow' to the tenant. In *Charles Follet Ltd v Cabtell Investment Co. Ltd* (1986) 55 P&CR 36, CA, the judge assessed the market rent as being £80,000; the current rent was £13,500 and the interim rent was fixed at £40,000. A 50 per cent reduction should, however, be regarded as exceptional. A reduction of 10 per cent is likely to be closer to the norm (see *Janes (Gowns) Ltd v Harlow Development Corpn* (1979) 253 EG 799).

Date from which interim rent is payable

26.189 Where the landlord has given notice under s 25 the interim rent determined by the court will be payable from the earliest date that could have been specified in that notice (s 24B(2)). If the determination was made following the request for a new tenancy by the tenant under s 26 the interim rent will be payable from the earliest date that the tenant could have specified as the date the new tenancy was to begin (s 24B(3)).

I WHERE A NEW TENANCY IS GRANTED

The terms of the new tenancy

The court will determine the terms of the tenancy only where the parties are unable to **26.190** come to an agreement. This can happen where the landlord has opposed the tenant's application for a new tenancy but has failed to establish any of the grounds, and the court has ordered the grant of a new tenancy. In such a case the court is likely to adjourn to give the parties time to negotiate. If they fail to agree, the matter will have to come back before the court. It can also happen where the landlord does not oppose the grant of a new tenancy but the parties are unable to reach agreement as to the terms of the new tenancy. If the parties are able to agree some terms of the tenancy but not others, the court will resolve the un-agreed matters but will not interfere with the other terms.

The property

If the parties cannot agree what property should be included in the new tenancy, the court **26.191** will resolve the matter. Normally the new tenancy will be of the holding (see 26.50). If the parties are unable to agree what constitutes the holding then the court will designate the holding by reference to the circumstances existing at the date of the order (s 32(1)).

In two situations the tenancy will not be of the holding: **26.192**

(a) Where the landlord has opposed the grant of a new tenancy on ground (f) and by virtue of s 31A(1) the tenant has agreed to accept a tenancy of part of the holding, in which case the court will order the grant of a new tenancy of that part only.
(b) Where by virtue of s 32(2) the landlord requires the new tenancy to be a tenancy of the whole of the property comprised in the current tenancy.

Section 32(2) can be of considerable importance to a landlord where the tenant is not occu- **26.193** pying the whole of the premises, for example where the current tenancy is of a shop with a flat above it and the tenant has sub-let the flat. Under the 1954 Act the tenant only has a right to a new tenancy of the holding, namely the shop; but in such a situation the landlord may well have no interest in recovering possession of the flat on its own. In this case the landlord can require that all the property comprised in the current tenancy is included in the new tenancy. Returning to the example of Jim's tenancy of Western House at 26.51, if at the end of Jim's tenancy he applies for a new lease his landlord, City Property Ltd, can insist that Jim takes a new lease of the whole of the property, including the residential flats. If City Property Ltd does not insist that the flats are included in Jim's new lease the status of the tenants of the flats will not be affected. City Property Ltd will become their immediate landlord instead of Jim, and the tenants will continue to occupy under residential rather than business tenancies (*Wellcome Trust Ltd v Hamad* [1998] QB 638).

Section 32(3) further provides that where the current tenancy includes rights enjoyed **26.194** by the tenant in connection with the holding, those rights shall be included in the new tenancy unless the parties agree to the contrary. If the parties cannot agree, the court will determine which rights should be included. For example, in *Re No. 1 Albermarle Street WI* [1959] Ch 531, [1959] 1 All ER 250, the tenant had the right to display advertising signs on the outside of the premises under his current tenancy and this right was included in the new tenancy. Any rights that have been granted separately from the lease (for example a right to park that was granted under a separate agreement) will not be ordered to be included in the new tenancy (*Picture Warehouse Ltd v Cornhill Investments Ltd* [2008] EWHC 45, (QB), (2008) 12 EG 98). Similarly, an option to purchase the freehold that had been contained in the original lease but had expired would not be repeated in the new lease because the right was not in existence at the date of renewal (*Kirkwod v Johnson* (1979) P&CR 393).

The duration of the new tenancy

26.195   If the parties are unable to agree the length of the new tenancy, the court will determine its duration. The tenancy should be 'such a tenancy as may be determined by the court to be reasonable in all the circumstances'. The court therefore has a wide discretion. The new tenancy can be a periodic tenancy or for a fixed term, but if it is a fixed-term tenancy the term must not exceed 14 years (s 33). The duration of the old tenancy will be a factor in determining what the length of the new tenancy should be, as will be the nature of the property and the nature of the tenant's business (see *London and Provincial Millinery Stores Ltd v Barclays Bank Ltd* [1962] 2 All ER 163). The court may also take into account the relative hardship caused to both parties. Where a landlord has been able to establish a bona fide intention to redevelop the property but has failed to satisfy s 30(1)(f), the court may grant the tenant a relatively short term (*Reohorn v Barry Corpn* [1956] 1 WLR 845, [1956] 2 All ER 742, CA); or, if applicable, the court may order the inclusion of a break clause in the new tenancy (*McCombie v Grand Junction Co. Ltd* [1962] 1 WLR 581).

Rent

26.196   In the majority of cases the most difficult term to settle by agreement between the parties will be the rent to be payable under the new tenancy. Where the parties fail to reach agreement, s 34(1) of the 1954 Act provides that the rent payable:

> … may be determined by the court to be that at which, having regard to the terms of the tenancy (other than those relating to rent), the holding might reasonably be expected to be let in the open market by a willing lessor…

26.197   In assessing the open market rent of a property the court has a wide discretion. In practice, however, the evidence of expert witnesses such as surveyors or valuers will be most persuasive, as will evidence of suitable comparables in the area (see *English Exporters (London) Ltd v Eldonwall Ltd* [1973] Ch 415, *per* Megarry J at 423). Where there are no relevant comparables, the court may look more broadly at the general increases of rent in the area (*National Car Parks v Colebrook Estates Ltd* (1982) 266 EG 810).

26.198   The court must also have regard to the terms of the tenancy. If any terms of the tenancy have been altered, this may well have consequences for the amount of rent that should be payable. Thus, where the court has also to determine other terms of the tenancy, these other terms should be fixed first before the court considers the rent (*Cardshops Ltd v Davies* [1971] 1 WLR 591, [1971] 2 All ER 721, CA).

26.199   In assessing the rent the court must disregard certain factors (s 34(1)):

(a)   Any effect on rent of the fact that the tenant has or his predecessors in title have been in occupation of the holding. Thus, the fact that the tenant is already in occupation of the premises does not permit the landlord to charge a rent higher than the market value because the tenancy is of greater value to the current tenant than to a new tenant. Neither is the tenant able to claim that as a sitting tenant the rent payable should be below the market value.

(b)   Any goodwill attached to the holding by reason of the carrying on threat of the business of the tenant (whether by the tenant or by a predecessor of the tenant in that business). Thus, the fact that a tenant has built up goodwill in the current premises does not enable the landlord to charge a rent above the market value.

(c) Any effect on rent of an improvement. By s 34(2), the improvement must have been carried out by a person who was at that time the tenant and it must not have been carried out in pursuance of an obligation to the current landlord. The improvement must either have been carried out during the current tenancy, or:

(i) it was completed not more than 21 years before the application for the new tenancy was made; and

(ii) the holding or any part of it affected by the improvement has at all times since been comprised in tenancies to which Pt II of the 1954 Act applies; and

(iii) at the termination of each of those tenancies the tenant did not quit.

(d) In the case of a holding comprising licensed premises, any addition to its value attributable to the licence, if it appears to the court that having regard to the terms of the current tenancy and any other relevant circumstances the benefit of the licence belongs to the tenant.

By s 34(3), the court may, if it thinks fit, include a provision varying the rent. The court may therefore require a rent review clause to be included in the new tenancy.   **26.200**

Other terms

Where the parties cannot reach agreement as to the terms of the tenancy other than duration and rent then those other terms 'may be determined by the court; and in determining those terms the court shall have regard to the terms of the current tenancy and to all relevant circumstances' (s 35).   **26.201**

Where one party wishes to introduce terms different to those in the current tenancy, the burden is upon that party to establish reasons for the change; and furthermore the proposed change must be fair and reasonable in all the circumstance (*O'May v City of London Real Property Co. Ltd* [1983] 2 AC 726, [1982] 1 All ER 669, HL). In the *O'May* case the landlords wanted to introduce a term into the tenancy requiring the tenant to pay a service charge, the result of which would be to shift the cost of repair and maintenance of the building on to the tenants. In return the landlords offered a small reduction in rent. The court held that such a change in the terms was unjustified, for it would require the tenants to accept risks that were unpredictable and significantly different from their obligations under the current tenancy. Likewise, where the tenant dealt in both new and second-hand clothes and the landlord sought to introduce a user clause prohibiting the sale of second-hand clothes the court did not permit the introduction of the new clause (*Gold v Brighton Corpn* [1956] 1 WLR 1291, [1956] 3 All ER 422). Where the original tenancy contained a break clause the court permitted the landlord to include a break clause in the new tenancy (*Leslie & Godwin Investments Ltd v Prudential Assurance Co. Ltd* [1987] 2 EGLR 95). However, where the original tenancy contained an option to purchase, a similar option was not included in the new tenancy (*Kirkwood v Johnson* (1979) 38 P&CR 392). The option in the original tenancy could be exercised by the tenant serving notice at least three months before the end of the term; when the tenant applied to the court for a new tenancy he no longer had the right to exercise the option. The effects on the tenants' continuing obligations of the Landlord and Tenant (Covenants) Act 1995 (see 9.03) can be taken into account when negotiating the new terms as the landlord may wish to introduce stricter controls on assignment. It is also possible for the new tenancy to include a term that a guarantor is required, even if this was not the case for the previous tenancy (*Cairnplace v CBL (Property Investment) Co.* [1984] 1 WLR 696, CA).   **26.202**

Carrying out of the order for a new tenancy

26.203 Where the court makes an order for a new tenancy, the landlord is bound to execute the new tenancy embodying the terms as agreed between the parties or as determined by the court, and the tenant is bound to accept it (s 36(1)). There are two exceptions to this rule. First, the landlord and tenant are free to agree not to act upon the order. Secondly, the tenant may apply to the court within 14 days of the making of the order for the order to be revoked (s 36(2)). This gives the tenant a last chance to back out of the tenancy if he or she decides that the terms are unacceptable. If the tenant applies to revoke the order under s 36(2), the current tenancy will come to an end at a date agreed or determined by the court so as to give the landlord a reasonable opportunity for re-letting or otherwise disposing of the premises.

Further information

26.204 Useful guidance on the procedures for extending and renewing business tenancies is contained in the government publication *Business tenancies: new procedures under the Landlord and Tenant Act 1954* (Office of the Deputy Prime Minister) April 2004. The appendices to the guidance include draft agreements to exclude security of tenure, draft s 40 and s 25 notices, and draft surrender agreements. The guidance and the appendices are available free online from <http://www.communities.gov.uk>.

J COMPENSATION FOR IMPROVEMENTS UNDER THE 1927 ACT

26.205 Part I of the Landlord and Tenant Act 1927 (as modified by Pt III of the Landlord and Tenant Act 1954) contains provisions giving the tenant the right to claim compensation for certain improvements made to the premises when he or she quits the premises. This right is not extensive; it is limited only to authorized improvements: and even if the improvements do fall within the Act, the amount of compensation payable is calculated in a way that is usually favourable to landlords. Furthermore, it is generally easy for a landlord to avoid the consequences of the 1927 Act by including an express covenant in the lease requiring the tenant to reinstate the premises at the end of the term.

Eligibility

Is the holding within the Act?

26.206 The provisions of the 1927 Act apply only to holdings where the premises are held under a lease and are used wholly or partly for carrying out upon them any trade or business (s 17(1)). 'Lease' here includes any under-lease (s 25). It should be noted that, in contrast to the 1954 Act, the carrying out of a profession on the premises does not automatically bring the holding within the protection of the 1927 Act. However, any profession regularly carried on on the premises is included as a 'trade or business' so far as Pt I of the 1927 Act relates to improvements (s 17(3)). Another difference between the 1927 and 1954 Acts is that under the 1927 Act, 'trade or business' does not include the business of sub-letting premises as residential flats (s 17(3)(b)).

26.207 The following premises are excluded from the 1927 Act:

(a) premises let under a mining lease (s 17(1));

(b) agricultural holdings (s 17(1));

(c) service tenancies (if the service tenancy was created after 24 March 1927, it will be excluded only if the contract is in writing and sets out the purpose for which it was created) (s 17(2));

(d) premises used to carry on a profession, where the profession is not regularly carried on on the premises (s 17(3)(a));

(e) premises which are used for the business of sub-letting as residential flats (s 17(3)(b)).

Where the premises are used partly for business purposes, and partly for other purposes, **26.208** compensation for improvements is available only for improvements made in relation to the business purposes (s 17(4)).

Is the improvement within the Act?

By s 1 of the 1927 Act, the tenant of a holding to which the 1927 Act applies may claim **26.209** compensation from his or her landlord upon quitting the holding at the end of the tenancy for any improvement on the holding made by the tenant or the tenant's predecessors in title. The improvement must add to the letting value of the holding at the end of the tenancy. Improvements do not include a trade or other fixture which the tenant is by law entitled to remove.

The following improvements do not attract a right to compensation: **26.210**

(a) improvements made before the commencement of the 1927 Act (25 March 1928) (s 2(1)(a));

(b) improvements which were begun before 1 October 1954 (when the 1954 Act came into force) and were made in pursuance of a statutory obligation;

(c) improvements which the tenant or his or her predecessors in title were under an obligation to make in pursuance of a contract entered into for valuable consideration (s 2(1)(b)).

Procedure

The greatest restriction upon the right to claim compensation is the fact that, in order for **26.211** the improvement to qualify, the tenant must have observed the correct procedure at the time at which the improvement was made. The right to compensation does not arise automatically simply because the tenant has carried out the improvement. The improvement must be an authorized improvement; if the preconditions have not been fulfilled the tenant will not be able to claim compensation at the end of the tenancy.

If a tenant wishes to make an improvement, his or her first step is to serve a notice of **26.212** intention upon the landlord. This notice should include a specification and a plan showing the proposed improvement and the part of the existing premises affected. Once a notice of intention has been served the landlord has three months in which to serve a notice of objection. If the landlord does not serve a notice of objection within this time the tenant can go ahead and carry out the improvement. The improvement will be authorized and will attract compensation at the end of the tenancy. It is possible, where a lease requires the tenant to obtain the landlord's consent to an improvement, that the obtaining of consent from the landlord within the terms of the lease will amount to compliance with the statutory procedure.

If the landlord does serve a notice of objection, the tenant must apply to court for a cer- **26.213** tificate authorizing the improvement as a 'proper improvement'. The carrying out of an improvement upon a property will, in the long term, affect not only the tenant's immediate landlord, but also, where there is a chain of landlords, any other person with a superior interest in the property. All superior landlords should therefore be notified and are entitled to be heard. Note that this is different from the procedure under the 1954 Act where notice has to be served on the competent landlord (see 26.79 and 26.92).

26.214 Where there is a chain of landlords it will be the tenant's immediate landlord who has to pay compensation at the end of the tenant's tenancy, for it is the immediate landlord who will then benefit from the improvement. However, when that landlord's term comes to an end he or she will then be entitled to receive compensation from the next landlord up in the chain for the improvements carried out by the original tenant (s 8).

Procedure

26.215 The application should be made in the county court using CPR Part 8 procedure. The new provisions contained in CPR Part 56 and PD 56, para 5.2, set out the rules for the contents and form of the application. As with an application for a new tenancy, any application for compensation under the 1927 Act should not be commenced without reference to Part 56 and its accompanying Practice Direction.

26.216 Where an application is made to the court, the court must give a certificate if it is satisfied that:

(a) the improvement is of such a nature as to be calculated to add to the letting value of the holding at the end of the tenancy;
(b) the improvement is reasonable and suitable to the character of the holding;
(c) the improvement will not diminish the value of any other property belonging to the landlord or to any superior landlord.

26.217 The court may also make any modifications to the proposed plans and specifications that it thinks fit and may impose any conditions it thinks reasonable. In carrying out the improvements the tenant must comply with any requirements imposed by the court including any timetable set out for completion of the works: if the tenant does not comply he or she will not be able to claim compensation.

26.218 The landlord can prevent a certificate being granted to the tenant if he or she offers to carry out the improvements himself or herself in consideration of a reasonable increase in the rent. No certificate will be granted unless the landlord fails to carry out the proposed undertaking.

When the claim should be made

26.219 The timing of the claim depends upon the way in which the tenancy comes to an end:

(a) If the tenancy is terminated by a notice to quit or by a s 25 notice, the claim must be made within three months of the service of the notice.
(b) If the tenancy is terminated by a tenant's request for a new tenancy under s 26, the claim must be made within three months of the service of the landlord's counter-notice or, if no counter-notice is served, within three months of the last date upon which such a notice could have been served (ie two months after the service of the tenant's request).
(c) If the tenancy ends by effluxion of time, the claim must be made between three and six months before the term date.
(d) If the tenancy ends by forfeiture or by re-entry, the claim must be made within three months of the date of the possession order, or, if there is no order, within three months of the date of actual re-entry.

26.220 It should be noted that the right to compensation arises only when the tenant quits the holding when the tenancy is terminated. The security of tenure offered by s 24 of the 1954 Act has therefore reduced the significance of the 1927 Act, because the tenancy will automatically be continued and the tenant will be entitled to remain in occupation. All the same, even if the tenant wishes to apply for a new tenancy, it is still sensible to make a claim under the 1927 Act if the right to do so has arisen: first, because the landlord may success-fully object to the granting of a new tenancy by establishing one of the grounds contained in s 30(1) of the 1954 Act; and, secondly, because even if a new tenancy is granted the tenant will then be able to have the increased value of the property disregarded when the rent is determined for the new tenancy under s 34 of the 1954 Act. Again, the contents of the claim form should follow the provisions set out in CPR PD 56, para 5.2.

The amount of compensation

If the amount of compensation cannot be agreed between the parties it will be determined **26.221** by the court. Section 1(1) of the 1927 Act provides that the amount of compensation shall not exceed:

(a) the net addition to the value of the holding as a whole which may be determined to be the direct result of the improvement; or

(b) the reasonable cost of carrying out the improvement at the termination of the tenancy, subject to a deduction of an amount equal to the cost (if any) of putting the works constituting the improvement into a reasonable state of repair, except so far as such cost is covered by the liability of the tenant under any covenant or agreement as to the repair of the premises.

Section 1(2) provides that in determining the amount under item (a), regard shall be had to **26.222** the purposes for which it is intended that the premises shall be used after the termination of the tenancy. If it is shown that it is intended to demolish, or to make structural alterations to or to change the user of the premises, regard shall be had to the effect of these acts on the additional value attributable to the improvement, and to the length of time likely to elapse between the end of the tenancy and the demolition, alteration, or change of use.

Section 2(3) further provides that compensation should be reduced to take into considera- **26.223** tion any benefits which the tenant or his or her predecessors in title may have received from the landlord or his or her predecessors in title in consideration, expressly or impliedly, of the improvement.

The result of these provisions will often be to reduce the amount of compensation pay- **26.224** able significantly. If the landlord intends to demolish the premises, it may mean that no compensation is payable at all. However, if the landlord does not carry out the proposals within the time specified, the tenant may apply again to the court to vary the amount of compensation determined.

The form of the claim

The claim must be in writing, be signed by the tenant or his or her agent, specify the **26.225** holding and the business, and state the nature of the claim, the cost and particulars of the improvement, the date it was completed, and the amount claimed.

Avoiding the effect of the 1927 Act

Landlords can avoid the effect of the 1927 Act by: **26.226**

(a) putting in a covenant obliging the tenant to carry out any improvement to which the landlord agrees;

(b) putting in a covenant obliging the tenant to reinstate the premises at the end of the tenancy;

(c) deciding to demolish or change the use of the property at the end of the tenancy.

Since December 1953 it has not been possible for landlords and tenants to contract out of the provisions of Pt 1 of the 1927 Act.

K CODE FOR LEASING BUSINESS PREMISES

26.227 The Code for Leasing Business Premises in England and Wales 2007 has been developed as a result of collaboration between commercial property professionals and industry bodies representing both landlords and tenants. The stated aim of the Code is to promote fairness in landlord and tenant relationships. The Code provides guidance for both landlords and tenants entering into negotiations for a lease on the essential elements that should be considered. It also provides a model Heads of Terms for a commercial lease.

26.228 The Code is voluntary. Whilst commercial landlords are encouraged to be 'code compliant' neither party is obliged to use it. Failure to comply with the Code will not mean that a lease (or any term of a lease) is unenforceable. The Code does, however, provide extremely helpful guidance, particularly for the tenant, in suggesting clauses that are fair to both parties and explaining the implications of the commitments that the tenant will be making when entering into the lease. The Code is available free online from <http://www.leasingbusinesspremises.co.uk>.

L COMMERCIAL RENT ARREARS RECOVERY

26.229 When they come into force, ss 71 to 87 of the Tribunals, Courts and Enforcement Act 2007 will introduce a new regime called commercial rent arrears recovery (CRAR) to replace the old common law right of distress for rent. The regime will only apply to the recovery of rent arrears due under leases of commercial premises. CRAR will allow commercial landlords to employ an authorized enforcement agent to recover and sell the tenant's goods if the rent arrears exceed a prescribed amount. The Act will also allow a landlord to recover rent arrears from a sub-tenant of the defaulting tenant. At the date of writing CRAR procedure is still undergoing the process of government consultation but the system is expected to come into force in the near future. Until then the old common law rules for distress will apply (for a brief overview of these rules, see 6.35 to 6.38).

KEY DOCUMENTS

Landlord and Tenant Act 1927

Landlord and Tenant Act 1954

Landlord and Tenant Act 1954, Part 2 (Notices) Regulations 2004, SI 2004/1005

Regulatory Reform (Business Tenancies) (England and Wales) Order 2003, SI 2003/3096

Printed copies of all legislation can be ordered from The Stationery Office at <http://www.tsoshop.co.uk>. All legislation from 1988 onwards and most pre-1988 primary legislation is available online at <http://www.legislation.gov.uk>.

The Civil Procedure Rules are available online from <http://www.justice.gov.uk/courts/procedure-rules>.

A great deal of helpful advice and information about business tenancies can be found on the Communities and Local Government website: <http://www.communities.gov.uk>.

27

AGRICULTURAL HOLDINGS

A INTRODUCTION

Two statutory codes govern the commercial letting of agricultural land. The first of these, **27.01** the Agricultural Holdings Act 1986, is the subject of this chapter. The second code, the Agricultural Tenancies Act 1995, is dealt with in Chapter 28. The two codes are mutually exclusive and the crucial date to remember when determining which code applies is 1 September 1995. Tenancies granted before 1 September 1995 will fall under the Agricultural Holdings Act 1986. Tenancies granted on or after 1 September 1995 (subject to a few transitional exceptions) will fall under the Agricultural Tenancies Act 1995.

The two codes, while both dealing with the same subject matter, take very different **27.02** approaches. The 1986 Act is a lengthy statute, a consolidating Act that pulled together existing legislation and provides extensive security of tenure and, for tenancies granted before 12 July 1984, rights of succession. The 1995 Act, in comparison, is brief. Its aim is substantially to deregulate the letting of agricultural land and to permit the relationship between agricultural landlord and tenant to be governed by market forces and freedom of contract. Both Acts, however, contain similar provisions for dispute resolution. The majority of disputes between agricultural landlords and tenants are to be dealt with by the Agricultural Land Tribunal or, more frequently, referred to an arbitrator. The intervention of the courts will be rare.

27.03 Before looking at the provisions that govern the letting of agricultural land it is worth considering just what it is that makes agricultural land different. Farming, after all, is in many respects a business like any other business. However, unlike most other businesses its success or failure is dependent upon the treatment of the land itself. A working farm cannot spring up overnight like a light industrial unit or a shop. For land to function properly as agricultural land it will take many years of tending and nurturing. Farming is also dependent upon the yearly cycle of the seasons. Any system of letting that did not permit this yearly cycle to function would find few takers among agricultural tenants. After all, who would wish to invest time and money planting and tending a crop only to have the landlord take possession of the land before the crop could be harvested? For this reason, as we shall see, it is the tenancy from year to year (a yearly periodic tenancy) that is the paradigm of an agricultural tenancy.

27.04 Despite the fact that since 1 September 1995 very few tenancies of agricultural holdings will be granted, the 1986 Act and its complex provisions will remain significant for quite some time to come. Many tenancies granted before that date will have acquired security of tenure under the Act and will continue in existence. Furthermore, though the succession rights introduced by the Agriculture (Miscellaneous Provisions) Act 1976 were abolished in 1984, they provided for two successions and so a significant number of older tenancies of agricultural holdings will continue long beyond the lifetime of the original tenant.

B WHAT IS AN AGRICULTURAL HOLDING?

27.05 The statutory definition of an agricultural holding for the purpose of the 1986 Act is a rather complex, cumulative definition which relies on the interrelation of a number of different terms, each of which will be considered in what follows. However, the first question to ask is when tenancy started. If the tenancy began on or after 1 September 1995 it will not be an agricultural holding (unless it belongs to one of the exceptional cases set out in the Agricultural Tenancies Act 1995, s 4, see 28.03). A tenancy starting after 1 September 1995 may be a farm business tenancy (see Chapter 28).

Agricultural holding

27.06 Section 1(1) provides the core of the definition of an agricultural holding. It states that an 'agricultural holding' is the aggregate of the land (whether or not agricultural land) comprised in a contract of tenancy which is *a contract for an agricultural tenancy*. This land must not be land let to the tenant during his or her continuance in any office, appointment, or employment held under the landlord.

A contract for an agricultural tenancy

27.07 A 'contract for an agricultural tenancy' is defined by s 1(2) as a contract of tenancy where the whole of the land comprised in the contract, subject to such exceptions only as do not substantially affect the character of the tenancy, is let for use as *agricultural land*, having regard to:

(a) the terms of the tenancy;
(b) the actual or contemplated use of the land at the time of the conclusion of the contract and subsequently; and
(c) any other relevant circumstances.

A contract of tenancy, as we shall see at 27.18, is strictly defined by s 1(5). **27.08**

Agricultural land

'Agricultural land' is defined by s 1(4)(a) as land used for *agriculture* which is so used **27.09** for the purposes of a trade or business. (It can also be land that has been designated as agricultural land by the Minister of Agriculture, Fisheries and Food under s 109(1) of the Agriculture Act 1947.)

Agriculture

Section 96(1) defines 'agriculture' to include horticulture, fruit growing, seed grow- **27.10** ing, dairy farming, and livestock breeding and keeping, the use of land as grazing land, meadow land, osier land, market gardens, and nursery grounds, and the use of land for woodlands where that use is ancillary to the farming of land for other agricultural purposes.

Thus, the initial question to determine is whether the land is 'agricultural land' in that it **27.11** is land used for agriculture which is used for the purposes of a trade or business, then to determine whether the tenancy in question is an 'agricultural tenancy' within the meaning of s 1(2) by looking at the terms of the tenancy, the actual or contemplated use of the land at the time of the contract and subsequently, and any other relevant circumstances and deciding whether the whole of the land comprised in the contract (subject to minor exceptions) is let for use as agricultural land. If this is the case, the land will be an agricultural holding provided it is not let to the tenant during his or her continuance in any office, appointment, or employment held under the landlord.

These requirements do not mean that an 'agricultural holding' must be wholly and **27.12** entirely made up of agricultural land, for s 1(a) defines an 'agricultural holding' as the aggregate of the land (whether or not agricultural) comprised in the agricultural tenancy. Section 96(5) defines the use of land for agriculture, in relation to land forming part of an agricultural unit, and includes any use of the land in connection with the farming of the units.

Thus, an agricultural holding can include some land that is not agricultural (eg a residen- **27.13** tial farmhouse) provided that agriculture is the main purpose of the tenancy. How this is determined in practice will always be a question of degree to be decided on the particular facts of the case. In *Howkins v Jardine* [1951] 1 All ER 320 a lease of seven acres of farmland that included three cottages that were sub-let to non-employees was held to be an agricultural holding. Similarly, in *Dunn v Fidoe* [1950] 2 All ER 685, CA where 12 acres of land used for crops and grazing was let together with a pub it was held to be an agricultural holding. A garden centre may be an agricultural holding but an important factor will be whether the plants sold in the centre are grown on the premises (*Short v Greeves* [1988] 1 EGLR 1, CA).

Changes in use

27.14 If land was not originally let as agricultural land but the tenant subsequently puts the land to agricultural use, the land may become an agricultural holding. However, the subsequent use will not make the land an agricultural holding if the change of use breached the terms of the tenancy unless the change of use was effected with the landlord's permission, consent, or acquiescence (s 1(3)).

27.15 If the use of the land changes away from agriculture, the protection of the Act may be lost if agricultural activity is completely or substantially abandoned. Whether this is the case will be a question of fact and degree, but a landlord will need strong evidence to support a claim of abandonment. The time at which the use of the land should be considered will be the time at which the tenant seeks the protection of the Act (*Weatherall v Smith* [1980] 1 WLR 1290, [1980] 2 All ER 530).

27.16 If the use of land is changed from agricultural use to residential use, the tenancy will not acquire protection under the Rent Act 1977 or the Housing Act 1988 because both codes require the property to be let as a dwelling. The agricultural and the residential codes of protection are mutually exclusive (Rent Act 1977, s 10 (13.66); Housing Act 1988, Sch 1, paras 6 and 7 (15.30 to 15.33)).

The nature of the tenancy

27.17 We saw in the introduction how farming is dependent on the cycle of the seasons. Traditionally, agricultural tenancies have usually been granted on a yearly basis. What amounts to a 'contract of tenancy' for the purposes of the 1986 Act is therefore defined by s 1(5) to fit in with the yearly nature of agricultural lettings.

27.18 A 'contract for a tenancy' means a letting of land, or an agreement for letting land, *for a term of years or from year to year*. This is a restrictive definition which would, were it not qualified, make it very easy for landlords to evade the 1986 Act. Only yearly periodic tenancies and fixed-term tenancies for a term of two or more years would fall within the Act; weekly, monthly, quarterly, and six-month periodic tenancies, licences, and fixed-term tenancies for a term of less than two years would all be excluded. Section 2 of the Act, however, brings shorter tenancies and licences within the protection of the Act.

A tenancy for less than a year

27.19 By virtue of s 2(2)(a) an agreement under which any land is let to a person for use as agricultural land for an interest less than a tenancy from year to year will take effect (with the necessary modifications) as if it were an agreement for the letting of land for a tenancy from year to year, provided the circumstances are such that if the interest were a tenancy from year to year the tenant would fall within the protection of the Act. Thus, s 2 effectively converts tenancies for a period of less than a year to yearly tenancies.

Licences

27.20 Section 2(2)(b) provides that if a person is granted a licence to occupy land for use as agricultural land the licence will also be converted into a yearly tenancy. This, however, will only apply where the licence grants exclusive possession on the occupier (*Bahamas International Trust Co. Ltd v Threadgold* [1974] 1 WLR 1514, HL; *McCarthy v Bence* [1990] 1 EGLR 1). This provision was originally introduced by the Agricultural Holdings Act 1948 and is of considerably reduced significance today since, following the rule in *Street v Mountford*, a licence which grants exclusive possession will usually create a tenancy (see 2.10 to 2.12).

Grazing or mowing agreements

Section 2(3)(a) excludes from the operation of s 2 an agreement for the letting of land, or **27.21** the granting of a licence to occupy land, which is made in contemplation of the use of the land only for grazing or mowing (or both) during some specified period of the year.

A tenancy of two years or more

By virtue of s 3 special provisions apply to fixed-term tenancies for a term of two years or **27.22** more. Such tenancies will not expire at the end of the term but will automatically continue as yearly tenancies on the terms of the original tenancy (so far as applicable). In order to prevent this automatic continuation either the landlord or the tenant must give written notice to the other party of an intention to terminate the tenancy not less than one year nor more than two years before the term date. If the tenant dies within one year of the term date and no notice has been given, the tenancy will only be continued for one year beyond the term date (s 4). (This applies only to tenancies granted after 12 September 1984; before that date more extensive rights of succession apply, see 27.78.)

Fixed-term tenancies of between one and two years

Tenancies of an interest of less than from year to year, which will include a fixed term of **27.23** less than a year, will be converted to yearly tenancies by s 2 (see 27.19). Fixed-term tenancies for a term of more than two years will fall within the definition of a term of years for a contract of tenancy for the purposes of s 1 (see 27.18). This leaves fixed-term tenancies with a term of more than one year but less than two years. These tenancies will not acquire security of tenure under the Act. It is therefore relatively easy for a landlord to evade the protection of the Act by granting a tenancy for a period of, say, 23 months (*Gladstone v Bower* [1960] 2 QB 384, CA; *EWP Ltd v Moore* [1992] 2 EGLR 4, CA).

C THE TERMS OF THE TENANCY

Right to written tenancy agreement

There is no requirement under the 1987 Act that a tenancy of an agricultural holding **27.24** should be in writing. The tenancy may be created by an oral agreement or, if there is a written tenancy agreement, its terms may not cover all the relevant matters. Schedule 1 to the Act sets out a list of the matters for which provision should be made in a written tenancy agreement. If the tenancy is oral, or if it does not make provision for the matters set out in Sch 1, the tenant or the landlord may request the other party to enter into an agreement embodying the proper terms. If agreement cannot be reached, both parties have the right to refer the terms of the tenancy to arbitration (s 6).

The model clauses—liability for maintenance, repair, and insurance of fixed equipment

By virtue of s 7 of the Act the Minister may by regulations make provisions prescribing **27.25** terms as to the maintenance, repair, and insurance of fixed equipment. These terms (the model clauses) will be implied into every contract of tenancy except in so far as they would impose on one of the parties to a written agreement a liability which under the agreement is imposed on the other (s 7(3)). 'Fixed equipment' includes buildings and structures affixed to the land and works on, in, over, or under the land (eg ditches, drainage, and roads). It can also include things grown on the land which are not used or consumed after they have been severed from the land (eg hedges) (s 96(1)). The current regulations are contained in the Agricultural (Maintenance, Repair and Insurance of Fixed Equipment) Regulations

1973, SI 1973/1473, as amended by the Agriculture (Maintenance, Repair and Insurance of Fixed Equipment) (Amendment) Regulations 1988, SI 1988/281.

27.26   If the written agreement effects substantial modifications in the operation of the Regulations, the landlord or the tenant may request the other party to vary the terms of the tenancy to bring them into conformity with the model clauses. If agreement cannot be reached, the relevant terms of the tenancy may be referred to arbitration (s 8(2)). The arbitrator should consider whether (disregarding the rent payable for the holding) the terms referred to arbitration are justifiable in the circumstances. If they are not justifiable, the arbitrator may vary them in such a manner as appears reasonable and just between the landlord and tenant (s 8(3)) and may also vary the rent accordingly to reflect the changes in the terms (s 8(4)).

27.27   Where the effect of any of the provisions dealing with written agreements and model clauses (ss 6, 7, and 8) is to transfer the liability for the maintenance or repair of any item of fixed equipment from the landlord to the tenant or vice versa, either party may claim compensation in accordance with the provisions of s 9.

Landlord's obligations

27.28   In brief, the landlord is liable to:

(a)   repair and maintain the structure and exterior of the farmhouse, cottages, and farm buildings. In the case of certain items (eg floorboards, internal staircases, doors, and windows) the landlord is entitled to recover one half of the reasonable cost from the tenant (Sch 1, para 1(1));

(b)   repair and replace underground pipes, wells, sewage disposal systems etc (Sch1, para (1(2)));

(c)   replace worn out fixtures and fittings which it is the tenant's responsibility to repair under para 5 (Sch 1, para (1(3)));

(d)   keep the farmhouse, cottages, and farm buildings insured (Sch 1, para 2);

(e)   carry out external decoration required to prevent deterioration of the farmhouse, cottages, and farm buildings at least every five years. In the case of certain items (eg doors, windows, guttering, and downpipes) the landlord is entitled to recover one half of the cost from the tenant (Sch 1, para 3).

27.29   If the landlord fails to execute repairs or replacements for which he or she is liable within three months of receiving a written notice from the tenant specifying the repairs or replacements and requiring the landlord to execute them, the tenant may carry out the repairs or replacements and recover the cost from the landlord forthwith (Sch 1, para 12(1) and (3)). In the case of underground water pipes the landlord has only one week in which to carry out the repair (Sch 1, para 12(2)). In the case of replacements, the tenant's right to recover costs from the landlord is limited to £2,000 or the rent of the holding for that year, whichever is the smaller (Sch 1, para 12(3)).

27.30   If the landlord wishes to contest his liability to execute any repairs or replacements specified in the tenant's notice, he should serve a counter-notice on the tenant within one month of receiving the tenant's notice. The counter-notice should specify the grounds on which and the items of repair or replacement in respect of which the landlord denies liability and require the question of liability to be settled by arbitration (Sch 1, para 12(5)(a)). Once counter-notice has been served the tenant's right to recover the reasonable cost of repairs specified in the counter-notice will not arise until the question of liability is determined by arbitration in favour of the tenant (Sch 1, para 12(5)(c)).

Tenant's obligations

In brief, the tenant is liable to: **27.31**

(a) repair and keep and leave clean and in good tenantable repair the farmhouse, cottages, and farm buildings (Sch 1, para 5(1));

(b) repair and keep and leave clean and in good tenantable repair all fixtures and fittings, boilers, drains, sewers, fences, hedges, field walls, gates, ditches, roads etc (the list is extensive and there are special requirements with regard to certain items such as sewage disposal systems, guttering, hedges, and watercourses) (Sch 1, para 5(1));

(c) use carefully so as to protect from wilful, reckless, or negligent damage items which the landlord is responsible to repair or replace and to report any damage to such items to the landlord immediately (Sch 1, para 5(4));

(d) carry out the internal decoration of the farmhouse, cottages, and farm buildings at least every seven years (Sch 1, para 7);

(e) renew or replace broken, cracked, or slipped tiles or slates up to an annual cost of £100 (Sch 1, para 8).

If the tenant fails to execute repairs or replacements for which he or she is liable, the **27.32** landlord may serve written notice on the tenant specifying the repairs or replacements and requiring the tenant to execute them. If the tenant fails to start work on the repairs or replacements within two months, or fails to complete them within three months of receiving the notice, the landlord may enter and execute the repairs or replacements and recover the reasonable cost from the tenant forthwith (Sch 1, para 4(2)). The tenant may contest liability by serving a counter-notice within one month of receiving the landlord's notice requiring the question of liability to be referred to arbitration (Sch 1, para 4(3)(a)). Once counter-notice is served the operation of the landlord's notice is suspended until arbitration determines the question of liability (Sch 1, para 4(3)(b)).

Tenant's right to remove fixtures and buildings

A fixture is an object (eg machinery, fencing, or a greenhouse) that has become attached **27.33** to the land. At common law, an object attached to the land becomes part of the land and therefore belongs to the landlord, in contrast to a chattel which remains the tenant's property. Whether or not an object is a fixture is a question of fact that should be determined by looking at the degree of annexation and the object of annexation to the land. An object so securely attached to the land that it cannot be removed without damaging the fabric of the land will be a fixture. Similarly, if the aim of attaching the object to the land was to improve the land, rather than for the purpose of using or enjoying the object, the object will be a fixture (see *Leigh v Taylor* [1902] AC 157; *Berkley v Poulett* [1977] 1 EGLR 86).

By virtue of s 10 of the Act a tenant has the right to remove fixtures or buildings from **27.34** the agricultural holding. Section 10 applies only to fixtures and buildings which the tenant has installed or erected and which therefore remain the tenant's property. It does not apply to buildings or fixtures erected or installed in pursuance of some obligation or to buildings in respect of which the tenant is entitled to compensation (see 27.101) (s 10(2)). The tenant must give notice of his or her intention and must have paid all rent owing and satisfied all other obligations under the lease (s 10(3)). The landlord may, by counter-notice, elect to purchase the fixture or building instead of permitting the tenant to remove it (s 10(4)).

Provision of fixed equipment necessary to comply with statutory requirements

27.35   Section 11 permits a tenant of an agricultural holding to apply to the agricultural land tribunal for a direction that the landlord should provide, alter, or repair fixed equipment to enable the tenant to comply with statutory requirements.

Permanent pasture

27.36   Where a tenancy agreement provides for specified land, or a specified proportion of the holding, to be maintained as permanent pasture, s 14 permits either the landlord or the tenant to apply to arbitration to vary the tenancy in order to reduce the area of permanent pasture in the interests of the full and efficient farming of the holding.

Disposal of cropping and produce

27.37   Section 15 gives the tenant, subject to certain restrictions, the right to dispose of the produce of the holding (other than manure) and to practise any system of cropping on the arable land on the holding. This right takes effect notwithstanding the tenancy agreement, any other agreement regarding the cropping or disposal of crops, or any custom of the county.

Record of the holding

27.38   Section 22 of the Act provides that at any time during the tenancy either the landlord or the tenant may require the making of a record of the condition of the holding and fixed equipment. This may be important if a tenant, when he or she quits the holding, wishes to claim compensation for adopting a special system of farming (see 27.109).

Good husbandry

27.39   There is no provision in the Act implying a term into the contract of tenancy requiring the tenant to farm the land in accordance with the rules of good husbandry or good estate management. Nevertheless, both concepts are referred to in several sections of the Act. In particular, a landlord may obtain a certificate of bad husbandry in order to terminate the tenancy (see 27.62). Section 96(3) therefore states that the Agriculture Act 1947, ss 10 and 11 apply for the purposes of the 1986 Act. These sections specify the circumstances in which the responsibilities to manage the land in accordance with the rules of good estate management or good husbandry will be fulfilled.

D RENT

27.40   At the beginning of an agricultural tenancy the parties are free to negotiate the rent that is payable for the holding. If the tenancy is a fixed-term tenancy, they may choose to include a contractual provision providing for rent review on specific dates or after specific periods. If a fixed-term tenancy provides no contractual mechanism for reviewing the rent, the rent will remain as fixed at the beginning of the tenancy throughout the course of the term unless the parties can agree between themselves voluntarily to vary the rent.

27.41   However, the Act provides for security of tenure that can last long beyond the expiry of the original fixed term and either the landlord or tenant may wish to vary the rent from that which was originally agreed. If a voluntary agreement cannot be reached, s 12 of and Sch 2 to the Act permit either party to the tenancy to refer the rent to arbitration. This statutory machinery is designed to bite only on yearly periodic tenancies; however, as we saw earlier, tenancies created for terms of less than a year will take effect as yearly periodic tenancies (27.19) and fixed-term tenancies for more than two years will be continued as yearly periodic tenancies on the expiry of the term (27.22).

To refer the rent to arbitration either the landlord or the tenant must serve notice in writing **27.42** on the other party (s 12(1)). This notice must demand that the rent payable in respect of the holding as from the next termination date shall be referred to arbitration. The 'termination date', for the purposes of s 12, means the next day following the date of the demand on which the tenancy of the holding could have been determined by notice to quit given at the date of the demand (s 12(4)). In general, this will mean that the notice must be served at least a year before the variation in rent is to take effect.

Frequency of arbitration

References to arbitration are only usually permitted every three years. A demand for arbi- **27.43** tration will not be effective if the next termination date following the date of the demand falls earlier than the end of three years from:

(a) the commencement of the tenancy; or
(b) the date from which there took effect a previous increase or reduction of rent (whether made under the provisions of s 12 or by agreement between the parties); or
(c) the date from which there took effect a previous direction of an arbitrator that the rent should stay unchanged (Sch 2, para 4).

The three-year period shall be disregarded where: **27.44**

(a) an arbitrator has varied the rent after the tenancy agreement has been referred to arbitration under s 6(3) (see 27.24) or s 8(4) (see 27.26);
(b) the rent has been increased under s 13(1) or (3) on account of the landlord's improvements (see 27.49);
(c) the rent has been reduced under s 33 on account of the landlord resuming possession of part of the land.

Once notice has been served on the other party the demand for arbitration remains effec- **27.45** tive until the next termination date unless either an arbitrator is appointed by agreement between the parties or an application is made to the president of the Royal Institution of Chartered Surveyors for the appointment of an arbitrator (s 12(3)).

Determining the rent

When the rent is referred to arbitration, the arbitrator determines what rent should be **27.46** properly payable in respect of the holding at the next termination date following the date of the demand for arbitration (s 12(2)). The complex provisions for determining the amount of rent are set out in Sch 2. The basic principle is that the rent should be the rent at which the holding might reasonably be expected to be let by a prudent and willing landlord to a prudent and willing tenant taking into account all relevant factors. These will include:

(a) the terms of the tenancy;
(b) the character, situation, and locality of the holding;
(c) the productive capacity and related earnings capacity of the holding;
(d) the current level of rents for comparable lettings (Sch 2, para 1(1)).

27.47 In considering the current level of rents for comparable lettings the arbitrator should disregard:

(a) any element of the rents that is attributable to scarcity value;

(b) any element of the rents that is due to the tenant having other land in the vicinity of the holding that might be occupied together with that holding;

(c) any effect on the rents which is due to any allowances or reductions made in consideration of the charging of premiums (Sch 2, para 1(3)).

27.48 The arbitrator must also disregard:

(a) tenant's improvements or fixed equipment other than those executed or provided under an obligation imposed by the terms of the tenancy (Sch 2, para 2(1)(a)). If the tenant held a previous tenancy of the holding, tenant's improvements carried out during that tenancy will also be disregarded except those for which the tenant received compensation at the end of the tenancy (Sch 2, para 2(3)). If the tenant has adopted a system of farming more beneficial to the holding than the system of farming required by the tenancy this should be treated as a tenant's improvement (Sch 2, para 2(4));

(b) landlord's improvements for which the landlord has received a grant from Parliament or local government funds (Sch 2, para 2(1)(b));

(c) any effect on the rent due to the fact that the tenant is in occupation of the holding (Sch 2, para 3(a));

(d) any dilapidation or deterioration of, or damage to, buildings or land caused or permitted by the tenant (Sch 2, para 3(b)).

Landlord's improvements

27.49 If a landlord carries out an improvement to the holding, he or she is entitled to increase the rent to reflect the increase in rental value attributable to the improvement regardless of the rule that there should be a three-year period between variations in the rent. The improvement must be one that is carried out:

(a) at the request of, or in agreement with, the tenant; or

(b) in compliance with a direction given by the tribunal under s 11 (ie where the tenant has applied to the agricultural land tribunal for the provision of fixed equipment in order to comply with statutory requirements and the tribunal has directed the landlord to provide that equipment, see 27.35);

(c) in pursuance of a notice served by the landlord under s 67(5) (ie where a tenant has sought consent for an improvement from the tribunal and the landlord has elected to carry out that improvement himself, see 27.104);

(d) in compliance with a direction from the Minister or in order to comply with other statutory requirements (s 13(2)).

27.50 The landlord must serve notice in writing on the tenant within six months of completing the improvement (s 13(1)). If the landlord and tenant cannot agree the new rent, the dispute can be referred to arbitration (s 13(7)).

E SECURITY OF TENURE

27.51 As we shall see, the Agricultural Tenancies Act 1986 provides security of tenure for the tenant by providing a statutory framework which severely restricts the operation of a landlord's notice to quit once it has been served. First, however, there are strict rules as to when a notice to quit can be served at all.

Service of notice to quit

Agriculture is a long-term endeavour that operates on a yearly cycle and, as we saw earlier, **27.52** most tenancies under the Act will be converted to yearly tenancies (27.19). Under the common law a yearly tenancy would require only six months' notice to quit.

Section 25 of the Act therefore modifies the length of a notice to quit to accord with the **27.53** yearly regime. A notice to quit an agricultural holding or part of an agricultural holding shall (notwithstanding any provision to the contrary in the contract of tenancy of the holding) be invalid if it purports to terminate the tenancy before the expiry of 12 months from the end of the then current year of tenancy (s 25(1)). This provision applies not just to landlords who are seeking to terminate a tenant's tenancy; the same notice periods must be observed by a tenant who wishes to quit.

This 12-month notice period does not apply: **27.54**

(a) where the tenant is insolvent (s 25(2)(a));
(b) where notice is given in pursuance of a provision in the tenancy authorizing the resumption of possession of the holding or some part of it for some specified purpose other than agriculture (s 25(2)(b));
(c) where notice is given by a tenant to a sub-tenant (s 25(2)(c));
(d) where the rent has been referred to arbitration under s 12 and the arbitrator has increased the rent (see 27.41), in which case the tenant can give six months' notice (s 25(3));
(e) where, following an application to the tribunal for a certificate of bad husbandry under Case C (see 27.62), the arbitrator has specified a shorter period of notice (not being less than two months);
(f) where an arbitrator has specified a date for the termination of the tenancy following a notice to do work (Agricultural Holdings (Arbitration on Notices) Order 1987, SI 1987/710).

Landlord's notice to quit

There are two types of notice to quit that a landlord can serve on the tenant. The landlord **27.55** may serve a notice to quit specifying one or more of the statutory grounds of possession, or cases, set out in Pt I of Sch 3 to the Act. If the landlord serves this type of notice to quit, the tenant's right to serve a counter-notice is excluded (see 25.57). Alternatively, the landlord may serve a notice to quit which does not specify one of the statutory cases. In this case, the tenant has the right to serve a counter-notice. We shall consider this latter possibility first.

It should be noted that in serving a notice to quit the landlord is under no obligation to **27.56** inform the tenant of his or her right to serve a counter-notice. A notice to quit served on one of a number of joint tenants (subject to the statutory restrictions on its operation) will be sufficient to determine the tenancy (see 10.50). Where joint tenants wish to serve a counter-notice, that counter-notice must be served by all of them.

Tenant's counter-notice

If the tenant wishes to contest a notice to quit that has not specified a case, he or she **27.57** can serve a counter-notice in writing on the landlord within one month of the giving of the notice to quit. The effect of serving a counter-notice is to prevent the notice to quit from having effect unless the landlord applies to the agricultural land tribunal (ALT) and obtains consent to its operation (s 26(1)). The landlord must apply to the ALT within one month of receiving the counter-notice (Agricultural Land Tribunals (Rules) Order 2007, SI 2007/3105, art 39). The ALT will only consent to the operation of a notice to quit if it is satisfied that the landlord can make out one of the grounds set out in s 27(3), namely:

(a) that the carrying out of the purpose for which the landlord proposes to terminate the tenancy is desirable in the interests of good husbandry as respects the land to which the notice relates, treated as a separate unit;

(b) that the carrying out of the purpose is desirable in the interests of sound management of the estate of which the land to which the notice relates forms part, or which that land constitutes;

(c) that the carrying out of the purpose is desirable for the purposes of agricultural research, education, experiment, or demonstration, or for the purposes of the enactments relating to smallholdings;

(d) that the carrying out of the purpose is desirable for the purposes of the enactments relating to allotments;

(e) that greater hardship would be caused by withholding than by giving consent to the operation of the notice;

(f) that the landlord proposes to terminate the tenancy for the purpose of the land's being used for a use, other than for agriculture, not falling within Case B.

27.58 Even if the tribunal is satisfied that one or more of these grounds is made out it still does not have to consent to the operation of the notice to quit if, in all the circumstances, it appears to the tribunal that a fair and reasonable landlord would not insist on possession (s 27(2)).

Landlord's notice specifying cases

27.59 If the tenant wishes to contest a notice to quit that has specified a case under Sch 3, the tenant does not have the right to serve a counter-notice. If the notice to quit relies upon Case A, B, D, or E, the tenant must serve on the landlord a notice in writing requiring the question to be determined by arbitration. Such a notice must be served within one month of service of the notice to quit (Agricultural Holdings (Arbitration on Notices) Order 1987, SI 1987/710, art 9). A notice to quit relying on Case C, F, G, or H cannot be referred to arbitration. A notice to quit may be invalid if it contains fraudulent statements even though the tenant did not refer the notice to arbitration (*Rous v Mitchell* [1991] 1 WLR 469, [1991] 1 All ER 676).

The cases set out in Sch 3 are as follows:

Case A—compulsory retirement of smallholder

27.60 Case A is of limited application. It applies only to a holding that was let as a smallholding by a smallholdings authority or the Minister under Pt III of the Agriculture Act 1970 on or after 12 September 1984, and where:

(a) the tenant has attained the age of 65; and

(b) if the notice would deprive the tenant of living accommodation occupied under the tenancy, that suitable alternative accommodation is available; and

(c) the tenancy agreement contains an acknowledgement that the tenancy is subject to the provisions of Case A; and

(d) the notice to quit states that it is given under Case A.

Case B—land required for use other than agriculture

The notice to quit is given on the ground, and it is stated in the notice, that the land is **27.61** required for a use, other than agriculture:

(a) for which permission has been granted on an application made under the enactments relating to town and country planning;
(b) for which permission is granted by a general development order;
(c) for which permission is deemed to have been granted under an Act other than the town and country planning legislation;
(d) which any such provision deems not to constitute development for the purposes of those enactments;
(e) for which permission is not required under the town and country planning legislation by reason only of Crown immunity.

Case C—certificate of bad husbandry

Case C applies where, not more than six months before the giving of the notice to quit, the **27.62** tribunal granted a certificate under para 9 of Pt II of Sch 3 that the tenant of the holding was not fulfilling his or her responsibilities to farm in accordance with the rules of good husbandry, and that fact is stated in the notice.

Therefore, in order to rely upon Case C, the landlord must first apply to the tribunal for a **27.63** certificate of bad husbandry. The tribunal will only grant a certificate if it is satisfied that the tenant is not fulfilling his or her responsibilities. In making its decision the tribunal must disregard any practice adopted by the tenant in pursuance of any provision of the tenancy or any other agreement with the landlord which indicates that its object is the furtherance of:

(a) the conservation of flora or fauna or of geological or physiographical features of special interest;
(b) the protection of buildings or other objects of archaeological, architectural, or historic interest;
(c) the conservation or enhancement of the natural beauty or amenity of the countryside or the promotion of its enjoyment by the public (Sch 3, para 9).

Case D—non-payment of rent and remediable breaches

Case D contains two grounds of possession both of which are important. A landlord can **27.64** only give a notice to quit relying on Case D where that landlord has first served notice in writing on the tenant and the tenant has failed to comply with that notice. That notice must be either:

(a) a notice requiring the tenant within two months from the service of the notice to pay any rent due in respect of the agricultural holding to which the notice to quit relates; or
(b) a notice requiring the tenant within a reasonable period specified in the notice to remedy any breach by the tenant that was capable of being remedied of any term or condition of his tenancy.

A notice to pay rent must be in the prescribed form (Sch 3, para 10(1)(a); Agricultural **27.65** Holdings (Forms of Notice to Pay Rent or to Remedy) Regulations 1987, SI 1987/711, Form 1). If the tenant fails to pay all the rent due within the two-month period, the landlord is then entitled to serve a notice to quit. The only way in which a tenant can challenge a notice to pay rent is to wait until the landlord serves a notice to quit and then, within one month, refer the matter to arbitration.

27.66 In the case of notices to remedy other breaches, the prescribed form will depend on the circumstances. A notice to remedy which requires any work of repair, maintenance, or replacement must be in Form 2 of the Agricultural Holdings (Forms of Notice to Pay Rent or to Remedy) Regulations 1987. Any other notice must be in Form 3. The notice must specify the breach and, in the case of a notice to do work, give particulars of the work required to remedy it. The notice must also specify the time within which the notice is to be complied with. Where work of repair, maintenance, or replacement is required, a period of less than six months will not be treated as reasonable (Sch 3, Pt II, para 10(c)). If the tenant wishes to contest the notice, he must serve written notice requiring arbitration on the landlord within one month of the service of the notice to do work. The tenant's notice must state:

(a) any items in respect of which the tenant denies liability;

(b) any items or parts of items which the tenant claims to be unnecessary or unjustified; and

(c) any method or material in respect of which the tenant desires a substitution to be made (Agricultural Holdings (Arbitration on Notices) Order 1987, art 3(3)).

27.67 The tenant may also refer other matters arising under the notice to do work (such as the time limits for completing the work) to arbitration by serving written notice on the landlord within one month. The arbitrator has broad powers to alter the notice to do work; he or she may, for instance, delete unnecessary or unjustified items, substitute different materials for those stated in the notice, or extend the time limits. However, if the tenant fails to comply with the notice within the time limits the landlord will be entitled to serve a notice to quit relying on Case D.

27.68 Even if this is the case, the tenant has one further line of defence. The tenant may, under s 28, refer the notice to quit to arbitration by serving a counter-notice in writing on the landlord within one month. The tribunal must then give its consent to the operation of the notice to quit and it will not do so if it appears to the tribunal that having regard:

(a) to the extent to which the tenant has failed to comply with the notice to do work;

(b) to the consequences of his or her failure to comply with it in any respect; and

(c) to the circumstances surrounding any such failure,

a fair and reasonable landlord would not insist on possession.

Case E—irremediable breaches

27.69 Like Case D, Case E deals with breaches of terms or conditions in the tenancy agreement. However, under Case E, the breach in question must be one which is not capable of remedy. Consequently, there is no requirement for a landlord relying on Case E to serve a notice to remedy upon the tenant before serving a notice to quit. The landlord may serve a notice to quit on the tenant where at the date of the giving of the notice the interest of the landlord in the agricultural holding had been materially prejudiced by the commission by the tenant of a breach, which was not capable of being remedied, of any term or condition of the tenancy that was not inconsistent with the tenant's responsibilities to farm in accordance with the rules of good husbandry. The notice to quit must clearly state that the landlord is relying on Case E. The most common examples of irremediable breaches will be breaches of covenants not to assign or sub-let. However, even where a breach has taken place, the landlord will only be able to rely on Case E where his or her interests have been materially prejudiced. For example, an unlawful sub-letting to a company was not held to 'materially prejudice' the landlord in *Pennell v Payne* [1995] QB 192, [1995] 2 All ER 592, CA.

Case F—insolvency

27.70 Case F applies where, at the date of the giving of the notice to quit, the tenant was a person who had become insolvent, and it is stated in the notice that it is given by reason of the said matter. Insolvency for the purposes of the Act is defined by s 96(2).

Case G—death of tenant

The notice to quit is given: **27.71**

(a) following the death of a person who immediately before his or her death was the sole (or sole surviving) tenant under the contract of tenancy; and
(b) not later than the end of the period of three months beginning with the date of any relevant notice,

and it is stated in the notice to quit that it is given by reason of that person's death.

For the purposes of Case G, 'tenant' does not include an executor, administrator, trustee in   **27.72**
bankruptcy, or other person deriving title from a tenant by operation of law (Sch 3, Pt II, para 12(a)). The 'date of any relevant notice' means:

(a) the date on which notice in writing was served on the landlord by or on behalf of an executor or administrator of the tenant's estate informing the landlord of the tenant's death; or
(b) the date on which the landlord was given notice by virtue of s 40(5) of the Act or any application with respect to the holding under s 39 or 41; or
(c) where both of these events occur, the date of whichever of them occurs first.

Case H

Case H applies where the notice to quit is given by the Minister in order to enable him to   **27.73**
use the land to effect an amalgamation scheme and the tenancy agreement acknowledges that possession might be recovered for this purpose.

Notice to quit part of the holding

At common law a notice to quit only part of the land would be bad. However, by s 31 of   **27.74**
the Agricultural Holdings Act 1986, a notice to quit part of the land will not be invalid if it is given:

(a) for the purpose of adjusting the boundaries between agricultural units or amalgamating agricultural units or parts of such units; or
(b) with a view to the use of the land for any of the objects listed in s 31(2). (These include such things as the erection of cottages or houses for farm labourers, the provision of gardens for cottages or houses for farm labourers, the provision of allotments, the letting of land as a smallholding, the planting of trees, or the making of a watercourse or reservoir.)

If a landlord serves on the tenant a notice to quit part of the holding, the tenant can, on   **27.75**
serving a counter-notice within 28 days, accept the notice as notice to quit the whole of the holding (s 32). If the landlord does resume possession of part of the holding, the tenant is entitled under s 33 to a reduction of rent proportionate to that part of the holding that the landlord has repossessed.

Sub-tenants

Most agricultural tenancies will contain a covenant restricting sub-letting. A covenant not   **27.76**
to assign or sub-let without the landlord's consent is one of the matters contained in Sch 1 for which provision must be made in a written tenancy agreement (see 27.24). If a sub-tenancy is created in breach of covenant, the landlord will be able to terminate the tenancy under Case E and the sub-tenancy will be ended with the head tenancy. However, even where a sub-tenancy is authorized by the landlord the position of the sub-tenant is

precarious. A sub-tenancy may attract the protection of the Act as against the sub-tenant's intermediate landlord (the tenant). In which case, if the intermediate landlord seeks to terminate the tenancy the statutory rules restricting the operation of a notice to quit will apply. However, where the head landlord serves a notice to quit on the tenant and successfully determines the head tenancy, the sub-tenancy will also be terminated (*Barrett v Morgan* [2000] UKHL 1, [2000] 2 AC 264).

Joint tenants

27.77 If a landlord serves a notice to quit on one of a number of joint tenants, or one joint tenant serves notice to quit on the landlord, this will determine the joint tenancy (see 10.50).

F SUCCESSION

Succession on death of tenant

27.78 Part IV of the Agricultural Holdings Act 1986 contains complex provisions enabling a relative of a tenant to succeed to an agricultural holding. These provisions, unless they fall within the four exceptions listed, will apply only to tenancies granted before 12 July 1984 and are therefore of waning importance. However, Pt IV of the Act permits two successions to an agricultural holding and so will continue to be relevant in limited cases for some time to come.

27.79 A tenancy granted after 12 July 1984 will have succession rights where:

(a) the tenancy was obtained by virtue of a direction of the tribunal under s 39 or 53 (ie where there has already been one succession (on death or retirement) and that was obtained following an application to the ALT);

(b) the tenancy was granted (following a direction under s 39) in circumstances within s 45(6) (ie where the landlord granted the tenancy to a person or persons entitled to succeed following a direction of the ALT);

(c) the tenancy is written and the parties agree that Pt IV should apply;

(d) the tenancy was granted to a person who, immediately before 12 July 1984, was a tenant of the holding or of a substantial part (by reference to either area or value) of the land comprised in the holding (s 34(1)(b)).

27.80 Succession under Pt IV of the Act does not happen automatically. A person who wishes to succeed to an agricultural tenancy must apply to the tribunal within three months of the death of the tenant for a direction entitling him or her to a tenancy of the holding (s 39(1)). Before making an application that person must give notice of his or her intention to do so to all interested parties in accordance with the provisions of art 40 of the Agricultural Land Tribunals (Rules) Order 2007, SI 2007/3105. That person must also be eligible to succeed, and to be eligible to succeed he or she must satisfy the three important tests considered below.

Close relative

27.81 Only a 'close relative' of the deceased can succeed to an agricultural holding. A 'close relative' is defined by s 35(2) as:

(a) the wife or husband or civil partner of the deceased;

(b) a brother or sister of the deceased;

(c) a child of the deceased;

(d) any person (not within (b) or (c) above) who, in the case of any marriage to which the deceased was at any time a party, was treated by the deceased as a child of the family in relation to that marriage.

Principal livelihood

27.82 The close relative of the deceased must also show that in the seven years ending with the date of death his only or principal source of livelihood throughout a continuous period of not less than five years, or two or more discontinuous periods together amounting to not less than five years, derived from his agricultural work on the holding or an agricultural unit of which the holding forms part (s 36(3)(a)). If the close relative is the deceased's wife or civil partner, 'agricultural work' shall be read to mean agricultural work carried out by either the wife or civil partner or the deceased (or both of them) (s 36(4) and (4A)). For the purposes of the principal livelihood test, any period (to a maximum of three years) during the seven years preceding the death of the tenant in which a close relative of the deceased was in full-time, higher, or further education will be treated as counting towards the five-year qualifying period (Sch 6, para 8).

27.83 From 19 October 2006 'agricultural work' may include other work carried out by the potential successor on or from the holding or an agricultural unit of which the holding forms part, provided this work is of a description approved in writing by the landlord (s 36(6)). This provision, introduced by the Regulatory Reform (Agricultural Tenancies) (England and Wales) Order 2006, SI 2006/2805, is designed to make it easier for close relatives to succeed where a significant part of their income comes from non-agricultural activities, but only where the landlord has voluntarily given written permission for such activities. Defra (Department for Environment Food and Rural Affairs) recommends landlords to view tenants' proposals for diversification in the light of its 'Code of good practice for agri-environment schemes and diversification projects within agricultural tenancies' (available from <http://www.defra.gov.uk>).

27.84 If the principal livelihood test is not fully satisfied, but satisfied to a material extent, by a close relative, then that close relative may apply to the tribunal within three months of the death for a determination that he or she is to be treated as an eligible person (s 41).

Non-occupation of a commercial unit of land

27.85 The close relative of the deceased must not be the occupier of a commercial unit of agricultural land (s 36(3)(b)). The aim of this test is to prevent persons who are already entitled to farm other land from succeeding to the holding. A 'commercial unit of agricultural land' means a unit of agricultural land which is capable, when farmed under competent management, of producing a net annual income of an amount not less than the aggregate of the average annual earnings of two full-time, male agricultural workers aged 20 or over (s 36(5) and Sch 6, para 3(1)).

27.86 Ascertaining whether agricultural land amounts to a commercial unit shall be done by reference to the provisions of orders made by the Minister of Agriculture (in so far as they are relevant) as to how to assess the productive capacity of land and how to determine the net annual income from a unit of land (Sch 6, para 4). Schedule 6 to the Act also sets out extensive rules to determine what counts as occupation for the purposes of s 36(3)(b); including, among others, the following provisions. If the close relative occupies the land under a tenancy for more than one year but less than two years or as a licensee, it will not count as occupation (Sch 6, para 6(1)(b) and (e)) because the close relative does not have a secure right to occupy the land (see 27.23). However, this will not be the case if the tenancy or licence is granted to the close relative by his or her spouse or civil partner or by a company controlled by the close relative himself or herself (Sch 6, para 2).

27.87 Where the land is occupied with one or more other persons as joint tenants or tenants in common this will be treated as occupancy provided that the close relative's share of the income is sufficient (Sch 6, para 7). Occupation by the spouse or civil partner of the close relative or by a body corporate controlled by the close relative shall also be treated as occupation (Sch 6, para 9).

Two successions

27.88 Even if the close relative is eligible to succeed on the criteria discussed, he or she will not be able to apply to succeed where two successions have already occurred. This rule will obviously apply where there have been directions by the tribunal under s 39 (or s 45(6)) providing for succession (s 37(1)(a)). However, it may also apply where there have been no formal directions by the tribunal: first, where the landlord, in the absence of a direction, grants a tenancy to a close relative of the deceased who was or had become the sole remaining applicant for such a direction (s 37(1)(b)); secondly, where, with the agreement of the landlord, a close relative of the tenant acquires the tenancy before the death of the original tenant as a result of a new grant of the tenancy or by virtue of an assignment of the current tenancy, such a situation will be deemed to be a succession (s 37(2)). Events occurring before the succession provisions originally came into force on 14 November 1976 will not count as a succession (*Kemp v Fisher* [2009] EWHC 3657 (Ch)).

Notice to quit

27.89 If the tenancy is already subject on the date of death to a notice to quit served under s 26(1) (ie a notice to quit that does not specify one of the cases from Sch 3, see 27.55) and the tenant has not served a counter-notice within the prescribed month or the tribunal has consented to its operation, then the eligible person will not be able to apply to succeed to the tenancy (s 38(1)). Similarly, if a notice to quit relying on Case B, C, D, E, or F has been served, and provided the time limits set out in s 38(3) have been complied with, succession will be excluded.

Suitability

27.90 Even where the tribunal is satisfied that the applicant is an eligible person, it must still determine whether or not he or she is, in the tribunal's opinion, a suitable person to become the tenant of the holding (s 39(2)). In doing so the tribunal should have regard to all relevant matters including:

(a) the extent to which the applicant has been trained in, or has practical experience of, agriculture;

(b) the age, physical health, and financial standing of the applicant; and

(c) the views (if any) stated by the landlord on the suitability of the applicant (s 39(8)). (The tribunal must afford the landlord an opportunity for stating his or her views on the suitability of the applicant before making its determination (s 39(7)).)

27.91 If there are two eligible applicants, the tribunal will choose between them by considering them both on the criteria listed as though each were the only applicant (s 39(3)). However, if the deceased has validly designated one of them as his or her successor in his will, the tribunal shall consider that applicant first and only go on to consider the second applicant if the applicant named in the will is not, in the tribunal's opinion, a suitable person to become a tenant of the holding (s 39(4)). Where both applicants are suitable the tribunal must determine which, in its opinion, is the most suitable (s 39(6)). However, in such a situation, the tribunal may, with the consent of the landlord, direct that two (or more) applicants are entitled to a joint tenancy of the holding (s 39(9)).

Resisting succession

27.92 If the landlord wishes to resist succession and reclaim possession of the holding he or she must serve a notice to quit under Case G (see 27.71) within three months of the death of the tenant. If no application to succeed has been made to the tribunal within three months of the death, the notice to quit shall have effect (s 43(1)(a)). Similarly, if the tribunal determines that none of the applicants are, in its opinion, suitable to succeed to the holding, the notice to quit shall have effect (s 43(1)(b)). If the tribunal does decide that the applicant is suitable, provided a notice to quit under Case G has been served, it must give the landlord an opportunity of applying to the tribunal for its consent to the operation of the notice (s 44(1)). The procedure for such an application is set out in Pt 6 of the Agricultural Land Tribunals (Rules) Order 2007. However, in considering the landlord's application the provisions of s 27 shall apply (s 44(2)). In other words, the application under Case G will not be treated as a mandatory ground of possession and the tribunal must consider all the factors set out at 27.57 including whether greater hardship would be caused by withholding than by giving consent and whether in all the circumstances a fair and reasonable landlord would insist on possession.

The terms of the new tenancy

27.93 Where an application to succeed to a tenancy of the holding is successful the new tenancy (or tenancies in the case of joint tenants) will take effect from 'the relevant time' (s 45(1)). The 'relevant time' will usually be the end of the 12 months immediately following the end of the year of tenancy in which the deceased died (s 46(1)(a)). If the landlord served a notice to quit under Case G, the relevant time will be the date on which that notice to quit would have terminated the tenancy had it been permitted to operate (s 46(1)(b)).

27.94 In general, the terms of the new tenancy (or tenancies) will be the same as the terms of the deceased's tenancy at the end of his or her term (s 47(1)). However, if the deceased held a tenancy for a fixed term of years this will be converted to a tenancy from year to year (s 47(2)) and, if the deceased's tenancy did not contain a covenant against assigning, sub-letting, or parting with possession without the landlord's consent, such a covenant will be included in the new tenancy (s 47(3)).

27.95 Both the landlord and the tenant may refer the terms of the tenancy to arbitration by serving notice demanding arbitration on the other at some time in the period from the giving of the direction entitling the successor to a tenancy up to three months after the relevant time (or three months after the direction if that occurs later) (s 48(3)). Where the terms of the tenancy (not including rent) are referred to arbitration the arbitrator may make what variations are justifiable having regard to the circumstances of the holding and the length of time since the holding was first let on those terms (s 48(4)(a)). Where the rent is referred to arbitration the arbitrator may determine what rent should be or should have been properly payable in respect of the holding at the relevant time (s 48(4)(b)). The arbitrator may also include provisions entitling either the landlord or the tenant to recover compensation (either under the Act, agreement, or custom) from the other party (s 48(5) and (8)).

Succession on retirement of tenant

27.96 If the agreement of the landlord can be obtained, it is open to the tenant of an agricultural holding to arrange to pass that holding on to a close relative during that tenant's lifetime either by assignment or under a new tenancy granted by the landlord. (We saw in 27.88 how such an arrangement will be treated as a succession for the purposes of the Act (s 37(2)).) Sections 49 to 58 of the Act provide a procedure whereby the tenancy can be transferred prior to the death of the tenant without the agreement of the landlord. The tenancy must be a tenancy from year to year and have been granted before 12 July 1984 or fall into one of the exceptions set out in s 34(1)(b) (see 27.79) (s 49(1)(a)). In order to take advantage of these provisions the tenant must serve a retirement notice on the landlord indicating that he or she wishes a single eligible person to succeed him or her as tenant of the holding (s 49(1)(b)).

The retiring tenant

27.97   To be able to apply to the tribunal, the retiring tenant must be at least 65 years old at the retirement date (ie the date specified in the notice from which the succession is to take place). The retiring tenant may only be younger than 65 if he or she is or will be incapable, by reason of bodily or mental infirmity, of conducting the farming of the holding in accordance with the rules of good husbandry, and such incapacity is likely to be permanent (s 51(3)).

The eligible person

27.98   To be eligible, the person named in the notice must be a close relative who satisfies both the principal livelihood test and the non-occupation test (s 50). These requirements are the same as in the case of the death of the tenant (see 27.81 to 27.87); however, in the case of succession on retirement, a close relative has no right to apply to the tribunal to be treated as eligible under s 41 if he or she cannot completely satisfy the principal livelihood test.

Exclusions

27.99   As in the case of succession on death, the right to succeed on retirement will be excluded where the tenancy is a smallholding or was granted by a charitable trust, where there have already been two successions (see 27.88), or where the tenancy is already subject to a valid notice to quit (see 27.89) (s 51). Furthermore, the right to succeed on retirement will only arise once: if the tenant has served a retirement notice on the landlord and any person has applied to succeed on retirement, the right to apply again is excluded (s 51(2)), though if the application was withdrawn or abandoned, it will be treated as though it had never been made (s 51(10)). It should also be noted that under the provisions to succeed on retirement there is no right to apply to succeed to part of the holding.

Application to tribunal

27.100   Applications must be made in accordance with the provisions of Pt 6 of the Agricultural Land Tribunals (Rules) Order 2007. The tribunal must then decide whether the applicant is a suitable person to become the tenant of the holding. The provisions are the same on succession as on death (see 27.90). If the applicant is held to be suitable, the tribunal must consider the question of greater hardship. So long as it does not appear that greater hardship would be caused by giving the direction than by refusing the application, the tribunal may then give a direction entitling the applicant to a tenancy of the holding as from the relevant time (s 55(1)). The 'relevant time' will generally be the retirement date specified in the retirement notice (s 55(8)). If the tribunal decides against the applicant and refuses to give a direction, the retirement notice shall be of no effect (s 55(9)) and the tenant may serve another retirement notice in the future.

G COMPENSATION

Compensation for tenant's improvements

The tenant of an agricultural holding is entitled, on the termination of the tenancy and on **27.101** quitting the holding, to obtain compensation from his or her landlord for certain improvements carried out on the holding by the tenant. These improvements must be improvements specified in Sch 7 or Pt I of Sch 8 to the Act and they must have been begun on or after 1 March 1948 (s 64).

Schedules 7 and 8 divide these improvements into three categories. **27.102**

Improvements requiring landlord's consent

For the improvements listed in Pt I of Sch 7 the tenant will not be entitled to compen- **27.103** sation unless the landlord has given his or her consent in writing to the improvement (s 67(1)). Consent may be given unconditionally or conditionally on terms as to compensation or otherwise as may be agreed in writing between the landlord and the tenant (s 67(2)). There is no requirement that the consent has to be given before the carrying out of the improvements; however, it would be advisable to do so, for if the landlord refuses consent to an improvement listed in Pt I of Sch 7 the tenant has no right to refer the decision to the tribunal. The improvements listed in Pt I of Sch 7 include the making of water meadows, watercress beds, osier beds, and gardens; the planting of hops, orchards, or fruit bushes; the provision of underground tanks; and the warping or weiring of land.

Improvements requiring landlord's consent or consent of tribunal

For the improvements listed in Pt II of Sch 7 it is also necessary for the tenant to obtain **27.104** consent from the landlord. However, if the improvement concerned falls within Pt II of Sch 8 and the landlord refuses to give his or her consent, the tenant has the right to apply in accordance with the provisions of the Agricultural Land Tribunals (Rules) Order 2007 to the ALT for approval of the proposed improvement (s 67(3)). The tribunal may refuse to give its approval, make the approval conditional on terms, or grant unconditional approval (s 67(4)). If it does grant approval, the landlord has the right to serve notice in writing on the tribunal and the tenant, within one month, stating that the landlord intends to carry out the improvement himself or herself (s 67(5)). Part II of Sch 7 contains an extensive list which includes such items as the erection or alteration of buildings, the making or improvement of roads, the erection or removal of fences, land drainage, and repairs to fixed equipment.

The measure of compensation for an improvement specified in Sch 7 shall be an amount **27.105** equal to the increase attributable to the improvement in the value of the holding as a holding, having regard to the character and situation of the holding and the average requirements of tenants reasonably skilled in husbandry (s 66(1)).

Short-term improvements and tenant-right matters

For the improvements listed in Pt I of Sch 8 no consent is required from either the landlord **27.106** or the tribunal. It is not even necessary for the tenant to give the landlord notice of his or her intention to carry out an improvement (except in the case of para 1 (mole drainage)) (s 68(1)). The improvements listed in Pt I of Sch 8 include the protection of fruit trees against animals, clay burning, liming, the application to land of purchased manure and fertiliser, and the consumption of feeding stuffs not produced on the holding.

27.107   Part II of Sch 8 contains a further extensive list of what are entitled 'tenant-right matters'. These are generally acts of good husbandry that are carried out on the holding (eg the sowing of seeds, the growing of crops, the laying down of pasture) which will leave behind some benefit to the holding when the tenant leaves.

27.108   The measure of compensation for an improvement or matter specified in Sch 8 shall be the value of the improvement to an incoming tenant calculated in accordance with the prescribed methods (set out in Agriculture (Calculation of Value for Compensation) Regulations 1978, SI 1978/809, as amended) (s 66(2)).

Special systems of farming

27.109   Where the tenant has increased the value of the holding by the adoption of a special system of farming which has been more beneficial to the holding than the system of farming required in the contract of tenancy or the system of farming normally practised on comparable agricultural holdings, the tenant is entitled on quitting the holding to obtain compensation from the landlord of an amount equal to the increase (s 70(1)). This right will not arise unless the tenant has:

(a)   given the landlord notice in writing at least one month before the termination of the tenancy of his or her intention to claim compensation under s 70 (s 70(2)(a)); and

(b)   a record has been made under s 22 (27.38) of the condition of the fixed equipment on the holding and of the general condition of the holding (s 70(2)(b)).

27.110   Compensation will not be recoverable in respect of any matter arising before the date of the record made under s 22 (s 70(3)). Compensation under s 70 is an additional right and so in assessing the increase in value of the holding, due allowance will be made for any compensation awarded to the tenant for improvements or tenant-right matters (see 27.106 to 27.108) (s 70(5)).

Compensation for disturbance

27.111   A tenant will be entitled to compensation for disturbance where the tenancy of an agricultural holding terminates by reason of:

(a)   a notice to quit the holding given by the landlord; or

(b)   a counter-notice given by the tenant under s 32 after the giving to him or her of such a notice to quit part of the holding as is mentioned in that section (ie where a tenant is given notice to quit part of the holding and elects, by serving notice on the landlord, to quit the whole of the holding, see 27.74),

and the tenant quits the holding in consequence of the notice or counter-notice (s 60(1)).

27.112   However, if in the case of (b) the notice to quit affects less than a quarter of the holding and the rest of the holding is reasonably capable of being farmed as a separate holding, then compensation for disturbance will only be payable for the part of the holding to which the notice to quit relates (s 63(3)).

27.113   Compensation for disturbance under s 60 is payable in addition to any other compensation to which the tenant may be entitled (s 60(7)). Compensation under the Act is payable notwithstanding any agreement to the contrary (s 78). Under s 60 there are two types of compensation for disturbance: *basic compensation* and *additional compensation* (see 27.115 and 27.116). Neither basic nor additional compensation for disturbance will be payable where the tenancy is terminated under Case C, D, E, F, or G (see 27.62 to 27.71) (s 61(1)).

Sub-tenants

It should be noted that it is a requirement of obtaining compensation for disturbance that **27.114** the tenant quits the holding. However, this rule does not apply where the tenant has sub-let the holding and because of a notice to quit given by the landlord becomes liable to pay compensation to the sub-tenant. The tenant may recover compensation for disturbance from the landlord notwithstanding the fact that, because he or she is not in occupation of the holding, he or she cannot quit it (s 63(2)). A sub-tenant may also claim compensation for disturbance where the sub-tenancy is terminated by operation of law because the head tenancy has been terminated by notice to quit or counter-notice under s 60(1) (s 63(1)).

Basic compensation

Basic compensation can be calculated in two ways. It can be an amount equal to one **27.115** year's rent of the holding at the rate at which rent was payable immediately before the termination of the tenancy (s 60(3)(a)). However, if the tenant feels that this sum is too low, he or she may seek to claim the actual loss incurred up to a maximum of two years' rent (s 60(3)(b)). The tenant's actual loss means the amount of the loss or expense directly attributable to the quitting of the holding which is unavoidably incurred by the tenant upon or in connection with the sale or removal of his or her household goods, implements of husbandry, fixtures, farm produce, or farm stock on or used in connection with the holding and includes any expenses reasonably incurred by him or her in the preparation of his or her claim for basic compensation (but not the cost of arbitration) (s 60(5)). If the tenant wishes to claim the actual loss, he or she must give the landlord written notice of his or her intention to do so not less than one month before the termination of the tenancy (s 60(6)(a)) and give the landlord an opportunity to make his or her own valuation of the goods, stock etc before they are sold (s 60(6)(b)).

Additional compensation

The amount of additional compensation is an amount equal to four years' rent of the hold- **27.116** ing at the rate at which rent was payable immediately before the termination of the tenancy of the holding (s 60(4)). No additional compensation will be payable where the tenancy is terminated under Case A or H (s 61(2)). Similarly, no additional compensation will be payable where the tribunal has consented to the operation of a landlord's notice to quit on the grounds of good husbandry, sound estate management, agricultural research (see s 27(3)), or greater hardship (s 61(3)).

Compensation to landlord for deterioration of holding

As well as the extensive provisions with regard to tenants' compensation, the Act also pro- **27.117** vides a statutory mechanism enabling the landlord to recover compensation from the tenant for deterioration of the holding. The compensation available under the Act is divided into two classes.

Compensation for deterioration of particular parts of the holding

Section 71(1) of the Act provides that, on the tenant's quitting of the holding, the landlord **27.118** shall be entitled to recover from the tenant compensation in respect of the dilapidation or deterioration of, or damage to, any part of the holding or anything in or on the holding caused by non-fulfilment by the tenant of his or her responsibilities to farm in accordance with the rules of good husbandry. The amount of compensation payable will be the cost, as at the date of the tenant's quitting the holding, of making good the dilapidation, deterioration, or damage (s 71(2)).

27.119 *In lieu* of claiming compensation under s 71(1) the landlord may alternatively claim for deterioration of particular parts of the holding in accordance with the written contract of tenancy. Such a claim can only be exercised on the tenant's quitting the holding on the termination of the tenancy (s 71(4)(a)) and the landlord is not permitted to claim both under statute and under the contract of tenancy (s 71(4)(b)).

27.120 Whether claiming under s 71(1) or under a written contract, the amount of compensation shall not exceed the amount by which the value of the landlord's reversion in the holding is diminished owing to the dilapidation, deterioration, or damage in question (s 71(5)).

Compensation for general deterioration of holding

27.121 In addition to claiming for deterioration of particular parts of the holding, a landlord may recover further compensation from the tenant where the landlord can show that the value of the holding generally has been reduced by reason of dilapidation, deterioration, or damage (as set out in s 71(1)) or otherwise by non-fulfilment by the tenant of his or her responsibilities to farm in accordance with the rules of good husbandry (s 72(1)). The amount of compensation payable under s 72 will be the decrease in the value of the holding having regard to the character and situation of the holding and the average requirements of tenants reasonably skilled in husbandry (s 72(3)). A claim made under s 72 for general deterioration is in addition to a claim under s 71 and so any compensation under s 71 will be taken into account.

H DISPUTE RESOLUTION

27.122 As we have seen, the majority of questions arising under the 1986 Act are to be referred to the ALT or, more commonly, to an arbitrator. The Act provides for the appointment of a single arbitrator, who may be chosen by the parties. If the parties cannot agree, either party may apply to the President of the Royal Institution of Chartered Surveyors for an arbitrator to be appointed (s 84). Under the Act, all claims which arise on the termination of a tenancy must be referred to an arbitrator (s 83(1)). Various other matters arising during the term of the tenancy must also be referred to arbitration (eg issues involving rent and improvements: see 27.41 and 27.103). As a result of these requirements the involvement of the courts in disputes concerning agricultural tenancies will be limited. The county court has jurisdiction to enforce awards (CPR r 70.5; CCR r 25.12), and to remove an arbitrator, or remit his decision for reconsideration (CCR r 44.1). The High Court also has jurisdiction to determine questions of law referred to it by the ALT (CPR r 52.22.7). As we shall see in the next chapter the importance of the role of the arbitrator has been reinforced by the Agricultural Tenancies Act 1995.

KEY DOCUMENTS

Agricultural Holdings Act 1986

Agricultural Holdings (Forms of Notice to pay Rent or to Remedy) Regulations 1987, SI 1987/711

Regulatory Reform (Agricultural Tenancies) (England and Wales) Order 2006, SI 2006/2805

Agricultural Land Tribunals (Rules) Order 2007, SI 2007/3105

Defra's 'Code of good practice for agri-environment schemes and diversification projects within agricultural tenancies' (available from <http://www.defra.gov.uk>)

Printed copies of all legislation can be ordered from The Stationery Office at <http://www.tsoshop.co.uk>. All legislation from 1988 onwards and most pre-1988 primary legislation is available online at <http://www.legislation.gov.uk>.

28

FARM BUSINESS TENANCIES

A INTRODUCTION

In many quarters the extensive regulation of agricultural letting by the Agricultural Holdings **28.01** Act 1986 and its predecessors was held responsible for a marked decline in agricultural land available to let. The main culprits were regarded as the provisions as to security of tenure and succession, but an additional problem was the strict definition of an agricultural holding which discouraged tenants from diversifying into non-agricultural activities for fear of losing the protection of the 1986 Act.

The change of emphasis effected by the Agricultural Tenancies Act 1995 was apparent in **28.02** the change of name given to agricultural lettings. From 1 September 1995 (apart from a few transitional exceptions) no more tenancies of 'agricultural holdings' could be granted and agricultural lettings were instead known as 'farm business tenancies'. Farming was to be seen as a commercial activity—a business—and in many ways the 1995 Act has more in common with the Landlord and Tenant Act 1954 (see Chapter 26) than it does with its agricultural predecessors. At the heart of the 1995 Act is the principle of freedom of contract. The parties are to be free to negotiate their tenancy on whatever terms they can agree between them. The Act imposes no more than minimal security of tenure beyond the length of the tenancy agreed between the parties. There are no rights of succession. Furthermore, a more flexible approach is taken to the definition of a farm business tenancy which permits tenants, if they so wish, to diversify their business into non-agricultural activities without losing the protection of the Act.

B WHAT IS A FARM BUSINESS TENANCY?

28.03 A tenancy will be a farm business tenancy for the purposes of the 1995 Act if it meets the *business conditions* together with either the *agriculture condition* or the *notice conditions* (s 1(1)(a)). It cannot be a farm business tenancy if the tenancy began before 1 September 1995 or if the tenancy is an agricultural holding (s 2(1)). Certain tenancies beginning after 1 September 1995 may be agricultural holdings if they fall within the exceptions set out in s 4. These will include:

(a) where the tenancy begins after 1 September but pursuant to a written contract of tenancy entered into before that date which indicates that the 1986 Act is to apply in relation to that tenancy (s 4(1)(a));

(b) where the tenancy was obtained under the rights of succession contained in the 1986 Act (see 27.78 to 27.100); whether the tenancy was obtained by a direction of the agricultural land tribunal (ALT) under s 39 or 53 of the 1986 Act, granted by the landlord under s 45(6) of the 1986 Act, following a direction of the ALT, or granted by a written contract of tenancy following an agreement with the landlord (s 4(1)(b), (c), and (d));

(c) where the tenancy was granted under the 'Evesham custom';

(d) where the tenancy was granted to someone who immediately before the grant was the tenant of the holding (or a substantial part of the holding) under the 1986 Act and the new tenancy was not expressly granted but had effect as an implied surrender followed by the grant of the tenancy because of an agreement reached between the parties (s 4(1)(f));

(e) where the tenancy was granted to someone who immediately before the grant was the tenant of the holding (or a substantial part of the holding) under the 1986 Act and that tenant is granted a new tenancy agreement which indicates (in whatever terms) that the 1986 Act is to apply (s 4(1)(g)).

The business conditions

28.04 There are two *business conditions*:

(a) that all or part of the land comprised in the tenancy is farmed for the purposes of a trade or business; and

(b) that since the beginning of the tenancy, all or part of the land has been so farmed.

28.05 Both of these conditions must be satisfied. Basically they mean that at least part of the land must be farmed for the purposes of trade or business throughout the life of the tenancy. Of course, it would be difficult for a tenant to demonstrate that the land (or at least part of it) has been continuously farmed for the purposes of a trade or business since the beginning of the tenancy without an interruption. Section 1(7) therefore sets up a presumption in favour of the tenant that in any proceedings (ie at the time the status of the tenancy is challenged), provided it is proved that all or part of the land is being farmed for the purposes of a trade or business, then it will be presumed that it has been so farmed from the beginning of the tenancy unless the landlord can prove the contrary. Furthermore, for the purposes of determining whether a tenancy satisfies the business or agriculture conditions, any breach of the terms of the tenancy will be disregarded unless the landlord has consented to the breach (s 1(8)). Thus, if a tenant, in breach of the terms of the tenancy, ceases to use the land solely for agricultural purposes, the tenancy will still satisfy the business condition provided the landlord has not consented to the change of use.

28.06 It should also be noted what the business conditions do not require. They do not require that the same part of the land is always farmed for the purposes of a trade or a business;

they will be satisfied even if different parts of the land have been used for commercial farming at different times, provided that at all times some part of the land has been farmed for the purposes of a trade or a business; nor do they require that farming has always been the predominant use of the land.

'Farmed' for the purposes of the Act is defined in s 38. Farming of the land means carrying **28.07** on agricultural activity in relation to the land (s 38(2)) and 'agriculture' is defined as it is in the Agricultural Holdings Act 1986 to include horticulture, fruit growing, seed growing, dairy farming, and livestock breeding and keeping, the use of land as grazing land, meadow land, osier land, market gardens, and nursery grounds, and the use of land for woodlands where that use is ancillary to farming of land for other agricultural purposes.

As well as satisfying the business conditions the tenancy will also have to satisfy either the **28.08** *agriculture condition* or the *notice condition*.

Change of use

If during the course of the tenancy a tenant ceases to use the land for agricultural activity, **28.09** the business condition will cease to be satisfied and the tenancy will fall outside the 1995 Act. However, if the land continues to be used for commercial purposes, it may qualify as a business tenancy under Pt II of the Landlord and Tenant Act 1954 (see Chapter 26). A change in the other direction will not bring the tenancy within the protection of the 1995 Act because the business condition requires that at least part of the land has been farmed for the purposes of a business since the beginning of the tenancy.

The agriculture condition

Section 1(3) states that the agriculture condition is that, having regard to: **28.10**

(a) the terms of the tenancy;
(b) the use of the land comprised in the tenancy;
(c) the nature of any commercial activities carried on on that land; and
(d) any other relevant circumstances,

the character of the tenancy is primarily or wholly agricultural.

Unlike the business condition the agriculture condition does not need to have been satisfied **28.11** since the beginning of the tenancy; it only needs to be satisfied at the time of proceedings. However, it does require that, taking into account a broad range of factors, the tenancy is *primarily* or *wholly* agricultural. The section is drafted in broad terms and therefore gives the court considerable discretion in determining the nature of the tenancy.

The notice conditions

Rather than leaving it up to the court to decide in the event of a challenge to the status of **28.12** the tenancy the parties may avoid uncertainty by satisfying the notice conditions. This will make sure that, regardless of the subsequent use to which the land is put and provided that it continues to satisfy the business conditions and any express covenants in the tenancy agreement, the tenancy will remain a farm business tenancy.

To satisfy the notice conditions there are two requirements. The first requirement is that on or **28.13** before the relevant day, the landlord and the tenant each gave the other a written notice:

(a) identifying (by name or otherwise) the land to be comprised in the tenancy or proposed tenancy; and

(b) containing a statement to the effect that the person giving the notice intends that the tenancy or proposed tenancy is to be, and remain, a farm business tenancy (s 1(4)(a)).

28.14 The 'relevant day' is defined by s 1(5) as whichever is the earlier of the following:

(a) the day on which the parties enter into any instrument creating the tenancy, other than an agreement to enter into a tenancy on a future date; or

(b) the beginning of the tenancy.

28.15 There are no prescribed forms for the notice but s 1(6) states that it must not be included in the instrument creating the tenancy. (Section 36 contains further rules governing the service of notices under the Agricultural Tenancies Act 1995.)

28.16 The second requirement is that, at the beginning of the tenancy, having regard to the terms of the tenancy and any other relevant circumstances, the character of the tenancy was primarily or wholly agricultural (s 1(4)(b)). Unlike the agriculture condition, which must be satisfied when the tenancy is challenged, this requirement of the notice conditions needs only to be satisfied at the beginning of the tenancy. With regard to satisfying the notice conditions, therefore, the important thing is that the use of the land is primarily or wholly agricultural at the beginning of the tenancy. Provided notice has been properly served, it will not matter if subsequently the use of the land moves away from agriculture. The tenancy will remain a farm business tenancy as long as part of the land remains used for agriculture, though, of course, if the agricultural use of the land stops altogether, the tenancy will cease to satisfy the business condition.

28.17 In general, where, having held a farm business tenancy that satisfied the notice conditions, the same tenant is granted a subsequent tenancy of the land, it will be necessary for the landlord and tenant to serve notice again in order to satisfy the notice conditions. However, in certain limited circumstances where there is surrender and re-grant of the tenancy, s 3 of the Act will deem the notice conditions to have been complied with. This can only occur provided that:

(a) the original tenancy complied with the notice conditions; and

(b) the terms of the new tenancy are substantially the same as the terms of the old tenancy; and

(c) either:

(i)   the new tenancy is the same as the land comprised in the old tenancy, apart from any changes in area which are small in relation to the size of the holding and do not affect the character of the holding; or

(ii) the old tenancy and the new tenancy are both fixed-term tenancies but the term date under the new tenancy is earlier than the term date under the old tenancy.

C TERMINATING A FARM BUSINESS TENANCY

28.18 The 1995 Act provides only minimal security of tenure for farm business tenants. What protection there is functions by imposing statutory restrictions on the common law periods for serving a notice to quit. A landlord does not need to give advance notice nor make out any grounds of possession; provided the notice to quit is valid and accords with the statutory periods set out in ss 5, 6, and 7, the landlord will be able to terminate the tenancy.

Fixed-term tenancies of two years or more

28.19 Section 5(1) provides:

A farm business tenancy for a term of more than two years shall, instead of terminating on the term date, continue (as from that date) as a tenancy from year to year, but otherwise on the terms of the original tenancy so far as applicable, unless at least 12 months before the term date a written notice has been given by either party to the other of his intention to terminate the tenancy.

Thus, as in the Agricultural Holdings Act 1986, the 1995 Act ensures the automatic continuation of longer fixed-term tenancies. Such tenancies can only be terminated by serving a notice of intention to terminate at least a year before the date on which it is to take effect. It is not possible to contract out of the provisions of s 5 (s 5(4)). It should be noted, however, that the provisions apply both to the landlord and the tenant. A tenant who wishes to be released from his or her tenancy must also give at least 12 months' notice and, in any case, such notice will not be effective to terminate the tenancy before the term date. If a tenant wishes to terminate the tenancy during the term, the only option is to surrender the lease and this can only be done with the agreement of the landlord. **28.20**

Fixed-term tenancies of two years or less

Fixed-term tenancies of two years or less have no protection under the 1995 Act and will simply expire at the end of the term. Tenancies of a period of less than a year will not be converted into yearly tenancies as they are under the 1986 Act (see 27.19). **28.21**

Tenancies from year to year

Section 6(1) provides: **28.22**

Where a farm business tenancy is a tenancy from year to year, a notice to quit the holding or part of the holding shall (notwithstanding any provision to the contrary in the tenancy) be invalid unless:
  (a) it is in writing,
  (b) it is to take effect at the end of a year of the tenancy, and
  (c) it is given at least twelve months before the date on which it is to take effect.

Thus, tenancies that were granted as yearly periodic tenancies or tenancies that were granted as a fixed term of over two years and are being continued past the term date by s 5 must be given at least 12 months' notice. **28.23**

Other periodic tenancies

There are no provisions in the Act dealing with tenancies of other periods, eg weekly, monthly, or quarterly tenancies. These tenancies can be terminated according to the normal common law rules (see 10.32 to 10.50). **28.24**

Option to terminate

A fixed-term farm business tenancy, particularly one for a longer term, may contain a provision permitting either the landlord or the tenant to terminate the tenancy of the holding before the full term has run its course. Such an option to terminate (or break clause) may apply to the whole holding or to part of the holding. However, if the tenancy is for a term of more than two years, s 7 will override any other provisions in the tenancy agreement and require that a notice to quit must be in writing and given at least 12 months before the date upon which it is to take effect. **28.25**

Sub-tenants

Like the 1986 Act, the 1995 Act gives no protection to sub-tenants. If the head tenancy is terminated by a notice to quit the sub-tenancy will be determined at the same time (see 27.76). **28.26**

Joint tenants

28.27 If a landlord serves a notice to quit on one of a number of joint tenants, or one joint tenant serves notice to quit on the landlord, this will determine the joint tenancy (see 10.50).

Licensees

28.28 Under the Agricultural Holdings Act 1986 exclusive licences would be treated as tenancies by virtue of s 2(2)(b) (see 27.20). There is no equivalent provision in the 1995 Act and licences will fall outside the protection of the Act. However, under the rule in *Street v Mountford* an agreement that grants exclusive possession but purports to be a licence will usually create a tenancy (see 2.10 to 2.12).

Forfeiture

28.29 Because of the statutory provisions in the 1986 Act with regard to the service of notices to quit where a tenant breaches a covenant in the lease (see Cases D and E, 27.64 to 27.69), the law of forfeiture had little application to agricultural holdings. In the 1995 Act there is no comparable statutory mechanism and so a landlord's ultimate sanction in the case of a tenant breaching the terms of the lease will be to seek to forfeit the lease. (During the course of a fixed term the landlord cannot terminate the tenancy by notice to quit.) The normal rules of forfeiture will apply to farm business tenancies (see Chapter 11). To be able to rely on forfeiture a landlord must make sure that a right of re-entry is included in the tenancy agreement.

D RENT

28.30 The position with regard to rent under a farm business tenancy is again rooted in the underlying principle of freedom of contract. The parties are free to agree between them what the level of rent should be, whether or not it can be varied, and how any such variation should be determined. The Act does provide a statutory rent review procedure permitting either party to refer the rent to arbitration but it also enables the parties to contract out of these provisions if they so wish. The statutory rent review provisions will not come into play in three situations:

(a) where the tenancy agreement expressly states that the rent is not to be reviewed during the tenancy (s 9(a));

(b) where the tenancy agreement expressly provides that the rent is to be varied at a specified time or times during the tenancy by a specified amount (s 9(b)(i));

(c) where the tenancy agreement expressly provides that the rent is to be varied at a specified time or times during the tenancy in accordance with a specified formula. This formula must not preclude a decrease in rent. It must also be an objective criterion which does not require or permit the exercise by any person of any judgment or discretion in relation to the determination of the rent of the holding (s 9(b)(ii)).

28.31 For provisions in tenancy agreements made after 19 October 2006 further exceptions were introduced by the Regulatory Reform (Agricultural Tenancies) (England and Wales) Order 2006, SI 2006/2805. The agreement will also be excluded from the statutory rent review provisions where it does not contain any provision which precludes a reduction in rent during the tenancy and:

(a) expressly states that Pt II of the Act does not apply; or

(b) makes provision for the reference of rent reviews to an independent expert whose decision is final (s 9(c)).

Of course, such arrangements will not always be satisfactory to both parties. All of them **28.32** have the advantage of certainty, but, on the other hand, neither the landlord nor the tenant, particularly in tenancies of a relatively long fixed term, may wish to tie themselves into an inflexible arrangement regarding the rent. They may, instead, choose to agree in writing that the rent will be reviewable on specified dates or at specified intervals. Alternatively, they may make no written agreement as to rent review and choose to rely on the statutory provisions. In which case, as under the 1986 Act, either the landlord or the tenant will be able to demand a rent review every three years. This is done by serving a 'statutory review notice' on the other party requiring that the rent to be payable in respect of the holding as from the review date be referred to arbitration (s 10(1)). The review date must be at least 12 months but less than 24 months after the day on which the statutory review notice is given (s 10(3)).

Where there is no agreement in writing, the review date will be the anniversary of the **28.33** beginning of the tenancy (unless the landlord and tenant agree in writing that it is to be some other date) (s 10(6)(a)) and the three-year period will run from the latest of the following dates:

(a) the beginning of the tenancy;
(b) the date as from which there took effect a previous direction of an arbitrator as to the amount of rent;
(c) the date as from which there took effect a previous determination as to the amount of rent made by a person appointed under an agreement between the landlord and tenant; and
(d) the date as from which there took effect a previous agreement in writing between the landlord and the tenant, entered into since the grant of the tenancy, as to the amount of rent (s 10(6)(b)).

If there is an agreement in writing to review the rent on specified dates or at specified inter- **28.34** vals, either the landlord or the tenant may also serve a statutory review notice and refer the rent to arbitration, in which case the review date must be a date as from which the rent could be varied under the agreement (s 10(4)).

Severance of the landlord's reversion

Section 11 makes special provisions with regard to the severance of the landlord's rever- **28.35** sion. If the landlord sells part of his or her estate which is let to a tenant under a farm business tenancy, and as a result of severing the estate a new tenancy of part of the land is granted to the tenant, the three-year period between statutory rent reviews will run from the granting of the original tenancy, not from the creation of the new tenancy.

Arbitration

Once a statutory review notice has been served the parties may agree the rent between **28.36** them, agree to appoint an arbitrator to determine the rent on an open market basis, or agree to appoint some other person to determine the rent on a basis agreed between them. If the parties are unable to agree on one of these courses of action then either party may apply to the president of the Royal Institution of Chartered Surveyors for the appointment of an arbitrator. Such an application must be made in the six months preceding the review date (s 12).

Where an arbitrator is appointed in pursuance of a statutory review notice he or she shall **28.37** determine the rent properly payable in respect of the holding at the review date and shall, with effect from that date, increase or reduce the rent or direct that it should remain unchanged (s 13(1)). The rent properly payable in respect of a holding is the rent at which the holding might reasonably be expected to be let on the open market by a willing land-lord to a willing tenant, taking into account all relevant factors including the terms of the tenancy. The fact that the tenancy agreement either includes or does not include a provision for reviewing the rent should be taken into account, but terms which preclude a reduction in the rent during the tenancy should not (s 13(2)).

28.38   Any increase in the rental value due to a tenant's improvements should be disregarded other than:

(a)   any tenant's improvements carried out under an obligation imposed on the tenant by the terms of the tenancy;

(b)   any tenant's improvement to the extent that any allowance or benefit has been made or given by the landlord in consideration of its provision; and

(c)   any tenant's improvement to the extent that the tenant has received any compensation from the landlord in respect of it (s 13(3)).

28.39   The arbitrator should also disregard any effect on the rent of the fact that the tenant is in occupation of the holding (s 13(4)(a)) and should not reduce the rent because of any dilapidation or deterioration of or damage to the buildings or land caused by or permitted by the tenant (s 13(4)(b)).

E FIXTURES AND COMPENSATION

28.40   One of the aims of the 1995 Act is to revive the rural economy by encouraging agricultural tenants to invest in their farm business. Such investment may well involve the purchasing of machinery or equipment or the erection of buildings upon the holding. Obviously, however, where there is no security of tenure, tenants will only be willing to make such investments if they know that at the end of the tenancy they will either be compensated for the improvements made to the landlord's land or will be entitled to remove the equipment and take it with them.

Tenant's right to remove fixtures

28.41   Under s 8(1) of the Act a tenant under a farm business tenancy has the right to remove any fixture affixed, whether or not for the purposes of agriculture, to the holding by the tenant and any building erected by the tenant on the holding. Section 8 will also apply to fixtures and buildings acquired by the tenant (eg where a tenant has purchased a fixture or building from the preceding tenant) (s 8(5)). Section 8 will not apply to fixtures or buildings:

(a)   affixed or erected in pursuance of some obligation;

(b)   affixed or erected instead of some fixture or building belonging to the landlord;

(c)   in respect of which the tenant has obtained compensation under s 16 of the Act or otherwise; or

(d)   in respect of which the landlord has given his or her consent under s 17 on condition that the tenant agrees not to remove it (s 8(2)).

28.42   The right to remove fixtures or buildings may be exercised at any time during the continu-ance of the tenancy. The right may also be exercised after the termination of the tenancy but only when the tenant remains in possession as a tenant (whether or not under a new tenancy) (s 8(1)). In removing a fixture or building, the tenant should not do any avoidable damage to the holding (s 8(3)) and should immediately make good all damage caused to the holding by the removal (s 8(4)). (For a definition of fixtures, see 27.33.)

Compensation for improvements

Section 16 gives a farm business tenant the statutory right, provided certain conditions are fulfilled, to be entitled on the termination of the tenancy, on quitting the holding, to obtain from his landlord compensation in respect of any tenant's improvements (s 16(1)). **28.43**

A tenant's improvement means: **28.44**

(a) any physical improvement which is made on the holding by the tenant by his or her own effort or wholly or partly at his or her own expense; or
(b) any intangible advantage which:
  (i) is obtained for the holding by the tenant by his or her own effort or wholly or partly at his or her own expense; and
  (ii) becomes attached to the holding (s 15).

This right, however, will not arise in respect of any physical improvement which is removed from the holding, or any intangible advantage which does not remain attached to the holding (s 16(2)). The Act does not permit the parties to contract out of the provisions of Pt III (s 26(1)). **28.45**

Landlord's consent for improvements

Compensation for a tenant's improvement will only be available if the landlord has given consent in writing for that improvement (s 17(1)). Such consent can be given in the tenancy agreement or in a separate document (s 17(2)) and can be given either unconditionally or on condition that the tenant agrees to a specified variation (relating to the improvement) in the terms of the tenancy (s 17(3) and (4)). There is no requirement that the consent must be given before the making of the improvement. **28.46**

If a landlord: **28.47**

(a) refuses to give consent to an improvement;
(b) fails to give consent to an improvement within two months of the tenant requesting consent in writing; or
(c) requires the tenant to agree to a variation in the terms of the tenancy as a condition of giving the consent,

the tenant may give notice in writing to the landlord that he or she wishes to apply for arbitration under s 19.

Section 19 will only apply if the tenant gives notice before beginning the improvement except where the improvement in question is a 'routine improvement'. A routine improvement is defined as a physical improvement made in the normal course of farming the holding or any part of the holding which does not consist of fixed equipment or an improvement to fixed equipment (s 19(10)). 'Fixed equipment' is given effectively the same definition as in s 96(1) of the Agricultural Holdings Act 1986 (see 27.25). Routine improvements will include the normal acts of good husbandry such as growing crops, sowing seeds, and laying down pasture. **28.48**

Landlord's consent for planning permission

Where the tenant's improvement consists of the obtaining of planning permission, special conditions apply regarding the landlord's consent. The tenant will only be entitled to compensation if: **28.49**

(a) the landlord has given his or her consent in writing to the making of the application for planning permission; and

(b) that consent is expressed to be given for the purpose:

    (i) of enabling the tenant to make a specified physical improvement to the holding; or

    (ii) of enabling the tenant lawfully to effect a specified change of use; and

(c) on the termination of the tenancy, the specified physical improvement has not been completed or the specified change of use has not been effected (s 18(11)).

28.50 Consent can be given unconditionally or on condition that the tenant agrees to a specified variation in the lease (s 18(2)). However, in contrast to improvements that have actually been made, the tenant cannot appeal to arbitration if the landlord refuses consent or makes consent conditional on a variation in the lease.

Amount of compensation for improvements

28.51 The amount of compensation payable to the tenant for a tenant's improvement is an amount equal to the increase attributable to the improvement in the value of the holding at the termination of the tenancy as land comprised in a tenancy (s 20(1)). This amount will be reduced where the landlord and tenant have agreed in writing that the landlord should make a contribution towards the tenant's improvement (s 20(2)) and where a grant has been made to the tenant out of public money (s 20(3)).

28.52 From 19 October 2006 the parties may agree in writing to place an upper limit on the amount of compensation payable (s 20(4A) and (4B)). This provision was introduced by the Regulatory Reform (Agricultural Tenancies) (England and Wales) Order 2006 to assist landlords who may previously have been discouraged from granting consent to improvements because they could not be sure how much compensation would be payable at the end of the tenancy.

Amount of compensation for planning permission

28.53 The amount of compensation payable to the tenant where the tenant has obtained planning permission for an improvement shall be an amount equal to the increase attributable to the fact that the relevant development is authorized by the planning permission in the value of the holding at the termination of the tenancy as land comprised in a tenancy (s 21(1)).

Settlement of claims

28.54 Where the parties are unable to agree the amount of compensation between them the tenant may then take the claim to arbitration under the provisions set out in s 22. In order to do so the tenant must give notice to his or her landlord of his or her intention to make a claim and the nature of the claim within two months from the date of the termination of the tenancy (s 22(2)). Once notice has been given, the parties may settle the claim by agreement in writing or agree to appoint an arbitrator. If, after four months, they have failed to agree on either of these steps, either party may apply to the president of the Royal Institution of Chartered Surveyors for an arbitrator to be appointed (s 22(3)).

Successive tenancies

If, at the end of his or her tenancy, a tenant does not give up possession of the holding but is **28.55** granted a further tenancy, the right of that tenant to claim compensation for improvements made during the earlier tenancy is preserved by s 22. The tenant may claim compensation at the end of the second (or further subsequent) tenancy or may agree with the landlord that compensation is paid at the end of the original tenancy (s 22(2)). However, if the tenant is entitled to compensation at the end of the original tenancy and then remains in possession under a further tenancy, that tenant will be precluded from claiming again for improvements made during the earlier tenancy (s 22(3)).

Resumption of possession of part of holding

Where the landlord under a farm business tenancy resumes possession of part of the hold- **28.56** ing in pursuance of a provision in the tenancy entitling him or her to do so or because the landlord's reversion has been severed and the person entitled to the severed part resumes possession of that part, then the part which has been repossessed (the relevant part) will be treated as if it were a separate holding which the tenant had quitted in consequence of a notice to quit (s 24(1)). In such cases compensation is calculated on the basis of the increase in value to the entire original holding which is attributable to the tenant's improvement to the relevant part (s 24(2) and (3)). Similarly, if the improvements are made on the land retained by the tenant, compensation is again calculated on the basis of the value which the improvement had for the entire holding (s 24(4)). However, if the parties have agreed a limit under s 20(4A) (see 27.52) the total amount of compensation should not exceed this limit (s 24(4A)). The reason for these provisions is not as obscure as it might first appear. Improvements upon one part of the land may well affect the profitability and value of the whole holding. For example, a dairy farmer might erect a milking shed on his or her land; this milking shed would be essential to his or her whole business. If, having erected and equipped the shed, the reversion is severed and the new landlord serves a notice to quit the part on which the milking shed is situated, the value of the shed to the whole original holding would be greater than the value of the shed to the severed part.

KEY DOCUMENTS

Agricultural Tenancies Act 1995

Regulatory Reform (Agricultural Tenancies) (England and Wales) Order 2006, SI 2006/2805

Defra's 'Code of good practice for agri-environment schemes and diversification projects within agricultural tenancies' (available from <http://www.defra.gov.uk>)

Printed copies of all legislation can be ordered from The Stationery Office at <http://www.tsoshop. co.uk>. All legislation from 1988 onwards and most pre-1988 primary legislation is available online at <http://www.legislation.gov.uk>.

29

RESIDENTIAL PROTECTION OF AGRICULTURAL WORKERS

A INTRODUCTION

In the preceding two chapters we considered the two statutory codes (the Agricultural **29.01** Holdings Act 1986 and the Agricultural Tenancies Act 1995) that deal with the commercial letting of agricultural land. In this chapter we shall be dealing with the protection available to agricultural workers. It is important to be clear that these are very different things. The subject matter of this chapter is the *residential* protection that may be available to an agricultural worker in a specific situation: namely where the worker's accommodation goes with the job. In such a case the relationship between the worker and the person providing the accommodation will not simply be one of landlord and tenant or of licensor and licensee but it will also be one of employer and employee (or 'master and servant'). As we shall see later, in order for an occupier to acquire an assured agricultural occupancy or protection under the Rent (Agriculture) Act 1976 it is an essential requirement that the accommodation is either owned or arranged by the occupier's employer.

However, it is important to bear in mind that this will not always be the case. Many agri- **29.02** cultural workers will be tenants like any other tenants and may acquire protection under the Housing Act 1988 or the Rent Act 1977 depending on when the tenancy was granted. The fact that they work in agriculture will make no more difference to the status of the tenancy than if they were a lawyer, an architect, or a cab driver; in which case, reference should be made to Chapters 12 to 16 of this book. It is only where the agricultural worker occupies 'tied accommodation' or is a service occupier that the provisions considered in this chapter will be relevant.

These provisions are necessary because without them agricultural workers could well find **29.03** themselves with no security at all. First, this is because under a service occupancy they may well not have a tenancy at all. As we saw in Chapter 2 most licences that grant exclusive possession to the occupier will be tenancies under the rule in *Street v Mountford*. However, one of the key exceptions to this rule is where the occupier is in a relationship of 'master and servant' with the person who provides the accommodation (see 2.21). Secondly, even if there is a tenancy, it may well fall foul of the rules that exclude tenancies at a low rent from the Housing Act 1988 or the Rent Act 1977. Where accommodation goes with the job, the employee's wages will be adjusted to take into account the provision of accommodation and commonly only a low rent, or no rent at all, will be payable. Thirdly, both the 1988 Act and the 1977 Act specifically exclude a tenancy of a dwelling-house which is comprised in a farm business tenancy or an agricultural holding which is occupied by the person responsible for the control of the farming of the holding (see 13.66 and 15.30 to 15.33). Thus, for example, where a tenant rents a farm under one of the commercial agricultural codes and then sub-lets the farmhouse to his farm manager, the farm manager would find himself or herself without any residential protection.

29.04   The two primary statutory codes that we consider in this chapter are contained in the Rent (Agriculture) Act 1976 and in Ch III of the Housing Act 1988. In broad terms the 1976 Act provides similar protection for qualifying agricultural workers as is available for residential tenants under the Rent Act 1977. Tenancies and licences granted after the Housing Act 1988 came into force on 15 January 1989 (with a few transitional exceptions) do not have their own separate statutory code but are brought within the 1988 Act and treated as assured tenancies.

B THE RENT (AGRICULTURE) ACT 1976

29.05   Tenancies and licences granted before 15 January 1989 will be governed by the Rent (Agriculture) Act 1976. In order to fall within the protection of the 1976 Act a number of definitions must be satisfied. The agricultural worker must be a 'qualifying worker', the tenancy or licence under which he holds his or her dwelling-house must be a 'relevant tenancy or licence', and the dwelling-house itself must be in 'qualifying ownership'.

Qualifying worker

29.06   A person is a qualifying worker for the purposes of the 1976 Act at any time if, at that time, he or she has worked whole time in agriculture for not less than 91 out of the preceding 104 weeks (Sch 3, para 1). A person may also fall under the protection of the Act if he or she is incapable of whole time work in agriculture in consequence of a qualifying disease or injury. A qualifying disease or injury is one prescribed, in relation to employment in agriculture, by s 76(2) of the Social Security Act 1975, or an injury caused by an accident arising out of the course of his or her employment as a whole time worker in agriculture (Sch 3, para 2). (There are also special provisions for 'permit workers' who have been granted special dispensations under s 5 of the Agricultural Wages Act 1948.)

Agriculture

29.07   'Agriculture' is defined by s 1(1) of the 1976 Act to include dairy farming, livestock keeping and breeding, the production of any consumable produce, and the use of land for grazing, pasture, orchards, market gardens, nurseries, and forestry. It should be noted that the definition is not the same as the definition of agriculture used in the Agricultural Holdings Act 1987 and the Agricultural Tenancies Act 1995, nor is it an exhaustive list. A person employed to repair and maintain farm machinery is employed in agriculture (*McPhail v Greensmith* [1993] 2 EGLR 228, CA) but a gamekeeper is not (*Normanton (Earl of) v Giles* [1980] 1 WLR 28, HL).

Qualifying ownership

For the purposes of the 1976 Act a dwelling-house will be in qualifying ownership at any **29.08** time when the occupier is employed in agriculture and the occupier's employer either:

(a) is the owner of the dwelling-house (ie the occupier's immediate landlord); or

(b) has made arrangements with the owner of the dwelling-house for it to be used as housing accommodation for persons employed by him or her in agriculture (Sch 3, para 3).

Relevant licence and relevant tenancy

A 'relevant tenancy' is a tenancy of a separate dwelling which would be a protected ten- **29.09** ancy under the Rent Act 1977 but for the provisions of the 1977 Act listed in 29.11. A 'relevant tenancy' may not be a tenancy which falls under Pt II of the Landlord and Tenant Act 1954 (business tenancies, see Chapter 26), Pt I of the 1954 Act, or Sch 10 to the Local Government and Housing Act 1989 (long leases, see Chapter 22), or is an agricultural holding or farm business tenancy.

A 'relevant licence' is any licence under which a person has the exclusive occupation of a **29.10** dwelling-house as a separate dwelling which, if it were a tenancy, would be a protected tenancy under the Rent Act 1977 but for the provisions of the 1977 Act listed in 29.11.

The provisions of the Rent Act 1977 are: **29.11**

(a) s 5 (which excludes tenancies at low rents, see 13.47) (Sch 2, para 3(2));

(b) s 10 (which excludes a tenancy of a dwelling-house which is comprised in an agricultural holding and occupied by the person responsible for the control of the farming of the holding, see 13.66) (Sch 2, para 3(2));

(c) s 7 (which excludes a tenancy where the rent includes payments for board or attendance, see 13.52). The 1976 Act modifies this section to make it clear that meals provided in the course of a person's employment in agriculture do not constitute 'board' (Sch 2, para 3).

Protected occupier

Section 2(1) and (2) of the 1976 Act provide that a person will be a protected occupier in **29.12** his or her own right (as opposed to by succession) where:

(a) he or she holds a relevant licence or a relevant tenancy in relation to a dwelling-house, and

(b) the dwelling-house is in qualifying ownership or has been in qualifying ownership at any time during the subsistence of the licence or tenancy (whether or not it was, at the time, a relevant licence or tenancy), and either:

(i) he or she is a qualifying worker; or

(ii) he or she has been a qualifying worker at any time during the subsistence of the licence or tenancy (whether or not it was, at the time, a relevant licence or tenancy); or

(iii) he or she is incapable of whole time work in agriculture in consequence of a qualifying injury or disease.

It is important to note that s 2 does not require a person to be a qualifying worker, nor a **29.13** dwelling-house to be in qualifying ownership, throughout the entire course of the tenancy. A person's protection under the Act will not end if the tenant or licensee changes job or retires, nor will it end if his or her employer/landlord sells the dwelling-house to somebody else. Provided the person was a qualifying worker and the dwelling-house was in qualifying ownership at some point during the course of the tenancy or licence, that person will be a protected occupier. A person will also be protected under s 2(3) if immediately before the licence or tenancy was granted, he or she was a protected occupier of the same dwelling-house or if the tenancy or licence was granted in consideration of that person giving up another dwelling-house of which he or she was a protected occupier.

Security of tenure

29.14 The system of security of tenure offered under the 1976 Act is very similar to that offered by the Rent Act 1977 (see 13.91 to 13.107). First, s 4(1) of the 1976 Act provides that when a protected occupier's tenancy or licence is terminated, and the tenant or licensee continues to occupy the dwelling-house as his residence, a statutory tenancy will arise. The protected occupier's licence or tenancy may be terminated by a notice to quit, a notice of increase of rent under s 16(3) of the Act, or otherwise. In the case of many protected occupiers their right to occupy their accommodation will depend upon their employment, so if their employment is terminated their tenancy or licence will be terminated too. Schedule 5 to the Act contains detailed provisions as to the terms of the statutory tenancy. In particular it should be noted that if the original contract was a licence this will become a weekly tenancy (para 3) and any term of the original contract which made the right of occupation dependent upon the occupier's employment will be disregarded (para 1(2)).

29.15 Secondly, the court may not make an order for possession of a dwelling-house subject to a protected occupancy or a statutory tenancy unless the landlord can establish one of the statutory grounds of possession set out Sch 4 (s 6(1)). As under the Rent Act 1977 these are divided into discretionary and mandatory grounds. In the case of the discretionary grounds the court will not make an order for possession unless it considers it reasonable to do so (s 7(2)). The court also has wide powers to adjourn and, if a possession order is made, to stay or suspend the execution of the order or postpone the date of possession (s 7(3)).

29.16 To rely on one of the discretionary grounds of possession the landlord must show:

(a) That suitable alternative accommodation is available for the tenant, or will be available when the order for possession takes effect (Sch 4, Case I). (Provisions as to what will be deemed suitable alternative accommodation are similar to those set out in Sch 15, Pt IV to the Rent Act 1977, see 14.08 to 14.24.)

(b) That the housing authority has offered to provide or arrange alternative accommodation and the landlord can show that the tenant accepted the offer, or, if not, that the tenant acted unreasonably in not accepting the offer (Sch 4, Case II).

(c) That the tenant has not paid rent that is lawfully due or has breached an obligation of the tenancy (Sch 4, Case III).

(d) That the tenant is guilty of nuisance or annoyance or has been convicted of using the premises for immoral or illegal purposes (see 14.32 to 14.36) (Sch 4, Case IV).

(e) That the condition of the dwelling-house has deteriorated owing to acts of waste by the tenant (see 7.77 and 14.37) (Sch 4, Case V).

(f) That the condition of the furniture has deteriorated owing to ill treatment by the tenant (see 14.38) (Sch 4, Case VI).

(g) That the tenant has given notice to quit and the landlord would be seriously prejudiced if he or she could not obtain possession (see 14.39) (Sch 4, Case VII).

(h) That the tenant assigned or sub-let without permission (Sch 4, Case VIII).

(i) That the dwelling-house is reasonably required by the landlord for occupation as a residence by the landlord or a close relative (Sch 4, Case IX). (In this case the court must be satisfied that no greater hardship would be caused by granting a possession order than by refusing it, see 14.47.)

(j) That the tenant is overcharging a sub-tenant (see 14.48) (Sch 4, Case X).

To rely on one of the mandatory grounds the landlord must show: **29.17**

(a) That before granting the tenancy the person who granted the tenancy (the original occupier) occupied the dwelling-house as his or her residence and the court is satisfied that the dwelling-house is now required as a residence for the original occupier or for a member of his or her family who lived with the original occupier when he or she last occupied the dwelling-house as a residence and the original occupier gave notice to the tenant before the start of the tenancy that possession might be recovered under this Case (Sch 4, Case XI).

(b) That the person who granted the tenancy acquired the dwelling-house with a view to occupying it as a residence on his or her retirement, that person has now retired and requires the dwelling-house as his or her residence or that he or she has died and it is required for a member of his or her family, and that notice was given to the tenant before the start of the tenancy that possession might be recovered under this Case (Sch 4, Case XII).

(c) That the dwelling-house is overcrowded within the meaning of Pt X of the Housing Act 1985 in such circumstances as to render the occupier guilty of an offence.

Rent

It will usually be the case that during the course of a protected occupancy only a low rent   **29.18**
or no rent at all will be payable for the accommodation that goes with the job. However, when the protected occupancy is terminated and a statutory tenancy arises under s 4(1), the relationship between the occupier and the landlord/licensor will often change significantly. In many cases, the reason for terminating the protected occupancy will be because the occupier has ceased to be employed by the landlord/licensor. Nevertheless, unless the landlord can establish one of the cases in Sch 4 (eg by arranging alternative accommodation) the occupier will have the right to continue residing in the dwelling-house as a statutory tenant; in which case the landlord may well want to increase, or start charging, rent. No rent will be payable under a statutory tenancy until either the landlord and the tenant fix the rent by agreement under s 11 or the landlord serves a notice of increase of rent under s 12 or 14 of the Act (s 10(2)).

As under the Rent Act 1977, both parties have the right to apply to register a fair rent   **29.19**
(see 13.131) and s 12(2) and (3) of the 1976 Act set out which provisions of the 1977 Act will apply. Once rent has been registered the amount of rent payable must not exceed the amount registered (s 11(3), s 12(7)).

Succession

The 1976 Act provides for a single succession. Where the deceased was a protected occu-   **29.20**
pier in his or her own right (ie not by succession), his or her spouse or civil partner, provided he or she was residing with the deceased immediately before his or her death and has a relevant licence or tenancy, will succeed to a protected occupancy (s 3(2)). If there is no spouse or civil partner, a member of the deceased's family may also succeed to a protected occupancy provided he or she was residing with the deceased for six months before the death (s 3(3)). Where the protected occupancy has been terminated and the deceased was a statutory tenant, the situation is a little different. A spouse or civil partner may succeed to

a statutory tenancy (s 4(3)) as may a family member who has resided with the deceased for two years prior to his or her death. However, a family member, in contrast to a spouse or civil partner, will succeed to an assured tenancy under the Housing Act 1988 (s 4(4)).

C ASSURED AGRICULTURAL OCCUPANCIES

29.21 Tenancies and licences granted to agricultural workers after 15 January 1989 will be governed by Ch III of the Housing Act 1988 (unless they fall within one of the transitional exceptions set out in s 34, see 13.03). Rather than setting out a whole parallel code, as in the 1976 Act, Ch III of the Housing Act 1988 functions by bringing agricultural workers within the assured tenancies scheme by creating the specific category of the assured agricultural occupancy. It should be noted, however, that the 1988 Act has adopted a number of definitions from the 1976 Act.

Relevant tenancy or licence

29.22 In order to be an assured agricultural occupancy the tenancy or licence of the dwelling-house must be:

(a) an assured tenancy which is not an assured shorthold tenancy (see 15.03 and 15.106); or

(b) a tenancy which would be an assured tenancy but for the fact that it is excluded by:

    (i) the provisions of Sch 1, paras 3, 3A, and 3B which exclude tenancies at a low rent (see 15.26); or

    (ii) the provisions of Sch 1, para 7 which excludes a tenancy of a dwelling-house which is comprised in an agricultural holding or farm business tenancy and occupied by the person responsible for the control of the farming or management of the holding (see 15.33); or

(c) a licence under which a person has exclusive occupation of a dwelling-house as a separate dwelling which, if it were a tenancy, would satisfy (a) or (b) (s 24(2)).

29.23 For the purposes of (b) a tenancy may not be an agricultural holding or a farm business tenancy (s 24(2A)).

Agricultural worker condition

29.24 The first requirement of the agricultural worker condition is that the dwelling-house must be in qualifying ownership or have been in qualifying ownership at any time during the subsistence of the tenancy or licence (whether or not it was at that time a relevant tenancy or licence) (Sch 3, para 2(a)). Qualifying ownership is defined as under the 1976 Act (ie that it is accommodation provided by the tenant or licensee's employer, see 29.08).

29.25 The second requirement is that the occupier (or where there are joint occupiers, at least one of them):

(a) is a qualifying worker or has been a qualifying worker at any time during the subsistence of the tenancy or licence (whether or not it was at that time a relevant tenancy or licence); or

(b) is incapable of whole time work (or work as a permit worker) in agriculture in consequence of a qualifying injury or disease (Sch 3, para 2(b)).

29.26 The definition of qualifying worker and qualifying disease or injury is the same as under the 1976 Act (see 29.06).

Where the agricultural worker condition is fulfilled and the tenant or licensee is granted **29.27** another relevant tenancy or licence of another dwelling-house in consideration of giving up possession of the original dwelling-house, or where the tenant or licensee is granted a new tenancy of the same dwelling-house, the tenant or licensee will continue to satisfy the agricultural worker condition (Sch 3, paras 4 and 5).

Succession

The agricultural worker condition may also be fulfilled by succession. This will occur where **29.28** a dwelling-house is subject to a relevant tenancy or licence and an occupier who satisfied the agricultural worker condition has died (Sch 3, para 3(1)). A spouse or civil partner may succeed where he or she was residing with the deceased at the time of his or her death and, if there is no spouse or civil partner, a member of the family may succeed if he or she was residing with the deceased for the period of two years before his or her death (Sch 3, para 3(2) and (3)).

Security of tenure

Where the tenancy or licence is a relevant tenancy or licence and the agricultural worker **29.29** condition is fulfilled, that tenancy or licence will be an assured agricultural occupancy. An assured agricultural occupancy which is not an assured tenancy will be treated as if it were an assured tenancy (s 24(3)) with the following alterations:

(a) a landlord will not be entitled to seek possession of the dwelling-house under Ground 16 (ie where the landlord can show that the dwelling-house was let to the tenant in consequence of the tenant's employment and that employment has now ceased, see 16.69) (s 25(2));

(b) if the tenant gives notice to terminate his or her employment, that notice shall not constitute a notice to quit notwithstanding any agreement to the contrary (s 25(4));

(c) when an assured agricultural tenancy is terminated and a statutory periodic tenancy arises by virtue of s 5 (see 15.46), that statutory periodic tenancy will be an assured agricultural occupancy as long as the agricultural condition is for the time being fulfilled with respect to the dwelling-house in question (s 25(1)(a));

(d) if no rent is payable under an assured agricultural occupancy, the statutory tenancy that arises on termination of the occupancy will be a monthly periodic tenancy (s 25(1)(b)).

The details of security of tenure under the 1988 Act and the grounds of possession avail- **29.30** able to the landlord are dealt with in Chapters 15 and 16.

Rent

Under the Housing Act 1988 there is only limited control of rent. This is dealt with in **29.31** Chapter 15 (see 15.79 to 15.88).

Assured shorthold tenancies

Assured shorthold tenancies provide a simple and convenient way for a landlord to grant **29.32** a tenancy to an agricultural worker without providing any long-term security of tenure. However, if a tenant satisfies the agricultural worker condition (see 29.24 to 29.27) the landlord must serve notice on the tenant before the tenancy is entered into stating that the tenancy is to be a shorthold tenancy (Sch 2A, para 9). Assured shorthold tenancies are dealt with in Chapter 15 (15.106 to 15.132).

D PROTECTION FROM EVICTION ACT 1977

29.33 By no means all agricultural workers will fall within the provisions we have already considered. On the one hand, as we stated in the introduction, they may acquire full protection under the Housing Act 1988 or the Rent Act 1977 provided they have a tenancy and pay sufficient rent. On the other hand, they may fail to qualify under the Rent (Agriculture) Act 1976 or Ch III of the Housing Act 1988 (eg because they have not worked long enough in agriculture to be a qualifying worker). However, in this latter case, a person employed in agriculture (as defined by s 1 of the 1976 Act, see 29.07) is given a limited degree of protection by s 4 of the Protection from Eviction Act 1977. This provides that where a possession order is made against such a tenant or licensee that order must be suspended for a period of six months from the date on which the contractual right to occupy the dwelling-house came to an end, unless the court is satisfied:

(a) that other suitable accommodation is, or will within that period be made, available to the occupier; or

(b) that the efficient management of any agricultural land or the efficient carrying on of any agricultural operations would be seriously prejudiced unless the premises are available for occupation by a person employed or to be employed by the owner; or

(c) that greater hardship would be caused by the suspension of the order until the end of that period than by its execution within that period; or

(d) that the occupier, or any person residing with the occupier, has been causing damage to the premises or has been guilty of conduct which is a nuisance or annoyance to persons occupying other premises;

and the court considers that it would be reasonable not to suspend the execution of the order for the remainder of that period.

KEY DOCUMENTS

Rent Agriculture Act 1976

Housing Act 1988 (Ch III)

Printed copies of all legislation can be ordered from The Stationery Office at <http://www.tsoshop.co.uk>. All legislation from 1988 onwards and most pre-1988 primary legislation is available online at <http://www.legislation.gov.uk>.

30

YOUR PRACTICE

A INTRODUCTION

The relationship of *landlord and tenant* can arise in a wide variety of circumstances, be it **30.01** between an individual tenant and a local authority, a commercial landlord and a business tenant, a farmer and a landowner, or between two private individuals. *Landlord and tenant* is therefore a large area of law and its boundaries are not always clearly defined. What is of concern to commercial tenants may often be very different from the preoccupations of residential tenants. And the concerns of residential tenants will also differ considerably; there is a great difference between an occupier with a six-month shorthold assured tenancy and the holder of a long lease. Similarly, therefore, it cannot be assumed that landlord and tenant advisers will be a particularly homogenous group: there will be those that specialize in property and commercial tenancies, those that specialize in residential public sector housing, and those that specialize in disrepair, long leases, or leasehold enfranchisement.

In this chapter, therefore, we have sought to provide a little initial guidance for a legal **30.02** adviser approaching a landlord and tenant issue: first, with regard to library and information resources; and, secondly, with respect to further training courses and continued professional development.

As with any large body of law it is inevitable that many aspects of landlord and tenant will **30.03** be subject to development and change. In fact, this is particularly true of landlord and tenant law at the moment. Those advising tenants of social housing providers in England will need to be aware of the provisions of the Housing and Regeneration Act 2008 and the Localism Act 2011. Advisers should also be alert to the recent developments in Human Rights Act case law which have had a major impact on public sector possession proceedings.

B LIBRARY AND RESEARCH MATERIAL

Practitioners' texts

There are two multi-volume looseleaf updatable practitioners' texts dedicated to landlord **30.04** and tenant law: Woodfall's *Landlord and Tenant*, published by Sweet and Maxwell, and Hill and Redman's *Landlord and Tenant*, published by Butterworths. Both are comprehensive and cover all areas of landlord and tenant law in considerable detail. They contain all the statutes, statutory instruments, and forms that are likely to be required in practice, as well as an extended commentary on the principles of landlord and tenant law. Either of these practitioners' texts provides an excellent source of information when dealing with virtually any landlord and tenant problem.

30.05   Both Woodfall and Hill and Redman are updated quarterly and will therefore include most new developments in the law, and one or other of them will usually be available in any good law library, though care should always be taken to make sure that the updates have been carried out regularly.

30.06   Woodfall is available online as part of Sweet and Maxwell's *Westlaw UK Landlord and Tenant Service* (which also includes the *Landlord and Tenant Review* and the *Property Law Bulletin*). Details can be found at <http://www.sweetandmaxwell.co.uk>.

Law reports

30.07   Most significant landlord and tenant cases will be featured in either the *All England*, *Times*, or *Weekly Law Reports* and will be available in any law library. The *All England* and *Times Law Reports* are also available online as a subscription service from <http://www. butterworth.co.uk> and the *Weekly Law Reports* from <http://www.justis.com/database/ weekly_law_reports.html>. More specialized cases will usually feature in the *Housing Law Reports*, *The Estates Gazette Law Reports*, or the *Property and Conveyancing Reports*. Many cases are now available free online. An extremely useful site is run by the British and Irish Information Institute <http://www.bailli.org>.

30.08   Leasehold valuation tribunal decisions are available free on the Leasehold Advisory Service's website at <http://www.lease-advice.org.uk> and direct from the Residential Property Tribunal Service at <http://www.rpts.gov.uk>. Decisions of the Upper Tribunal (Lands Chamber) are available from the Tribunals Service at <http://www.landstribunal.gov.uk>.

Statutory material

30.09   Landlord and tenant law is a large area and covered by a wide variety of statutes. These are available in print form from The Stationery Office at <http://www.tsoshop.co.uk> or, for all statutes from 1988 onwards, online from the Office of Public Sector Information at <http://www.opsi.gov.uk>. All the statutory material covered in this book can be found in the appendices of Woodfall or Hill and Redman.

Civil Procedure Rules

30.10   The full text of the Civil Procedure Rules is available free online from <http://www.justice. gov.uk>.

Forms

30.11   Court forms are available online from <http://www.hmcourts-service.gov.uk>. Leasehold valuation tribunal applications forms are available from the Residential Property Tribunal Service at <http://www.rpts.gov.uk>.

Keeping up to date

30.12   The monthly *Current Law Digest* is always a good place to start when looking for new developments in landlord and tenant law. Its landlord and tenant section provides a brief summary of new case law in the area and any significant statutory development. With regard to public sector tenancies the housing section should also be checked. *Legal Action*, the monthly journal of the Legal Action Group, has a section entitled 'Recent Developments in Housing Law' which covers private as well as public sector tenancies. *Legal Action* also includes a bi-annual feature on disrepair. The *New Law Journal* includes a regular property law update.

When looking at new case law it is important to bear in mind that many of the cases fea- **30.13** tured will often be at first instance and in the county court, and advisers should be wary of giving such decisions too much significance until they have been subject to a hearing in the Court of Appeal or House of Lords/Supreme Court.

With regard to new statutory developments, the full text of all new legislation is avail- **30.14** able from the Office of Public Sector Information at <http://www.legislation.gov.uk>. Similarly, for those interested in the future development of the law, the text of the bills before Parliament can be obtained from <http://www.parliament.uk>. Law Commission reports (the report on renting homes is of particular interest) are available from <http://www.lawcommission.justice.gov.uk>.

It is also important, particularly with regard to the Commonhold and Leasehold Reform **30.15** Act 2002, to keep an eye not only on primary legislation but also on statutory instruments. All new statutory instruments can be viewed at <http://www.opsi.gov.uk>.

Journals

There are a number of journals that feature articles which may be of interest to the land- **30.16** lord and tenant advisor; of particular note are *Estates Gazette*, the *Landlord and Tenant Review*, and the *Journal of Housing Law*. Furthermore, many of the more general legal journals, such as the *Solicitors' Journal*, *New Law Journal*, and *Law Society Gazette*, will often contain articles relevant to landlord and tenant issues. The landlord and tenant sec- tion of the *Current Law* monthly digest always contains a useful round-up and brief sum- mary of recent articles.

C FURTHER PROFESSIONAL TRAINING

There are now a number of organizations that run accredited continuing professional devel- **30.17** opment courses. The CPD Foundation (<http://www.cpdfoundation.com>), CLT (<http://www.clt.co.uk>), and Progressive Legal Training (<http://www.progressivelegal.co.uk>) all run courses dedicated to landlord and tenant issues. The Legal Action Group <http://www.lag.org.uk> runs an excellent course on recent development in housing law. The Bar Council provides information on continuing professional development courses run by the Inns of Court at <http://www.barcouncil.org.uk>.

INDEX